DATE DUE

DEMCO 38-296

WOMEN, CULTURE, AND COMMUNITY

Sacred Heart Church in Galveston just after the storm of September 8, 1900. Courtesy Rosenberg Library, Galveston, Texas.

R

. . . .

WOMEN, CULTURE, AND COMMUNITY

Religion and Reform in Galveston, 1880–1920

ELIZABETH HAYES TURNER

New York   Oxford • Oxford University Press   1997

Oxford University Press

Oxford   New York
Athens   Auckland   Bangkok   Bogota   Bombay   Buenos Aires
Calcutta   Cape Town   Dar es Salaam   Delhi   Florence   Hong Kong
Istanbul   Karachi   Kuala Lumpur   Madras   Madrid   Melbourne
Mexico City   Nairobi   Paris   Singapore   Taipei   Tokyo   Toronto   Warsaw

and associated companies in
Berlin   Ibadan

Copyright © 1997 by Elizabeth Hayes Turner

Published by Oxford University Press
198 Madison Avenue, New York, New York 10016

Oxford is a registered trademark of Oxford University Press

"Second Fig" by Edna St. Vincent Millay. From *Collected Poems*, Harper Collins. Copyright 1922, 1950 by Edna
St. Vincent Millay. All rights reserved. Reprinted by permission of Elizabeth Barnett, literary executor.
"As I Grew Older" by Langston Hughes. Copyright 1994 by the Estate of Langston Hughes. Reprinted by
permission of Alfred A. Knopf, Inc.

Library of Congress Cataloging-in-Publication Data
Turner, Elizabeth Hayes.
Women, culture, and community : religion and reform in Galveston,
1880–1920 / Elizabeth Hayes Turner.
p. cm.
Includes bibliographical references and index.
ISBN 0-19-508688-0; ISBN 0-19-511938-X (pbk.)
1. Middle class women—Texas—Galveston—History.   2. Middle class
women—Texas—Galveston—Social conditions.   3. Middle class women—
Texas—Galveston—Political activity.   4. Social problems—Texas—
Galveston—History.   5. Social action—Texas—Galveston—History.
6. Galveston (Tex.)—History.   7. Galveston (Tex.)—Race relations.
8. Galveston (Tex.)—Social conditions.   I. Title.
HQ1439.G35T87   1997
305.4'09764'139—dc21   97-13014

1   3   5   7   9   8   6   4   2

Printed in the United States of America
on acid-free paper

For Al, Meg, and Laura

. . . .

ACKNOWLEDGMENTS

This book has been over ten years in the making. In that time I have accrued a good many debts both professional and personal. I want to give thanks to those who have been a part of this process and by doing so acknowledge that historians are never solely responsible for a book. It is the accumulation of the thoughts, ideas, suggestions, and scholarly work of many. I wish to thank the archivists at the Center for American History in Austin, the Austin Public Library, the Houston Metropolitan Research Center, the Southern Historical Collection, and the William R. Perkins Library at Duke University for their kind assistance. Most especially I owe a large debt of gratitude to the archivists at the Rosenberg Library in Galveston, where I spent many delightful hours. Casey Greene, Jane Kenamore, Margaret Schlanke, Julia Dunn, Anna Peebler, and Lisa Lambert aided greatly in my search for materials related to the history of Galveston women. Editors, too, make a difference in the progress of a book, and I want to thank Andrew Albanese and Thomas LeBien for their seemingly endless patience and good counsel and advice. Karen Wolny, Jeffrey Soloway, and Sheldon Meyer also helped see this project to completion.

I am indebted to Rice University for its financial aid as a graduate student, to the East Texas Historical Association and the Ottis Lock Foundation for providing a grant to help fund the computer programming for this project, and to the University of Houston–Downtown for two Organized Research Committee grants that gave me release time and funds to explore the history of African American Galvestonians. Also, the Southern Association for Women Historians has provided me opportunities for leadership and scholarship for which I am extremely grateful.

A number of former and present Galveston residents have been most helpful in allowing me the use of their materials and their expertise: Vernon Bennett, Debbie Bond, Mrs. Henry Cave, Izola Collins, Elizabeth Head, Mary MacGregor, Helene Levy, and Diana Rasmussen. Father John Donovan of Trinity Episcopal Church let me see the parish records when they were still stacked in boxes in an attic closet. Father Rick Benson kindly allowed me to photograph the stained glass windows of Grace Episcopal Church on two different occasions. Several friends and colleagues—Izola Collins, Jean Friedman, Jacquelyn Dowd Hall, Gillian Hanson, Linda Macdonald, Sally McMillen, Anne Firor Scott, Amilcar Shabazz, and Ruthe Winegarten—read various chapters and offered their expertise and advice. Edward Ayers, Elizabeth Fox-Genovese, Nancy Hewitt, Elizabeth Hanson, and Judy McArthur read the whole manuscript and made cogent recommendations for changes. I am especially grateful to Nancy Hewitt, whose collegiality knows no bounds. She offered superb advice and a helpful oppositional perspective to the notion of women's culture.

Thanks are also tendered to those within and outside the profession who gave insightful comments at conferences or who offered encouragement: Paula Baker, Ginger Bernhard, Kathleen Berkeley, Patti Bixel, Sidney Bland, Fitzhugh Brundage, Betty Brandon, Patricia Burgess, Jane Turner Censer, Catherine Clinton, Cita Cook, Flip Cuello, Janet Coryell, Mary Donovan, Mike Eldridge, Elizabeth Enstam, Wayne Flynt, Joanna Gillespie, Michele Gillespie, Glenda Gilmore, Louise Greenhouse, Joan Gundersen, John and Janet Hayes, Jim and Christine Hayes, Sam Hill, Darlene Clark Hine, John Inscoe, Dean James, Nancy Baker Jones, Martha Turner Keber, Sebastiaan Klaassen, Beth Langdon, Karen Leatham, Kent Leslie, Mary Lou Lewis, Ken Lipartito, Ginna and Larry Littrell, William Love, Antonio and Bettina Magro, Don Mathews, Michael McGerr, Rusti Moore, Evelyn Nolen, Rosslyn Terborg-Penn, Joan Priory, Richard Rankin, Robin and Judy Rudoff, Connie Schulz, Rima Schultz, Megan Seaholm, Stephanie Shaw, Tommy Simons, Anastatia Sims, Harold Smith, Randy Sparks, Bev and J Taylor, Wallace and Barbara Turner, Marjorie Wheeler, Charles Reagan Wilson, and the late Catherine Prelinger. Thanks to my former colleagues at the University of North Carolina at Charlotte—Julia Blackwelder, Dan Dupre, Cynthia Kierner, David Goldfield, and Carole Haber—I was able to write in an entirely supportive environment. Because Karen and Lex Youngman offered me a place to live, I was able to finish the last chapters of the dissertation in comfort. Colleagues at the University of Houston–Downtown—Garna Christian, Linda Gratch, and Jim McCaffrey—offered valuable advice. Karl Byas, Bob Greene, and Kathi Mahan made computer technology seem easy. Christa Sherwood cataloged books for me, and Juan Maldonado generously offered to take photographs.

I am especially indebted to Harold M. Hyman, whose counsel and advice I sought throughout this project. My greatest intellectual debt is to John B. Boles, whose instruction has encouraged in me a lifelong interest in southern history, whose guidance and foresight led me to Galveston, and whose keen intellect kept me from straying into swampy ideological terrain.

My greatest personal debt is to my family. To my parents Harry and Mildred Langston Hayes and to my aunt Kathryn Langston Francis I owe a great deal, because it was through their love of history that my own began to develop. My deepest thanks go to Meg and Laura, who helped track down entries in city directories, labored over the photocopier, and traveled with me to Galveston summer after summer while they were young. As for my husband Al, he and I both know that without his good humor, patience, love, and unlimited and unreserved support this project never would have been completed.

CONTENTS

WOMEN, CULTURE, AND COMMUNITY

INTRODUCTION

The Multiple Meanings of Culture, Community, Religion, and Reform

This book is about women who made a difference in a New South city. Except for one or two, they remain unheralded in the annals of history. They are ordinary, many are middle class, most are wealthier, but all are representative of southern women who left the private realm of their homes, entered the public arena, and thereby transformed the cultural and political landscape of their communities.

Three major questions drive this study: The first asks about the identity of these southern women — black and white. In the nation's most conservative region, which southern women became committed to founding public organizations, their work eventually culminating in a woman suffrage movement, and why? The second question inquires into the importance of religion, class, and race for women's emergence into public cultural, benevolent, civic, and reform organizations. The third explores the consequences of women's civic activism — how white women mobilized a progressive women's community into a politically powerful bloc and how African American women, affected by the deterioration in race relations, mobilized a women's progressive community to combat the numbing effects of disfranchisement and segregation.

I

Focusing on a trans-Mississippi seaport like Galveston for the purpose of studying women's organizations has certain advantages not found in a study of older southern seaboard cities. Texas offers fertile territory for the investigation of reform, particularly since the state produced Populist, Prohibitionist, and Progressive movements and concluded a successful woman suffrage campaign.[1] By 1880, Galveston had become the state's largest city, but its population of only 22,000 makes it a manageable site for study. It was also a dynamic city and, unlike other southern seaports, such as Charleston and Mobile, did not decline in commercial importance between 1865 and 1900. Before the hurricane of September 1900 the city had grown in population to nearly 38,000. True, by 1910 Galveston was no longer the largest city in the state, but the sheer grit of its citizens in reconstructing their home suggests a certain resilience that statistics alone cannot capture. Galveston offers special importance for black history as it was the home of Norris Wright Cuney and Adelina Cuney, who fought for race equality in the face of increasing segregation. Galveston also carries special meaning for Texas women's history as the base of the Daughters of the Republic of Texas and the site where the state's most influential suffragist, Minnie Fisher Cunningham, got her start. Finally, because we know much less about the cities of Texas and their connections to southern values and southern politics than we do about cities of the Southeast, it is time for a closer look at the South's most western region.[2]

Galveston was part of a larger network of cities across the South. Culturally, the Island City belonged to the South; regionally, it bordered on the West and on the Gulf Coast. Its history predates the chartering of the city in 1839. A Native American tribe known as the Karankawa occupied the island when Europeans in 1519 first explored the region. The island and the bay were named in the 1780s for Bernardo de Galvez, who governed Louisiana for Spain during the American Revolution and later commissioned cartographers to survey the coast of Texas. Smugglers, privateers, and pirates used the island and the bay often for illicit purposes; the most notorious of these characters was the French pirate Jean Lafitte, who smuggled slaves into Louisiana after 1808. He and his followers departed the island in 1821 after the U. S. government sent a Navy warship and made it clear that his presence was a nuisance.[3]

American and European immigrants began to settle the island after Texas declared its independence from Mexico in 1836. By 1839, with about 1,000 residents and 250 structures, the city incorporated and began self-governance. Slaves from Africa as well as other parts of the South provided labor with skills necessary for urban life. By the 1850s, there were an estimated 1,500 slaves on the island. Trade winds brought sailing ships ladened with merchandise for planters. The first ships to leave for northeastern and European ports went out with their hulls full of cotton, "hides, sugar, molasses, cattle, pecans, and cottonseed." In the antebellum years Galveston served as the official port of entry for the state of Texas; its exports, however, far exceeded its imports. Entrepreneurs found trade more lucrative than manufacturing, and Galveston remained primarily a trading city, with profits plowed into improving the wharves, funding railroad projects, and establishing banks. The connections to towns and cities in the interior of Texas, such as Austin, San Antonio, Dallas, and Fort Worth, were possible in these early years only by overland wagon; that is, until railroads unevenly crossed the plains in the 1850s. Houston remained Galveston's closest partner in urban development and its strongest rival. Steamers plied north daily to Houston via the cities' connecting waterways, the Galveston Bay and Buffalo Bayou. The Civil War put a halt to much of Galveston's commercial activity, but not to the city's prospects for the future. The antebellum elites, whose fortunes had been made in trade, were ready to begin anew in 1866, often in partnership with eager and promising newcomers. As one evidence of this startling change, the population doubled between 1861 and 1873 to 13,800.[4]

Urban historians have been mindful of the differences between postwar southern cities, in their growth rates, social organization, and cultural values. Don H. Doyle argues that interior New South railway centers, such as Atlanta and Nashville, attracted into civic-commercial leadership younger men who differed from the more relaxed, liquor-imbibing businessmen found in the seaport cities of Charleston and Mobile. In the interior cities advancement to elite status depended upon individual achievement, but in the older seaports an entrenched upper class stemming from antebellum days dominated business and social life. Galveston, fell somewhere between the two types. In the area of economic vitality and upward social mobility for enterprising individuals, it competed favorably up to 1900 with such vibrant interior cities as Atlanta, Nashville, Louisville, Memphis, Houston, and Dallas–Fort Worth. But a social elite, composed mainly of Protestants, dominated the largely Catholic city.[5]

Denominational preferences clearly present a pattern consistent with Doyle's claims of differences in social organization between younger interior cities and older seaport cities. Atlanta, Nashville, and also Louisville, Memphis, Montgomery, Houston, and Dallas had greater numbers of white Protestant communicants in the evangelical (Baptist, Methodist, and Christian) denominations than did the seaport cities of Charleston and Mobile, as well as New Orleans and Galveston. More important was the fact that the white civic elite of hinterland cities were most often Methodist, while the white civic elite of seaport cities were more often Episcopalian.[6] (See tables 1. 1 and 1.2.)

Inland cities seemed to allow greater upward social mobility; newcomers who ventured into the trades of wholesale produce, dry goods, lumber, iron, textiles, and other manufacturing interests seized opportunities to rise to positions of commercial and civic leadership. Many of these young men and their wives belonged to the less prestigious but faster growing Baptist and Methodist churches. Despite the fact that in 1916 92.4 percent of Baptists and 89.8 percent of Methodists still resided in the countryside, in cities that sprang up out of the farming hinterlands Baptists and Methodists flourished.[7]

Coastal cities saw greater numbers of Catholics and a more sizable Episcopal presence. In each of the seaboard cities in 1906, the largest percentage of white Protestants were Episcopalians, followed in three cities by Lutherans and members of the Methodist Episcopal Church [North]. In all but Mobile, Baptists and members of the Methodist Episcopal Church, South, were the least prevalent. Seaboard cities had higher percentages of Irish and German Catholics and other immigrant groups than did the interior cities of the South (Kentucky and Texas excepted). A more tolerant attitude toward drinking prevailed in cities where seamen found recreation and, on another level, where urbanites easily adopted the habits of Europeans.[8] Status belonged, moreover, to the more firmly entrenched social elites who were primarily of the nonevangelical denominations; in Protestant circles this usually meant Episcopalian.[9]

In its religious composition between 1880 and 1920, Galveston more nearly resembled the coastal cities of Charleston, Mobile, and New Orleans. By 1906, Galveston Roman Catholics outnumbered Protestants three to one, but few Catholics achieved elite status. Of the city's Protestants, Episcopalians were the most

TABLE 1.1. Protestant Denominations by Inland City, 1906

Denomination	Atlanta (%)	Nashville (%)	Louisville (%)	Memphis (%)	Montgomery (%)	Houston (%)	Dallas (%)
Baptist	19.5	11.6	16.8	8.6	9.4	9.1	17.7
M.E.C.S.	21.4	22.1	8.9	17.6	12.4	19.9	19.4
Dis. Ch.		10.8	8.4	4.2	2.5	4.9	9.8
Pres. U.S.	7.5	8.5	6.3	9.9	5.1	8.4	7.0
Episcopal	4.3	4.1	5.9	7.1	4.4	8.3	5.6
G.E.			15.2			3.1	
Total Protestant population	53,644	37,908	60,680	31,623	21,502	15,860	22,917
Total Catholic population	5,079	5,865	85,170	5,270	3,006	13,743	9,284

Source: U.S. Bureau of the Census, *Religious Bodies: 1906.* Pt. 1: *Summary and General Tables* (Washington, D.C., 1910), 410–494.

Notes: Totals include black congregants; with the exception of the Episcopal Church, white communicants only are included in percentages. Protestant totals include members above age twelve; Catholic totals include members above age nine.
Baptist = Baptist–Southern Convention
M.E.C.S. = Methodist Episcopal Church, South
Dis. Ch. = Disciples of Christ and Churches of Christ
Pres. U.S. = Presbyterian Church of the United States
Episcopal = Protestant Episcopal Church
G.E. = German Evangelical Synod of North America

numerous, and most of the white socially elite families were either Episcopalians, Presbyterians, or Jews. In 1906, 45.6 percent of Galveston Protestants belonged to the more liturgical Episcopal, Presbyterian, and Lutheran churches. White Baptists and Methodists comprised 33.5 percent of Protestants, but among them may be found fewer elite families. The remaining 20 percent of Protestants included African American Methodists and Baptists and members of an assortment of other churches. Because Galveston combined the dynamic elements of a young, rising New South city with the denominational and class structure of an older port city, it provides an opportunity to test and evaluate the origins of progressive women reformers whose attitudes were not informed or shaped by churches usually associated with the evangelical South.[10]

Here it may be best to sort out the meanings behind terms such as *evangelical* and *liturgical* in reference to churches. The South as a region has been labeled evangelical, meaning, in the words of Samuel S. Hill, that "the evangelical family of Christians is dominant." Evangelical churches hold to four basic convictions: the Bible is the ultimate authority; all people are naturally corrupted sinners, but God is accessible and all welcoming; morality is more an individual than a societal affair; and worship is informal and enthusiastic. Of the mainline southern Protestant denominations, Baptists, Methodists, and Disciples of Christ are considered

TABLE 1.2. Protestant Denominations by Port City, 1906

Denomination	Charleston (%)	Mobile (%)	New Orleans (%)	Galveston (%)
Baptist	5.1	7.1	2.6	9.7
M.E.C.S.	7.5	12.0	6.3	11.3
Pres. U.S.	4.5	6.6	9.9	7.2
M.E.C.	12.7		9.0	12.3
Lutheran	8.7(a)		13.6(b)	13.7(c)
Episcopal	14.3	12.7	14.0	23.2
Total Protestant population	20,030	19,451	36,875	5,504
Total Catholic population	7,602	13,579	148,579	14,872

Source: U.S. Bureau of the Census, Religious Bodies: 1906. Pt. 1: Summary and General Tables (Washington, D.C., 1910), 410–494.

Notes: Totals include black congregants; with the exception of the Episcopal Church, white communicants only are included in percentages. Protestant totals include members above age twelve; Catholic totals include members above age nine.
Baptist = Baptist–Southern Convention
M.E.C.S. = Methodist Episcopal Church, South
Pres. U.S. = Presbyterian Church of the United States
M.E.C. = Methodist Episcopal Church [North]
Lutheran = (a) United Synod of the Evangelical Lutheran Church in the South; (b) Evangelical Lutheran Synodical Conference of America and Evangelical Joint Lutheran Synod of Ohio and Other States; (c) General Council of the Evangelical Lutheran Church in North America and Evangelical Lutheran Synod of Iowa and Other States
Episcopal = Protestant Episcopal Church

evangelical. In rural areas, many Presbyterian churches fall into this category as well. Liturgical churches follow a pattern of worship that is formal, that is guided by a common liturgy, and that includes the celebration of the eucharist, often on a weekly, sometimes daily, basis. This is especially true for the Roman Catholic church. Among Protestant denominations, the Episcopal and Lutheran churches fall under this definition. Presbyterian churches by strict definition are considered classical or stemming from the Reformation, though heavily influenced by evangelicalism. In Galveston, Presbyterian churches appeared to be more like the liturgical denominations with their reserved form of worship. There is a sense in which the entire point of the worship service in an evangelical setting is to bring the unconverted to Christ, while the worship service in a liturgical setting is more focused on the worship experience of those already converted. That is, the difference is one of both mood and emphasis. Yet all denominations in the South have to a degree been subject to evangelical influences—all reach out to the unchurched through missionary efforts, Sunday schools, and youth programs.[11]

This discussion of New South cities, male elites, and denominational differences is relevant to the study of white southern women activists and reformers, most of whom were wives, daughters, and sisters of men wielding commercial or political power. Before 1900 in those interior cities and towns where Baptists and Methodists predominated and their members achieved upper-middle- and upper-class status, women of the evangelical missionary societies and the Woman's Christian Temperance Union (WCTU) were accorded positions of leadership within white women's clubs and associations. But in Galveston, and possibly in other southern seaport cities, Baptist and Methodist women seldom achieved elite status and, therefore, did not generally participate in the leadership of women's reform organizations beyond those with a religious orientation. In Galveston, most white female civic activists emerged from Episcopal and Presbyterian churches and the oldest Jewish synagogue. What this study suggests is that elitism more than evangelicalism drove the southern women's reform movement, especially in such secular reforms as the equal suffrage movement.[12] It also suggests that when studying the composition of such movements, we must take into consideration not only denominational predominance in cities but also geographic and economic factors, class structure, and opportunities for upward social mobility.

In the 1880s, Frances Willard, president of the Woman's Christian Temperance Union, toured the South and encouraged southern women, mostly from Baptist and Methodist churches, to form unions, creating an alliance for the first time with a national women's organization. Motivated by basic human compassion and perfectionist theological tenets to engage in public reforming activities and, yet, frustrated over unresponsive legislatures, southern evangelical women found that they needed the vote to effect their plans. Historians have depicted evangelical women moving from the protected enclosures of Baptist and Methodist churches to the more worldly realm of public prohibition. Recognizing the difficulty of enacting reform by moral suasion and the unlikelihood of prohibition legislation passing without the vote, the WCTU endorsed woman suffrage as early as 1879. A number of WCTU members joined the ranks of the suffragists secure in the goal of perfecting the community and guarding the home. A model emerges of southern women issuing forth from evangelical societies to join the WCTU and then marching toward membership in their state's Equal Suffrage Association.[13]

This structural model helps to explain how women from a religiously conservative South were able to foster women's social reform movements that addressed the problems of intemperance, child labor, prison reform, early childhood education, and the white slave traffic without abandoning an evangelical heritage. It has the advantage of providing an ideological explanation for the coexistence of such diverse elements as foreign mission, prohibition, and suffrage societies. Through direct conversion experiences, belief in the perfectability of men and women, and hope of adoption of domestic values, evangelical women were encouraged to follow the path already outlined toward reform. This model may very well help to describe some female reform activities at the state level, in communities where Methodists and Baptists predominated, or where the WCTU was organized early and grew vigorously. But the South is not monolithic, and the model does not account for the origins of women's activism and reform in many New South cities, including Galveston.[14]

Galveston belied the stereotype of the Bible Belt; it was a coastal city that tolerated gambling dens, bordellos, and saloons. Hence, evangelical women's mission societies and the WCTU had a difficult time getting established there and played virtually no role in the creation of a coterie of volunteer progressive female reformers in Galveston. The WCTU never enjoyed the popularity there that it did in interior Texas cities, in part because there were fewer members of evangelical denominations in Galveston, and because in this port city, saloons, as well as immigrants' drinking customs, were accepted as too profitable to oppose. Moreover, Methodists and Baptists, who were largely of the middle and lower-middle classes, provided most of the membership of the WCTU, giving that organization a middle-class but not an elite status.

In Galveston, the foundations of white women's reform rested on women's church societies that had actively pursued community relief for twenty years, women's benevolent institutions designed to care for the city's dependents — orphans, widows, and children of the factory district — and women's clubs, which educated women in a Progressive curriculum. Reform in Galveston was engendered by elite women from nonevangelical congregations who responded to the urban conditions peculiar to that city between the 1870s and 1920.

II

This history begins with a study of white elite and upper-middle-class Protestant women and their churches mainly because these women dominated the cultural, benevolent, and civic affairs of the city both prior to and after the turn of the century. But a question remains: Why did some white women in Galveston identify with civic reform movements or, more radical still, become suffragists and campaign openly in their communities for the right to vote? Understanding the evolution of activist women from domestic circles to churches and then to more public realms requires observing them in groups. Although individual women occasionally appear at center stage, reminding us that societies are really composed of unique persons, the focus remains on women's organizations formed mostly between 1880 and 1920. To comprehend more fully white Galveston women in all their particularities, including denominational membership, I devised a Galveston Women Database of 370 white activist women (see appendix A, "An Essay on Methodology"). With this data we are able to ask detailed questions about the origins and composition of the many women's organizations. Which churches and church societies served as forums for women's social activism? Did links exist between women's congregational societies and the asylums they founded, the literary clubs they initiated, or the progressive reform groups they created? What agents, agencies, or events helped women to organize? Who were these women, what was their economic status, and what experiences did they bring with them? And were there connections from pre-1900 benevolence and club work to a Progressive Era community of white women reformers?

A similar statistical study for African American women was impossible to complete because few records from black institutions survived the storm of 1900. Instead, I followed Galveston's African American history through black and white newspapers, white city directories, transcribed oral interviews, a few archived manuscript collections, mortuary ledgers, church records, and privately held records.

Perhaps more important to this study than to document all of the names of African American activists is to adumbrate the evolvement in Galveston of a women's community, an informal alliance of politically and socially active black women who challenged racism and sustained progressive reform.

When we focus on these two women's communities and the urban environment from which they evolved, patterns begin to emerge that may shape our understanding of the path that led to the southern women's Progressive movement. Also, by using this Gulf Coast city as a case study and by employing the technology devised by urban historians to complement the already well-established gender-related methodologies of women's historians, I hope to explore four broad yet interrelated themes regarding the emergence of southern women into public life — culture, community, religion, and reform.

For many white women, the pattern of their emergence into public activism followed a trajectory that began in the home and led to eventual evolvement from church to relief society to benevolent institution to women's club to civic activism and finally to the suffrage movement. For Jewish women living in Galveston, the pattern of evolution into public civic life was similar to that of elite Protestant women. This study found that very few Catholic and evangelical Protestant women joined in organized civic activism. Episcopal, Presbyterian, and Jewish women moved early into urban cultural and relief organizations and continued to maintain their interest in community affairs. Middle-class African American women also began their organizational life in churches, which remained the mainstay of the black community. There they taught Sunday school, led youth groups, organized missionary societies, founded ladies' aid societies, and formed literary clubs. Outside of their churches they created benevolent and charitable organizations. But once African American women began to organize civic clubs and associations, much of their work concentrated on countering the debilitating effects of segregation, which was increasingly imposed upon them after 1902. African American churches offered a far more radicalizing influence toward women's civic activism than did white churches.

The cultural world that upper- and middle-class women made for themselves in churches and in synagogues became the starting point from which they created benevolent institutions; literary, musical, and patriotic clubs; civic reform groups; and, finally, suffrage leagues. The concept of culture in this study evokes several meanings. If upper- and middle-class women did hold a culture or values of their own distinct from men, then it stemmed from the domestic world that they knew best and evolved outward to affect every institution they touched and every organization, club, or association they founded.[15] But culture has other meanings — it delineates the essence of a people's sense of themselves and may encompass expressions in music, art, and literature. It can include rituals that celebrate life and commemorate the dead; it may be seen in religious iconography and in the symbolism presented in parades and festivals. Galveston women used culture as an entrée into public life; they sought and won approval for their efforts from politically powerful men. Once citizens identified women with positive public contributions, fewer barriers were left to prevent them from actively engaging in civic reform movements. Cultural representations differed because of race, but the role women played in creating culture for their communities was an important dimension for both black and white women. Understanding the cultural element of women's public roles is integral to interpreting their aesthetic tastes and moral values, but it is even more important to discern culture's connection to civic reform.[16]

Mention of communities, which brings us to the third area of study, comes laden with many meanings. White women and most African American women created parallel roles vis-à-vis their male counterparts in community building. Women and men interacted with one another at all levels and in various organizations. Women, however, encountered the larger community of Galveston first by forming needed organizations and benevolent institutions that countered the business and political interests exhibited by men. Women seemed to care more about orphans, the elderly, and the education of preschool children. In the process of entering public life, they transformed it, altering it with organizational ideas and agendas that reflected their values and their worldview.

Other types of communities—women's communities—evolved out of their benevolent institutions and club life. This can be seen in much bolder relief after 1900, when the crucible of the great hurricane brought women activists together to create white and black progressive communities. They were clearly distinguishable from other coalitions of women within the city, in part because of their class structure and reforming goals. These two progressive women's communities were critical because they provided leadership for the city far out of proportion to their numerical representation and they helped to shape the public face and private resources of the city. Moreover, the white women's community was remarkable, not so much for its class and race privilege, but for its religious particularity—its willingness and ability to embrace Jewish as well as Episcopal and Presbyterian women and yet its reluctance to include Baptist, Methodist, Catholic, and African American women of roughly the same social and economic status.

III

The great storm of 1900 served as a catalyst for women's civic activism; out of destruction and ruin came a remarkable flowering of women's creative energy and organizational genius. White women founded the first Progressive Era civic reform organization, the Women's Health Protective Association, followed a decade later by the Galveston Equal Suffrage Association and the Young Women's Christian Association (YWCA). These three organizations provided a community of activists who greatly improved the health of the island, sought to help working women, and challenged men for the right to vote. But the storm's political consequences— for white male elites, for black officeholders, and for white women reformers— were equally important. In the aftermath of the storm, white elite businessmen consolidated the city's board of aldermen and mayor into a single five-member commission. This act virtually eliminated African American officeholding in Galveston and continued the process of concentrating white power in the hands of a few men. White women leaders, often related by birth or marriage to male leaders, were given far more attention as a nonthreatening political presence, and their issues, perhaps because they were promoted by white women, were given a hearing denied to blacks who sought similar consideration for their causes.

The elevation of white women into politics through the founding of the Women's Health Protective Association took place at the expense of African American men, who before 1900 had been a political counterweight to white control. Blacks as a political presence were replaced after 1900 by white women, not as voters, but as influential complements to the white power structure. The demand, therefore, for women's voting rights was never seriously challenged by city leaders because they saw in enfranchised white women political allies and compatriots. On the other hand, the threat of black women voting, which might have challenged white control, was reduced by such voting "reforms" as the poll tax and the white primary.

Along with this position of privilege for white women came undeniable notions of superiority. Their relative silence on issues of race, nonetheless, tells us something about their attitudes. Privately, white and black women spoke and interacted, many on a daily intimate basis in the homes of white employers, where African Americans worked as domestics, or in shops and stores, where the races might mingle. In semipublic discourse within women's clubs, benevolent societies, and civic organizations, however, the dialogue was either muted or nonexistent, and women's groups remained segregated. By excluding African American women from charitable institutions in the 1880s and 1890s, by not inviting dialogue with African American churchwomen or clubwomen in the Progressive Era, and by marching forward with a woman's agenda for the city but not fully including African Americans, white privileged women showed that they held the color line as firmly as did their male peers. Although sympathies may have existed toward African Americans, they were guarded, suggesting that white social concern had its limits.

As African Americans prospered in towns like Galveston before 1900, race relations became more strained, suggesting that white elites were uncomfortable with the economic competition, the political power, the educational advancement, and the struggle for equal citizenship that blacks exhibited. At precisely the time white women moved to contribute to the cultural climate of the city, black Republicans experienced a very visible struggle to maintain political ground. In many ways the heyday of black activism in Galveston rose and fell with the fortunes of one exceedingly bright political star, Norris Wright Cuney. But with his death in 1898 and with the diminishment of black voting rights through the poll tax and white primaries after 1902, there came a rather rapid decline in the political fortunes of black men.

The black community thereafter suffered the indignities of de jure segregation on street cars and in other public places and received paternalistic treatment with regard to school and library facilities. African American women, many of whom had achieved privileged status in their own community, showed remarkable resilience in an era of increasing discrimination. Thriving churches, women's church societies, women's clubs, festivals and celebrations, and vocal protests countered the demoralizing effects of disfranchisement of black male voters and segregation of public facilities. African American women, responding to the fact of segregated facilities, worked to mollify the worst aspects of it and, thus, after the turn of the century supported a progressive and race-conscious agenda of their own.

Attitudes of white elites toward white working-class men and women, though difficult at times to decipher, were not invisible. When privileged white women created relief societies, orphanages, old-age homes, and kindergartens for factory children in the 1880s and 1890s, they indicated a desire to shield working-class families, especially mothers and children, from the ravages of an uncertain economy. When they formed the YWCA in 1914, they indicated a concern for young single working women in the city. Although class differences remained and often presented a barrier to true understanding, white working-class women often evoked a sympathetic response from privileged women. Race solidarity played a role in the interaction, but so did a desire to see the transmission of middle-class values to working-class families.

The story of the emergence of a southern Progressive movement, which we more often see in regional studies, is here captured at the local level. Few studies of reform movements in the South have given much attention to the urban environment as a catalyst, particularly for organized women. This book attempts to understand in rather close detail how the movement for change by women in the South played out in a local setting where they lived and worked. Southern women, who may have been slow to respond to national entreaties for a social gospel movement or a feminist revolution, were, nonetheless, stirred to action on behalf of their own communities. The surprising results of this study show that women became politicized even as they continued their roles as guardians of traditional domestic values. At the same time, regional attitudes toward race and class prevailed wherever slavery had existed. White women, however subtly, played the race card to their advantage in gaining political power. African American women countered this with resilience and an investment in their own community. Galveston offers us something of a laboratory for understanding the complexities of gender and race. What follows is a more detailed description of the city and the crisis that created a Progressive Era Galveston.

PART ONE

· ·

GILDED AGE GALVESTON

. . . .

DISASTER STRIKES THE ISLAND CITY

Safe upon the solid rock the ugly houses stand:
Come and see my shining palace built upon
the sand!

—Edna St. Vincent Millay, "Second Fig"

The city of Galveston in 1900 shimmered off the coast of the Gulf of Mexico, a tiny jewel precariously perched on the edge of the continent. Vulnerable to tropical heat and storms, Galveston rested at the end of a long, slender, low-lying island off the coast of Texas. On the gulf side of the island, sandy beaches beckoned summer visitors by the hundreds; on the north side of the island facing Galveston Bay, shipping wharves, a railroad, grain elevators, and warehouses brought in teaming workers and proclaimed the city's busy commercial life. In between the beaches and the wharves stood monuments to prosperity: banking houses, the cotton exchange and trade center, a U.S. customshouse, and a commercial emporium called simply The Strand. Here also lived the city's 38,000 residents, a few in elegant mansions, most in modest, even humble, dwellings. Some said the island was little better than a sandbar, "a mere wave-built cay or key—made by the waves of average storms during a few centuries."[1] But Galveston had a history, an elegance, and a style that set it apart. To Texans the city that sprang up out of the gulf symbolized the amazing growth and prosperity of the Lone Star State in the aftermath of the Civil War.

"Galveston is primarily a seat of good living," noted Julian Ralph, a roving reporter for *Harper's Weekly* in 1895.[2] So tourists, visitors, and residents had been saying for years. Edward King made the same discovery more than twenty years earlier when on his grand tour of the postwar South he described Galveston as enchanting—"a thriving city set down upon a brave little island which has fought its way out of the depths of the Gulf, and given to the United States her noblest beach, and to Texas an excellent harbor. . . . It is a city in the sands; yet orange and myrtle, oleander and delicate rose, and all rich-hued blossoms of a tropic land shower their wealth about it."[3]

There were some detractions to be sure. Tropical storms, hurricanes, epidemics, and insects all plagued the island at one time or another. One visitor complained, "You have to tie yourself in bed at night to keep the cockroaches and other insects from carrying you off bodily. And I am told the 'skeeters' soon eat up a bar [mosquito net] trying to get at you. If you attempted to sleep without a bar, I can truly say, there would be nothing but the bones of a person left in the morning." Bouts of yellow fever scourged the island from time to time; the last really nasty episode occurred in July 1867; eleven hundred people were carried away by a disease brought in by migrants from other infected areas. When Thomas Seargent penned these words, he had no idea they would be among his last: "The fever is getting pretty bad indeed—we had twenty-four burried [sic] on Saturday; about the same Sunday and today I fear it will be equally as fatal." Amelia Barr, living behind a military encampment that fateful summer, dolefully recorded, "I saw long lines of carts filled with rude boxes and tarred canvas pass the house. They were carrying the dead to the long trenches. . . ." Her family of seven all contracted yellow fever; she lost her husband and her only two sons in the epidemic. Years later she dubbed Galveston, the "city of dreadful death." Storms, of course, were an ever-present danger, and Galveston's history is so closely tied to hurricanes that it inspired one author to lament: "Galveston has an implacable enemy. Like Torre Annunziata and Herculaneum, the great seaport lives in the shadow of possible destruction."[4]

Despite the dangers, Galveston found plenty of admirers, and the city grew charming in its recovery after the Civil War. Its attractiveness was built upon several foundations: a mild climate, sandy beaches, fertile soil, a good harbor, admirable mercantile prospects, and enterprising people for whom commerce was only one pursuit in life.

The Gulf Coast city sported a "salubrious" and healthy climate, where sea breezes usually tempered the heat from the Texas interior in summer and warmed the island in winter. "The heat is never disagreeably intense in Galveston; a cool breeze blows over the island night and day," reported Edward King to the nation's readers.[5] He obviously had not experienced a 95-degree day in the middle of August, when most of the city's wealthier residents headed for the mountains of Virginia or for the Northeast. As in most southern towns close to the equator, heat plus an average forty-five inches of rain per year yielded summer days dripping with humidity. "An hour or two of pouring, beating, tropical rain, and then an hour or two of such awful heat and baleful sunshine, as the language . . . has no words to describe," complained Amelia Barr in 1867. In winter the occasional "Blue Norther" from the Midwest blew in cold so severe that twice in the city's history the bay froze. "It was the funniest sight in the world, as it was the first snow that any one had ever seen before," remembered Margaret Sealy Burton, daughter of prominent businessman George Sealy, of the 1886 freeze. "All sorts of costumes appeared and cow bells were tied onto horses attached to huge piano boxes turned upside down and filled with children going for a sleigh ride." Despite an occasional seasonal extreme, Galveston had the advantage of gulf winds to help warm the air to an average 49 degrees in winter and cool it to an average 87 degrees in summer.[6]

Thirty-one miles of sandy beaches, "laved by the restless waters," flanked the island in the days before concrete seawalls and stone riprap. "It is only a few steps from an oleander grove to the surf, the shell-strewn strand, and the dunes," wrote

King.[7] Leslie Brand informed his mother in Los Angeles that compared to the Pacific Ocean, the warm gulf waters provided splendid bathing. "The breakers roll in oftener and the water is much warmer. I remained in for an hour and enjoyed myself more than I ever did before in water. For I did not get cold. And then the numerous beaches make it exciting." Average water temperatures of 84 degrees made bathing in the gulf and the bay the most popular summer sport. Swimming was not the only recreation on the beaches. "From my window," wrote one island visitor, "I watch the sea all day, and in the afternoon I walk or drive on the finest beach in the United States." Promenades, horse and buggy rides, and later excursions by car on the hard sand delighted tourists and residents alike.[8]

Rich prairie soil for the sustenance of oleander groves, chinaberry trees, colorful gardens, and overarching oaks kept the city shaded and roseate. "On the whole it is a very pretty place, . . . [with] large and beautiful lawns and lovely flowers and shrubbery. . . . Oleanders can be seen bordering sidewalks nearly everywhere," noted one sojourner. So abundant were the colorful shrubs that Galveston called itself the Oleander City. Others noticed the towering oaks shading visitors from the relentless sun. Julian Ralph praised the "marvelous abundance of . . . salt-cedar trees, . . . oleanders, magnolias, gums, palms, huge laurels, and cloudlike water oaks and live-oaks." He ended by declaring "her gardens . . . semi-tropical and gorgeous." Wollom's Lake, at the end of the West Broadway trolley line, provided a peaceful nature refuge from the city's bustling center. "Surrounded with trees, winding walks and overhanging boughs," the lake sported "gayly painted row boats [that] wended their way through the tiny canals. There were rustic bridges and islands for flower gardens and cages for scarlet and purple parrots. White swans and wild Mallard ducks swam about at ease and trailed the canoes for the cracker crumbs that the passengers threw to them." Margaret Sealy Burton opined that "it is almost impossible to visualize such beauty as once existed in this lovely city before the terrible devastation in 1900."[9]

Physical amenities aside, Galveston boasted the best harbor in Texas. The only deep water port between New Orleans and Tampico, Mexico, the city had since its beginnings in 1839 relied on the harbor and shipping for its prosperity. In the years before the Civil War, Galveston became the principal port of entry for the state. In 1854 wealthy citizens combined to form a Galveston Wharf Company, consolidating individually owned wharves into a profitable collective, one third of which was owned by the city. As Texas cotton production leaped forward in the postwar years, wharf owners and the city were in a position to benefit from the increased trade. Galvestonians foresaw their city's dependence on shipping and began to look for ways to improve the entrance to the harbor, which at times was obstructed by an annoying sandbar lurking twelve feet below the water's surface. In 1874, U.S. Army engineers began to build two jetties, extensions of the channel to the harbor, that jutted out into the Gulf of Mexico. The jetties were intended to help the tide and currents scour the channel of any sand, but the plan was not successful. Realizing that a massive project entailing federal funds would bring the necessary improvements, a Deep Water Committee, comprising leading Galveston entrepreneurs, petitioned both state and federal representatives for help in constructing a first-rate port. In 1890, Galveston citizens, led by Colonel William

L. Moody, who stood to gain a fortune in the cotton trade, secured $7.5 million in federal aid for the construction of a deep water port. After that, large vessels frequented the harbor and required the improvement of the Galveston wharves. The Galveston Wharf Company, owned partly by private interests and partly by the city, extended its wharves, built new warehouses and elevators, and earned the reputation "of having the best wharves and warehouse accommodations of any city." With deep water and improved wharves, Galveston by 1898 shipped 64 percent of the Texas cotton crop to world markets and by 1900 "was the leading cotton port of the nation."[10]

Shipping required railroads and steamship lines, and Galveston already had both. The Galveston, Houston, and Henderson rail line, which ran to Houston, was built in 1858 and by 1876 was in the hands of John Sealy, who standardized the track gauge, linking Galveston to the transcontinental railroads. Eventually the Gulf, Colorado and Santa Fe Railway—financed in part by citizens who resented the power Houston wielded over rail traffic—stretched from Kansas City to the Island City bringing grain, cattle, and cotton from the great Midwest. These were carried away in freighter vessels owned by various individuals and companies, among them the Texas and New York Steamship Company, Harris and Morgan line, and the C. H. Mallory line, which served the city for more than fifty years.[11]

Galveston led the way in technology that advanced business and improved living comfort. Communication from the island to markets outside the city and the state began in 1854 when the first telegraph service opened. Far more practical items came over the wire, however, as Galveston began to receive national weather reports. John Downey, as if forecasting dreadful events, wrote to his sister in 1885: "Before RR and telegraph lines we seldom knew of the weather far off until weeks or months. Now we hear all about the weather in extreme sections and are warned by signal service reports by telegrams and the signal lights (of different colors according to the weather looming) are seen all nights as a warning. . . . We know at once or in a few minutes, what weather to expect the coming day and ships stay in harbor till the danger is over." More advances came with the telephone. Galvestonians claimed that they introduced telephones to the state of Texas in 1878 and opened the first telephone exchange in 1879. The two earliest patrons were cotton brokerage firms, but within a month 101 subscribers had joined the telephone exchange, and in 1883 the first long distance service to Houston opened. Soon proprietors of smaller businesses, shops, and groceries, as well as the police station found the telephone a valuable asset, especially when the idea caught on for home use. Gas for heating and artificial lighting came to the city in 1856; electrification superseded gas in January 1882 when the Brush Electric Light Company cranked up twenty-eight arc lamps at the old ice house at Twenty-Sixth and Post Office streets. John Downey fairly exulted: "We have electric lights over most of the city except when we have bright moonshine." Businesses, city street lamps, trolley cars, and homes were all using the "new urban power source" by 1891.[12]

The harbor, railroads, shipping lines, and communication networks provided excellent export-import prospects for enterprising capitalists. Dry goods wholesalers and retailers, printers and lithographers, book binders, furniture dealers, piano sellers, jewelers, luggage purveyors, and boot and shoe makers, not to mention the more commonly found butchers, grocers, cigar and tobacco vendors, liquor sellers, coal dealers, dressmakers, grain dealers, and auctioneers, all benefited from the city's premier trading position. A sizable commercial base preceded the Civil War, when entrepreneurs like Henry Rosenberg, George Ball, Joseph Osterman, James Moreau Brown, John Henry Hutchings, and John Sealy began trade that carried over into the postwar period. With commercial opportunities flowing into town, the wholesale and retail business worth approximated $50 million by 1885. Successful businesses, such as Marx and Kempner wholesalers, Clarke and Courts printers, and the Galveston Dry Goods Company, continued to grow, adding to their capital stock, their facilities, and their prospects for trade in the greater South and Midwest. As Walter Grover reminisced, the "Strand [was] lined with next-door to next-door wholesale business houses that supplied not only all of Texas but the western part of Louisiana, Arkansas, Indian Territory, New Mexico and the Northern part of Old Mexico, with all the merchandise and commodities they needed." The result, he found, was that within fifteen years after the Civil War the city had become wealthy, "with more millionaires than any city of comparable size." Boosterism aside, statistics show that long-term prospects for the city were indeed good. Galveston in 1915 (even after the hurricane destruction of 1900) exported nearly $230 million worth of cotton, cattle, grain, and crude oil while importing more than $10 million in manufactured items and luxuries.[13]

Cotton, of course, was the major export item. As railroads began to enter Texas, linking the interior of the state with cities to the north and east, Galveston merchants sought ways to keep cotton flowing through their hands rather than through factors in midwestern cities. In 1873, twelve cotton brokers gathered and formed the Galveston Cotton Exchange. They adopted standards of classification, adjusted controversies between members, and maintained uniform rules, regulations, and usages, thereby collectively helping Galveston's up-and-coming cotton dealers. Soon after, the Exchange contracted with the Western Union Telegraph Company for service at a cost of $565 per month; thus, the brokers were connected by telegraph to world cotton markets.[14]

The moment of Galveston's departure from frontier status to sophisticated city came in 1879, when wealthy citizens dedicated the new Cotton Exchange Building, an ornate, four-story structure at the corner of Twenty-first and Mechanic streets. A formal ball, the society spectacle of the year, marked the occasion. Wives and daughters of the city's elite, as if to announce their own entrance into a world of respectability, danced in finery never before seen in this southern town. Ten years later, members changed the name to Galveston Cotton Exchange and Board of Trade, indicating that the Exchange had expanded to include a market for futures and for wholesalers of grain, coffee, and produce. Brokerage firms within the Exchange prospered until "exports reached the 1 million bales mark in 1891." Out of the Exchange developed the Galveston Maritime Association, a company of ship agents who inspected cotton for its uniformity. "It is an age of venture and recklessness," wrote one fellow working in a cotton brokerage on the Strand, "it is the rule rather than the exception for men to steal themselves rich when opportunity offers. . . . It requires a firm and fixed character to go safely through the strife and take the position of 'poor but honest' and to follow the 'golden rule.'"

Whether acquired honestly or ruthlessly, fortunes were made through cotton and its related industries for a few enterprising Galvestonians: William Moody, P. J. Willis, Julius Runge, J. G. Goldthwaite, William F. Ladd, and Bertrand Adoue, to name a few.[15]

Cotton factoring and brokering gave rise to another lucrative business: compressing. Competition swelled in the postwar boom between cotton press owners, many of whom forged companies as newly invented mechanical devices improved the compression of bales. With the invention of the Taylor press in 1876, vessels were able to carry 25 percent more cotton. By 1893, five major cotton presses worth more than $1 million were able to handle 6,000 bales a day, 300,000 bales a year; employ 550 men; and store cotton in warehouses that covered fourteen city blocks. Without exaggeration, in postwar Galveston, cotton was king.[16]

Railroading, shipping, merchandising, and cotton factoring brought in enough capital for Galveston to become a banking center as well. The interdependence of commerce and banking dates to the antebellum period, when banks, especially those controlled outside the state, were looked upon with suspicion by Texas legislators. Banking houses in Texas's early years were more likely extensions of cotton factor and commission houses. By 1866, Galveston banking concerns were complying with the 1862 federal National Banking Act, and legitimate banking houses opened on the Strand, the city's main trading street. The First National Bank, founded in 1866, "commenced business with a cash capital of $200,000, with authority to increase to $500,000." In 1869 the directors elected to the bank presidency Henry Rosenberg, whose business acumen and enormous philanthropic gifts to the city are now legendary. The local but important Ball, Hutchings & Company (later Hutchings, Sealy & Company), which opened as a banking enterprise in the 1850s, by 1885 was rated as "having greater resources than any bank in the South." It was responsible for taking the plans for the Gulf, Colorado & Santa Fe Railroad in hand in 1879 and seeing the road to completion; it continued its financial interests in the Galveston Wharf Company and handled accounts for cotton, grain, and other staple commodities in connection with shipping. Cotton and banking joined hands in the firms of W. L. Moody & Company; in City National Bank, founded in 1907 by William L. Moody, Jr.; and in the Texas Bank and Trust Company, which later became United States National Bank under Isaac H. Kempner. The three principal families of wealth in twentieth-century Galveston — Sealy, Moody, and Kempner — were tied directly to banking.[17]

Some of Galveston's wealth spilled over into industries and manufacturing, but the city never claimed manufacturing as one of its primary commercial pursuits. In 1880 Galveston ranked among the lowest ten in the top 100 manufacturing cities of the nation; its net product reached just over $1 million. City manufactories did increase in the years between 1880 and 1900 from 170 establishments to 295, and the additional establishments more than doubled the labor force and the gross value of products. Galveston supported a brewery, a baggage and cordage company, several cotton oil mills, a vinegar and pickle works, a cracker company, a candy factory, several foundries, and ice and cold storage plants. City manufactories made hats, soap, barrels, bricks, asphalt, sashes and blinds, brooms, lime, and apple cider. Texas Star Flour and Rice Mills, which processed grains for shipment to the West Indies and Central America, became one of the largest food processing mills in the state. The Galveston Cotton and Woolen Mills, a West End (of the island) manufacturing plant headed by local elites, provided employment for 650 textile workers, most of whom earned pitiful wages for long hours of tedious work. The fact that Galveston had so few of these textile sweat shops (and the Galveston Cotton and Woolen Mills closed before 1900) added somewhat to the illusion that life in the city was pleasant for almost all of its citizens. Most manufacturers served the local market by supplying the city with such necessities as boots, saddles and harnesses, clothing, bread and confections, furniture, guns and locks, smithing of all sorts, printing and publishing, carpentering, carriages and wagons, bottling works, cooperage, tombstones, lumber, and ironworks.[18]

For skilled workmen Galveston offered multiple avenues of employment on ships, wharves, railroads, ironworks, and in carpentry, metalwork, and in lumber mills. The proliferation of trade unions toward the end of the century gives a clue to the diversity of the laboring population. Among the strongest and oldest were the Screwmen's Benevolent Associations, separate organizations for blacks and whites, which protected the interests of men who stowed bales of cotton in the holds of ships. Longshoremen, pilots, typesetters, tailors, painters, marine engineers, tinsmiths, mechanics, sheet iron and cornice workers, boilermakers, and barbers, to name a few, had formed some thirty trade unions by 1895. But most of the unskilled remained unorganized as manufactories increased in number. Industries employed 1,600 workers in 1890 and more than 2,000 in 1900; among these were 333 women and 132 children. The average annual wages of the women were $235; the average salaries of the children were $171, compared to the 1,593 men who averaged $553 per annum. Over time the salaries decreased and the hours lengthened. In 1895, women textile workers earned ninety cents a day for a sixty-six-hour week, eleven and a quarter hours five days a week and nine and a quarter hours on Saturday. Owners docked their pay as much as five to fifteen cents for errors made usually at the end of their shifts. As more women entered the workforce, they did so at greatly reduced wages and in harsher conditions, which may help explain why Galveston also had a thriving red light district.[19]

Women with other skills found a slightly wider range of opportunity among the usual sex-segregated jobs. Eight midwives and five hairdressers advertised their services in the 1875 business directory. The millinery and dressmaking professions had "reached an exquisite degree of perfection . . . given the closest study by . . . ladies of rare taste"; so oozed Charles Hayes in 1883. Of the thirty-nine boarding houses listed in the business directory of 1881, thirty belonged to women. In this same decade more women owned private schools than did men, and more women in religious orders managed schools than did male clerics. Of the seventy teachers hired by the public school system in 1887, fifty-eight were women — fifty-one white women to four men; seven African American women to eight men. Of the six principals in white public schools, two were women. African American women, on the other hand, were outnumbered by male colleagues: male principals presided over all three "colored public schools." The only private school listed for African Americans in the city directory was owned by a man. Nobody said women had to be excluded from the commercial life of the city, and in 1881 one woman owned a tobacco store, another an oyster market, and two others coffee and chocolate stands; of the 105 grocery stores in the city, women owned seventeen. The truly lucrative businesses — cotton factoring, railroading, shipping, and banking — listed no women as owners or members of the boards of directors.[20]

Galveston's commercial base was a male enterprise, and, while wealth was mainly derived from cotton, shipping, and banking, such other concerns as law firms, insurance companies, newspapers, utility plants, waterworks, electric trolleys, hospitals, the public school system (1881), the University of Texas Medical School (1891), and fire and police departments all contributed to employment in a thriving city. Small shops, dairies, fishing businesses, drayage and livery services, mortuaries, and many more of the accoutrements of urban life provided income for hundreds of families.

As a seaport Galveston attracted a good number of merchant seamen and sailors who came ashore looking for adventure and usually found it in numerous "pleasure dens." The Reverend Ralph Albert Scull recalled that "the majority of the laborers drank and played cards"; he added candidly that saloon keeper "Ike Rector had a flourishing place at Post Office and 25th. Rector added the women to his place and did a rushing business." In 1880, Galveston offered up 489 liquor saloons — more saloons than any city of its size and more than any port on the Gulf Coast, including New Orleans. Disgruntled citizens voiced their complaints in newspapers to little avail: "Every one who lays claim to decency regards [the Belle Poole Saloon] as a nuisance and at times deafening noises emanate from its portals and shock the ears of pedestrians." Although the evidence is difficult to acquire, the Island City probably had as many as fifty-five brothels. Drunkenness and prostitution were illegal activities, but citizens tolerated vice, no doubt for the profits associated with these dens of iniquity. Instead of closing down houses of ill fame, police arrested the ladies of the night; the courts fined them and set them free, giving the city a little extra revenue. Through whatever means, Galvestonians by 1891 boasted that theirs was "the wealthiest city in the world of its size."[21]

On the other hand, Galvestonians were worshipful people. In 1900, the city claimed no fewer than forty-five congregations: eight black and four white Baptist churches; four black and four white Methodist churches; one black and four white Episcopal parishes; one black and four white Catholic parishes; four Presbyterian and three Lutheran churches, two Jewish synagogues, and an assortment of Disciples of Christ, Christian Scientists, Swedenborgians, and Spiritualists. Likewise, citizens enjoyed one another's company to the extent that they created several hundred societies and clubs. The city directory listed no fewer than sixty-five white church and synagogue societies (of which thirty-one were women's and twenty were youth's led by women), six charitable institutions (all managed by women), and clubs of every description for men and women. These listings do not begin to show the full extent of associational life in Galveston, for these directories seldom included the organizations of African Americans beyond churches and schools.[22]

Galveston by 1900 supported an urban elite accustomed to sophistications beyond the reach of most southerners. Those who belonged to this privileged group (probably less than 10 percent of the city's population) represented a greater cross section of the world's populace than one might think, as foreigners and Americans alike moved up from humble beginnings to wealthy status. A swell of immigrants entered the island in the 1850s; many stayed and were joined by others after the Civil War. Swiss-born Henry Rosenberg, Harris Kempner of Poland, Mor-ritz Kopperl of Moravia, Samson Heidenheimer of Württenberg, and J. L. Darragh of Ireland were just a few of the Europeans who added to the native-born American mix. Among African Americans, who composed approximately 20 percent of the city's population, Norris Wright Cuney and his brother Joseph should be consid-ered "aristocrats of color." Dr. Mary S. Moore, Dr. James Moore, Dr. J. H. Wil-kins, newspaper editors William H. Noble and W. H. Bearden, and educators John R. Gibson and the Reverend Ralph Albert Scull were representative of an educated black middle class. The city's ethnicity more heavily reflected the heri-tage of northern and western Europe than that of Mexico and Latin America; approximately 40 percent of Galveston's residents claimed English, German, Irish, or French ancestry, whereas the 1900 census shows only 156 foreign-born residents from Latin America.[23]

The German influence was so strong in Galveston that for years the Lutheran and German Catholic churches performed services in their native language; German newspapers flourished, and beer gardens, open to the public, hosted bands, family recreation, and, of course, beer. Schmidt's Garden "was planted out in large mulberry, chinaberry and straggling cedar trees. Under these were long tables and benches, a band stand was at one end of the garden where a splendid German Band played and there was an open dance floor, and swings for the little children, at the tables foaming glasses of beer could be had[,] sour kraut, wiener-wursts and liver sandwiches with heaps of pretzels." The Garten Verein Pavilion, built in 1876 as an exclusive social club by the "best German families," boasted membership by the city's white elite regardless of ethnicity. Margaret Sealy Burton remembered that every Wednesday afternoon and evening, her family and their servants went to enjoy the park; the children came "to play on the swings, see-saws, sliding pole or the trapeze." The young adults danced inside the pavilion to the tune of a "splendid orchestra." Young ladies showed off their finery of "ruffled organdies, point de sprit, lawns and embroidered East India princess frocks." The mothers, nurses, and grandmothers "sat under the spreading trees at green tables and yellow benches, listening to the music. . . . tiny tots sitting in their baby bug-gies, lined with pink and blue . . . bouncing up and down to the strains of the music." Often families brought their dinners in huge picnic baskets but were assisted by German waiters "with flowing yellow mustaches and red perspiring faces, carrying black trays with platters of cold meats, salads, and steins of beer. Their long white aprons flying out before them in the wind like bellied sails on a schooner."[24]

Travelers noted that the privileged classes were intent on making Galveston a city for living the good life southern style. To reach a state of gracious leisure required honing talents for amassing wealth with seeming ease. Julian Ralph found members of the prestigious Aziola Club, "well-to-do men of cosmopolitan tastes and experiences, gourmets, lovers of art and literature, music, and such ease as

FIGURE 1.1. Garten Verein Pavilion and Park before 1900. Courtesy Rosenberg Library, Galveston, Texas.

our best element gets in America, where every one works hard six days in the
week." Leslie Brand thought he had the last word on Galveston's denizens: "The
place strikes one as a sleepy, old fashioned, lazy and easy going little city, whose
inhabitants live for ease more than for money."[25] Actually, white-collar Galvestonians worked long hours to acquire a standard of living that allowed them to seem
at ease, affording them the appearance of cultured southern gentility. The point
was to make money as rapidly as possible so one could enjoy its fruits, build
architecturally interesting dwellings, travel, attend cultural events, invest in civic
benevolence, and be at home in polite society.

Cultural entertainments, many of them locally produced, added to the city's
image of refinement in this, "the most southern of all Texas cities." The Artillery
Ball, grandest and oldest of Galveston's exclusive events, resembled the St. Cecilia
Society Ball of Charleston for its exclusivity and snobbery and remained a gate-
keeper for the city's upper social classes. Mardi Gras, created for the masses but
enjoyed in exclusive parties by the wealthy, reminded longtime residents that Gal-

FIGURE 1.2. Garten Verein Pavilion and Park before 1900. Courtesy Rosenberg Library, Galveston, Texas.

veston was at heart a Catholic city, even if its civic leaders were mostly Protestant and Jewish. Beginning in 1867, Mardi Gras captured the romantic imaginations of young women fortunate enough to be invited to the masquerade ball. Invitations came by coach; Margaret Sealy Burton remembered "the blast of the long coach horn, from the trumpeter that stood at the back of the golden coach drawn by six snow white horses, as it dashed up to each favored door. . . . The herald, who delivered the golden card . . . was dressed in red velvet; the postillions were in silver cloth[,] and the King, as he sat inside, was [a] triumph in Turquoise satin, embroidered in heavily precious jewels. . . . It was a regular Cinderella coach . . . Oh! for the days of romance once more, roses, Valentines, and love letters of poetry, gallantry, chivalry, modesty and deference."[26]

Not everyone agreed. "There is a constant succession of attractions going on

in Galveston—I think more than is good for the quiet and prosperity of the pleasure seekers," counseled John Downey to his sister in North Carolina. "The theater
goes on all the winter and the Rolling Scating [sic] rink near the Beach Hotel has
been the cause for months[,] and in the summer Ball play in the Beach Park is
all the go[,] and even Sunday does not conflict with many of these amusements."
As the state's center of trade and culture, Galveston offered up theater at the
Tremont Opera House just after the war and at the Grand Opera House after
1895. Lawrence Levine writes that "the theater, like the church, was one of the
earliest and most important cultural institutions established in frontier cities." Performances by Lillie Langtry and Sarah Bernhardt dazzled genteel audiences, while
variety shows, minstrels, troubadours, circuses, and traveling performers offered
the masses of Galvestonians more excitement than did most southern towns. More
frequently, however, the city's histrionic societies, glee clubs, quartettes, and or-
chestras—filled with women—helped introduce "culture" to Galvestonians while
giving voice to local performers.[27]

The Island City had always provided spectacular palm tree and ocean vistas,
but, with the accumulation of wealth, its structural environment became equally
arresting. James Moreau Brown, a hardware store owner, banker, and president of
the Galveston, Houston & Henderson Railroad, in 1859 built the finest and most
expensive house on the island. Ashton Villa, a three-story brick Italianate "subur-
ban residence," cost $14,000, not including the $4,000 lots on the corner of Broadway and Twenty-fourth. It stands today, a museum home, a symbol of the wealth
that accumulated early in the city and carried over into the postwar years. With

FIGURE 1.3. Ashton Villa, built by James Moreau Brown in 1859. Courtesy Rosenberg
Library, Galveston, Texas.

war and depression behind them and with cotton bringing in unimaginable sums, antebellum elites, as well as postwar Galvestonians who achieved elite status, changed the architectural character of the city after 1873 to reflect the new prosperity. By then Nicholas Clayton, a native of Ireland, had arrived to begin his career creating solid buildings lightened by the ebullience of stone tracery. He was the first professional architect to remain in Texas; his initial design, the Block-Oppenheimer Building on the Strand, began his long commitment to embellishing the city's natural beauty. Over a period of thirty years he designed buildings for the mighty and the humble, from the Hutchings Sealy Bank building and the Gresham House (Bishop's Palace) to the city's poor farm. As architects added a touch of class to the commercial district, so too were common neighborhoods transformed. Elegant, fanciful, and thoroughly Victorian, the city's residential sections took on the flavor of the era of carpenter Gothic, as wooden gingerbread ornaments adorned simple frame houses. Architectural historians identify a typical Galveston style that included variations of Victorian design combined with the practical necessities of sleeping porches and galleries (verandas) for the warm climate. John Downey took pride in his "upstairs room with north and south galleries and doors and windows for the most delightful sea breeze,"and he gloried in his view of the "finest streets and Beach drives and street cars and the Gulf and ships and steamers, all in full view." With thousands of buildings in place by 1900, surrounded by an azure sea and a calm harbor, Galveston resembled a glistening jewel—a "shining palace built upon the sand."[28]

There was little to suggest that 1900 would prove to be the worst year of Galveston's history or that the city would receive a blow from which it would never entirely recover. As in most midsized towns, citizens of the Island City had welcomed the new century with romantic expectations of renewed prosperity. The twentieth century—the modern century—promised a continuation in growth. City population had climbed from a mere village of 7,000 in 1860 to a city of 38,000 in 1900. The depression of the 1890s was over, William McKinley and fiscal conservatism reigned in Washington, and businessmen glowed expectantly over the prospects of increased trade. Since cotton production was on the rise, importers and traders saw nothing but high times ahead. Nobody guessed that the good fortune of the principal port city of Texas would be devastated by the weather.

Newspaper accounts just prior to the storm of September 8, 1900, gave no hint of the disaster to follow. Headlines chronicled the news: Americans were concerned over Russian aggression in northern China and feared the threat of attack by Chinese Boxers in Peking. While the U. S. government had committed 5,000 Americans troops to China, in another part of the world the Taft Commission had declared the Filipinos incapable of ruling themselves. On the domestic front, the papers showed concern over William Jennings Bryan running again on the Populist and Democratic tickets. Locally, city officials quibbled over the latest census report that placed the city at 37,789 citizens—too low a figure according to the compilers of the Galveston city directories. No headline indicated that a cataclysm was approaching. No front-page weather reports of impending disaster penetrated the calm.[29]

FIGURE 1.4. Bishop's Palace, built by Walter Gresham in 1893. Courtesy Rosenberg Library, Galveston, Texas.

News that a storm was brewing in the Caribbean reached the island as early as Tuesday, September 4. By Friday, September 7, the storm, now a hurricane, was in the Gulf of Mexico and storm-warning flags went up as Dr. Isaac M. Cline, chief of the Galveston Weather Bureau, issued news of the approaching hurricane to telephone callers. No defenses lined the coast except for a few salt cedars planted at shore's edge; no seawall protected the densely packed houses upon an island whose elevation stood no higher than nine feet at its tallest point. No lessons had been learned from the hurricane of 1875 that brought winds of over 100 miles per hour and left 176 dead.[30] The city stood naked and vulnerable to nature's cruel might.

Saturday morning brought mother-of-pearl skies and a mild wind that reached twenty-four miles per hour by 10 A.M. Isaac Cline noted that the barometer was dropping and the tide had begun to invade the lowest parts of the island. Worried, he harnessed his horse and wagon and rode up and down the beaches warning playful sightseers of the danger that lurked at sea. Although the temperature at 11 A.M. was a pleasant 82.8 degrees, heavy rain began to fall; the barometer at 29.417 was still plummeting, and winds of thirty miles per hour whipped the red and black storm warning flags atop the Levy Building. By 2 P.M. the tide, now six feet above normal and driven by a north wind, slammed against the wharves and railroad tracks facing Galveston Bay. The last train filled with unsuspecting passengers drove into the city sometime after noon; none followed because the tracks on the west end of the bay went under water, effectively cutting off the island from the mainland.[31]

The flooding of homes and businesses began that afternoon. When the waters came over the doorsill of her home, Louisa Rollfing begged her husband to find them a safer place. He hired a driver and buggy, who took Louisa and their three children toward the West End to relatives. "It was a terrible trip, we could only go slowly for the electric wires were down everywhere. . . . We got as far as 40th Street," but "the water was so high . . . the horse was up to his neck in [it.]" John Newman reported that the waters in the streets of the business section came up to his waist. Ida Austin, who only the night before had given a "beautiful and well-attended moonlight fete" at her home on Market Street, heard a man running and shouting, " 'My God! The waters of the bay and the gulf have met on Fifteenth Street.' . . . In an incredibly short time," she noted, the salt water "surged over the gallery driven by a furiously blowing wind. Trees began to fall[;] slate shingles, planks and debris of every imaginable kind were being hurled thro the air. We brought our cow on the gallery to save her life," she wrote, "but soon had to take her in the dining room where she spent the night." Ida Austin opened all the doors of her house and let the water flow in. Three feet of salt water covered the downstairs floors; the wind ripped at the frames, blinds, sashes, and draperies, leaving no protection from the driving rain. Water poured in through the damaged upstairs windows and then dripped through to the lower levels bringing down a mess of plaster and paper.[32]

Wind velocity increased to possibly 120 miles per hour that evening. The wind gauge atop the weather bureau registered 100 miles per hour before blowing away at 5:10 P.M. The barometer dropped to 28.48 inches, its lowest point, between 8 and 9 P.M. on September 8, but the storm raged on until morning. Louisa Rollfing and her three children found refuge with relatives, where they nailed ironing boards and table tops across the doors and windows downstairs. As the water rose inside the house, the families retreated to the upstairs hall, where they witnessed the devastation. "We soon heard the blinds and windows break in the rooms upstairs. . . . It sounded as if the rooms were filled with a thousand little devils, shrieking and whistling. In the rooms downstairs the furniture, even the piano, slid from one side of the room to the other and then back again." The kitchen broke off from the house when the water reached seven feet inside, and finally the whole house jolted off its pillars, but the families remained unharmed. Henry M. Wolfram, after securing safety for his wife and children in a brick building, returned to his home only to find it lurching off its foundations. He managed "to grasp the rafters" and there spent the next five hours.[33]

Not all were as fortunate. In the howling darkness homes were shattered, their occupants flung into the roily sea, some to survive, many to perish beneath the collapsing structures. Isaac M. Cline, after warning citizens of the impending disaster, found his own home at Twenty-fifth Street and Avenue Q in trouble. The water climbed ten feet above ground until finally, knocked off its base by debris, wind, and water, the house with fifty sojourners inside collapsed into the sea. Thirty-two of the fifty, including his wife, drowned. Later, workers recovered the body of Mrs. Cline under the structure that had once been her home. Cline, along with his three children and brother, clung to the floating debris for three hours, dodging flying timbers, resisting tearing wind and rain, hoping to find shelter in the utter darkness. Cline reports that many people were "killed on top of the drifting debris by flying timbers after they had escaped from their wrecked homes." At St. Mary's Catholic Orphanage, next to the sea on the island's West End, Mother Superior Camillus prepared the children for rescue by tying several of them together with pieces of clothesline. But before 8 P.M. the roof blew in on the innocents, and the orphanage vanished completely, ninety-one of the children and all ten of the sisters gone. One of the sisters was found with nine orphans tied to her cincture. Two other sisters' bodies were found at the far north end of Galveston Bay. Three teenage boys, sole survivors of the orphanage, were thrown into the water and managed to stay afloat on a drifting tree for two days.[34]

Others were luckier; they found safety in the city's more substantial houses and public buildings. Ashton Villa, at Broadway and Twenty-fourth, one of the highest points of the island, became a sturdy refuge for those who could make it to her doors. Even so, the flood waters climbed to six feet inside the first floor. Down the street the Sealy mansion, Open Gates, was transformed into a way station for 400. The Tremont Hotel, near the Strand, sheltered 1,000 people; the Union Passenger Station housed 100. Henry Johnson recalled running away from his collapsing boarding house on Avenue I, grabbing a broom to push away floating debris as he made his way to rescue teams. "Dere was a lot of de men what live in de neighborhood helping de people to leave. . . . Dere was one thing 'bout those men, white or colored it didn' make no diffrunce wit' 'em. Dey treat 'em all 'like." Johnson was taken to the train station where he observed "white people an' colored people . . . all bundled up dere together." Daniel Ransom formed a one-man rescue operation. He had built his own home on Avenue R near the beach and practiced swimming across the bay from the island to the mainland. The house began to rock about four o'clock that afternoon, when he jumped into the water and swam out over his picket fence into the maelstrom. "I swam for two and one-half hours and rescued forty-five people from houses that had blowed down or was just about to, and swam with them to a brick building where hundreds of people were." Finally, John Newman found refuge in a "public house" near the Strand. He recounts, "As I stood on the floor the water reached me up to my neck, and the barman was standing on the counter serving customers with drinks. Talk about devotion to duty!" Newman stayed only long enough to fill his flask with brandy; venturing out into the night, he swam until he could climb onto the upstairs balcony of a private home. He talked his way into the house, paid thirty cents for a room with a bed, and slept the rest of the night "whilst outside, the elements seemed to have gone stark crazy."[35]

Catholic churches, hospitals, convents, and monasteries took in more refugees than any other temporary asylums. St. Mary's Infirmary became a hospice not only for its own patients but also for the patients of the county hospital, many of whom were carried a quarter of a block to safety through waist-deep water. Sacred Heart Church and St. Mary's University, which adjoined each other, secured 400 refugees. The Ursuline Convent gathered 1,000 people into its sheltering walls, including four women in labor who delivered live babies in the midst of the howling storm. The infants were christened immediately as no one could foresee the outcome of that dreadful night. While death pulled many into its grasp, life forces, sometimes in astonishing ways, resisted. One child, William Henry Heideman, born that night represents the triumph of life. His mother, in the throes of labor, was tossed out into the waters after her house collapsed. She landed on a cottage roof but was thrown from the roof into a floating trunk where she traveled with the current until colliding into the convent walls. Rescuers brought her into the convent and several hours later William Henry was born. Meanwhile, Mrs. Heideman's brother, trapped in a tree outside the convent, heard the cry of a child afloat and caught the little fellow by the hand. It was Mrs. Heideman's other son. Again rescuers brought the pair into the safety of the convent where the family—what was left of it—reunited.[36]

When the survivors emerged from their shelters Sunday morning, they were greeted by the pealing bells of the Ursuline convent amidst scenes of incredible destruction. Sarah Littlejohn, daughter of school principal E. G. Littlejohn, described in wonderment the view from her home at Thirty-seventh Street and Avenue O 1/2: "We looked out of the window and of all the beautiful homes that were between our house and the beach not one was left. It is just a clean sweep; nothing but desolation." When Louisa Rollfing's husband reached their own neighborhood, he found, "Nothing! Absolutely nothing! The ground was as clear of anything as if it had been swept, not even a little stick of wood or anything for blocks and blocks." Gid Sherer exaggerated only slightly when he wrote that "every house in the East End went in the storm, except a few large Buildings. You would not know the city now if you should see it." Henry Wolfram, grateful that his family had survived, wrote sadly, "Here we stand father, mother and seven children, looking upon the ruins of our once cozy home, all that was left us, excepting the few clothes upon our backs and barefooted. . . . The period of our married life, its cherished accumulations, all these years of toil , thrift, devotion and ambition, to see them ruthlessly crushed and torn from us, the feelings, the emotions and all that this inspires, is best imagined by you, than pictured by me." Despite his sorrow, he knew he had been lucky; among those he met the morning after the storm, many who had ventured out to help others had lost their entire families and were left to recover alone.[37]

Sunday dawned bright and pleasant as if to mock the horror over which the day presided. "Oh what a glorious morning it was," wrote John Newman.

> The sun spread its golden robe over a new creation. . . . huge areas were entirely denuded of houses and trees, and the general aspect completely changed. Here and there were tangled masses of telephone wires and overhead electric cables. Huge piles of timber flung here, there, and everywhere by the raging elements during the previous night—demolished human dwelling houses, stables, byres, and warehouses, under which were buried beneath the debris both man and beast. Sorrow and sadness everywhere. Parents searching for their children, among the dead and injured. Weeping children looking for their parents. Husbands inquiring for their wives, and heartbroken almost hysterical women [searching] for their beloved ones.[38]

Survivors sought food while those who had not lost their all, including hotel kitchens and cafes, proffered nourishment to the destitute. Cook stoves still standing were put to work and smells of coffee wafted across the sodden ruins.

Nothing like this had happened to any American city. The storm killed at
least 6,000 of 38,000 citizens in a fifteen-hour period. It demolished or damaged
beyond repair approximately 4,000 or nearly two-thirds of the city's structures, and
it destroyed between $17 and $30 million worth of property. Water had completely
covered the island and flooded the city to a level, in some places, of fifteen feet
when the tide from the Gulf of Mexico met Galveston Bay.[39]

Not a single public structure in Galveston escaped damage. The hurricane
blew away the bridges to the mainland and damaged the central water works
system, so the city had no water for days. The wharf suffered severe wreckage;
ships anchored in the bay were sent reeling off in the raging storm to land ten—
even twenty-two—miles away from deep water. The Marx and Blum Building on
Mechanic Street was reduced from four stories to one; city hall lost its roof and
much of its upper story; the Galveston Orphans' Home and the Letitia Rosenberg
Women's Home, large stone structures, stood but with their roofs caved in. School
after school on the island reported damage—and this with the fall term just beginning. One entire wall of the Bath Avenue School dropped away, exposing a
collapsed third floor with pupils' desks still attached in neat rows. The storm destroyed East District School for African American children and drowned seven of
the teachers. The pupils from East District and the damaged Central High School
doubled up for the fall term at tiny West District School at Thirty-fifth Street, the
only safe public school structure available to black students. Black citizens complained nearly one year later that trustees of the school board had not yet rebuilt
the East District School.[40]

Hardest hit, ironically, were the churches. African American churches—fourteen in all—suffered the most; every single structure was demolished. Among the
white Protestant churches, the storm destroyed totally twenty-two (five of them
brick) and damaged twelve. Those religious structures that sustained less damage
became host sanctuaries for neighboring congregations: members of the African
American St. Augustine Episcopal Church met in Eaton Chapel, the only usable
part of Trinity Episcopal Church; Methodists met in the Central Christian
Church; and members of First Baptist met in the Jewish synagogue. Martha Poole
remembers sadly but gratefully the neighborliness of the congregation at Temple
B'nai Israel. "The awful storm of 1900 swept away all our church buildings and
50 of our members. . . . We were in despair, but God helped us. Our neighbors,
the Jews, opened the doors of the synagogue to us, like genuine Christians; although their building was greatly damaged. I changed my seat there four times
one Sunday, to escape a wetting." No Catholic church sustained more damage
than the towering St. Patrick's Church at the city's West End. Its lofty spire, 220
feet tall, broke in half and came crashing down upon the nave of the church,
slicing through brick, lumber, and tiles, exposing the interior of the sanctuary to
utter ruin. Only four small stained glass windows and two altars remained. At one
of the altars, "every morning since the storm the priest of the parish has held
service," wrote Father James M. Kirwin. St. Mary's Cathedral, the oldest church
on the island, sustained the least damage among Catholic churches. Parishioners
took hope from the revelation that the statue of Mary, Star of the Sea, placed atop

FIGURE 1.5. Bath Avenue School, 1900. Courtesy Rosenberg Library, Galveston, Texas.

the cathedral after the storm of 1875 as a guardian, remained in place even though a two-ton bell was torn from its fastenings within the cathedral tower.[41]

The area of the city that suffered the most damage stretched in a 1,500-acre crescent from the far east end of the island at Eighth Street diagonally across Broadway to the shore and away to the west end of the island beyond Forty-fifth Street. As if some huge arm had moved across the island, the storm swept away whole neighborhoods and left only a denuded stretch of land from the beach to Avenue P. Structures closest to the gulf had had the least chance of survival; winds drove fifteen- to thirty-foot waves against small clapboard houses, most of which could not withstand the force of water and wind and collapsed with their hapless occupants either buried under the debris or flung out into the tide. Over half of those living near the beach, an estimated 8,000 people, had chosen not to seek shelter within the city's more substantial buildings, leading to extraordinary loss of life. Even more lives were lost when victims ventured or were tossed out in the storm's midst late Saturday afternoon. The hurricane winds loosened from roofs slate tiles, which acted as lethal missiles mutilating those caught in their path. Then, as the houses collapsed, their shattered remains, driven by 100-mile-per-hour winds, acted as battering rams against the buildings north of them. Like a giant scythe, the storm scraped away traces of habitation until it deposited the refuse in a great three-mile-long mound of shattered buildings south of Broadway.

FIGURE 1.6. St. Patrick's Church. The 220-foot spire fell, destroying the church nave. Courtesy Rosenberg Library, Galveston, Texas.

Within this two-story mountain of detritus rested the remains of houses, barns, furnishings, machinery, dead animals, and sodden human corpses.[42]

When the waters had receded to expose the work of the storm, survivors spoke of the horror awaiting them in the streets and in the denuded land beyond town. "I hope I never see nothing like dat 'gain," remembered Ella Belle Ramsey. "De whole town was tore up. . . . An' dead people was all over de street an' everywhere." Father Kirwin, on his day-after inspection, found forty-three mangled bodies caught upon the framework of a railroad bridge. A row of salt cedar trees as far west as Heard's Lane held in its branches the twisted bodies of 100 victims. "The horror of such spectacles was increased by the fact that all of the bodies were stripped of clothing." At first residents underestimated the numbers of dead, thinking the storm had taken perhaps 100, maybe 500. But the enormity of the tragedy unfolded as people began to search for relatives, friends, and neighbors and found bodies littering the streets, floating in waterways, or intertwined within the storm debris. Not all were recognizable, so battered and broken were the remains. Later estimates had it that 3,000 corpses lay buried beneath the mountain of rubble in the middle of the island. Another 1,000 covered the streets and yards; 500 swept out to sea with the receding tide and 500 more were blown to the north end of Galveston Bay. Probably 1,000 on the mainland drowned. Searchers continued to find skeletal remains months later.[43]

The problem of removal soon became pressing. Survivors sought their dead

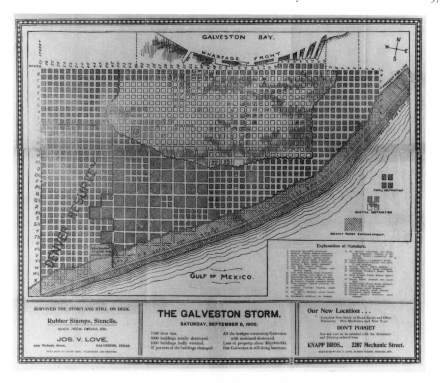

FIGURE 1.7. Map showing the damage from the Galveston, Texas, storm of September 8, 1900. Shaded portion of the map shows the area of total destruction. Enhanced from an image reproduced courtesy of the Rosenberg Library, Galveston, Texas.

and buried them in shallow graves in any available plot of ground. Disposal of the unclaimed was left to the hastily devised Central Relief Committee. At first the bodies were taken to a makeshift morgue near the docks. Volunteers searched for identification and allowed survivors to view the remains for signs of their loved ones. But as the day heated up, and as the numbers of dead swelled past 500, the futility of providing decent burial became apparent. Initially, volunteers tried interment, but the ground was too saturated for mass graves. Despite a shortage of horses and willing hands to carry the dead, the first 700 bodies collected in the makeshift morgues were gathered and sent out on barges for burial at sea. But the remains washed ashore. Ida Austin captured the moment: "The mournful dirges of the breakers which lashed the beach, the sobbing waves and sighing winds, God's great funeral choir, sang their sad requiem around the dead. The sea as though it could never be satisfied with its gruesome work washed these bodies back upon the shore, the waves being the hearses that carried them in to be buried under the sand."[44]

In the 88-degree heat of September corpses quickly reached a state of putrefaction before the workers, bribed with whiskey, could remove them from the tangled mounds. Finally, at the insistent demand of the city's medical community, the Central Relief Committee decided to burn the bodies in great funeral pyres across the devastated wasteland of the once-thriving port city. The ghastly charnal mounds, as many as twelve at a time, burned for six weeks. Observers said that eyewitness descriptions were inadequate, although many tried to report the desolation. "They gathered up all the dead bodies they could find," noted Daniel Ransom. "Then they piled them up, just like you cross-pile cord wood, and pour oil all over them and burn them. It sure was a awful sight, but I guess it was all they could do." Fannie B. Ward of the American Red Cross observed these scenes from across the bay, "Over on Galveston island, a long line of flame, mounting to the heavens, marked the burning of ruined homes and corpses; while other fires, in all directions on the mainland, told of similar ghastly cremations. . . . Early in the morning a strange odor drew attention to a fresh funeral-pyre, only a few rods away. . . . That peculiar smell of burning flesh, so sickening at first, became horribly familiar within the next two months, when we lived in it and breathed it, ate it and drank it, day after day." Teams of men were pressed into working to clear the island of bodies and debris. They even worked on Sundays because, as the *News* reported, "It is a holy office to care for the dead and the health of the city demands that the work be continued without interruption until finished."[45]

It is difficult to measure the shock and grief that citizens experienced in the aftermath of the disaster. Everyone had lost something; some had lost everything. Some went out of their minds, but more often people responded with determination to carry on. A certain stoicism marked the columns of the *Galveston Daily News* as it editorialized about the city and its citizens:

> The sorrows of the past few days are overwhelming and we all feel them and will continue to feel them so long as we live. It could not be expected that our friends and relatives and loved ones should be so suddenly torn from us without leaving scars from which those in the ranks of maturity can never recover. But it is all in the past now. We can not recall our dead thousands. Whereever they sleep . . . we will love their memories and recall as long as we live the unspeakable and mysterious tragedy which destroyed them. But it must be remembered that we have more than 30,000 living, and many of these are children too young to have their lives and energies paralyzed by the disaster which has overtaken us. Our homes must be rebuilt, our schools repaired, and the natural advantages of the port must sooner or later receive our earnest attention. We have loved Galveston too long and too well to desert her in the hour of misfortune. Our distress and destitution are going to be relieved. . . . We must look to the light ahead.[46]

Hard work was one way of dealing with grief. Ida Austin may have seemed prideful when she described the survivors at labor, but she was not inaccurate. "Galvestonians are a brave people and they are taking heart again and are busy trying to rehabilitate their city and their homes. The necessity of work for all classes has been the salvation of the city. . . . Galveston will be rebuilt more beautiful, more massive, more enduring than before."[47]

Building the city and reshaping its government consumed the efforts of its remaining citizens. Just hours after the storm had blown itself out over New England, survivors organized emergency relief, districted the city by wards, and moved ahead with burial, cleaning, and food and supply distribution. Out of the catastrophe also came political reformers who would shape a new generation of civic leaders. The storm had been the great catalyst for this. It demanded the creation of an emergency Central Relief Committee made up primarily of entrepreneurs; brought an elite faction of capitalists openly into politics; stimulated the creation of a city commission form of government; mobilized African Americans to strengthen churches, schools, and civic organizations; and drove white women survivors to create a permanent organization to promote their goals for a better community.

This last group, formed to help shape the future of the city, was the Women's Health Protective Association. Founded in March 1901, six months after the day of wreckage, the WHPA planned a voluntary program to inspect and safeguard the city's cemeteries, streets and alleys, markets and restaurants, sewers, dairies, schools, jails, hospitals, and parks. Within days they launched a vigorous campaign to reinter the remains of storm victims; then they moved to revegetate the island after the city constructed a seawall and raised the island with sand dug from the bay. Their most challenging years came with the campaign to secure pure milk for the infants and children of Galveston, for here they battled the forces of entrepreneurial independence and public indifference. Their civic activism continued through the 1920s, and their efforts spawned other women's civic organizations, not the least of which was a woman suffrage association whose leader, Minnie Fisher Cunningham, went on to become president of the Texas Equal Suffrage Association.

The women who founded the WHPA in 1901 had not suddenly materialized without warning. They were among the most visible white upper- and middle-class women in the city. More important, they responded to the crisis of the storm as they had to other needs within the city: collectively and with a sure sense that theirs was an important role to perform in civic betterment. Where did this confidence come from? Where do we find these reforming origins?

It came from a long legacy, at least thirty years, of activism by the women of Galveston. They had begun to minister to community needs first through their churches and synagogues, then through their own benevolent institutions, and finally through Progressive Era organizations. Reform in Galveston was engendered by genteel women who transformed their churches to accommodate their concerns, created benevolent institutions to care for city dependents, formed women's clubs for edification and to tackle urban problems, and campaigned for equality of voting rights and protection of working women. As we shall see, however, the development of women's confidence and public acceptance came before all reforming efforts. And it began in the city's religious institutions.

. . . .

WOMEN, CULTURE, AND THE CHURCH

Memorials, Cemeteries, and Music

> No woman is really an insider in the institutions fathered by masculine consciousness.
>
> —Adrienne Rich, Commencement Address at Smith College, 1979

Mollie Ragan Macgill Rosenberg was considered a character among her friends and acquaintances in Galveston. Second wife of Henry Rosenberg, one of the wealthiest men in town, Mollie had met Henry before the Civil War as a young girl. She married him when she turned fifty after spending more than twenty years in his household as companion to his invalid wife Letitia. Born in Hagerstown, Maryland, in 1839, she became a staunch defender of the Lost Cause and president of the local chapter of the United Daughters of the Confederacy. In a fundraiser for the Galveston monument to soldiers of the Confederacy, Mollie (at sixty-six), clad in bonnet, pantaloons, and short skirt, performed the role of Jerusha in a little drama, "The Deestrick Skule." Gossip had it that when she and Henry had been members of Trinity Episcopal Church, they had grown angry with the rector Reverend Stephen M. Bird and his wife for declining to name their last child after Mollie. In a pique the Rosenbergs headed off to tiny Grace Episcopal Church in the western part of the city, taking several important families with them. If this were all there were to say about Mollie Rosenberg, we would conclude that she was just another southern eccentric, fascinating, perhaps, but important to neither the cultural climate of Galveston nor to those who worked so steadily to improve the position of women within the community. But, of course, there was more to Mollie than this brief glimpse. There was her gift in 1895 to Grace Episcopal Church.[1]

The stained glass windows, which she commissioned for Grace Church, depict women in the New Testament and their close affiliation with Jesus or with Christian teachings. Besides bringing stunning pieces of art to this town on the fringes of the South, Mollie made sure that the artists glorified faithful believing women, showing them to be disciples as well as servants of the church. The windows become ideologically useful in that they remind the viewer that women's domestic world, unimportant in the realm of theological higher criticism, was the stuff out of which Jesus created homilies, parables, and stories. His wisdom found sanctuary not only in Bethany, home of Mary and Martha, but in the hearts of women, who, through identification with domestic tasks, understood that their female world was as much a part of Christian tradition as the crucifixion and resurrection. Resonating through this glass artistry is the message that God blessed individual women selectively throughout history for their spiritual insights but in doing so placed value on all women called to a religious life. Women were exalted in their roles as homemakers, caretakers of families, and nurturers of children as well as for their acceptance of divine intervention and spiritual discernment. Stained glass windows to the glory of God but to the memorialization of women called forth a subtle but very real statement about the worth of women, and they represent Mollie's most important contribution to the community. They also spoke volumes about the interconnectedness between family, home, and the church.

Family and home life were, of course, central to the lives of southern women and of women who migrated to the South. As Galveston matured from a village to a commercial center in the postwar era, middle-class families exemplified domestic patterns established by the change. The physical distance between home and the workplace and the ideological accompaniments to this economic shift resulted in the apotheosis of the home as a "haven in a heartless world." Father assumed the role of bread winner and benign patriarch, while children, nurtured in religious and artistic values, were raised for a life of independence. Women, especially wives and mothers, took the elevated position of domestic, religious, and moral authority to become a "counterforce to commercialism and self-interest." Although periodicals such as *Godey's Lady's Book* described the ideal woman as pious, chaste, submissive, and domestic, true womanhood also required skills in nurturance, healing, artistry, and above all mothering.[2]

For middle-class women, the home was the undisputed domain for the cultivation of culture, education, and piety. Books, pianos, parlors, organs, wallpaper, draperies, wall hangings, and curios defined the household as a center of refinement that benefited from a woman's touch, sensitivity, taste, and values. Homes for the wealthy and the middle classes became objects for consumerism in the late nineteenth century, and women were the principal purchasers of furnishings and adornments. Aware of the importance of piety in family life, women introduced religious iconography into the home in the form of framed biblical pictures, memorial prints, crosses, punched paper mottos, embroidered samplers, and hair art. Material culture experts claim that women brought religious artwork into the home when they began to join churches in ever greater numbers. But the reverse was also true; domestic concerns and feminine artistic themes entered the churches as more and more women created a comfortable place—a church home—within congregational walls.[3]

Before the Civil War, Galveston churches were devoted to worship, prayer meetings, business meetings, and not much else. Eventually, churches changed to provide an essential refuge from society—a house of worship for the faithful, a haven for the traveler or the stranger, a source of community for families and single adults, and a place bubbling with activity for children and mothers. As women's participation in church life increased, they brought to it attributes and characteristics of their domestic lives. The result: churches grew to become more homelike and more comfortable for women and their families as they insisted upon edifices and programs complementary to their tastes, sensibilities, and needs. In the years between 1870 and 1920 Galveston churches changed from simple wooden structures to elaborate architect-designed stone complexes with church-yards, Sunday school rooms, nurseries, parlors, libraries, choir rooms, parsonages, offices, halls, meeting rooms, and cemeteries. Women's groups within the church often raised money for these projects through dinners, entertainments, bazaars, and fairs filled with handmade goods. Women made significant modification to church aesthetics, including architecture, memorial furnishings, cemeteries, and music. Familiar with decorative arts, laywomen transformed the interiors of churches, softening the contours of stone and wood with fabric and carpeting, embellishing bare walls with stained glass, and dignifying the sanctuary with care-fully crafted works of art. Churches began to resemble homes physically, not only figuratively as the "church home" or "congregational family," terms used by many southerners today. The domestication of Galveston's Protestant churches was a direct consequence of the transference or extension of women's interests originat-ing in the home to a semipublic institution.

Much of what women brought to churches was reflective of woman's sphere, a sphere to which upper- and middle-class white women had been consigned by societal convention, but out of which women had shaped distinctive tastes, be-haviors, and values. Some of the most important aspects of their world included not only artistic sensibilities but also nurturing capacities and interest in and de-votion to family and spiritual life. As women began to extend their talents from home to church, the (mostly Protestant) churches shifted to accommodate the influx of females. Church programs — Sunday schools, youth leagues, adult Bible classes, missions, and fundraising — expanded with increased female membership. Sunday schools and church youth leagues grew as congregations placed greater importance on children and families, an emphasis for which women were partly responsible. Women volunteered to lead youth groups and teach Sunday school, some so successfully that they displaced focus from the pastor to the Sunday school teacher. They learned to work together in all-female groups, gained confidence through leadership, and sometimes challenged male authority. They saw the mis-sion field as the responsibility of Christian women such as themselves. And in some congregations they recognized early on that, while the poor would always be with them, they were obligated to share whatever resources they could. Middle-class, mostly non-wage-earning women increasingly considered church a part of their world in ways that the commercial houses and business offices of the Strand were not. Church was an institution separate from home, yet it was one that accepted their ways, their values, their tastes, in short, their culture. The conse-quence was a transformation of churches before the turn of the century that was profound and lasting.

Women's involvement in church life changed them as well. It exposed them to values and behaviors that were not conventionally assigned to women. Traits attributed to men — competitiveness, striving for power, public recognition, and authority — were presented in unexpected ways: through games and prizes in Sunday school, by strategical maneuverings on committees and in Sunday school, via independent Bible classes, and by decisions over expenditures. Involvement in church life brought women into a closer relationship with men outside the family, and with that came the opportunity for internalizing principles of so-called male assertiveness. Women also learned through their sisterhoods and all-women societies about independence — financial and organizational — that allowed them to develop skills appropriate for administrative leadership and accountability. Women learned through church life how to exert authority while being denied formal access to power.

No doubt laywomen pushed religious leaders to accept their vision of an institution that could move beyond worship, theology, and liturgy to embrace programs essential to Christian life. Women knew what families needed; women knew what they wanted in church life and were willing to exert pressure to see their values accepted. The result was twofold: churches became more accommodating to women and families, while at the same time they served as a place from which women could launch into community activism. Programs were designed with women and children in mind, and, having asserted themselves in the one institution outside the family amenable to their desires, women learned how to press on into the world, taking their talents to secular areas outside the church. As Rima Lunin Schultz writes, "In the late nineteenth century religion became a bridge for women that brought them from the ideal of a sheltered domestic life of the home . . . to the public sphere of the workplace, the school, the hospital, the mission, and the social welfare agency." Rather than arguing solely that religious institutions held women back or kept them "in their proper place," this study seeks to understand how women changed the church and how the church broadened women's world without drastically altering basic nineteenth-century gender prescriptions.[4]

Protestant churches became more humane as a consequence of the involvement of women, more accepting of human needs, and more adaptive as programs and structures broadened to include resources for families. Charitable outreach increased enormously in the late nineteenth century as laywomen formed church-related benevolent societies. Sunday schools, initially intended to bring literacy to working-class children, were broadened by women to include Bible study and worship. Church structures expanded, largely through the fundraising of women, and became more inviting as church leaders attempted to accommodate to new programs and growing numbers of parishioners.

As women took more active roles in church maintenance, programs, and missions, they moved from the private enclosures of their homes to the semipublic forums of churches and eventually into community organizational work. Historians of southern women, especially Anne Firor Scott, have always maintained that the roots of female evolution into public life began in church societies. Evelyn Brooks Higginbotham has given us the most comprehensive look to date at the activist roles of black women in Baptist churches and has argued convincingly that the foundation for civil rights activism was in "the sacred space of black churches." In many respects, Protestant churches supplied the nursery for the growing roles that upper- and middle-class women would play upon a public stage. But in this nursery of white Protestant southern churches we are not necessarily going to find the seedlings of a feminist movement. Some churches by their doctrine and mission *did* encourage, perhaps unwittingly, the evolution of feminist consciousness. Others did not; thus, those scholars who insist that "only through a study of women's culture can we assess nineteenth-century feminist consciousness and activity" will be disappointed in the knowledge that laywomen seldom voiced aloud so-called feminist views, that is, beliefs in the political equality as opposed to the spiritual equality of women.[5]

But if studying one of the institutions most important to women in the nineteenth century has merit to scholars, it is in understanding the way women shaped that institution to fit their values, transformed it according to their visions of piety, and added to it avenues for individual and collective activism; in short, it is in witnessing the creation of a women's world within an institution protected and managed by men. Then our understanding increases of how women shaped and molded a woman's community of their own *outside* the church, built upon many of the experiences developed within churches. If one accepts the idea that any attempt by women to act on their own values, or to transform an existing institution to reflect their standards, demonstrates resistance to male dominance (or, at least to male tastes and preferences), even devout churchwomen may be seen as challengers to patriarchal control.

Church life is one aspect of southern culture that found ready acceptance among southern women. From the origins of the Great Revival in 1805 to the creation of separate southern denominations in the 1840s, women flocked to churches in greater numbers than did men.[6] In the years after the Civil War, southern churches continued to grow, with women still dominating the membership. In Galveston, Protestant church membership climbed from 4,000 communicants in 1890 to 10,000 in 1916. In 1906 Protestant women outnumbered men 3,200 to 2,000.[7] Even with their disproportionate majorities, women still were offered very few avenues for leadership on a par with men. Denied admission to the pastorate, the diaconate, the vestry, or the boards of elders and stewards, women appear only occasionally in church minutes as "workers." So, why did women comprise the majority of church members?

The beauty, sanctity, and fellowship of church life drew them in. The roles women played in churches—as choir members and directors, organists, Sunday school teachers, youth leaders, philanthropists, and committee members—give evidence not only of their piety but also of their growing influence within churches.[8] The emergence of women's talents from home to church to the larger community is a theme that will be introduced here but shown more thoroughly in later chapters. This and the next two chapters will describe and interpret those aspects of church life in which women's influence changed the church or in which their participation changed the women, that is, in the areas of church decor and memorials, cemeteries, church music, Sunday schools, independent Bible classes, and, finally, autonomous women's church societies.

Memorials, Decor, and Stained Glass Windows

As a few women in the 1880s and 1890s in Galveston began to inherit wealth from their successful merchant husbands or fathers, they sought ways, just as male philanthropists did, to benefit society with memorials and bequests. Rarely did individual women leave gifts to the city as men did in the form of outdoor monuments, drinking fountains, hospitals, or schools. Instead, especially in the decades before 1900, they spread their gifts and bequests throughout the island, some to women's charities but most to churches and synagogues.[9] In many ways the gifts that men and women left to the community continued the pattern of separate spheres and separate space. Men designated funds to build public structures; women more often left money privately to charities or for the purpose of embellishing interior space.[10]

In the years between 1880 and 1910, church sanctuaries in Galveston underwent dramatic changes from simple wooden structures to architect-designed stone and brick edifaces. T. J. Jackson Lears has labeled this phenomenon "aesthetic religion" and has connected it to "the growing acceptance of wealth," the maturing of urban churches, and the reliance on "priestly authority." Seeing a "gilded religion for a gilded age," Lears equates the revival of medieval architecture in church design with the adherence to ritual and the otherworldliness of Catholic forms. In Galveston, Protestant churches became modest repositories of fine art rather than splendorous edifices devoted to invoking the mysterious. Local architects, such as Nicholas Clayton, emulated the great cathedrals of New York and Chicago. But other stone churches were simpler affairs, reminiscent of their rural southern roots. Contractors, architects, and masons may have put the buildings in place, but they did not create the final touches; women did this by defining and delineating interior space on their own terms to meet their tastes and sensibilities. The combination of women's wealth and interest in the decorative arts with end-of-the-century reconstruction and refurbishing of the island's churches allowed women the opportunity to create a sacred visual world.[11]

The same wealth that allowed parishioners to give liberally to church building campaigns first appeared in the mansions and substantial homes that adorned Broadway and the East End. Galvestonians of wealth, carefully encouraged by merchants and capitalists, had become part of the consumer culture of the late nineteenth century. Architecturally designed homes, many with cavernous rooms, needed to be tastefully furnished with items that represented "stability and grace" and that were commensurate with the nouveau riche status of their owners. "Where architecture leads, decorative art follows," pronounced Candace Wheeler, a leader in the decorative art movement and delineator of male and female artistic roles. Knowing which items to order from New York or European manufacturers required study or sound advice. Although Galveston was not yet a department store town where many ideas for decorating emerged, its wealthier residents traveled frequently to New York, where they beheld the marvels of the emporium. In an advance over the dry goods stores of the South, Samuel Lord and George Taylor, A. T. Stewart, and John Wanamaker created palaces of commercial enticement, where women of refinement became discerning consumers. These stores appealed directly to elite women as culture conservators. Many Galveston women, too sophisticated to ignore the influences of the Gilded Age, became interior designers and decorative artists first for their homes and then for their churches.[12]

At the same time, there developed a movement for purity within the world of art and culture. Highbrow culture, wrested from the teaming masses by professional musicians, museum directors, artists, and dramatists, became evermore the province of the well educated and the wealthy. Turning away from the ugliness and grotesque artifacts of industrialization, connoisseurs of art, such as Charles Eliot Norton, professor of fine arts at Harvard, preached a message of artistic wholesomeness, authenticity of materials, and the aesthetics of carefully crafted items. Elite American women were educated by tastemakers who articulated an ideal of integrity of material for furnishings and decor. The association of aesthetics with morality in the minds of many Victorian Americans centered around domesticity and religion. To be gracefully artistic in reworking one's environment suggested a higher moral authority and thus led to changed homes and churches. The trends of consumerism and concern over the elegance of ornamentation, coming as they did at a time of greater church construction, flowed together as architects finished their work and churchwomen, often the only designers congregations used, took up the task of furnishing and decorating the interiors of houses of worship. The effect was an emphasis on decorative pieces that were well made, hand crafted, and of the finest materials. The result was a greater definition of class structure, elite values, and gendered preferences through church architecture and design.[13]

As church construction increased dramatically throughout the nation so did the production of stained glass windows. By the end of the century, glass making had risen to new stature mainly through commercial demand and through the artistry and technical genius of famous glaziers, such as John La Farge and Louis Comfort Tiffany, and lesser known artists, such as Mary Tillinghast, Clara Burd, D. Maitland Armstrong, and Joseph Lauber. Techniques that created opalescent glass, known in Europe as American glass, modernized the stained glass industry and brought beauty and grace to home and church windows. American Protestant theologians by the mid-nineteenth century no longer objected as strenuously to images of biblical figures, and no longer worried as much about idolatry or "popery" or fretted about the luxury of stained glass. Victorian religious themes predominated in sacred windows, depicting scenes mostly from the New Testament rather than the Old, showing women and men of the gospel in an optimistic light, giving more attention to Mary and the infant than to the suffering crucified Christ, and featuring hosts of angels: avenging angels, heralding angels, comforting angels, annunciatory angels, celebrating and serenading angels. Scenes were often set against a background of nature; not the ensnaring nature of Calvinistic thought but a nature in which God was manifest, a peaceful natural world beautiful to behold and reminiscent of America's idealized natural spaces.[14]

Themes of artistry, beauty, and integrity of materials resonated with churchgoing women of wealth. Even though Suzanne Lebsock cheerfully announced that " 'Woman's sphere' was never a fixed space," the wealthier ladies of Galveston, who wanted to be remembered for their devotion to the church (if not for their piety), tried, indeed, to fix a place for women within and upon the church walls.[15] Why individual women of means should choose to leave gifts to the churches or synagogues and not to the city's public spaces is an interesting question. Possibly the boundaries of male and female spheres were as tightly drawn in the symbolic sense as they were in the areas of politics, economics, and the law. Places where women had virtually no roles to play as leaders would have been inappropriate loci for their endowments. By contrast, religious institutions presented an altogether suitable site for the memorialization of individual women. Here they taught Sunday school, funded and kept in repair the cemeteries, sang in choirs, played the organ, supported mission schools that eventually became new churches, refurbished and financed the church structure, and most important, established their own societies and relief associations of benefit to themselves as leaders and to other women as supplicants. Besides the home, where else had women and their values been so liberally accepted? In the continuing attempt to expand women's realm beyond their own houses, where their tastes and preferences were in evidence, women found in churches a repository for the symbols of their world.

Testaments to this fact can be seen in church interiors via plaques, windows, furnishings, organs, even whole structures, dedicated to the glory of God but given in memory of women or in memory of those loved by women. Martha Poole, in reminiscing about the Baptist church built in 1883, recalled that W. R. A. Rogers was the first to be baptized in it. "I shall never forget his mother's happiness that day. She died suddenly, to our grief, and John D. her husband gave an organ to the church in her memory." In the newly built First Methodist Church of 1901, eight of the fourteen Gothic lead glass memorial windows and the baptismal font were given in memory of the "consecrated Christian" women who had served the church. One sanctuary window depicting a nurturing Christ with his lambs was commissioned in memory of Etta Toothaker, who had been secretary of the Texas Conference of the Epworth Leagues but who had perished in the 1900 storm. Five of the ten stained glass windows of the First Presbyterian Church were donated as memorials to women. The pipe organ, a $7,000 gift from Sarah Ball, whose husband gave Galveston its first high school in 1885, surrounded the communion table, chairs, and offering plates. These sacred implements were carved with religious symbols in 1894 by Virginia Hutches Austin, wife of a Presbyterian minister and sister-in-law to Ida Austin. Among the carvings were lilies, representing the resurrection; a loaf and a cup from the last supper; a crown of thorns; and a descending dove symbolic of the Holy Spirit. Taken from the New Testament, they represented the sacrificial nature of Christ, a model for both men and women, but one that mostly women aspired to emulate.[16]

In Trinity Episcopal Church a treasury of stained glass windows illustrates the tie between women and church art; nine of the sixteen windows memorialize women or girls who either served the church or died young. Angels provide a familiar theme for these windows; they sometimes symbolized the feminine nurturing side of humankind but with transcendent otherworldly powers. In Victorian parlance women were often referred to as angelic creatures, ministering angels, or the angel in the home. Not surprisingly, angels appear as subjects chosen by women also to commemorate women and girls. The 1886 window in memory of Bessie Haden shows an angel serenading two saints below with a harp. Given by her grandmother, the memorial creates for the modern viewer a poignant reminder of the vulnerability of life in the nineteenth century, for while Bishop Alexander Gregg confirmed the fifteen-year-old girl, Bessie fainted and died on the spot. Angels are in evidence in two other windows memorializing women who died leaving behind grieving loved ones. Mary and the Christ child are represented in three more. The remaining windows, also in memory of women, show the three women at the tomb and another with Mary at the feet of Jesus on the cross. Windows depicting Jesus as a youth teaching in the synagogue, as the Good Shepherd, and teaching the little children were all reminders of the self-denying, nurturing, encouraging, comforting Jesus, who possessed the traits most often ascribed to and valued in women.[17]

Few ladies had the means to spend sizable donations in remembrance of their loved ones, yet eleven of the sixteen stained glass windows in Trinity Episcopal Church were given by women consecrating the memory of husbands, daughters, parents, sisters, brothers, grandchildren, and grandparents. Furthermore, nearly three-fourths of the sanctuary furnishings and ornaments were presented by women or were presented by men in memory of women or female children. As family and close female friendships were considered important to women, they, more than men, honored family and friends in the personal yet public environment of their churches. The gifts were, for the most part, objects that contributed to the beauty of the interior space—portraits, candlesticks and candelabra, desks, lecterns, prayer books, Bible altars and altar hangings, altar vases, kneeling benches, and baptismal shells. Even the altar, the focal point of the ritual of the eucharist, was furnished in memory of Colonel and Mrs. William Stafford by their daughter Margaret. By the mid-twentieth century, when the window installation was completed, Trinity's sanctuary had been transformed with the artistic and material evidence of women and their aesthetic choices.[18]

Permanent memorials served another purpose—compensation. All the visual reminders lent symbolic but not actual power to women. In an institution where women were not allowed to preach, stained glass windows spoke for them, compensating for their powerlessness. Dispensing with the harsh patriarchal attitudes of the Old Testament in favor of the liberating message of a New Testament Christ, the images shown through stained glass windows translated the gospel into language understood by women. We have no record of what the men thought of all of this. Perhaps, given the inegalitarian position of women in an institution based on the premise of spiritual equality, men encouraged all manner of symbolic grandisement for women. Better to let women adorn the walls in symbolic immurement than to allow them positions of real power as vestry board members, stewards, elders, or deacons, governing offices from which women were excluded. Public, visible recognition within the house of God solemnized and sanctified the gifts of service and stewardship that women had imparted without threatening male leadership.[19]

As artistic representations and symbolic reminders of women, the windows provide a counter statement to a waning but nonetheless powerful Victorian fascination with female victimization as seen in American ideal sculpture. Women as captives, women in peril, women in death scenes held in thrall the imagination of mid-nineteenth-century artists who tapped into societal fears over the changing role of women. Passivity, enslavement, and victimization provided the drama of sculpture, but implied in their rendering was the possibility of triumph through female goodness and spiritual power. Unlike sculptures of chained nudes, shipwrecked mothers and children, or of captured queens of antiquity, the women portrayed in church art were projected as active agents, not passive victims. Their nobility was not in triumph over captivity, but in freedom of movement in the face of death and loss. These are conservative scenes, for they do not threaten family stability or warn of impending danger to women who cross the boundaries of their sphere. Rather they project images of women in active response to God's calling—tending to the poor, listening to Jesus, caring for children. In the face of Christ's death, the women at the tomb were active: preparing the body for burial, receiving the message of resurrection, telling the others, meeting Christ's spirit on the highway. They were not imprisoned in the home nor made passive by their grief (or by their sin); rather, they were made active by the Holy Spirit, facing death with courage, maintaining self-control in the face of the supernal. Whatever lessons may have been imparted by these windows, they offered a very different perspective—agency rather than passivity—from the midcentury art world on the place of women in a rapidly changing culture.[20]

Some might argue that the windows and sanctuary furnishings given in memory of loved ones represent yet another example of the Victorian fascination with death and conclude that women were no longer concerned with this world. On the other hand, gifts to the church in the form of memorials represent an all too worldly perspective—the display of privilege and wealth. There are elements of truth in each. But more important than either of these perspectives is the notion that women of means were acting on a traditional view of their responsibilities as women to uphold and honor the family. The fact that they chose themes that elevated women or woman's nurturing traits gives credence to the possibility that they valued their own sex. Women felt they had fewer arenas within the community to display tastefully but prominently their particular beliefs about women's talents. Men, by contrast, felt no such limitations.

Take, as a perfect example of the difference between the giving of men and women, the case of Henry and Mollie Rosenberg. Their story illustrates not only the power of money but also the manner in which members of the same family divided their gifts along gender lines.

Henry Rosenberg , born in 1824 the son of a shoemaker in Bilten, Switzerland, came in 1843 to the primitive but potentially prosperous port of Galveston, where he joined another Swiss émigré in a dry goods business. In Horatio Alger fashion, Henry advanced from clerk at eight dollars a month to owner of the store in a matter of three years. Diversifying his profits, he bought lots in the commercial section of Galveston, rented one to a young woman who wanted to open a millinery shop, found her charming, and in 1851 married her. Letitia Cooper Rosenberg became a diaphanous, shadowy figure in Henry's life; for more than twenty years she remained an invalid cared for by a young friend of the family, Mollie

Macgill from Hagerstown, Maryland. By 1859 Henry's dry goods business had become the largest in Texas.[21]

Henry's vigor contrasted sharply with his wife's pallor. Serving as president of the Board of Harbor Improvements and director of the Galveston Wharf Company, he was in a prime position to move into railroading, banking, and politics. As the city had prospered him, so he returned the favor—first in 1882 to his church, Trinity Episcopal, with a gift of $10,000 to complete a chapel in memory of the church's first rector, the Reverend Benjamin Eaton. Then in 1889 he gave $75,000 to the Board of School Trustees for an elementary school, which they named after him.[22]

In 1888 Letitia died, and the following year Henry married the no-longer-young Mollie Macgill. They enjoyed married life together less than four years; Henry Rosenberg died in 1893. Although he had already donated funds for the chapel and the school, the city was overwhelmed by the generosity found in his will. He bequeathed to Galveston $645,000, two-thirds of his entire estate. This legacy funded the charitable works of the Ladies' Aid Society of the First Lutheran Church, the creation of a seventy-four-foot monument to the heroes of the Texas Revolution, seventeen city drinking fountains for "man and beast," and the erection of five structures—the Galveston Orphans' Home, the Old Woman's Home (renamed the Letitia Rosenberg Women's Home), the YMCA building, the Rosenberg Library, and, for our story, Grace Episcopal Church. Rosenberg's will

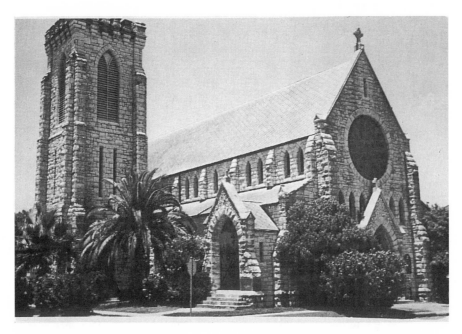

FIGURE 2.1. Grace Episcopal Church, built in 1895. Courtesy Rosenberg Library, Galveston, Texas.

read, "I desire to express in practical form my affection for the city of my adoption and for the people among whom I have lived for so many years." He might just as well have stated that he wanted the bulk of his money to be invested in brick, stone, and concrete, for while the intent of his will cared for the lives of strangers, the substance of it demonstrably, overwhelmingly favored public buildings.[23]

Mollie Macgill Rosenberg, by contrast, chose to use her legacy to embellish, decorate, and furnish the interior of Grace Episcopal, the little church that Henry's money had built. Rather than bestow her gratitude upon the public domain, or upon the city that fostered her husband's success, she chose to create a lavish, intimate memorial, an internal gift of beauty and adornment, and a fitting, even feminine, embellishment to the white stone Gothic structure. She chose as her designer and craftsman architect Silas McBee, an Episcopal churchman from the South, who in 1894 had served as interior architect for Christ Church Cathedral, Houston. Born in 1853 in Lincolnton, North Carolina, and educated at the University of the South, McBee set up his studio at 105 E. Seventeenth Street in New York. He would become editor of *The Churchman* from 1896 until 1912, and founder and editor in 1913 of the *Constructive Quarterly*, a journal of "faith, work and thought of Christendom."[24]

Mollie Rosenberg commissioned McBee to install a hand-carved solid oak altar and reredos from Switzerland, her husband's native country. Described as "probably the richest that has ever been put into any church in the south," the Gothic-style reredos features a bronze centerpiece depicting the birth of Christ and above it Christ on the cross. Covering the reredos is a canopy that casts a shadow on the picture of Christ's suffering and humiliation. The brass plate at one end of the altar dedicates the furnishings to Henry Rosenberg; lest one forget the benefactress, a plate at the other end reads: "This altar and reredos are erected by Mollie R. Macgill Rosenberg, Anno Domini, 1895."[25]

Mollie Rosenberg used Grace Church as a repository for the memorialization of the personal—for her husband, her mother and father, her brother and sisters, Henry's mother and father, Letitia Rosenberg, and her friends—but she used it to redeem women from their inferior position within church teachings as well. The three windows above the altar, given in memory of Mollie's father and two sisters, depict the three women at the tomb receiving from an angel the first news of Christ's resurrection.[26] As if to compensate for their humble status, the women on the left are clothed in rich colors of maroon and blue, the woman on the right, whose image takes up the entire panel, is in deep red. Portrayed against a rugged natural background, two of the women seem to be looking inside the tomb, the third, kneeling, looks expectantly toward the messenger.

In the synoptic gospels there are but two supremely important scenes for the elevation of women: the magnification of Mary and the announcement of the resurrection to the women at the tomb. Mary's magnification was a singular event for a specially anointed woman. The choosing of Mary to be the mother of God was unique, impossible to be duplicated. The gospels tell us Mary proclaimed her own apotheosis by announcing that all generations would call her blessed. The women at the tomb did not share Mary's sacred, singular destiny. By contrast, the gospels of Mark, Luke, and Matthew portray a group of ordinary women—at least two, possibly more—performing a domestic function, the preparation of the body with spices and ointments. At the moment they were about to commence their work, they experienced a special divine message from God, the first news of Christ's resurrection, and they were instructed to go and tell the disciples. The synoptic gospels agree that Mary Magdalene was present at the tomb; theologian Elisabeth Schüssler Fiorenza argues that "Mary of Magdala was the most prominent of the Galilean disciples, because according to tradition she was the first one to receive a vision of the resurrected Lord." While Mary, the mother of Jesus, would be forever blessed, the women at the tomb were disavowed of their knowledge of Christ's return by the disciples. Today, feminist theologians are well equipped to reconstruct the role of these female "apostolic witnesses" from androcentric sources and to understand the radical nature of Jesus' ministry by his inclusion of them.[27]

Nineteenth-century churchwomen, however, understood the gospel in symbolic terms and were able in their own minds to magnify and identify with Christ's female followers. Those women, in the performance of their gender-based duties, had received a particular, albeit private, dispensation from God, yet they were denied credibility by men. Analogously, churchwomen, who felt called by God to serve as the women at the tomb had done, were denied full parity of discipleship by men in the church. For women to see their circumstances reflected through the magnificence of stained glass, to understand that men might relegate them to inferior positions while God upheld them with a special call, no doubt provided them a redeeming and salvific satisfaction. What makes the choice of this window by Mollie Rosenberg even more demonstrative of her special intention to glorify faithful women was the fact that in many Episcopal churches the windows above the altar were reserved for the depiction of the celebration of the holy eucharist—usually the last supper—a communion of men and a closed male preserve that denied even symbolic representation to women.[28] Through the scenes of the three women at the tomb, faithful women were reminded of their special importance in the body of Christ while being denied inclusion in the body politic.

All the stained glass windows in Grace Church from this period portray women in various roles in the New Testament gospels. Furthermore, where scenes of Christ are shown, he is always in the company of women, not his male disciples. The large window on the south side of the church, dedicated to Henry Rosenberg's parents, presents two scenes: first, a man shielding a youth, under which the inscription reads, "To visit the fatherless and widows in their affliction," and, second, a woman, presumably Tabitha, distributing bread to the hungry, "full of good works and alms, deeds which she did." Known as the "Good Works" window, it represents in symbolic form the lives of Henry and Mollie Rosenberg. Henry had served on the Board of Trustees for the Galveston Orphans' Home and had bequeathed funds to build the home as well as the Letitia Rosenberg Women's Home. Mollie, who served as past president of the Grace Episcopal Ladies' Aid Society, also sat on the Board of Lady Managers of the Galveston Orphans' Home and the Rosenberg Women's Home.[29] Another window, with an inscription from John 3:16, shows Mary with the Christ child and a friend, possibly her cousin Elizabeth, with several children. A third window remembers Jesus as a youth in

FIGURE 2.2. Stained glass window in Grace Episcopal Church depicting Mary and the Christ Child with a woman and three children. The inscription below the window is from John 3:16, "For God so loved the world that he gave his only begotten Son." Photograph by Juan Maldonado.

the company of his parents, but with Mary in the foreground and Joseph behind her. A fourth shows only women, the wise virgins, in a parable taught by Jesus to show the value of spiritual preparedness. A fifth window shows Martha serving and Mary of Bethany listening while sitting at the feet of Jesus. This last window was especially popular with Victorian followers of the decorative arts, but its importance to women cannot be underestimated, for it claims their spiritual liberation. At first, the passage from the gospel of Luke appears to make Jesus insensitive to women's roles. Here was Martha serving up lunch while Mary listened intently. Martha asked Jesus, "Don't you care that my sister has left me to serve alone?"

Jesus answered, "Martha, you are troubling yourself about many things, but only one thing is needed and Mary has chosen the good portion which cannot be taken from her."[30] It would seem as though Jesus did not appreciate Martha's sacrifices. But taken on another level, Jesus' words freed women from servitude. For centuries families and society had thought women were there to cook, serve, and clean up. Jesus in one short statement said that women, too, may choose the "good portion," and become students while seeking sacredness.

The opening of Grace Episcopal Church was a greatly anticipated event; the city felt itself enriched by the infusion of precious artwork and handcrafted religious objects. Silas McBee spoke at length about the use of real materials and the honesty this represented in Christ's church. "The bronze is bronze, the oak is oak, the carving is carving, the stone is stone, the stained glass windows are stained glass, the pine is pine—everything shows itself to be what it absolutely is." Lost in the eloquent description of materials and design was one important fact: Mollie Rosenberg had consciously chosen to depict in the most prominent places scenes from the New Testament that elevated women. There was nothing particularly radical about her actions, *except* that by donating windows she pushed aside patriarchal icons in favor of women's images—women specially ordained not by men but by God.[31]

In the symbolic discourse of art, faithful believing women stood glorified, showing them to be disciples as well as servants of the church. Here we see cultural language used to build a sense of community among faithful women and at the same time to rebel against patriarchal norms—a dialectic between "language as social mirror and language as social agent." If ever there was a place of grace for women, it was within those walls. If ever there should be a question of what a church would look like if furnished only by women, Grace Church is a stunning example.[32]

Cemeteries

In all of the important rituals surrounding the great events of life—birth, marriage, death—tradition finds families coming together to affirm, to celebrate, and to eulogize. These special events, made more meaningful by religious observances, mark off the milestones of one's life. As Mary S. Donovan has pointed out, services commemorating these events in the antebellum period and into the late nineteenth century were held in homes, especially in the South.[33] Baptisms and weddings by custom were the "special province of women" (although presided over by male clergy) because women have long been guardians and caretakers of cultural traditions. By destiny and biology women are linked in every case to birth and marriage and are therefore inextricable from the preservation of their rituals. But since women did not attend funerals, they were denied equal participation with men, even in the death of a woman. In the hundreds of obituaries collected for this study, not one woman was appointed pallbearer or honorary pallbearer in a funeral service. The weight of the coffin prevented them from assuming this duty, one surmises. A 300-pound load divided among eight women would require each to carry about thirty-seven pounds, not an impossible task for a woman accustomed to lifting a two-year-old child, but not one that women were invited to assume. Given the fact that women had equal or stellar roles in the other two "events" of life, it seems odd that lifting a coffin from platform to hearse should prove to be the barrier to granting women equal honor in life's last ritual.

In the nineteenth century pallbearing was an honor reserved for men; it signified trust and friendship. Pallbearers' names were printed in newspaper obituaries. Depending on who the deceased was, status and stature could be gained by appointment to the deceased's funeral entourage. Fraternal orders often conducted funeral ceremonies with a full cast of members decorated with the symbols of their order. The Masons were especially in evidence at Galveston funerals, as were other fraternal orders, immigrant protective societies, and labor unions. The Galveston Screwmen's Benevolent Association, a labor group vital to the transport of cotton, not only paid funeral expenses of deceased members but also ruled that all members attend; absences were fined one dollar, and drunkeness and disorderly behavior were fined ten dollars by the union. These were male ceremonies; women might in some cases have control over who served as pallbearers, but they were not invited to become public participants.[34]

Women accepted this, it seems, and found other ways collectively to solemnize and mark the passage of life to death. Grieving customs required respectable widows to wear black clothing for one year, mottled gray or purple in the second year. Jewelry was optional but custom dictated that only black beads, black stones, or brooches, bracelets, and lockets containing the dearly departed's hair were acceptable. The mourning period for other family members — parents, children, grandparents, or siblings — lasted fewer months, but the cards and stationery women used in their year of mourning properly required a black border on letter and envelope. One grief custom for the very privileged was to memorialize loved ones in stained glass or other sanctuary decor. Another was to mark the pages of women's organizational minutes with resolutions to the good works of the deceased, most often women members. Many times the resolutions, formal and proper in their solemnity, were reprinted in newspapers the following day. Finally, women cared for the grounds in which loved ones were buried. Informally and often in family units, women took on the maintenance of individual gravesites and family plots.[35]

As towns grew, church and synagogue cemeteries replaced private family gravesites. Because grave tending was seen as women's responsibility, and since churches and synagogues offered proper burial grounds, congregational graveyards then came under the care of women members, who served at first not in any official capacity but as interested guardians, cajolers of the church sexton, and later as cemetery committee members. Tending graves was not as prestigious a calling as pallbearing, but it fit in well with female traditions of honoring the family and caring for those within the family circle; it also meshed with the increasing domestication of church structure, function, and membership.

Because cemetery maintenance brought to religious institutions one more aspect of their world, women often left provision in their wills for the founding or upkeep of a synagogue or church cemetery. The first evidence of such a gift came in the will of Rosanna Dyer Osterman. The Ostermans, of German-Jewish background, had immigrated to Galveston in 1839, when the city was still unincorporated. A merchant of considerable skill, Joseph Osterman retired four years later a wealthy man. His death by accidental gun charge in 1861 left Rosanna with a sizable fortune. Her life had been taken up with routine domestic tasks interrupted by outbursts of disease and war. She nursed yellow fever victims in the great epidemics that periodically scourged Galveston, and she nursed both Union and Confederate soldiers during the Civil War. Devoted to her faith as well as to her adopted city, she longed for the establishment in Galveston of a synagogue, regular worship services, a Hebrew benevolent society, education for poor Jewish children, a home for orphans, and, among other things, a larger Hebrew cemetery. In the years that she had been in Galveston, the Jewish population had grown from four families to 105 in 1868. After her own tragic and accidental death in 1866, her will provided money for these enterprises, including $1,000 for the expansion and upkeep of the Galveston Hebrew Cemetery. Her bequest was exceedingly timely, for, unfortunately, the worst yellow fever epidemic to plague Galveston hit in the summer of 1867, lasted five months, and carried away at least forty Jews. The original Hebrew cemetery proved too small to accommodate all of their burial needs. The following year, the Hebrew Benevolent Society, with Osterman funds, purchased a larger tract of land at Avenue K and Forty-third Street and established the Hebrew Rest Cemetery.[36]

Although no evidence remains to show that Christian women prepared the dead for burial, Jewish records indicate that the women of the Ladies' Hebrew Benevolent Society, a synagogue organization that had its beginnings in 1868, continued to wash and anoint the dead for interment until the establishment of Jewish mortuaries. Functions common to the home and family became necessarily functions of the synagogue when religious services were invoked to sanctify important life events.[37]

The Episcopal cemetery, in contrast to the Hebrew, had its origins in 1844 without the direct involvement of women. Benjamin Eaton, rector of Trinity Episcopal Church, accepted a donation from the Galveston City Company of a city block for the purposes of establishing a church cemetery, which was desperately needed. Prior to that time bodies had been covered over in the sand hills south of the city. That first primitive cemetery as described by Francis Sheridan merged into "a swamp & some of the graves in consequence [were] filled with & destroyed by water." Even more grisly scenes—"several large Turkey Buzzards in close consultation round a grave that had just fallen in"—prompted churchgoers to demand a proper cemetery.[38]

Although Trinity Episcopal was fortunate in receiving its own burial space, caring for cemeteries was not a priority among churchmen, who, busy with the commerce of life, had little time to devote to the maintenance of last resting places. The Episcopal ladies admitted as much when they petitioned the vestry in 1878 for permission to form a "standing committee" to assume the care of Trinity's church cemetery. "We know that gentlemen have other duties to perform that their vocations do not admit of their devoting valuable time to the details of such affairs. While we ladies can spare the time and delight in being of some use in our small way, a speedy and favorable reply will much oblige."[39]

Vestry minutes indicate how appallingly churchmen kept up the graveyard; women acted out of a sense of urgency, as storms and erosion in Galveston continually threatened the integrity of graves. The women who approached the vestry had already solicited $880 worth of subscriptions "for the purpose of improving the condition of the Episcopal Cemetery" and were asking that the vestry's cemetery committee cooperate with their standing committee. Although the petition sounded deferential, the women firmly stated that they would need money from the Cemetery Fund (which was granted) and cooperation from the cemetery committee to proceed "with the improvements we contemplate." Thus, two cemetery committees within the church, an official one formed by the vestry and an unofficial one comprised of laywomen, worked together, the women taking on the greater share of responsibility but without authority to act on their own. Vestryman W. H. Nichols was ardent in his praise of the "ladies," to whom "all honor is due" and who "accomplished in one week what your committee had hardly hoped to under twelve months."[40]

Honor rather than power rewarded women workers. The dual committee system continued to function until 1884 when apparently the women's committee dissolved. The vestry, taking note that repairs were needed again, addressed the Sisterhood (formed in 1875) "asking their cooperation with the cemetery committee in having the cemetery kept in better condition." The women, this time in a separate and, one presumes, more powerful organization, agreed to help with the maintenance of and the fundraising for the cemetery only if care of all church property came under female supervision. Apparently unsatisfied with the way vestrymen were keeping up the property, the Sisterhood requested more involvement in the affairs of the church grounds. Need one be reminded that lawns, yards, flower beds, and trees lent aesthetic appeal to a dwelling or a cemetery and were of enormous concern to women? The vestrymen acted as though they had discovered willing women workers for the first time and stated in 1886 that the treasury showed "a fair surplus owing principally to the good work of the Guild [Sisterhood] which came nobly to our relief at an opportune moment, and bids fair to prove a valuable acquisition to the board of managers in the near future."[41] Once invited to help, the work mainly devolved upon women.

After the devastating storm of 1900, all church properties needed repairs; it took nearly one year for a new women's cemetery society to raise funds necessary to repair the cemetery, and another year before the work costing $768 was completed. By then, women made the decision with the vestry's approval to select a sexton. Again in 1904 the ladies' cemetery association raised $745 by subscription to care for the cemetery; consequently, the vestry granted them "full power to act in the premises." Women all along had sought greater control over cemetery affairs. Their chance came briefly in 1911 when the vestry decided to invest "the management and control of the cemetery in Trinity Church Cemetery Association" headed by Mrs. Agnes F. Erhard, longtime member of Trinity, and two other Trinity women; five members of the vestry served as ex-officio members. But just at the point when laywomen were about to gain permanent control, the concept of perpetual-care cemeteries reached the ears of the ever-businesslike vestrymen. Cemeteries across the nation were adopting "Forest Lawn"–type arrangements that would alleviate volunteer efforts and maximize efficiency under an orderly arrangement. The adoption of this idea by the vestry board served to move women out of the maintenance and control of cemetery upkeep, thus eliminating care of graves from their cultural world within the church.[42]

Still, as an indicator of the importance of the cemetery to them, women gave money for its upkeep in greater portions than did men. As early as 1907, bequests began to accumulate for a perpetual care fund; the first came from a woman, and over a period of forty-two years, twelve out of thirteen donors to the fund were women, who gave a total of $8,450 (the fund eventually reached $48,000 through the sale of lots). Because the vestry never entirely relinquished its right to govern the cemetery, in 1913 it voted to issue perpetual care contracts "for the care of graves in the cemetery." The following year the Cemetery Fund, which eliminated the need for fundraising for its maintenance, was created from the sale of lots. It seems that in the years before 1914 the sale of cemetery lots went directly into the parish treasury to be used for general parish expenses. This necessitated frequent appeals to the ladies to raise funds to keep the grounds in repair. Fortunately for the women, their role as fundraisers kept them active in the decisions regarding cemetery affairs. But in 1914, when the vestry finally decided to use perpetual care contracts, the sale of lots, and bequests from individuals to form a cemetery fund, the women were no longer needed to raise money, and they lost their advantage. After 1914, all power over cemetery matters was given to the vestry cemetery committee, and women were no longer consulted or even asked to share in its maintenance.[43]

This example of cooperation with women followed by a closing off of their participation under the aegis of efficiency is a familiar tale to followers of women's history. The vestry cemetery committee, like all other vestry committees (music was the one exception in the years before 1920), never appointed laywomen to its ranks, even though women clearly held a profound traditional and cultural interest in the affairs of the cemetery. Perhaps the fact that the vestry controlled the ownership of church cemetery property made committee work in the eyes of its male guardians unsuitable legal terrain for women to traverse. When laywomen created their own separate cemetery association, one that they themselves insisted on forming as early as 1878, the vestry was more or less coerced into cooperating with them. As the ladies' fundraising became an ever-present necessity, vestrymen were obliged to consider them unequal partners. But as so often happened to women once the issue of money was taken out of their hands, their involvement, even with its cultural heritage, was diminished and their efforts subsumed under a so-called integrated professional system where there was no future for women. Men needed women to raise funds for cemetery upkeep, but sexism still prevented women, even in affairs that had culturally and traditionally belonged to them, from gaining control. Perhaps this helps to illustrate why the women's societies, which remained independent of vestry interference, were such valuable and important arenas for women's work within the church.

Church Music

Three areas where women found their musical talents useful to pastors and elders were in church choirs, choir directorships, and service on church music committees. To belong to the select group of singers, or to direct a choir, or even to be appointed to the committee that supervised music suggested a public acceptance of women's cultural and artistic talents.

For women, the performance of sacred music often afforded them their first opportunity to participate in public worship. When women formed or joined church choirs, they enhanced worship, whether the service was a simple Baptist "divine worship" or an elaborate Episcopal mass. Not long after Martha Poole began attending Galveston's First Baptist Church in 1861, she was asked by the "leading ladies" to help create a choir. "Mrs. Guy Bryan asked me to help her form a choir; she to play the reed organ, I to sing soprano, and her German cook, alto. We had no bass, no tenor; the men all sang soprano. But we sang with hearts as well as voices, and so worshipped until the fall of [Fort] Sumpter." Because music was central to her life and since she "had been trained vocally, and loved to sing," she joined the Methodist choir while the Baptist church remained closed during the Civil War.[44]

One of the ideals of an educated young lady of the upper and middle classes in the nineteenth century was the development of musical talents, principally piano playing and singing. Parlor skills long had entertained, amused, even impressed guests and suitors. In some cases, these little performances served as auditions to the larger role of properly educated wife and mother. Although usually seen by modern-day historians as the ultimate trivialization of a woman's life within her "sphere," the development of musical talent was, in fact, an endeavor that women took seriously as their means of adding refinement to the home.[45] It is only seen as trivial in its confinement to the parlor. Musical gifts upon the larger stage of life, in the theater or in worship services, were seldom mocked or trivialized by contemporaries. Small wonder that women of great talent sought the stage, while those of more modest gifts found fulfillment in the artful enhancement of worship.

By the 1880s, Galveston churches were offering women the chance to perform musically challenging pieces and to display their talents before public audiences. It no longer seemed strange to see an Episcopal choir loft, for example, filled with women and men singing the *kyrie* and the *gloria in excelsis*. Appreciation was spread out upon the pages of the *Galveston Daily News* in 1884 when it trumpeted:

> The morning service was an artistic model of sacred music. Mrs. Adoue, Mrs. Sealy have been rarely heard to sing with the spirit of praise so perfectly realized as they did yesterday. With the rich contraltoes of Mrs. Ladd and Mrs. Roeck . . . the service was uplifting to the realm of true art. When it is known that the choir is entirely a voluntary one, no one receiving a penny for the services rendered; on the contrary, sacrificing much to produce such results . . . one can but congratulate the congregation of Trinity Church, and the city, in having a local prize wholly their own.[46]

Choir directors continued to train women (and men) without cost to choir members. The exchange was a beneficial one to girls who might not have been able to afford private lessons and to wealthy ladies who needed a venue for their trained voices. The church, on the other hand, was the greater beneficiary, as more beautiful worship services created by a trained choir brought a dignity and elegance that Galvestonians seemed to enjoy. The church with the best choir was more likely to attract members; more members meant more tithes and a more generous church budget. A more generous budget could include a salary for an organist or choir director, positions that were sometimes filled by women.

The benefits for women did not end there. Choir members and soloists often took their church-trained gifts to the community, usually under the auspices of separate women's choirs, glee clubs, and ensembles. At a time when the only music heard was that performed live, the pleasure gained in hearing women sing was no small aesthetic contribution to the city. And, as so often occurred when women found a ready audience for their talents, they learned they could earn a profit either to further their group's musical ambitions or to benefit a cause. The payoff for the very talented woman was exposure in church to a critical audience and a chance to further a career in music. Just how many Galveston women made musical debuts before their congregations cannot be determined, but one young talent, Etheldreda Aves, daughter of the rector of Trinity Episcopal Church, sang first to her father's parish before signing a contract with the Metropolitan Opera Company in New York, where she performed the lead roles in "Carmen" and "Aida."[47]

Of course, the church's discovery and use of musical talent was not limited to women. Men were better able than women to find musical opportunities in the church. A boys' choir was organized that first performed at Trinity Episcopal in December 1878, but there was no equivalent girls' choir. Men singers, composers, and conductors found it easier to advance their musical careers in the workplace through churches than did women. When choosing musical leadership for the parish, the vestry of Trinity nine times out of ten hired a male organist and choir director.[48]

In an age when conducting (and composing) was a field dominated by men, women had very few avenues through which to channel their talents. Often, women conductors fine-tuned their skills by directing church choirs and later found work directing women's city choruses. Iola Barns Beers, a member of Trinity Episcopal, found that by exchanging her choir robe for the directorship of the Galveston Girls' Musical Club, she substantially advanced her credits in the community.[49] Such was also the case for Louise Fowler Parker, who acted as music director of the Ladies' Musical Club of Galveston, one of the oldest performing groups in the city, while at the same time serving as music director and choir director at Trinity. During her tenure at Trinity, the music "reached the peak of excellence and the sacred concerts were eagerly attended by the music lovers of the city."[50]

Louise Parker, Trinity's first woman choir director, was clearly an exception to the long line of men directors hired by the vestry. While she chose a career as a professional musician, she also remained active in the women's cultural life of

Galveston — her affiliations extended to the Wednesday Club, the city's most prestigious literary club — until the birth of her son in 1904. Then she dropped her membership in the Wednesday Club but continued as director of both choirs and as a private voice teacher. Her actions implied a conscious choice concerning her professional life, for given her family's position she did not have to work. On one side, her brother, Charles Fowler, occupied officerships in no fewer than five city civic and commercial enterprises and eleven philanthropic, social, and political associations, in addition to his membership on the vestry. On the other side was her older sister, Mary Fowler Bornefeld, an activist in the women's cultural and literary world, whose interest in woman suffrage ultimately led her to become the first president of the Galveston Equal Suffrage Association. Louise Fowler Parker chose to remain true to her musical talents, preferring salaried employment as Trinity's choir director and voluntary directorship of the Ladies' Musical Club to membership in a women's literary club.[51] Her affiliation gives us some clue about the priorities that she set for herself and the value she placed on using her talents. Churches served as important conduits for women whose music would eventually fill more than just the sanctuary.

Louise Parker was also the beneficiary of a network of women within the church who supported her role as choir director and helped her win that position. Her employment began at a time when laywomen were gaining access to parish and vestry committees, a rare moment at Trinity before 1920. At the same time, women had founded several critically acclaimed choirs in Galveston, where their performances gave them public visibility. Talented voices sang not only in Trinity's choir but also in the Girls' Musical Club and the Ladies' Musical Club. Many Trinity members were officers of these organizations and had proved their capacity to prepare and manage up to four concerts a year, bringing in professional talent from New York and Europe, and presiding over a virtual renaissance of choral music in the years between 1894 and 1920. Even though women's talents were displayed publicly, churchmen were slow to appoint women to positions of authority on music committees equal to their own. So in 1901, fifteen years after the founding of the first women's city chorus, Episcopal rector C. M. Beckwith finally wrote to Clifford Groce, also president of the Ladies' Musical Club, Magnolia Sealy, Kate Ebbert, Horace Nugent, and John Sealy that he had appointed them an ad hoc committee "to take in charge all matters connected with the music of Trinity Church." The rector hoped they would "accept the responsibility as a privilege."[52] In the years between 1904 and 1910, when Louise Parker began work as Trinity's first woman choir director, women also served on the vestry music committee. Clearly, the admission of women to the rector's ad hoc music committee and the vestry's music committees had been a significant factor in her employment.

Music belongs exclusively to neither a man's sphere nor a woman's sphere, but in Galveston at the turn of the century musical talent and musical performance were considered an important cultural component of women's lives. Women with musical abilities and an interest in its performance made their talents available to the church, and choir leaders responded by training both female and male voices for sophisticated enhancement of worship. The exchange of talent from church to community commenced when women formed musical organizations, brought concerts to the public, and kept alive interest in musical achievement. Then realizing women's administrative and professional talents, churchmen opened committees to women artists and gave women like Louise Parker space for development as professional musicians. Their musical talents, long confined to family settings, became visible first through sacred service and later through women's choral organizations—an extension of their cultural gifts from home to church to community.

Galveston after the Civil War evinced a remarkable commercial energy, transforming a small Gulf Coast town into a prosperous city in a matter of twenty years. Wealth, unimaginable in most rural sections of the South, drove Galvestonians to seek within their houses and within their houses of worship a splendor befitting the nouveau riche. Women, usually the silent partners in the creation of cultural distinction, took an especially active role in creating not only elegant sanctuaries but also places for female artistic symbols, magnifying and giving honor to the roles of womanhood in an institution otherwise devoted to the glorification of men or male dieties.

It was normative for women to memorialize family and friends and to be memorialized through the gifts of musical instruments, decorative furnishings, and stained glass; to regard cemetery upkeep as their province within church life; and, if able, to seek musicianship in church choirs and individual performances. Their actions betokened a symbolic discourse that elevated women's roles while demonstrating subtle and covert opposition to the patriarchal system of church hierarchy. They laid claim to the church as a protean institution amenable to their interests and accepting of their values. For many women, defining church decor, pursuing church cemetery upkeep, and performing in sacred worship represented a partial mirroring of women's unique roles in the home. And while artistry and symbolism do not represent real power in ecclesiastical realms, they suggest that women were much more than mere shadows; they exhibited choices in the work they chose to do and in the art they selected for perpetuity. Women gained a sense of worth, self-esteem, and confidence, allowing them to enter areas of church life that required action, decisiveness, and stamina. To find out how women handled their increased roles we must turn to the next chapter.

3

. . . .

CHURCH PROGRAMS

Sunday School, Bible Classes, and Women's Societies

> *The gratification to be earned from progressively learning how to engage,*
> *control, and reap the rewards of the social order are inextricably linked*
> *to women's self-insertion into society.*
>
> — Margaret R. Miles, "Theory, Theology, and
> Episcopal Churchwomen"

When Margaret Riddell McCullough entered the city of Galveston in spring of 1870, hers was a journey of despair. Widowed in January and left with nine children on a piece of ranch land in Caldwell County, Texas, south of Austin, she did the only thing she could do. She packed up her family, traveled by wagon train to the Island City, and sought refuge at the hand of her brother, John Riddell. As with so many women of her generation, Margaret brought with her the fundamentals of a patriarchal Calvinist faith. From Pennsylvania Presbyterian stock, she and her family valued above all the teachings of the covenant and endeavored to live by them even in sorrow. Admonitions to keep the faith ran strong within her family; kinsman William McCullough freely offered her direction in the way of the Lord.

> My dear Cousin, your loss and mine may seem hard but let us submit with
> Christian fortitude and be like our departed friend, also ready. You can, if spared,
> bear testimony to your children that their father loved God and proclaimed the
> righteousness of Christ as the only hope of salvation, and it is hoped that they,
> even in the morning of life, will give their hearts to the Saviour. This charge God
> in his providence has placed upon you. . . . It will be your privilege and your duty
> to pray with and for your children, teaching them by precept and example to
> walk in the ways of holiness. . . . [1]

First things first; once Cousin William had defined Margaret's spiritual duties, he then concerned himself with her temporal well being. "I hope your brother will be faithful . . . and comfort and console you in your sore bereavement. Tell him for me that God will look to him to minister in your behalf, and that he would be unworthy of the name if he fails to assist you at all times and under all circumstances."[2]

Heavy handed, laden with promises of heavenly rewards, tempered with family pride and guilt, William McCullough did his best to impart the cultural and religious values of his age. Although peppered with patriarchal language, there were also in William's words the hint of a larger role for women in leading children to walk in faith. He had firmly established that the most important element in life was the acceptance of Christ's saving grace. Nine little souls were at stake here. If indeed this mission — to bring a soul to salvation — took preeminence over every other aspect of life, then William had just informed Margaret that God had assigned her the most important task a person could fulfill.

The implications of this message for women were enormous. As Mary Beth Norton has pointed out, the elders' stand on the importance of nurturing children in the faith made direct impact on the role, the responsibilities, and, ultimately, the elevation of women, first within the family and then within the church.[3] Margaret McCullough lived up to these religious and familial expectations, and in the course of her forty-one years in Galveston created a much wider role for herself within the church than she or her cousin could have imagined in 1870.

Fortunately, she had a safe harbor in a brother who willingly aided her; she had a church that took her in as one of its own; and she lived at a time when women transformed churches by their active involvement. Returning to Galveston after an absence of sixteen years, she found that survival required the cooperation of helpful relatives and friends. Her late husband, the Reverend John McCullough, who trained at Princeton Theological Seminary, had founded Galveston's First Presbyterian Church in 1840. Though he was described by an early observer as "a young man with very moderate abilities," he, nonetheless, came to be revered by later congregants as a founding pillar of the church. Margaret found a home and a "church home"; in return for this good fortune, she set to work following the prescriptions of her faith, entering into church life, and above all keeping the children involved.[4]

Eight years after her sad return to Galveston, reports to the Pennsylvania relatives stated that "Cousin Margaret is getting along very well." She was not the type of woman to remain dependent for long; her life experiences had supplied her with a fortitude common to many women who accompanied their husbands to the frontier. While looking after her nine children, who by 1880 ranged in age from ten to twenty-six, she kept (as many widows did) fifteen boarders at her home on the corner of Nineteenth Street and Avenue M. While she maintained middle-class respectability, frugality no doubt prevented her from hiring any live-in servants, and hard work filled her days.[5]

Still, William's admonitions continued to follow her. "I imagine," he wrote, "her nine children all seated at table at once. . . . I hope they are all healthy and good looking, and what is better, that they are all children of the covenant and growing wise in things belonging to their everlasting peace." Again, William placed the responsibility for their salvation squarely on Margaret's shoulders. "As a mother's teachings is the most potent agency in the training of children, I have no doubt she is making good use of her opportunity and pointing those whom God has committed to her care to the 'Lamb of God, who taketh away the sins of the world.' "[6]

Cousin William need not have worried. In addition to Margaret's teachings

FIGURE 3.1. Margaret McCullough and her nine children, 1883. Courtesy Rosenberg Library, Galveston, Texas.

at home, the church rosters show all the McCullough children enrolled in Sunday school. Emma, the oldest, taught Sunday school in 1878, a year in which 262 scholars passed through First Presbyterian's program. For several years, Margaret and her daughter Lou spent Sunday afternoons giving Bible lessons to Chinese children. Although gaps in the Sunday school records leave us to wonder if Margaret may have begun earlier, she is shown teaching Sunday school in 1895, the year her youngest child turned twenty-six.[7] As long as the McCullough children lived at home, they remained active in their church. At the very least, Margaret had been successful in "pointing [them] to the 'Lamb of God.'" In return, others within the church helped her raise her nine children, a task she pursued without remarrying.

Perhaps out of a desire for female companionship or from her own sense of moral order, by 1883 Margaret had joined the Ladies' Aid Society of the First Presbyterian Church, an agency committed to relieving the poor. In 1890, she was elected president of this group, a position of honor and respect that she enjoyed until her death in 1911. Although Margaret began life in Galveston as a widow, dependent on male succor and advice, hers was not a life of dependency. As soon as she was able, she became self-supporting, using her domestic skills in a commercial venture to sustain the family. When her children were nearly grown, she began to associate with churchwomen in weekly meetings where the misfortune of others was the chief concern. She spent the latter days of her life an independent woman, surrounded by the company of women.[8] Margaret McCullough's brief biography, culled from the minutes of the Ladies' Aid Society, Sunday school records, census records, and private papers, provides but a glimpse of life for a single Galvestonian before the turn of the century; it hints at the existence of a women's world within churches and at the shadow of an emerging women's community in Galveston. This nascent community of women within Protestant churches managed to gain a measure of influence, even power, by teaching Christian beliefs and values to the young and by forming indispensable Bible classes and women's societies. They encountered male pride in their efforts but also male resistance to their independence. By learning how to turn their sacrifices into positions of privilege, activist churchwomen discovered ways to resist male dominance while establishing a women's agenda for the church—and eventually for the city.

Sunday School

For the women who came with their families to the outposts of the South's postwar frontier, churches offered an escape from loneliness and isolation. Town life fostered churches and hence provided an important place for women to gather in groups outside of their homes. As women joined churches, they saw before them opportunities for creative expansion. They could join a Sunday school class or teach one, form a Bible class or belong to one, begin a mission, lead a youth group, or, most important, they could create their own societies.

When women moved into church teaching positions in postwar Galveston, they found themselves in a vortex of change. A Sunday school movement, begun before the Civil War, experienced a renewed "forward surge" in the postwar years.[9] Churches embraced Sunday schools for several important reasons: to gain new adherents to the faith, thus adding families to the church roll; to stem the tide of secularism that threatened to undermine the morals of society; and to give vocation to those women and young adults who felt called to service in the church. As women joined Sunday school teams, they assumed leadership roles in church training and acted as spiritual guides to those ready for religious conversion. They created positions for themselves as nurturers of young children, as trainers of adolescents in youth leagues, and as religious and moral mentors in a rapidly changing world. Many of these attributes they brought from the home, transferring their concern for the religious education of their own children to the children of others. They altered drab classrooms into inviting places and made the lessons accessible to children. Women teachers believed that they held a special calling to lead the young into paths of righteousness; thus, teaching became a religious vocation for many women, particularly given the fact that they were denied the opportunity to preach from church pulpits.

Becoming a Sunday school teacher had many more consequences than simply moving domestic skills to a new forum; women who taught in mission Sunday schools actually helped initiate the growth of new churches—from single classes to full-fledged parishes or congregations. Churchmen, especially clergy, aware of the talents, enthusiasm, and dedication that lay at their direction, often called upon women teachers to spearhead the founding of missions. This meant offering to the unchurched, usually on the fringes of town, Sunday school classes, which, if successful, would be followed by worship services conducted by male preachers or rectors. Consequently, women founded new churches.

Fortuitously for southern women, the Sunday school was beginning to take on new importance in the postwar years just as women were entering the church volunteer workforce in sizable numbers. Of course, for evangelical churches (Baptist and Methodist) the overriding purpose of Sunday school in the postwar years was not just to study the Bible but to win sinners to Christ. As Sunday school teachers, women, especially mothers, were entrusted with the responsibility of bringing children to the point of conversion or profession, followed by joining the church body. Toward the end of the century, adult classes emerged, and scholars who had already been converted found Sunday school a vehicle for encouraging a revitalization of their faith or a movement of letter (membership) from one church to another. In the last three decades of the nineteenth century, Sunday school stood at the critical juncture between sin and salvation, and women teachers became the principal agents in the process of conversion.[10]

In the antebellum years, sermons, both published and performed, revivals, and camp meetings had served the purpose of reaching sinners and reaping conversions. In rural areas of the antebellum South, where revivals lasted for days, people came in wagons from miles around prepared for a religious encounter that would "awaken hardened and indifferent sinners to the precariousness of their unregenerate condition." Randy Sparks writes that camp meetings took on the intensity of a major battle, as preachers fought the forces of evil, wrested sinners from the clutches of Satan, and literally fought off brigands who tried to break up the meetings. Such opposition only stiffened the resolve of evangelical frontiersmen and women. After the Civil War, in urban areas such as Galveston, revivals and protracted meetings took on an institutional flavor that, while not lacking in intensity, hardly resembled the communal encampments of the rural South or held the immediacy of revivals in southern military camps and communities on the edge of battlefields. Revivals held in urban churches competed with all of the other distractions of city life. By the 1880s, moreover, Protestants, including non-evangelical congregations, had begun to sense that they were losing ground in the contest with secular influences to determine the course of the nation. Even though churches continued to grow numerically in the South, fear of secular influences compelled southern believers to look to Christian education as the key to maintaining ecclesiastical hegemony. Competition from rising public school systems (Galveston established its in 1881) only meant a corresponding decrease in denominational secondary schools, which had provided not only Bible study but also an antidote to secularism.[11] Clearly, Sunday schools and the rise of religious youth organizations in the 1890s — weekly lessons instead of seasonal revivals — came to assume a central position in the edification, conversion, and retention of young people within southern churches.

Astoundingly little has been written about Sunday schools and even less about youth organizations in the New South.[12] Sally McMillen, investigating the Southern Baptist drive for universal Sunday schools, found that fear of external worldliness, crime, poverty, Catholicism, and foreign influences all contributed to the point of view that the Sunday school should stand as an institution for moral reform. With an emphasis on reshaping individual behavior, Sunday schools provided a source of hope that southern youth, through appropriate Christian education, would save the nation and "offset declining values."[13]

The same fear of the decline of moral values that led to the establishment of Sunday schools created church youth groups in the 1890s as well. No doubt their influx can be traced to a general sense of insecurity among parents, teachers, and ministers that adolescents were vulnerable to vice and sin. Ed Ayers notes that family life was "often the subject people worried about most." Certainly, the temptations of adolescence — sexual relations, smoking, drinking, and rebellious behavior — created anxieties among adults, especially in urban areas where city delights beckoned. Members of evangelical denominations railed against dancing, card playing, gambling, even the theater. Fears about African Americans and drinking played a part in this. If inhibitions were lowered by the use of alcohol, no telling what kind of social interaction might follow. As an antidote to temptation churches devised youth programs and attempted to offer a forum of sociability for youth under adult supervision. The Baptist Young People's Union (BYPU) of Galveston's First Baptist Church, organized in 1890, boasted seventy-five teenagers by 1900. They met every Tuesday night at the church, elected their own officers, and offered a variety of programs and entertainments. A younger version, called the Junior Union of First Baptist Church, with a membership of thirty, organized preteens, but with the understanding that they enter the BYPU in their teenage years. The Sunbeam Missionary Society, with a membership of ninety, took children as young as five and prepared them for youth activities, although the express purpose of the organization was to interest children in supporting missionaries. Songs ("I'll Be a Sunbeam for Jesus") and stories acculturated children at an early age to identify with their youth group and their denomination. Thus, Protestant churches, by engaging young children and adolescents in church-supported programs that provided fun and entertainment, hoped to counter the image of church as a somber institution while at the same time attempting to stem the tide of secularism, save the young from indiscretions, and keep them loyal to the church of their childhood.[14]

Women played an important role in the execution of these goals. In Galveston by the 1890s, every denomination for both races had church programs designed especially for youth — the Epworth League, Juvenile Missionary Society, Young People's Society of Christian Endeavor, Luther League, Altar Guild, Daughters of the King, Daughters of Erin, and the like — which continued the work that children's Sabbath schools had begun. Supervision for the Epworth League of the Methodist Episcopal Church, South, for example, came first through the Sunday schools where women volunteers helped in their establishment. Symbolic of the importance of a woman's teachings, the Epworth League was named for the parsonage where John Wesley had received his mother's religious instructions. Epworth Leagues were organized to promote piety and loyalty to the church, to educate young people in the Bible and in church history, to encourage charity, and to provide a safe place for youth to congregate, but they also offered important leadership training for young women.[15]

Galvestonians, especially Protestants, showed an enormous enthusiasm for organizing Sunday schools in a systematic manner. All of the white Protestant churches, all of the black Protestant churches (more about them is in chapter 8), nearly all of the Catholic churches, and even Temple B'nai Israel organized Sunday schools. By 1900, a Chinese Sunday school had been added to the First Presbyterian Church, and all of the denominations had organized some type of youth group. In 1906, 5,088 scholars attended some 41 Sunday schools; Protestants offered the best teacher-pupil ratio: 343 teachers to 3,254 students (9.5 per teacher) as opposed to 40 Catholic teachers for 1,398 students (35 per teacher).[16]

The Presbyterians, who claimed that Sabbath school "preceded the Church in point of age," as early as 1869 were following a curriculum outlined on a quarterly basis that included lessons, home readings, central thoughts, and topical analyses of scriptures. Teachers met monthly for lesson study and weekly for prayer and were encouraged to visit their pupils. All teachers were expected to turn in written reports on the spiritual condition of their students as well as their attendance habits, promptness, and the quality of their responses to the lessons. In 1875, the Presbyterian Sunday school boasted nine male officers, eight male teachers, nineteen female teachers, and 137 scholars (73 females, 64 males). Although top heavy with male officers, women demonstrated greater concern for their pupils' advancement and nurture. Women were more often in attendance at the monthly meetings, and they were better at keeping up with the children outside of class.[17]

In the First Baptist Church, the congregation and the board of deacons relied on churchwomen to keep the Sunday school open and growing. Although Sabbath school had been established as early as 1846, when half the teachers were women, immediately after the Civil War no Sunday school existed. By 1874, the church recovered a membership of 120 and supported two Sunday schools: one of its own and another at their newly established East End Mission at Fourteenth Street and Avenue K. In both Sunday schools Baptist women provided the motivation for continuation. But the mission school, which had no pastor to preach the service, was on its own. Hence, in January 1874 a committee of three, including Martha Poole, raised money to purchase new hymn books and the necessary equipment for the mission school. The women's efforts allowed the school to become an independent operation based on tithes and contributions.[18]

At about this time, the Methodists began to consider evangelizing the poorer and more sparsely settled western end of the city. Acting as "spearheads" in the evangelizing process, experienced female Sunday school teachers set off to begin a new Sunday school. Only after the women had broken ground, both structurally and spiritually, and after a sufficient number of adults also had begun to desire worship services, would a pastor from the home church offer worship or prayer meetings. The significance of this cannot be understated; women who taught Sunday school and who performed mission duty formed new congregations. Had they been able to seek seminary training and ordination, they most assuredly would have pastored those congregations as well. But women founders settled for the knowledge that they had obeyed a call to servanthood, teaching instead of preaching. This was the case in 1885, when Eliza Perkins, a teacher in St. James' Methodist Church, held the first mission Sunday school in her home in the city's West End. Both St. James' and St. John's Methodist Episcopal Church, South, supported the mission endeavor, but when Mrs. E. G. Foster, a teacher at St. John's, joined Eliza Perkins, they raised $200 for a small classroom built on land owned by Mrs. Foster. Once students started coming to Sunday school, parents soon followed. A pastor from St. James' blessed the infant congregation with prayer meetings, and by July 1888 a new church was established, which, of course, called a man to be its spiritual leader.[19]

Founding missions also became a top priority for Trinity Episcopal Church, which sponsored a West End parochial mission. Rector Stephen M. Bird, imagining a mission Sunday school, sent young Effie Raymond to head one up. In a schoolroom on Forty-second Street and Broadway in 1874, she and an assistant opened a Sunday afternoon class for seven scholars. Soon after, Trinity Guild bought a lot and built Trinity Chapel for the continuance of the mission Sunday school and the commencement of occasional services. Within a year, Episcopal women had increased the Sunday school to 100 scholars and the chapel to fifty members. In this case, as in the others, women had again created a new parish. By January 1876, members of the congregation of Trinity Chapel petitioned for independent parish status with the Diocese of Texas under the name Grace Episcopal Church, the same church that Henry and Mollie Rosenberg adopted as their own parish. Two other missions for whites, St. Andrew's and St. Michael's, began in 1880 and 1884 with teachers from Trinity Church, but they did not survive the 1900 storm. St. Augustine Episcopal Church, the city's only African American Episcopal church began as a mission in 1884. There is no indication that Trinity women or men taught Sunday school there, and why that is so remains a puzzle. Racism must be considered as a possible explanation, but church historian Lawrence Brown suggests that there may have been resistance to white intrusion on the part of St. Augustine's congregants, who were Jamaican immigrants, members of the Church of England, and accustomed to autonomous parishes governed by black parish officers and clergymen.[20]

Many Protestant women were intensely interested in the establishment of missions and in working in Sunday schools. There were excellent reasons for their concerns. Given moral legitimacy by churchmen, who praised their nurturing abilities, their central influence on children, and their tender Christlike nature, women were called to a special mission to reach the young and lead them to discipleship within the Christian community. Postwar Sunday schools nationwide were affected by the teaching of Horace Bushnell, author of *Views of Christian Nurture*, first published in 1846, and advocate of advancing a child's growth with proper religious instruction. Mothers and Sunday school teachers, Bushnell said, were eminently suited to bring a child to the point of conversion through Bible stories and by acting as affectionate models of God's love. Home was the initial setting for nurturing, and in the postbellum period Christians considered home a little bit of heaven on earth. It afforded a mother the opportunity to become a kind of secular angel.[21]

Probably one reason the home took on such importance as the arena for consistent Christian nurture in Galveston was that postwar churches were ill prepared to offer children an environment comparable to a loving home presided

over by an angelic mother. Sunday schools were decentralized, notoriously un-
derfunded, understaffed, and conducted in buildings that provided few delights
for the child. Martha Poole, a teacher in Galveston's First Baptist Church Sunday
School for at least forty-seven years, described her early teaching years in the 1870s.

> The Sunday School was an unorganized body, with no adult members excepting
> the superindendent and the teachers, without song-books or literature. Scripture
> lessons were given and each teacher followed her own method of teaching. Dr.
> Howard [pastor] . . . asked me to take charge of the little tots. Before that, however,
> Judge Cole brought me a simple song in a paper, and asked me if I could sing
> it, and then teach it to the school. So I had become music-teacher, and intro-
> duced the first Gospel Songs. There was a small house used as the pastor's study,
> for we had no parsonage. Into that I took my class, a bare room with no accessories
> whatever. I found my own subject matter, and taught my own way, and I was
> never happier than when with my little tots. . . .

One student remembered with affection that "each class had its separate corner or place in which to meet. At the tap of her bell all assembled to hear her
give a summary of the lesson for that day. The Bible stories, so simply told by her,
were taken in by small minds and the seeds of truth therein inplanted are now
bringing forth fruit."[22] The physical structure improved during Martha Poole's
time; she eventually received her own classroom, which she made into a comfortable space for her little learners.

The atmosphere within Sunday schools changed when women introduced
the nurturing qualities of the home into the classroom. Teaching emboldened
them to shape the environment for children, and they took increasing responsibility for the design and furnishing of Sunday school rooms, buying child-size
tables and chairs, cushions, carpets, and books and raising the money for Sunday
school projects through bazaars and fairs. They transformed austere church structures into attractive settings. The result was a form of domestication of the church,
which, even with its male hierarchy, provided women a supportive semipublic
domain and a familiar space for children. Women teachers often provided children
with gentle remonstrances of affection, unlike male Sunday school superintendents
who sometimes remained aloof. Superintendent Oscar Farish likened his role at
Trinity Episcopal Church to that of a "general at the head of an army, his teachers
his lieutenants, and the scholars his soldiers." His military imagery was misplaced,
however, for in actuality he "never interfered with the School farther than occasionally visiting it, catechising the children, and delivering those pleasing and
interesting adresses, always making the officers, teachers and scholars glad at his
appearance and grateful by his recognition and encouragement." Farish took on
the role of kindly father, benevolent, supportive, generous, but uninvolved, not
unlike the perceived role of a father in the home.[23]

Episcopalians and members of evangelical churches took different approaches
to Sunday school and missions. Evangelical laity in the South, concerned with
bringing the uncommitted to Christ, saw Sunday schools and missions (along with
revivals and weekly preaching) as a means to conversion. Episcopalians thought
of Sunday school and mission outreach as a way to teach children and potential

communicants the "church system." Because many Texans were converts to the Episcopal church, the purpose of Sunday school was not only to save souls but also to inform, instruct, and catechise members, especially children, in church doctrine, discipline, and worship. This required a patient approach, as emotional exhortations from the pulpit or individual evangelizing had no place in the church's "orderly round of observances." Theoretically, as time went by, with consistent biblical and creedal teaching, and with instruction in the services, life, and "holy work of the Church—the living, mystical body of Christ," individually and collectively parishoners would bring forth the desired results, a church whose every member would grow up into "Him who is the Head."[24] Training children and youths in the church system required not only weekly catechism but also the use of *The Book of Common Prayer* for worship services; in short, Sunday school imparted churchman(woman)ship to the uninitiated.

The roles that Episcopal women assumed as Sunday school teachers differed from those in evangelical churches. Evangelical teachers, by virtue of their belief in original sin, were given the immense responsibility of leading to conversion a child who was considered unredeemed and, in the Baptist tradition, unsaved until submission, profession, baptism, and redemption. Episcopal women teachers took under their tutelage children who, because of infant baptism, had had the sin of Adam erased and who were ready to be trained through religious education.[25] The differences in these approaches—evangelism versus church training—would eventually result in profound dissimilarities in the way churchwomen of different backgrounds addressed community outreach and reform. Women from evangelical churches were more concerned about poverty of the spirit rather than a person's material well-being. Consequently, among evangelical women "soul work" took precedence over poor relief. But within the classroom, the *process* of teaching, organizing, nurturing, and training was remarkably similar. Evangelical and Episcopal women were needed to nurture, love, and train children, and over time, the Episcopal Sunday school changed to reflect the influence of women teachers.

Trinity Episcopal Sunday school, founded in 1843, was probably the oldest among the island schools. Antebellum vestry minutes, which discuss mostly the finances of the parish, are absolutely silent on the subject of Sunday school and whether its teachers were men or women. In the post–Civil War years, "ladies of the Episcopal Church" put their domestic talents to work on a Sunday school fair and fundraiser at the courthouse. Revenue came from the efforts of "the ladies," who donated a "great variety of articles which had been prepared by the needles of the girls and their mothers." Cakes and "viands," fishponds and fruit compote stands (complete with Gail Borden's condensed milk), and, finally, lotteries and auctions netted the Sunday school enough money to reorganize. By 1867, the Sunday school was in "an unusually flourishing condition." It boasted an excellent library, "comprising many standard works of elegant literature," available to all parish members. In the days before free libraries, a parish full of books offered communicants something more than sermons, ritual, and sacred music. As another example of the domestication process, private libraries, first introduced in homes, were replicated in churches in Galveston before the advent of a free library in 1879.[26]

The Episcopal laity understood very early the need to create an environment attractive to children. One way to do that was to promote a sense of Sunday school as family, to hold parties and outings, and to praise students and reward them with the kind of recognition that built self-esteem. To that end, three annual festivities marked the traditional Sunday school calendar—a summer picnic, a Christmas party, and an awards ceremony and Easter processional. The whole Sunday school family celebrated the advent of summer as teachers and superintendents herded the children aboard the Galveston, Houston, and Henderson train to Dickinson Bayou on their annual summer picnics. There the children played croquet, roamed the woods, wandered up and down the bayou, and danced as a band played. The yearly Christmas party held in a rented hall included square dancing, feasting, and game playing.[27]

The Easter celebration, which was covered in detail by the city newspapers, displayed to the church and to the community the achievements of the little scholars (and the Sunday school) in a stately atmosphere designed to impart dignity, pride, and honor. After an elaborate ceremony, the rector read aloud the names of those students who were to receive honors and prizes for their performance in Sunday school. Eighty-one honor roll recipients heard their names announced to the assembly. Prize winners went away with books, except for the two children who won the rector's prizes—two gold crosses. That year eight children were eligible for this highest award, but the prizes went to two little girls: Annie Scoby, a "little orphan girl, from Trinity Church Sunday School," and Daisy Bell of Trinity Chapel Sunday School in the West End. Whatever else may be said of the Easter Sunday awards ceremony, apparently it pleased the community because Sunday school enrollment increased to 400 by 1885 and to 667 by 1894, exceeding other Protestant Sunday schools in the city.[28]

The type of pageantry displayed on Easter was specifically designed to win the loyalty of children to the church and to impress upon their hearts the special symbolism of their new life in Christ on the day of resurrection. Along with this spiritual message was another: hard work and constancy will be rewarded. In this commercial city and in a church where the fruits of success in commerce were most clearly visible, the lessons of competition and reward were made applicable to the life of the church. Although there are no records to indicate who planned the ceremony with its attendant awards, most likely competition and prizes were introduced because they had been successfuly used in other Sunday schools and in grammar schools and because they fit well with concepts of advancement in the business world. By 1879, a point system had been introduced, and the little scholars were graded on church attendance, Sunday school attendance, and lessons and deportment for the year.[29]

How children responded to the use of competition in church life raises a host of questions, all of which are complicated by issues of gender. Well before introduction of the concept of Muscular Christianity, a late nineteenth-century ideology that imagined a strong, manly Jesus and a robust faith, Galveston children were asked to apply rigor to their Bible study and their church life. Could it be that competition for prizes used by parents, elders, schools, and Sunday schools contributed to the culture of capitalism? Did awards, ceremonies, point systems, and pageantry, intended to bring a sense of pride in self and in church work, teach children lessons equally applicable to the world of commerce or politics? For boys, at least, the message imparted through Sunday schools was complementary to masculine notions of work, achievement, and advancement. Just as evangelicalism in northern churches had its message of respectability and time management for working-class men, the southern Episcopal church system offered a corresponding message for middle- and upper-class boys destined to assume not only vestry duty but also the commercial and civic leadership of the town and state.[30]

How did *girls* respond to the message that hard work, constancy, and competition brought rewards? The education of women before 1875 in Galveston and in the South had been reserved primarily for those families that could afford the expense of educating daughters. This limited group of young women, through private schools and seminaries, was taught not so much to compete as to accommodate. Lessons in aesthetics, complementary to but opposite from the lessons in the disciplines for men, left women with few skills and little incentive to compete in the public realm. Theirs was an education designed to fill the home with refinement. Between 1875 and 1920, education for women went through a transition of great importance as public schools, especially high schools, were adopted in cities across the South and as education became somewhat more equal for both sexes. Women's colleges in the Northeast and in the South, which a few Texas women attended, opened with the intention of granting an education as rigorous as the men's.[31]

Public schools and the improved Episcopal Sunday school, both of which reinforced systems of work and rewards, were introduced to Galveston at about the same time. Perhaps the young women who heard this message felt some sense of confusion. How were they to act on messages that applied to a male ideal? Yet they too were learning these lessons as if they had similar access to public work. How young women dealt with the issues of competition, public recognition, and the consequences of educational opportunities is not easily sorted out. But the girls in the 1875 Easter Sunday processional had already imbibed the competitive spirit—forty-eight of the eighty-one scholars on the honor roll were girls, and the two highest prizes went to girls. The years ahead for these young women would prove to be full of enormous change for the position of women in society. In looking over the list of girls and young women, at least four names leap from the page as those who, twenty-five years later, would become some of the city's most energetic leaders. Within the church, girls and adult women found themselves increasingly exposed to patterns of "masculine" behavior, values reflective of those who seek achievements in a public forum.[32] Perhaps it was an amalgamation of women's traditional values and the psychological acceptance of standards applied to men that formed a more independent and assertive female body within the church. This was reflected most clearly in the autonomous women's societies, but it was also reflected, as we shall see, in the way individual women leaders created "powerful" roles for themselves in independent adult Bible classes.

Independent Bible Classes—A Tale of Two Women

Occasionally, an adult Bible class within a Protestant church took on a life of its own. When this happened, an institution within the church was established that, while not superseding the authority of the Sunday school superintendent or the pastor, in reality became more powerful than the superintendent's office and certainly had the potential for challenging pastoral authority. Independent classes such as these usually were named after and taught by women.

Since female teachers in Protestant churches before the turn of century (and some well into the twentieth) were usually under the authority of male superintendents, they had little chance to exert leadership skills beyond the classroom, except perhaps as assistant superintendents. Seen as nurturers rather than administrators, women were seldom offered the opportunity to supervise Sunday schools, even though some worked as principals in elementary schools.[33] A few determined women with impeccable church credentials managed to earn places of honor and independence within their congregations by remaining primarily Sunday school teachers. In these cases, the reward for service amounted to an independent Bible class, a base of respect that could not be duplicated in the home, but which commanded the veneration of men and women within and outside of the church. There were several such Bible classes in Galveston, two of which are illustrated here.

The Martha Poole Bible Class had become an independent institution in the post–Civil War all-white First Baptist Church. Poole was never its teacher; rather the class was named in her honor before she joined it. How did she come to have a class named for her that continued long after her death? The answer lies in the extraordinary length of service and depth of commitment that she gave to her church at a time when it had experienced drastic changes.

Arriving in Galveston as a bride from New York on January 1, 1861, Martha Poole and her husband, Valentine, attended church at the first opportunity. She found a handful of "people worshiping in the simplest manner," singing "old fashioned hymns of praise." Soon after their visit, the pastor and a contingent of ladies called on her to unite with their congregation. The women invited her to join their church home, an act of outreach and potential friendship for which members of evangelical denominations were well known. Besides, they wanted new members. This was the sort of overture that strangers to a new community needed in order to integrate into town life. It was essential for wives, who, if they remained homemakers, had few formal ties to organizations outside the home. For most women in the immediate postwar period, integration into a semipublic community of women also began in a congregation (church or synagogue).[34]

For Martha Poole, church was the first, and arguably the most important, contact outside her family in this new city. Apparently, she alone held up the churchgoing traditions. Perhaps the visitors invited her husband to seek fellowship with them as well, but Martha's reminiscences do not mention him again, and the records do not indicate that he joined the church.[35] Rumor had it that Valentine was an emotionally abusive husband. For women with insensitive or unkind spouses, the evangelical community with its emphasis on love and redemption offered the kind of environment wives sought in their own homes but often did not have. The "church family" in a sense liberated women from the confines of spiritually dulling relationships, broadened their opportunities to perform creative and fulfilling work, and rewarded them with the praise and adulation they lacked at home. Piety had a great deal to do with the initial search for such a community; Donald Mathews labels this a "fervent search for maturity." But the need for emotional succor also played a role. In a world dominated by secular institutions headed by men, women found in church a community that honored their religious commitments, and included, accepted, and encouraged them within the limits of their sphere.[36]

In her reminiscences Martha recalled that she began her association with other churchwomen by joining a small choir. No sooner had she done so when the Civil War forced the church doors to close, and members departed for the interior. Martha remained on the island for a time worshipping with the Methodists, singing in their choir, and making friends among the Methodist and Presbyterian women. Meanwhile, she kept an eye on the Baptists' small clapboard church, which was used alternatively as a sanctuary for soldiers' services, a barracks, and a school for freedmen. Apparently, without regard for the freedmen who would lose their school, she made the first overtures to the Union military commander for return of the church to its congregants. Unsuccessful on her own, she returned with a committee of three churchmen and petitioned the Freedmen's Bureau for repossession. "The building was in a horrible condition, . . . carpets and cushions had been taken by our own soldiers. Dirt and grease covered seats and floor. The roof was worn out, and fences for the three lots gone," she wrote. "But we set ourselves resolutely to work to restore our former place of worship. Every Saturday afternoon, early, we sisters met there, and while one sat at the sewing-machine, others cut and basted all manner of every-day wear until compelled to leave. Each one took home work to be finished. We found ready sale, and at length repairs were made."[37] Painting, repairing, and replacing window sashes fell to the men; women handled all of the decorating, refurbishing, and "domesticating" of the church interior *plus* all the costs involved in the restoration.

It also was in 1866 that Martha Poole began her long teaching career in the Sunday school, beginning with the "Infant Class" and leading in 1901 to her superintendency of the "Junior Department," a position of authority few women in Galveston achieved. In 1913, when her younger Baptist sisters formed the Martha Poole Bible Class for adult women, she wrote, "I appreciated the unexpected honor, and occasionally said a few words to them. When my health failed so I could no longer conduct my work as I felt it ought to be conducted, I resigned, and of course, joined my class. . . . It cheers many an hour that would otherwise be lonely, while I wait for release from my worn-out body, and the spiritual body that will again enable me to be an active servant of my Lord." On her ninetieth birthday, class members hung her portrait in the room where her class met; they gave her a party "showered with beautiful flowers." The Sunday following her death in 1927, the congregation eulogized her in worship service as one of the sainted ones, printed her likeness in the church bulletin, and praised her as the mother of the church Sunday school where she had trained most of its teachers.

FIGURE 3.2. Martha Poole at age ninety. Courtesy Rosenberg Library, Galveston, Texas.

Deacon Charles Sherwood offered an address entitled "Martha Poole: What Made Her Great," and pastor Thomas Harvey preached on "Heavenly Recognition." Spread across the church bulletin and the *Baptist Standard* were "Resolutions of Respect" by four class members.[38] Martha Poole was honored as the most luminous of its devoted servants. At no time had anyone, man or woman, inspired such attention within the First Baptist Church.

The illustration of Martha Poole's unwavering sacrificial life raises questions regarding the place of women in the church relative to men. Randy Sparks writes, "The doctrine of Christian equality was in one sense a double-edged sword, for while it struck effectively at hierarchy, it implicitly undercut patriarchy as well. Evangelicals were unwilling to pursue the doctrine of the equality of all believers to its logical conclusions." In denying equal authority to women and in perpetuating fundamental inequality of opportunity for women, churchmen formed a policy at odds with the doctrine of equality in Christ. But women remained in churches, even dominated them numerically, despite the asymmetry of authority. Why women should choose to belong to and support patriarchal institutions may be explained by a theology that awarded power to some and privilege to others. Men who practiced piety and service were rewarded positions of power within the church — as stewards, deacons, vestrymen, elders, and clergy — but for women the same dedication, even sacrifice, more often brought rewards of honor rather than authority. Feminist theologian Margaret R. Miles has labeled this "privileged subordination," wherein women who project an image of "humility, submissiveness, and attentiveness to others' needs" are honored in Christian tract literature, sermons, and artwork. As meager as this compensation seems, this was, after all, one of the few areas where women found any public recognition at all. Of course, newspaper obituaries proclaimed Martha's earnest involvement in the Sunday school, and prior to her death journalists had recounted her many sacrifices. But if we are to believe the devotional literature of the time, women who followed the precepts of self-sacrifice in Christ's name were to take delight only in Him and not in earthly prizes such as power or money. "Lay not up for yourselves treasures on earth," spoke of material possessions, but everyone knew that Jesus' dictum included eschewing power in order to walk humbly with God. Love, sacrifice, and humility were ideal Christian qualities ascribed to women that bound them to a subservient role in the temporal church while elevating them to a higher position within the theologically idealistic "body of Christ." We must assume that most women adjusted to their status by accepting this dual position. A theology based on power to men and privilege to women was familiar to them as Christians and as women who knew and understood their place in this dualistic hierarchical system.[39]

The authoritarian, patriarchal, and sometimes Calvinistic position of southern evangelical churches constituted only one side of the picture; the reverse side was an understanding of the Resurrection in terms of Christ's overpowering, unlimited, unconditional love. Depicted as the weaker sex, sacrifices by women of the sort seen in churches across the South constituted the earthly manifestation of Christ's love, a love so encompassing that even death could not end it. To be Christlike was not only to be self-sacrificing but to teach the gospel, to console the mournful, and to accept those within the Christian community regardless of station or need. The qualities that attracted many women, working-class folk, and blacks to the evangelical denominations was not fear but love. Christians of both sexes were reminded that they should "make love their aim" but that "love is not . . . arrogant" and "does not insist on its own way."[40] Because women embodied love, a condition assigned to them as a component of their gender role, they saw themselves idealistically closer to a Christlike model than men. Out of humility came honor; from sacrifice, privilege. Martha Poole, through her years of teaching, singing, and faithfulness created a position of respect for herself within the congregation. Her reward, however, came as a gift, unsought and unexpected. She never cashed in her sacrifices for greater access to power.

There were women, however, who, unwilling to accept marginality, understood that rewards were possible and made the system of privilege work to bring them a measure of authority. As Margaret Miles writes, "by the exercise of individual creativity some women were able to use the condition of privileged subordination to play roles in the patriarchal church and in society that they might otherwise not have achieved."[41] Ida Smith Austin was such a woman; she fashioned her rise in church affairs through years of devotion and hard work within First Presbyterian Church and, thus, was able to take the system of reward and privilege about as far as a woman could go. The wife of Valery Austin, a prominent real estate dealer and city commissioner, she presents another picture of a Sunday school teacher whose class became an institution unto itself.

Born in 1858 in Lexington, Virginia, and educated at Mary Baldwin College in Staunton, Ida Smith came to Texas in 1881 to teach public school. Three years later she began her Sunday school teaching. When she married in 1885, she gave up public school teaching to set up housekeeping and to devote her talents to Sunday school. One dedicated to the role of teaching could make much or little out of a Sunday school position. Ida Austin, who remained childless, transferred her enormous energies and enthusiasm for teaching to the church. In 1884, she began with a class of five girls; the next year five boys lost their teacher and asked to join her class. She recalled that "there was some opposition in the minds of our church fathers as to the propriety of allowing the goats and the sheep to graze in the same spiritual pastures together." Acting out of good sense, Ida took a firm stand against the "fathers" in her quest for independence. "Realizing that if unpresbyterian it was not unspiritual, [she] went on in the even tenor of her way."[42]

Sometime in the years between 1884 and 1909, her students changed from children to a mixture of young people and adults. At the end of that time the class members "christened" it the Ida Austin Bible Class, chose class colors of maroon and gold, and subscribed to this motto: "With God everything, without God nothing." In 1912, one of its members, Josephine English, gave in memory of her husband enough funds to construct the English Memorial Chapel for use as a classroom by the Ida Austin Bible Class. Women often raised money for or dedicated funds toward a Sunday school building as part of the domestication process of the church complex. But this was different. A single gift from one woman to construct a Sunday school class for another seems to have been unique in Galveston and may speak volumes about Ida Austin's prestige. The congregation dedicated the structure that same year before a "large gathering of God's people." Between 1909 and 1934, 5,000 visitors registered with the class secretary, and through the years the class elected nine presidents, and seven secretaries and existed through the terms of seven pastors. Ida Austin remained its teacher for fifty-three years until her death in 1936.[43]

Obviously, this class had a profound impact on its members, who, the promotional literature proclaimed, went forth "well trained and grounded in the Faith of Our Fathers to spread the Gospel message and win souls for Christ." But what did such a class do for women within the church? First, it allowed other women to see that there were ways to achieve authority within the patriarchal hierarchy. Second, it empowered Ida Austin to such a position of almost reverential awe that several students remarked she made them feel as if they needed to curtsey.[44] Denied access to the ministry, excluded from ordination as an elder or deacon, there were but two avenues for women to pursue who felt called to proclaim the gospel — missionary service or Sunday school teaching.

Finally, the class over time evolved into a group of adults, giving Austin a position of substantial influence over men. She was the teacher of ministers and missionaries, deacons and elders, becoming, thereby, one of the most influential women in the church. The tribute of one young member claimed "he felt that the foundation of his life and character, and its greatest influence was through the guidance of his Mother and Mrs. Austin's teachings." Convinced of their mission to spread the gospel and using Sunday school as a vehicle, women like Ida Austin found that time and perseverance were their best allies. As the numbers grew, as the coffers filled with offerings, and as the reputation of the teaching spread, Austin's personal worth rose. Assuming the aura of a minister, Austin created a separate enclave within the church, making herself indispensable and thereby untouchable to those who might challenge such a position for women. Her stately rank was enhanced by wealth, her husband's political career, and her own involvement in a number of other voluntary associations outside of the church. In this important period of transition for women, Ida Smith Austin gathered to herself adherents, admirers, and supporters, using her talents to build a powerful base within the church and expanding upon it into the community. She never strayed outside of the boundaries of women's sphere, but she stretched them to include a potent role for herself in an institution that denied women professional standing.[45]

Both Martha Poole and Ida Austin embodied the sacrificial nature of Christ in their willingness to devote years to teaching the gospel. Both were honored, but where one accepted honor almost passively, the other turned privilege into opportunities for authority.[46] Class and a sense of power derived from status may have played a role. Perhaps Martha Poole's humility stemmed in part from her middle-class status in a city where elite Episcopalians and Presbyterians dominated polite society; Ida Austin's sense of importance came in part from her more elite background and education. Wealth and status helped elevate dedicated Christian women within the church and the community. Austin's many volunteer roles outside the church, in contrast to Martha Poole's few, were another indication of the enhancement gained through class status. For those with means, honor and privilege could be used as a vehicle for assuming limited authority in the secular as well as the sacred world.

Women's Church Societies

If power existed at all for the majority of women in churches, it resided in groups — but only in some groups and only elusively. Laywomen did not form women's church societies necessarily to gain power; rather, they joined together to accomplish tasks and to find companionship. In some cases, the work they set out to do and the way they managed it led to a certain amount of leverage within the congregation, a certain portion of control, even a certain respect, perhaps a moment or two of power. At times they offered a challenge to the male governing boards and clergy, at others they remained helpmeets and church housekeepers.

Women's church societies did not of themselves provide liberation to women, but as Rosemary Keller writes, the "entrance of women into lay leadership decisively changed the status and role of females in Protestant churches during the nineteenth century," and through their "self-created separatist organizations, females enlarged their churches' programs."[47] Occasionally, a church society provided women contact with the crueler dimensions of life in the city, gave them a glimpse of life beyond their sheltered walls, and helped project them onto a larger stage. These groups, and there were but three identifiable ones in Galveston by 1880, formed relief societies, which served as springboards for women into civic responsibilities.

In the early days of Galveston's existence, just after its legal incorporation in 1839, Protestant women formed prayer groups and sewing societies. Although these groups were not the only societies fostered by women—immigrant aid groups and Jewish synagogue societies offered equally valuable forums for women's interests—churches were for the majority of Galveston women the first institutions outside the home to offer a place to gather purposefully.

By the 1880s, every church had its women's society, but these groups differed, each according to its stated purposes.[48] Invariably, there were six types of women's church societies in the postwar years: prayer groups and sodalities, altar guilds that prepared the chancel for worship, ladies' aid societies that raised money for church improvements, home mission societies that raised money for denominational missions within the United States, foreign mission societies that raised funds for missionaries, and benevolent or poor relief societies (discussed in chapter 4).

Quite often, in the beginning of organized church life, a sole women's society fulfilled more than one of these functions. But as the opportunity for women's ministry expanded, greater "specialization" occurred and several different groups might coexist within a single church. As a new generation of young women entered into volunteer church life, many preferred to start their own societies in order to be with women their own age. Eventually, there grew to be so many societies, guilds, leagues, sodalities, auxiliaries, and unions that the Galveston city directory in 1914 stopped listing them all. And by the 1920s, every denomination took steps toward consolidating the many groups that women had formed—some adopted the circle plan (dividing the women of the church into small groups or circles), others simply brought all women together under one rubric and called them the Women of the Church. Most church societies eventually allied themselves with state- or regional-level women's associations, which enabled them to affiliate with women beyond their single church.[49]

Despite the variety, it is important to understand how collectively the societies expanded within the churches or into public life, how women labored to create a world for themselves inside the church, how they stretched the limits of their woman's sphere to issues and activities outside the church, and, finally, how they came to understand the incompetence of some male leaders and to challenge their own subordinate role in church governance. More should be said about denominational differences among white churches as well as class distinctions, because these shaped the ways in which many women approached their church-womanship and their relations to the world outside the church. Some denominations emphasized certain aspects of ministry and limited women to roles that did not encourage their worldly involvement or encouraged it only in certain directions. Then, too, wealth, or the lack of it, dictated choices. It is commonly understood that denominations followed class lines and that practices and customs among the different denominations influenced the routes women took within their societies. How women reacted to needs outside of the church and how they came to see themselves as potentially equal partners in church affairs was in part determined by their economic status and their denominational choices. All of these forecast their involvement in future civic affairs.

Prayer Groups, Altar Guilds, and Catholic Lay Societies

No one could deny the value of prayer groups and sodalities in fostering a more spiritual environment; hence, women were made to feel useful to the church in solemnizing their faith through prayer and regular assembly. Catholics tended to formalize their prayer life into sodalities. Sodalities for children in connection with St. Mary's Cathedral and the Society of the Sacred Heart were listed in city directories beginning in 1880 and 1883, respectively. By the following decade, sodalities for women and young ladies and altar societies sprang up in connection with St. Mary's Cathedral, St. Patrick's Church, St. Joseph's German Catholic Church, and the Parish of the Sacred Heart. Although men performed the celebration of the eucharist, women in altar guilds carved out ancillary roles for themselves by attending to the implements surrounding communion, by decorating the site with flowers and embroidered coverings, and by making or mending the priests' vestments. Episcopal women formed the Guild of the Blessed Virgin Mary in 1887, later known as the Altar Guild, which trained young women in the "history, observance, and meaning of the church building itself." In taking care of the altar, the chancel, and the implements needed for the eucharist, women found a way to participate in this sacred celebration, a ritual originally limited to and traditionally presided over by men. While nonliturgical churches often did not have altar guilds, women in these churches purchased the communion chairs, made the communion bread, and bought, distributed, and washed the communion sets before and after the Lord's supper.[50]

The association of Catholic laywomen into church aid societies began in 1871 with the founding of the Society of the Sacred Heart, an association that primarily served the parish. By the 1890s, in addition to women's sodalities, altar societies, and Christian mothers' societies, there appeared Leagues of the Sacred Heart, St. Paula's Reading Circle, and a Benevolent Society of Sacred Heart Church. Thirteen such church-related Catholic laywomen's societies existed in 1910. The first Catholic laywomen's organization founded outside a parish in Galveston was the Catholic Daughters of America, which was an auxiliary to the Knights of Columbus and served social, literary, and charitable purposes. In 1916, laywomen formed a women's auxiliary to aid the Sisters of Charity of the Incarnate Word in the work of caring for the children of St. Mary's Orphanage. On the whole, Catholic laywomen contributed to the life of the church through sodalities, altar guilds, primary parish care societies, and auxiliaries to Catholic men's associations or to women's religious orders. It seems that Catholic laywomen devoutly served these organizations and institutions but without forming their own women's societies free of clerical control.[51]

When evaluating who stepped out of women's societies into public service, we see that Catholic women had several obstacles in their way. First, their associations were tied to a church that valued parochial over secular institutions. For example, when free public schools opened in Galveston, Catholic children flocked to them. Alarmed over the loss of their schoolchildren and desiring to keep parishioners from secular influences, Bishop Nicholas A. Gallagher in 1883 announced that no child in public school would receive the sacraments of first communion or be confirmed; moreover, parents of children in public schools would receive no sacraments. In other words, attending public schools was a sin.[52] Catholic religious orders set up institutions — hospitals, schools, cemeteries — to care for their own in every aspect of life, creating an insular community that needed little from the city beyond public services and freedom for businesses. Although Catholic families lived among non-Catholics, worked beside them, and tendered care to non-Catholics in times of crisis, they kept to themselves, a fact that was reflected in the women's parish societies.

Other impediments remained to discourage Catholic women's involvement in secular women's activities outside the parish. Laywomen were supposed to raise large families and, short of that, to support Catholic institutions, but they were not encouraged to seek wider fields of service in the same way that women in religious orders were. Moreover, Catholic families, though outnumbering Protestants sometimes two to one, were largely of working-class or immigrant origins, a fact that impeded the access of women into socially elite semisecular clubs and boards of lady managers for benevolent institutions. Then too, although Galvestonians professed a liberal tolerance and lived in harmony with whites of varying ethnicity, the dominant Protestant/Jewish elite still discriminated socially against members of the working classes and especially against Catholics.[53] Social acceptability, that is, a combination of economic well-being, education in the refinements of society, and inclusion in certain congregations became important criteria for the admission of women into clubwork or benevolent institutions. A few Catholic women transcended the barriers and entered into Galveston's women's civic community after 1900, when secular women's organizations became somewhat more democratic. But out of 370 women who were active in civic affairs from 1880 to 1920, only 21 or 5.7 percent were identified as Catholic, well below their numerical representation in the city (see table 3.1). Alongside discrimination, it is probable that Catholic insularity, discouragement on the part of the clerics, and few experiences in directing their own choices tended to inhibit the movement of Catholic laywomen into secular civic and reforming activities.[54]

Missionary Societies

Women understood the Great Commission, or the spreading of the gospel to all the lands, in concrete terms. They aided home and foreign missions by raising money for those who worked in mission fields; they educated the congregation and especially children in mission work, and prayed for the support required for each of these endeavors.[55]

TABLE 3.1. White Congregational Membership and Activist Women by Denominations in Galveston

Denomination	No. 1890	% 1890	No. 1906	% 1906	No. 1916	% 1916	No. Activist	% Women
Baptist	734	(5.3)	534	(2.5)	1,220	(5.2)	21	(5.7)
Catholic#	8,200	(59.6)	14,872	(69.6)	11,299	(48.6)	21	(5.7)
Dis. of Christ	50	(.3)			379	(1.6)	3	(.8)
Episcopal#	670	(4.9)	1,278	(6.0)	815	(3.5)	136	(36.8)
Jewish	650	(4.7)	200*	(.9)	1,000	(4.3)	36	(9.7)
Lutheran	787	(5.7)	758	(3.5)	1,152	(4.9)	7	(1.9)
Methodist**	1,280	(9.3)	1,308	(6.1)	2,098	(9.0)	39	(10.5)
Presbyterian**	485	(3.5)	475	(2.2)	617	(2.6)	54	(14.6)
Unknown							49	(13.2)
Other#	892	(6.5)	1,932	(9.0)	4,642	(20.0)	4	(1.0)***
Total	13,748		21,357		23,222		370	99.8

#Includes black congregants.
*Heads of families only.
**Northern and Southern.
***Christian Science = 1 and Swedenborgian = 3.

Sources: U.S. Census Office, *Report on Statistics of Churches in the United States at the Eleventh Census: 1890* (Washington: Government Printing Office, 1894), 112–13; U.S. Bureau of the Census, *Religious Bodies: 1906*. Pt. 1 (Washington: Government Printing Office, 1910), 442; U.S. Bureau of the Census, *Religious Bodies, 1916*. Pt. 1 (Washington: Government Printing Office, 1919), 405–407; Galveston Women Database.

In 1881, members of First Baptist and the Methodists of St. James and St. John's churches formed missionary societies of about thirty women that met monthly for the purpose of helping missionaries financially.[56] Later, the St. John's "Light Bearers" Young Ladies Missionary Society, organized in 1891, sent two young women, Edith Park and Mary Minor Tarrant, to the mission field. By then there were no constraints against single women serving, and these two joined some 700 other single women missionaries in foreign lands. Edith Park, born in Galveston, attended Laredo Seminary and chose as her field of work in 1896 Chihuahua, Mexico. Later she went to Saltillo, Mexico, where she ministered for thirty-five years until her retirement. Mary Tarrant, who grew up in St. John's Methodist Church, enrolled at Scarrett Bible and Training School and graduated in 1898. In 1900, she sailed to Shanghai and later became principal of the Virginia Atkinson Academy for boys in Soochow, China, until well into the 1940s.[57] With two graduates in the foreign mission field, Galveston Methodist women maintained a strong incentive to continue supporting foreign missions almost exclusively.

The emphasis on foreign and home missions in the evangelical denominations cut two ways for women. On the one hand, missions were the logical extension of an evangelizing process that concentrated on salvation and conversion. Sending the gospel into all the earth was a mandate that called to women as well as to men. Foreign mission societies elevated women above the rather confining duties of primary parish care and allowed them to assume responsibility for enterprises beyond their everyday existence. In this sense, foreign mission work provided women with a vocation that was church-related yet did not threaten the custom of male authority. It was, in the words of church historians, a "respectable" or "pragmatic feminism" that espoused action in the mission field. And it provided experience in administering funds, programs, and connections to statewide and denominational boards of missions. On the other hand, the challenges presented by mission work diverted attention away from the problems of their own city. Home mission work, which could have gone in the direction of city activism, did not in Galveston because women donated money and clothing instead to statewide Methodist institutions and programs in other cities. Not until 1905 did Galveston Methodist women begin a project of their own within the community by forming a Wesley House, or daycare center for children of families from the factory district. This program came ten years after the formation of a free kindergarten for children of the factory district founded by women from nonevangelical churches.[58]

The overall emphasis on evangelizing foreign continents was not conducive to bringing numbers of Methodist and Baptist women into Galveston's secular civic reform in the years between 1880 and 1920. With the Baptists, moreover, opposition by men to women's organizing in general tended to inhibit their activism both in church and without. Patricia Martin argues that "resistance to women's organizing, even to fill a traditional supportive role, continued in Texas until the 1890s and in the S[outhern] B[aptist] C[onvention] well into the twentieth century."[59] This is evident when looking at the statistics. (See table 3.1.) Of the 370 women active in secular organizations outside of churches, Baptists numbered 21 (5.7 percent) and Methodists 39 (10.5 percent), which, although within range of their numerical representation in the city, did not, as in the case of the Presbyterians and Episcopalians, exceed it. Economic reasons, along with foreign mission emphasis, explain the mediocre showing. Most Baptist and Methodist women were not among the elite members of Galveston society. Their families filled the ranks of the middle and lower-middle classes, and only occasionally do we find wealthy Baptists or Methodists entering into civic reform.

Ladies' Aid Societies

As the Marthas of the church, members of ladies' aid societies (and some Episcopal guilds) shouldered heavy burdens because their tasks were manifold and the requests for funds many. As ecclesiastical housekeepers, these women often supervised janitors, cooked church suppers, baked for bazaars, and fashioned fancy work for sale. The proceeds from their fairs, teas, and "entertainments" brought in hundreds of dollars. When they were not earning money, they sewed garments for the poor or sheets and pillowcases for the hospitals. If they controlled their own funds absolutely, they chose the projects that interested them, and — the pleas of the pastor notwithstanding — were seldom subjected to outside interference. In fact, earning money gave them a controlling edge when the all-male governing bodies responded too slowly to projects the women deemed important or did not take seriously the opinions of the women members. With these societies the potential existed for physically adapting the church structure to the needs of its women teachers, seamstresses, embroiderers, choir members, and decorators. Ladies' aid societies, or their equivalents, were often responsible for raising the money to build mission chapels, Sunday school structures, parlor rooms, and parsonages. As Suzanne Lebsock noted, women worked to build structures because these became lasting monuments to "the labor and values of women."[60]

Lutherans organized a Ladies' Aid Society in 1882 that served multiple roles. Its primary function was to act as a poor relief society, and its secondary purpose was to lend aid to the pastor and raise money for structural and domestic improvements. Lutheran women devoted their energies almost exclusively to supporting poor relief efforts until the storm of 1900, when church repairs claimed their attention. In 1916, a group of younger Lutheran women formed a Ladies' Auxiliary that at first took on the responsibility of raising money for a new church and helping Lutheran soldiers stationed in the Galveston area during World War I. In a sense, the Lutheran church, which conducted its services in German until 1892, acted as an immigrant association; the majority of its congregants were native Germans. The fact that the women of the church were engaged in bringing "spiritual comfort and material assistance to the needy in the name of the Lord and his church" (and that they continued to speak German in their meetings until 1924), was a response to the special needs of the German community. Lutheran women, unlike Catholic women, many of whom also were immigrants from Ireland and Germany, were not tied solely to supporting religious institutional structures, but they may have been limited from entering secular women's groups by their immigrant status.[61] Only seven (1.9 percent) of 370 activist women were Lutherans, making them the most underrepresented of all the Protestants in women's activities outside the church. (See table 3.1.)

Presbyterian women organized the First Presbyterian Ladies' Aid Society soon after the war in 1869 and reorganized it in 1880. Records show that the forty or so members of this group wore four hats: they served as congregational housekeepers, supported a missionary family in China, raised money for a mission in the West End of the island and later for a parsonage, and met weekly to sew and distribute aid to the poor. In a typical meeting in 1890 they discussed the fact that their tea, a fundraiser for foreign missions, had netted $170. Events of this type were no small affair. Missionary teas required 600 sandwiches, twenty-three cakes, eight dozen crullers, and four dozen cinnamon "sticks" to be washed down with a pound of tea, and six gallons of coffee accompanied by a dozen lemons, nine pounds of sugar, and a gallon and a half of milk. People paid for the privilege of sampling the ladies' fine delicacies. Since the tea was pronounced a financial success, the pastor met them with another appeal for money, this time to build a West End mission chapel. Members of this multipurpose society took appeals for aid in their stride, but by 1890 they had become sensible businesswomen who trucked no nonsense when it came to requests for money.[62]

Pleas for funds to build the West End mission is a good case in point. The ladies were happy to donate funds to the decorating of the mission, a domestic task that women often performed. But they were willing only so long as they felt their pledge would be matched by other funds and so long as the elders held up their end of the work. This brings up the all-important issue of contol over earnings and the choices women made with it. Perhaps because they had handled money successfully for poor relief, raising it themselves and carefully distributing it, the Presbyterian women displayed an uncommon independence when it came to funding projects for the laity.

In 1891, tired of waiting for the West End mission chapel to be built, the women voted "with a hearty unanimity" to "advise the gentlemen that if nothing was accomplished in this direction by the end of the year, that this society would feel privileged to devote their work to some other cause." The secretary was "directed to write a strong letter which would 'stir the gentlemen up.' We want that church building to go up now, and show that the Presbyterians are *alive*." The chairman of the Business Committee replied that building delays were caused by "the stringency of the times." Still, by January 1892 no building had been erected, and the elders were again soliciting money for a building fund. The women were annoyed and dug in their heels further. Do not bother us with requests for money, they counseled, until such time as the mission "should be completed, free of debt." Eventually they gave in at the behest of their pastor and donated $600 to the building fund and $400 to the interior (or 34 percent of the total costs for the chapel), probably out of a conviction that the mission chapel was more important than the stand against the elders.[63] Nonetheless, in the matter of money, when women had control over it their power increased along with their choices. In a limited world where women were restricted on many other fronts, there was might in having their own income, even if it did go to charitable causes. A sense of self-respect and a certainty that projects could be accomplished, outreach administered, and lives saved spiritually and physically were the result of this fiduciary independence.

Did independence learned in the Ladies' Aid Society transfer to the world of civic activism and urban reform? Probably it did. Presbyterian women were more active in women's groups outside of churches than women from most other denominations. They comprised 54 (14.6 percent) of the 370 white women found active in other organizations, or were five times more active than their small numerical presence in the city would suggest. The economic status of Presbyterian women seemed to range from middle to upper class, indicating that women who wanted to move out into the world, even in circumscribed fashion, found it easier to do when combined with the experience of financial control over funds and advantaged social position. (See table 3.1.) Then, the Ladies' Aid helped the poor, as we shall see in the next chapter, and this greatly enhanced the women's understanding of the community's needs and led many of them into civic work. They presented models to succeeding generations of young women, who followed their example of community activism.

Episcopal women in Galveston were undoubtedly the most privileged of all churchwomen in terms of status and economic security. Out of the 370 activist women already mentioned, 136 Episcopalians (36.8 percent) were involved in other women's organizations. Their entrance into civic affairs was nearly eight times greater than their denominational strength, which averaged 4.7 percent of all faiths in the years 1890, 1906, and 1916. (See table 3.1.) If we only count Protestants active in civic affairs, the percentage of Episcopal women involved jumps to 43 percent, or put another way, nearly half the Protestant women engaged in women's civic affairs were Episcopalian. Surely class, status, and privilege worked in favor of these women, but so too did the structure, the emphasis, and the opportunities offered by the Protestant Episcopal Church.

The first recorded organized efforts of Episcopal women came in 1867 when the women of Trinity Episcopal Church gathered to fund a "chapel," or structure that would encompass the domestic functions of church life, including Sunday school classrooms, meeting rooms for the guilds, and a parlor in which to entertain and socialize. Named the Ladies' Parochial Society by their rector, Benjamin Eaton, the women worked to raise funds to build the chapel, continuing even after Eaton's death in 1871. But ten years later, they had raised only about one-half the funds needed. Henry Rosenberg came to their rescue with $10,000 to complete the project, and together they called it Eaton Memorial Chapel—the first evidence of structural domestication to occur to old Trinity Church. The women were justly proud of their long-awaited accomplishment and in February 1882 brought this statement to the vestry:

> Gentlemen,
> With pleasure the Ladies of the "Parochial Society" announce that the Eaton Memorial Chapel for which they have labored to obtain funds for its erection for the past ten years is now about ready to be given into the hands of the Vestry of Trinity Church. They can but look at the completion of their work with a feeling of pride and gratitude to those who have so generously assisted them in this great enterprise. . . . *they are justly the Stewards of this beautiful building* and answerable to those kind donors. . . . The ladies of the Parochial Society feel that *their beautiful edifice* should be preserved in its present perfect condition. . . . [64]

The announcement was signed by sixteen ladies with the request that they be allowed to rent out the schoolroom and parlor in order to pay the insurance and the janitor and to make repairs. Obviously, the women felt a strong sense of proprietorship over the building even as they symbolically handed it over to the vestrymen. This was their building; they funded it, and they expected to use it for their needs. But they also saw it as a benefit to the whole parish. If gender relations between men and women had been equal, these parochial ladies would have been awarded higher political office, such as terms on the board of vestry. But church governance was a patriarchal affair, so, in fact, women gained strength at Trinity (as was true with other churches) not by insisting on serving on "men's" boards but by forming women's societies, developing and exercising leadership potential among themselves, and gaining leverage by occasionally challenging the vestry with a refusal to cooperate if their conditions were not met. Domesticating the church through structural changes was just the beginning. What follows is the history of a growing awareness of power in solidarity among Episcopal women.

Perhaps nowhere was the presence of women felt more strongly than with the forming in 1875 of the Sisterhood, which became Trinity Church Guild by 1885. Their major project, like that of the Presbyterian women, was to provide systematic charity to the urban poor, but they also acted as primary parish caretakers and "agreed to help in maintenance of church property," from the cemetery to the church bell tower. Not long after the Guild had become a women's organization, the vestrymen congratulated themselves on the quality of their work. "Our exchequer . . . shows a fair surplus owing principally to the good work of the Guild which came nobly to our relief at an opportune moment, and bids fair to prove a valuable acquisition to the board of managers in the near future." Indeed, only four years later the vestry was again gloating that the Guild had given them $2,300 to clear the church debt; by the next year the debt was reduced by one-half, thanks to the Guild. In the next round with the vestry in 1893, the women were not quite as free with their gifts. They let the men know that they had $1,200 for church improvements, but they chided the vestry into forming a building committee to get on with the plans for a new church. Unfortunately, the storm of 1900 ended talk of a new church; it was all they could do to repair the one they had.[65]

Because the women took on extensive projects for the church in a separate women's organization, they actually constituted a parallel "vestry." Although not recognized as such, the women, nonetheless, understood the potential influence, even power, that they exercised in conjunction with the all-male governing body. They may not have been sufficiently subversive to challenge the sovereignty of the vestry, but they did require its accountability. An illustration of this came in February 1915. Senior Warden Fred Catterall called a meeting of the vestry and relayed a complaint that the women had put to him: they were "dissatisfied with the present administration of the Vestry; this dissatisfaction seemed to be centered in two or three particular matters . . . namely, the notable absence of vestrymen from church services, the seeming inability of the vestry to have regular meetings, and the poor showing of the parish in financial matters that lie without the home circle." Embarrassing as this must have been for the men, they resolved to study their duty toward the parish and to forthwith expand the "envelope system," a means of bringing in the tithe, and explain the need for systematic giving in a letter to the parish. Finally, they commissioned the Senior Warden to "see to it that two vestrymen are present at every regular Sunday service."[66]

Tensions between vestrymen and guild members, or, in the case of the Presbyterians, between ladies' aid members and elders, were signs of the very real progress that women had begun to make in asserting themselves into church politics. It seems that women in societies had very few complaints about their pastors. The trouble came with the Episcopal vestrymen and Presbyterian elders; they neither visited with the women in their meetings, affirming and applauding them as pastors did, nor always acted in such a way as to give the women confidence in male governing abilities. Trinity Episcopal and First Presbyterian were not the only churches where tensions existed; similar developments were also taking place at Grace Episcopal Church.

The women of Grace Episcopal established their Ladies' Aid Society sometime in the 1880s. Averaging a membership of thirty, the women raised money for the church by making and sewing dolls, aprons, and other fancy work and holding an annual doll show that included the sale of candy, cakes, and ice cream — the usual domestic items. They also developed another strategy for raising money; they owned a rental house and used the $216 annual rent, which comprised one-third of their income, to aid the parish. It was truly a woman's project. The rental property on Broadway had been bequeathed to the Ladies' Aid from Sarah Pear-

son, one of its members, and owning it required a certain business acumen—
collecting rent, paying taxes, ordering repairs, housecleaning, and contracting for
paving the sidewalk.[67]

To illustrate how seriously the women in these societies took their responsibilities and the importance they attached to their opinions, one need only look to
the case of Irene Saunders and the selection of a new rector. Having endured four
intermittent years without a priest, the vestry finally chose in 1917 to call the
Reverend Gaynor Banks, whom the ladies endorsed with their signatures. Apparently, the vestrymen changed their minds without informing the members of the
Ladies' Aid and decided at the last minute to call another candidate, the Reverend
S. G. Porter. Needless to say, there was consternation in the Society the following
week. President Saunders and one other member tendered their resignations because "the vestry had shown little regard for the opinion and labour of the women
of the Church, by totally ignoring them in their selection of a rector." This was
particularly galling since the ladies had disbursed to the vestry $300, one-half of
their income for 1917. It may have been an unwise move on the part of the men—
akin to killing the golden goose—for after December 1917 the minutes end, and
there is no evidence that the Ladies' Aid continued; six years later, parish instability
caused a return to mission status.[68]

Resigning from office in a women's church society in protest over the actions
of the men's governing board constituted radical action. Criticizing or complaining
about the actions of male church leaders was more common and grew even more
frequent in the years when a viable and strident woman suffrage movement over-
took the city and influenced women in the direction of equal rights. As one might
expect, these altercations occurred in churches where women had become indispensable to the solvency of the church treasury.

This brings us back to women controlling their own money and making decisions based on their own priorities. Where women had invested heavily in the
maintenance of church structures, grounds, and programs, they were more likely
to expect in return a form of partnership, if not equality, in the way things were
run. This was not necessarily true with churches where women emphasized missions—the money was sent out to causes beyond the church treasury. In the case
of the Presbyterians and the Episcopalians, however, where their funds were critical to church revenue, they chose to confront the men on issues of accountability—putting up their fair share for a West End chapel, attending to basic
churchmanship, and consulting the women before imposing a rector upon them.
Underlying each confrontation was a hidden issue, the power of the purse. That
is not to say that women used money instead of piety to gain influence, but they
knew that their earnings provided them leverage, if only to move the men to hear
and act on their complaints. Not surprisingly, these women were also the most
active in women's societies outside the church; the majority of suffragists also
came from these churches.[69] Their activism no doubt cut two ways. Probably
their involvement in secular organizations lent them the courage or experience to
stand firm in their own congregations, just as solidarity in church life gave some
women the desire and confidence to enact reform through secular women's
groups.

From the city's earliest frontier beginnings, women had been active in church life, teaching, singing, praying, donating, and finally organizing among themselves. Most elite and middle-class white women found abundant life within churches. The sacred beauty of worship service, the fellowship, and the opportunities for service drew women inside church doors. There they showered the sanctuary with memorial gifts, sang in choirs, served on church committees, tended church cemeteries, taught little ones and adults the essentials of a Christian life, formed youth groups, and aided the church in all-woman societies. Their roles as choir members and directors, organists, donors, committee members, Sunday school and adult Bible teachers, and laywomen volunteers signify the increasing responsibilities that women shared in church affairs. Denied access to positions of ecclesiastical authority, women, nonetheless, shaped a world for themselves within church walls. By their presence, women made profound changes in church structures, furnishings, programs, and patterns of decision making. They brought their cultural values to a forum that, although firm in patriarchal governmental construct, was yet malleable to the influences of women's skills.

Women who joined in the cultural transmission were changed too, but none more so than those who invested in the financial and physical improvement of the buildings, grounds, and programs of their churches. As women began to move into areas outside the home, so women's aspirations for a more equal partnership in church affairs increased. At the local level, this led to conflict that only resulted in a reevaluation of old customs. Whereas women made questionable gains in areas of church governance, they took tremendous strides in advancing their vision of a more caring church. When they found no avenue of advancement into positions of parish leadership, they instead looked to other women to broaden and strengthen their power within the denomination. Rather than finding alliance with men, they sought and gained common purpose with women across the state and at the regional and national levels. In every denomination a parallel women's church evolved to unite those who found few opportunities for integration and policy making.

For some, uniting with other churchwomen was not the only answer to women's limited participation in positions of authority; becoming an officer in a church society was the beginning step in a journey toward greater community activism. The now-familiar phrase penned by Anne Firor Scott that by 1900 "the public life of nearly every Southern woman leader . . . began in a church society" is indicative of the common assumption that participation in church societies led to community activism. While this has the ring of truth to it, there are qualifications and adjustments that need explaining. In Galveston, the evidence shows it to be a half-truth; at least 193, or 52 percent, out of 370 women who were officers of women's secular clubs and societies were also members and officers of a church society. There may have been more, but the records for many women's church societies no longer exist.[70] Moreover, for those women who did advance from church society to civic life, it depended on the church, the society, and the individual. Some laywomen's associations were not very conducive to integrating women into secular organizations. Women from Catholic, Lutheran, and evangelical church societies were far less likely to enter the realm of women's secular

TABLE 3.2. White Activist Women in Congregational Women's Societies, Galveston, 1880–1920

Church or Synagogue	No. Women in Congregational Societies		Percentage of Women in Cong. Societies		Percentage of Total Women Activists* N = 370	
Baptist	15		7.77		4.05	
First Baptist		14		7.25		3.78
Broadway Baptist		1		.51		.27
Catholic	7		3.62		1.89	
Sacred Heart		2		1.03		.54
St. Mary's		4		2.07		1.08
St. Patrick's		1		.51		.27
Disciples of Christ	1		.51		.27	
Central Christian		1		.51		.27
Episcopal	85		44.04		22.97	
Trinity		74		38.34		2.00
Grace		11		5.69		2.97
Jewish	25		12.95		6.75	
Temple B'nai Israel		25		12.95		6.75
Lutheran	2		1.03		.54	
First Lutheran		2		1.03		.54
Methodist	24		12.43		6.48	
St. John's		7		3.62		1.89
First Methodist		15		7.77		4.05
West End		2		1.03		.54
Swedenborgian	2		1.03		.54	
New Church		2		1.03		.54
Presbyterian	32		16.58		8.64	
First		31		16.06		8.37
Fourth		1		.51		.27
Total	193	193	99.96			

Percentages do not equal 100 due to rounding.
*Unchurched women not included in this table.

Source: Galveston Women Database.

activism, as evidenced by the fact that 25.4 percent of the 193 women active in both secular and church societies belonged to or were officers of those church groups. The figure is even smaller when based on the total 370 women activists, equaling 13.2 percent for Catholic, Lutheran, and evangelical women. (See table 3.2.) Those from the Episcopal and Presbyterian women's societies tended to dominate women's clubs and associations. Nearly one-half (44 percent) of all women active in church and secular societies came from the Episcopal churches (38.3 percent from Trinity Church Guild alone). This figure constitutes 23 percent of all activist women. Presbyterian women accounted for 16.1 percent of women active in church societies and 8.6 percent of overall active women. The remainder belonged to Jewish and Swedenborgian congregational groups.

The church societies that seemed to encourage women to form public associations were those that afforded them the best opportunity to experience firsthand the enormous problems of urban life. Pressing in upon them in the late nineteenth century were distressing glimpses of poverty and destitution caused by industrialization. All of this contrasted sharply with the wealth created by a growing commercialism. Women with means, especially from churches, responded to the disparity in conditions in a variety of ways. As we shall see, Trinity Church Guild and the Presbyterian Ladies' Aid Society functioned not only as parish caretakers and housekeepers but also as relief societies for the poor; their members, who did not care if the supplicants were of their faith, were most likely to enter the secular world of women's civic responsibilities.

Almost every aspect of women's life within the church became replicated in women's semireligious or secular volunteer associations outside the church. Women found voice in city choruses, artistic expression in art leagues, gravetending in patriotic and civic societies, teaching in literary clubs, children's work in benevolent institutions, and youth work in the WCTU and the YWCA. They transferred their talents to worlds beyond the home and church, and in the process they changed their community and were changed by it. Most valuable of all to women's independence and autonomy were church societies that were free from male dominance. But even conflicting relationships with men in churches provided important experiences for women as they learned to exert their own agendas. As churchwomen emerged into more public and political roles, they would encounter opposition from male leaders—from benign paternalism to outright hostility. Women's church societies provided the kind of solidarity needed to face the struggles ahead. The steps women took toward reform in the city began in women's church societies, but how they fashioned these societies, bending them to serve their goals of poor relief within the city, is the subject of the next chapter.

4

"A BLESSING UPON OUR LABORS"

Women's Benevolent Societies and Poor Relief

You shall give freely, and your heart shall not be grudging when you give, because for this the Lord your God will bless you in all your work and in all that you undertake. For the poor will never cease out of the land; therefore I command you, You shall open wide your hand to the needy and to the poor in the land.

—Deuteronomy 15:10–11

In July 1893 a Mrs. Brown appealed to the Ladies' Aid Society of the First Presbyterian Church for help. She had suffered an unwarranted fate; her husband had abandoned her without any resources for herself or her three small children. Fittingly, Margaret McCullough, who also had been in desperate straits twenty-three years earlier when left a widow with nine children, pleaded Mrs. Brown's case before the society. "Having been a telegraph operator before her marriage," she began encouragingly, "this woman is now trying to again fit herself for a position in a telegraph office." The ladies discussed the case, as they did those of all supplicants who came for aid, and decided that because "she shows her willingness to help herself" they would pay her rent and provide her with necessities until she "can earn a support for herself and her little ones." Members of the Ladies' Aid Society strove to bring the victims of life's vicissitudes back to independence and, therefore, dignity. It did not always work out as they hoped, especially during the depression years of 1893 to 1895, but they, better than most women of privilege, knew the uncertainties that befell hapless women like Mrs. Brown.[1]

One month later, the case came up again, and this time the ladies enlisted the support of another benevolent society, Trinity Church Guild. "Mrs. Brown, who is courageously fighting life's hard battle and trying to fit herself to provide for herself and her little ones as it is impossible to do this and take care of the children at the same time, the ladies agreed to help to take care of the little ones for two months."[2] The society arranged to pay for child care with a trusted woman in the community, and Trinity Guild promised $10 toward her expenses. But Mrs. Brown's problems did not disappear. By November she had once again sought the good offices of the ladies when she asked them to provide money to allow her to go to Fort Worth to put her children in the orphanage there.

94

So it had come to this. Mothers without means and with little chance for earning immediately were at times forced to make the greatest sacrifices of all. The only hopeful sign in this dreadful tale was the plan that Mrs. Brown determined to follow and the aid she received from those who knew the full sorrow of her situation. A loan for a three-month "college education in telegraphy" at a school in Waco and money to outfit her were provided by the Ladies' Aid Society. All of this was complicated by the fact that she sought and obtained a divorce from her runaway husband yet needed character references for admission to the school. The ladies gave her the needed recommendations with a notation in the minutes that read, "she has the sympathy of all of our ladies in her severe trials and it is thought best to see her through." Three months later, the Galveston ladies heard that Mrs. Brown had been unable to keep her children and had given her two little girls away to a couple in Waco "relinquishing all maternal rights upon her children."[3]

The ultimate fate of Mrs. Brown, unlike that of her supporter Margaret McCullough, is unknown, as her name does not reappear in the society's minutes. We may wonder if she ever reclaimed her children and started life anew as a wage-earning woman. Actually, McCullough's straits in 1870 had been far more desperate, with nine children and no livelihood beyond housekeeping. Except for the fact that widowhood proved more respectable than abandonment, she had one thing that Mrs. Brown did not—family on which to rely in Galveston. Support from kinship or neighborhood networks could make the difference in a family's survival as a unit. By the 1880s, Galveston was experiencing an increasing influx of wayfarers, travelers, jobbers, and transients as well as working families seeking employment in the city's manufacturing and shipping concerns—but most of them were strangers to each other. As traditional kinship networks declined, the need for support groups rose. A host of fraternal organizations, labor unions, benevolent societies, church charities, and immigrant self-help groups—some of them formed by women—had long taken care of *their own* in the city. As postwar needs mounted, however, Galveston's elected leaders saw a rise in a class of indigent poor, who belonged to no self-help groups and who had no means of relief. Hoping to both assist those in need and prevent the formation of a permanent class of dependents, county commissioners and city aldermen searched for solutions to their care. The remedy—almshouses and a poor farm—was less than humane and left destitute people with few choices.

It fell to the genteel women from several of the Protestant churches to recognize that in order to prevent the formation of a class of permanent poor, rescue efforts must be made available to those who might fall into the abyss of permanent dependency. They acted on the knowledge that besides the lame and the destitute were those needy who sought temporary support to get back on their feet. Thus did the white "ladies bountiful" of the Protestant churches find a niche for themselves and in doing so redefine the nature of charity in Galveston. They supported the unattached and the unconnected, the abandoned, and the wayfarer, many of whom were women. By organizing benevolent societies through their churches and by assuming the task of urban poor relief, Galveston white middle- and upper-class ladies took their first lessons in civic responsibility. They projected themselves onto a public stage, established their right to public works, and found that they too had a public voice. Along the way, they more clearly defined what it meant to be respectable, not only for themselves but also for those whom they served. Although their charity was couched in the language of the gospel, it was directed in such a way as to establish middle-class moral ideals of sobriety, industry, and piety over those less fortunate than themselves. Thus, one of the legacies of benevolence was the creation of a greater awareness of class differences and more social stratification.

In the earliest days of the city, the concept of charity and relief were heavily dependent on the notion of self-help. In an underinstitutionalized society, as the South was in the years before the Civil War, relief came primarily from self-help organizations: fraternal orders, synagogues, immigrant societies, labor organizations, and sometimes churches — but for their own members only.[4] The charitable aims of these associations, many of which were formed by men as a hedge against future uncertainties, provided the city's first model of benevolence. The ideal was for the individual to join a group, contribute to its relief fund, and hope that a need for charity would never arise. Models of benevolence changed, however, when white Protestant churchwomen sustained charitable relief for those not connected to churches, labor unions, or ethnic communities. Benevolent ladies asked little from the supplicants in the way of dues but asked a great deal of them in their behavior. For a better understanding of the role of gender in aiding the city's poor, this chapter explores the various forms of organized benevolence: self-help groups, almshouses and the poor farm, women's benevolent societies, and finally the United Charities, established as an overall city relief system in 1914.

Even before Galveston had been legally incorporated in 1839, the Masons had formed two associations, and they were soon followed by the International Order of Odd Fellows. The post–Civil War period saw the formation of several more chapters of Masons and Odd Fellows as well as Knights of Pythias, Druids, Knights of Honor, and Chosen Friends, which served primarily as an insurance organization. By 1892, some twenty-three chapters of the secret and fraternal orders and six chapters of Chosen Friends stood solidly in place, evidence of the city's growing business and professional life.[5] Fraternal orders gave to their Protestant and Jewish male members certification of individual respectability, provided an arena for ritual and pageantry within a liberal religious context, and gave members a semblance of security at a time when health, burial, and accident insurance were hard to come by. Should a member fall prey to illness, bad fortune, even death, the fraternal organizations provided "nurses to wait upon the sick," relief "not exceeding ten dollars," and "necessary arrangements for burial of the dead." One historian has labeled fraternal orders "predecessors of modern life insurance agencies."[6] By forming associations that took care of their own members in time of need, middle-class men set the pattern of relief in Galveston for thirty years.

Just as fraternal associations provided a safe haven for middle-class Americans, so immigrant and African American benevolent societies created life-sustaining enclaves within the larger city. Hostility, ignorance, and prejudice often hindered these residents from gaining a toehold on economic security. Some associations helped members find jobs and homes, and most provided sickness and death benefits.[7] By 1876, at least five Galveston immigrant groups had formed societies for mutual association and for the purpose of benevolence.[8] African American citizens of Galveston by 1883 had formed at least twenty-one separate organizations for relief, fraternity, and culture—two separate Masonic lodges (1870 and 1880) with a combined membership of sixty-five in 1881, two Odd Fellow lodges by 1880 with 130 members, and several secular and religious societies to aid those in need. Black organizations were instrumental in helping freedmen and women adjust not only to freedom but to a society that was becoming increasingly concerned with separate institutions. Lodges and other societies became critical strongholds to withstand the ever-increasing reality of racial separation and inequality.[9]

Labor, too, had its own benevolent associations. From 1860 to 1895 no fewer than seven workers' associations, mostly connected with the city's shipping industry, formed to protect white workmen from the worst bouts of unemployment and illness. One of the oldest of these, the Screwmen's Benevolent Association, began operation in 1866 with twenty-three members who paid $5, or a day's wages, to join together for mutual benefit.[10] As time went on, the Screwmen, so called because they compressed (screwed) cotton bales more compactly into ship holds, doubled their annual dues and became better organized, forming a relief committee that "waited upon" sick members. They used dues, fines, and the proceeds from rental property owned by the association to relieve sick members and pay for funerals. At the end of the century, the Screwmen had amassed $45,000 in assets, allowing them to continue to grant on average $25 in sick benefits to each member. Even more important, in the worst moments after the 1900 storm, which took the lives of forty of its members, the association appropriated $10,000 for the relief of its members.[11] African American workers sought protection through separate labor unions. Black dockworkers organized the Longshoremen's Benevolent Association and two more locals between 1870 and 1880. The all-white Screwmen's Benevolent Association considered and rejected several times before 1900 the admittance of black workers. Thus, in 1876 African American screwmen formed their own union, the Negro Screwman's Benevolent Association, followed three years later by the Cotton Jammers' and Longshoremen's Association No. 2. Skilled working men and their families were fortunate when mutual benefit societies provided for their members and eased the burden of financial insecurity.[12]

Not everyone had the safety of a well-run beneficence agency. Most workers were uninsured and unprotected. Here the churches and synagogues played a role in aiding their members with no formal connections to fraternal, ethnic, insurance, or labor organizations. Pastors, priests, and rabbis often solicited monies for the poor from their congregants, as did congregational benevolent organizations founded by the laity.[13] In 1866, Jewish men founded the Hebrew Benevolent Society with $1,000 bequeathed for that purpose by Rosanna Dyer Osterman. By 1868, when Temple B'nai Israel was chartered, 105 Jewish families had become permanent residents of Galveston in time to help with the overwhelming influx of Jews from Germany, Alsace, Poland, and Russia. Osterman's will provided fifty shares of stock in the Galveston wharves to be used, "for the support of indigent Israelites, if any there be, if not, of any other denomination residing in Galveston."[14] This was the first hint that funds designated for a religious organization may have been used for persons other than those of the benefactors' faith. Other Jewish organizations also provided relief. A chapter of B'nai Brith formed in 1875, and as immigrants from eastern Europe began arriving toward the end of the century, they formed a Hebrew Orthodox Benevolent Society.[15] Catholic men founded two St. Vincent de Paul societies in 1872 and 1873. The more successful of the two was formed by the men of St. Joseph's German Catholic Church and had fifty members in 1895. Episcopal men created Trinity Church Guild in 1873 to aid the rector, to support missions, and to serve "the sick, the poor, and the afflicted." Religious institutions sponsored and gave aid to respective members but left open the possibility of occasionally rendering aid to indigents outside their own denominations. The suggestion that benevolence might reach beyond cultural, class, and ethnic boundaries came first from these religious groups.[16]

Although few records exist for the Galveston Methodists, similar relief societies may be found among the white Baptists. Pastor William Howard, concerned over the influx of newcomers to the First Baptist Church in 1869, appointed a relief committee of two men and two women "whose duty it shall be to attend to all cases requiring material aid from the church." Poor relief before 1900, however, was not a major consideration among evangelical Protestants, who held to a theology that emphasized individual salvation and conversion over other aspects of ministry. While strongly identifying with one another in community, they tended to look toward a person's "soul" worth, refraining from assessing the material condition of the unsaved. Actually Baptists (and Methodists, too), were more interested in foreign and home missions than in poor relief, as shown in the 1888 budget for the First Baptist Church, which allocated $335 for missions and $10 for the poor fund.[17]

Against this background of multivaried private responses to the problems of economic insecurity, infirmity, poverty, and destitution were city and county governments, which also shared responsibility for those unable to maintain themselves. There were few provisions for indigents in the city ordinances, just the usual vagrancy laws providing for the arrest and fine of persons "likely to become chargeable to the city as paupers," and allowance for the establishment of one or more workhouses or houses of correction "where vagrants, stragglers, idle, suspicious and disorderly persons . . . may . . . be kept therein, subject to labor and confinement." With the demise of the Freedmen's Bureau in 1868, care of the impoverished under Texas law fell to the county commissioners, who benefited only those who had been residents of Texas for one year and of Galveston County for six months. Short-term residents, recent arrivals, or those whom the county court did not find "so indigent, so infirm, sick, or disabled as to become an object of public care and support." were ineligible for county relief.[18] Most who sought aid were not interested in public support, for the county could offer them only a pittance in outdoor relief (money) or a humiliating existence within the almshouses and then, after 1887, on the county poor farm.

Nationally, public attitudes toward the poor were hardening between 1870 and 1900, and like government officials to the north, Galveston County commissioners demonstrated their hostility to public assistance at taxpayers' expense.[19] The commissioners' minutes present a grim picture of financial calculation toward the impoverished. Indigents who were eligible for public assistance either petitioned the commissioners directly for aid or their cases were presented to the commissioners' court (board) by the county charity committee. Either way, the commissioners disbursed funds in dribbles of from $3 to $10 per month, always "during the pleasure of this Court." Commissioners gave away just enough to keep sufferers from starving in hopes that they would find other means of support. True paupers, unable to sustain themselves except through the grace of the court, lived in two almshouses owned by the county and operated by hired caretakers. The unfortunate inmates, many of whom were aged or infirm, were given no money but were supplied food and clothing at the request of the caretakers.[20]

Almshouses of this type were typical relief institutions for the late eighteenth century or even into the 1840s, but almshouses were being replaced in the Northeast by the harsher and more controlling system of indoor relief known as workhouses or poorhouses. The Texas Constitution of 1876 allowed for each county to provide "a manual labor poor house and farm for taking care of, managing, employing and supplying the wants of the indigent and poor inhabitants."[21] By December 1886, the Galveston County commissioners were ready to move to the workhouse-asylum-farm concept for all county dependents—not only for county indigents but also for criminals, the insane, and the dependent sick. They needed county dependents to somehow earn their keep.

The commissioners decided to buy a farm across Galveston Bay on the mainland—a train ride away from the city. Removing county dependents to a poor farm would consolidate the county's indoor relief and correction efforts and render the inmates invisible to the good citizens of Galveston. It would also save money by moving these charity cases and criminals to an income-producing farm owned by the county. The Sisters of Charity of the Incarnate Word, who managed St. Mary's Infirmary, charged the county $.60 per charity patient per day in the 1880s. Because many of the patients were chronically ill with tuberculosis or were helpless cripples, they stayed in the hospital for months until recovery or death. One month's bill for eight county charity hospital patients reached $113. Keeping prisoners in the county jail was even more expensive, requiring $1 a day for food. Clearly, financial efficiency was a factor in the decision to buy a poor farm. Plans for the buildings were drawn up by Galveston's most famous architect, Nicholas Clayton, and were built at a cost of close to $6,000. Finally, by September 1887 the almshouses were emptied of their paupers, who were sent to the 200-acre farm. The commissioners instructed county judges "to have committed to the poor farm all persons fined by the Justice's Court, or fined and imprisoned by the Criminal District Court"; and all patients at St. Mary's Infirmary "at the charge of the county" who "can be properly moved to the Poor Farm" to be "moved at once."[22] By March 1888, the poor farm inventory showed the acquisition of four mules, three cows, six hogs, ten paupers, and nineteen convicts. One year after the poor farm had been in operation, the commissioners requested a subcommittee to file a report comparing the costs of maintaining the paupers before and after the purchase of the farm.[23]

In the beginning, the farm may have been an improvement over the almshouses. An informal inspector from the Ladies' Aid Society of the First Presbyterian Church, who wanted to know if the farm was suitable for the poor, reported that the buildings were "clean and comfortable. The occupants were cheerful and contented, being well cared for particularly in sickness. The food given them was good and plentiful, the same as the attendants were supplied with. When in good health, they were expected to help with the work. The men and women had separate buildings, really comfortable, nice homes for the helpless."[24]

The darker side of the operation became evident, however. In the short time that the farm had held its inmates, twenty-four convicts had been released, indicating that the farm may have served as a half-way station for convicts from the county jail. It was a convenient way to get them out of town before their release. For those convicts who would help themselves to freedom, however, the commissioners fortified the farm by sending out three guards and two bloodhounds. They fined the convicts for any medical treatment received and for the expense of recapturing them if they ran away. They ordered the superintendent to alter the asylum house "in such a manner as to fit it for a work house," where among other forms of labor, the inmates' clothes (uniforms to identify them as convicts or paupers) were to be made. The commissioners required the manager to supply a list of paupers so that they could be hired out and to hire convicts out to other persons "residing in the neighborhood." Small wonder that those who could walked away from the place—approximately one-third of the paupers left the farm in the first year.[25]

Considering the treatment afforded the poor at the hands of the government, private relief organizations served as essential alternatives for those struggling to maintain independence. Men's organizations within fraternal orders and labor organizations, the most exclusive of such agencies, provided benefits for the family only through its male members. Ethnic or immigrant aid societies minimally benefited those of their own race or native culture. Churches and synagogues, led by the spirit of charity, were more apt to benefit those of their own faith except in emergencies such as storms, fires, or epidemics. In each of these endeavors, women as benefactors were either nonexistent or were ancillary to the men. The need for female benevolent societies was acute, especially since many, and arguably most, of those who needed aid were poor women. In this age of commercialism, separate spheres, and increasing stratification, questions arise regarding the function of women's benevolence and its influence on the city. How did women of means respond to those of their own and of the opposite sex who were in need? How did white benevolent women treat African Americans in their city? How did the women's benevolent societies influence the delineation of class? And finally, how did these societies benefit the women who labored on behalf of the poor?

Women's Earliest Benevolence

The history of benevolence imparted by southern women most often begins with the Civil War. But Galveston appears unlike older cities in the South, where women formed what may be called emergency organizations—collectives that brought the women into homefront action on behalf of soldiers and that, in some cases, continued into the postwar period.[26] Instead, accounts of individual heroism mark the pages of Galveston's Civil War days; Rosanna Dyer Osterman remained on the island, turned her home into a hospital, and nursed the soldiers on both sides of the conflict. The Ursuline Sisters, educators rather than nurses, also stayed and opened their academy to the wounded.[27] Probably one-half of the town's residents, on the other hand, fled to the interior when news spread that Galveston faced a Union blockade. Whole families moved to Houston for the duration of the war and were wise to do so, for Galveston experienced the occupation first of Union soldiers, and, after the Battle of Galveston in 1863, occupation by the Confederates. Undisciplined soldiers of both stripes vandalized property and disrupted the peace. Bread riots broke out in the later years of the war and were quelled only by martial law. The civilian population sank to 2,500 in 1864 from a peak of 7,000 in 1860. Finally, after defeat, the occupation forces allowed some semblance of order to return. With hopes for a Confederate nation gone, Galveston families began returning to resume the business of export and import. As the city's residents returned, so did the amenities of a social life. Citizens sponsored a benefit for returning soldiers in 1865, and the proceeds went to a committee of women, who collected clothing for needy veterans. By 1868 the city began to show signs of recovery, and in 1870 the population climbed to 13,800. Life began once more for the returnees.[28]

Apparently, no women's organizations from the war years survived to continue charitable deeds; rather, the first women's benevolent societies were organized in the booming 1870s by immigrants, 3,614 of whom resided in the city in 1870. By 1880, the foreign born reached 5,046 or nearly 23 percent of the population. Not much is known about the Ladies' German Benevolent Society founded in 1874, except that it met once a month in Eaton Chapel and included both Christian and Jewish women. With an average of about forty members, it peaked in 1895 with eighty-two members. Agnes F. Erhard, a widow of German descent but of Episcopalian upbringing, presided over the society from 1898 until the 1920s. Those aided were primarily German-speaking persons and their descendants, but, as with many societies, the German ladies in times of crisis sent out appeals to the city for clothing to distribute to the needy.[29]

Jewish women formed in 1868 the Ladies' Hebrew Benevolent Society (LHBS), which ostensibly acted as an auxiliary to the men's benevolent society but was in reality quite separate and rendered the kind of personal aid to women that no male association could offer. Jewish women either acted as midwives or procured midwives for Jewish newcomers to Texas; they cared for "indigent, infirm or sick Jewesses," and "upon the death of a Jewess" prepared "the body for burial according to Jewish custom." Like the men's society, the ladies met once every quarter. But committees for membership, visiting ("the sick women of the Jewish faith"), employment, and distributing clothing among the poor occupied the women between meetings. They limited their donations to the needy to $20 per person, except in special cases. There is no way of knowing how many or in what varied ways Jewish women were helped by the Ladies' Hebrew Benevolent Society, but we can learn something about the members and the course the society took.[30]

Of all the women's benevolent societies in the city, the Ladies' Hebrew Benevolent Society in its earliest days was the most exclusive. Because most Jewish
women were themselves the object of discrimination on account of religion, ethnicity, and gender, it was important for them to establish beyond a doubt the
society's respectability and middle-class morality. A new recruit was accepted by
the members if no more than two votes were cast against her; thus, this society
was composed of about fifty women from the more prosperous economic echelons
of Galveston society. Although women resigned and were replaced by new members throughout the years before 1900, the period between December 1889 and
February 1894 brought few new members to the society. Three times in a row the
women had no quorum (10) for a meeting, which meant the society did not meet
as a whole for nine months. Then in 1894 a quarrel erupted over initiation costs
and was finally resolved by reducing initiation fees for older applicants and by
eliminating them entirely for young women. The result in 1898 was a flood of
thirty new members to carry on the work of the society.[31]

The desire on the part of the older women to maintain the LHBS as it had
always been points to a problem of generational resistance to new faces, new ideas,
and younger women with less wealth. Just as men clung to power and social status
in their organizations, so did women. But on a more positive note, many Jewish
women found other organizations to join. There was actually competition for
women's involvement during the doldrum years. A Ladies' Auxiliary Society,
which met twice a month with seventy members, had been organized in 1882 to
help with temple affairs. Then, too, because wealthy Galveston Jewish families
were an integral part of polite society, many Jewish women served on the boards
of lady managers for the orphanages and the Rosenberg Women's Home, while
others joined literary and culture clubs after the 1890s. Galveston Jewish women
enjoyed a high degree of assimilation with others of their economic station, and
the variety of choices available to them had actually increased by the turn of the
century. With new leadership at the helm in 1903, with a bequest of $1,000 from
Isabella Dyer Kopperl in 1902, and with eighty-one members recruited to carry on
the work there came a marked resurgence in the LHBS's community benevolence.[32]

The Storm of 1875

The first Christian women's relief society arose through the Episcopal church in
the aftermath of one of Galveston's worst storms. In September 1875 a terrific
hurricane battered the city, leaving its victims in need of food, money, and clothing. The disaster gave Episcopal women a chance to demonstrate their usefulness
to the parish and to the community through the distribution of relief supplies.[33]

Residents remembered storms ravaging the city in 1837, 1842, 1854, 1867, 1871,
and 1874, but they commented that "the water was never so high as it was . . .
Friday morning, the 17th" of September 1875. The storm of seventy hours duration
brought eighty-mile-an-hour winds, dropped 10.53 inches of rain, and flooded the
city mostly with sea water; "breakers . . . were rolling into the city from the Gulf,"
and the tide covered the island to the level of a horse's "arched back."[34] In the

aftermath, a reporter from the *Galveston Daily News* estimated the monetary loss at $21,000 damage to the city's cotton presses and an estimated $200,000 to ships and property. The east end of the island, which had been covered with "shanties by the negroes and poor whites, were all gone, and the place where they had stood was one sheet of water." These people lost everything they owned, including their clothing—"all washed out to sea."[35]

The first relief for storm victims in Galveston and along the Gulf Coast came from private groups. A meeting at the African Methodist Episcopal Church on East Broadway resulted in the creation of a relief society with plans to coordinate efforts among the city's black pastors and congregations. Simultaneously, at the Cotton Exchange white citizens called an emergency meeting to aid in the relief of storm victims in Indianola, Velasco, Matagorda, and other towns to the southwest of Galveston. The German Ladies' Benevolent Society pleaded for clothing for storm victims so that they could "faithfully attend to their distribution among the families who need aid." Baptist pastor William Howard "personally attended to the distribution of over five hundred changes of apparel, principally to women and children." The Louisiana Relief Committee sent $2,500 for the purchase of blankets and groceries, while the citizens of Boston gave $5,000 for the Gulf Coast victims.[36]

The Galveston Board of Aldermen five days after the storm still had not yet risen to the emergency. The mayor had been out of town, and the remaining aldermen saw no need to move hastily to relieve suffering. A *Galveston Daily News* editorial excoriated the public officials for being "either unprepared or incompetent to do anything in reasonable keeping with the emergency" and for adjourning "without any definite provision for the destitute and suffering poor, without any action towards the protection of the city on the Gulf shore, and without any measure of disinfection and purification with reference to a horrible miscellany of carrion and offal left by the subsidence of the flood." The *News* editors found the officials "a hopeless embodiment of incapacity for any good whatever."[37]

Soon after, talk of erecting a "permanent seawall" filled the columns of the *News*. Again the editors challenged the city council to give it their immediate attention. When the city's representatives took the matter to Austin, state legislators refused to aid with the construction of a breakwater. Instead of a seawall, the city planted salt cedars along the shore line. Several years later, a Deep Water Committee of city entrepreneurs sucessfully petitioned the federal government for funds to build two strong jetties as entrances to the harbor and to dredge the bay for a deep water port. Protection of the island would have to take a back seat to the advancement of commerce. This meant that the relief efforts from the storm of 1875 would serve as a rehearsal for a greater and more lasting disaster in 1900.[38]

In this city of sand and insecurities caused by tropical storms and tropical diseases, women learned the value of responding swiftly and effectively in groups to the existing crises. As the men prepared donations and gifts of supplies to the destitute in Galveston and cities along the coast, all the while hailing the continuance of trade and commerce, women took lessons in how to mobilize for a citywide emergency. Most southern women who lived in cities learned these organizational techniques in response to the privations and sufferings caused by the Civil War. In Galveston, weather and disease set the course for their involvement.

Trinity Church Guild, among the more effective emergency relief agencies in 1875, collected and distributed clothing, food, and money from a temporary headquarters at the courthouse. The members divided the city into four districts with a committee in charge of each, a technique that would be repeated by benevolent women for consistent aid to the poor in less trying times.[39] Working together, the women of Trinity Episcopal were capable of accomplishing a great deal more in the way of charity than had been possible before.

Having benefited from the experience of organized emergency relief, thirty-three ladies decided to form their own permanent relief organization as an auxiliary to the guild. The Sisterhood of Trinity Church Guild met weekly for the dispensing of regular, systematic charity. They disbursed funds to dozens of "destitute widows and orphans . . . every month." The annual report of their activities five years later (1880) credits the women with $569 "disbursed in provisions applied to the poor" and shows the extent to which the women had reached out into the community beyond the walls of their own church.

> The Sisterhood have visited and relieved not less than 260 indigent families, given away 483 garments to the worthy poor, supplied work to sewing women and furnished many suffering and needy with fuel and shoes, also material for work. The Industrial School held every Saturday in the Mission is attended by 30 scholars. . . . The object is to teach little girls to sew and make their own clothing and to supply needy children with materials for dresses.[40]

The laity apparently had full faith in their sisters' accomplishments because by 1885 the men's guild ceased to exist and the women took over the name Trinity Church Guild. In short, the church had turned over to its women the entire task of benevolence. It seems that Trinity's vestrymen in the critical 1870s had come to accept the fact that women could and should be raising and distributing money for the sake of the poor, and the women, too, found a vocation for their interest in community welfare.

White women who chose relief of the urban poor as part of their mission formed at least two other benevolent societies in the late 1870s and early 1880s: the Ladies' Aid Society of the First Presbyterian Church and the Ladies' Aid Society of the First Evangelical Lutheran Church. The charters for the three benevolent societies were remarkably similar in breadth of purpose: the Lutherans determined "to help poor and sick people when in need, to assist in church and mission work"; the Presbyterians wanted "to help aid and encourage charitable work according to their judgment"; and the Episcopalians desired "to help on Church work . . . in serving the sick, the poor, and the afflicted."[41] Benevolence, then, was but one part of their ministry, and it was entirely up to the women how much of their funds and time would be spent in aid to the poor.

It is difficult to know in those years exactly how much time and money Lutheran women spent on poor relief; no records exist for their society. But we know from secondary histories that their main "sphere of activity" was in "the ministry of mercy, helping the poor and unfortunate, visiting of the sick and suffering, offering them aid and comfort."[42] It is equally difficult to determine the extent to which African American women organized benevolent societies before 1900. All their church records were destroyed by the storm. For Episcopal and Presbyterian women, the years between 1880 and 1900 were the most important for emphasizing poor relief. After the 1900 storm, all women's societies for a time were pulled away from poor relief to primary parish care, that is, helping the church to recover and to raise money for repairs and refurnishing. Later, in the second decade of the twentieth century, other agencies coopted their roles as early social welfare workers. But in the years prior to 1900, poor relief constituted the main object of women's ministry.

Churches and synagogues were absolutely crucial in the second half of the nineteenth century for pushing southern women out into community life. But without developments in their urban dwelling place, the opportunity for community benevolence might not have presented itself. Fifty years earlier, women in northern cities had discovered this too and sought effective channels for their energy and piety in benevolent work. Urged on by the forces of modernization that helped to create class strata, economic differences, and an unending stream of working poor, women in New York, Boston, Philadelphia, and the towns emerging along the Erie Canal felt compelled to aid the poor, and they did so largely through the auspices of their most viable institutions, their churches and synagogues.[43]

In many ways, Galveston in the 1880s, though booming, was just entering the commercial and industrial age. The city's youthfulness, its rapid urbanization in the postwar years, the influx of immigrants and native-born Americans, and the creation of manufacturing concerns that attracted laboring families all contributed to increased numbers of working poor.[44] Because Galveston remained a walking city where all types of people lived in integrated neighborhoods, the have-nots were never out of sight of the haves. Those who had the means to help viewed those in need not as distant problems but as neighbors. As Kathleen D. McCarthy has pointed out, at least among the pious, "wealth was inextricably linked to public service from the outset."[45] The awakening of moral stewardship—in Chicago as well as in Galveston—arose under just such conditions.

Rationales

The forces of women's benevolence stemmed not only from witnessing scenes of distressing poverty but also from individual religious conviction. Whereas Old Testament commandments for ethical behavior, moral concern, and social justice moved Jewish women to perform acts of charity, Christians found inspiration in the gospel of Matthew: "Inasmuch as ye have done it unto one of the least of these my brethren, ye have done it unto me." The ladies of the First Presbyterian Church echoed these sentiments when they recorded that their pastor, Dr. William Scott, "asked a blessing upon our labors for the coming year . . . that we in ministering to the needy and suffering might through our sympathy with them be brought into closer kinship with Him whose earthly life was passed amid scenes of sorrow and suffering, thereby leading both us and them to a higher spiritual life." They drew hope from Christ's ordeal, sought a blessing for themselves and their ministry, and anticipated that by their deeds they would find themselves and their petitioners closer to the spiritual throne. Hence, out of a sense of moral stewardship Presbyterian and Episcopal women broadened their charity to include even the unchurched and unaffiliated.[46]

Episcopal women also gained approval for benevolence through the encouragement of their clergy. When the Reverend Stephen Moylan Bird rendered a memorial sermon to Trinity Church after twenty years as its rector, he gave special praise to the laywomen, singling out three by name and calling attention to the Ladies' Parochial Society for the building of Eaton Chapel. The tenor of the sermon spoke throughout of deeds and organizations—baptisms, Sunday schools, guilds, brotherhoods. For the Reverend Bird all "have made our Parish a sweet savour and blessing to many hearts and homes of the poor—where the orphan has been tended, and the widow's heart made to sing." Any woman church worker hearing this sermon would have understood the clerical emphasis placed on helping the poor; it was a message designed to become a personal commandment.[47]

Edgar Gardner Murphy, the reform-minded southern Episcopal priest, who long has been heralded as a great theologian and modernist spokesman for the South, believed that "to be fully human is to be in community"; blessings of habit and service were best expressed through the "institutions of human community: church, family, corporation, and voluntary service." Service and sacrifice to the community good were ideals to which those who belonged to the privileged classes or "wealth-worthy" should give priority. He believed that philanthropy should be personal, an ecclesiastical form of the gospel of wealth that did not necessarily challenge the hierarchy of the social classes but called for a caring distribution of resources to ameliorate suffering. How much of Murphy's theology found its way to the hearts and minds of Episcopal women in Galveston is difficult to determine, but as a spokesman for the church, his theology fit well with southerners' conservative notions of social concern.[48]

Episcopal women in the South relied on their connection to a national church for inspiration, guidance, and for models of progressive action with regard to urban problems. Mary Donovan writes that Episcopal women created models for ministry in urban settings that offered them "a broader range of activities than in most other denominations" and provided examples for their southern sisters. Episcopal doctrine that emphasized good works and responsibility for the poor, particularly in the context of community, encouraged women to minister to those in need. Donovan demonstrates that Episcopal women shared a "unique attitude toward social service," wherein laywomen assumed active servanthood following Christ's commandment to minister to the poor and suffering. Evangelism leading to conversion and possible membership was not their primary concern. And witnessing, so popular among evangelical sects, was left to the priests. Women educated others, organized, and served, only later insisting on theological training to carry on that side of ministry.[49]

It is hard to know just how these examples may have influenced the Episcopal women of Galveston. Did they receive stimuli from their northern sisters? The answer must be a qualified yes, based on circumstantial rather than direct evi-

dence. But like their northern co-religionists, Galveston churchwomen were probably inspired more by the conditions at their doorstep and by the call of local
rectors to remember their sacrificial duty to the poor than by pronouncements of
distant theologians for a social gospel or by examples of charity in other cities.

Religious motives and emergency relief efforts were not the only reasons that
some women plunged themselves into charity work. Most felt that helping the
poor was decidedly a function of woman's nurturing role. Since women were
"naturally" more tender hearted, more caring, and more concerned with the well-
being of their own sex and children, they were better suited to serve those in
poverty, especially widows and women and children. The notion of woman's moral
superiority complemented nineteenth-century concepts of ennobled womanhood,
which both men and women wrote about and acted upon. Women who served
in benevolent societies believed that they fulfilled a feminine ideal of Christlike
self-sacifice and were thus memorialized at death with eulogies to their womanly
virtues. "Her life, so full of good deeds will ever be memorable to us for the
sweetness and tenderness of her nature, for manifold duties faithfully performed,
for her ernestness and readiness in all good work and for her unselfishness, and
her many charitable deeds to the poor and unfortunate," wrote Margaret Mc-
Cullough when Helen Thurmond, a member of the Presbyterian Ladies' Aid Society, died. Similar sentiments were expressed by members of the Ladies' Hebrew
Benevolent Society when Mrs. Jake Cohen departed in 1908: "Heaven is enriched
by her noble and kindly spirit and to this extent has our, and similar organizations,
[been] impoverished. Her life . . . so bright, vivid and beautiful [will] be forever
engraven on our hearts."[50]

The concept that women were special, morally superior, yet fragile, worked
to the advantage of some of the societies' supplicants, as well. Widows who petitioned for aid were given characteristic sympathy, as it was thought that women,
especially mothers, who had spent their days in toil were robbed by poverty of the
respect and dignity they deserved. Benevolent ladies believed that mothers, regardless of station, shared the noble values of self-sacrifice. Poor mothers trying to
raise children as best they could deserved help even more than unemployed men
or single women. Sentimental as these notions may have been, they represented
a middle-class identification with working-class women. Motherhood was a positive
female attribute, an exclusive category that crossed class lines and that in symbolic
ways was analogous to male inclusion in benevolent associations. As men were
taken care of by the alliance to fraternal, laboring, or immigrant groups, so mothers
could find a source of support in time of need among women.[51]

Little better illustrates the notion of the nobility of motherhood than the case
of Eleanor (Nellie) Roeck Thompson. Nellie was raised in an elite Galveston
home where she and her brother received affection tempered with discipline.
When Nellie was almost seventeen, her mother, Kate Waters Roeck, died, and
Nellie's bereft father wrote an aunt that the death of his wife "left a void in this
community, that is not easily filled. She took a prominent part in all charitable
and church work, and not the least touching incident of the two days, during
which she lay before interment, was the influx of the many poor people whom
she had helped & cared for, and who have lost in her a friend that cannot be

replaced."[52] Nellie thereafter took on the role of mother to her nine-year-old brother and assumed the duties of mistress of the house. A short story written by her in 1892 and accepted for publication in *The Youth's Companion* illustrates the enduring sentimentality of ennobled motherhood.

The story, entitled "Nino," is set in the coastal mountains of northern Italy and describes a peasant mother, Tessa, and her only child, Nino, a blind boy of about ten. The boy is described in overly sentimental tones as patient, pathetic, beautiful, and yet ailing. The mother, however, is the true heroine of the story. "She was only a simple, ignorant, hard worked peasant woman, but she was a mother, and would gladly have borne her child's infirmity always, if by so doing, she could give him a glimpse of the sunlight he so often talked of. . . ." Nellie went on to point out that the mother's "own life had not been happy, it was too full of grinding poverty to admit of much happiness, and at thirty she was quite wrinkled and withered and brown, from toil and exposure." Because the local sage had told Tessa that her boy could be made whole again in sight and body by a doctor in the city, she labors for an entire year to earn fifty lire to pay for the doctor's cure. The day arrives for their trip to the city, and the mother takes the boy on an arduous journey to see the physician, who, as it turns out, can do nothing for a boy blind from birth. Devastated, she carries Nino up the hills to their peasant cottage, where the child breathes his last.[53]

Aside from the maudlin theme so typical of nineteenth-century fiction, the point here is that a well-placed young southern woman idealized a peasant mother and acted on the belief that women, especially mothers, were morally superior creatures. On the strength of that identification, Eleanor Roeck Thompson went on to become a mother of eight herself and one of the city's greatest workers in defense of the underprivileged. Soon after her marriage to Dr. James Thompson in 1896, she joined Trinity Church Guild, assuming the presidency from 1915 to 1918. Following her mother's example of investment in the community, she became in 1917 the first woman elected to the Galveston School Board, enabling her to influence directly children's lives through education.[54]

Women in Need

White genteel Galveston women regarded the poor as objects for their religious and humanitarian sensibilities, but the poor desperately needed them. In 1885 a great fire devastated the business section of the city, creating requests for aid beyond the norm.[55] Those who petitioned the Protestant women's societies for assistance were for the most part persons who had no connection to any of the other benevolent associations in the city and were ineligible or unwilling to go to the county commissioners for support. This included stranded travelers, temporarily disabled working-class men and women, abandoned women with children, sick mothers with small children, working girls, and widows without family or funds — in other words, the poor for whom existing private agencies provided no relief.

Among the needy who petitioned the ladies' aid societies, the largest group of those helped were poor women. The records of the First Presbyterian Ladies' Aid Society show that over a ten-year period between 1890 and 1900, more than

TABLE 4.1. Recipients of Aid from the First Presbyterian Ladies' Aid
Society, 1890–1900

Year	Black Men	Black Women	White Men	White Women	Total No.
1890	0	2 (8%)	4 (16%)	19 (76%)	25
1891	0	3 (16.7%)	4 (22%)	11 (61%)	18
1892	1 (10%)	0	1 (10%)	8 (80%)	10
1893	0	2 (10.5%)	5 (26%)	12 (63%)	19
1894	1 (2%)	3 (6%)	2 (4%)	44 (88%)	50
1895	0	3 (4%)	19 (25%)	54 (71%)	76
1896	1 (1.6%)	7 (12%)	4 (6.8%)	47 (79.6%)	59
1897	0	4 (7.5%)	11 (20.7%)	38 (71.7%)	53
1900	2 (5.4%)	8 (21.6%)	2 (5.4%)	25 (67.6%)	37
Total	5 (1.4%)	32 (9.22%)	52 (14.9%)	258 (74.3%)	347
Mean per year	2.1%	9.6%	15.1%	73.1%	38.5

Black and white women total average = 83.5%

Sources: Minutes of the Ladies' Aid Society of the First Presbyterian Church, Galveston, 1890–1900,
First Presbyterian Church Records (Rosenberg Library, Galveston).

80 percent of the supplicants aided were females while less than 20 percent were
males (see table 4.1).[56] Of all society's needy, women had the fewest connections
to private charity. If a woman was not a member of an ethnic community or
church, or if her husband, brother, or father had not been a member of a fraternal
order or a labor union, there was only one other possible source available before
succumbing to public aid—the women's benevolent societies. In a city where the
economic station of nearly every woman bordered on dependency, middle- and
upper-class women tried to cut across class barriers to support and help others of
their sex. Thus, the role filled by female benevolent societies was not that of just
another charitable group but was that of an essential safety net for poor women
and for the city's unattached and unconnected.

Admittedly, the overall safety net worked best for white women. On average,
nearly 75 percent of those helped were white women, while less than 10 percent
were black women. In fact, more white men (15 percent) were aided than black
men and women combined (10.6 percent). (See table 4.1.) Although African Americans made up 20 percent of the population in Galveston, they were given aid in
numbers far below their actual representation. This obvious discrepancy is com-
pounded when one realizes that undoubtedly more black than white Galvestonians
were in need. Racism on the part of the ladies is the most obvious answer but not
necessarily the only one. Institutional segregation by 1890 was well established in
Galveston, and many black charities were in place. When Sallie Warner applied
for help, the ladies first asked, "Can she get aid from the colored people?" Without
an immediate answer to that question, the women decided to pay for her medicine
in the meantime. It may have been that most African Americans hesitated to ask
for aid from white women, finding it more comfortable to seek help from black
benevolent societies. Perhaps the records did not include every supplicant's race,

although those who were recorded as other than white were usually mentioned in the minutes by race, sex, ethnicity, and sometimes approximate age. "A poor old German woman applied for aid," read one entry, and "found a woman (who is colored) at the corner of 18th and Mechanic . . . She was sick in bed, and attended by a Catholic priest. . . . who said that the church had no fund which he could use in such a case," read another. Black supplicants were usually not turned away as undeserving, although plenty of whites were. In fact, blacks were treated with a form of paternalistic patience. When a Mr. Holmes, a janitor in a black church, applied for help, the ladies found him in a "destitute condition" and promised to buy groceries and recommend him to the John Sealy Hospital as janitor. Within two weeks Mr. Holmes got the job at the hospital for ten dollars a month. Perhaps because most African Americans attended Protestant churches, the Presbyterian Ladies' Aid felt a religious kinship despite racial difference. Conscious contempt for blacks simply does not come out through the minutes, though it may have existed.[57]

What is obvious is that white Protestant benevolent ladies harbored a disdain for supplicants they considered unworthy—loafers, "imposters," and those who had succumbed to vices such as drinking and gambling. Middle-class moralisms pervaded the worldview of benevolent ladies, rendering them powerful judges of those in wretched straits. While on the one hand sentiments of Judeo-Christian charity drove their efforts, class prejudices informed by impressions of the vices of the working classes limited their gifts. They applauded the efforts of families who made the appearance of industry but who simply had fallen on hard times. When a Mrs. Simpson applied for aid, the ladies found her "destitute" and "too frail or ill to work" and gave her $5, two blankets, and a comfortable pair of shoes. When they investigated her case further, they found that her husband had been crippled while working on the Santa Fe Railroad and of her five children, the oldest, a boy of seventeen, was supporting them. The ladies then paid the family's rent, rounded up some used clothing, and presented them with another $5. These were the kind of working-class people benevolent ladies were willing to help because they met the standards of middle-class probity. In passing judgment on others, by withholding charity from those labeled unworthy, benevolent ladies helped to articulate a notion of middle-class superiority. This attitude echoed the beliefs of the county commissioners, who, although ready to support county dependents, wanted them to pay for their upkeep. Benevolent ladies did not expect their supplicants to repay their charity (nor did they sanction permanent dependency), but they did expect a semblance of respectable behavior from the needy; thus did they control relief and demand that the working class mirror bourgeois moral assumptions. The effect was to accentuate class differences.[58]

The rules were equally tough when it came to alcoholics who showed little incentive to recover. "No assistance should be given to Mrs. Andrews who is a victim of the drinking habit." Although recognized as a victim, the pronouncement on this condition brokered no sympathy. On the other hand, "fallen women" and morphine addicts were given an unusual degree of sympathy, especially when the ladies heard from members of the Woman's Home in Fort Worth and the Bethesda Door of Hope in Galveston, both rescue homes for "fallen and distressed women."[59] One of the greatest problems in the eyes of genteel women was the possibility of sexual ruination followed by prostitution. Young women of the factory district who had no family and worked at low wages were at greatest risk. "Mrs. [Sarah] Ball reported the case of a young girl named Mary Ferris who is in our city alone and unprotected and who wished to go to her mother in Kentucky. As we all recognize the temptations that a friendless young woman without strength of character is exposed to, it was decided to send her back to her mother under whose protecting care she will be kept from all harm." Underlying assumptions of moral weakness among working-class girls allied with notions of nurturing motherhood led the ladies to send the young woman home. Mary Ferris at least escaped the fate of Lizzie McKeskie, whom the ladies described as "a sad case . . . who had been ruined by a married man in Bolivar and whose infant was sick." They voted to pay for the board of her child while the woman worked. When a woman of fallen virtue did apply for aid ("Mrs. Lawson's case came up . . . it was found her life was not what it should be. . . ."), the ladies referred her to Mrs. E. W. Nichols of the Bethesda Door of Hope. When Mrs. Gussie Killough visited a Mrs. Foster in November 1892, they learned that "the woman [was] addicted to the use of morphine," but was "endeavoring to be cured of her disease." The Ladies' Aid referred her to a physician and gave her groceries, shoes, and money for rent. In late December, Mrs. Foster was still not doing well, and the ladies talked about referring her to the Keeley Institute in Houston for treatment. In January they found her improving, and by February they wrote that she was "cured of the morphine habit." Once on the mend Mrs. Foster reapplied to the Ladies' Aid; this time she sought a suit of clothes, as she had taken a job as a traveling companion. The society gave her $15 and hoped that she would "not apply to us for aid again."[60]

Women deemed worthy were helped in ways other than direct relief. Episcopal and Presbyterian benevolent ladies held teas for factory girls and nursing students and made sheets, dressing gowns, and sacks for the John Sealy Hospital. They subsidized training for working women, set up "industrial schools" to teach girls sewing or other domestic skills, and, as in the case of Mrs. Brown, supported working women who chose to divorce runaway husbands. This type of activity differed from direct relief and constituted an advancement in upper-class perceptions of women and the world of public work. Rather than ignoring the reality of women working in industry, as most other societies had done, benevolent ladies served as employment facilitators.[61]

The Ranks of Working Christian Women

In order to lend a hand to those in distress, the ladies themselves had to work and, in fact, considered themselves among "the ranks of working Christian women." Although the kind of work they did—sewing, selling their fancy work, and giving teas, lawn parties, oyster roasts, and chrysanthemum shows—were extensions of domesticity brought to the semipublic forum of church parlors and social halls, this should be viewed as a step forward into public life for middle- and upper-class women. Visiting the poor constituted another foray into the public realm. This required maintaining a visible presence in neighborhoods other than one's own, calling on the needy in their homes, ordering drugs from the apothecary, and seeing the woodman, clothier, and grocer on behalf of the poor. The differences between the purely domestic work that women practiced in the home and the associational benevolence proffered through churches and the synagogue were organizational technique, control over their own money, and public exposure — all related to business concerns. While many of their tasks were domestic, the women themselves seemed to prefer organizational work. As one member noted, "our society has kept every pledge, met every call for funds, paid all its bills promptly, has had money flowing into its treasury steadily all summer and that without being compelled to give one lawn party."[62]

Raising and handling their own funds constituted for married women a form of independence seldom found in the home. The ladies were adamant about money. Trinity Guild members "voted the Guild be the custodian of its own funds." And the Presbyterian Ladies' Aid Society became quite huffy when it was suggested that the male trustees handle their savings: "we [are] 'neither infants nor invalids[,]' that while we [are] glad of any advice or suggestions from the Trustees it [is] advisable that our securities be allowed to remain in [the] charge of the Society."[63] As important as the care of the poor was to the women, the experience in money management remained valuable for the sense of independence and confidence it gave them in their own abilities. All this would seem to suggest that women who helped the poor materially and saw their work as social service considered themselves in a career commitment to the community, presaging the day of the career social worker or the "professional altruist."[64]

The women of the First Presbyterian Ladies' Aid Society wrote their own constitution and bylaws and elected officials, including the position of first directress, who oversaw the sewing work and sales. They met weekly for two hours, the first hour for sewing and socializing, the second for business and social work. The officers appointed seventeen women out of forty-five in 1883 to "Charity Committees" and divided the city into three parts — northeast, southeast, and west. Teams of women, headed by a captain, were responsible for referring cases of need to the society. Those who applied for aid were "investigated" by a member of the petitioner's district committee. Home visits were common to evaluate need as well as to establish worthiness. Relief was not usually given in money but in kind: fuel, shoes, groceries, clothing, linens, furniture, stoves, medical assistance, and the payment of rent and hospital bills. Exceptions were made for former members, however, who occasionally would fall on hard times and need help. When the ladies found such a case, they invariably provided the former member with a healthy monetary outlay, often $25 at a time. Perhaps out of a sense of class loyalty were former members allowed this discretion, making service in a women's aid society something of an insurance policy against an uncertain future.[65]

Between February 1893 and March 1896, Presbyterian women dispersed $2,751 in aid.[66] Money and supplies were not the only services provided; the Ladies' Aid commissioned a physician (a female!) to attend the sick and a druggist to fill orders. Occasionally, an elderly white woman would be judged incapable of living alone and recommended for admission to the Rosenberg Women's Home. Elderly men and African Americans were advised to go to the poor farm, the only institution that accepted men and women of both races. Orphans and half orphans were urged upon the privately endowed Galveston Orphans' Home or the Home for Homeless Children; children of sick, disabled, or abandoned women were provided a nurse who went to the house at the request of the society, or the children were sent to boardinghouses where temporary care was provided. No one was coerced; the society merely facilitated these transactions. Those institutions, although judged clean and hospitable by the ladies, were seen as asylums of last resort. Keeping families together, giving temporary relief, and returning people to their former positions of independence were the society's first goals. Indeed, Mary Gale, a young woman on her way to the Huntsville Normal School to become a teacher received $15 dollars to buy clothing. This was justified on the grounds that "she'll become independent." In short, the ladies practiced a combination of outdoor (aid directly to the supplicant) and noncoerced indoor (placing individuals in asylums) relief.[67]

The ladies knew that they held positions of responsibility, as indicated in their minutes. "It is pleasant and delightful to know that we have it in our power, through the beneficence of one who loved his fellow men . . . to help those who wish to help themselves." At that time, few other voluntary institutions in Galveston gave middle and upper-class women the opportunity to learn sound organizational and business techniques and to develop methods of raising and dispersing funds without the direction of men. While acknowledging Christ's hand in their endeavors, power belonged to them, and they used it to establish their importance within the community. Some of their actions were socially controlling—they wielded the ability to refuse aid and to dispense it at their discretion.[68] But for the most part, benevolent ladies sought to return the displaced to a functional position in the community and the elderly and dependent to a more secure place. Concern with social welfare took first priority. Yet class-based biases dictated the awards. Arguments, such as those advanced by Paul Boyer, that varying approaches to charity were part of a larger scheme toward moral and or social control, tend to view women's charity work as stemming from the same motives as men's. As we have already seen, men did not offer charity as a gift; it came laden with dues, fines, memberships, or taxes, in the case of the indigent. It is more likely that volunteer benevolent women approached charity (as they did politics) differently than men, raising money with their own labor and giving it according to their moral imperatives. While their class and economic status may have been the same and their moral assumptions the same, women's reasons for involvement and methods of benevolence were not based primarily on issues of efficiency and control but on sentiments of nurture, amelioration, protection of the disadvantaged, and the desire for their independence.[69]

This does not mean that middle- and upper-class ladies did not perceive and react to class differences among their clients or label some of their claims fraudulent. The emphasis of benevolent societies was on aid, not social acceptance. Sisterhood existed only among the members. When one woman petitioned the Presbyterian Ladies' Aid Society for $10 to return to Natchez, the recorder carped, "she was dissolved in tears, but . . . tears with that class of people was not to have too much weight as it is the usual concomitant of appeals for money. Indeed we ought to bear this in mind having had so many examples; there seems to be no bar to the deep water of their eyes when they have a petition to float in." In actuality the rise of church and synagogue benevolent societies differentiated class more clearly, separating women of privilege from working-class women and ascribing notions of greater moral authority, which should be read as power, to middle- and upper-class women. Advantaged white women formed societies with one another where none had existed before. As if to announce to the city the existence of a middle- and upper- class identity, these benevolent ladies articulated a value system that was decidedly class as well as gender based. Notions of domesticity, nurture, and piety were women's values *and* middle-class Victorian values. As Lori Ginzberg states, "benevolent work and rhetoric were vehicles for the emergence of a new middle-class identity." Clashes were bound to occur between recipients of aid and their benefactors over these values, showing more pointedly the distance between the classes.[70]

Ironically, however, the more elite the church, the more involved its women's benevolent society was with poor relief. Episcopal and Presbyterian women, certainly, and Jewish women to a lesser extent were the most likely to encounter destitution and more likely to do something about it in cooperation with one another. Presbyterian and Episcopal women began to meet together on a monthly basis to exchange lists and coordinate efforts. Other white Protestant women's societies did not focus on the plight of the poor with the same intensity and hence were not as fully engaged in an emerging reforming women's community.[71]

With the advent of the 1893 depression, the worst the nation had seen with 20 percent unemployment nationwide, the need for systematic aid and cooperation between benevolent societies was greater than it had ever been before. In 1894, the Pullman Strike, which began in Chicago, reached Galveston portending a breakdown in rail service. The mayor, the police, and the militia "forced the trains through" and averted more economic loss. But the depression hit working-class people the hardest, and early in February 1894 Rabbi Henry Cohen of Temple B'nai Israel asked the Presbyterian Ladies' Aid for $20 to buy 200 meals for unemployed mechanics. In December of that year, as the cases mounted and monies dwindled, the Presbyterian ladies eagerly awaited the Ball Charity Fund gift of $500 to be parceled out in drops of from $3 to $5 for each petitioner. In 1895, women from the cotton mill, who earned 90 cents a day, petitioned the mayor and aldermen for an adjustment in their thirteen-hour days. The aldermen failed to bring about a resolution with the factory owners, so fifty women requested $1,000 for return tickets to their homes. The aldermen raised a measly $175 for transport. So the employees of the Galveston Cotton Mill applied to the Ladies' Aid for assistance and were helped on an individual basis. Things got so bad that when the pastor and later the elders asked the ladies to take charge of the janitor, they replied that they "could not undertake any more work in connection with the church." Their days were filled with raising money to feed the unemployed. Finally, in 1897 the ladies lamented that times were so hard and honest work so difficult to find that absolutely no charity cases would be refused.[72] The depression of 1893–1897 may well have been the benevolent societies' most constructive years of service to the community. A steady rise in the numbers of applicants for aid to the Presbyterians proves the point. Beginning in 1894, requests for aid nearly tripled and by 1895, the society gave help to the largest number of recipients in the society's history. (See table 4.1.)

Twentieth-Century Charity

The devastating storm of September 1900 was a blow that substantially affected the women's benevolent societies. Approximately one-half of the surviving residents left the city; some never returned. At first, few individuals reported to the various women's charities, because a Central Relief Committee created in the wake of the disaster, the American Red Cross, and donations from around the world supplied the homeless. The minutes of the various societies appear spotty even months after the disaster as the ladies tended to their own problems. Then, too, with damage to many of the churches and the synagogue, the women concentrated on rebuilding and refurbishing congregational interiors.[73]

The momentum for poor relief among women's benevolent societies had been severely impaired by the overpowering currents of the disaster. Hundreds were without homes, food, and clothing. No catastrophe of that magnitude had afflicted the island before, and the women's benevolent societies, attached as they were to the care and upkeep of their churches as well as poor relief, were simply overwhelmed by the need. Moreover, the kind of fundraising the women did to earn money for charity—sewing dainty items for sale, holding teas and bazaars—could not be sustained in a community coping with massive debris removal and homeless camps on the edge of town. Fortunately, emergency relief agencies, spawned in the wake of the disaster, carried the city's homeless through the worst part of the recovery.

Still, after 1901, all of the women's benevolent societies continued some form of poor relief, but either their methods of fundraising became more labor saving or they sought distance from the subjects of their charity. Rather than come together for sewing, Lutheran women bought two rental houses on Winnie Avenue, the income from which went toward aiding the needy and earning money for missions work.[74] Jewish women quickened their activities to accommodate the needs of charitable organizations of Jewish origin or that cared for Jewish children rather than deal directly with the Jewish poor. They continued to give $50 at a time to the New Orleans Orphans' Home, donated $250 to the Jewish Kindergarten begun by the Council of Jewish Women in 1914, and contributed monthly charitable allotments to the Lasker Home for Homeless Children to help poor Jewish children therein. In 1915, Josie Marx Blum suggested reinstituting a sewing society to make garments for the poor, indicating that the society had long ago abandoned that kind of work.[75]

Trinity Church Guild members were persuaded to reorganize their charitable pursuits, creating charity subcommittees and hiring a professional "investigator" to check on the worthiness of recipients. But they were not able to continue systematic charity to the poor. Rather, in 1912, they turned their attention to making garments to be given away by other agencies—to patients in the tubercular and

John Sealy hospitals and to the poor through United Charities, which was formed in 1914.[76]

As the war years approached, Trinity Church Guild began donations to the Red Cross and bought Liberty Bonds, but they ran out of money and, finally, members. "The Guild find they cannot possibly get up a sale of work or do anything to make money at present, there are so few members who can work, so decided to ask the members to pay their dues for 1918." The problem of carrying on the charitable work of the parish, that is, of visiting the sick, assisting in the Sunday school, and setting an example for those women not in the guild, could be aided, said Magnolia Sealy, if the parish would call (hire) a deaconess for $1,200 a year with funds raised by the women. Mrs. Sealy offered to give the first $250. When the matter of a deaconess was taken before the vestry, they voted against it, and the women tabled the idea. Although many Episcopal parishes did hire deaconesses to perform parish tasks, thus freeing laywomen for charity work, the vestrymen preferred to save the money and allow poor relief to languish.[77]

The Presbyterian Ladies' Aid Society suffered a slow decline in the years between 1900 and 1920. In the first months after the storm of 1900, few women managed to come to the meetings and even fewer supplicants asked for aid. Assembling at times with only eleven members in 1911, the women spent more time and money on foreign mission work than on home missions or poor relief. The treasurer's report for 1911 shows no line item expense for charity, and the subsequent years' reports show decreasing membership and little activity. Finally, in 1923, a group of younger women, the daughters and granddaughters of many of the original members of the Ladies' Aid Society, called for a revitalization of the apparently defunct society.[78]

Ironically, as the older benevolent societies moved away from poor relief, members of the Women's Missionary Society of the First Methodist Episcopal Church, South, who earlier had not ventured into poor relief, in 1906 opened a Wesley House, or a religious settlement house, for factory workers on the island's West End. Mothers were invited to leave their children under the care of a Methodist deaconess who taught them "Christian ideals." Located across the street from the old brewery, the Wesley House for several years provided daycare in an age when the city lacked such necessities for working mothers. One of the few evidences of any organized attempt to improve race relations came with this society when it appointed five members (three of whom were active in other women's organizations) to a "Negro and Immigration Committee." Methodist women also stretched their activism to include religious services for inmates of the county jail and the clothing of several children at the Home for Homeless Children. The sixty-three-year-old widow and matron at the county jail, Susan C. Russell, was also president of the Ladies' Aid Society of St. John's Methodist Church in 1900 and no doubt paved the way for the introduction of Methodist ministries to prisoners.[79]

As time went on, Episcopal, Presbyterian, and Jewish women (with singular exceptions) distanced themselves from actual contact with the poor and relied instead on monetary donations and the making and distributing of garments through other institutions. The reasons for the shift were many and varied. Kathleen D. McCarthy's example of Chicago women moving away from direct and personal involvement in poor relief offers lessons for understanding a similar phenomenon among Galveston women. McCarthy attributes the decline in direct relief to problems of sprawling slums filled with immigrants that were no longer manageable by teams of charity ladies.[80] For Galveston, the problem was not city growth — in fact it had lost population — rather, the crisis had created needs beyond their abilities. The storm of 1900 overwhelmed the benevolent societies, which, able to function adequately in normal times with approximately forty members per society, were not equal to the task of modern emergency relief on a par with the Red Cross. Moreover, churches and synagogues were in some cases totally destroyed, requiring herculean efforts by the benevolent societies, which still served as congregational housekeepers, refurbishers, and decorators.

Equally important was the fact that women's benevolent societies had traditionally given assistance to the poor at a time when there were fewer options available to women of means, talent, and incentive. By 1900, a plethora of other women's associations existed that took volunteer time and resources away from benevolence. Those women most likely to enter into civic reform activities after 1900 came from the churches that had directly served the poor. Poor relief had given them exposure to community activism, but the very women most likely to engage in poor relief were those who chose more comprehensive and progressive women's associations that addressed needs of the larger community. Essentially, they gave up benevolence for civic reform, leaving the women's poor relief societies in the hands of older members whose principal volunteer careers had been devoted to charity. In every case after 1910, the societies show evidence of aging despite attempts to interest younger women in poor relief. And, as McCarthy points out, the newer generation of women entered into other avenues of community improvement, where more public visible roles allowed reforming women to shine. Public exposure replaced private sacrifices as a means for well-intentioned women to gain self-esteem.[81]

Perhaps the most important underlying reason that benevolent societies declined after 1910 was the rise of secular organized charity organizations that took away the need for women's personal relief efforts. The United Charities, organized in 1914, originated as a clearinghouse for relief work. Its creators were men active in the commercial life of the city, but its canvassers for the initial fundraising were thirty-four women, who ward by ward solicited $7,000 as a base endowment. The first board of directors, representing various denominations, was composed of five men and two women from the community. The two women, Margaret Sealy Burton and Sally Trueheart Williams, were members of the Episcopal and Presbyterian churches, respectively, which had "invented" relief for sufferers without connections. Soon after its organization, the United Charities hired a secretary, Mary E. Wood, who, as an experienced social worker, took charge of city relief work. She coordinated the efforts of at least twelve church benevolent societies and petitioned the county commissioners for aid to individuals in need. In 1916, the United Charities disbursed $10,680 in aid and found work for 150 unemployed.

In the two years between 1914 and 1916, it helped 2,300 transients and 984 family cases. These charitable gifts went far beyond the means of the women's benevolent societies.[82]

Two years after its initiation, the United Charities saw more women appointed to positions of administrative power. Miss Mary Martin, a Catholic, was advanced to the board of directors, and four women and one man of different faiths composed the advisory board. Although community relief was now taken over by bureaucracy, it was still in the hands of women, many of whom learned their first lessons in civic responsibility in women's benevolent associations. Complete separation between welfare services and churches did not occur before 1920. In fact, an appeal sent out by the United Charities' secretary to the congregations sounded very much like the goals advanced by the women's benevolent societies. It announced that the new organization strived for "a united effort to relieve the unfortunates who have been submerged in life's struggle, and [to] give them another opportunity for gaining independence, self-respect and usefulness." Major breakthroughs were the interracial and nonsectarian policies adopted by United Charities.[83] In effect, organized secular benevolence that coordinated the efforts of a host of poor relief societies coopted the work of benevolent ladies. A bureaucracy, with hired administrators, handled the needs of the poor in an efficient, business-like manner, making sure that the truly needy received the care they deserved.

Poor relief in Galveston evolved from a combination of relief efforts put forward by both men and women. Early efforts came from men's fraternal organizations, labor unions, and male ethnic and religious societies to care for their own members. This was followed by women's ethnic societies that also ministered to the needs of their own kind. Although government agencies existed for the care of the poor and indigent, most agreed that the poor farm was an institution of last resort for the ambulatory poor in financial distress. By the mid-1880s, every church and synagogue of any size had some means for helping the poor, and most had women's societies as well. But Episcopal and Presbyterian women's benevolent societies filled a need as safety nets for those, mostly women, who had access to no other forms of relief and who were not eligible for or desirous of county aid. These groups, which served the worthy poor beyond the doors of their own church, did not try to evangelize or proselytize the supplicants; rather, they sought to assert Christian humanitarianism. Women's benevolent societies among these churches evolved as urban and industrial conditions, including decreasing wages particularly for working women, created greater hardships for the working poor.

The rise of women's benevolence in Galveston should be viewed as an organizational effort that returned to the community as productive members those who might otherwise have fallen into permanent destitution. As an integrating force, women's benevolent societies strengthened the link between individual and community, both for benevolent ladies and for the poor. Their acts of charity, whether in the form of German immigrant groups aiding ethnic kinfolk, German Jewish settlers aiding transient newcomers from Russia and Poland, or Protestant women confronting the age-old problem of the poor at their doorsteps, arose out of their own sense of personal involvement in the community, from a sense of class differentiation, from religious convictions that demanded social action, and from societal values that portrayed women as gentle caretakers.

True, there were shortcomings to the women's system. It did not adequately address the source of the problems or attempt to rearrange the social order better to accommodate the working poor. It did not measure poverty as a consequence of race discrimination and did little to alleviate the great discrepancy in wealth and social acceptance between the races. There is little or no evidence that these Galveston women viewed their charitable deeds as scientific or effective in eradicating pauperism. And no vision of the northern brand of the social gospel—the transformation of society to relieve conditions that created poverty—graced the pages of their ledgers. Southern benevolent ladies coveted no grand designs for overturning the social order; they were too much a part of that order.[84]

Most women who joined the benevolent societies grew old within them and never ventured into areas of public life. A few women boldly "graduated" from church-related societies to the managing boards of semireligious benevolent institutions—orphanages, a home for elderly women, and a kindergarten—and to women's clubs, civic groups, United Charities, and reforming associations. Although a description of this process will supply the subject for the next chapters, suffice it to say that a female voluntary hierarchy was being developed in Galveston for women who were both charitably, socially, and, some might say, politically ambitious. The shaping of a reforming women's community, which would emerge full grown in the Progressive Era, began as early as 1870 with certain women's societies that devoted their energies to helping stem poverty. Already we can begin to see the contours of this community of reformers: elite women from Presbyterian, Episcopal, and Jewish congregations tended to be more visible in secular reform groups later in the century than white women from Baptist, Methodist, and Christian (Disciples of Christ) churches. Class, an ever present articulator of reality, became more defined through women's benevolent societies, both for working-class folk and for the would-be elite.

There is no doubt that most women who joined the benevolent societies acted out of piety and were clearly moved by scenes of suffering and destitution. They never lost their patronizing air, nor did they openly criticize an economic system that left women underpaid. Instead, they helped working women to adapt to the realities of the workplace, providing a type of insurance for employees at a time when sick pay and unemployment compensation did not exist. For the dependent young and aged they made temporary and permanent arrangements for care. They developed the case system of social welfare in Galveston long before the advent of professional social workers, and they crossed denominational lines to establish a citywide women's ecumenical charity system. Perhaps more important than any aid given was the fact that the ladies of these benevolent societies took weekly lessons in human depravation, coming into immediate contact with the truly desperate within the community. Instead of closing their eyes to the need and want, they sought ways to further their effectiveness, to aid more than just those who came to their church parlor doors. They began to reach out and gather in those who needed shelter, food, or education in homes or schools built especially for those least able to care for themselves. Their main targets, as we shall see in the next chapter, were women and children. And their involvement was just the next step in their journey into civic affairs. Parallel institutions, formed by women to care for the city's dependents, became public edifices and public endeavors, which paid homage to female effectiveness. To say, as Anne Scott did, that women invented the welfare state may be only a slight exaggeration.[85]

5

. . . .

BENEVOLENT INSTITUTIONS AND
THEIR LADY MANAGERS

*Every man who has reached middle age begins to realize that women will
take hold of and accomplish by labor what men would never dream of.
. . . Animated by a desire to do good, they take hold of it and possess
greater force than the men.*

—Colonel Marcus F. Mott, at opening of the
Letitia Rosenberg Women's Home

By 1880 the women's benevolent societies were firmly in place, dispensing aid
on a regular basis; they served a critical need as proto-welfare agencies in a
time when few such institutions existed. By ministering to the poor, however,
benevolent ladies came to understand the degree of dependency that had been
created by increased industrialization and the growth of the city. The answer to
the problems of orphans and the aged poor came through the creation of benevolent institutions, homes, or asylums. In order to care for white Protestant and
Jewish dependents, Galveston citizens, mostly white women, created their own
benevolent institutions; thus began a new chapter in Galveston's history of poor
relief. Individual women's church and synagogue societies chose not to sponsor
these asylums for the city's dependents.[1] Instead, elite women from various congregations formed an interfaith female force by binding the energies of the city's
most affluent women to the task of institution building. Thus, for the first time
women moved from the safe and sanctioned enclosures of church and synagogue
to the larger secular world, transferring their concerns for dependents from home
to church to city. The importance of this shift cannot be overstated, because by
moving into the public sector women with means created an opening for themselves that would continue through the twentieth century.

Drawing upon their experience with congregational societies, white genteel
Protestant and Jewish women between 1878 and 1894 founded or helped to found
four permanent benevolent institutions that were administered by boards of lady
managers. Two orphanages, the Galveston Orphans' Home (1880) and the Lasker
Home for Homeless Children (1894); a home for aged women, the Letitia Rosen-
berg Women's Home (1888); and the state's first free kindergarten, the Johanna
Runge Free Kindergarten (1893),[2] were added to the already existing St. Mary's
Catholic Orphan Asylum and the County Poor Farm.

Members of the Protestant and Jewish communities were not the first to build benevolent institutions in Galveston; Catholic women's religious orders were. Very early in the city's history, Ursuline nuns accompanied Bishop John Mary Odin to Galveston and formed the Ursuline Academy and convent. These sisters, although educators, acted as nurses while yellow fever epidemics raged, and during the Civil War they converted their convent to a military hospital. After the war, Bishop Claude Marie DuBuis of Galveston summoned three Sisters of Charity of the Incarnate Word from France to establish an infirmary and an orphanage in Galveston. In 1867, St. Mary's Infirmary became the first Catholic hospital in Texas; in its infancy it also housed twenty orphans. Finally, in 1874 St. Mary's Orphan Asylum became a separate institution managed and cared for by the Sisters of Charity.[3] The Catholic orders, missionaries to the Southwest, established institutions in the city before there was a substantial population to support them, and the struggle to maintain their schools, hospital, and orphans' home was heroic given the few resources available to them.

A brighter period came with the 1880s, and the rise in institution building at that time is attributable to the increase in population and prosperity on the island. In the twenty years before 1900, the population steadily climbed from 22,248 to 37,789. More important was the tremendous rise in commercial activity leading boosters to point with pride to the fact that Galveston by 1880 was the third largest cotton export center and fourth largest coffee market in the United States.[4] Fortunes were being made in cotton merchandising, railroading, banking, manufacturing, and real estate. As capital accumulated, men with investment instincts sought to improve the city by creating institutions worthy of the island's growing prosperity and increasing population.

In these years, public institutions with state and city funding accepted private donations by wealthy citizens. In fact, private investments were often used to induce state or local governmental appropriations. The public school system, which opened in 1881, was helped substantially when Henry Rosenberg paid for the construction of Rosenberg School, when George Ball gave funds for the erection of Ball High School, and when Isidore Lovenberg bequeathed money to build Lovenberg School. In the same manner, John Sealy offered $50,000 for the construction in 1890 of a charity hospital with the strict proviso that the state open the University of Texas Medical Branch and use John Sealy Hospital to train student doctors and nurses. The city in turn made an annual appropriation of about $40,000 to the hospital, which did not cover its costs. The deficit was made up by John Sealy's son and daughter, who also expanded the hospital and eventually created a foundation for the care of patients.[5]

Other institutions created to benefit the public in these years were private and were established or were substantially aided by men of wealth. A free public library had been the goal of Henry Rosenberg when he died in 1893. In the tradition of the "Gospel of Wealth" espoused by Andrew Carnegie, Rosenberg left $400,000, the bulk of his estate, to the erection of a public library in hopes that succeeding generations would be morally and intellectually uplifted. The Rosenberg Library opened its doors finally in 1904. The Young Men's Christian Association (YMCA) struggled to maintain itself in the years before and after the Civil War, but it remained underfunded until 1884, when a permanent organization took root. Then

Henry Rosenberg left $65,000 to construct a YMCA building, which, when completed in 1898, ensured its success. University Hall, a dormitory for women students at the Medical Branch, was built in 1897 with a gift from San Antonio's George W. Brackenridge. There were other societies that, with the help of generous donors, after 1900 became established institutions — the Adoue Seamen's Bethel and the Young Women's Christian Association (YWCA) are two notable examples.[6]

Galveston's middle- and upper-class women sought to capitalize on the wave of pride and donations to build institutions of their own — for children and old women. Remaining within their sphere by offering "homes" to orphaned children and elderly women and a kindergarten to the children of factory workers and immigrants, privileged white women avoided challenging the common assumptions about woman's proper place or her duties as homemaker. After all, women in church and synagogue societies benefited the poor without offense to conventional notions of woman's place. Moreover, women had gained experience in handling poor relief, and it was evident that relief could not adequately compensate for lack of wages for single mothers whose children were suffering privations. Rather than address the issue of decent wages for working women, elite women and men followed the path of nineteenth-century child-saving experts, who recommended institutions to rescue children from poverty and lack of skills. The elderly, too, came to be seen in these years as different from the ordinary poor. Because of their helplessness, inability to earn their way, or poor health, they were perceived as needing special institutional protection. Galveston's benevolent ladies, by offering sanctuary to the victims of capitalism's iron laws, contributed to the redistribution of resources among whites without challenging either male egos or bourgeois sensibilities. These women in return gained a foothold in the public sphere that eventually led them to initiate women's civic reform movements.[7]

In the minds of many citizens, the city needed decent asylums for homeless waifs and the elderly. No state "homes" existed in Galveston at the time. Moreover, the state legislature did not appropriate enough funds to care for dependents. According to the 1904 census report on benevolent institutions, Texas ranked a surprising fifth after New York, Pennsylvania, Illinois, and Ohio in the number of institutions per population, even though the state ranked fourteenth in the absolute number of institutions (83 as compared to New York's 659, Pennsylvania's 409, Illinois's 257, and Ohio's 267). Texas, however, ranked thirty-fifth out of fifty states and territories in the number of inmates (125.2) per 100,000 population in benevolent institutions. This fell well below the average of 347 per 100,000 nationally, indicating the state's conservatism when it came to spending money on welfare. It seems that institutions were available in Texas, but the legislature declined to fund them adequately.[8]

The state assembly appropriated even less for black citizens. No institution for the care of orphans and the elderly was provided before 1929, although the legislature established an institute for Deaf, Dumb, and Blind Colored Youths in Austin in 1887. In Galveston, the bitter fact remains that white philanthropy was woefully inadequate to help meet the needs of African American dependents. The black community, as will be seen in chapter 8, was forced during this time to fall back on its own resources to provide help for orphans and the elderly. Although elite white women were willing to cross class lines in an effort to provide homes and kindergartens for working-class families, they were unwilling before 1900 to found homes—either on their own or in conjunction with middle-class black women—for African Americans.

Members of Galveston's elite were no different from other white Texans in their indifference to the needs of black citizens, but one must ask why whites chose to withhold this particular form of charity. It is more difficult to interpret why an event did not happen than why it did, but the answer may lie in the establishment of a powerful class of elites in cities like Galveston, who, either through experience or in theory, supported the goals of the Confederacy and were dismayed or angered in the postwar era to find ex-slaves seeking jobs, housing, and access to public facilities. As late as 1881, letters from white readers to the *Galveston Daily News* suggested that the needs of freedpeople should be taken care of by the federal government since it was a Union dictate that emancipated them. Southern whites felt resentment that now they, not the nation, were given responsibility for persons whom they felt were an expense to white taxpayers. Speaking of the presence of the "colored race" as a burden that should not be imposed on the South, one writer stated, "Northern speculators and Northern ships brought the negro from his jungles in Africa, and Northern men and Northern bayonets made him a citizen and placed the ballot in his hand. Thus the South sees only fairness in the appeal to the Federal Government for assistance in the gigantic undertaking so urgently demanded." No amount of logic seemingly could transcend the boundaries created by a mentality that resented the presence of free blacks. Without federal aid, southern whites chose to ignore the needs of African Americans and felt justified by their inaction. By law, white taxpayers were forced to support black schools, but they felt that it was up to African Americans to provide for their own dependents. White benevolent ladies, therefore, contributed to this mindset and to the neglect of black children and elderly by establishing homes and kindergartens for whites only.[9]

The Galveston Orphans' Home

White benevolent ladies mobilized themselves behind nearly every effort to care for white dependent children and the elderly; men, in the beginning, still felt the need to be in charge. Later on, that would change as women gained confidence and experience in the business of raising money and managing institutions. In the case of the orphans' home, a man and a woman, both interested in the relief of suffering, combined forces to found a temporary refuge. George B. Dealey, a Baptist tea merchant who lived in the city from 1870 to 1889, took the commandment for servanthood seriously. He served on the church communion committee, taught Sunday school at the Baptist East End mission, and often visited the hospital, where he read to the patients, conducted religious services, and distributed religious tracts. There he met Mrs. E. M. Arnold, one of the matrons of the city hospital, and together they devised a plan to found an orphanage. The reports are vague on the particulars of the arrangement, but it would appear that Dealey convinced Mrs. Arnold to take charge of the home while he acted as corresponding secretary, rented the house, provided for the children, and, presumably, paid her salary.[10]

They opened a home at Eighth Street and Broadway Boulevard in October 1878 but later, because the landlord objected to the orphans, moved it to a more hospitable abode at Eleventh and Market streets. No information exists today on how the orphans were brought in, but a year later twenty boys and girls occupied the home. They survived the first year on donations gathered from merchants and businessmen "one of the first being . . . Henry Rosenberg who indorsed [sic] warmly the effort." The founders then realized the need for wider community support and sought a regularly organized, albeit temporary, board of directors. The first overtures were to men prominent in the community who would help with legal and financial matters.[11]

In May 1880, the male board of directors procured a charter for the orphanage, which they named the Island City Protestant and Israelitish Orphans' Home because it admitted Jewish and white Protestant children only. In July, at the home of George and Sarah Ball, the directors elected a permanent board of thirteen trustees, which acted in a supervisory capacity by handling the legalities of adoptions and nonpayments but which otherwise had little involvement with the children.[12] Most important to this study, the directors also elected twenty-eight women to the board of lady managers and named as governess Hallie Ballinger, the wife of jurist William Pitt Ballinger, and as vice governess Sarah Ball, who was prominent in charitable work, with Mrs. Clara Ritter as matron (no mention of Mrs. Arnold).[13] It seems that Galveston was ready for the home, for in a matter of two years, the orphans' home had grown from a house run by a couple of well-meaning individuals to a community-funded, congregation-supported, trustee-supervised, woman-managed affair.

A combination of wealthy citizens quickly raised the necessary funds to provide a permanent home for the orphans.[14] The board purchased the Bolton Place at Twenty-first Street and Avenue M, while Henry Rosenberg filled the position of president of the trustees. Upon his death, he bequeathed $30,000 for the building of a larger orphans' home. That structure, a two-story brick Gothic mansion 104 feet by 94 feet, stood completed in 1895.[15] The children and managers enjoyed five years in their new abode before the hurricane of 1900 hit the island. The orphans' home sheltered the children and hundreds of refugees from the ravages of the storm, but after the children had been safely removed to Dallas and an inspection made of the grounds and building, the relatively new asylum was declared profoundly damaged.

The orphanage underwent several name changes before it settled on the Galveston Orphans' Home. It had remained the Island City Protestant and Israelitish Orphans' Home until 1895 when, without explanation, it dropped the "Protestant and Israelitish." Apparently there was no disagreement between the Protestant and Jewish members of the boards of trustees and lady managers, for the two remained integrated, and the Kopperls, who were Jewish, continued to give the home their wholehearted support. In fact, a legacy of Jewish support for community enterprises

FIGURE 5.1. Galveston Orphan's Home, built in 1895. Courtesy Rosenberg Library, Galveston, Texas.

continued through Isabella Dyer Kopperl, the niece of Rosanna Dyer Osterman. Undoubtedly, Isabella Kopperl was an inheritor not only of her aunt's fortune but of her boundless goodwill and philanthropy toward the island city.[16]

The duties of the board of trustees and the board of lady managers for the home in the 1880s and 1890s fit the rigidly defined roles for men and women in their separate spheres. The men assumed responsibility over the "financial affairs, property, and business of this corporation," invested the funds, supervised the property, handled the legalities of adoptions, and met four times a year. The lady managers were assigned tasks related to the "internal and domestic affairs," making rules, admitting and disciplining children, hiring and firing employees, supplying the home with food, clothing, and fuel, inspecting both the home and potential inmates, arranging for schooling, choosing adoptive parents, and raising money. They met twice a month as a board and as often as needed in committees. The women ran the orphanage much the same way a genteel lady would orchestrate the management of a large home and family. Children and servants were under her supervision and subject to her discipline, her rules, her inspections for a clean and tidy dwelling, and her provisioning. The men graced the home as would a paternalistic father, who handled the finances and legal arrangements but distanced himself from domestic entanglements in a posture of benign neglect.[17]

As with most households, the amount of work each put into keeping a family well fed, housed, clothed, disciplined, and educated divided along severely disproportionate lines. Men oversaw, while women did the work. It was no different with the orphanage. The lady managers met more often, took more pains with their decisions, and watched more closely over the residents of the home. In the "woman's work is never done" category, the lady managers divided themselves into committees for Ways and Means, Furnishing, House, and Children. Reports were due at every meeting by the chairperson who had sent members of her committee to attend to their assigned tasks. In addition, weekly inspections by appointed "visitors" meant that every manager at least twice a year ran a white glove over the entire house. Most visitors reported favorably that everything was in order, but not always. "The floors were dirty and needed scrubbing," read one uncomplimentary report in the middle of winter. "The house was dirty and cold. The weather was so bad that the matron claimed she could not keep the place clean. Mrs. Lytle had never before thought the House looked like an orphan asylum, but on this occasion of her visit it did — unmistakably." The stove had gone out in the hall and in the nursery and the flues needed cleaning. An endless litany of "needs" cropped up over the years — a new water closet for the girls, a repaired cistern, a new window blind, new beds, mattresses, sheets, and mosquito bars, drain pipes for the back yard, repairs of leaky pipes and falling plaster.[18] These complaints were referred to the House Committee, but often the ladies prevailed upon the trustees for the repairs; in a sense forcing the men's involvement when the women could have called the repairmen themselves.

The two furnishing committees took care of all of the food, fuel, and clothing needs of the home and children. Expenditures for shoes, stationery, dry goods, groceries, meat, bread, milk, vegetables, kerosene, coal, oil, and wood amounted to $1,075 for 1884. House Committee members reported expenses of $952 for the salaries of the matron, assistant matron, nurse, cook, laundresses, and miscellaneous repairs. The matron earned $300 that year and the nurse less than half that amount for living in the home and watching, supervising, and caring for children on a twenty-four-hour basis with only a short annual vacation.[19] Matrons were hard to keep; the low salary and demanding work were undoubtedly the cause. Managers had little choice but to keep looking for suitable matrons at low wages, because the costs of running a home kept them all scrambling for extra funds.

Whereas caring for the needs of the home and paying the bills fell under the rubric of general housekeeping by the managers, admitting children constituted at once a more sensitive and a more elevated task. Members of the children's committee held more powerful roles than women in benevolent societies, who may have denied aid to the undeserving poor, but who did not in that decision determine the life course of an individual. Not so with the lady managers; their determinations were critical to the lives of the children and to the families that requested admittance of children. Lady managers acted as proto-welfare agents, commanding respect for their important offices and wresting power for themselves in areas outside their own homes and the church.

The orphans' home was established for white full orphans and half orphans only, and on these points the managers based their decision for admittance. In the years before 1900, a parent paid $5 a month for the care of the child and was allowed to bring the child home only with the permission of the lady managers, usually twice a month. Parents could remove their children at any time with the approval of the managers, except in those rare cases where parents allowed the home to adopt their child. Parents who summarily removed children because of displeasure could not return them without special permission. Charity cases were considered by the lady managers and accepted only after a thorough investigation as to the impoverished condition of the parent or the complete indigency of the orphan. At times the parents of charity cases were asked to work for the home in order to make some kind of payment. About forty children occupied the home before 1900; on average, twenty children per year were admitted, three or four were lost to death, about ten were removed by relatives, four were adopted out, and about three were dismissed each year due to bad behavior or graduation.[20]

Once admitted, children fell under the control of the lady managers, who saw to their needs; hired qualified matrons, nurses, and cooks; made sure that they were sheltered, fed, clothed, educated, trained, allowed free choice of worship, and given special celebrations or outings at holidays. In the early days, a board member even took a child into her own home for a while. Lady managers worked long hours to see to the needs of the home. In return, they expected the children to learn good work habits, self-discipline, cleanliness, and tidiness — qualities assigned to the middle classes. Pleasure with the children was usually expressed in connection with the fulfillment of these expectations. When the house was "clean and nice," the inspector would often comment that the children had also been working. "Some girls busy with patch work," read one entry, or "girls were ironing," "children were sewing," "the girls were scrubbing the dining room." One weekly visitor commented that "the boys were cheerfully chopping and sawing wood." Praise for the children was rare but always accompanied tasks that they had performed well. When the boys helped clean the cistern in order to repair the leak, they were rewarded with a trip to the beach and a picnic.[21] Keeping children busy and teaching them "habits of industry" was part of the psychology of asylum management. It was also the role assumed by a diligent housekeeper and mother who understood it as her duty to raise children to become self-supporting citizens. Lady managers projected the cultural expectations of their roles as mothers, and as middle-class matrons and insisted on good deportment by the orphans.[22] The fact that most of the children came from underprivileged classes meant that, in the minds of the managers, training was essential to keep these future citizens from falling back into lower-class impoverishment. While the institution had these children, the ladies would do everything they could to teach usefulness, order, and self-discipline.[23]

More frustrating for the managers was the lack of success they experienced in adopting out full orphans and in placing adolescents in apprenticeships. In the years between 1884 and 1886, only eight children were given out for adoption or apprenticeship. Because of religious differences, the managers would not allow a child to go to a Catholic family, and too often the children came back, rejected by Protestant or Jewish guardians. When the managers sent young Pat Newport by himself to Austin on trial with a Mrs. L. C. Rease, she rejected him, and Pat returned the next year. His sister, Myra, shuttled from home to home seemingly always on trial. When the girl protested leaving her last assignment, she was told that the woman she was with would not take out guardianship papers. With two adoptees sent back in one week, the managers finally admitted "the matter of permanently replacing our orphans seems hedged with difficulty, and requires . . . reform." These episodes of rejection could be devastating for the children and represented failure for the lady managers. Volunteering for service on the board of an orphanage required dedication and stamina.[24]

Teaching self-sufficiency leading to independence was uppermost among the goals of the managers. But when lessons in self-discipline failed, the women resorted to punishment. Although the managers did not administer the punishment—the matron usually did—they still authorized it. Often the troublemakers were the older boys and girls between twelve and fourteen.[25] By adolescence the necessary regimen of an orphan's agenda—studying, obeying, doing chores—were all frustratingly familiar. For those youths ready for the world but afraid of the rejections awaiting them there, the orphanage proved authoritarian and limiting, more an institutional prison than a home. When the youngsters rebelled, the managers responded with surprising harshness. Pat Newport ran away after not learning his lessons. The matron, Mrs. Delano, had threatened to punish him if he did not study. Interviewing the matron but not the child, the managers decided to call both the parties before the board to inform Pat that Mrs. Delano had the "authority to punish." Pat was asked to apologize, which he did. But troubles with this young man were not over. The problem with one boy showing his independence was that it often led others to follow. Two months later, four boys ran away, and Mrs. Delano threatened to quit if "something is not done to control unruly boys." Two weeks after the incident, the managers were still debating what they should have done. Some wanted the boys whipped by the police, but, fortunately, the policeman said that no law permitted him to do so. He could send an officer out to frighten them, came the helpful suggestion.[26]

The boys' rebelliousness continued. In June the minutes reveal that the matron had to whip sixteen boys for throwing chunks of dried mud at a neighbors' house and hitting her child. With community favor at stake, those in authority could take no chances of a repeated outbreak of high spirits. One parent, embarrassed by her sons' outburst, gave them a licking. But not all parents agreed with the action. "Mrs. Hearst who had two children in the Home without charge, vexed that they should be whipped, removed them," an action that would lose her the chance for readmitting the children. Anthony Rotundo labels adolescent boys' group behavior "boy culture." Peer group antics were part of an adolescent need for self-assertion and independence. Mischief making, disregard for private property, and pranks of all kinds elevated boys from childhood to positions of semiautonomy as they approached adulthood. Confrontations, writes Rotundo, came from the community over minor acts of vandalism. Using military imagery, boys waged guerrilla warfare against an adult world in order to lay claim to their own values and independence.[27] When all attempts to correct and train were at a loss, the managers expelled those with a living parent or relative and simply asked to leave those who would not cooperate.[28]

The discipline may have been harsh in this orphanage because corporal punishment was accepted as a part of southern upbringing. Whipping does not seem consistent with the image of women as gentle, pure, and nurturing, nor does it accord with a national middle-class belief that instilling internal control in children was preferable to external control—guilt versus shame. Middle-class adults hoped to teach self-control to youngsters and adolescents, for so they believed lay the path to success in life. Their methods began with the imposition of rules and usually resulted in psychological manipulation and guilt production. Physical punishment as a method for maintaining order was more common to working-class families nationwide.[29] But, as Linda Gordon points out, the subject of punishment is not easily generalized and must take into account its "different contexts, . . . the victims' infractions, . . . and personal networks of support." To smother the question of the managers' attitudes toward orphans under the theoretical blanket of social control also does not shed much light on the subject. Ninety-four percent of the children in the orphans' home had one living parent whose relationship with his or her offspring was in some cases harsher and less nurturing than that of the managers. Certainly the lady managers felt concern for the children, and in many ways they provided a more congenial environment than the fabled orphanage warehouses of the Northeast. Each child was given an identity, mentioned by the managers by name, not required to wear uniforms, and provided education through the orphanage kindergarten and through the public schools. But the managers were willing to allow corporal punishment for the orphans, perhaps because they saw these children as social inferiors and for whom strict discipline was a necessity. Or they may have feared that without it unruly behavior would land these children in trouble as adults. Although little is known about the child-rearing techniques of Galvestonians, most elite children in Galveston in the 1890s were held to a standard of behavior that honored authority and allowed few avenues for independence. Dr. James Thompson wrote his fiancée that her younger brother, Fred, was "one of the nicest and best mannered boys I have ever met. . . . [but] take my advice, don't curb him too much. . . . He is rather too much inclined to petition whether he may do this or that; and does not seem yet to know instinctively what he may do and what he may not."[30]

Assumptions concerning class may have influenced their attitudes toward discipline, but the lady managers made sure that among the orphans there was no discrimination between charity cases and children with paying parents. It is difficult to know exactly how many charity cases there were, because with the largest category (44 percent) of children admitted there was no mention of either payment or charity. In a count of applicants between 1887 and 1893, a total of 102 children were admitted by fifty-one parents. (See table 5.1.) Thirty children were admitted by nineteen mothers without indication if they were paying or charity cases. Men who accepted aid comprised but 7 percent of the fifty-one parents seeking admission for their children. The managers gave an extra hand to mothers and female children regardless of class differences. As in the case of the benevolent societies, those who were most often helped by benevolent institutions managed by women were women: 20 percent of parents admitting their children were women who were given some form of charity by the managers. In a southern city where few jobs with decent pay for married women existed, widowed mothers from middle to working classes became a segment of society at risk. A more telling statistic gives

TABLE 5.1. Charity and Noncharity Half Orphans and Orphans Admitted to the Galveston Orphans' Home, 1887–1893

	Full Charity		Some Charity		Full Payment		Unknown Payment		Orphans
	M	F	M	F	M	F	M	F	
Sex of Person Admitting	2	1	3	2	1	2	2	1	1
	2	4	2	2	1	1	1	2	1
	4	5	5	2	4	3	3	1	1
				2	3		2	1	4
				2	1		1	1	7
			4		1		2	1	
			1		1		3	2	
			3		3		14	1	
			18		1			3	
Total No. Children Admitted = 102					16			3	
Total Known Charity Children and Orphans = 39								1	
Total Women Admitting Children = 31								1	
Total Men Admitting Children = 20								1	
								2	
								3	
								2	
								2	
								1	
								1	
								30	

Each number indicates a separate admission of from one to four children by a male or female relative under conditions of full payment, full charity, or partial charity. No indication of sex of relatives was given for full orphans.

Source: Minutes, Galveston Orphans' Home, Galveston Orphans' Home Records, 1887–1893 (Rosenberg Library, Galveston).

a glimpse of the lengths to which the managers went to help impoverished women. Of all those receiving charity, women were aided two and a half times more often than men in order for their children to stay in the home. Moreover, of the ninety-five children admitted by parents, 59 percent belonged to women. Finally, in the annual reports of the board of managers, girls nearly always outnumbered boys as residents of the home. In the end, the managers favored rescuing underprivileged parents and children of their own sex.[31]

Most of the orphans in the home could have remained with their own parent if a decent wage scale had been introduced for working women or if governmental aid to dependent children had existed.[32] Industries in 1890 employed more than 300 women and 132 children. Women earned on average $235 a year; the average salaries of the children were $171, compared to male factory workers who averaged $553 a year. Over time the salaries decreased and the hours lengthened. As more women entered the factories, they actually lost ground economically. It is difficult to know how many of these women were single mothers, but because only 7 percent of the children admitted between 1887 and 1893 were full orphans, the orphanage, in fact, acted to aid single parents. No crisis of children without parents existed, but a crisis of single mothers without adequate income did. Southern conservatism, trust in the system of laissez-faire economics, belief in the iron law of wages, and allegiance to unfettered individualism prevented a revolution in the wage-earning capacity of women. Lady managers would have considered it un-thinkable to involve themselves in wage and labor problems. For them, the pur-pose of charity was to return to self-sufficiency those who had become dependent. Barbara Bellows in comparing orphanages in antebellum Charleston run by men and by women found that the women managers "encouraged the poor to become self-sufficient," while male managers, upholding a patriarchal order, encouraged obedience leading to dependence. Galveston lady managers, then, were subverting the patriarchal system of dependency by insisting on self-sufficiency and by run-ning the orphanages themselves, thereby proving their own independence. At the same time, by educating their charges for blue-collar or domestic work, they often seemed to enforce old social codes and the existing social order.[33]

In the case of the orphans, gaining self-reliance required educating them until age fourteen, providing them with a skilled livelihood, and caring for them until they were able to support themselves (or until they became intractable). A few talented girls were given encouragement to continue their studies until certified to teach. By not allowing children to finish high school or by not encouraging them to continue to higher levels of study, critics claim, the managers were as-suring their lack of social mobility. Yet these criticisms may unfairly censure the lady managers of that time, for Galveston had no public school system until 1881, a year after the orphanage was chartered. After that time, however, connections between poor relief, child-saving institutions, and public education became quite strong. At least those were the intentions of the philanthropists and the lady man-agers. Sarah and George Ball, benefactors and providers of a $50,000 charitable fund for poor relief, also—as we have seen—gave $75,000 for the construction of a high school in 1883. The first public high school, Ball High, which cost $100,000, did not come into existence until 1884. Although this does not preclude possibil-ities that they were educating orphans for a subordinate position in society, as soon as they could, lady managers made sure that their charges were afforded a sec-ondary education at the public high school.[34]

Whereas much of what has been said pertains to the duties of the managers of the Galveston Orphans' Home and the orphans and their parents, we need to ask who the managers were, what their connections to the women's benevolent societies were, and how their service on the board influenced the acceptance of public activities for women. Of a total of eighty-four activist women with known religious affiliation who served on the self-elected board of managers from its inception in 1880 until 1920, thirty-six (43 percent) were Episcopalian, sixteen (19 percent) were Presbyterian, twelve (14 percent) were Jewish, nine (11 percent) were Baptist, eight (9.5 percent) were Methodist, and three (3.5 percent) were Lutheran. Ideally, the twenty-six or so members every year represented equally each Protes-tant church and Congregation B'nai Israel, yet overall more came from the Epis-copal, Presbyterian, and Jewish congregations. Changes occurred as each decade passed; the average age of the women on the board increased from forty-one in 1880 to fifty-six in 1910, indicating not only the aging of the board but also the conservatism of a membership unable or unwilling to attract younger women.[35]

TABLE 5.2. Members of the Board of
Lady Managers of the Galveston
Orphans' Home by Religious
Affiliation, 1880–1920

Episcopal	36	43%
Presbyterian	16	19
Jewish	12	14
Baptist	9	11
Methodist	8	9.5
Lutheran	3	3.5
Total	84	100%

Sources: Minutes, Board of Lady Managers, Galveston Orphans' Home Records, 1885–1914 (Rosenberg Library, Galveston); *City Directories,*
1880–1920; and Galveston Women Database.

(See table 5.2.) The board held elections each year, and an incumbent board reelected itself unless someone resigned. To become a member, a woman was chosen by the board because she had served her time working in her own church or synagogue, or she was accorded the right to sit on the board by virtue of her station as wife of one of the city's elites. Usually, even wealthy ladies "earned" their place by first serving the church or synagogue. It is clear, however, that this body of women comprised an elite segment of society, and the board grew more prestigious over time.

The number of lady managers who were also members of women's church and synagogue societies totaled fifty-five over the years. The greatest number, twenty-one, came from Trinity Guild, followed by twelve members of the Presbyterian Ladies' Aid Society, and seven from the Ladies' Hebrew Benevolent Society. Over four decades, the number of managers associated with church or synagogue society work declined, indicating both the secularization of society by 1920 and the wider opportunities for volunteerism in other than church societies. Still, the connection between managers and women's congregational societies constituted an important network for benevolent-minded women and the supplicants they served. There is no doubt that the managers depended on their peers in the women's societies to support their efforts in maintaining orphans through various benefits and entertainments and in acting as investigative or referral agents in specific cases. In fact, those church societies whose primary mission was poor relief—Trinity Church Guild and the Presbyterian Ladies' Aid—were the very societies that were called on more frequently for aid. To a lesser extent, the Jewish synagogue and evangelical church societies were also asked to lend a hand. Indeed, each denominational society on a rotating basis provided the orphans their Thanksgiving dinner. In this manner, reciprocal relationships developed between societies that favored charity for the urban poor and boards of managers that sheltered this same constituency. Between the representatives of the various denominations there also developed friendships and a breakdown of sectarian barriers. Although elite and possibly exclusive, a woman's charitable network, or a woman's community, outside the churches was beginning to form.[36]

Just as Kathleen D. McCarthy found that Chicago women after several decades separated themselves from the day-to-day management of their orphanages in favor of charity fundraisers, so too did Galveston lady managers in the 1890s tend to step away from the detailed management of the home. Eventually, quarterly reports by the matron begin to fill the minute books, suggesting that more and more of the detail work for the orphanage was left up to the matron and her assistants. Problems were still handled by the various committees, but by hiring more workers under the matron's supervision, the managers freed themselves for fundraising. Once they hit upon the idea of an annual charity ball as their principal fundraiser in 1890, the managers began to invest a great deal more time and energy on this grand "society" event than on the daily operations of the asylum. As a point of prestige, Miss Bettie Brown, daughter of railroad magnate John Moreau Brown, donated a tapestry painting to be raffled at the ball. Despite the low admission price—tickets, supper, and cake cost only $2—the charity ball brought in $1,225 in 1892. After 1900, the ball grew to enormous proportions requiring teams of people preparing for weeks to bring to the ballroom Japanese lanterns, a candy stand resembling a flower shop, wisteria bowers, a bazaar, a series of seven tableaux preceding the ball itself, and the usual orchestra, dance cards, ball gowns, and debutantes—all enjoying elaborate press coverage in the next-day news.[37]

Connections to high society in New York City were evident when, in October 1900, William Randolph Hearst, after hearing of the structural damage to the orphanage, organized a benefit bazaar at the Waldorf Astoria "for the homeless orphans of Galveston," and raised over $50,000 for a new home. The bazaar lasted three days, was opened with Texas governor Joseph D. Sayers as the principal speaker, and was closed by novelist Mark Twain. Most of New York's elite, among them Mrs. Stuyvesant Fish, Mrs. Joseph Choate, and Mrs. John Jacob Astor, were in attendance. National attention and a circle of well-established philanthropists brought to Galveston a new orphans' home dedicated March 30, 1902, but they also brought a moment of glory to the Galveston women who served as managers and who had begun to think of themselves as among Galveston's finest.[38]

The results of working on the board of lady managers led to a surprising amount of public approbation; the names for the entire board were spread out across the city directory in a three-inch entry. Moreover, the board provided women the opportunity to "advance" in a semipublic arena parallel to their husband's positions in the world of commerce. In time, the board constituted a privilege afforded only to women of wealth or civic prominence; a position on the Galveston Orphans' Home board held the highest prestige value of all the benevolent institutions.[39]

The Letitia Rosenberg Women's Home

"It is a sad enough sight to see an old man tottering down the rugged mountain path of life under such adverse conditions, but how infinitely more touching it is to see a dear old woman, bereft of home, of kindred and of friends, sinking down upon the stony path, crushed by the weight of years of sorrow, of misfortune. . . . it is . . . a picture that must cause your hearts to throb . . . with loving sympathy."[40] Although spoken by a man, his thoughts resonated with hundreds of women, who saw themselves in old age in an urban area where kinship networks were rapidly breaking down. In postwar Galveston, families remained the primary caretakers of the aged. But for those without family (and this included the foreign born especially), unable to care for themselves, and without resources to hire help, there remained only the county poor farm, an alternative that, as we have seen, combined criminals, the poor, and invalids in inaccessible surroundings.

The rationale for founding a home for aged white women differed from the justification for creating orphanages. Orphans were expected to become self-reliant, but contemporary medical theories assumed that with increasing senility the aged never would. The problem of rising senescence and mental and physical debilitation forced many hospitals to refuse admission to aged, senile patients who suffered no treatable illness. Poor farms were inappropriate for those who no longer were able to work. Forming homes for the elderly, then, required a different rationale, namely that of affording a place of rest for the aged rather than a home for teaching independence.[41]

Alarming numbers of widows and single aged women had applied for relief from the women's charitable societies. When it became obvious that old women were suffering in the same way that orphans had in the years before 1880, benevolent ladies and a male board of trustees hurried to establish a home for aged white women. The idea for an Old Woman's Home, a practical if not attractive title, was first conceived in 1888 by a set of privileged women who, for the most part, differed from those who had founded the orphans' home. For one thing there were not as many of them. In the years between 1888 and 1920, forty-five activist lady managers, nearly half the number of the Galveston Orphans' Home board, ran the Women's Home; only eight lady managers of the orphanage crossed over to the Women's Home board and worked with both institutions. For another, not as many of them made it into the 1896 Blue Book for Galveston—an average 50 percent for the Orphans' Home members but not quite 30 percent for the Women's Home board. Again, more Episcopal women, twenty-four, constituted members of the board, followed by six Presbyterians, five Jews, three Baptists, seven with unknown affiliation, and no Lutherans or Methodists. More than half the women, twenty-six, belonged to church and synagogue societies, seventeen to Episcopal societies. The board members aged along with their inmates from an average age of forty-two in 1888 to fifty-three by 1910.[42] (See table 5.3.)

In the first year of the home's organization, the ladies drew up a roster of seventeen directors composed entirely of women. They rented a house at Thirty-first Street and Avenue I for $25 a month; within a year, twenty-three elderly white women lived there. Payment for bills came from subscriptions of the women who composed the board of directors. By donations, small legacies, and the help of friends, the home survived without a permanent endowment. Finally, in 1893, Henry Rosenberg bequeathed to the board a gift of $30,000 for the "building and furnishing of a woman's home."[43]

FIGURE 5.2. Letitia Rosenberg Women's Home, built in 1895. Courtesy Rosenberg Library, Galveston, Texas.

Even with this enormous legacy, however, fundraising was a constant and nagging worry for the lady managers. In 1894, at each biweekly meeting ideas and suggestions for earning money were considered. A series of teas brought in barely enough to pay for postage. Donations from individuals, the *Galveston Tribune*, and baby shows helped some. Eventually the women hit on an idea that Galvestonians found quite popular and that catapulted women into the commercial section of the city as visible and aggressive solicitors. They institututed Tag Day. Several of the charities united by sending out teams of ladies to "tag" passersby in the downtown area for donations. A tagged person, or donor, sported a badge that demonstrated support for the cause and allowed a respite from the constant female harassment. By taking their campaign to the Strand, women volunteers created a visible advertisement for themselves as fundraisers and for the cause they served.[44]

By January 21, 1896, the elderly women moved into a three-story Victorian Gothic stone structure 80 by 120 feet on Rosenberg Avenue not far from the gulf. Renamed the Letitia Rosenberg Women's Home after Henry Rosenberg's first wife, the asylum was home to at least fifty-one elderly women between the years 1896 and 1917. Their average age was sixty-five, their average length of stay four years. Of the fifty-one inmates, thirty-nine were widows, eleven were single women, and

TABLE 5.3. Members of the Board of
Lady Managers of the Letitia
Rosenberg Women's Home by
Religious Affiliation, 1894–1911

Episcopal	24	53.5%
Presbyterian	6	13.3
Jewish	5	11.1
Baptist	3	6.7
Methodist	0	
Lutheran	0	
Unknown	7	15.5
Total	45	99.9%

Source: Minutes, Board of Lady Managers, Letitia
Rosenberg Women's Home, 1894–1911 (Rosenberg
Library, Galveston); City Directories, 1880–1920; and
Galveston Women Database.

one was married. More striking is the fact that thirty-six (70 percent) of the women
were charity cases, while ten (20 percent) made some sort of payment for board
according to their means. The percentage of aid for elderly women was twice as
high as aid for orphans and half orphans. Elderly women without resources were
in some ways more needy than half orphans whose one parent could help support
them. Widows composed a larger percentage of charity cases than did single
women. Of thirty-six women receiving charity, thirty (83 percent) were widows.
But of the ten who were paying for their keep, half of them were single despite
the fact that single women composed but 22 percent of the total inmate population.
(See table 5.4.) It is tempting to speculate that marriage and subsequent widowhood provided little financial security for a good portion of the female population—so much for the protection that went with the legal status of feme covert.
Single women, who all of their lives were either wage-earning women or acted to
safeguard their legacies, were more apt to remain solvent into old age.

Then, too, women of foreign birth were the most likely to be living in the
home in their old age. Of forty-seven women with known birthplaces, better than
half were not native Americans, while the foreign population citywide was 22
percent. Moreover, twenty of the foreign women were charity cases, most from
Ireland and Germany. These women constituted 55 percent of all those who received charity and 74 percent of foreign inmates in general. What does this signify?
Were family ties too far away to be of help in an immigrant's golden years? Or
was the struggle for a better life in this country for some in vain? It certainly
suggests that Galveston was the home of many more indigent foreign women, who
in old age were unable to call on family for help. It also suggests that the native
white American board members, who had control over admissions, did not discriminate against charity cases or foreign women when they were aware of the
distress level of this group.

Separated as middle-class white board members were from long-term contact

TABLE 5.4. Women Inmates of the Letitia Rosenberg Women's Home, 1899–1917

Total inmates = 51   Widows = 39,   Single = 11,   Married = 1

Charity Cases	= 36	Charity widows	= 30 (83%) of charity cases
Pay cases	= 10	Paying widows	= 5 (50%) of pay cases
Unknown payment = 5		Charity singles	= 5 (14%) of charity cases
		Paying singles	= 5 (50%) of pay cases
		Charity married	= 1
		Unknown payment widows =	4
		Unknown payment single =	1

Average Age = 65.78   Lowest age = 51,   Highest age = 88

Nativity
Foreign = 27
  England = 2, Ireland = 9, France = 2, Germany = 10, Mexico = 1, Scotland = 2, Spain = 1
American = 20
  South = 11, North (New York) = 4, Region unknown = 5
Unknown nativity = 4

Average length of stay in the home = 4.76 years
Shortest stay = 1 month, Longest stay = 20 years

How left? 25 died, 14 left voluntarily, 6 were asked to leave, 6 unknown

Source: Register of the Letitia Rosenberg Women's Home, 1899–1917, Letitia Rosenberg Women's Home Records (Rosenberg Library, Galveston).

with those outside their social circles, the Women's Home represented an opening in cross-class association. Raising money for the home, interviewing the applicants, and visiting immigrant inmates regularly constituted a form of sustained charity work across class lines that fundamentally opened the avenue for a more sympathetic attitude toward foreign-born and Catholic disadvantaged. Although there were still no Catholic lady managers, the acceptance of foreign and Catholic women into the home was an opening that would continue to widen.

For the lady managers, there was always the possibility that the home would be a refuge for them if they needed it. Carrie Finlay, the home's first president and wife of a lawyer who also served on the board of directors, knew this firsthand. She maintained an abiding interest in the home, and in 1905, when she could no longer afford to volunteer her services as president of the board of managers, she applied for and was accepted as matron of the home, where she worked until 1914. When failing health prevented her from laboring at all, she and her husband were allowed a "room [in the home] that a grateful board of lady managers and of directors had dedicated to her use forever during the term of her natural life."[45]

Perhaps too much may be interpreted from these glimpses of life for women inside a sanctuary for the elderly, but it would appear that this was no warehouse with impersonal caretakers and faceless inmates. Emerging from the lifeless pages of the minute books and register is a picture of a humanitarian community for women supported in large part by a sympathetic, even grateful, city willing to support the home if not for charitable reasons, at least for personal ones. As Colonel Mott said in the keynote address for the opening of the new home, "our mothers, sisters, wives and daughters may some day knock at the gate of the Letitia Rosenberg home for women, and God grant that they may not knock in vain."[46]

Benevolent institutions founded in Galveston in the 1890s differed significantly from those chartered in the 1880s; these differences, consequently, led to changes in the way elite women approached community activism. First, the earlier homes had much greater male participation in the founding; male boards of trustees held positions of authority denied to the lady managers. The later institutions were conceived and established entirely by women with help from men supporters. From one decade to the next, benevolent ladies had grown confident and experienced in their abilities to found and manage institutions for dependents.

Second, the orphanage and kindergarten formed after 1890 were much more child-centered, focusing on the needs of children rather than on the moral propriety of the parents. Lady managers of the later institutions were more concerned about keeping the family unit together and set rules to allow parents greater access to their children or devised programs to bring parents into the institutional fold with instruction and moral support. Attitudes of inclusiveness toward the working classes foreshadowed more democratic tendencies in women's organizations.

Third, the older institutions presented a fortresslike mentality, separating orphans and elderly women from their families and the larger community in great stone edifices with large ascending stairs and imposing entrance hallways. The later institutional buildings were more modest, less intimidating, more like the dwellings of the clients they served. The overriding philosophy of training children to be self-reliant, preparing them for reintegration into society, remained. But the lessons were administered with greater sensitivity for the needs of families, and, after 1900, with a progressive spirit.[47]

It is possible that some of the changes may be attributed to generational differences in the women board members. The average age of the women who founded the Galveston Orphans' Home and the Rosenberg Women's Home were 41 and 42, respectively, in the 1880s, but by 1910 their average ages had risen to 56 and 54. The women who created the Home for Homeless Children in 1890 were on average about 41, rising to 50 by 1910. Still younger women formed the Johanna Runge Free Kindergarten; in 1890 their average age was 37, and by 1910 they topped out at 45, a good ten years younger in age and outlook than the ladies of the Galveston Orphans' Home. Younger women and modern philosophies of child saving improved institutional life for children substantially. These also brought greater awareness to lady managers of the potential for a more inclusive women's community that would serve the whole city and all of its citizens.

Lasker Home for Homeless Children

At the close of the 1880s, it became clear that the city needed another orphanage. In 1894, eight women chartered the Society for the Help of Homeless Children, whose object was "to establish a day nursery," and a "temporary home for [white] homeless children until suitable arrangements can be made for the welfare of such children." Well in advance of anything Galveston had seen up to that time, the initial board of women "directors" began a new enterprise—a day nursery to tend babies and toddlers and a home for children who needed shelter from sick, negligent, or abusive parents.[48]

The differences between the two orphanages were great. Because the trustees of the Galveston Orphans' Home had decided in 1880 not to admit a child whose parent had deserted the family, and because they required proof of marriage, there were many children unable to enter Galveston's first orphanage. Looking back to the sad tale of Mrs. Brown, the abandoned mother of three children who applied for help from the Presbyterian Ladies' Aid Society, we see that in 1893 the Galveston Orphans' Home would not take her children even on a short-term basis while she sought employment. Unable to endure the economic pressures, she eventually gave up her children through adoption to another family. Hardships such as these abounded; in 1885, more than eighty applicants were rejected by the lady managers of the Galveston Orphans' Home, most because they did not fall strictly under the charter guidelines. With the creation of a second orphanage, the city received an institution more relaxed in its admission policies and able to accommodate children from more varied backgrounds.[49]

Whereas the Galveston Orphans' Home was created by a male board of directors, the opposite was true of the Society for the Help of Homeless Children. Here women were in charge. First, a founding group of eight women secured a charter and incorporated the association; then they elected thirty women to serve on a board of managers; last they elected "twelve gentlemen, to be called an Advisory Board." Article after article in the home's constitution indicated that women ran the corporation—from admitting children to investing funds. The president was to "sign all certificates, papers and legal instruments in behalf of the Society," while eight standing committees carried on the management of the home. Fourteen years after the founding of the first orphans' home, women had advanced to the level of founding, running, and chartering their own benevolent institutions. Those who ran the home were considered respectable women in the community, but collectively they did not have as high a social standing as women in the first two benevolent institutions. Of the forty-seven women identified as activist and serving on the board of managers, only 10 percent were listed in the 1896 Blue Book. Presbyterian women were more heavily invested in the home than any other religious group; thirteen, or 28 percent, were Presbyterian; eleven Episcopalian; eight Methodist; three Jewish; three Catholic (!); one Baptist; one Lutheran; one Swedenborgian; and six unidentified religiously.[50] (See table 5.5.)

Probably one reason that the society from its inception was a woman's enterprise was the fact that Rebecca Henry Hayes stood among the original eight founders. Best known for her feminism before the South was ready for such a thing, Hayes, a professional journalist, remained president of the Texas Equal Suffrage Association from 1893 to 1895, coinciding with the founding of the orphan society. She also organized one of two mutual benefit associations exclusively for Galveston women with a capital stock of $3,000 in 1897. Her fiery speeches and determined efforts toward achieving women's rights to full political equality and financial in-

FIGURE 5.3. Children from the Home for Homeless Children before 1900. Courtesy Rosenberg Library, Galveston, Texas.

dependence found practical expression in the constitution of the Society for the Help of Homeless Children.[51]

The orphanage's first structure at Thirty-seventh Street and Avenue R came to be known as the Home for Homeless Children and was unique in that it took in three classes of children totaling as many as seventy before 1900. The first category constituted children whose bill was paid in full by relatives; the second, usually children of widows and abandoned wives, remitted a portion of their bill; and the third, destitute children often received from the foundling hospital or from the streets, were supported minimally by the county commissioners. In the first two classes, the parents were required to obtain an agreement from their employers to assume responsibility for payment should the parent default. In this way, the home protected itself while requiring a certain amount of accountability from capitalists upon whom parents depended for their wages. In the third class, the home took in children whom the Galveston Orphans' Home refused and who were technically wards of the county.[52]

The day the census taker came by in 1900, a total of thirty-nine children lived at the home. Six employees staffed the orphanage: a matron, an assistant matron, a head nurse, an assistant nurse, a cook, and a laundress—all white. The children ranged in age from less than one year to thirteen years. Only one baby was in the nursery, but there were fourteen children between one and five years and nineteen children over the age of six. Five of the children had no ages recorded. Just months

TABLE 5.5. Members of the Board
of Lady Managers of the Lasker
Home for Homeless Children by
Religious Affiliation, 1894–1920

Presbyterian	13	28%
Episcopal	11	23
Methodist	8	17
Jewish	3	6
Catholic	3	6
Swedenborgian	1	2
Baptist	1	2
Lutheran	1	2
Unknown	6	13
Total	47	99%

Source: Lasker Home for Children Records,
1894–1920 (Rosenberg Library, Galveston);
City Directories, 1880–1920; Galveston Wom-
en's Database.

after the census taker had visited the home, the storm hit and demolished the building. The head nurse and at least ten of the children perished in the hurricane. After the storm of 1900, the lady managers struggled to regroup their efforts, but through the assistance of the city and county governments they bought property for the construction of another home at Sixteenth Street and Avenue K. Even disaster could not stem the enthusiasm for adding "progressive" programs. Hayes, in petitioning the mayor and county commissioners in 1904 for the deed to the property, stated that the lady managers desired "to establish a kindergarten in the home and also provide for a common school literary education supplemented with industrial training."[53]

Rebuilding, expanding the grounds, and admitting more children required a substantial outlay of funds, and, while women could found, manage, and improve their institutions, the economic discrepancy between the sexes limited their abilities to fund them. With no endowment, the managers were dependent on the community's goodwill for their recovery. Damage to the city was so great that it was years before their dreams would be realized. In the meantime, the women invented ways to keep from sinking financially. Managers of benevolent institutions across the city were beginning to find ways to raise money while cutting back on intensive domestic labor. Tag Day, first used by supporters of the Women's Home, became an efficient means of raising money, and it did not require long hours of sewing, baking, or creating entertainment.

By joining forces with the Johanna Runge Free Kindergarten, the lady managers of both institutions in 1908 chose a sunny day in April to canvass the downtown streets, soliciting donations and rewarding donors with a tag that read, "I Am Tagged to Help the Children of Galveston." The *Galveston Daily News* reported inaccurately that this was "the first trial in this city of this novel and highly successful method of raising money for charity." Noting the difference in bazaars or other sales for charitable purposes, the writer simply stated, "what you gave you gave . . . what you got in return was the pleasure of knowing that you were giving to a cause as worthy as any that exists—the feeding, clothing, housing and education of poor and homeless children." The results were effective: the amount collected in one day came to $1,909. Solicitations of this nature represented a decided departure from women selling homemade items and foreshadowed future large-scale community fund drives.[54] It also appeared more democratic—instead of promoting exclusive balls to raise money, women engaged the public at large in charitable donations while putting themselves squarely in the public forum.

Even with Tag Day events, money for a new home seemed impossibly out of reach. The home needed a philanthropist, who, like Henry Rosenberg, would contribute a substantial sum for improving their structure. The man who came to the rescue was Morris Lasker. Of East German Jewish descent, Lasker immigrated to the United States in 1856 at the age of sixteen and literally peddled his way across the South to Texas on a one-eyed horse. After service in the Confederate army, he recouped his business by setting up trading posts across Texas. He then came in 1867 to Galveston, where, after working for the wholesale grocers Marx and Kempner, he formed the Lasker Real Estate Company, ventured into banking, and in 1906 became owner of the Texas Star Flour and Rice Mills.[55] As an indication of his stature in the community, he was elected to the Texas legislature in 1895. Along with Bertrand Adoue, he provided $30,000 for the establishment of the first "manual training and domestic science" classes in the public schools. In 1912, Lasker gave to the home $15,000 for the expansion and renovation they sought. In return, the managers renamed it the Lasker Home for Homeless Children. A pattern of dependence on philanthropists such as Henry Rosenberg and Morris Lasker was one aspect of institution management that did not change for women. Economic realities barred the homes from becoming entirely self-supporting.[56]

Kindergartens

One of the last major benevolent institutions founded by women from various churches and synagogues before the turn of the century was the Johanna Runge Free Kindergarten. In keeping with current theories of child development, Galveston mothers sought the establishment of kindergartens in the city. These advances in education coincided with women's increasing confidence in their abilities to manage child-centered institutions and with their interest in uplift among working-class and immigrant families. No longer content to take just the indigent child from its impoverished surroundings and place it in an orphanage to teach it self-reliance, those who favored kindergartens saw the entire family at risk and hoped to sensitize children and their parents to middle-class values.

Although not a home or an asylum, the Johanna Runge Free Kindergarten was an institution, nonetheless, inspired and originated by women interested in the quality of early education for the children of factory workers. Its founder, Johanna Runge, of German Lutheran ancestry and wife of cotton magnate Julius

TABLE 5.6. Members of the
Board of Lady Managers of the
Johanna Runge Free
Kindergarten by Religious
Affiliation, 1893–1920

Episcopal	10	42%
Jewish	6	25
Presbyterian	2	8
Baptist	2	8
Lutheran	2	8
Catholic	1	4
Methodist	0	0
Unknown	1	4
Total	24	99%

Source: City Directories, 1880–1920; Galveston Women Database.

Runge, conceived of a school for underprivileged preschoolers when, in 1892, she enrolled her own child in a private kindergarten. Impressed by the beautiful environment, and the songs, games, and delights for children, she determined to create a charity kindergarten. Probably Johanna Runge had thought little of the implications of this type of social outreach either for the community or for herself; she admitted that "up to that time [1892], I never had entered into any public life, although belonging to the different aid societies, had never taken an active part, but devoted all my time to my home and children."[57]

Most women took on such projects after years of experience in organizations, but naïveté wrapped in enthusiasm plunged Johanna Runge into the factory district, reputedly the poorest in the city. Since no other benevolent society or institution at that time centered its project in the midst of the working poor, Johanna Runge simulated the actions of settlement house workers by offering kindergarten classes to the children of working mothers. In a city where charity was conservatively managed and distributed from the safety of church parlors or from "the well-ordered asylum" and where lady investigators seeking the truth about a supplicant's poverty stayed but a few minutes in the homes of the poor, Johanna Runge's venture into the lives of the working class constituted a radical departure. Of course, as the wife of one of the directors of the Galveston Cotton and Woolen Mills, where the parents worked, she fit the image of a lady bountiful rather than a Jane Addams.[58]

To begin her venture she convinced eight "influential ladies" to serve as a board of directors and hold a money-raising drive. They netted $1,300—enough to buy an upright piano, tables, and chairs and to sustain the school for four years. The board of managers was a small but socially select group. In the years before 1920, twenty-four activist women assumed board membership: ten (42 percent) Episcopalian, six (25 percent) Jewish, two Baptist, two Lutheran, two Presbyterian, one Catholic, and one unknown religiously (see table 5.6). The women's social status, according to Blue Book representation, was nearly as high percentagewise as those belonging to the Galveston Orphans' Home; half the members were listed. And this board invited the most experienced women: fifteen belonged to other boards; Isabella Kopperl and EllaMae VanName serving on three. Yet this was also the youngest group; forty-one was the average age.[59]

Beginning with a trip to the factory district at the northwest end of the city, Johanna Runge and her husband, who supported this venture with affirmation and funds, obtained permission to use a church for their kindergarten; the mill where the parents worked agreed to buy the fuel for heat. As she recounted, "Before opening the kindergarten my friend, Miss [Anna] Wilkens, and myself had gone from house to house to visit the families, ask about their children, and see whether they would care for it." Having met with the approval of the parents, they opened the kindergarten January 1, 1893. Fifty children showed up.[60]

The women who came to teach that day were not prepared for the encounter. The children presented to the women a stereotypical image of working-class ur-chins—"unkempt and dirty" and "needing much attention after coming there." The helpers gave the children clothing, aprons, and handkerchiefs, but disillu-sionment persisted. Johanna Runge recalled, "I took home nineteen of the most neglected in sets of two and three at a time to our home, and they always re-sponded with beaming faces when asked to run home and get their parents' per-mission. The nurse gladly bathed and combed these poor children and after dinner the house girl took them home again."[61]

What the parents thought of these incursions into their lives will never be known, for stories such as these are always told by the donors, not by the recipients. They responded, according to Johanna Runge, by making "every effort to improve the physical condition of the children." To her credit, she did not blame the poor for their condition; rather, she saw them heroically struggling to meet the demands of industrialists. "These poor mothers working day by day in the factories came home at night exhausted. A mother['s] heart is ever the purest reflection of divine love, and these mothers no doubt thought many times of the threefold develop-ment—mental, moral, and physical—of their children, but using all their strength to get the bare necessities they could not give to their children the attention they wished."[62] Here it was again, ennobled motherhood creating commonalities be-tween capitalists' wives and factory mothers.

Even with the 1893 depression, the kindergarten grew and they needed more space. The women received word that two adjoining cottages owned by the cotton mill would be available to them if the lady directors bore the expense of con-necting them, which they accepted. This allowed enrollment to increase to sev-enty-five children on the books, age three to six, with an average attendance of sixty. The unmistakable philosophy of progressive education pervaded—"the games of children are their most serious occupations. In the employment of games, the children imitate the parts they themselves will have to fill in after years." The children were given materials to stimulate their "power of doing, inventing, and creating." Music, rhythm, stories, and "chatting" encouraged children "to think." Teachers became increasingly sophisticated as they took summer training classes in Grand Rapids, Michigan, paid for by Morris Lasker.[63]

In 1893, when the Runge Free Kindergarten opened, there were but two other private kindergartens. By 1898, white women had opened eight kindergartens and black women had opened one under the auspices of St. Paul's Methodist Church. It was the direct result of Johanna Runge's influence that a kindergarten opened with fourteen preschoolers at the Home for Homeless Children. Johanna Runge's kindergarten remained one of the only free preschools in the city until the establishment of the Jewish Free Kindergarten in 1913. After the storm of 1900 damaged the kindergarten cottages, the Texas Federation of Women's Clubs made it possible for the school to reopen in December of that year. In 1911 a new schoolhouse went up, and in 1921 the kindergarten merged with the Galveston Public School system in advance of the establishment of kindergartens in all of the elementary schools in the city.[64]

Kindergartens, first envisioned by German educator Friedrich Froebel as enchanting gardens for eager but privileged little learners, became something more to middle-class American women reformers. They believed that if they could reach underprivileged children early enough, teach them in kindergarten habits of cleanliness and industry and channel their innate curiosity into wholesome learning, educators would be "saving" the next generation of working-class citizens. No longer were underprivileged children seen as inately inferior; their surroundings were to blame for their poverty. Create a beautiful environment early enough and children would be transformed by the beauty and "truth" of nature's garden. Whether in factory districts, orphanages, or settlement houses, kindergartens were considered not just educational experiments for the young but the first battleground in winning the child to the progressive middle-class perception of life. Claims for kindergarten at the close of the Progressive Era were weighty; the Runge Free Kindergarten "became a leaven for bettering conditions in the west end," counseled one observer. "Kindergartens minimize the need of juvenile courts, peace officers, and reformatories," went another. Teachers moved beyond the classroom in their efforts: "visiting the homes, organizing mother's clubs to meet in the school building and in every way working long and devotedly for the uplift of the needy."[65]

Johanna Runge was unable to raise wages in her husband's factory or lessen the hours for working mothers. Many of the same working women who petitioned the city aldermen for a decrease in their workday of thirteen hours in 1895 were the mothers of these children. Unable to leave the island with families to support, they could only submit to the awful pressures of economic hardship. In the conservative South, however, it would be years before middle-class women became radicalized enough to champion the rights of workers. In the meantime, they provided charity, asylums, and a free kindergarten for the children, ameliorating somewhat the harshness of the factory village. With grand philosophies suggesting that kindergartens could alter the lives of the working poor, women sympathizers believed that they were instituting momentous changes and had found a cure for urban poverty. Perceptions such as these were slow to change, slower even than the rise in industrial wages. The fault lay in trying to put patches on a ragged industrial system. As idealists, they hoped to bring middle-class values to those who would imbibe their message of uplift.[66]

"Uplift," of course, was a term used consistently in the nineteenth and early twentieth centuries by more privileged classes toward the working poor and recent immigrants. The notion of uplift entered the discussion of members of the Ladies' Hebrew Benevolent Society when they convened in May 1913 to discuss plans for a Jewish Free Kindergarten "for the uplifting of the Orthodox children." The records, unfortunately, do not give details of the "lively discussion" that followed, but the society voted to donate $100 the first year toward the school. The kindergarten was the project of the Council of Jewish Women, a chapter of which had formed in Galveston in 1910. Following the model of the national organization founded in 1893 for aid to immigrant women arriving by the thousands to Ellis Island, the Galveston chapter responded to the recent arrival of orthodox Jews to their city.[67]

The kindergarten "for orphans of the Jewish faith" opened in October 1913 in the rooms and yard of Temple B'nai Israel with only eight children. It soon grew to forty pupils with an average attendance of thirty. Elizabeth Kempner, wife of entrepreneur Harris Kempner, furnished most of the equipment, while a committee of three oversaw the operation and hired the teachers. The purpose of the kindergarten, explained the teacher, is "to give each child the environment that is needed most for his development and growth." She went on to say that through social interaction and play children learned to cooperate. "Each game has its laws, which must be obeyed, and the child soon learns to love fair play. Kindergarten is a child['s] world of small citizens learning the true meaning of citizenship."[68] Had the teacher substituted "Americanization" for "citizenship," the true meaning of her speech would become evident, for, in fact, Americans feared that the influx of immigrants, even in small cities like Galveston, would somehow change the character of the nation. Kindergartens for immigrant children gave "Americanizers" a means by which to teach foreign children national values, habits, customs, and language.

Reaching beyond the children to their families, managers of the Jewish kindergarten organized clubs for older children, where they learned arts and trades through crafts. Mothers, who suffered the greatest isolation from the language and customs of the new country, could then be reached through the children, as the young led the way in adapting to the values of the middle classes or of older immigrant groups. Mothers' clubs for the parents of the kindergartners were intended "to bring the mothers and kindergarten into closer relationship; that the mother may be more in sympathy with the child's work." Programs were planned around "child welfare work," where mothers learned, for example, the fundamentals of hygiene given by the local feminist physician, Dr. Ethel Lyon Heard.[69]

Families, not just preschoolers, were targeted for classes, acculturation, and uplift. From the perspective of the teachers and benefactors, their efforts were intended to turn the kindergarten into a community center. In effect, the movement to establish kindergartens in underprivileged neighborhoods was an attempt to modify the habits of the poor through education, example, and encouragement. Although that sounds meager, it was a far sight more progressive than having the poor travel across town to the rich for aid or having destitute mothers give up their children to an asylum.

The kindergarten movement influenced elite women as well, for it invited them to think in terms of the total community, not just their privileged neighborhoods. This would eventually culminate in a Progressive Era civic league whose primary goal was to beautify the total city environment for uplift just as the beautiful kindergarten uplifted disadvantaged children. More immediately, the establishment of kindergartens in Galveston paralleled activities sponsored by the women's club movement, which by the 1890s had spread across the South like wildfire. Indeed, Johanna Runge's observations on forming a free kindergarten were presented to a meeting of the Texas Federation of Women's Clubs in 1899. Just as benevolent women were beginning to construct preschools for little learners, so were they developing schools of their own through literary clubs. Beyond kindergartens and women's clubs, however, the elite women of Galveston were beginning to shape a women's community borne of their experience in helping the working poor, the elderly, the orphan, and the immigrant.

The creation of a white women's community in Galveston evolved over time through various institutions and organizations, beginning with churches and benevolent societies, proceeding to the benevolent institutions, and followed later by women's clubs. The connections between the women's benevolent societies, the Galveston Orphans' Home, the Women's Home, the Home for Homeless Children, and the Johanna Runge Free Kindergarten existed on at least two levels. On one level, women's church and synagogue benevolent societies acted as important referral agencies for the needy seeking asylum in one of the homes. To be referred, even subsidized, by a benevolent society virtually assured the applicant's acceptance. The societies, then, constituted an initial channel for the feeble or the helpless to find a more permanent form of aid. Cooperation between societies and institutions ensured more than just nodding support for the inmates. Women in church and synagogue societies took turns providing services and special care for the children and elderly women.[70] Of supreme importance was the fact that Jewish and Protestant men and women acted in concert in creating benevolent institutions. This climate of interfaith cooperation continued into the twentieth century.

On another level, the benevolent societies acted as stepping stones for elite women with ambitions beyond home and church; those who sought public approval advanced to the boards of managers of the benevolent institutions. Those most likely to serve on the boards of lady managers were from the Episcopal, Presbyterian, and to a lesser degree Jewish congregations—those congregations where the women's benevolent societies had specialized in city poor relief—indicating of continuum of purpose by community-oriented women.[71] The boards of the four benevolent institutions became self-perpetuating; new members were recruited by the presiding managers from the Protestant churches and the synagogue. In order to become a board member of the older institutions, a woman had to be actively engaged in church or temple work or belong to an elite family that practiced philanthropy. Boards of lady managers constituted a female hierarchy, a power structure parallel to that of men in commerce and professional life, a religious voluntary elite where status was as important as piety. The members' responsibilities as caretakers of orphans, aged women, and children from the factory district were commensurate with their stature within the community, and though they may have used the boards for their own social purposes, there is no doubt that they also advanced their roles as semipublic servants while allowing broader application of women's domestic values.

There were important differences between the early institutions and the later ones that resulted in significant distinctions for the women who administered them. The Orphans' Home and the Rosenberg Women's Home, the earliest institutions outside the home managed by women, most resembled homes in the conventional sense. The lady managers, representing a slightly older generation of activists, were given responsibilities that accompanied their parallel roles in the home. The guidelines for male trustees and women managers more nearly approximated traditional work roles for men and women. Moreover, in the orphans' home, the board of lady managers preferred to adopt the children and, therefore, have control over the child in loco parentis. Children were carefully isolated from their parents in hopes of creating a new family or a better family within the orphan home. And parents were never given much in the way of encouragement. The women tried to keep their charity charges from returning to the poverty from which they had come, even if it meant limiting contact with the family. Insulated from poorer neighborhoods, the lady managers prevented the orphans from interacting with working-class types whom the managers felt subverted the goals of the home. Children of women who were unmarried or divorced or abandoned had no access to the Galveston Orphans' Home, whose constitution written in the 1880s still had not changed by the 1930s. Exclusive rules and elitist assumptions manifested in carefully prescribed sex roles for the managers resulted in an institution out of step with the changing times, always accommodating fewer children than its spacious halls would allow and managed by an increasingly older group of women. This cream of Galveston society practiced a lofty approach to benevolence with charity ball fundraisers and connections to New York "society." Their intentions were sincere, but their methods were elitist.

By contrast, the Lasker Home for Homeless Children and the Johanna Runge Free Kindergarten, both conceived in the 1890s, emerged as undertows of the progressive spirit pulling women toward a greater sense of civic and community responsibility. The institutions themselves, although homelike, were not intended to replace the child's home. They were temporary shelters for children whose families were in turmoil or unable to offer an education. These institutions started off in neighborhoods where poor parents could reach them. Parents were welcome to leave their children in the day nursery or kindergarten and pick them up again. Children of divorced, unmarried, and abandoned women were not turned away from the Lasker home nor was the poorest child of a factory worker denied access to the free kindergarten. The women who managed these institutions cared little for stereotypical sex roles and did what needed to be done without male supervision or circumscription. Even their fundraising methods were more democratic, taking to the streets rather than to the ballroom. Tagging everyone who worked

in the commercial sector brought in about as much as the elaborate fancy gatherings of the older homes. And like the Sunday school missions that preceded
them by a decade or two, the kindergarten movement hoped, through the children,
to win over parents and families to the new gospel of community-centered progressive improvement and uplift. The later benevolent institutions arrived on the
cusp of changing philosophies with respect to child saving: families were now the
target of their self-help designs. This included less control over the child and more
help for the parents in their own homes and communities. The founders and
managers of the later institutions represented a more modern-thinking segment of
Galveston society. Unafraid to associate with the working classes in their own
environment or to help the whole family, these women heralded the civic leagues
of the next century as well as change for the future of the city and for themselves.

6

. . . .

WOMEN'S CLUBS

I would be true, for there are those that trust me;
I would be pure, for there are those who care;
I would be strong, for there is much to suffer;
I would be brave for there is much to dare.
I would be friend of all—the foe—the friendless,
I would be giving and forget the gift;
I would be humble for I know my weakness,
I would look up—and laugh—and love—and lift.

—Harold Arnold Waters, motto found in the
Wednesday Club Records

Suddenly in the 1880s, as if zephyrs from the Northeast had brought notions of self-improvement to the flatlands of the Southwest, women in Texas set about taking stock in their own learning. Years of benevolence to others had edified them to pressing social needs, urging them to act, but the time had come for women to see to their own education. A desire for better education by southerners was part of a national phenomenon. Beginning with the lyceum and culminating in the Chautauqua movement, self-improvement for adult women, who, especially in the South, may have had no access to public schools, betokened a wish for higher learning, culture, and edification. Southern universities, some in existence with the founding of the republic, were slow to accept women. And, although by 1870 eight midwestern and western state universities had admitted women, only seven southern universities, including the University of Texas, had done so by 1912. The number of women students in institutions of higher learning increased slowly nationwide. In 1900, only 2.8 percent (85,000) of women between the ages of eighteen and twenty-one attended college. Higher education was elitist for everyone in this era, and that 2.8 percent of young women represented more than one-third (36.8 percent) of all students enrolled.[1]

No dissembling could mask the fact that education for Texas women was woefully inadequate to meet the demands of the 1880s, and few women born in the unsettled 1860s could afford to be educated in female seminaries (schools) or universities. With a few important exceptions, the first generation of activist Galveston women born in the 1850s and 1860s missed opportunities even for attending finishing schools. Women born in the 1870s, however, were able to attend Ball High School, which was completed in 1885. Daughters of the wealthy were sent off to female seminaries or to art and music instructors outside of Texas, including New York and Europe. Children born in the 1880s looked out upon a world with wider openings for women's education, but only a few women gained a liberal arts degree or training in a profession.[2]

Thus, the women's club movement, which jelled in the South in the 1890s, began as an educational and cultural self-improvement plan for black and white middle-class and elite women whose lives had formerly been privatized in the home, or whose organizational experiences consisted of church or synagogue societies or boards of lady managers. Learning to focus on intellectual matters, handling abstractions, coping with contradictory ideas, dealing with written assignments, delivering papers before a club and then a larger assemblage of women, speaking before mixed groups, arranging annual conventions, traveling to the conventions unaccompanied by male escorts, assuming responsibility for committee work, and leading others into the public arena confronted and challenged middle- and upper-class women as they sought self-improvement together.

The *Galveston Tribune* captured some of these challenges women faced in club meetings: "No anguish ever compares with that first time a woman reads a paper or makes a speech in public. Though she may have the eloquence of a Hypatia and the self-confidence of a Mary Ellen Lease, she is doomed on that debut to a torture which, if known to Dante, would have inspired him to establish an extra purgatorial circle." For women who persevered, such experiences brought rewards. The women's club movement became the largest and most widely accepted national women's movement in the late nineteenth and early twentieth centuries. Its membership eclipsed the Woman's Christian Temperance Union by 1900 and represented for many women in small towns their only affiliation outside of churches and families.[3]

Women's club beginnings trace back to the antebellum period when outcroppings of isolated study groups organized by women dotted mostly New England towns. Among the earliest of self-improvement clubs were those formed by black women in communities north of the Mason-Dixon Line. Study clubs in the South were rarer, but Galveston women in 1856 organized their own scientific club, the Electro Auto-Biological Society, which was inspired by a course of lectures at the Galveston Courthouse by Professor Lawrence Hale. Undoubtedly, this was one of the first secular women's clubs in the city, for the children who accompanied their well-bred mothers to the meetings found mysterious "the arrival of the members unattended by masculine friends."[4] The Civil War, historians argue, provided further stimulus for women's organizations. While literary clubs declined in the face of pressing war needs, women's voluntarism increased. The postwar period brought renewed concern for professional, legal, and educational rights, hence the spread of literary clubs accompanied a host of organizational drives by women. The first women's club, which brought into being a national club movement, began in 1868 when New York journalist Jane Cunningham Croly and other women founded Sorosis, a secular club for the purpose of study and friendship.[5]

The increasing need for education and cultivation of the fine arts was at the heart of the appeal to women in Texas. Yet no progress on this front was made until the state experienced sufficient urbanization. By 1900, Texas boasted three of the largest cities of the former Confederate South. Towns along shipping routes and railroads, where increasing population brought a measure of prosperity, provided the first setting for the women's club movement in Texas. Luxuries such as gas lighting, electricity, telephones, and servants eventually relieved the genteel woman in urban areas of the constant drudgery of housework, freeing her for cultural pursuits.[6] Women in professions, the few that existed in the 1880s and 1890s, sought companionship with women interested in pursuing topics beyond dishes and diapers. Women who had already invested in volunteer groups sought another avenue for their public interests that combined the opportunity for self-improvement with female fellowship. They accepted the notion that white women of different faiths had much to offer in a forum for ideas.

Eventually, word of clubs begun by women in other states spread through Texas. Galveston had a direct connection to New York and cities on the New England coast through shipping and family networks. Sorosis was not an unfamiliar group to Galveston women; their own Anna Maxwell Jones had moved to New York and become a member. By 1892, the General Federation of Women's Clubs had organized with 495 club affiliations and 100,000 members. Very few of the clubs within the GFWC admitted black women. This obvious racial prejudice on the part of white women led to the development of a separate African American women's club movement at about the same time. Many black women's clubs formed under the auspices of the National Association of Colored Women founded in 1896, and the Texas Association of Colored Women's Clubs, which formed in 1905.[7]

Beyond all of the practical explanations for the rise of women's clubs nationally and in Texas, historians have come to understand the movement as the last great moment of exalted womanhood—the epitome of the notion of a separate, superior, more cultured, spiritual, and cultivated women's sphere. Upper- and middle-class women grew to take pride in themselves as women, no longer apologizing for an inferior status; indeed, finding an elevated moral position, they preached the virtues of truthfulness, purity, strength, courage, democracy, generosity, humility, and uplift. Women also gathered unto themselves the mantle of cultural appreciation for art, drama, and music as well as literature, because "culture and the arts were, by the late nineteenth century, like religion in that they were widely considered female terrain."[8] In short, middle- and upper-class white club women challenged late nineteenth-century notions of privatized domesticity and broadened their domain to include art, music, history, and literature. Once embarked on a combined course of self-improvement, that is, self-understanding and learning, women at the turn of the century could not ignore societal problems or blatant sex discrimination. The majority of club women in the United States may have been far more sensitive to the problems of their community and to the exclusion that they felt from public policy formation, but they were often less sympathetic, especially in the South, to the discrimination of others based on class or race. So, by 1900, while the club movement shifted its emphasis on literature and learning to the pressing needs for women's worldly involvement, focus on improvement in race relations followed, but much more slowly.

Art and Literary Clubs

Clubwomen believed that all educated, refined women "had an inherent interest in culture," that women were innately attracted and were sensitive to music, art, and drama. Stemming directly out of what they considered "woman's domain," the world of the belle arts was appropriated by women in the same way that community politics at the turn of the century became the province of men. While women would eventually find themselves involved in politics as well, they never did relinquish the notion that somehow the bond between women and "high culture" was graced with a certain spiritual content divorced from the workaday world.[9]

The connection between intelligent, well-traveled, sophisticated women and the fine arts allowed women to believe in their own sensitive natures, elevating them above men to higher realms of moral superiority. But it also elevated them above the masses. The fact that artistic study required money and taste meant that the consumers of culture were from the upper strata, thus emphasizing what everyone knew already, that "cultured" women were elite women. Less clear was the relation of men to cultural pursuits. Although the world's great artists were men, clubwomen strongly suspected that educated women had an affinity for the arts that their aggressive, materialistic menfolk lacked. Notions of elitism, moral superiority, and innate sensibilities provided women with a modicum of pride in themselves and acted as buffers to male attempts to trivialize women's artistic pursuits. Karen Blair has boldly stated that "women used culture to soften the reality of sexism."[10]

The fact is, women who studied painting, literature, or music during the 1870s, 1880s, and 1890s did so in part because access to an academic education in private or state universities seemed remote, and women were discriminated against when seeking admission. Even with the establishment of colleges for women in the Northeast—Vassar in 1861, Wellesley in 1870, Smith in 1871, Bryn Mawr in 1885, Barnard in 1889, and Radcliffe in 1894—only a few women from Texas were able to take advantage of opportunities for higher education. There were very few Texas female seminaries or institutions of higher education for white women; Mary Hardin-Baylor College in Belton was an exception. The University of Texas at Austin opened its doors as a coeducational institution in 1883; the Girls Industrial College (now Texas Woman's University) held its first classes in 1903. Baylor University became coeducational in 1886 but with different degrees for women; one could earn a Maid of Philosophy, a Maid of Arts, and a Mistress of Polite Literature in 1890. Southern seminaries and colleges for women, such as Sophie Newcomb College in New Orleans, more often attracted students from the southeastern states rather than from Texas.[11] Southern customs, moreover, worked against the idea of women entering universities for intellectual training. Enhancing musical or painting talent was considered a far more useful occupation for a woman than the rigors of academe. Concerts, recitals, and exhibitions were contributions to the community that did not compete with the worlds of business, law, or medicine or put women out of their proper place. And these talents could be used to raise funds for charities and churches. Many intelligent Galveston women of affluent families were directed or chose to take training in the arts instead of attending a college or university. As one Galveston journalist wrote, "Then the children of all the 'best families' were taught music along with their alphabet and the girls went to the continent after graduating from preparatory school to complete their musical training in Paris and Berlin instead of going to college to finish."[12]

More Galveston women from the upper economic strata chose to study art or music than attended institutions of higher learning. Galveston newspapers gave ample publicity to the phenomenon of genteel young ladies studying with great artists. "Studied under Famous Master: Many Galveston Girls Are Pupils of Celebrated Teachers of Music," announced a headline in 1914. "Miss Ethel Randall studied under Bruno Oscar Klein and Richard Burmeister of New York, the latter now one of the great teachers in Berlin . . . Miss Linda Fowler, with Mr. Sigismund Stojowski of New York and the famous Russian pianist, Mr. Ossip Gabrilowitch of Berlin (accepted as one of his few pupils). . . ." The article went on to list no fewer than seventy-five women who studied outside of Galveston under music masters.[13]

Musical training had its rewards. In some cases, it allowed women to pursue careers as vocal soloists, teachers, or as choir directors, though seldom as orchestra conductors. For others, the training provided them with cultural and entertainment skills useful to the community. Church choirs, open-air concerts, benefits, women's club meetings, and choral performances provided local musicians with exposure to the public and opportunites for advancement. Churches, incubators of women's talents, supplied the first entrée into the world of performance. Musically inclined young ladies, nurtured in youth choirs, were invited to sing or play before their church families rather than first attempting larger audiences.[14]

Open-air evening concerts at the Garten Verein provided Galvestonians with a welcome diversion from the heat and humidity of Gulf Coast summers. Frederick Roeck, who informally led Trinity Episcopal Choir, commented frequently to his wife Kate on the quality of individual local vocalists who were well known to the community. "Last night [was] a beautiful clear, cool, evening and all [were] enjoying themselves. At 8 o'cl. the concert began," he recounted, "and was quite good with a very large audience. They have built a stand in the middle of the hall for the orchestra but the recitations and singing were done on the stage. Carrie Bright sang 'Beware' very prettily, Mrs. Carothers sang better than I ever heard her (result of Rosetti's teaching) . . . Mrs. Mansfield . . . was in spendid voice and sang an air from Lucia."[15]

Ladies with musical talent were often invited to perform benefits. When Nellie Roeck, Frederick's daughter, journeyed to Lampasas, Texas, on a youth retreat, she wrote to her mother that Magnolia Sealy, the wife of Galveston's leading banker, had organized a benefit for a local church. "There is to be a concert in the hotel this evening for the benefit of the Episcopal Church which is being built here. I think Mrs. Sealy and one or two other ladies in the hotel got it up. Mrs. S[ealy]., Mrs. Byrne, and Mrs. Fowler will sing. Margaret [Sealy] will recite or play. Mrs. Arden will play and they will have several other things. The programme is quite long and select. . . . Mrs. Byrne is to sing 'Angel's Serenade' with piano and violin. She is practising it now below my room, it is a beautiful thing.

Mrs. Sealy will sing one of Helmund's new songs, I think 'The Daily Question' which is lovely too."[16] Significantly, it was a women's cultural evening designed and executed by the city's social leaders for religious and fundraising purposes.

Women's clubs also provided performance forums for all kinds of musical talent. It seems that every time women held a meeting or a conference they called upon local musicians to provide "the entertainment." The fact is that before the 1920s most Galvestonians only heard live music performed by residents of the city or by visiting artists. Galveston did not have a permanent professional symphony, nor, in fact, did any city before Boston entrepreneur Henry Lee Higginson founded the Boston Symphony Orchestra in 1881. Without local homegrown talent, there would have been little to recommend Galveston as a cultural center. But those were times when communities encouraged and admired local productions, grateful for the artists in their midst. Women felt keenly that they enhanced community living through these performances and understood that their training kept culture alive for the average and not so average resident.[17]

Most women of musical training and talent eventually joined with others of like interest to create women's musical clubs. The desire to sing could not be satisfied through the study of music in literary context but needed to be met with actual performance. Two clubs emerged at the close of the nineteenth century in Galveston, the Ladies' Musical Club and the Girls' Musical Club. The first, formed in 1888, limited its membership to thirty-five women who agreed to perform three "musicales" a year for the public. They met every Saturday afternoon for rehearsals and paid $6 for the privilege of joining. Louise Fowler Parker, director of Trinity's church choir, directed the Ladies' Musical Club performances, which consisted of a number of piano and harp solos, string quartets, arias and other vocal solos, and always a performance by the ladies' chorus.[18]

The programs gave Galveston its first women's performance group. Of the forty-nine chorus members also active in other clubs, thirty-two (65 percent) belonged to Episcopal churches where sacred music reached heights of elegance (see table 6.1). The officers were generally the same women who were active in other community endeavors, indicating that musical performance was as much a part of women's world as literary club life and benevolence. The fact that the arts took women out of the home while employing their talents constituted another means for women's escape from domestic confinement but did nothing, of course, for their real liberation from social stereotyping. Still, the visible nature of women's performances and their advancement of the arts went far toward winning them community approval.

A Galveston music teacher, Mrs. L. P. Gruenwald, with a highly successful private studio, helped to organize some of her pupils into the Girls' Musical Club in 1890; this group outlived the older Ladies' Musical Club, performing well into the twentieth century in Galveston. They scaled down their choral performances to one per year, bringing to the city at other times exemplary professional talent— Ignacy Jan Paderewski, Vladimir de Pachman, and Geraldine Farrar, among others. Reorganized in 1892 by Iola Barns Beers, a member of Trinity's choir, the club's purpose was to "provide the best facilities for musical culture of its members and the uplifting of the standards of music in the city of Galveston." As the girls

TABLE 6.1. Activist Women's Membership in Select Women's Clubs by Religious Affiliation, 1890–1920

	Wednesday Club		Ladies' Musical Club	
Episcopal	41	(46.59%)	32	(65.31%)
Presbyterian	11	(12.5)	6	(12.24)
Unknown	10	(11.36)	2	(4.08)
Catholic	7	(7.95)	1	(2.04)
Methodist	7	(7.95)	1	(2.04)
Baptist	5	(5.68)	1	(2.04)
Jewish	4	(4.54)	4	(8.16)
Christian Church	1	(1.14)		
Lutheran	1	(1.14)	1	(2.04)
Swedenborgian	1	(1.14)	1	(2.04)
Total	88	(100%)	49	(100%)

	DRT		DAR		UDC	
Episcopal	23	(44.23%)	28	(62.22%)	17	(38.64%)
Presbyterian	9	(17.31)	3	(6.67)	6	(13.64)
Unknown	6	(11.54)	3	(6.67)	6	(13.64)
Methodist	5	(9.62)	2	(4.44)	3	(6.82)
Baptist	4	(7.69)	5	(11.11)	3	(6.82)
Catholic	3	(5.77)	3	(6.67)	9	(20.45)
Jewish	1	(1.92)				
Swedenborgian	1	(1.92)	1	(2.22)		
Total	52	(100%)	45	(100%)	44	(100%)

Note: DRT = Daughters of the Republic of Texas. DAR = Daughters of the American Revolution. UDC = United Daughters of the Confederacy.

Source: Galveston Women Database.

who had been vested with expensive musical educations matured into adult women, they continued to sing, maintaining the club's original name. Performances provided the city with great "social moments," attracted capacity crowds, and displayed women as hostesses to the enhancement of culture. In their private meetings, the members studied music history and great composers. In 1916, for example, members of the Girls' Musical Club undertook the study of Russian music, beginning with a paper, "Eighteenth Century Music in Russia," read by Edith Fordtran and ending with illustrative musical pieces performed by three other members.[19] To maintain membership in the musical club, performing talent had to go hand in hand with an active mind. Crossovers between officers of the musical clubs and the literary clubs were common.

As the perceived bond between artistic culture and womanhood motivated women to found musical clubs and art leagues, so too did the search for "cultural authority" compel women to study literature.[20] The course of study was not the only good to come out of clubs, however; middle- and upper-class women achieved a certain intimacy as they shared their feelings about the works or risked criticism over their own intellectual capacities. Unlike boards of lady managers that administered institutions or musical clubs that emphasized performance, literary clubs drew women into discrete circles, inviting them for a time to abandon their domestic roles and travel down the path of mutual intellectual activity.

The generation of women who initially introduced literary clubs to Galveston was born in the 1840s and 1850s. Betty Ballinger (b. 1854), her sister Lucy Ballinger Mills (b. 1852), and Maria Cage Kimball (b. 1844) cofounded Galveston's first literary women's club. The two Ballinger women had enjoyed a privileged upbringing as daughters of one of Texas's finest jurists, William Pitt Ballinger.[21] With this illustrious background and with a library stocked full of books, Betty and her sister were able to gain an education despite the postwar struggle. The two were first sent to Miss Hull's French School in New Orleans until they advanced to the Southern Home School in Baltimore. Well educated and thoroughly genteel, the two Ballinger sisters in October 1891 persuaded Maria Cage Kimball, a professional artist, to join them in forming the city's first literary club—the Wednesday Club. For a time they met in Kimball's studio, where the women decided on a course of study that would eventually include new and classic works of literature. For the first year, however, they and twenty-two other invited members embarked on a thorough investigation of Texas history. Coinciding with the founding of the Daughters of the Republic of Texas, the idea to study Texas history complemented the women's desire not only to rescue Texas heroes from oblivion and to honor them as patriots but also to educate women about the Lone Star State.[22]

In subsequent years, the club joined first national then state federations. In 1894, the club affiliated with the General Federation of Women's Clubs (GFWC) and in 1897 sent Betty Ballinger and Mary Davis as delegates to the first convention of the Texas Federation of Women's Clubs (TFWC) in Waco. In April 1899, the Galveston Wednesday Club hosted the second convention of the Texas federation, at which time the Texas clubs formally connected with the General Federation. Maria Cage Kimball greeted the delegates with these words: "Our grandparents would have been scandalized at the thought of a convention of women, presided over and addressed from the rostrum by a woman, yet we are no whit less womanly than the purely domestic creatures of their day. It is the change in conditions and ideals, the result of evolution." Despite the fact that women had "evolved," Kimball still extolled the virtues of housewifery, remembering that homemakers made up the majority of the audience. Mentioning that inventions had lightened their labor, giving them leisure to devote to "doing good outside our own doors," Kimball averred that today's women had "more time to exert that womanliness in various channels." Later in the evening, the delegates were given a taste of this new combination of womanhood and culture when they visited Kimball's flower-bedecked studio, viewed her artwork, and sipped "frozen tea," while listening to the strains of the orchestra provided by the Wednesday Club.[23] Domesticity and artistic culture stood hand in hand.

At the third convention, held in San Antonio in April 1900, Maria Cage Kimball, by then president of the Wednesday Club for nearly ten years, presented an "interesting address" representing the art department, wherein she "deplored

the ignorance and apathy concerning art that prevailed in Texas cities where opportunities might be provided . . . for the enjoyment of culture in this direction."
She pointed to barren walls in schools and homes and suggested that these be
hung with prints of the great masterpieces "until the eye became trained to the
really true and beautiful in art." Libraries and assembly halls would make excellent
temporary art galleries for towns where artistic interests lay dormant, she counseled.
And for those places where paintings were hard to come by, the Wednesday Club
had established a fund to start a traveling picture gallery, akin to the traveling
library already established by the TFWC. All that was needed was a call from
other clubs to "start the collection on its rounds." Karen Blair explains that this
desire to spread art to children—"all immigrants, all poor, and all rural dwellers"—accompanied the Progressive movement for greater democracy, for more
accessibility to social institutions and especially to the arts. Included in this dream
was the longing to provide access to arts training "so that they [children] could
involve themselves with the joy of making a play or performing a song" or creating
a painting. Cultivation of art, music, literature: these had fallen to women, their
clubs becoming the academies of cultural pursuits.[24]

Wednesday Club women avidly pursued literary quests amidst a climate of
extended sisterhood. Although Episcopal and Presbyterian women still predominated, the club encouraged a wider representation among women from various
religious groups than did the boards of lady managers of the benevolent institutions. (See table 6.1.) The only surviving minutes for the Wednesday Club before
1920 extend from 1904 to 1909, but from these we can gain a glimpse of life inside
the club. Part of the unchartered mission of the club was to foster fellowship
leading to greater intimacy and friendship. The Wednesday Club met every other
Wednesday at 3:30 for study, discussion, and refreshments, but in months where
a fifth Wednesday occurred, the members planned an "entertainment." One such
event required that each member present an original limerick about another member as her ticket of admission to the party. Most of the rhymes were tributes to
one another, flattering and encouraging.[25]

The Wednesday Club served two distinct functions aside from fellowship. The
first was to promote "mutual improvement by the encouragement of individual
study, as preparation for discussion in the Club," and the second, to cooperate "in
any work which may advance the welfare of humanity."[26] These seemed to be the
members' only stated missions; besides sponsoring lectures and providing funds
for a traveling art exhibit, in the years between 1891 and 1920 they never took up
any sustained civic projects either locally or at the state level. Except from 1900
to 1901, when the club took up sewing for the storm victims, and during 1917–
1918, when they volunteered for war work, the members devoted themselves to the
study of literature. Saturated with American authors, the women in 1904 turned
to the works of Honoré de Balzac and Victor Hugo. The next year they tried
Scandinavian literature, which was followed by three years of Shakespeare, one
year of literary criticism, and two years of Greek drama. Eventually, they incorporated more current works of a "sociological" nature into their curriculum.

Several events conspired to lure them away from purely literary studies. First,
as soon as they united with the GFWC in 1894 and the TFWC in 1897 they began

to receive letters and information channeled to them through state and national officers concerning current issues important to women. Second, in 1901, progressive women formed civic reform associations that at once took the pressure to become reform minded off the Wednesday Club, while at the same time activating members' interest in reform topics. Third, the composition of the Wednesday Club changed from 1891 through the second decade of the twentieth century. At first, elite members who were wives of influential commercial types dominated the club, but later professional women—librarians, nurses, and especially teachers—joined. As the club matured, the women became younger and generational needs differed. Diversity, both within and without the Wednesday Club ultimately altered its curriculum and the women's outlook.

After the rise of progressive movements across the South, no club remained immune from news of the pressing need for greater protection for the environment, for libraries, for child-labor legislation, for protection for working women, and for the need for state agencies to regulate and control industries that affected women, their families, and the home. Not a meeting went by that there was not a communique from some level of the women's club movement asking for their support or endorsement.[27] In the years between 1897 and 1920, when Texas clubs not only federated but became interested in civic work, clubwomen clamored for action regarding the establishment of free libraries (85 percent in Texas were started by women's clubs), kindergartens, manual training centers in public schools and in state institutions, child labor laws, city beautification, women's prison reform, pure food and drug laws, hospitals for tuberculosis patients, parks and playgrounds, juvenile courts, civil service reform, and movie censorship.[28]

Many of these issues filtered to Wednesday Club members. They discussed the need for police matrons, a state industrial school for girls, kindergartens, pure food and drug laws, the creation of a state library commission, cooperation with the Anti-Tuberculosis Association, a juvenile court, and at the national level, support for a bill to protect children and animals. In many cases, endorsement for the state or general federation's action was requested and was usually granted. But as an indication of the club's lingering conservatism, the members tabled an endorsement of suffrage requested of them from the GFWC in 1906, pleading that politics should not enter club work. Then, in 1909, when the chairwoman of the district committee on laws affecting women and children sent information regarding "the all important but little understood subject of the legal status of women in Texas," the members moved to table the letter, filing the information away "for the future reference of any member of the club wishing to give the subject further attention."[29] Both topics would later find their way into the formal course of study.

In 1912, Wednesday Club members took up the study of "sociological subjects," including women in industry, the social settlement movement, modern educational movements, changes in municipal governments, Texas laws relating to women and children, socialism, and woman suffrage. By 1913, they had incorporated the problem of women and delinquent children into their curriculum. In subsequent years, they either returned to fiction or studied the problems of nationalism and democracy in Europe in response to World War I.[30]

If direct missives from state- and national-level associations were not enough to convince Galveston women to adopt a more progressive agenda, Wednesday Club members could read all about the actions of other women locally and nationally in the *Galveston Daily News*. Every Monday, a section called "The Woman's Century," conceived first by the *Dallas Morning News*, devoted itself to issues of national importance to women—from Texas clubwomen and WCTU members to homemakers with interests such as childrearing, nursing, teaching, and writing. Pauline Periwinkle [Isabel Calloway], graced the page with her syndicated column reciting the accomplishments of women in clubs and coaxing them to see issues and problems of concern to women long before women were ready to take action. With her prodding, cajoling, and needling about environmental, health, child-labor, and educational issues, Texas women could not claim ignorance of the problems or the tasks before them.[31]

Progressive Era Galveston saw the formation of several reform-minded women's civic associations before 1911: The Women's Health Protective Association, the Juvenile Protective Association, the Council of Jewish Women, Mothers' Clubs, and a reorganized chapter of the WCTU. The gradual accumulation of women's civic groups had the affect of encouraging Wednesday Club members to study issues important to women. Also, as women moved in and out of the club, the presence of these other groups infused the staid Wednesday Club with members whose experiences had already been shaped in reform-minded ways.

By 1907, members such as Annie Hill, a suffragist who taught civics at Ball High School, began to assert that the club "should broaden the scope of its activity and fall in line with the work being so generally done by other clubs in sociology."[32] As more teachers, librarians, and nurses entered the ranks of the Wednesday Club, it lost some of its old-guard prestige and took on a more liberal air. After all, teachers made wonderful members: they already were professional educators, many taught in schools the subjects studied in the club, and they motivated women to see the connection between literary training and professional life. Librarians were useful for their full range of knowledge of current books. Women in the medical profession saw problems that society women missed. But, most important, professional women were generally eager to pursue topics such as women's legal status or women's right to vote.

Although the members of the Wednesday Club let no civic projects interfere with their study of Balzac, Shakespeare, and Euripides, the result of the above-mentioned incursions did bring changes over time in their coursework—some literary, some sociological—as they absorbed current issues. Inevitably, they adapted the study of literature to their own purposes. The first evidence of a glimmering of understanding of woman's subordinate position in the eyes of men, for example, was addressed in the November 1905 study of Henrik Ibsen's *A Doll's House*. It was telling that the woman presenting the paper on the play's indictment of man's trivialization of woman was Jean Scrimgeour Morgan, one of the most active progressives in the city. As each woman was required to give a paper discussing the work just read, she also chose a quotation from that work to be printed in the club's annual program. Jean Morgan chose as her exemplary quotation this statement from the play, "Why, my Nora, what have you to do with serious things?"[33] In 1905, Galveston women were heavily engaged in a host of "serious things" including the aforementioned benevolent enterprises and recovery from the disastrous 1900 hurricane. In addition, by 1908 Jean Morgan had begun her four-year presidency of the Women's Health Protective Association, the city's foremost civic reform association.

In 1914, women turned in their volumes of Shakespeare for books and stories authored by women. One such was "The Revolt of Mother," the story by Mary Wilkins Freeman of a farm wife's quiet rebellion against an autocratic husband. They chose to study the "Proud Women" of George Meredith's novels, which confirmed the existence of "the new world for women."[34] They devoted time to the problem of unhappy marriages in literature — perhaps with personal lessons for themselves.

Was it coincidental or purposeful that Wednesday Club members chose subjects that would eventually draw them into public life? Minnie Fisher Cunningham, who later became president of both the Galveston and Texas suffrage associations, chose to discuss woman suffrage in 1912, the year the club decided on "sociological" subjects and the year a Galveston Equal Suffrage Association formed. Her authoritative sources were *History of Woman Suffrage* the four-volume work edited by Elizabeth Cady Stanton, Susan B. Anthony, and Matilda Joslyn Gage, and the *Progressive Woman*, a journal published in Washington, D.C. "Since women have so much at stake in the community," she stated in the club program, "and since they possess a point of view and information which is sometimes not possessed by the men, it is desirable from the standpoint of their own welfare as well as the welfare of the community as a whole, that they should be given the right to vote."[35] For Minnie Fisher Cunningham, the Wednesday Club served not so much as a source of her own edification as a forum for her passion for woman suffrage. Probably Cunningham's goal was to convert the members of the club because they represented the influential leaders of the women's community.

Lois Haines, using Edith Abbot's text, chose to present a study of "Women in Industry," which apparently fit her particular interests. Two years later, she joined the building committee of the Young Women's Christian Association, an organization whose initial design was to protect working girls from the uncertainties of the city and the workplace. She educated the members to the fact that in 1900 over five million women were gainfully employed in the United States, an increase of 33 percent over the previous decade. Solutions suggested in the program included protective legislation for women, trade unions, and an increase in wages.[36]

Melanie Pimstein, an unmarried Jewish teacher, presented a paper in 1913 on "Modern Educational Movements." In that year, the Council for Jewish Women opened a free kindergarten for immigrant Jewish children; Pimstein recounted the advantages of instruction beginning with kindergartens and leading eventually to "manual training." One of the three Lasker sisters, all of whom became suffragists and professional social workers, chose as her topic of discussion in 1912 "Delinquency in Children," using Jane Addams and Sophonisba Breckenridge's, *The Child in the City* as her authoritative sources. Helen Winter McMaster, suffragist and wife of the publisher of the *Galveston Tribune*, brought forward "The Problem of Woman," illustrating her paper with quotations from Olive Schreiner's *Woman and Labor* and Charlotte Perkins Gilman's *The Un-Sexed*. She concluded with the question, "What's wrong with the world?" Wednesday Club members went on to discuss the Mother's Pension Law in Illinois and eventually entertained the provoking notion of the origin of the double standard between men and women. No modern topic seemed to escape their notice after 1912—settlement houses, changes in municipal government, Texas laws concerning women and children, and a lucid discussion of socialism led by the redoubtable Betty Ballinger all entered the agenda.[37]

While the club members remained staunchly opposed to any form of civic activism, their course of study served as a wellspring for the community of women who sought to open the door for progressive reform. Just as educational institutions seldom ventured into the political arena to lobby for social change, so the Wednesday Club, Galveston's women's institution for "higher learning," taught its pupils the principles of critical reasoning, discipline, logic, and debate, informed them of the issues at hand, and then sent them *out* into the battle for progressive change. Other Galveston women's clubs took to the streets and alleys, challenging power and authority in the seats of government.

There may have been one other reason why the Wednesday Club chose to remain aloof from civic activism—by doing so its members avoided conflict with the codes of social convention. Although after 1900 the membership changed to include professional women, the Wednesday Club remained exclusive if not aristocratic. Its membership was limited to twenty-five active women who were received into the club by the recommendation of two members and a vote that did not exceed two blackballs. Not all who applied were accepted, and there were always more who wanted to join than the club could accommodate. Founded in an era when Galveston boasted a number of patrician families and published directories to identify them, the Wednesday Club remained imbued with racial exclusion and class pretensions.

Blue Books and Social Conventions

Women's clubs after 1900 gradually became more open to women of the middling classes; however, elitism remained an important factor in the life of Galveston's women's societies before that time. This was reflected in the appearance in 1896 of *The Galveston Blue Book*, claimed to be the first of its kind ever issued in Texas. Adding prestige to novelty, it professed that "in every *fin de siecle* city of both Europe and America a Blue Book is given a welcome place in all the best families. It finds no lodgment elsewhere." Listing prestigious families as well as organizations, the blue book served notice that Galveston and its elite clubs had "arrived," their places in society secure. But just in case Texas "society" proved a diamond in the rough, a section entitled "Social Code" was included to serve as "a pleasant reminder to polite memory and gentle breeding."[38] The Social Code consisted of twenty pages of instructions in how to navigate through "society"—from the shallows of male and female introductions to the white water rapids of calling cards, at homes, dinner parties, balls, and weddings. Confessing that the code was "sometimes extreme in its formality," it was also, according to the publisher, based on "kind feeling and good sense. The conventionalities of society restrain and direct merely to remove friction and assist life to freer and easier movement."[39]

Every instruction that detailed social intercourse between the sexes guarded and protected women in ways that restricted them, serving notice that, while men were free to move about inquiringly after women, women were free only to accept or reject such attentions. Anthony Rotundo writes that young men who entered into courting invariably realized that they were "passing back into women's world," where their sense of mastery and control slipped. Small wonder that blue books were useful; they prescribed a way for men to overcome their hesitation and take command and explained to young women how to respond. Calling on one another and using cards involved complicated rules of etiquette that, as usual when between the sexes, cloistered women. "A gentleman having been introduced to a lady may be uncertain whether she desires to continue the acquaintance. If he wishes it, he leaves a card, and her mother or chaperon sends an invitation to visit the family, . . . after which he is expected to call and pay his respects." She might have liked to see him again, but if the woman was unmarried, convention forbade her from telling him so. Moreover, the book counsels, she may not accompany him to the parlor door as he takes his leave. These arrangements, the authors apologized, provide a "wall of defense against strange and unwelcome visitors," a fact that every "true gentleman" will recognize, for they erect "barriers across the sacred threshold of home."[40]

The rules for crossing over the sex barriers for elite Galvestonians in 1896 were elaborate and complicated, based on the assumption that polite society needed guides to maneuver between the two worlds—home as an enclosure for women, and the world outside for men. Once the rules were internalized, proper behavior became a matter of habit, an unthinking response to the position of woman as unfree, the object of protection, a prisoner of social convention. True, blue books simply prescribed behavior; whether ladies and gentlemen followed them is quite another matter. But references to New York society reinforced the pattern, and with the names of elite Galveston families printed in the same book with the code, the inference was powerful. Galvestonians of this social class should bring themselves up to the standard of New York society, the mecca of social chauvinism.

Blue books served another purpose in the postwar South—they indicated who had moved up the social ladder. According to Don Doyle, mug books, a corollary to blue books, were not to be found in cities such as Charleston and Mobile, where elite society remained static and newcomers were a rarity.[41] Everyone knew who was who; there was no need for guides. In cities with bustling economies, where upward (and downward) mobility changed the social register with each passing decade, those interested in society matters needed a guide to who was new and successful. There were powerful incentives not only to make the acquaintance of the old and new elites but also to follow the regimen of social etiquette: to use calling cards, to isolate women in the home, to treat the worlds of men and women as separate. The space between became a treacherous field mined with social faux pas.

Wednesday Club members both acquiesced to some of these rules and acted to alleviate women from these straitjacket conventions. By remaining exclusive, by inviting to membership those listed in the social register, and by conforming to the rules of separation between men and women, the members acted in accord with the spirit of the code. But by bringing women out of the home into a club of their own, by introducing each other to worlds beyond the drawing room, and by encouraging independent thinking, the Wednesday Club counteracted the pull toward social suffocation for women. There were no blue book rules for women speakers at public conventions (even if the assemblants were mostly women), so the women invented their own guidelines free of male proscriptions. There were no regulations as to the course of study except those devised by the women themselves. Yes, there were formal proceedings, and *Robert's Rules of Order* was strictly followed, lest anyone accuse the women of frivolity of intentions, but Henry M. Robert, who wrote the rule, did so in order to take arbitrary power out of the hands of the chairperson, allowing everyone at the meeting an opportunity for participation. Its intent was democratic; its usage by women almost universal.[42]

It is ironic that just as ascriptive rules of behavior were foisted on Galveston — by then at the height of its wealth and social prominence — the woman's club movement should be making simultaneous forays against the codes that insisted on cloistering women. In fact, it would appear that the 1896 blue book, with its directions for cards, calling, and visiting customs, was the last defense for a fading world. Coming as they did at the end of the century, blue books tried to counter the democratizing trends of society as a whole. Women's artistic and literary clubs represented transitional vehicles — at once reflecting society's desire to limit women to separate sphere type functions yet acting to move upper-crust women beyond restricting conventions.

At any rate, Galveston's second blue book, published in 1914, carried no social code and listed men and women in the community whose status depended as much on professional position as on received social station. The publication read like an endorsement from the Chamber of Commerce; it advertised Galveston as "The Ultimate City" — "a wide-awake, hustling and progressive city of approximately 40,000 people." Clearly the scent of business profits had come to replace old-fashioned notions of social snobbery. By the 1930s and 1940s, Galvestonians published "mug books," historic elegies to those (mainly men, of course) who had been or were successful, a who's who for the community that endorsed hard work over high birth.[43]

Patriotic-Hereditary Organizations

If the women's club movement acted as at least a partial counter to elitist trends, other groups of women countenanced the world that blue books signified. The Daughters of the American Revolution (DAR, 1895), the Daughters of the Republic of Texas (DRT, 1891), the United Daughters of the Confederacy (UDC, 1895), and the Society of Colonial Dames appeared in Galveston in the 1890s as organizations that perpetuated class pretensions and racial exclusivity.

Of course, patriotism, reverence for fallen heroes, and the extension of family loyalties were the ostensible reasons for the outcropping of women's patriotic-hereditary organizations, but racial and social separatism were unspoken desired ends. As the tide of immigration into this country from eastern and southern Europe swelled into a tidal wave and as African Americans jousted for middle-class respectability, Anglo-Saxon nativism—inconsistently juxtaposed with national values of freedom, democracy, and opportunity—broke forth into foreign and ra-cial discriminations. These were manifested in various ways—in laws to restrict immigration, in labor-union bashing, in psycho-social theories of superior and inferior races, in Jim Crow laws and lynchings, and in exclusive clubs. Despite the fact that women were at times the objects of discrimination by those who justified exclusion, they too formed patriotic-hereditary societies that perforce ex-cluded the recent immigrants along with African Americans and other racial mi-norities.

Some Americans responded more sympathetically to immigrants and blacks, setting up societies and settlement houses to aid in their assimilation. Others, threatened by the fear that these newcomers could not absorb patriotic sensibilities, formed organizations that established rules of hereditary exclusivity, thus assuring themselves they were perpetuating true American values that would eventually drown out the din of foreign voices. They created elite enclaves, far above the teeming masses, justified on the grounds of patriotism and loyalty to country.

Southern patriotic and hereditary organizations for women fit in well with southern upper-crust society. Reverence for family and ancestors constituted a nat-ural part of a southern young lady's upbringing.[44] Pride in ancestral accomplish-ments became even more pronounced after the Civil War, as southerners sought to rebuild a sense of regional honor. They held on to the assumption that good breeding could not be bought and, in fact, remained a priceless treasure that one trotted out at appropriate times along with the family heirlooms. These notions validated women with tap roots in colonial American or southern soil and set them apart from the recent immigrant and the nouveau riche. Defeat heightened the need to find solace in genealogy and provided a distorted antidote to grief and disappointment. Southerners would be hard pressed to confess shame over the events that nearly severed a nation, but they could admit anger and resolve to keep alive the spirit that led to the forming of a nation, the founding of a republic, or the fomenting of a war to preserve states' rights. Ancestor worship and adoration of fallen heroes—of the American Revolution, Texas War for Independence, Civil War—were means of turning sorrow, even wrath, into what they considered con-structive uses.

Pride was the main item being dispensed, and southern ladies with a penchant for glorifying the past needed it more than men. Unable to glory in tales of combat, women patriots sought honor for themselves vicariously. Patriotic societies, more-over, served to elevate the members in an age when other women were moving beyond the Old South plantation legends. The transition to New Womanhood, still in its infancy, acted as a countervailing force to the pull of the past. As the 1890s found southern ladies running orphanages, dispensing welfare, presenting concerts, and staffing the churches with volunteers, rural idylls seemed overrun by the needs of the present.

For urban women who felt sentimental over the loss of the role of plantation mistress along with the war, however, patriotic hereditary clubs connected to the Confederacy restored to them a sense of ennobled southern womanhood based on Old South values. This allowed them to grieve over their sullied regional honor, to reminisce about lost "civilizations," or to celebrate past victories in the context of modern club life. Always southern women extolled the virtues of a past "southern life" that they sensed was slipping away from them by the changes in technology as much as through defeat. Among the more truthful aspects of women's glorification was the picture put forward of hard-working mistresses laboring beside their husbands in the cooperative economic effort that plantation life demanded. Among the hallowed memories were southern belles, energetic plantation mistresses, and wives, sisters, and daughters who sacrificed for the war effort or tended wounded soldiers.[45]

What makes the study of exclusive patriotic clubs for women fascinating if not infuriating are the contradictions that the organizers readily accepted. Denied admission to the military and hence to men's veteran organizations, women nonetheless made war and soldiers the object of their veneration. Gratitude for the sacrifices made in their behalf, one supposes, motivated women to be content with their auxiliary status in return for a measure of the glory that veterans reflected. From our twentieth-century perspective, their actions appear absurd—women were asked to accept society's glorification of men as the stronger, more intelligent sex, while at the same time finding contentment in woman's moral superiority. Morally superior beings would not countenance war, would in fact beat swords into plowshares, and yet these peace-loving women honored warriors. Because men made little attempt to allow women an equal sense of participation in the remembrance of decisive military events, patriotic ladies created their own associations and withall still ended up lauding men. Without ever sanctioning glory for themselves, members, nonetheless, garnered the pride that before their collective action had been missing.

There was more to it, of course. Veterans and their descendants in Texas were long on celebrating and short on monument raising. In the viewpoint of the women, monuments to fallen heroes validated sacrifices made, and if women could not fall beside their soldier brothers, they could at least memorialize them with monuments. Moreover, these ladies were able to call themselves members by virtue of the fact that their ancestors fought or lived at the time. Few traced their lineage to generals or colonels, yet even the common soldier or laborer deserved recognition. Hence, they churned out genealogical lists, not only to verify membership credentials but also to find and honor the unsung heroes of the past. Women had the time to pursue such tasks, and because these ventures had to do with family, they fell well within woman's cultural domain.

Preserving the past took on multidimensional properties: the women encouraged the writing of histories according to the principles of patriotism, they placed heroes' pictures in schoolrooms to instruct children visually; they saved the birthplaces or the homesteads of notable statesmen, rescuing them from demolition and preserving them for future generations. This went along with their goal of educating the public and especially youth on the history of sacrificial events, to impress the young with the knowledge of their past and the proper respect for its symbols. It served, moreover, to place women, mothers, wives, and sisters, who were guardians of the hero's domestic circle, in strategic positions. Thus, families of heroes became heroic too, and women in particular were elevated along with the men.[46]

In the matter of beneficence, some women's patriotic groups built and maintained homes for aged veterans or for aged women connected with the organization. And concerns for fallen soldiers or patriots brought them into graveyards, where, before the advent of perpetual care cemeteries run by corporations, women considered themselves guardians. In whatever manner women chose to remain close to the font of liberty, we can be sure that their projects were still connected to traditions of the home. It is true that only a small percentage of women became members of these groups. But like the elite of any community, their influence outweighed their numbers. As they worked their influence on statehouses, educating politicians in the art of patriotic politicking, erecting statues and monuments, caring for veterans, and educating the young, their deeds were given ample attention by the press.

Daughters of the American Revolution

Historians generally consider the Daughters of the American Revolution among the most elite of the patriotic organizations, because the older the event the more status was attached to requirements for membership. Julia Washington Fontaine, the great-great-niece of General George Washington, formed the George Washington Chapter of the DAR in Galveston in 1895. Julia Washington's father, Dr. Lawrence Augustine Washington of Winchester, Virginia, had come in 1850 to Texas, where he continued cotton planting in Colorado County. Julia was born in 1852 on the plantation surrounded by wealth and tutored in music, art, and literature. She married a native Texan, Colonel Sydney Fontaine, moved to Galveston, and remained there for thirty-eight years. She was appointed State Regent for Texas from 1900 to 1902. The first meeting of the DAR, convened by Julia Fontaine, took place in the home of Maria Seeligson, who married the scion of one of the oldest families in the city. This home, a model of Galveston wealth in the 1890s, was resplendent with towering cupolas and carpenter Gothic gables and represented old money and status. Nineteen women became charter members of the DAR; by 1908, their numbers had increased to sixty. If membership in the Episcopal church may be taken as a sign of elitism, then the DAR was indeed the most prestigious of all patriotic groups (62 percent were Episcopalian).(See table 6.1.) Of the fifteen first regents (presidents) of the local chapter, twelve were Episcopalian.[47]

The George Washington chapter was instrumental in making sure that every Galveston school had a U.S.flag, in researching and writing biographies of notable women from Galveston before 1864, and in preserving antiquarian relics from historic sites. Members collected bits of memorabilia, transforming them into objects of veneration. "Our greatest treasure is our gavel," read a report to the state association. "The wood of the mallet is a piece of the framework of the original 'North Bridge' at Concord, Massachusetts, over which was fired the first shot in the war for independence. . . . The handle is a piece of flooring from the old house occupied by General Washington as his headquarters at Valley Forge. . . . It is banded in silver from a spoon once owned by General Washington, and given by Mrs. Julia Washington Fontaine, our founder."[48] Representing both war and domesticity, the gavel brought together in one object the stirring events of the American Revolution with the role of women as domestic caretakers of the treasures of the past. Banners and flags embroidered by members punctuated the connection between historic events and women's handiwork. The members of each patriotic organization found ways to connect the duties and rituals of their domestic world with glories of the past. It allowed them to celebrate the prosaic and to experience "ego magnification" in connection with the creation of a nation.[49] Managing to integrate women's values with national culture satisfied their need to feel included rather than separated, important rather than insignificant. Although practiced in separate organizations, members symbolically and ritualistically used objects from the home to insert themselves into a venerable past, thereby transcending gender limitations.

Daughters of the Republic of Texas

Most women were ineligible for the rarified atmosphere of the DAR, but membership in the Daughters of the Republic of Texas (DRT) was even more uncommon. No more than fifty women in the years between 1891 and 1921 belonged to this exclusive group because most people had emigrated to Texas after the Civil War. The fact that this group honored Texas heroes was not lost on most of the citizens of Galveston, who, after allegiance to God and nation, made Texas an object of veneration.

It was with pride, then, that citizens observed the founding of the Daughters of the Republic of Texas, the first patriotic-hereditary association to become a part of Galveston society. The women who founded the DRT created a local chapter and at the same time a state organization. Several events led to the founding of both organizations. Inspired by the 1891 reunion of the Texas Veteran Association, Betty Ballinger and her cousin Hally Bryan, both descendants of veterans of the 1836 Texas Battle for Independence, met to discuss their discovery of the forsaken graves of two Texas heroes—David G. Burnett, first president of the Republic of Texas, and General Sidney Sherman, a hero at the decisive Battle of San Jacinto. Tending graves was a role that fell to women within the family and in the churches, a component of their ties to family and kin (see chapter 2). Extending the tradition and custom of grave maintenance from home to church to secular patriotic organization suggests the continuity and reshaping of southern women's traditions.[50]

According to folk wisdom, the cousins next took to reading Henderson King Yoakum's *History of Texas* in Ballinger's law office and library, which was built away from the house, so the story goes, in order for him to escape "feminine chatter." This library (ironically, ever after associated with women) later was consecrated "The Cradle," wherein the idea of the DRT was born. The cousins, in sympathy with the forgotten heroes of the republic, began a campaign to reclaim past memories, tidy up and memorialize their last resting places, and spread the study of Texas history throughout the state. Rescuing the Alamo in San Antonio from destruction and commercial exploitation would eventually follow, as women across the state organized chapters of the DRT.[51]

To accomplish their goals, the two women planned to solicit support from other women of Texas whose husbands or ancestors had helped the republic achieve and maintain its independence. Hally's father, Guy M. Bryan, president of the Texas Veteran Association, introduced the women to Mrs. Anson Jones, widow of the last president of the Republic of Texas, and to Mrs. Andrew Briscoe, widow of the Texas patriot. The organization was approved, and on November 6, 1891, seventeen women assembled in Houston to form the Daughters of the Lone Star Republic. Betty Ballinger was chosen a member of the Executive Committee that drew up the organization's constitution and by-laws. From November until April of the following year, the charter members sent out circular letters to each member of the Texas Veteran Association and to "prominent ladies in different localities who [were] eligible, urging them to qualify and organize local chapters in their communities."[52]

The first annual meeting of the DRT took place on April 20, 1892, in Lampases in concert with the Texas Veteran Association. Meeting separately at a Methodist church, they decided to change the name to the Daughters of the Republic of Texas. Mrs. Anson Jones became the DRT's first president, Mrs. Briscoe its first vice president, while Betty Ballinger agreed to serve, fittingly, as historian general. The official purposes of the organization were then spelled out: to perpetuate the memory and spirit of the men and women who achieved and maintained the independence of Texas, to encourage historical research into the earliest records of Texas, and to promote the celebration of Independence Day (March 2) and San Jacinto Day (April 21).[53]

The next year, Betty Ballinger delivered the keynote address in Houston to the DRT in which she explained the rationale behind the forming of such an organization of Texas women. Her words are instructive in that they display the longing that women felt to be a significant part of the celebration of patriotism.

> Houston and San Jacinto! What Texan can hear those words and not feel his heart beat higher? A woman in this generation must be deaf indeed who does not hear from all sides appeals to her to come forward and bear her fair share of the heat and burden of the day. The dullest of us is set to wondering where lies woman's duty to the State.[54]

Having established that women wanted to be included, indeed had a duty to bear part of the burden, she outlined how, within the confines of convention, Texas women could accomplish this. "The material welfare of Texas is secure," she mused, "her future is in the hands of her sons. Daily they go forth to achieve great things, and we must not blame them if, strong in their own strength, dazzled by the splendor of the present, they have somewhat forgotten the . . . past." Not so with women, she announced. She mistakenly concluded in 1893 that women would have no part in creating the material future of the state, for women's work lay at home with the family. The future of Texas should be left to the men, she announced; the daughters of Texas will guard its "holy past." Therefore, "let us love to study Texas history and teach it to her children until they shall have learned that Goliad is as glorious as Marathon, and San Jacinto as sacred as Bunker Hill."[55]

Then she adumbrated the rest of woman's duty: "Let us seek out the graves of our heroes and having found them, let us care for them with grateful reverence. Be ours the duty to visit it and mark the spots where Texas was won for us, Gonzales, the Alamo, Goliad, San Jacinto—milestones along the bloodstained path to freedom." Betty Ballinger in her elegy to womanhood gave credence to the sharp contrast between men and women in the nineteenth century. Anthony Rotundo explains that nineteenth-century middle-class males were driven by competition and pursuit of individual interests, taking their identity from their achievements in the workplace. But he writes that, "with the male tradition of public usefulness fading, men would no longer protect the bonds of society." Thus it was that "women became guardians of civilization." But there was a catch: "women could not participate in all the privileges of individualism, as men did." So, women moved *collectively* to renew the concept of public virtue by acts of memorialization and commemoration.[56] The clear exposition of women's patriotic responsibilities was borne out of woman's cultural experience—home fires, children, reverence for family, grave tending, and glorification of historic heroes.

Betty Ballinger and other patriotic ladies in Galveston lost no time in forming a local group, the Sidney Sherman chapter. The organizing meeting took place at the home of General Sherman's daughter, Caroline Sherman Menard, who also assumed the presidency of the chapter but due to illness relinquished the office to Betty Ballinger.[57] Before a year was out, the little chapter had removed the remains of General Sherman and President Burnett from the abandoned cemetery on the east end of the island to a plot donated by the Lake View Cemetery Association. By 1894, the Daughters had raised enough money to place a twenty-three-foot stone obelisk over their graves, and they celebrated the event in one of the first public outpourings of patriotic fervor expressed by the newly formed Daughters.

The ceremonial day, March 2, 1894, began with the arrival of a trainload of guests from Houston, who were brought to the Garten Verein veranda, where a "dainty" breakfast of fried oysters, trout, potatoes, quail, green peas, fruit, and assorted cakes for some sixty invited guests had been prepared by the Sidney Sherman chapter. Afternoon exercises began promptly at 2:30 with a procession of mounted police; a band; the Daughters and their guests; clergymen; the mayor; aldermen; veterans of the Texas, Confederate, and Union armies; school children; the Screwmen's Benevolent Association; Carpenters and Joiners; Painters and Decorators; the Texas Labor Conference; the fire department; and all of the city's orphans (in that order), who marched in a body to the cemetery. The unveiling ceremonies attracted an estimated 1,600 people. Catholic bishop Nicholas Gallagher offered prayer, and Judge Norman G. Kittrell of Houston eulogized the two patriots. Afterward, the DRT members pronounced the affair "an interesting and important event."[58]

It was exactly the kind of recognition the women so desperately needed and sought, always couching the desire for pageantry, ritual, and symbolism not in terms of enhanced self-esteem for women, which it represented, but in terms of patriotism. Women had hit upon memorializing heroes as a means of elevating themselves in the eyes of a world that they admitted rewarded with material favor men's roles of aggression over women's roles of nurturance. By taking patriotic sentiment from their brothers and pushing it further, they hoped, in symbolic if not in real ways, to find equal prestige with men—not to be men, but to be valued as women the way men were valued by society.

It worked for a time, but the enthusiasm of leaving the future of Texas to the men while the women picked up the pieces of the past, for Galveston women at least, did not last. Membership in the Sidney Sherman chapter dipped from a high of forty-eight to a low of thirty-one after the storm. Projects, such as dedicating monuments to Sherman and Burnet, were not as grand thereafter in Galveston; the glory was transferred to other parts of the state that had bigger, more impressive sites to preserve—Goliad, the Alamo, and the San Jacinto battleground. Unveiling the Texas Heroes' Monument at Broadway and Rosenberg Avenue on April 21, 1900, as part of the bequest of Henry Rosenberg, proved to be a momentous occasion for the city but not for the Texas Veterans or for the Texas DRT, who, except for the Sidney Sherman chapter, were meeting in convention in San Antonio. Of course, the local chapter promised to care for the heroes' monument, championed the cause of Texas history to the Galveston schools, convinced the school board to name elementary schools for Texas sites and heroes (Alamo, San Jacinto, Sam Houston, and Goliad schools), every year placed flowers and flags on the graves of Texas warriors, and began a project to place a marble slab marker on each Texas veteran's grave.[59]

Women from Galveston with time and money to spare on the DRT usually involved themselves in projects at the state level. Betty Ballinger and Cornelia Branch Stone, for example, pushed state senators to have statues of Sam Houston and Stephen F. Austin sculpted by the best known artist in Texas, Elisabet Ney, and erected in Statuary Hall at the Capitol in Washington, D.C., in 1903.[60] In this way, patriotic-hereditary societies provided some women with a channel into state-level forums. The proximity to politicians and politics must have enhanced their desire to see women in the assembly, for Betty Ballinger eventually took the position that, indeed, women should be there.

Betty Ballinger stopped believing in the nonsense of leaving the future of Texas to its sons alone. She understood better than most the value of women's active participation in community life; not only did she join the male-dominated board of trustees of the Rosenberg Library and the Red Cross, she belonged to more women's groups than any other woman in the city. Each association she joined represented a different aspect of woman's public role: as president of the Ladies' Aid Society of the First Baptist Church, she understood women's church work; from membership on the board of lady managers of the Johanna Runge Free Kindergarten, she understood women's benevolence; through membership in Colonial Dames, the DAR, and of course the DRT, she came to know women's longing for a share of patriotic pride; by founding the Wednesday Club and remaining an officer in the Women's Health Protective Association, she learned well to appreciate both types of women's clubs—literary and civic; and by proclaiming the right for women to vote before an audience of 150 and serving as the suffrage

FIGURE 6.1. Monument to the Heroes of the Texas Revolution, funded by Henry Rosenberg and dedicated by the Sidney Sherman chapter of the Daughters of the Republic of Texas, April 21, 1900. Courtesy Rosenberg Library, Galveston, Texas.

society's first vice president in 1912, she signaled to the state that women also would share in the future of Texas.

Born in the antebellum South, where cultural proscriptions confined ladies to the traditions of family, children, domesticity, and church, Betty Ballinger, an exemplar of white southern womanhood, changed with the rise of a New South. Ironically, women's organizations such as the DRT, whose functions perpetuated domestic values, in fact encouraged women to gain greater exposure to public life, animating them to participate in the future of Texas through emphasis on education and maintenance of historic sites. Ironic, too, is that fact that southern women were complicated, did not fit into neat categories of progressive or conservative, and somehow lived with contradictions as great as blue book social codes and suffrage speeches. Yet they shared with women all over the nation the idea that they, as women, were culture carriers and transmitters. Men, they believed, would abandon the past for the future, would ignore the aesthetic for the practical, and would rather drive a hard bargain than teach a child poetry or history.

United Daughters of the Confederacy

This notion that men would abandon the past was especially troubling to women who bore scars from a more recent national upheaval, the Civil War. The animus that drove women to join the United Daughters of the Confederacy was in many ways similar to that which impelled women to join the DRT—the desire to educate the young with proper histories lest they forget the sacrifices of their fathers and mothers, to tend and mark the graves of fallen heroes, and to erect in regal monuments symbolic gestures of gratitude for sacrifices. But there were other concerns for Confederate daughters: aged veterans and female survivors of the war suffering from neglect needed care, and, of course, overarching all was the fact that there had been heroic struggles for nationhood but no ultimate victory. Theirs was a Lost Cause in fact; Confederate Daughters would not let it be a cause lost to memory.

Nothing worried southern women more than to think that southern children might be subjected to "distorted" views contradictory to the "true" picture as presented by the UDC, guardians of the region's past. Mary Hunt Affleck, chairwoman of the textbook committee for the Texas Division of the UDC, exhorted her audience to concern itself with the selection of books for schools and town libraries. "Southern schools should use such books bearing on literature that give proper emphasis to Southern productions; on civics, that discuss the deeper constitutional questions, as did the ante-bellum statesmen and jurists; on history that recognizes the great war of the sixties as a civil war, in which both sides were equally patriotic and both honest defenders of unsolved national questions, and in which neither was in rebellion."[61] Histories that did not make the grade were "condemned," their expulsion from southern schools insisted upon by the UDC and often acted upon by veterans of the Civil War in towns across Texas. Resolutions were passed in 1905 that propelled the Texas UDC, under the guidance of its president, Ida Smith Austin—First Presbyterian Bible class teacher, YMCA auxiliary and future YWCA president—to use its influence "as a body to have books teaching Southern authors and their works . . . in our public schools." The result was a purging from southern schools and libraries of books that did not present a "true history for the children of the South."[62]

The Daughters of the Confederacy put substantial pressure on women's clubs in Texas, which were beginning to establish libraries in little towns across the state, to select carefully those histories, biographies, novels, magazines, and volumes of literary criticism that were acceptable to southern views. The report from members of the Fortnightly Club of Brenham, Texas, to the annual meeting of the UDC stated boldly that its members were "true Southern ladies, all of whom are eligible to the Daughters of the Confederacy. Its policy has ever been to place upon the library shelves the very best of Southern literature. Especial attention has been paid to juvenile books pertaining to the growth and true history of our beloved Southland."[63] The urgency Texas clubwomen felt in establishing libraries involved not only educating the public but also educating them according to southern prescriptions. The library movement was propelled by women who maintained a form of censorship over the ideas, literature, and history that might reside upon library shelves.

Open-mindedness that accompanies intellectual inquiry never presented itself for adoption among members of the UDC. Their goal was propagandistic and was aimed at children who had never lived with slaves or experienced the war. UDC members worried that the new generation might at some future point endanger the region's collective memory with views critical of slavery or of the Lost Cause. Hence, the justification of nationhood and secession and the description and adulation of "southern civilization" for the future of the region remained the UDC's most important missions. Mothers were singled out for special admonition. "I urge upon you as Southern mothers the sacred duty of teaching your children the truths of history and ask you to use as a home textbook the UDC Catechism written by our beloved Mrs. Cornelia Branch Stone. Its truths will sink so deeply into their young hearts that their after lives will be firmly imbued with the belief in a cause that was just."[64]

Cornelia Branch Stone, prominent Galveston clubwoman and former president of the General UDC, wrote for the Texas Division a question and answer booklet, the "U.D.C. Catechism for Children." Its sale contributed substantially to the UDC monument fund and was widely used among Galveston households to train and instruct young people in the proper history of the South. Typical passages included:

QUESTION: What causes led to the war between the States?
ANSWER: The disregard on the part of the States of the North, for the rights of the Southern or slave-holding States."
QUESTION: What were these rights?
ANSWER: The right to regulate their own affairs and to hold slaves as property.
QUESTION: How were the slaves treated?
ANSWER: With great kindness and care in nearly all cases, a cruel master being rare, and lost the respect of his neighbors if he treated his slaves badly.
QUESTION: What was the feeling of the slaves toward their masters?
ANSWER: They were faithful and devoted and were always ready and willing to serve them.
QUESTION: How did they behave during the war?
ANSWER: They nobly protected and cared for the wives of soldiers in the field. They were always true and loyal.[65]

To suggest that southern men would unnecessarily lead the region into a disastrous and futile war would bring dishonor on the family; to admit that slaves were mistreated or that they proved their objections to slavery by disloyalty during the war would bring into question the racial order upheld by white supremacy. When viewed from the perspective of racism as well as of "home and family protection," which southern women upheld as their duty, the dissembling becomes more clear. The notion that southern honor and race superiority were male ideals needs to be broadened to include women, especially given the evidence manifested by members of the UDC. Southern women simply could not admit to themselves or to their children that their forebears had erred or that African Americans had suffered in bondage; to do so would bring shame upon white southerners. The logical extension of this cultural trait was to invest an entire region with glory and honor.[66]

A stereotypical lecture given in 1916 by Mildred Lewis Rutherford, historian general of the UDC, justified, whitewashed, and carefully revised southern history. She baldly stated that "the selling of slaves in the South did not separate mother and child as often or with as much cruelty as did the slave trafic [sic] in Africa. . . . There was no such thing as chattel slavery in the South." Reconstruction came in for severe criticism. "This unwise policy [Reconstruction government] was the real blow aimed at the overthrow of the civilization of the Old South. The men of the South were then put under military discipline which actually tied their hands and only the Ku Klux, the 'Chivalry of the Old South,' could break these bonds that fettered them."[67] The seriousness of the fact that southern men perpetrated violence in the form of war and later in vigilante groups compelled southern women (including Galvestonians) to practice a kind of self-delusion, to pretend that the South held no imperfections, to insist that slaves were treated fairly and that violence on the part of whites was fully justified. It was a subterfuge that produced no guilt, for the women were convinced they were correct. Moreover, they again were duty bound by southern cultural traditions to preserve the honor of their ancestors and family. Caught up as they were in the traditions of cultural transmission, white southern women chose to defend, preserve, and protect southern civilization wherein their ancestry, family, and pride resided. The motives for producing shibboleths for southern schools and libraries was a very personal one, bound inextricably with the imperatives of family honor, protection of the home and homeland, and grave site memorialization of loved ones.

Galveston women took seriously the admonition to train children in southern truths. Agnes D. Killough set up in 1910 a children's auxiliary to the local UDC chapter, where children of UDC members attained proper southernizing at least once a month. James S. Hanna recounts that his boyhood was filled with such attempts to construct his thinking along proper channels. Apparently it worked, for he wrote of the "shameful atrocities that occurred during the period of Reconstruction." But his reminiscences betray a certain cynicism toward the method of indoctrination. "I, and my sister Margaret, Dorothy and all of the other children of the prominent Southern families of Galveston were drafted into [the children's auxiliary of the UDC], and for several years had to attend monthly meetings where we were compelled to listen to accounts of the brave deeds of our ancestors, and wind up the meetings singing 'Dixie.' "[68]

Southern songs, ballads, and patriotic anthems were essential to the preservation of oral traditions from the Old South, and members of the UDC, also caught up in the musical culture peculiar to women, understood this better than most. Attempts to revive and bring into popular usage songs of their childhood were facilitated by their own singing and by their admonition to others. Annual meetings rang with renditions of the "Bonnie Blue Flag," whose stanzas repeat

"Hurrah for Southern rights," and old ballads such as "Annie Laurie" and "Ben Bolt and Lily Dale." Children needed to learn these songs, the members insisted, for emotional ties to the old homeland are often best bound through music and lyric. They romanticized the "old songs that black mammy crooned to drowsy children, when gray heads were golden, and starlit dusks [were] odorous with lilacs, clove pinks, and old-fashioned Southern roses." "Oh Daughters of the Confederacy," they pleaded, "open your old music books before your descendants, and strike upon the harps of the past, and teach them in home and school, the fireside songs and grand old battle hymns of the Southland, while time plays softly on the pipes of peace."[69] Music had its patriotic uses as well.

The Galveston UDC chapter, known as the Veuve Jefferson Davis chapter, was established in 1895 at the instigation of Mollie Macgill Rosenberg, who remained its president until she died in 1917. Within three years it had enrolled 100 members and by 1908 had reached its peak membership of 390.[70] The timing is notable, for it coincides exactly with the elimination of black male office holders, the disfranchisement of black male voters, the rise of Jim Crow laws, and the transfer of political influence from minority and working-class voters to white women. The UDC and its philosophies, then, provided politically powerful white men and potential women voters with rhetorical assurances that the emergent Jim Crow politics contributed to the restoration of Old South values. By publicly justifying the past violence of whites in the defense of southern civilization, they articulated a rationale for discrimination. Divorced from the actual political process as they were in 1895, women supporters of the Confederacy ideal, nonetheless, employed a falsified version of history to win converts to a political agenda that supported white supremacy. The fact that they did this aggressively, influencing the selection of reading material for libraries, inculcating children with notions of white superiority, and reviving music and memories of a time when whites owned slaves, puts them squarely in the camp with apologists of the emerging racial order.

In this way, members of the UDC used the past to construct elaborate rituals filled with political and gendered meanings. Mollie Rosenberg, widow of financier philanthropist Henry Rosenberg, is best known for two things: for furnishing and supplying the interior artwork in Grace Episcopal Church and for presiding in queenly fashion over the Veuve Jefferson Davis chapter of the Daughters of the Confederacy. Like many of her contemporaries in the UDC, she was born and raised in comfort, living her childhood in the ancestral home in Hagerstown, Maryland. Her family endured deprivation and hardship during the war as four brothers fought under southern skies and as she and her sisters survived Union "occupation." It was through these experiences that she came to live a life devoted to the perpetuation of southern cultural values. Grace Episcopal Church received the benefits of her spiritual devotion to an aristocratic southern church, and the local UDC gained its most generous and ardent patroness. As if epitomizing a genteel feminine culture, Mollie Rosenberg spread her fortune only among select semiprivate organizations. In both cases, she made sure the emphasis was on women and family. While we cannot pretend that this constitutes a feminist political perspective, it does represent, nonetheless, a concentration on women's values that tended to enrich women's self-esteem while at the same time locking them into an ecclesiastical and regional conservatism.

Mollie Rosenberg expressed her devotion to the Lost Cause through her maternalism over the local chapter.[71] As president she not only presided over meetings and influenced the agenda and activities of the chapter but she also showered the chapter with gifts. Her authority allowed her to play the role of lady bountiful—supplying items from stationery to pianos—without appearing to "buy" the chapter. "Again our gracious president has given us evidence of her continued and generous care, and at her own expense provided official stationery, of beautiful quality, and complete and personal design, for the use of her official family," wrote one grateful member, who saw more in the term "daughters" than simply the official appellation.[72]

Rather than meet in a church parlor or in a home, Rosenberg built a fully furnished meeting hall on her property, named it Macgill Memorial Hall for her parents (her mother's wedding dress remained on display there), and insisted that the chapter conduct its business under her wing. Cornelia Branch Stone best described the scene:

> Her boundless generosity gave no pause, but filled [the hall] with one hundred
> chairs, a cabinet in oak for relics, a handsome bookcase, a beautiful and conven-
> ient desk, . . . and then she crowned this wonderful bounty by the splendid gift
> of a piano that our lives here may be full of melody. In the corner closet . . . will
> be found the brooms in two sizes, which is a reminder that royal gifts require
> royal care.[73]

Symbols of the home abounded: a cabinet for relics, a piano for musical entertainment, and brooms to suggest a tidy house. Karen Blair writes that a movement for clubhouses did not gain momentum until after World War I. Mollie's gift to the local UDC was well ahead of the national trend, but it betokened a need felt by women to pursue their interests in their own space. Most clubhouses became focal points of artistic display, but the Macgill Hall became a reliquary for Mollie's family mementos and a meeting place for members away from individual homes or the impersonal rooms of the YMCA.[74]

Although the officers of the local UDC were elected annually, Mollie Rosenberg's office may as well have been self-perpetuating. One indication of the group's conservatism rests on the fact that no other women's club surviving to the twentieth century allowed one "patron saint" to dominate its activities. Yet, no one dared oust their patroness from her position. In effect, the organization not only revered the culture of the Old South, it practiced it as well, perpetuating a form of matriarchy, and, as long as enthusiasm lasted for the club, a conservative hierarchy among women that would barely be challenged by New South progressivism.

Besides Mollie Rosenberg, the local chapter's two most influential and prominent members were Ida Smith Austin, who became president of the Texas Division of the UDC in 1905, and Cornelia Branch Stone, president-general of the UDC from 1907 to 1909.[75] Ida Austin remained the teacher of the Bible class named for her at the First Presbyterian Church; the class motto, "With God everything; without God nothing," was adopted by the Veuve Jefferson Davis chapter of the UDC, every chapter letterhead containing this imprint. While it is well known that the connection between religion and the Lost Cause found expression in civil religion, in this case the direct transference of the Ida Austin Bible class motto to the Daughters of the Confederacy, surrounded by the symbols of the Confederate flag, confirmed for women the sanctity and religiosity of their cause.[76] Just as Mollie Rosenberg had provided a home so that the Daughters would never be far from the hearth, so Ida Austin reaffirmed their close affiliation to the church and legitimated their mission with the symbols of divine guidance. As heirs and guardians of family traditions, as enthusiastic participants in church endeavors, and as preservers of "southern civilization," the Daughters of the Confederacy wove a conservative tapestry of blue and gray, heavily decorated with gendered symbols of religion, home, and ancestry.

Cornelia Branch Stone, born in Nacogdoches in 1840 and already mentioned for her work in creating the "U.D.C. Catechism," spent much of her time in establishing memorials for Confederate soldiers and sailors (she sold more than 1,000 copies of her catechism in one year, which helped pay for the monument in Galveston), in promoting the Confederate Veterans' Home in Austin, Texas, and in serving on the board of managers for the Home for Wives and Widows of Confederate Veterans, also in Austin.[77] Although memorials honored the dead — and women particularly felt the need to perpetuate the memory of fallen soldiers — homes served the living. The need for a home for Confederate women, indeed, the need for benevolent institutions of any kind for elderly women, was great. Although imbued with exclusivity, allowing only relatives of veterans to reside in the home, the UDC was one of few organizations that cared about the future of its elderly women as well as its veterans. Every annual meeting brought tales of hardship for women who had once served the Cause but who had ended up poorly. "Grandma Harold . . . who ministered to the wounded soldiers after the Battle of Lookout Mountain . . . finally died in the Bexar county poor house and was buried in a potter's field, all for want of this Home and the proper care of the U.D.C." The women passed biblical injunctions recounting the buried talents that "have never been dug up yet" and admonished the chapters to send in their donations. Land for the home was finally purchased in Austin in 1906, and a $10,000 structure was built to house the women.[78]

Although remembered for her involvement in Confederate homes, Stone's most important connection was to the women's club movement. As first vice president of the Texas Federation of Women's Clubs (TFWC), she chaired the committee to secure a poll tax, one-third of which was paid to the school fund of Texas. Women not only believed the rhetoric of the day — that a poll tax would help fund public education and elevate the electorate by ridding the state of "unqualified" voters — they produced it. Behind the rationale of increasing funds for public education lay race and class prejudice. Stone also served as chairperson of the TFWC's education committee and worked indefatigably for clubs to increase their interest in education and to provide scholarships for students to universities. Her work toward education bespoke of her interest in the future, but it was a future tinged with the cultural baggage of the past. In her position as both UDC president and an officer in the Texas women's club movement, she was able to

FIGURE 6.2. Mollie Macgill Rosenberg, president of the Veuve
Jefferson Davis chapter of the United Daughters of the Confederacy. Courtesy Rosenberg Library, Galveston, Texas.

marshal an impressive following for the UDC's brand of truth. In this, she managed through her affiliations to influence a generation of young southerners in
the "verities" of southern civilization.[79]

The Daughters of the Confederacy have been credited with perpetuating behavior that epitomized southern womanhood. Well-educated, upper-middle-class
women banded together to raise money for commemoration, rituals, and education and to keep alive the memory of heroic service rendered by men and women
during wartime. Members who assumed officerships took their responsibilities to
the Lost Cause far more seriously than one would expect, which resulted in deadly
earnest elections for the honor of presiding over the organization at state and

FIGURE 6.3. Mollie Macgill Rosenberg as "Jerusha" in the "Dees-trick Skule," a drama given November 29, 1905, by the Veuve Jefferson Davis chapter of the United Daughters of the Confederacy as a benefit for the monument to the Galveston Confederate soldiers and sailors. The bonnet was worn in 1839, the year she was born. The doll belonged to her sister, who died in 1851. Courtesy Rosenberg Library, Galveston, Texas.

national levels. In the process of campaigning and promoting themselves for candidacy, albeit with the trappings of gentility, some abandoned their traditional ladylike decorum and acted more like the aggressive leaders they in fact were. Mollie Rosenberg conveyed genuine shock when she unmasked as "unladylike" the actions of a candidate for state president from another city. "Miss Adelia A. Dunwant has been most insulting to Mrs. Sampson. She tried to 'walk over her with both feet' . . . and threatened to *tear her to pieces* in her own home, did you ever hear of any thing more dreadful? . . . Col. Dunwant says his sister shall be the next state president if it takes every cent he has. Can you inform me how money can buy votes of a true Southern lady?"[80] Of course, Mollie Rosenberg knew very well how money bought votes; she practiced it every year to win her own election as chapter president, but her methods employed the usual device of benign benevolence rather than aggressive vote mongering.

Even within the Galveston chapter, "male" rivalries erupted between Ida Austin and Cornelia Branch Stone, when Stone sought the office of president-general of the UDC in 1906. Ida Austin served as a delegate to the twelfth annual meeting of the UDC and carried with her a number of votes from members of the Texas delegation. When Stone's name was proffered for election, it became clear that Ida Austin would not give those votes entrusted to her to Stone; in fact, the proxies had been specifically pledged to another candidate. Stone declared that if the Texas delegation did not vote for her unanimously, then she would withdraw her name from nomination, which she did. Although Stone finally won her election in 1907, she never forgave Ida Austin for her "principles" and circulated a "defamatory" letter criticizing Austin's work in the chapter and as Texas division president in 1905. This put Austin in the position of having to exonerate herself among the 390 members of the local chapter and among the 5,000 Texas members. Aside from the unpleasantness of the whole situation, it points to an interesting fact: that in contests for high office, southern ladies, even Daughters of the Confederacy, displayed a telling aggression in battling for positions of authority. As women entered public space, whether in schools, churches, or associations of both men and women, they were exposed to competition, aggression, and politicking. Although heavily imbued with the philosophy of woman's peaceful nurturing nature, which in effect directed their goals toward women's interests in asylums, education for children, and the arts, in fact, some of them entered heated election contests, struggled for power within organizations, and pursued public acclaim. One probable reason that Mollie Rosenberg condemned the aspirations of another UDC member as unladylike was that it too blatantly crossed the boundaries of expected female behavior. On the other hand, the exposure to the machinations of politics for some turn-of-the-century clubwomen increased their political awareness, sharpened their parliamentary skills, and honed their talents for larger battles outside the arena of an all-woman's world. As Anne Scott stated: "Clubs also became a training school for women who wanted to serve in public life."[81]

In the halcyon years of the 1890s, wealthy Galveston families enjoyed the fruits of their merchant capital. They lived in elegant homes that towered over boulevards lined with palms and oleanders and sent their daughters to Europe for musical and artistic training. Women from this class ventured into the world of secular clubs. The Ladies' and Girls' Musical Clubs, the Wednesday Club, the Daughters of the American Revolution, the Daughters of the Republic of Texas, and the United Daughters of the Confederacy emerged to grant women a separate but elevated world of refinement in a rapidly changing society. These organizations differed entirely from benevolent institutions; their principal purpose was not charity. And while they differed from one another, as well, in mission, they shared a commonality in bringing well-to-do women together for esteem building and education. Altogether, the estimated number of white women in clubs of the type mentioned here reached 300 in 1900. In the pre-1900 period, women's clubs remained small, just large enough to be accommodated by a drawing room or a church parlor. By 1915, with the introduction of four large and more democratic women's organizations, the numbers swelled to approximately 3,500.

Musical and artistic emphasis found expression in clubs where performance and edification raised their art to community-level acceptance. Women's artistic cultural pursuits were legitimated via churches, women's clubs, and public community concerts. A call to self-improvement brought a select number of women together to explore first the great literary masters and later the world at their doorsteps. Interest in the position of women turned them into careful articulators of the needs for progressive change, even as they remained firmly embedded in the social and racial hierarchy. Finally, an urge to join in the great patriotic celebration and to exclude the déclassé led Galveston women to found and to join patriotic societies wherein the great celebrations of history could be domesticated. Each woman sought elevation for herself in the protected environment of exclusivity. Certainly culture and self-improvement were the common themes of these late nineteenth-century associations, but the clubs retained their nineteenth-century "blue-blood" identification.

Beyond elitism and self-edification, however, there were major differences between literary clubs and patriotic-hereditary groups. Members of choral and literary clubs introduced music, plays, novels, and histories into their club work and, hence, into their lives. They tried to use this material to change women's attitudes, behavior, and world outlook. Literary clubs invited women to prepare themselves for emergence into the public realm. Consequently, literary clubs provided unconscious training for their members in the world of ideas and public action, a world that would encompass their future. Patriotic club women incorporated into their world the battles, treaties, constitutions, and heroes of the past — a past that for the most part favored men. In attempting to integrate these subjects into their club life, the Daughters first turned them into symbols — relics, flags, portraits, histories. Then they transformed the symbols into feminized vestiges of male events by shrouding them in the winding cloths of domesticity. Rather than allowing the events of the past to change them, the Daughters sought to domesticate past events, to interject symbolically, ritualistically, and religiously the importance of womanhood into the patriotic celebration. To say that they domesticated patriotism does not go far enough. They sought no important future for women with these acts; they sought instead to entomb the events of the past, symbols really, in feminine caskets. The metaphor of death, used here to illustrate their worldview, surrounded their activities as well — marking graves, memorializing fallen heroes, erecting statues, building homes in which to die, and perpetuating racist ideologies. Southern elite women needed at that point to transform themselves for the twentieth century, not change history to fit a version of their domestic and hierarchical ideal. In terms of preparation for the future, literary clubs served women better, not just for what they studied but for the way they handled and dealt with the material in their midst.

The early women's clubs and the boards of lady managers for benevolent institutions were not democratic in nature. The women continued their exclusivity either by limiting the size of the organization, by voting on new members, or by imposing ancestral safeguards. True, the Wednesday Club after 1900 included more teachers and other genteel working women; the Daughters of the Confederacy had the potential for greater openness than the older patriotic-hereditary organizations, but their bylaws insisted upon some form of exclusion. Throughout the Progressive Era, therefore, some club women maintained a conservative or even reactionary posture to the progressive ideals of direct democracy or to the inclusion of women from all classes as equals in their own organizations. With the advent of progressive civic reform clubs open to all white women, Galveston female elitism was challenged. The shift for clubwomen from self-educators to progressive civic reformers occurred at different times in communities across the South.[82] In Galveston, none of the women's clubs or boards established before 1900 ventured into what may be called civic reform work after the dawning of the twentieth century. They had not yet discovered political activism; rather the 1890s proved to be a wellspring decade, as women gathered together and focused on self-improvement and commitment to the preservation of patriotic ideals. Perhaps this class of self-satisfied women needed to be shaken from their sunny complacency, for models of progressive reform work in other cities seemed not to disturb their serenity. It would take an enormous disaster before Galvestonians saw the opportunities for women's civic activism and reform.

PART TWO

. . . .

PROGRESSIVE ERA GALVESTON

7

AFTER THE STORM

Women, Public Policy, and Power

*And the rain descended, and the floods came, and the winds blew and
beat upon that house; and it fell; and great was the fall of it.*

—Matthew 7:27

Probably the best known fact about Galveston, Texas, besides singer Glenn
Campbell's lyrics about its "sea winds blowin'," is that the city was nearly
demolished by hurricane in 1900—the worst natural disaster in the history of the
North American continent. Historians of the Progressive Era will quickly recall
that out of the destruction citizens implemented structural reform and turned a
formerly aldermanic governing body into a five-man city commission. Hence city
commission government was born, a practical and utilitarian method of governance that took the nation, if not by storm, at least by drizzle as some 500 mostly
small- to medium-sized towns and cities across the nation adopted the efficient
and "progressive" plan.[1]

Less well known, indeed lurking in obscurity, is the fact that the adoption of
this governing political body was not the only change to follow the storm. Six
months prior to the installation of the five city commissioners, sixty-six upper- and
upper-middle-class white women survivors of the storm created the city's first civic
reform organization, the Women's Health Protective Association (WHPA). Although accustomed to working in groups quietly for the public good, these women
found that after the storm they, too, held a vision for a restored Galveston. Through
their newly created reform association they began to vie openly with city hall for
the power to shape public policy. Hence in Galveston, progressivism begins in
1900 with a great hurricane, but as others have already noted: "Progressivism
emerged from the confluence of two broad streams of political action—one largely
male and the other largely female, each with its distinctive aims, values, tactics,
and style."[2]

Some may view public policy as determined solely by decisions from officially
appointed or elected bodies and individuals. The definition of public policy employed here is broader and includes the actions of private groups and voluntary
associations that ultimately affected city life. Urban historians have traditionally
asked how members of powerful and influential urban groups, who were not

elected city officials, have "realized their own will in a communal action."[3] This is an especially appropriate question when considering the activities of influential upper- and middle-class white women's organizations of the Progressive Era and their ability to effect change. Probably at no other time in the history of organizational life were women better able to implement their vision of civic improvement. Yet few scholars outside the realm of women's history have given much attention to the political and quasi-political activities of women in urban areas and related their actions to the creation of public policy.[4] Those who have write that "the traditional boundaries of political history will no longer do. What we call politics must be expanded beyond electioneering and the conduct of formal governance to encompass the colossal efforts of organized women."[5]

Considerable debate exists over who held power at the community level during the Progressive Era: Did a single elite or competing elites retain power? Was power invested in a ward-boss system? Or was power more widely dispersed among laboring, immigrant, charitable, and women's groups, especially with the advent of rapid urbanization?[6] The debate shifts slightly when discussing cities of the New South, which in most cases were not governed by professional politicians or by city bosses and their machines, but rather by merchants, tradesmen, and professionals.[7] Even though local governance after 1900 may have been in the hands of legally elected or appointed officials, Progressive Era groups with a host of new issues emerged to challenge city hall. Labor unions, commercial associations, chambers of commerce, even private cabals of well-placed businessmen and lawyers influenced and shaped the direction of city life. Against this milieu of competing interest groups, white women in organizations emerged as relative novices, yet they, nonetheless, composed a privileged group in some ways, as they married or had close personal relationships with male leaders, found money, education, and domestic help available to them, and could afford to spend time on civic activism.

In Galveston after the storm, the arrival of the American national Red Cross proved to city leaders that privileged white women were capable of leadership in a crisis. At the same time, other groups—black men and women, working-class women—found themselves portrayed as unequal to the task of governance. When Galveston voters and the Texas legislature implemented structural reform through city commission government, they opened the way for privileged white women—rather than enfranchised black men—to gain access to public policy making despite the fact that women were not voters. The disfranchisement of black male and poorer white voters across the South was a deliberate attempt to solidify power for white male voters of the civic elite (professional men, white collar workers, clerics, and businessmen). But the admittance of professional women and wives of civic elites to policy making was unintentional, perhaps even unforeseen, as these women were already disfranchised and constituted no seeming threat to power. Only later, when women demanded changes in policies, did overt resistance grow.

The progressive movement greatly influenced privileged classes across the nation. Those women who read the agendas of national women's clubs and associations gained access to a woman's progressive agenda, giving them a vision of reform beyond their own community. How Galveston women managed to choose their own goals and to gain experience in their implementation, how successful they were in achieving them, how they interacted with the city commission, what tactics they used, and how the process of politicization affected them is the subject of this chapter. Employing Galveston as a case study has advantages, for, while there were older interest groups at work in determining public policy after 1900, the storm was a catalyst in the creation of two new influential bodies—the much-discussed city commission and the Women's Health Protective Association. Although the WHPA was a private voluntary association outside the formal political structure and was concerned primarily with domestic issues, it gained sizable influence, even power, in the creation of public policy.

We left our story of the hurricane of 1900 in its aftermath. In addition to problems of disposing of the dead, an estimated 10,000 were left homeless; the city lacked water, electricity, and gas, plus rail line, telephone, and telegraph connection to the mainland; moreover, looting became a problem. The morning after the disaster, Mayor Walter C. Jones met with a number of surviving civic leaders at the Tremont Hotel, where they planned to get the word out about Galveston. Getting help was imperative, and somebody was going to have to cross the bay and traverse the fifty miles to Houston. W. L. Moody's steam launch, one of the few seaworthy vessels available, left Sunday morning with a volunteer crew of five. They made it to Texas City, rode a cart to La Marque, found a rail hand car, and cranked their way to League City, where they met a train coming from Houston. They convinced the train to turn back to Houston and, thus, got the word out to Texas governor Joseph D. Sayers and President William McKinley that the city was nearly prostrate. Houston's response was admirable. Within a day, the city had gathered a force of 250 volunteers, three train carloads of supplies, and 100,000 gallons of water in huge tanks.[8]

Also on Sunday, September 9 at 2 P.M., Mayor Jones called a meeting of "prominent citizens"at the Chamber of Commerce rooms in the Tremont Hotel "for the purpose of organizing to relieve the suffering and to bury the dead." He appointed nine of the city's leading businessmen to form a Central Relief Committee with himself as chairman. Eventually, six of the men were assigned specific tasks heading up subcommittees or departments of general relief, finance, burial, hospitals, correspondence, and property protection. The Relief Committee (a subcommittee of the Central Relief Committee), headed by W. A. McVitie, became a focal point of industry. On Sunday evening and Monday morning, the Relief Committee met to "district" the city by its twelve wards, to requisition food from local warehouses and grocers, and to elect a chairman for each ward who would be responsible for the establishment of supply stations for the distribution of food and for the removal of debris from the ward. Ward chairmen also had to organize a working force with horses and drays. "Any able-bodied man who will not volunteer for this work must not be fed," cautioned the committee instructions. For months, members of the relief and other temporary committees, including those added for clean-up and transportation, saw Galveston through the worst of the emergency. Thus, in the crisis, a prototype of a city commission was born.[9]

An equally important prototype for women workers emerged from the American National Red Cross, led by the indomitable Clara Barton. On September 25, an item appeared in the *News* indicating that "a number of ladies met yesterday at the headquarters of the Red Cross society, on Twenty-fifth and Mechanic streets, to assist in the distribution of stores sent through that organization to the Galveston flood sufferers." Twenty-six women leaders, all active in Galveston's women's organizations, gathered to help where needed. Clara Barton paid them high tribute: "The ladies of the city, in spite of the shock, grief, and mutilated homes, came grandly to the work of relief, asking to form a Red Cross auxiliary and take charge of the distributing stations in the various wards of the city, under the name of the Red Cross."[10]

Attaching itself to the already established ward relief system, the Red Cross began to supply the twelve wards, each headed by a woman volunteer, with goods coming in from around the nation. In order to eliminate duplication, on September 27 the city "committee on relief, of which Mr. W. A. McVitie is chairman, . . . and the ladies' relief committee, were amalgamated, and the Galveston auxiliary of the American National Red Cross was launched." It was decided to elect a "lady chairman in each ward, the gentlemen chairmen of the wards who have been working under the relief committee . . . to continue their good work." But McVitie thought that the ladies should "predominate," as they could "do this work better than the men." It was true that women's benevolent societies had traditionally investigated the resources of the poor by direct visitation, and women were thought to be better suited for this sensitive work. But at a meeting the next day, McVitie made it clear that involving the women was also a means of reducing expenses. Within the relief stations, assistants had been paid, and he wanted women volunteers to do the work for free, thus reducing the emergency payroll. Women ward leaders found themselves, not for the last time, obliged to cooperate with the men in their traditional volunteer roles.[11]

Still, gains were made for the women. White women leaders since the 1870s had discovered need and distributed goods through church, synagogue, and private charities. Now civic leaders gave these actions official recognition. Male leaders drew these women and their talent for charitable relief into the orbit of local government. This had two extremely important consequences for the city. First, it provided a model for activism and led to the creation of a Women's Health Protective Association; second, it moved the city to establish a United Charities (see chapter 4), which would render systematic relief to indigents under the direction of women administrators.

In the short term, women volunteers joined men officially in the distribution of food, clothing, and materials for temporary shelters and the removal of the dead. The women were responsible for going out among the people of their wards to determine need; they helped compile a census and distribute clothing and supplies in a much more organized fashion. As quantities of supplies poured into the city, the massive task of sorting, labeling, and distributing became a shared task for women and men. The operation of providing clothing and supplies for the destitute continued until October 25, when ward relief stations closed. This left the city with the immediate problems of providing housing for the homeless and disinfecting what was salvageable. By the end of the year, national Red Cross workers were winding down their operations, moving to help the counties on the mainland, and sending Clara Barton back to Washington. This association had been a catalyst for privileged Galveston women who had wanted to help in the recovery. No means had existed for their entrée into the relief system until a national agency, accustomed to putting able-bodied women into positions of leadership, had shown Galvestonians how to do it and, in addition, had provided the good name of the American National Red Cross as "protection" for women serving in the ward relief stations. Clara Barton made sure that the women relief chairs were recognized for their public work: "The accession of the Red Cross ladies to the distribution committee is hailed with great satisfaction by the chairmen of the committees, nearly all of them being leaders of the different wards." The opportunity to work in the wards provided the white women leaders of Galveston *their first official positions* within the structure of emergency governmental relief and became a significant forerunner to their entrance into civic reform politics.[12]

No one could have doubted their leadership capabilities. Of the eleven women ward leaders identified in the newspaper, eight had had extensive experience with women's organizations. Six had served on the boards of lady managers of the city's orphanages, suggesting interest in the welfare of children, who, along with the children's mothers, would be most helped by the ward relief stations. Two of the women were officers of the hospital aid society, and four belonged to women's patriotic societies. Their average age was approximately fifty; they were not a young group but one with stature and experience. As in most cases of civic involvement in Galveston, Episcopalians predominated: there were four, along with three Presbyterians and one Methodist. Of this group, two would later become active suffragists. Five of the twelve chairwomen assigned to wards later became officers and members of the Women's Health Protective Association.[13]

At this point in the city's poststorm history, events dictated public policy; and citizens responded with a sense of urgency seldom seen in city council meetings. The volunteer Central Relief Committee, momentarily more powerful than the city council, collected $1,258,000 in donations from around the world and used this eventually to replace 483 homes and more than 1,500 private plumbing systems. The committee spent at least $500,000 in providing food, clothing, and household supplies, in removing the dead and insuring public sanitation, in rebuilding private homes, and in replacing lost tools, including 222 sewing machines. A temporary city of several hundred families, labeled the "white city on the beach," appeared as tents donated for shelter, and a camp hospital was created in the storm's aftermath. Residents of this camp built floors and furnished their tents with wood and furniture (some of it their own) found in the great debris piles. Under the direction of Rabbi Henry Cohen, the camp supervisors provided a dining tent and prepared meals for the refugees. City officials felt comfortable with the situation, but as soon as they expressed this sentiment, they heard from Clara Barton: "I am constrained to address you upon the subject . . . of some fixed plan of action." Barton urged the Central Relief Committee to find out how many were homeless, living in tents provided by the camp or on their own, sheltering with others, or residing on the mainland with relatives. Then she counseled them to let the American people know how many houses, modest but fitted out with do-

FIGURE 7.1. The "White City on the Beach" for homeless victims of the 1900 hurricane. Courtesy Rosenberg Library, Galveston, Texas.

mestic amenities, the city planned to build. "Our experience teaches us that it is only necessary to inform the public in a business-like way the exact needs . . . and the efforts will at once be earnestly directed in such channels." She went further and suggested the city have its architects plan to rebuild "in a definite and comprehensive way." This may well have been the first time city officials heard such direct words of authority from a woman, who not only admonished them to enumerate their people's needs more efficiently but also recommended a comprehensive plan for city planning. We are left to wonder if women leaders in Galveston hailed her words as progressive and imagined themselves following her example.[14]

No comparable disaster had ever struck an American city, so no one knew for certain how quickly the city should or could recover. Through the diligence of carpenters, engineers, and alderman C. H. McMaster, by September 12 water was restored through the city's pumping plant and into the water mains. Those homes and businesses with intact pipes were able to receive water. Banking, brewery, ice plant, and telegraph services were restored within the first week; by the second week workers had cleared the streets for traffic, laid telephone lines underground, and resumed railroad service. And by the third week electricity returned, ships began to ply in and out of the harbor, and, as an indicator that the worst was behind them, saloons were allowed to reopen.[15]

While there is much to admire in the way Galvestonians rallied to the crisis and set to work with remarkable alacrity, there is also a darker side to the story.

Apparently, exploiters robbed the dead of their jewelry, looted unprotected buildings, and hoarded what they found for their own profit. This sort of thing often occurs in disasters, human nature being what it is. For this reason and for the general protection of the public, Mayor Jones considered asking the governor to send in Texas guardsmen. After several suspected looters had been shot by local patrollers, the mayor on September 13 requested the presence of Texas militiamen under the leadership of Brigadier General Thomas Scurry. He declared martial law, issued twenty-four general orders immediately, and sent guardsmen to help remove survivors—women and children first—to Houston and set up the tent city for the homeless. The troubling aspect in all of this is that looters, "ghouls" (those who cut off fingers from the dead or ransacked pockets for jewelry), and shirkers were more often than not identified as "negroes." The *Galveston News* reported on September 12 that "Quite a number of negroes were killed for looting." The impression given by the press at the time was that some men were unwilling to work at the clean up; again blacks were singled out as unresponsive. The *News* reported: "It was decided to take the bodies to sea, . . . But men refused to touch the bodies. This was especially true of the negroes. . . . Men were impressed at the point of a bayonnet to do the work that must be done." In a series of vignettes entitled "Grewsome Stories," reporters depicted a "colored man" as "drinking steadily" from a beer keg before being carried away by the storm. Another *News* story, filled with pathos, depicted a black worker, "an aged negro," who came across the remains of his own son. The work crews stopped; the man "cried like a child" but agreed to follow the health authorities' dictum to burn all the bodies, even after his fellow workers had offered to bury the lad. Conversely, white leaders were held up as morally superior models of industry, bravely soldiering on despite personal loss. Clarence Ousley of the *News* in writing a poststorm book did not vilify or infantilize blacks as his paper had done, but he held a patronizing attitude in many of his accounts. Final evidence that white leaders discriminated against African Americans came with the political decisions made in the wake of the storm. No black aldermen were appointed to the Central Relief Committee or its subcommittees, although black leaders were asked to work at the direction of whites. For example, the Reverend Frank Gary, pastor of St. Paul's Methodist Church, a black congregation, led a force of men in the poststorm cleanup of the East End. Seldom do we have evidence of the resentment that these racial exclusions created, but an angry L. C. Luke, writing in the black-owned Galveston *City Times*, spoke his mind:"The colored man is good enough to save the lives of the little white babes, white women and even men. Good enough to visit the sick, bury the dead, care for the helpless, and render noble assistance in every particular . . . and yet in all of that he has not been good enough to even be represented as a committeeman. He has lost everything he had and in two wards he was entitled to a committeeman."[16]

Working-class and African American women also came in for criticism by the city leaders and by the editors of the *News*. Complaints that "the supply depots are overrun with negro women[,] and white women and children have the greatest difficulty in getting anywhere within range of the commodities" were broadened four days later to include working-class white women: "bad female characters, both

white and black have been parading the streets and making themselves obnoxious."
Such outcries led to a ruling by the Central Relief Committee for the impressment
and detention "of all idle women found on the streets" in a camp under the
direction of General Scurry. The *News* editors labeled the camp "particularly for
negroes" and implied that these women had committed fraud in drawing rations.
Actually, some of the women had refused to take up housekeeping tasks for white
families, creating the illusion that they were "idle" and underemployed. "When
colored women are approached and asked if they want to work in many cases they
ask exorbitant wages or refuse to work at any price. . . . They must either remain
in the camp or go to work for private families or the public."[17]

The problems of distributing supplies, securing housing, and finding suitable
employment follow any such disaster. When scarcity exists, women have often
taken to the streets in disorderly contests with civic officials. Obnoxious behavior,
in the minds of officials, was just one step short of riots and constituted a foretaste
of what committeemen feared. Thus, the editors and the committee members,
removing the focus on the problem of supply and distribution, reverted instead to
racial slurs, accusing blacks of fraud. They painted a stereotypical version of black
working habits in the belief that blacks would not work unless compelled to do
so. By projecting this image, the relief committee justified to the public its move
to incarcerate "troublesome" black and working-class women. Gender was not a
protection for these women, mainly because their actions separated themselves in
the minds of the civic elites from the images reserved for genteel women. As a
postscript to this sad affair, the *News* reported twelve days later that donations of
clothing had come to one of the Red Cross distribution centers. In orderly and
controlled fashion the workers distributed the goods first to whites in the morning
and whatever was left over to blacks in the afternoon. African Americans were
reminded of what they already knew, white people in this society would always
be served first. And if black women should happen to arrive ahead of whites in
seeking supplies, they might be threatened with imprisonment for violating the
racial order.[18]

Whereas African American and working-class women came in for image bashing, African American men found themselves losing ground politically. This came
about both as a result of a southwide campaign to disfranchise and depoliticize
black voters and as a result of specific local laws set in motion as early as 1895.
The Galveston newspapers went far to encourage readers to think of black men
as less manly and more unscrupulous in the face of the city's need. Because this
was not a true depiction, it made the editors' attempts to discredit black citizens
all the more sinister. For in that moment of recovery, new civic leaders were being
shaped and plans for a new system of government were about to emerge. It is clear
that African Americans or working-class women were not going to be invited to
help shape the future of the city.

Ironically, just as blacks found themselves pushed out of politics and working-
class women belittled, upper- and middle-class white women found the door to
power open to them, just a crack. Civic leaders in the poststorm relief efforts
invited these women via the Red Cross to become involved as ward "co-chairmen"
for the purpose of relieving the destitute. Newspaper editors and committeemen

put white women in the best possible light, remarking as mentioned earlier that the "ladies" could do the work of relief in the wards better than the men. The key term here is "ladies," to connote genteel women of respectable station. Although the Red Cross claimed to take in "all good people" without concern for "distinction—religious, political or social," in reality, leadership positions in the South were reserved for elite and upper-middle-class whites. Just as the press worked to discredit working-class women and blacks, it helped to shape a public "new woman" image for southern ladies. Every accolade extended to these women was an endorsement of their new role in public life, even politics, as we have defined it earlier. The real test of the acceptance of this class of women into political life, however, would have to wait until after Galveston's government had been restructured.

Establishing City Commmission Government

Restoring the city's commercial position became paramount, and in order to do so, something had to be done about city government. Before the storm, Galveston had been the state's primary port, exporter of more cotton than any other city in Texas. Most citizens agreed that after the disposal of bodies the city's primary goal was to reestablish the port and resume business. The opportunity for survival as an important southwestern entrepôt still existed because the majority of Galveston's civic-commercial elite lived in the island's more sheltered neighborhoods and had been spared the worst ravages of the storm. The storm had attacked middle- and working-class neighborhoods, and there loss of life had been heaviest. Wealthier individuals, who resided either in more substantial homes or further from the beaches, suffered fewer deaths. The result of this peculiar "act of God" was the survival of most of the city's business elite. This group had also proved disarmingly capable in the emergency relief crisis. The mayor and the city aldermen, who actually had succeeded rather admirably in conducting city business during the crisis, *appeared* discredited when they offered no plan to protect the city from future assaults and when they ran into financial embarrassments. Consequently, the Deep Water Committee, a group of eighteen capitalists—bankers, corporation directors, and large property holders—who had long engineered public policy in Galveston from behind the scenes and who also had served on the emergency Central Relief Committee, took a proposal to the state legislature to establish the city commission form of government.[19]

Within a year after the storm, the Texas legislature had granted the necessary charter changes without a referendum by Galveston voters, and city commission government was in place. Founded on the principle of efficiency, the commission system, also known as the Galveston plan, consolidated power in a five-man board and rationalized government processes by allowing one commissioner to be mayor-president and the other four to head departments of finance, fire and police, waterworks and sewerage, and streets and improvements. Two commissioners were elected by city voters and three, including the president, were appointed by the governor; all served two-year terms. Although considered highly effective by citizens, the new plan actually eliminated a system of checks and balances and city ward representation, and it complemented the move toward disfranchisement of black and poor white voters. As states across the South legalized voting restrictions, black and lower-class white voting power diminished. Texas adopted the poll tax in 1902, making the burden of suffrage heavier on blacks and poor whites. Galveston, however, as early as 1895 had implemented structural changes that successfully terminated black officeholding on the city council, though not entirely working-class representation. The white Chamber of Commerce pushed through a charter amendment that allowed ward representatives to serve on the city council only if each had been elected by the city at large. "Consequently, the wards retained the appearance of direct representation but not the substance." Still, it was possible for council members to receive dual endorsement, that is, to be elected both by the ward and the city at large. In elections between 1895 and 1901, voters continued to return working-class representatives who often opposed the Chamber of Commerce crowd. Thus, steps had been taken toward domination by business elites, but power eluded them. The storm provided just the sort of momentum they needed to convince the state assembly to create a governing body made up of three appointed and two elected city commissioners, all of whom were drawn from the white middle and upper classes.[20]

On the one hand, city government had passed from a more broadly representative mayor-alderman system to a more narrowly representative city commission. Efficiency and businesslike "reform" structure had won out over a more democratic public body. Evidence for this can be seen in the way city commissioners voted for segregation of city streetcars in 1906. On the other hand, as the door to public policy influence was closing to working-class men and African Americans, it was opening to middle- and upper-class white women. The hypothesis that Progressive Era municipal reform encouraged the rise to power of middling businessmen backed by their wealthier silent partners and was, therefore, basically a closed movement does not take into account the important gains made by women in politics, who earlier had been consistently underrepresented in policy making.[21] Although it would appear that the increasing influence of elite white women meant solidarity within the ranks for that class, in fact women of this social station often carried with them priorities for urban reform at odds with those of their male cohorts.

Women approached politics differently than men did. Male voters used the franchise to protect or even to privilege their interests, which were usually their businesses, their families, their class, or their race. Because men's work roles, according to Anthony Rotundo, formed the essence of their identity, they channeled their voting behavior to protect themselves and their family's economic security. They worried less about community and more about individual pursuits, including the acquisition and maintenance of power. Women, on the other hand, were not voters, and therefore had either to promote their objectives through parlor politics (lobbying directly to or using their influence on male relatives or friends who were civic leaders) or by direct action, sometimes using confrontational tactics in hopes of winning voter support. Although not opposed to the advancement of commercial interests, security, or white supremacy, upper- and upper-middle-class southern women were more interested in issues of aesthetics, health, and protection of the community at large. Women's public activism had emerged first from their homes and churches and was imbued with values that fostered nurturing of dependents (orphans, elderly women, children of factory workers) and care for the unprotected. These charitable aims were given coherency and direction through the founding of benevolent institutions and through instruction provided by the women's club movement. A more beautiful environment and better health for city dwellers were extensions of the earlier goals of protection for the indigent and represented a broadening of women's outlook toward public policy making. No longer content to look after the orphan or the widow, the city became their mission field. If the truth be known, these same women were more willing than their male counterparts for government to exert control over businessess if these establishments threatened the health of the community.[22]

In Galveston, the storm was the great catalyst for political reform. It demanded the creation of an emergency Central Relief Committee made up primarily of entrepreneurs, brought an old elite faction of capitalists openly into politics, stimulated the creation of a city commission, and mobilized white women survivors of the storm to work for the National American Red Cross and then to create a permanent organization to promote their goals for a better community. But where these women had had very little public voice before the storm, with the nearly complete disfranchisement of blacks, with the creation of a city commission government, and with the rise of their own WHPA, they began to participate in the formation of public policy. Through Progressive Era governmental structural reform, middle-class white women were able to assert their own agenda. In many ways the four groups—Central Relief Committee, Deep Water Committee, the city commissioners, and the WHPA—were sympathetic to one another. Direct and informal connections between the male members of the Deep Water Committee, the emergency Central Relief Committee, and the city commission abounded. And the male leaders all had links to the women reformers. Four of the women appointed through the Red Cross to the relief committee of the emergency Central Relief Committee became officers of the WHPA. One-third of the wives of Deep Water Committee members became officers in the WHPA. Three of the five wives and one daughter-in-law of the first city commissioners joined the WHPA.[23] Connections of this kind were important for white women. They lacked voting power, but they held a position superior to blacks in the racial hierarchy. Replacing black male political strength with white female political influence created a potent coalition for white men, but it also opened the door to white female political activism.

For women, the September storm created the very worst kind of social disorder, especially with respect to burial of the dead, loss of vegetation, destruction of family homes, and unsanitary health conditions. Within a month after the storm, city officials had brought in from New York City sanitation expert Dr. George Soper, who advised them to continue with the cremation of bodies and the disposal of debris. But he also pointed to the need to "put [the city] in a very clean condition. The gutters and the alleys in which liquid filth has accumulated should be thoroughly cleaned out and disinfected. . . . Streets should be cleaned by sweeping and carrying away the matter collected, . . . the privies and stables should be

looked after and . . . the sewers should be investigated to see that they are in working condition." The danger to the citizens' health was "not from the dead but
from those living in crowded conditions." Soper advised the city council to add
more men to the city health department, which then numbered but twenty. The
council responded by asking the acting city engineer to provide manpower for
cleanup and by putting Dr. Soper and Dr. C. H. Wilkinson, city health officer,
in charge of "the entire sanitary work, both on the streets and private property."
The city health department provided disinfectant depots with cleaning solvents for
domestic purposes. Systematic removal of trash and debris from barrels or boxes
put out on the sidewalk or in the alley was implemented by cart garbage collectors.
If citizens did not dispose of their trash properly, inspectors cited them and threatened legal action. Those cases that went to court usually ended with the accused
removing the nuisance or paying a fine, but judges would not accept the excuse
that the defendant was too busy making a living. The message to women was clear:
if men were out working for the family, then "the good housewife [should gather]
up the refuse for collection by the health wagons," and women should take advantage of the availability of free cleaning disinfectants. In other words, cleaning
and clearing out trash *began* with the housewife and extended into the community.
The other message, forcefully applied, concerned the possibility of house by house
inspection and enforcement of health codes by city officials. Women activists
would rely on that model for future action against community health violators.[24]

The Women's Health Protective Association—The First Phase

The message that women were intimately connected with the sanitary condition,
indeed the health, of the city was not lost on women leaders. Consequently, on
March 5, 1901, six months before the establishment of city commission government, sixty-six women survivors, veteran organizers from the women's church and
synagogue societies, benevolent institutions, literary clubs, patriotic associations,
and the Red Cross, gathered to establish the Women's Health Protective Association (WHPA). The first officers represented the accumulation of years of women's
voluntary service and old-guard elitism. Among them, Magnolia Sealy, wife of the
city's prominent banker George Sealy; Lucy Ballinger Mills, daughter of Judge
William Pitt Ballinger and Hallie Ballinger, founder of the Galveston Orphans'
Home; and Isabella Kopperl, philanthropist in her own right and niece to the
founder of Temple B'nai Israel, composed the first executive committee. Elitism
may have launched the club, but after fifteen years of reform work, the association
evolved into a powerful 500-member investigative, inspection, and lobbying group
for a cleaner, healthier, more beautiful city. The name itself indicates the supreme
importance sanitation had taken in the wake of the hurricane, but it was not
original to the island women. As early as 1884, women of New York had created
the Ladies Health Protective Association to address the problems of slaughter-
houses and garbage scows. In 1893, a Woman's Health Protective Association in
Philadelphia set out to study the problems of public health and startled city voters
into adopting an improved water filtration system. A national organization of
Health Protective Associations emerged with forty clubs represented.[25]

In the formation of the WHPA Galveston women were greatly influenced by a former resident, Anna Maxwell Jones, who lived in New York, belonged to many women's clubs including Sorosis, and imbibed the progressive ideas of the Northeast. Anna and her sister returned to Galveston annually, and she, more than any other outside force, was responsible for advising the women on the creation of a citywide civic organization. Waldine Kopperl explained the connection in a letter to Margaret Sealy Burton, president of the successor organization to the WHPA: "I think Anna [Maxwell Jones] can justly be called the Inspirer and Founder of the Health Protective Association, for its spirit, its aims were hers. I remember so well the occasion the idea was born. It was . . . February 1901. Mrs. Isabella Kopperl had the first big 'Come get together' Friendship party after the Storm. Every one in Galveston was there. I was pouring tea. . . . When Anna got up everyone clapped." Referring to the work of the women who had served in the Red Cross ward relief stations, she said . . .

> 'You brave people of Galveston have buried the dead, clothed the naked and fed the hungry. Now you must not stop at that. You must safe guard the Beach of the City, plant trees and flowers, and make it again the City Beautiful.' We all caught fire from Anna's inspired talk, and I think each woman silently consecrated herself for further service for Galveston. *She* was the real Founder for we took fire from her idea. We all had worked so hard and were oh, so fatigued and stunned with the tragedy of it all, and we needed just that heart counsel that Anna so well knew how to give.[26]

Thus, Galveston women who were eager to bring their talents to bear and who had performed semiprivate acts of charity through the women's societies of their churches and synagogues and through serving on the boards of lady managers of benevolent institutions learned from Anna Maxwell Jones the concept of a national network of women's civic clubs. From Clara Barton they learned the efficacy of women's involvement in public work and the value of cooperation with or, if necessary, direct confrontation toward male leaders when the cause was just. Drawing upon this knowledge, they finally mobilized for action. The women declared that "the time had come when the Galveston women rich and poor, club women and non-club women, must work hand in hand and heart to heart to make Galveston a beautiful town and a law abiding place, and the only way to do this is to have the cooperation of every woman in the city."[27]

This call for a democratic organization for women was significant. Unlike the boards of lady managers of the benevolent institutions, which had been exclusive and self-perpetuating, the WHPA was open to all adult white women in the community, and members elected their own officers—ten executive officers and as many as seventeen committee chairwomen, not to mention the scores of women who chaired and served on ad hoc committees. The association combined the elements of elitism in its officer corps with an open democratic body. It appeared elite, however, because most of its elected executive officers were from the wealthier classes. Still, in the midst of crisis, the first democratic, citywide women's association had been created. It heralded the formation of a progressive women's community in Galveston.

One of the WHPA's first acts was a political one. Galvanized by the storm and determined "to inspire the women of Galveston to a realization of their municipal obligations," the members decided to support the bill to create a city commission government in Galveston. A subcommittee headed by Mary Landes, whose husband, Henry A. Landes, in 1905 would become mayor/commissioner, drew up a resolution asking "that the City Commission Government be formed." After "hundreds of women" had signed the resolution, it was sent to the state assembly in Austin. As the election approached for city commissioners, the WHPA made it clear in a public ceremony that they expected the men "to vote . . . for those men who will help to rehabilitate and restore the town to a place not hitherto attained." Next the WHPA decided its own mission and constitution in terms far different from any previous women's group; the language bristled with political objectives. The WHPA's purpose was:

> to promote the health of the people of Galveston and the cleanliness of the city by taking such action from time to time as may secure the enforcement of the existing sanitary laws and regulations by calling the attention of the proper authorities to any violation thereof, and to procure the amendment of such laws and regulations when they shall be found inefficient for the prevention of acts injurious to the public health or the cleanliness of the city; and to promote the beauty of the city of Galveston by encouraging the planting of trees, shrubbery, flowers and otherwise.[28]

While the storm of 1900 was the immediate catalyst that prompted the formation of the WHPA, there remain questions about the origins of the reformers and the influence of the pre-1900 women's congregational societies and benevolent institutions. Who were these women officers? Where did they receive their "training"? What role did religion, women's congregational societies, and benevolence play in the creation of this progressive women's club? Officers of the WHPA constituted an elite corps of Galveston women who had been active in public affairs long before 1901. Examination of the organizational histories of sixty officers of the WHPA between 1901 and 1911 show that the majority, 55 percent, were involved in a church or synagogue women's society; 42 percent belonged to Episcopal and Presbyterian women's societies—the very societies that had first directed their ministries to the city's poor. Also, 55 percent of the WHPA officers had once served on a board of lady managers for one or more of the four benevolent institutions founded and maintained by women in the 1880s and 1890s (Galveston Orphans' Home, Letitia Rosenberg Women's Home, Home for Homeless Children, and the Johanna Runge Free Kindergarten). More important, 89 percent, or twenty-five of the twenty-eight WHPA *executive* officers (president, vice president, secretary, treasurer, auditor, executive committee member) had served on boards of benevolent institutions. Of the congregation-affiliated WHPA executive officers, 100 percent had served on boards of lady managers for benevolent institutions, indication of the important link between church and synagogue, benevolence, and civic-reform leadership. Although the officers were elected, it is clear that women who had been active in leadership positions in the 1890s before the advent of the women's community continued to be sought for leadership in the city's first progressive reform association.

To understand the importance of church and synagogue affiliation to women in this southern city, we need to examine congregational rolls. Out of the sixty WHPA officers (twenty-eight held executive positions and thirty-two held committee chairs), only fourteen, or 23 percent, could not be identified by religious affiliation. The remaining forty-six officers, or 77 percent, belonged to eight religious groups: Baptist, Catholic, Episcopal, Jewish, Lutheran, Methodist, Presbyterian, and Swedenborgian. If the WHPA officers of unknown religious affiliation are removed, the number of officers who belonged to women's congregational societies reaches 72 percent, 54 percent of whom were affiliated with the Episcopal and Presbyterian churches. Again, it would appear that the combination of elite social status and membership in churches that emphasized relief for the poor outside of church membership provided training and incentives for Progressive-Era reformers.

The most striking evidence of the influence of the two community-oriented women's church societies (Trinity Church Guild and the Ladies' Aid Society of the First Presbyterian Church) and the four benevolent institutions can be seen in the histories of the first four presidents of the WHPA in the years between 1901 and 1911: Mary Elizabeth Landes (1901–1903), wife of the mayor of Galveston; Emily Clark (1904–1905), wife of a successful steamship agent; Albertine Adoue (1906–1908), whose husband owned extensive banking and industrial interersts; Jean Scrimgeour Morgan (1908–1912, 1914–1915), whose prominence in city life stemmed from her own and her family's civic benevolence. Clark, Adoue, and Morgan belonged to Trinity Church Guild; Adoue served as president of the Guild from 1875 to 1883, Clark became president in 1918, and Morgan belonged to both Trinity and Grace Episcopal sisterhoods, serving as president of Grace Episcopal's sisterhood in 1901. Landes had been a member of the Ladies' Aid Society of the First Presbyterian Church in the 1890s. All four of the WHPA presidents had been officers on one or more of the boards of lady managers for the benevolent institutions. In addition, all had extensive experience in women's clubs and patriotic societies. And two became active in the city's woman suffrage association.[29]

A continuum existed between the women's church societies that provided poor relief, women's benevolent institutions, and women's reform and suffrage organizations of the Progressive Era. Women who had been active in these societies were also more likely to belong to one of the city's secular women's clubs formed in the 1890s. Unusual for a southern city was the fact that evangelical women's missionary societies and the WCTU played virtually no role in the creation of a coterie of progressive female reformers in Galveston.[30] Wealth, of course, constituted a significant factor in determining which women had leisure to perform civic duties, and most evangelical women were not of the elite. But single professional women — teachers, librarians, lawyers, doctors, and real estate agents — also joined the progressive reformers. Generally, these women belonged to religious organizations that encouraged acts of charity beyond the church or synagogue doors. In the South, especially, the links between women, religion, and

reform were very close, but the notion that southern evangelical groups were usually responsible for their reforming impulses is challenged by this Galveston case
study.

This brings us to a discussion of class and religious belief. Was class more
important than religion in determining who would lead in women's progressive
activism? There is no way to know for certain. But we must ask why it was that
so many activist women came from specific congregations? What were the influences of those religious bodies? Among Christian women, what was it about the
Episcopal and Presbyterian churches that fostered an environment where women
felt free to pursue benevolence and civic reform? Perhaps it centers on the fact
that these congregations gave more latitude to women to work independently, and
that these denominations, as was true with Judaism, were theologically more concerned about the plight of people on earth than about salvation. More evangelistic
churches—Baptist and Methodist—placed emphasis on conversion and personal
salvation and less on the material well-being of the poor. Southern Baptists were,
and still are, more restrictive of women's freedom than most mainline Protestant
denominations. Methodists emerged after 1900 as a denomination conscious of its
mission toward social Christianity, but from 1880 to 1900, few Methodist women
volunteered for community benevolence in Galveston. By the same token, class
constitutes a factor. Lower- and lower-middle-class families, those least likely to
become engaged in civic affairs, were drawn to Baptist, Christian (Disciples of
Christ), and Methodist churches because education and cultural refinement were
not requirements for acceptance to the fellowship of those congregations. Nor were
a great many charitable gifts expected of them. Snobbery is difficult to document,
but it is also likely that elite women preferred the company of their own kind and
perhaps shut out some of the Baptist and Methodist women with the exception of
a very few prominent Baptists such as Betty Ballinger and Mary Scrimgeour, whose
sister-in-law was Jean Scrimgeour Morgan.

One of the least well understood motives for civic activism comes from an
individual's spirituality. Only on rare occasions do we find evidence of a woman's
faith as the basis for her civic reform activism. This may not be because the
occurrence is rare but rather because journals, diaries, letters, or public statements
seldom exist to reveal religious sentiment. Although no women's diaries from this
period in Galveston have been recovered, nonetheless, the papers of Jean Scrimgeour Morgan suggest that her civic activism was motivated by a deep spirituality.
As Trinity Episcopal's foremost progressive activist, for years she had led the way
toward civic involvement. Accepted among the wealthiest class of Galvestonians
as a peer, she and her husband, however, lived modestly on his earnings as a
manager and securities broker. In addition to serving as president of the WHPA,
she also began selling Red Cross Christmas Seals for the Texas Anti-Tuberculosis
Association. She worked through the war years for the Red Cross, and then, under
their auspices, founded in 1919 the Galveston Public Health Nursing Service,
which sent nurses to the poor and sick. She continued her affiliation with all of
these organizations and also became a member of the board of directors for the
YWCA.[31] Probably no one better represented Trinity Episcopal Church in civic

FIGURE 7.2. Jean Scrimgeour Morgan, president of the Women's Health Protective Association. Courtesy Rosenberg Library, Galveston, Texas.

affairs. In a report submitted to the Church Service League of her parish she tells us something about Christian beliefs as a motivation for social justice. "The responsibility rests upon us to give as much at least to the community as we receive from it. If we are using up more than we give we are parasites, and parasite and Christian are contradictory terms." Later still, she opined, "Christian Social Service is the Church at work; it is Christ in action through us."[32]

The spiritual call to community service was echoed by parish priests and church officials, who supported women's work in the city and who by 1921 had created the Church Service League, the Episcopal answer to a United Charities.

No other denomination on the island evidenced the same deliberate attention to servanthood. At work here was an Episcopal theology that affirmed serving humanity in its many areas outside the church and in its variety of needs. The result, Jean Morgan noted, was "Nearly every organization for good work among the poor, and others, is made up largely of members of Trinity Church, or those who are Episcopalian."[33]

The rise of organized groups of women pursuing cultural and civic activities is a common theme in historical literature. Perhaps less well known is how each local women's club came to choose its particular agenda of activity. Ideas and issues were available to clubwomen in southwestern cities through national and state women's club periodicals: those found to be in circulation among Texas women included *Club Woman*, *Texas Club Woman*, and *Club Woman's Argosy*, all of which published proceedings and provided guidelines for the WHPA. At first WHPA members appointed committees to survey a wide variety of community problems—the sanitary condition of stables, streetcars, markets (corner groceries and fruit stands), streets and alleys, cemeteries, dairies, fountains, esplanades, public parks and monuments, and beaches. They assigned committees to investigate school hygiene, jails, and the presence of a police matron. And for practical reasons they created ways and means, advertising, and special committees. As part of the structure of their bylaws, they printed the codes and city ordinances for each problem area. Whereas city council had passed a law against spitting in public conveyances (with a fine of up to $10), there was no ordinance regulating public school houses, jails, cemeteries, connections to sewerage mains, or the inspection of milk sold in the city.[34] When the WHPA chose its agenda for the first year, the areas of concern overlapped with official categories of city government. City councilmen were supposed to be overseeing these areas of municipal order listed by the WHPA, but their hands-off attitude toward regulation left them open to scrutiny from concerned citizens. "Municipal housekeeping" in the Progressive Era has been long been seen as a hallmark of women's activism, and often the rising concern of women for the city's hygiene and sanitation was portrayed as an extension of their domestic roles and their nurturing values. But since elected male officials were already in charge of this aspect of "public" life, we must wonder, when did women begin to see this as part of their realm? Answers to these questions are elusive, but several arguments suggest themselves: an extension of the concept of citizenship that included women; the rising concern over municipal problems stemming from expert analysis of city sanitation and muckraking journalists' horror stories, and the conservatism of elected officials who felt little compulsion to move toward stricter regulation.

All along, elite benevolent women and activists had established municipal institutions for the care of children and the elderly parallel to the official city departments of police, fire, water, streets, and public health. Before 1900, the public domain of women and of men were separate, and women's activism was not overtly political, although it did uphold race segregation. After the storm and with the founding of the WHPA, white women began to fix their attention on areas that had traditionally been under the supervision of men. On the one hand, women called this municipal housekeeping as if it were the special domain of women, but on the other, it had always been men's work, political men's work at that. Women activists wanted to take over these so-called housekeeping functions from men, whom they feared cared little enough for it to institute better regulations. By labeling it an extension of the housewife's role, they justified what was basically a power play, disguising it in the rhetoric of the women's sphere. The women did not have official power, but they had the power of righteous indignation, muckraking publicity, and extended notions of citizenship on their side. Without the vote, they had the right of petition and the right of public assembly, which, if accompanied by public support, could serve to grant them a measure of moral authority and, certainly, political leverage. Since the concerns of the WHPA and the creation of committees to "inspect" areas under the purview of city aldermen went into effect before the creation of city commission government, which the WHPA endorsed, we must wonder if the WHPA's reporting on the condition of streets, alleys, markets, stables, and other public areas had an influence on public opinion toward reform of city government? There seems to be no direct evidence, but the timing was appropriate for their influence to be felt. Once city commission was in place, the WHPA, while never relinquishing its pursuit of public health, concentrated on more pressing needs of the community, namely reburials and revegetating the island. Clearly there were avenues to pursue in strengthening local sanitation codes and their enforcement, but much of that kind of lobbying would have to wait until the more pressing concerns were resolved.

Despite the diversity of issues, the women chose first to concentrate on the reinterment of storm victims. The storm had provided a unique opportunity for the WHPA, on its own, to affect public policy and to extend influence over community rebuilding. Within the first year, members of the WHPA transported the remains of storm victims to a cemetery on the west end of the island. These bodies had been buried by relatives, often by stealth, before the work crews had found a chance to commit them to the flames. The appalling lack of decorum in the consignment of fellow citizens to their eternal resting places weighed on the consciences of WHPA members, many of whom, following southern tradition, had previously cared for the graves of their relatives. Because shock, grief, and death on such a massive scale nearly overwhelmed the community after the hurricane, citizens held few proper funeral services. Hence, the women of the WHPA conducted a memorial service one year after the tragic event. They chose to hold the ceremony atop the rubble of the Lucas Terrace apartments at the foot of Broadway Boulevard, where twenty-three had survived but fifty-three had perished. Flowers from all over the state, sent by relatives and friends of storm victims, decorated the rough scaffolding that provided a platform for speakers. Seven thousand mourners found places beside the demolished terrace and along the boulevard. Speeches — elegant, sad, quaint, and hopeful — followed from leading citizens who eulogized the 6,000 dead and complimented "these noble women [who] joined themselves together under the name of the Women's Health Protective Association." To rebuild the city was the underlying theme: "Few were here who did not for the moment despair. But out of the darkness of desolation and death the glorious sunshine of hope arises, and we have basked in its rays today.... We should build stronger and on higher ground. Elevate the Gulf front of the city, and construct a breakwater similar to our jetties." Following the ceremony, citizens symbolically began the rebuilding process. In keeping with the goals of the WHPA, the city's children, hope of the future, scampered off to the sand hills to plant salt cedars and oleanders.[35]

After the Central Relief Committee closed its operations, the WHPA continued to care for the removal of the dead from makeshift graves. Rather than contact city government, citizens who owned property on which bodies were interred as well as relatives of hastily buried storm victims petitioned the WHPA to help in removing the remains to a proper cemetery. When the grisly work was finished, the women voted "to take charge of the little cemetery of the unknown dead" and donated a memorial headstone to mark the common grave. As late as 1908, skeletons turned up in odd places, and the WHPA conducted the burial. Funding for this task was aided in part by the New York State Federation of Women's Clubs, which, through the urging of Anna Maxwell Jones, sent $1,000 to the Galveston association. The WHPA also applied for funds to Governor Joseph Sayers, who responded with over $1,148 for the work of "reinterment of storm victims not properly buried."[36]

Public health was a consideration, but decent burial and reverent memorialization were equally important. More often than we realize today, women were responsible for maintaining the traditions that accompany death. Not surprisingly, the WHPA, following female burial traditions, chose to continue the work of removing the dead to their final resting place long after the Central Relief Committee had disbanded. Although in most instances women in the Progressive Era sought to politicize their domestic concerns and make government more effective, in this case, women sought to reclaim from men the sensitive tasks related to death and burial. Thus Galveston women influenced public policy by removing from the all-male Central Relief Committee and city council work that they believed women were better suited to perform.[37]

In contrast to the desire to take from public control the tasks of burial and memorialization, the WHPA's campaign to create a more beautiful Galveston through replanting the island illustrates well the desire by the WHPA to give public forum to domestic tasks. Their work followed closely behind the immense structural changes made on the island by city and county governments. As soon as Mayor Jones and the councilmen passed the mantle of authority to city commissioners in late September 1901, the commission met to discuss how to protect the city from future storms. Through complicated bond and tax maneuvers involving the county, the state, and the U.S. Army, the commissioners were able to erect a seventeen-foot-high solid cement seawall for four miles along the coast. When this was completed in 1904, the island needed to be elevated to meet the wall, gradually sloping one foot for every 1,500 feet to the bay. To raise the grade of the island engineers lifted some 2,000 buildings—homes, churches, schools, businesses—on jacks and then pumped sixteen million cubic yards of sand from the bay under the structures. The grade raising was completed by 1911, but, as a result of both the storm and the fill, little survived in the way of plants. As Herbert Mason wrote: "Almost every sign of vegetation south of Broadway had been stripped away, and until the long and expensive business of relandscaping with trees, shrubs, and flower gardens was over, the once-lush city reminded onlookers of certain desert communities in the American West."[38]

There was obviously work for the WHPA to do in beautifying the city with new plant life, and they accomplished this with few funds from city hall. Fortunately, just as the women were about to embark on their plans for a complete replanting of the island, national trends for city beautification were beginning to excite urban reformers. The "City Beautiful" movement stemmed from the Columbian Exposition at the Chicago World's Fair in 1893. There, gleaming neoclassical buildings rose above a blue lagoon, and rich green lawns, statues, and marble bridges graced the landscape, suggesting to the American public that cities did not have to be simply utilitarian, grubby, unplanned, and unadorned. This new vision of urban beauty passed from the exhibition to municipal art societies and local improvement societies. Springfield, Ohio, in 1899 launched the first of many local improvement societies; a year later, the National League of Improvement Associations was formed to direct reformers toward the emerging ideals of beautification and sanitation. In addition to the efforts of many smaller communities, Washington, D.C., in 1901 launched an enormous urban beautification project that resulted in the now-familiar mall with its park and reflecting pool connecting the three architectural focal points—the Capitol, the White House, and the Washington Monument.[39]

How much WHPA members knew of these projects is difficult to determine, but in 1901 they did join the National League of Improvement Associations, thus indicating that their plans for a more beautiful city would be within the context of national City Beautiful campaigns. They set to work planting new growth as soon as they were granted access to newly filled land. "Once the filling was begun, the W.H.P.A. kept right behind the grade-leveling machine. When a section was turned over to the city, the WHPA turned its attention to beautifying the same." They began their operations by attending to the parks in the vicinity of the Strand, where commercial traffic was highest: the little square behind the Central Market House on Twentieth Street, the Isabella Kopperl Park in front of the Union Pacific building, Sidney Sherman Park in the East End, and Central Park at Winnie and Twentieth streets. As the grade raising commenced, they returned with oleanders, palms, and oak trees to the east end of the island and concentrated on tree plantings, especially palms, on Broadway and down the esplanade of Rosenberg Avenue. Gradually, they extended their work along the seawall, established a city garden and a garden for school children, inspired mothers' clubs throughout the city to begin tree and flower plantings on school grounds, and recruited benevolent institutions, churches, and the John Sealy Hospital to do their own landscaping with plants provided by the WHPA. In the first three years they spent $2,439. With this energy and investment, the News regarded the work of "woman" in "civic life" as full of "stability and permanence . . . a power for good in any community," apt words to describe the emergence of Galveston women into the Progressive Era.[40]

In order to accomplish their tasks efficiently, the women consulted agricultural experts to determine the best plants for the soil and climate; they operated their own nursery on land donated by J. C. League at Avenues M 1/2 and N, hired a gardener to tend the seedlings, and convinced the Gulf, Colorado, and Santa Fe railroad to transport without charge thousands of palms from Florida and Cal-

FIGURE 7.3. The Galveston Seawall in 1904. Courtesy Rosenberg
Library, Galveston, Texas.

ifornia. The WHPA became a clearinghouse for the free distribution of seeds and
for the sale of plants at cost to citizens, many of whom bought rose bushes for 10
cents apiece. Then they promoted the use of these plants by holding garden contests (first prize $75, $300 total). An award ceremony held at the YMCA and
attended by the officers of the WHPA, city commissions, and representatives of
the Business League had the effect of elevating the ordinary task of gardening to
civic improvement. Nine gardeners won cash prizes, and ten, including two African American residents, received commendation for their gardens. "The effect
of this was that people who had never kept a garden before were stimulated to see
what they could do. All of these did not receive prizes, but they had their reward
in learning that the beach sand is fertile. Like a miracle, the sand fresh from the
bottom of a salt water body, grew plants and flowers in abundance." The papers
reported that the fertility of the grade-raising fill was one of the great lessons
learned by the WHPA garden contests. Palm, oleander, and live oak plantings
commenced on the esplanades of Broadway Boulevard and Rosenberg Avenue
almost as soon as the curbing was in place. Schools organized auxiliaries, mothers'
clubs helped distribute the plants, and local businesses gave cuttings to every
school child on Arbor Day in December. The women raised money for seeds,

trees, and shrubs through rose bush sales (ordering 10,000 at a time), private sub-scriptions, sale of plants year round from their nursery, and benefits such as horse shows.[41]

The WHPA met monthly, and reporters gave them write-ups in the local newspapers, so the organization received plenty of publicity. But nothing could match the public exposure that came their way as a result of the horse shows, which were really more like county fairs. This large an appropriation of public space and time by women on the island had never before been tried. Not even tag day, with its ubiquitous feminine solicitors along the Strand, could compare to the enormity of the horse show project. The *News* crackled with the announce-ment: "The first annual Horse Show to be given by the WHPA will be held today at Sportsman's Park. The gates will be open at 9:30 A.M." The day, November 10, 1906, described as perfect, began with events scheduled every half hour until 5:30 P.M. with a two-hour break for luncheon (prepared and served by the women). The show featured such favorite categories as best coach team, best saddle horse for ladies or gentlemen, best high jumper, best driving team, best saddle pony for boys or for girls. A brass band played on for the crowds, and booths, decorated in yellow and white bunting, palm fronds, and flags, provided displays of fruit (lemons fourteen inches in diameter grown by islanders), vegetables (eggplants sixteen inches in diameter), potted plants, and flowers, especially chrysanthemums, the horse show flower. Box holders to the event read like a list of Galveston's *Who's Who*; the reservations were all made by women. Jean Morgan, chair of the adver-tising committee, opined, "This Horse Show is given for a cause, civic improve-ment, and accordingly is a popular event for the city; an inclusive feature, rather than exclusive. Some will aid the cause as box-holders; others of the same social position will don the kitchen apron and prepare the oyster luncheon." Fourteen committees comprising more than 100 people from the association and the com-munity worked to bring off the event. Children entered their ponies and worked at the lemonade stand, and businesses cooperated with donations. Segregation policies, a reminder that whites controlled the resources on the island, dictated that "a portion of the grandstand [be] reserved for colored people."[42]

Monetarily, the shows were a success; the first in 1906 netted $1,001; the next three brought about $2,000 each. Subsequent horse shows added more events and concessions: popcorn, ice cream, peanuts, cake, cider and lemonade, frankfurters, candy, a doll rack, a wonder well and recreational events—a cross country run, a barn dance, a cowboy dash, and, as a concession to modernity, an automobile parade. The shows became bigger and better, but by 1910 the WHPA lamented the demise of their best fundraiser: by then the automobile had displaced "Old Dobbin," and there were not enough horses on the island to hold the event.[43]

The success of the WHPA and the spirit of progressivism, as shown through their work, inspired others to organize: the Galveston Business League, the Com-mercial Association, the Young Men's Business Association, the Child Conserva-tion League, the Juvenile Protective Association, and such spin-offs from the WHPA as the Playground Association and the Young Women's Health Protective Association. Mothers' clubs to the various elementary and high schools (predeces-sor to the PTA) looked to the WHPA for help in planting and landscaping their grounds; in exchange, the mothers' clubs channeled saplings and seeds to children in celebration of Arbor Day and in school beautification. Mothers' clubs looked for other ways to improve the schools, acquiring paintings to adorn the walls cracked by the grade raising, earning money to build better playgrounds and parks for the children, and insisting with the help of the WHPA on hot lunch programs for the children. So much was being done by mothers' clubs that for a time the WHPA decided to suspend its inspection of classrooms. The Business League, always interested in promoting commercial gain, nonetheless began to concern itself with "securing better lighting for the city," a concept that was echoed by the WHPA when it began to realize that the city did not have "a sufficient number of street lamps . . . for a city of 40,000 people," and darkened streets and alleys were an invitation to crime. Members of the Commercial Association, which opened its first Cotton Carnival in 1908 to attract cotton brokers, manufacturers, and businessmen to the city, joined the WHPA as associate members and collaborated in petitioning city hall for civic improvements. The Young Men's Business League promised improvements for the West End Park at Fortieth and Avenue G, the second largest park in the city and playground to many of the city's factory children, but by 1913 they had not done anything. Women, it seems, were better able to accomplish these tasks. Still, a kind of progressive clubdom emerged that engaged the energies of men and women in community building or in improving schools for children, but in sex-separate organizations. White men could become associates of the WHPA, and the women members often met with the men's leagues after their formal meetings. An atmosphere of cross-organizational cooperation unfolded among whites, as the completed grade raising left citizens with ever more community projects.[44]

Thus in the first ten years of its existence, the WHPA enjoyed remarkable success in making known to Galveston the national trends toward city beautification, in encouraging numerous progressive clubs to spring up, and in garnering the cooperation of city commissioners. The city's governing body was quite happy for this volunteer organization of women to do the work and pay the expenses of planting, groundskeeping, and watering for the city. And city fathers allowed the WHPA freedom to plan, design, and plant whatever they deemed appropriate on city property.[45]

For a time, there appeared to be splendid cooperation between the WHPA and the city commission. Even when the members began to urge city government to take over tasks of watering and maintenance, the harmony continued. But the relationship between the city commission and the WHPA over planting city-owned property may seem curious to us today because, in effect, private citizens sought to give to the city improvements on publicly owned land. The fact that city government had no provision for the planting of city parks or esplanades meant that if the city was going to become beautiful it would be done either through changes in the city ordinances, possible tax collection, and salaried maintenance workers or through the efforts of private citizens or volunteer groups. The WHPA and its "helping organizations" took on this project instead of trying to insist on changes in local government. Naturally, the commisssioners accepted the offer, perhaps thinking that the organization would continue to maintain the plantings. The

WHPA, however, reasoned that, by example and design, the WHPA could convince city fathers and the rest of Galveston of the importance of planning, planting, and beautifying. Once WHPA members had spent several years in landscaping city boulevards, parks, and esplanades, however, they asked the city commission for a quid pro quo in the form of support. They wanted the commissioners to pay the gardener $75 a month and provide water for the nursery without charge, and they wanted the city to finance a watering system that included water taps every two blocks and to maintain the plantings. The commissioners hardly extended themselves: they agreed to rent the land on which the nursery stood for the cost of the taxes to the WHPA, and they agreed to purchase a water cart and employ a man and horse to see that the trees were watered by day. Because the city commisssion had not originally taken charge of landscaping city-owned property, the women presented them with a plan and then a fait accompli. Ultimately, the city would have to assume responsibility for maintaining the shrubs and trees. This agreement of private service given by the women in return for public control over the result of their efforts was to continue throughout the Progressive Era. By turning over the function of public property maintenance to city government, the WHPA would ultimately diminish its own control over beautifying public spaces. Nonetheless, the women knew they had exerted an important impact on public policy. They had envisioned a city beautiful, won support for its implementation, acted on their goals, and then brought city government into their scheme.[46]

In this case, cooperation between the women and the commissioners existed for several reasons. First, although beautification was a domestic issue and an attempt by women to make their city more homelike, it was also good for business. It boosted town pride, drew attention away from the scars of the 1900 disaster, and indicated resilience among the citizenry that invited investments in the rebuilt community. It was exactly what the town boosters had wanted when they launched their Greater Galveston campaign during the early years of physical reconstruction. The *Christian Science Monitor* editorialized:

> We find the women of Galveston, like advocates of beauty in other communities, laying much weight upon the contention that it pays a city to be beautiful. They are obtaining a hearing on this basis that otherwise might be denied them. By presenting beauty in the light of an investment that will pay a good rate of interest and pay it regularly—by holding it forth as an attainable and permanent asset—they are able to command the serious attention of many men of affairs to whom beauty in architecture, in street and square planning, in shaded walks and roadways, in watercourses, lawns and flower-beds does not appeal for its own sake.[47]

The second reason that WHPA members were successful in their dealings with city commission was that, unlike labor or immigrant groups, the WHPA officers and the commissioners were social equals, and parlor politics played no small role in winning cooperation from city commission for the women's vision of a beautiful environment. For example, the WHPA elected Mary Landes its first president; her husband, Henry A. Landes, served as mayor over the city commission in 1905 after the death of the governor's appointee, William T. Austin. The Landeses, like so many of their class, were related to the business elite: her brother and sister both married into families belonging to the Deep Water Committee. It is hard to know exactly what went on between elected city officials and WHPA officers outside of their official roles. But the gossip columns of the daily newspapers were filled with the reports of their social meetings. Because they were often family friends, city commissioners were accessible to and compatible with WHPA officers. Structural reform of city government had created an opening for white women civic activists that had not existed under the prestorm mayor and aldermanic system.

The third reason why cooperation existed between the two groups is related to the nature of the women's organization itself. Officers of the WHPA were elected by constituent members, and, for the first time in organizational life, white women from all classes, denominations, and economic stations were able to cast votes for their organizational officers. In a sense, the WHPA officers paralleled male elected officials; they were the city's highest elected women officials. Male voters elected their representatives to the city commission; women elected theirs to the WHPA. True, the WHPA was an extralegal body and able merely to influence public policy through activity, demonstration, and petition, but for the first time white women came together in a single body to act democratically and collectively upon their goals. Soon many of the women officers would be active in the suffrage movement. Male elected officials ignored or irritated this body only at their political peril.

Finally, cooperation lasted for ten years between the women and city hall because the WHPA had won enthusiastic support from progressive groups within the community. It had managed to generate an enormous amount of publicity through the years, enlisting progressives, and more important, voting support for its cause of beautification. But once the WHPA had nearly completed its work on land owned by the city, it looked at the rest of Galveston and saw the need to mobilize its citizens: to maintain respectable-looking, well-landscaped private premises, to sod their front yards, to plant shade trees along the street, and build sidewalks and curbing in front of their homes. Here the women ran into enormous problems. Apathy was one of their worst obstacles, and the fact that the city laid down streets but did not construct sidewalks and curbing led to a lack of uniformity or, worse, a lack of improvement whatsoever. Complaints began to be expressed in the WHPA meetings, and president Jean Morgan suggested that "the members interest themselves in the sidewalks in their neighborhoods . . . personal solicitation to be made in cases where property owners have been neglectful." The Galveston Commercial Association suggested that "perhaps the city would contribute the services of a police officer to act as sidewalk inspector." But the problem of homeowners refusing to put in a sidewalk in front of their property persisted. Next, the *Galveston News* came out with sensible articles on the cost of constructing a modest sidewalk with wooden curbing. "With mudshell sidewalk costing $10 and curbing costing $7.75, the entire work would not amount to more than $17.75." For a cement sidewalk, curbing, and gutter the cost was about $21.50, but the *News* suggested, "The combination curb and gutter is a good argument in favor of uniformity in the agitation of 'city beautiful.' " For many residents, the cost of constructing a sidewalk constituted a financial burden. Small wonder that citizens dragged their feet in improving their properties and lack of uniformity prevailed. The WHPA sought answers to the difficult problem of motivating private citizens. Rather than insist on a property tax to pay for city construction and maintenance of sidewalks, curbing, and gutters, the women embarked on a house to house campaign to enlist citizen cooperation. The Galveston Commercial Association rendered its approval by admitting that "nothing adds to the attractiveness of a city more than uniform, well-kept and improved sidewalks. This work also adds greatly to the value of property. . . . Each and every one who is interested in the welfare of our city should do his part."[48]

The problem was, however, that for some time the WHPA membership had been declining. Ten years of work had taken its toll on the numbers of volunteers, and it was going to prove difficult to take on the entire citizenry without more help. Thus, it was suggested that a membership campaign accompany the movement toward replacing citizen apathy with enthusiasm. Members present at the October meeting were to bring at least five new women to the November meeting with membership dues (ten cents a month) in hand. WHPA officers noted that the association had "embarked on a membership campaign . . . not only as a means of providing funds with which to continue the association's work, but to reach, if possible, every woman in Galveston." Unfortunately, this did not include African American women or women not "of good moral character," although it did mean that these residents should still install a sidewalk and curbing. By the end of the year, several hundred new members had been added to the rolls, giving the movement a certain momentum. The October 15 *News* headlines provided blaring coverage for the WHPA: "City Beautiful Movement: WHPA Launches Campaign of Interest to Every Property Holder in Galveston. Based upon Individual Effort. Committees Appointed to Interest Themselves in Practically Every Residence Block in the City." Using the city directory the women compiled a list of names and addresses of women in every block who were already willing to get their neighbors to comply with the mandate for "the planting of trees and flowers and the building of uniform sidewalks." Letters went out to prospective committee members in each block urging them to take on the task or assign someone in their place, and an updated list of representatives appeared in the pages of the *News* on November 5.[49]

Confidentiality was key to the success of the movement; if anyone could not afford trees or shrubs for the yard, the WHPA representative was to make note of that for the officers' consideration. But the businesss of enlisting citizen support was tricky: "it is no easy matter to accomplish what the ladies of the WHPA have set out to do," editors of the *News* wrote. "The plan announced . . . depends entirely upon the co-operation of the citizenship. Apathy not only can, but will, defeat the purpose. To Galveston . . . this movement is just as important as the seawall bond election, the grade-raising proposition, the causeway election, the good roads bond election." As if to pay the highest compliment, the editors intoned, "This line of endeavor opens to the women of Galveston an achievement commensurate to the accomplishment of their husbands, brothers and sons in the upbuilding of Galveston." The campaign reached a peak in December, when schoolchildren under the auspices of the mothers' clubs and the WHPA celebrated

Arbor Day. Harry A. Greene, president of the Federation of Tree-Growing Clubs of America, delivered an address to citizens in the Rosenberg Library. More than 5,000 children from twenty-one public, Catholic, and private schools "white and colored" celebrated the city's first Arbor Day on December 15 with "choruses, recitations, solos, . . . addresses by members of the WHPA and visitors" followed by principals and teachers. The next week 5,600 camphor trees arrived for distribution among the children; twenty members of the WHPA handled the organization and distribution. Achieving the cooperation of school administrators in the planting campaign was one more step in the advancement of the WHPA. As potential policy makers on more controversial issues, women needed to be seen as an established and accepted force for the good of the community. After ten years, Galvestonians had come not only to accept women's place in public policy decisions but also to depend on it.[50]

The *Galveston News* was unstinting in its praise. "With the appointment of a committee of one in practically every residence block of the city, . . . the Women's Health Protective Association . . . launched a city beautifying campaign. . . . wonderful results have already been obtained, organizations of the city, as well as children of the schools and individuals, endorsing the plan and entering actively into the work. The city beautifying movement, in short, has the undivided support of every loyal Galvestonian." In addition, the WHPA received the endorsement of the school board of trustees, the Business League, and the Commercial Association, which voted unanimously to become associate members of the WHPA.[51]

The final victory for the WHPA in its beautification campaign came in early 1912. Indications that citizens were responding to the tree and shrub planting theme came when a deluge of requests came to the WHPA. "More orders for trees are being placed than ever before in the history of the city," glowed the news report. Proudly, the women announced that nearly 8,000 sycamore, cottonwood, elm, oak, and hackberry trees, 2,500 oleanders, and 2,000 palms had been planted by the association since their work began in September 1911. Then, after the WHPA introduced a petition concerning unsightly sidewalks, city commissioners appointed a sidewalk inspector. Hailed as "one of the most important works this association has accomplished," it led ultimately to improved sidewalks. To put a club into the inspector's hands, city commission also adopted an ordinance that placed a lien against the property of individuals who took no action in installing sidewalks or improving alleys. Last, city fathers authorized more lights for Central Park and the paving of downtown alleys. These victories seem small compared to the tremendous outlay of volunteer energies expended. But there were important lessons learned by members of the WHPA in these years of intense city beautification. Had the women not been given signs of community support, city commissioners might have turned a deaf ear to the requests of the WHPA. But the commissioners realized their political futures, whether they liked it or not, were tied up with the women. So it became paramount for WHPA members to learn to work with various groups and established agencies, especially voters. WHPA members realized that persistent problems could be addressed and even solved by working on them through committees, bringing them to public attention, petitioning city hall for improvement, and lobbying for enactment of ordinances and enforcement. Power to change the city resided in the sagacious use of political strategy. Prophetically, the beautification campaign's success was summarized with an eye to the future: "Not only have the individual property owners been aroused to action, but the city and county authorities have given heed to the enforcement of laws looking to general betterment of conditions [trees, sidewalks, alleys]. Improved sanitary conditions will follow as a matter of course through the city." Without realizing it, members of the WHPA had become coworkers in the creation of public policy, politicizing their views and achieving encouraging results.[52]

The Women's Health Protective Association—The Second Phase

City beautification was not the only project adopted by the WHPA. By 1912 it had become a complex, departmentalized organization that supported reform in multiple areas of city life. WHPA members bought and placed in public places trash cans for refuse, supported a "Swat the Fly" campaign, urged citizens to use private incinerators, suggested the enactment of building codes for improved housing, demanded cleaner streets and alleys, railed against billboards, and requested the city to hire building, food, and milk inspectors, as well as police matrons. They organized inspection committees; members marched into meat markets, groceries, and bakeries to inspect the premises for sanitary conditions and then at the monthly meetings reported their findings, which were printed in the next day newspapers. They wrote letters to the Galveston Electric Company concerning the smoke nuisance at the power house on Avenue I and Twentieth Street. Worried about the spread of germs, particularly "La Grippe," they complained to the superintendent of the city railway that the ordinance regarding spitting was not being enforced. Jean Morgan, for the WHPA, sent a letter to the commissioner of police, A. P. Norman, griping that his policemen, despite repeated complaints from citizens, had ignored flagrant cases of spitting. A small sting operation was set in place when "a man of prominence who was unknown to the policeman, and in his presence, spat three times on the sidewalk to test the vigilance of the officer in this matter, resulting in no notice being taken of the offense." When citizens of the West End decried the cattle and horses let out to graze on their newly planted yards by insensitive neighbors, the WHPA wrote the commissioners about it. They lobbied for women on the school board of trustees (the city elected Eleanor Thompson in 1917) and sought hot lunches in the schools, regular medical examination of school children, better parks and playgrounds, women's restrooms in the downtown and on the beaches, and silent zones surrounding hospitals. The WHPA was responsible for establishing a Neighborhood (settlement) House in the West End and sponsored programs there for the neighborhood children. Through the WHPA, Jean Morgan began the sale of Red Cross Christmas seals for the prevention and cure of tuberculosis; sale of the seals aided in the establishment in 1913 of the Walter Colquitt Memorial Children's Hospital for Bone and Glandular Tuberculosis in Galveston and provided a modest income for the association. WHPA members invented ingenious new fundraisers to continue their work of city planting; they inaugurated bake contests, band concerts, and a profitable ($657) "Seed Day" in November 1912, during which teams of women and young ladies canvassed the commercial districts while the boy scouts "patroled" the residential neighborhoods. Finally, the WHPA agitated furiously for pure milk available to consumers at reasonable prices, and it acted on behalf of infant and child welfare through schools, visiting nurses, and well-baby clinics.[53]

The harmonious period of cooperation between city commission and the WHPA lasted until 1911, when, the grade raising completed, the women turned their full attention once again to public health and sanitation in the markets, restaurants, bakeries, and dairies. WHPA members had never entirely neglected the area of public health protection, but their concern for beautification, dictated by the grade raising, had taken first priority. Thus they entered a second phase in 1912 when they demanded *enforcement* by city authorities of the ordinances controlling sanitation in establishments that prepared food for public consumption and *enactment* of new ordinances in keeping with the advance of sanitation information and technology. This contrasted sharply with the superficial Greater Galveston promotional campaign that asked for voluntary citizen cooperation in planting trees, in clearing alleyways, and in using trash receptacles. The women were embarking on a confrontational campaign that demanded greater enforcement of the laws and punishment of fellow citizen offenders.

Reports of the monthly WHPA meetings bristled with a variety of problems needing attention. Citizens, instead of taking their concerns about sanitation directly to the city authorities, brought them to the WHPA, which became a clearinghouse for citizen complaints about garbage collection, trash in the streets, cases of ptomaine poisoning, and the like. One petitioner seeking garbage removal asked the WHPA to "stir up the health department in that direction." Petitioning Galvestonians, recognizing the former successes of the WHPA, empowered the women to act on the community's behalf. Thus, by 1914, the WHPA was in step with other women's civic clubs across the nation in its fight for improving public health.[54]

By contrast, the city of Galveston definitely lagged behind in the establishment of effective public health agencies for the enforcement of pure food and milk standards. For years the technology surrounding the purification of milk had been improving, and cities in the North were beginning to adopt advanced methods for the selling of clean, wholesome milk. The invention in 1890 by Dr. S. M. Babcock of a method for determining the amount of butterfat content in milk not only aided commercial milk purchasers in pricing milk; it also gave pure milk advocates a tool to test for unlawful skimming. In 1892, the first bacterial counts of milk in America were made for such deadly diseases as diptheria, scarlet fever, typhoid fever, and infant cholera, which caused severe diarrhea. Between 1892 and 1900, Theobald Smith had identified the germs of bovine tuberculosis in milk, and some milk industries had begun to pasteurize milk, at first in secret, as it was thought that boiling milk reduced its nutritional value. Simple procedures, such as the use of small-mouthed milking pails that kept dirt and manure out of fresh milk, advocated in 1903, helped cut down on bacteria. Then, in 1906, the thermal death point of pathogenic bacteria — temperature necessary for sterilization of milk — was discovered, and the industry had yet another study useful for the manufacture of pure milk.[55]

Following the discoveries of methods for identifying diseases in milk, twenty-seven medical milk commissions were organized in principal cities across the nation. The New York City medical milk commission, organized in 1900, determined after studying bacteria in the milk supply that contamination from healthy cows was occurring in transit due to unsanitary handling. The commission promptly called for certification of milk sold to the public. Just at the point when scientists were better able to understand the integrity of milk, the incidence of milk-related diseases rose. Typhoid epidemics caused by milk rose from a low of five per year in 1887 to a high of twenty-three in 1905. Thus, the need for better sanitation was made dramatically clear. The result: in 1907 New York City launched its own regulatory agency, the New York Milk Committee, which in the years following established infant milk depots to dispense clean, pasteurized milk. In 1908, Chicago adopted an ordinance for the pasteurization of all milk, and, in 1910, the American Public Health Association established standard methods for the bacterial testing of milk. This brought about standard testing procedures in cities across the country and the formation of a National Commission of Milk Standards. By 1912, New York City had adopted milk grading systems, enforced pasteurization, and was experimenting with the introduction of vitamins to milk.[56]

The technology for ensuring the purity of milk was already well known by the time Galveston citizens became concerned over their own milk supply. Moreover, other cities through regulatory agencies were already taking steps to enforce pure milk standards on the dairy industry. Galveston, by contrast, had no pasteurization laws, had no grading system, and lacked effective mechanisms to force local dairymen to clean up their barns and cattle. The lack of any regulatory agency meant that, aside from the health department's meager rounds, no single body was looking after the city's milk supply. Does this imply that, because Galveston and perhaps other cities in the South lacked regulatory agencies for pure food and milk, southern women had greater opportunities for public policy making? Possibly: this absence provided a fundamental opening for the members of the Women's Health Protective Association to act as if they constituted a regulatory agency. Women stepped in where no governmental body existed.

WHPA members concentrated their efforts where they knew they had severe problems locally and where they felt they could save the most lives. Their campaign for pure food and milk followed closely the battle for pure food standards in other cities. Much has already been written about the passage of pure food and drug laws at the state and national levels, but legal enactment was only the beginning; in Galveston, enforcement of the state Pure Food and Drug Act of 1907 and the Galveston ordinances of 1906 and 1907 in support of pure food claimed the attention of the WHPA from 1912 until its successful resolution in 1917.[57] The women employed political lobbying tactics in their campaign: they secured advice from sanitation experts; they drew support from men's [voting] civic groups, newspapers, and the consuming public; and they gained inspections and eventually appointments for themselves from state bureaucrats.

In 1913, anticipating resistance from the city health department, the WHPA, in concert with the Galveston Commercial Association, paid for a sanitation survey prepared by Dr. J. P. Simonds, head of preventive medicine at the University of

Texas Department of Medicine in Galveston. By then, sanitation surveys were becoming a national phenomenon, and often it was women professional "sanitary engineers" who handled the inspections. The Women's Municipal League in Boston hired a special "market inspector" and also conducted its own report; thus, Galveston was in step with national progressives. The survey claimed to be the first of its kind in Texas, and the plans " 'to make Galveston the cleanest city in Texas' [were] to be built on a scientific foundation." Dr. Simonds, with the help of a bevy of medical students, promised to investigate the city's water and milk supply, garbage collection, food handling in public establishments, conditions for the breeding of flies and mosquitoes, street cleaning, and housing problems.[58]

When the investigation was complete, a thirty-page survey concluded that Galveston, although a comparatively healthy city, indeed had sanitation problems. Fortunately, Galveston's water supply was deemed "almost ideal," one of the few bright spots in a long list of inadequacies. Because Galveston had no building code, the surveyors found some housing "deplorable" and one of the city's "crying shames." Conditions surrounding the disposal of rubbish and garbage were deemed "astounding"; the report called for more garbage collectors, more frequent pick-ups, better carts, and more citizen cooperation. The sewer system was "not up to the best standard of efficiency." The schools needed more and better playgrounds, the introduction of vaccinations and medical inspection of children, and abolishment of the common drinking cup. The surveyors found the condition of markets, bakeries, and groceries in "serious need of improvement" and suggested the appointment of extra inspectors. Alleys and streets should be cleaned up, the report said, as should stagnant pools that bred mosquitoes and manure piles that encouraged the breeding of flies.[59]

Finally, the survey gave its greatest emphasis to the problem of the city's milk supply, because milk was deemed "an essential article of food; one that is probably accountable for more sickness and more deaths than all other foods put together." The unsanitary condition of the city's dairies was to blame for the high bacteria levels found in the milk that led to infant intestinal disorders, dehydration, and even death. Thorough and to the point, the survey described appalling dairy conditions—inadequate water for washing cows, flies in the bottling room, manure falling into milk buckets, visible evidence of dirt in the bottled milk, and a primitive bottling technique in which a boy held milk bottles under a faucet of flowing milk while the overflow fell into a bucket: "When this bucket became full, this milk in which the boy had practically washed his hands was poured back into the large can, bottled and sold." The report pronounced unclean milk a contributor to tuberculosis and typhoid fever and gave statistics on the number of deaths in Galveston from these diseases. Cleaner dairies, markets, and restaurants were deemed essential to lower child mortality and improve public health. Moreover, vigilant inspection of milk that entered the city was necessary to prevent the two most common practices of milk adulteration—watering and removal of fat content, or skimming. This scientific report gave the women a tool with which to coerce commissioners to enforce existing pure milk, food, and sanitation laws and to enact tougher ones.[60]

Others began to clamor for action. Disgusted with the slowness of the city commissioners to compel downtown property owners to clean up the alleys behind their buildings, the editor of the *Galveston Daily Herald* proposed that commissioners appoint a WHPA member "with full pay" to inspect city alleys, streets, and yards. The results of the sanitary survey prompted the *Herald* to lambast the city health department and city health officer, Dr. C. W. Trueheart, in particular.

> We have no faith in the assertion of Dr. Trueheart that if convictions could be had the health department would clean up the city, for there are a dozen places in the down town districts which are daily passed by the officers of that department that are so unsanitary as to attract the attention of the buzzards and they make no arrests. . . . The trouble is that the health department is headed by an old fossil and that his assistants are relics of the stone age. . . . Appoint some woman on the police force and we will guarantee that she will see that these unsightly, these unsanitary places disappear.

Despite calls for their elevation to city office, the women had to continue lobbying for reform.[61]

Public education on the pure food and drug problem began to show up in the women's section of the newspapers. Citing examples of the outbreak of scarlet fever in Chicago due to bad milk and the death of soldiers in the Spanish-American War from adulterated canned meat, the columnist asked, "What does all this indicate?" The answer lay in legislation to obtain clean food, but "the women of the country are . . . responsible for feeding the family. It is to their door that this plea for a clean food supply should be carried and through their efforts it should be obtained. They should know the sanitary requirements of the drinking water, look into the housekeeping of the grocerymen and investigate the conditions under which foods are preserved and canned." Theoretically, as housekeepers, mothers, and *citizens* it was deemed their duty to perform the functions of a governing body, specfically, the city health department.[62]

By August 1913, Dr. Trueheart had been replaced by Dr. Walter Kleberg, who, prompted by repeated accusations of laxness within the department, launched a "fight for pure food." An announcement went out in September that investigations of bakeries and dairies would soon follow. An entourage of reporters, Dr. Kleberg, his city food inspector, Clara Ujffy (president of the WHPA), and several WHPA members trouped out to fourteen bakeries, where they found the conditions ranged from "the carelessly insanitary to the unspeakably filthy. . . . Pans into which dozens of eggs had been broken, small wooden tubs containing jam and the 'filler' for pies, brushes, used for glazing with eggs and sugar . . . greasy rags . . . and cake tins were found in various establishments, and in some instances were black with flies." They found bread prepared in shacks surrounded by stables, and "dilapidated toilets . . . in close proximity to the rooms in which troughs of dough were mixed. Screening in many instances was wholly inadequate and swarms of flies buzzed about the ovens, the bread pans and the dough troughs." The health department took photographs and instructed the bakers on how to improve their methods; they promised to return in ten to thirty days. In no instance was any bakery closed down.[63]

In the case of dairies, the health department opened the records of milk analyses to the public. Anybody could check on the lab tests of the dairies that supplied the city. Dr. Kleberg conducted inspections of the dairies on the island and the mainland accompanied by Clara Ujffy, Jean S. Morgan, and Agnes Cohen, chair of the dairy committee. But while conditions in the dairies were no better, again no citations were issued, for city commissioner H. O. Sappington believed in "educating the dairy men instead of raising thunder with them." By January 1914, dairy conditions were an urgent concern to the women. Promises extracted from city commissioners that the worst offenders would be arrested or fined were empty, for no citations were issued. Agnes Cohen reported in January that "the conditions were decidedly bad; that instead of improving in cleanliness, the dairies in some cases have retrograded and actually are worse at present than when the agitation for pure milk was started." Of the forty-seven dairies subjected to inspection, forty-two showed dirt and sand in the bottles; twenty-one exceeded the standard 100,000 bacteria per cubic centimeter in milk tested, and three showed over one million bacteria. And this in the middle of winter![64]

The WHPA by now had an ally in the city health department. Dr. Ethel Lyon Heard, who would become president of the WHPA (1916–1918) and vice president of the Galveston Equal Suffrage Association (1914–1915), received appointment as city pathologist in charge of testing milk samples. Her presence in both the health department and the WHPA provided a vital link for women progressives to the machinery of local government. With her scientific training, she legitimated the demands of women for pure foodstuffs for the sake of the community.

The WHPA gave wholehearted endorsement to the demand that city officials stop the leniency. WHPA members sent their own inspectors to check on the conditions of dairies, groceries, and meat markets and proposed circulating a "white-list," or a list of safe dairies. By publishing and distributing a monthly milk bulletin compiled by the city health officer, WHPA members hoped that "everyone may know which dairymen are supplying their customers with pure milk." Publicity was the key to resisting the dairymen's intransigence, and the agitation was beginning to show some success. The city health department responded by requesting more inspectors and tougher enforcement from city commissioners. The board of directors of the Galveston County Dairy Men's Association met to discuss hiring their own milk inspector, preferring self-regulation to law enforcement by city or county authorities. And by July 1914, WHPA members had convinced members of the Galveston Commercial Association to turn their attention to the pure milk problem. The men budgeted $500 to lobby city government for more effective punishments for milk offenders. Finally, it was decided that revocation of licenses would be more effective than fines, and the health department, after repeated urgings, adopted this policy.[65]

But conditions did not improve quickly enough. Dr. W. S. Carter, dean of the State Medical College, did his own research on Galveston's milk and found that one-fourth of the milk sampled showed over one million bacteria per cubic centimeter. He announced that "we are exactly where we were six years ago when the city adopted its milk ordinance. One-third of the milk sold in Galveston is dirty and should be condemned . . . half the milk sampled . . . showed visible dirt." And he continued, "I don't know of a single case of revoking a milk license in the six years since we have had our milk ordinance." Noting how easy it was for dairymen to pay a fine for dirty milk but continue their unclean methods, he counseled his listeners, "you can't reach a careless dairy man by fining him. You can reach him by revoking his license or by refusing to buy milk from him." After a city inspection from C. O. Yates, commissioner of the Texas food and drug department, in which he determined that "some of the milk could scarcely be worse," the WHPA declared war on "dirty foodshops" beginning with a sweeping boycott of any dairy or food shop not approved by the association.[66] The women wanted substantive changes not only in the way dairymen prepared milk for sale but also in the way shopkeepers handled perishable items sold to the public, such as bread, fruit, meat, ice cream, and especially milk. "In pledging ourselves not to buy food or milk from any dealer who will not conform to common standards of cleanliness, we can help create a public demand for sanitary conditions." Realizing that boycotts were too indirect a means of punishment for offenders, Caroline Waters Garrett, of the WHPA grocers' committee, suggested seeking deputization of the women as state inspectors. Echoed by Pauline Hawley Jones of the fruit stand committee, she noted that "the dealers met them with courtesy, promised to do everything they suggested, and did nothing. . . . the dealers seemed to take their visits as a joke."[67]

Meat, its preparation, and its sale, also came under public scrutiny. With sanitation uppermost in the minds of citizens, thanks to the WHPA, city commissioner I. H. Kempner brought a motion to the commissioner's meeting that the city determine if it had the right to deny a permit to butchers who did not practice sanitary methods as approved by the health department. Several months after this suggestion, the WHPA jumped ahead of city government and issued, through its meat inspection committee, a set of standards for butchers and meat markets. The rules were simple: screen windows and doors, provide adequate cold storage, keep meat covered to prevent people from handling it, wrap meat when transporting it, keep dogs or cats off the premises, outlaw spitting in butcher shops, and do not establish a shop near stables and barns. With rules in place, the WHPA inspection committees now had standards by which to judge vendors. The notion of standards spread to the fruit and vegetable, bakery, and grocery store committees. "Fruit and vegetables shall not be kept on the sidewalks, doors and windows shall be properly screened, . . . all decayed matter shall be gathered in metal cans and removed regularly," read some of the rules. Establishing standards was actually the job of the city health department, but the WHPA, always a step ahead, led the way, focusing on the vendor directly rather than relying on city hall. At a typical monthly meeting of the WHPA, the inspection committees made their reports and were frank about the specific problem areas. Reporting for the committee on markets, Emma Davis Gonzales said that in 1914 of fifty-three places visited, nine were found to be "excellent," twenty "fairly good," and the rest "bad." Each committee's report found its way to the newspapers, alerting the public to the good and the bad. Even with rules and standards, women held no authority to enforce them other than public opinion and boycott.[68]

Meanwhile, city commissioners were bombarded with demands by irate merchants to stop treating pure food offenders leniently. City health officer Walter

Kleberg, who had "promised to revoke licenses of dairy men and dealers who sold adulterated milk . . . ," by 1915 had listed eight dairies as in danger of losing their licenses. None did. Nor was there much progress in getting the health department to act against unclean bakeries and markets. So while city officials dragged their heels, WHPA took offenders to court, where defense attorneys interrogated the women about the cleanliness of *their* kitchens. Lawyers wanted to know if Caroline Garrett, WHPA bakery committee chair, "had ever baked 5000 loaves of bread in one day in her kitchen, and how she dared presume to tell about flies in a bakery when she couldn't remember whether there were people in it or not." Mrs. Garrett, retorted that she went to the bakery to inspect for flies not people, and as "for her housekeeping . . . she thought it was none of the lawyer's business." However, she countered, it was her "duty as a housewife to see that the bakery where she bought bread for her family was clean." Court appearances did not achieve much in the way of convictions. The women faced strong opposition from dairymen, their attorneys, and a hard-to-move city commission.[69]

Pure food advocates were pleased in February 1915 when the commissioners accepted the proposal to hire an extra inspector at the WHPA's expense. This resulted in another curious blend of public service paid for by private means: the WHPA legally shared the cost of policing city entrepreneurs. A small victory came in May, when the state pure food and drug commissioner appointed two WHPA members, Daisy League Davis, chair of the milk inspection committee, and WHPA president Maud Moller, as deputy state food and drug inspectors. The WHPA hailed this as a "notable victory in the fight for pure food," as the women "will have the right to go into any place in the city or county where food is produced or sold." But the right to inspect, or even to pay for inspection, was not the power to enforce; eventually, the women would have to combine public pressure with qualified voters in order to make city government ensure a pure food and milk supply.[70]

The power of inspection, public exposure, boycotts, court appearances, and whitelists gradually began to have an effect. Reports of improvements came in monthly installments as the WHPA monitored the city vendors' progress. And foodstuff purveyors professed that they were anxious to cooperate. Some dairymen were beginning to make strides toward better sanitation. The new city inspector reported that "Throughout the island dairymen were whitewashing their barns, sheds . . . and one dairyman was going to the expense of putting up a $3,000 barn to meet the desires of the WHPA and the public." But the problem of milk impurities remained. Thus, a joint delegation, comprising officers of the WHPA and the Galveston County Medical Society, went before the board of city commissioners to present their pleas for a new ordinance and more effective enforcement. "Plainly displayed grading of milk," insisted city pathologist and new WHPA president Dr. Ethel Lyon Heard, "was one of the main improvements desired: that all receptacles used by milk sellers be marked in classification of A, B and C, and that the city give wide publicity to the grades these letters stand for." That way, "all dairies would strive to have their milk in the highest classification." Dr. Heard voiced their request for a new ordinance and vented her disappointment with city officials by stating, "The only marked response obtained to efforts for better milk, was a little cleaning up and use of some whitewash by the offending dairies when they thought inspectors were coming to visit them." Prosecuting dairymen under existing ordinances, she noted, "has not accomplished anything in improving the milk supply of the city."[71]

The commissioners had the power to change the 1907 ordinance, and these recommendations were given: milk shall come from herds free of tuberculosis, as shown by regular veterinary tests; narrow-topped, hooded milk pails shall be used instead of cheesecloth strainers; all milk shall be cooled at the dairy before shipment to market; milk bottles shall be filled in a screened milk room, not on the milk wagon. The delegation wanted the inspectors to use a score card for dairies provided by the Bureau of Animal Industry in order "to give a reliable index for grading the sanitary condition of the dairies" and a grading system for milk once it reached the city. Faced with such an imposing delegation, which had the support of the Galveston Commercial Association, the Rotary Club, and the Galveston Labor Council, and such an organized outline for reform, the city commissioners declared their hearty approval. But within the next month, dairymen launched a campaign of their own to insist that the demands were too stringent. Dairies in this climate could not possibly cool milk to below 60 degrees Fahrenheit, they complained. Nor could some dairymen afford the dollar tuberculine test each year or the financial loss of destroying tuberculine cows. These objections were countered with suggestions that the tuberculine test be administered free of charge by the agricultural and mechanical college [Texas A&M]; the state reimburse dairymen for destroyed cattle; and restaurants, hotels, and soda fountains be held equally responsible for cooling milk at the proper temperature. With these objections answered, the city commissioners voted to adopt the plan as presented by the delegation. Hence, by 1917, the battle for pure milk had at last found victory.[72]

The struggle to convince the community, specifically bourgeois men's groups, dairymen, merchants, vendors, and finally the city commission, took the WHPA more than five years. As unenfranchised citizens, the women learned that parlor politics was no substitute for votes and that, by directing their campaign for pure milk toward voters, especially organized men's groups, they were able to accomplish collectively what they could not do alone. For obvious reasons, many WHPA officers were also officers of the Galveston Equal Suffrage Association. But, ironically, the association itself never endorsed votes for women. An explanation of sorts came through the Special Edition of the *Galveston Tribune* that featured the accomplishments of the city's women's organizations. "As originally constituted the WHPA was in itself a score of civic societies. At the time the women probably gave little thought to the ballot, for more pressing and urgent problems were before them: and today the 'votes for women' issue finds no place in the discussions of the organization."[73] Too busy, involved in too many other concerns, or finding the issue too controversial perhaps, the WHPA geared up for its pure food campaign at approximately the same time that the Galveston Equal Suffrage Association held its first viable organizational meeting. With a suffrage society in place, the heat was off of the WHPA to become embroiled in the issue of women's franchise. Thus, it is apparent that, although a progressive civic organization such as the WHPA may have demonstrated that its members practiced politics with savvy, it did not necessarily mean that as an organization they sought the vote. If, by getting city commisioners to cooperate with their goals and implement them, the members of the WHPA were exhibiting evidence of women's political culture, it does not necessarily follow that this led to seeking full voting rights except as individuals.

City officials had reacted slowly to the demands of the WHPA, in part because they thought they lacked voter support for civic improvements and in part because they were reluctant to interfere with free enterprise by regulating even small businessmen. Maud Moller reported that "for a long time they [WHPA] were unable to get any real assistance from the city authorities, for although the latter were willing[?], they appeared to lack support in enforcing the law." Women, who had formerly endorsed the spirit of free enterprise by creating a beautiful city more favorable to attracting business, changed their emphasis to promote health as a domestic ideal, even though it meant stricter control over dairymen, shopkeepers, and restauranteurs.[74]

In fact, one of the most important principles that the WHPA centered on was the issue of the enforcement of sanitation at all levels of production and consumption—even among upper-class hotel owners. After Isaac Kempner, Bertrand Adoue, John Sealy, and H. S. Cooper built the extravagant Galvez Hotel overlooking the gulf waters in 1911 and opened an elegant restaurant, the issue of inspection of restaurant kitchens came to a head. Daisy League Davis filed a report at the January 1914 meeting stating that the "kitchens of some hotels and restaurants [are] decidedly unsanitary." This led to the creation of a six-woman committee on hotel and restaurant kitchens with Daisy Davis in charge. The committee was authorized to "take steps at once to obtain a thorough inspection of the kitchens of public eating places and exert every effort to bring about a better state of sanitation where needed."[75]

Apparently, the notion of inspecting restaurants, especially those owned by members of the upper classes, struck a conservative nerve among some of the members, and a vote to rescind the action carried. Those who spoke against inspecting hotel and restaurant kitchens pointed to the fact that this was the duty of the city health department. WHPA president Clara Ujffy argued that women had no authority to make the inspections; unless invited, they were "not privileged to enter public kitchens for the sake of making inspections." Mollie Rosenberg, who represented old-guard Galveston, agreed and suggested that it was sufficient to inspect the bakeries, butcher shops, and groceries (which women could inspect uninvited); "the cleanliness of these places would insure the cleanliness of the food served by hotels and restaurants." Those who favored the inspection of all facilities that handled food were pointed in their response to the obvious class bias present. "The association must stand for protection against all bad food," said Nellie Ball League (Daisy Davis's mother) "and must not discriminate in favor of hotels and restaurants when the inspection of groceries, bakeries and other establishments is going on." Daisy League Davis counseled that "the whole work of the association would be useless unless the inspections were made to include the hotels and restaurants."[76]

A few weeks later, in a spirited meeting that lasted nearly three hours, Clara

Ujffy lost the presidential election to Jean Scrimgeour Morgan, who was returned to office after retiring from the presidency in 1913. The major election issue was inspection of hotels and restaurants. Opposition to Clara Ujffy had developed quickly after the January meeting and mounted in the women's election campaign in the following weeks. Waldine Kopperl and Daisy League Davis's sister-in-law, Emma Davis Gonzales, nominated Jean Morgan, who obviously sanctioned the inspections. Thus, the majority of WHPA members, understanding that there was no privileged class when it came to sanitation, took a stand against protecting owners of elite establishments from the humiliation of bad reports. Their positions as traditional guardians of the home, including the health of the family, overrode any allegiance they may have once held to men of the elite or governing classes who sought freedom for business pursuits. In other words, the coalition of upper- and upper-middle-class white civic leaders broke apart over issues peculiar to and important to women. In this case, gender asserted hegemony over class.[77]

No doubt, the issue of race and ethnicity could have entered the dialogue between the WHPA and the community. But it did not. The women did not use racist rhetoric to underscore the need for improved sanitation, and in only one instance did they mention an Italian shopkeeper, who seemed disgruntled by their inspection. This was so even though many of the shopkeepers, food purveyors, greengrocers, and fruit vendors were Italian, German, and African American. Why this should be true begs speculation. Perhaps the women were truly interested in building community rather than in building political coalitions based on race or anti-immigrant bias. The Arbor Day celebration included black schools as well as white, and Margaret Sealy Burton, who was responsible for soliciting funds to place decorative concrete benches on the seawall, asked if African Americans would contribute to the cause. Galveston had always been a port of entry for foreigners, many of whom stayed on in the city. Rabbi Henry Cohen supported the Galveston Movement, an immigration flow that brought Jews from Europe between 1907 and 1914 through the city to settle in the Midwest, but no mention was made of this or any other migrant population except in enumeration, and that occurred in 1917 with the West End neighborhood house. Equally interesting is the fact that black businesses did not come in for separate criticism, nor, on the other hand, was any protest raised by the WHPA against the segregating of public transportation that began in Galveston in 1906. Was there some code of decorum that simply did not allow white women to mention race or race relations? Was it their way of drawing the color line, treating with silence a segment of the population that historically had always been among the residents? The answers are elusive.[78]

In vying for a share of the power to direct public policy toward control of dairymen and shopkeepers, WHPA members adopted confrontational political tactics. Their strategies included conventional lobbying methods: they sought scientific evidence that Galveston indeed had a pure food problem, continued systematic inspections with published whitelists, attempted boycotts and initiated law suits against offending dairymen and other food purveyors, brought in state health officers and sought to legitimize their position through state inspector appointments, won editorial support from the city dailies, and finally sought coalition with sympathetic male organizations in petitioning the board of city commission-

ers. But the trouble with interest group politics is that once the issues have been
favorably decided, the reasons for remaining tied to politics disappear. Unlike
political parties, where the continuing point of their existence is to win office and
remain in control, interest groups such as the WHPA considered their political
work done when the commissioners voted in tougher laws. Turning the task of
inspection of markets and dairies over to a better managed public health department seemed the logical conclusion to the WHPA's political efforts. So they
(re)turned to goals that were long familiar to women: children and landscaping.

From 1917 until 1920, the WHPA began to focus more on the needs of children (perhaps as a result of their pure milk campaign), the war effort, and the
continuation of its planting program. The Galveston Child Conservation League,
which had hosted an annual Better Baby Conference, folded in 1917; its work was
assumed by the WHPA, which urged education regarding infant care. "Statistics
say one baby out of every seven born dies"; the slogan for the October conference
became "Save the Seventh Baby." The WHPA took even more direct action with
children by founding a "neighborhood house" in the West End and conducting
a survey of the West End residents. Called a "very complete human document,"
the survey counted 519 families with 1,361 children by race, ethnicity, and religion.
The association sponsored a picnic on the beach and a "moving picture entertainment," which 410 children and adults attended. What is missing in this report
of activism on behalf of the West End children is whether African Americans were
included. The survey notes that 52 colored families resided in the West End, but
no mention of a color line was made for the neighborhood house or the picnic.[79]

As the nation went to war, the WHPA found itself instructing others in the
creation of victory gardens. But the WHPA's most enduring contribution to the
city remained in landscaping. Palms, oaks, and oleanders planted throughout the
city and west on Broadway to the causeway remain today the most enduring legacy
of this women's organization. By the mid-1920s the organization changed its name
to the Women's Civic League, as if to say that the concern over public health
and sanitation was over; finally, they renamed it the Galveston Civic League, and
the organization lost complete identity with women. The winding down of the
organization into a garden club of sorts in the 1920s was probably not related to
the winning of the suffrage amendment but rather to the slowing down of activities
during the war years and the cessation of political activism. Women who had once
channeled energy into the WHPA felt that they had achieved their goals and
became engaged in other efforts. After 1912, there were many more women's organizations, and one single group, even one as powerful as the WHPA, could not
meet the many and diverse interests of women.[80]

The Galveston example should highlight the fact that a national women's
reform movement reached into New South cities. The WHPA's choice of agendas
was informed by national issues but decided by local needs and opportunities,
including a badly damaged economy, by a lack of regulatory agencies, and by
issues closely tied to women's interests. This particular group of organized women,
the first in the city to pursue political ends, met successes in its early years for
various reasons: They linked themselves politically to the 1901 city commission
government, which had consolidated decision-making power in the hands of com-

mercial-civic elites, a class from which the women also stemmed. Commissioners were more accessible to and more compatible with WHPA members than aldermen had been. Elite consanguinity existed between the two groups over burial of storm victims and city beautification. But the thornier issue of imposing domestic values of cleanliness on middling shopkeepers and dairymen brought women and city commissioners of the same class into conflict. Class cohesiveness broke down over gender issues. Power still resided with conventional civic-commercial elites, but, by the clever use of gender issues and lobbying techniques that enlisted the press and progressive male voters, even laboring men, women activists in Galveston gained, if not power, then substantial influence in turning domestic politics into public policy.

The Women's Health Protective Association's activities were considerable, especially given the city's destitution in 1900, and the rewards for the women leaders were manifold. They found that by acting collectively they had formed the rudiments of a white women's community, which, born of women's interests and nurtured in particular religious institutions, constituted a powerful lobbying force for municipal housekeeping. As leaders in the first democratic Progressive Era women's organization, they brought all the organizing skills learned in their earlier institution-building days to a more open organization and to a larger forum—the city. They transferred their concern for the indigent individual to the revegetation of a denuded island. This concern for the larger community compelled them to insist on decent burial for storm victims, beautification, clean streets and alleys, pure milk, and sanitary markets, even if it meant imposing progressive standards on reluctant dairymen and grocers. Their enthusiasm and energy spawned other progressive organizations for men and women. They learned the arts of inspection, of rhetoric, of petitioning for change, and of working around commissioners—in short, they learned practical politics, or, in the parlance of historians, they participated in a women's political culture. But without direct access to political power many (though not all) in the WHPA found their considerable organizing talents limited to mere influence. In the words of WHPA president Clara Ujffy, "without the ballot, [we] have little or nothing to say with regard to how such laws should be carried into effect. The day will come when we will have a voice, that's sure."[81] It was clear through their experience with city hall that women needed and deserved the vote.

8

$\cdot\quad\cdot\quad\cdot\quad\cdot\quad\cdot\quad\cdot\quad\cdot\quad\cdot\quad\cdot\quad\cdot\quad\cdot\quad\cdot\quad\cdot\quad\cdot\quad\cdot\quad\cdot\quad\cdot\quad\cdot$

"THE INTEREST HAS NEVER LAGGED"

African American Women and the Black Community

Help me to shatter this darkness,
To smash this night,
To break this shadow
Into a thousand lights of sun,
into a thousand whirling dreams
Of sun!

— Langston Hughes,
"As I Grew Older"

In 1865, at the close of the war, a young man, the son of a mulatto slave and a white plantation owner, came to Galveston. He had grown up along the Brazos River; his father had migrated from Louisiana to invest in the rich cotton lands of Texas. His mother bore eight children, all of whom were given their freedom, and three of the sons were educated in northern schools. Norris Wright Cuney, at nineteen, had come to Galveston to find his place in the commercial life of Texas; along the way, he discovered politics. His daughter wrote of him, "young, intensely patriotic, eager for service and possessing unlimited faith in the Negro race, [he] entered into public service during this troublesome period." Governor E. J. Davis gave him his first appointment as assistant to the sergeant-at-arms of the Twelfth Texas Legislature in 1870; from this position he met the political operators and the commercial lions who would make it possible for a black man to succeed in postwar Texas.[1] Cuney's life, from 1846 to 1898, became a beacon for many who hoped to find peace, security, and prosperity as freedpeople. But Cuney's life also represents the cycle of hope and despair common to blacks in the New South. His career, brilliant through the 1870s and 1880s, would end in defeat at the hands of a "lily-white" racist cabal within the Republican party. Cuney died before the full weight of "separate but equal" and "voting reform" could be applied; therefore, he never saw the nearly complete disfranchisement of his people or the abrupt decline of black political strength. Nor was he witness to the replacement of black aldermen with white female civic activists in Galveston's political landscape.

Cuney's death also brought the demise of an important bridge between the white and the black communities in Galveston. As the most politically influential black Republican in the state, he enjoyed the endorsement and support of Galveston's white business elites. Once gone, no single person took his place; members of the black community lost an ombudsman who had been able to navigate successfully through the tense currents of racial prejudice. After 1898, events conspired to diminish the freedom of black Galvestonians, with more evidence of petty and grand discriminations.

In the years following the Civil War, the Cuney family seemed to provide a measure of hope to African Americans living in Galveston. Cuney's presence, along with that of his brothers Joseph and Nelson, offered a pattern for middle-class respectability that fairly shouted the merits of hard work, honesty, and integrity. Cuney never turned his back on his African roots, nor did he accommodate to shabby treatment. The virtues of pride and resistance were also reinforced by his wife Adelina and transferred to his children. In standing up publicly to racists and demagogues, he and his family modeled the kind of courage that earned the respect of many, while at the same time he engendered resentment from whites unable to tolerate black achievements.

Adelina Dowdie, also the daughter of a white planter and his mulatto slave, migrated with her family to Galveston in 1864. There she met Wright Cuney; they married in 1871 and began family life at the same time Cuney began his political ascendancy. Adelina's life history, as revealed in daughter Maud Cuney's biography of her father, is shadowy and incomplete. We are told that she had aspired to become a teacher, had a lovely soprano voice, imparted the love of music to her daughter who became a concert pianist, tended the flowers in her yard, tenderly cared for her children, and was religious without being pious. She was not physically strong; indeed, she died of tuberculosis at age forty-one. But perhaps her most memorable characteristic is that she was steely, courageous, and resilient in the face of oppression.[2]

In the years between 1872 and 1875, Cuney managed to find success among white politicians and businessmen. He was elected a delegate to the National Republican Convention, was appointed inspector of customs for the District of Texas, and became secretary of the Republican State Executive Committee. White businessmen, impressed by Cuney's efficiency and dedication to the public good, invited him to deliberate with them in the Galveston Cotton Exchange over the future of the city, its harbor improvements, and its levees. The result was a nomination to run for mayor against a well-known Democrat in the 1875 election. He met with defeat but won the admiration of his opponent. This led to other endorsements by white civic elites. In 1876, when Cuney was summarily dismissed from his post as inspector of customs, Galveston's mayor and 100 other petitioners demanded his reinstatement. In 1881, he was appointed chief inspector of customs. At the same time, he was elected city alderman from the Twelfth Ward and, because he was not allowed to hold two public offices at the same time, resigned the federal position for the local one. It was in 1883 that he entered into a business of his own and created a longshoremen's company, employing 500 black men to work the wharves in competition with white longshoremen. Providing an alternative labor force to the most lucrative industry in the city brought its share of backlash and threats, but by introducing black longshoremen to shippers he guaranteed better paid jobs for hundreds of men. In 1883, Cuney was invited to become part of a Citizens Ticket for aldermen made up of the most prominent Galvestonians, men such as Henry Rosenberg, Charles Fowler, and J. G. Goldthwaite. He carried the Twelfth Ward in 1883 and again after a contested election in 1885. He remained on the Board of Aldermen until 1887, when he was appointed to the Board of Commissioners of Water Works.[3]

The triumph of Cuney's career came in 1889, when President Benjamin Harrison appointed him collector of customs at Galveston. It was the highest ranking post, in terms of position and salary, ever given an African American in the South. He was endorsed by hundreds of the city's leading citizens as well as his political friends within the Republican party. But white Republicans, angered over Cuney's patronage power and political clout within the party, began to express rumblings of discontent. Stirred by a southwide "lily-white" movement to diminish black political dominance in the party, some Texas Republicans organized a separate all-white party. To add to the insult, while he was still collector of customs, Cuney was refused the right to purchase a ticket for a berth in a Pullman sleeping car on account of his race. He later took suit against the Pullman company, but in the meantime the 1892 national elections brought a change in his political fortunes. Forced to resign as collector of customs with the ascendancy of Grover Cleveland to the White House and besieged by the lily-whites, Cuney spent the last years of his life fighting for his dignity, his political position, and the strength of black Republicans. But he was no match for the rising tide of racism in Texas. Within two years after his defeat, he was dead.[4]

Adelina and Maud Cuney, surrounded by the excitement of politics and nurtured in the spirit of democracy, found their own ways to combat discrimination. In 1883, when Wright Cuney introduced black longshoremen to the Galveston docks and broke the monopoly of white labor, his life and that of his family's was threatened with violence. Fearing that a mob would come in the night, he asked Adelina to take their two children, Maud and Lloyd Garrison, to his brother's home for safety. She refused and stood vigil at the back window throughout the night. Longshoremen and friends filled the house, surrounded the premises by hiding in the salt cedars, and by their presence prevented violence. Three years later, long after Cuney had been elected to the Galveston Board of Aldermen but before Texas had passed a separate coach law, Adelina tried to board the train to Houston. She was barred from entering the first-class car by a conductor who locked the door. Noting the racially motivated act, she simply asked her brother-in-law Joseph for a lift, climbed into the train through the window, and rode undisturbed to Houston. Maud faced unpleasant situations throughout her life, too, but relied on the model of equal treatment learned at home. While attending the New England Conservatory of Music at Boston in 1891, her father received a letter from the school's administration requesting Maud's removal from the conservatory dormitory. "We have a large number of pupils who are affected by race prejudices, and the Home must be conducted so as to insure the comfort and satisfaction of the largest number possible." Cuney wrote back a letter shaming the administrators into altering their intentions. By mentioning men such as William Lloyd Garrison, Wendell Phillips, and Charles Sumner, he deftly recounted Massachusetts's history of abolitionism. He wrote, "You request my co-operation in surrendering to the demands of prejudice, by withdrawing my daughter; I cannot help you." To Maud he wrote: "You were quite right, darling, when you said that you knew your father would tell you to stay." Maud graduated from the conservatory, then returned to San Antonio to nurse first her dying mother and later her father. After their deaths, she, like many other educated but disillusioned blacks, left the South, continued her concert career, and specialized in the presentation of African American history and music. She made glorious news in Galveston in 1914, when it was reported that she had given a recital at Howard Theater in Washington, D.C., under the auspices of the Washington Conservatory of Music. Critics wrote of her performance, "Mrs. Hare is a pianist of rare accomplishments . . . the concert was one of the most intelligent presentations of the Negro's advancement in music that Washington has ever enjoyed. . . . [Her] well prepared thesis dealt with the history of African and Negro Folk Music . . . songs of slavery [and] songs of Negro Minstrelsy."[5]

The example that this family provided Galveston cut two ways: integrity knew no color line; honor, loyalty, and race pride, however, could not prevent one from suffering indignities in a society imbued with racial prejudice. The central message of their lives seemed to have been that the best course to take was to build a place for oneself despite prevailing injustices and resist racial discrimination at every turn. This was the course that African American women and men in Galveston chose to take, but, just as the Cuneys experienced political good fortune and then decline as the forces of racial oppression grew, so too did Galveston blacks find their political and social aspirations diminished after the turn of the century.

Once Galveston voters decided to endorse at-large city elections in 1895, black officeholders were virtually eliminated, depriving the black community of city leadership. Proof of the effectiveness of at-large voting came in the 1891 election for school board trustees. J. H. Wilkins, the city's first black physician, ran against three other white men and lost primarily because white voters outnumbered black voters by ten to one. Coupled with the reorganization of city government into a single commission in 1901 and the introduction of a poll tax in 1902, disfranchisement and diminishment of black political power in Texas became nearly complete. Thereafter, a decided shift in the political landscape occurred in Galveston. White middle- and upper-class women, although not yet voters, allied themselves with the all-white male city commission after 1901, replacing the influence of black aldermen and supporting many of the policies that led to further "voting reform." The result was a rise of white female power and a decline in political power for black men. The move toward further separation of the races in public facilities seemed unstoppable, even though blacks continued to resist the ideology of Jim Crow on trains, and streetcars and in public libraries. Indignation meetings, which took place more often in churches than in public buildings after 1900, were common throughout this period and intensified with the state's rising tide of racial violence.[6]

African American women, although never accorded the same political clout as men, became more involved in civic affairs after 1900. Their activism followed a trajectory similar to that of white women who entered the public forum first through churches, then through benevolent societies and clubs, but it differed in several important ways. The core of middle-class African American women's activism evolved from churches, but it also followed their professional involvement as teachers. Moreover, black women addressed issues of gender equality quietly in their churches and in their separate club work, but they spoke and acted publicly for the redress of racial discrimination. While white middle-class women sought greater political force and gender equity in the community with city beautification, pure food and milk, and voting rights campaigns in the years before 1920, black women fought against the effects of segregation. African American women displayed the symbolic importance of ethnic celebrations when they organized Juneteenth parades to honor their heritage; they also formed women's charitable clubs, relief societies, and civic associations, which not only helped the community combat racism but also served to demonstrate middle-class respectability. They ameliorated the worst aspects of segregation by founding orphanages, homes for the elderly, hospital aid societies, mothers' clubs, and schools for delinquent girls. Joining with the men in national celebrations, community festivals, Central High alumni gatherings, and the National Association for the Advancement of Colored People (NAACP), women worked together to create race pride and solidarity and to dispel notions of powerlessness. In so doing, African Americans, women and men, became part of the progressive wave of reform that swept the nation.

African Americans and the Post Reconstruction Political Economy

The social, economic, and political lives of black families after the Civil War were tied together in an almost inescapable web. By 1880, the city's overall population had reached 22,250, of which 24 percent, or 5,350, were black. By 1900, the city's population surged ahead to nearly 38,000, and the black population grew to 8,300. Galveston in 1880 had become the third largest cotton market and the fourth largest coffee market in the United States. The most important economic "commodity" in Galveston centered around trade—merchandising, freight handling, exporting, and transportation. The value of exports leaving the port of Galveston was sixteen times greater than imports because Texas produced cotton for the world and Galveston was its principal port. White longshoremen and screwmen enjoyed a labor monopoly on the docks before 1876, in part because their trade union constitutions made it impossible to work alongside blacks. Breaking the monopolistic hold on this lucrative labor opportunity required convincing a shipper to contract with a black labor union for its sole employment rather than juxtaposing black workers against white on the docks. African American workers organized the Longshoremen's Benevolent Association in 1870, a Negro Screwman's Benevolent Association in 1876, and a Cotton Jammers' and Longshoremen's Association No. 2 in 1879; with these they were accorded sporadic work on the wharves. The first large break into longshoremen work occurred in 1883 when Norris Wright Cuney wrote to Colonel William L. Moody, president of the Galveston Cotton Exchange, explaining the need for more dockworkers and, in a sense, sought the endorsement of that body for an all-black company to work the

wharves. "Having observed that the commercial importance of Galveston has been
. . . jeopardized by the insufficiency of skilled labor necessary in loading seagoing
vessels with cotton, and having reason to believe that [labor] will not be large
enough to meet the demands of our growing commerce . . . , I have thought it
proper to call your attention to the fact that there are a large number of laborers
. . . to supply this necessity. I allude to those colored men who now find a scanty
livelihood by hard labor along shore." Cuney had 300 skilled laborers ready to
work at two-thirds the salary offered whites. The response from the members of
the Cotton Exchange was immediate and enthusiastic: "we heartily welcome the
new association, commend their enterprise, and wish them success." Of course,
white businessmen knew that by thus cutting costs to merchants they would be
antagonizing race relations. Cuney knew it, too, and anticipated retaliations from
whites as well as accusations of undermining black labor equality. Nonetheless,
with these competitive tactics, black longshoremen and screwmen were hired,
which brought $75,000 to $100,000 in wages to black workers and resulted in a
white walkout in 1883 and a general strike in 1885. It would be simply a matter of
time before white workers had a chance to retaliate.[7]

In the years following their entrée to the docks, the wage difference between
white and black longshoremen began to rankle, as did the incidences of discrimination. In the 1890s, disfranchisement and segregation began to take its toll on
workers' dignity—the city had altered the election process so as to virtually eliminate black ward leaders, the legislature had passed a law separating whites and
blacks on trains, and the U.S. Supreme Court in *Plessy v. Ferguson* had made a
"separate but equal" decision regarding interstate transit. This rising tide of racism
led workers to counter with the kind of economic clout the city understood. An
opportunity for raised wages presented itself with the opening of the Spanish-
American War, when the Mallory Company suspended all steamship transport
between New York and Galveston. The first ship to return to Galveston in August
1898 did more than cross a treacherous sea, it met a hostile crowd of 1,000 black
workers armed with clubs and pledging to stop the ship's unloading until the
Mallory Company increased their wages by ten cents an hour to the level of white
longshoremen. Arguing that Galveston dock men made more than workers in
other ports, Mallory officials refused to consider the raise and threatened to "send
our ships to some other port." The Mallory workers, all of whom were black,
compared their wages to white longshoremen in Galveston and to black screwmen.
Mallory officials responded by importing scab labor from Houston, which brought
a violent reaction from the strikers. Replying with a surprising show of force, Mayor
Ashley W. Fly called out the police and a citizen posse, which fired into the
crowd, wounding three and killing two others, a black striker and a white spectator.
J. Harvey Patrick, brother-in-law of N. W. Cuney and president of the striking
Colored Labor Protective Union, No. 7174, met with the traffic manager of the
Mallory Company, but to no avail, and more laborers from Houston were imported. The trouble escalated when a party of longshoremen made a sortie into
the sheds where the Houstonians were sleeping and fired over their heads, slightly
wounding one worker and accidentally killing one of their own. If the raid was
expected to discourage scab laborers from working the Galveston docks, the mob

action worked. The Houston workers were escorted home in special cars hired by the Mallory Company. Galveston longshoremen, however, ended up back at work for the same wages, while their union, in a face-saving gesture, vowed to continue the strike. Ultimately, the Mallory line won the dispute, and black laborers succeeded mainly in frightening white Texans into reconsidering the advisability of allowing them such wide economic and political power.[8]

White Backlash

The reaction to black gains in Galveston found reflection throughout the state in violence and in laws to limit black voting rights, to increase segregation, and to continue discrimination. These acts were met not with passive acceptance by African Americans but with resistance. Galveston black laborers, soldiers, store owners, teachers, and ministers, who worked steadily and showed growth in their respective endeavors, defied the notion that blacks could not succeed in freedom. Despite evidence to the contrary, for years the logic of white supremacy depended upon proving that blacks could not rise above a certain level and could not match the intelligence and competence of whites. To see blacks achieve economic ascendancy, however limited, or to see black laborers, black politicians, black educators, and black soldiers defy this myth with their achievements could not be tolerated by many whites. One way that white anger and jealousy found its outlet was in violence across the state. Texas held the third highest ranking for lynchings in the nation. Exact numbers are difficult to obtain, but the NAACP put the figure at 355 deaths (283 of which were black) between 1889 and 1918. Yet in the face of violence, Galveston African Americans vocally and insistently rallied in indignation meetings—in 1881 against mob violence in Orange, Texas, and against the deaths of three black voters by lynching in Washington County. In 1895, they protested a burning-lynching in Tyler and published antilynching resolutions. Governor James S. Hogg, appalled by it all, finally convinced the legislature to pass an antilynching law in 1897, and the violence decreased. Still, twenty-four died at the hands of the mob in 1908.[9]

At the same time, a southwide effort to remove blacks from the presence of whites on trains and in other public places led to a separate but equal conclusion. Protests by conventions of African American men brought attention to the demand for equal rights on railways, which was lengthened to include an appeal on higher grounds. "Surely our white fellow citizens, with their wealth and intelligence can afford to give us an equal chance with them in the race of life. We do not ask for special legislation, but we do insist upon being accorded the equal benefits and protection of the law." This plea was answered with a separate coach law passed by the Texas legislature in 1891 "for the convenience, benefit and comfort of both races alike." A state convention of African American men met in Houston and rebuked the act as

> unjust and pernicious . . . as the law was created on the presumption that the negro must necessarily be restricted in the enjoyment of his full citizen rights, in order to discourage social equality between the races; pernicious because of the

fact that the law is founded on wrong principles; that its origin was the result of race hatred fostered and unbridled by reason, because it proclaims to the world that the negro has not been progressive and that a necessity really exists in the south providing for an abridgment of the colored man's rights and a legal restriction of his full enjoyment of the same.[10]

Segregated public facilities had come first to *cities* across the South. By 1885, Galveston churches, schools, and most public buildings were separated by race. On rare occasions, black entertainers, such as the Black Patti Troubadours, performed at the Galveston Opera House to black audiences. But Opera House policy forced blacks to sit in the balcony when whites attended. Black women were not spared the humiliation of segregation in public facilities, of course. But like Adelina Cuney, some were not willing to be excluded without a protest. Two courageous black women in 1875 challenged the policy by sitting in the "white Ladies' circle" and were thrown out. In another incident involving the Mallory Steamship Company, which had hired black dockworkers in 1883, three Galvestonians, two women and a man, sued for damages. They had bought first-class tickets from Key West to Galveston on the Mallory line, but on the second day at sea they were humiliated by the attendants. When they went to the dining area, to which they had been directed earlier, they were ordered "in the presence of the other passengers to leave the table." After refusing, they were forcibly removed from the dining area, were forbidden to return, and were not given the first-class accommodations for which they had paid. Isabella E. Mabson, a teacher in Galveston's West District School, also sued in district court. She experienced similar treatment when she traveled from Kansas City to Galveston aboard the Missouri, Kansas and Texas Railway Company. After having bought two first-class tickets in Kansas City, she and her children rode in the "palace car" until they reached Denison, Texas, where they were ejected to a "dirty, common coach provided for negroes." Full impact of the separate coach law, upheld theoretically by the U.S. Supreme Court decision in *Plessy v. Ferguson*, in 1896, would discourage such suits. White unconcern for blacks who were poorly accommodated on the railways had already been seen in cases prior to the *Plessy* decision. When the Reverend W. T. Cain, rector of St. Augustine Episcopal Church, brought suit against the Great Northern Railway Company for exactly the same treatment, he won his case, but the jury awarded him $1 in damages.[11] These discriminatory actions were met by African Americans with dismay and then resistance. The result was more white backlash. African Americans suffered in Texas, as they did elsewhere in the South, at the hands of white politicians and lawmakers.

Galveston and Jim Crow

Democrats had been trying to eliminate black voters from the electorate for years before A. W. Terrell took the lead in advocating poll taxes for the state. Although some whites — Greenbackers, Populists, and Republicans — feared that a tax would disfranchise poor whites, the legislature, nonetheless, in 1902 passed a constitutional amendment requiring a poll tax for voting. With the diminishment of power

among African Americans within the Republican and the Populist parties — sometimes at gunpoint — voting declined. Black voting dropped from about 100,000 in
the 1890s to 5,000 in 1906. Difficulty with voting was deeply resented by active
citizens, who protested vigorously. "The colored voter cannot afford to lose any
strength," railed the Galveston *City Times* editor, "the *Times* has at all times been
opposed to restrictions on manhood suffrage . . . [but] while the law is in force . . .
go and pay your poll tax and arm yourself with a weapon." Despite firm admonitions by Galveston African American leaders, only 675 out of 4,000 (17 percent)
eligible black county voters were able to pay the tax. Of that number, 500 were
city voters. *City Times* editor William Noble continued to hammer away at the
need for citizens to pay the poll tax and exercise the right to vote. In 1908, a group
of potential voters organized a poll-tax club, "for the purpose of getting an interest
among the colored citizens to qualify for the necessary political standing in the
city." But it was hardly enough to turn the tide of repression.[12]

Once black voting power declined, the Texas legislature and local governments were able to increase racial restrictions with impunity. The years 1904 and
1907 became the nadir of deteriorating race relations in Texas: whites outlawed
black militias, segregated streetcars, continued to marginalize blacks in the Republican party, and rendered meaningless black votes with an all-white Democratic primary. White men left a trail of evidence indicating that they welcomed
disfranchisement and segregation and justified it on the grounds that it made for
"good government."[13] It rendered them more powerful and more controlling and
reinstated their opportunities for paternalism. When they displayed generosity toward blacks, as in the creation of a high school, for example, it was under white
aegis and control. Just how the majority of Galveston white women perceived
restrictions upon their black neighbors is difficult to determine; few left any record
of their thoughts on the matter. In the shifting sands of political opportunism,
white middle-class women found themselves by 1910 in a more advantageous position vis-à-vis black male voters and unenfranchised black women. Although white
women too were unenfranchised, their class position, their race, their friendship
with white men, and their club solidarity gave them greater leverage in accomplishing a "women's agenda" for the city. Excluded from open civic association
with whites, black women created their own goals, turned their attention to the
needs of their own people, and, by doing so, challenged the racism inherent in
segregation.

The loss of voting power led directly to the diminishment of African American
rights as citizens. The adjutant general of Texas claimed disingenuously that "the
colored citizens display no interest in the colored militia"; therefore, in April 1906,
he disbanded the "colored battalion of the State Guard," composed of companies
from Austin, Houston, and Galveston. The Hawley Guards of Galveston, which
had played a prominent role in city parades and celebrations, symbolized the
privileges of freedom and citizenship. This group, which had gained the right to
bear arms and form a militia, received the order to ship all state property back to
Austin. Evaluating the connection between disfranchisement and loss of power,
William Noble admonished that "where the colored citizens have the voice of
voting an honest man's ballot without the interference of unjust state restrictions,

he is respected as an American citizen. . . . do you think for a moment that in Illinois, the Adjutant General would order the colored troops disbanded as in Texas, Georgia and elsewhere?"[14]

Plans to segregate streetcars had been implemented in cities across the South but did not come to Galveston until 1906. The city of Houston had already segregated their streetcars, and blacks had successfully boycotted them by establishing their own hacks. The Houston city council imposed a $500 bond on hackmen before they could do business. William Noble again labeled it correctly when he wrote, "This piece of reprehensible dudgeon on the part of the council has for its devilish design the forcing of the self-respecting Negroes of Houston to ride in the Jim Crow cars." Three years later, Noble would meet before the Galveston city commissioners in an attempt to persuade *them* to vote against Jim Crow cars in his city.[15]

White citizens petitioned Galveston city commissioners to segregate the trolley cars in 1905. *New Idea* editors, sensing the mood early in July 1905, protested against the white-owned *Galveston Tribune* for allowing "the Jim-Crow-white-man" to advocate a separate streetcar for blacks, and in December they pleaded with black voters to pay their poll tax. "One reason you should pay your poll tax is because THE EVENING TRIBUNE wants the City Commissioners to pass a JIM CROW STREET CAR LAW against you." By March 1906, *New Idea* editors predicted that Galveston would soon have these laws. "The Separate streetcar discrimination, like a black cloud is spreading over Texas and will eventually reach Galveston. Dallas, Austin, Waco, Houston, Beaumont, San Antonio and in fact all the large cities have it." Arguing that only "poor white newspapers" that "represent the destructive elements of the community," were behind segregation, the editorial blasted black citizens who would ride on separate cars. "The Jim-Crow Nigger is among us, male and female, he is the handiest tool of the prejudiced white folks. They are what you call, 'Regular white-folks niggers.' They are the first to ride on separate cars and shame the race." *City Times* editor William Noble met before the commissioners and pleaded with them not to adopt this law. "I do not think it is right to discriminate against a people when they have not shown cause. . . . it is only a matter of plain prejudice against the colored people." Galveston city commissioners almost resisted the Jim Crow ruling, when commissioners Isaac Kempner and H. C. Lange voted against it. Kempner and Lange had both come from immigrant families and perhaps had personally known the sting of exclusion. Kempner noted his reasons: "I know of no concrete case that has been called to the attention of this board where there has been difficulty on the streetcars which would justify or warrant us passing this measure." Even though he gave the Jim Crow petitioners too much grace in saying that they did not mean to humiliate blacks, he vowed, "while that was not the design, it will be the result." When a final vote was taken, three of the five commissioners bowed to racism and, with a stunning piece of illogic, defended the decision. Mayor Henry Landes concluded by saying, "Well gentlemen, I regret very much that this question was ever brought up. We have a better class of colored people in Galveston in the way of deportment, character and civic duty than any other city in Texas or in the South, I believe. . . . there has been very little necessity for such an ordinance, but inasmuch as the matter has been brought up and discussed at such length, I believe that it is best for both parties under the circumstances, to adopt the ordinance." Thus, in civil and polite ways were racist rulings allowed to exist. When considering the banality of evil in a segregated society, one must remember that well-intentioned civic leaders often with much ballyhooed regret brought down upon the South this mantle of disgrace.[16]

Joseph Cuney, Galveston lawyer and brother of Norris Wright Cuney, launched in the pages of the *Times* a vehement protest, which was reprinted in the *Galveston Daily News*. But the result was the same and was later extended to buses. "Our mothers taught us what to do; go to the back of the bus," recalled Mrs. H. M. Smith and Mrs. L. Harrison, both residents of the city before 1920. They noted with irony that in their integrated neighborhood children often played together. "If children didn't mind, my mother would put them out of the yard—black and white." These same children would beg to come back and play. To keep the children happy, "Miss Sarah" would buy a bushel of oysters, "get one of the boys to dig a hole, put a grate over it and roast oysters." Despite segregation, children came for roast oysters, crackers, and companionship. But in other, more formal ways the separate doctrine prevailed. When 190 black citizens requested a permit to build a bath house in front of the seawall, first at Twenty-seventh Street, then, because of white protest, further west at Thirty-Seventh Street, the permit was discouraged. White citizens protested by arguing that property values would fall and, therefore, tax revenue would fall and that the bath house would prove to be a "source of trouble and vexation to our home people, and still more for visitors; that it would stop a great many enterprises, . . . that the beauty of the beach front would be marred." City commission, without an outright refusal, passed an ordinance that the petitioners must come up with $500 in ten days to secure the permit. This effectively quashed the request, and no bath house for black citizens was built.[17]

Solidarity within the African American Community

Despite the growing strictures on account of race, Galvestonians of African descent formed an ebullient, energetic community. During the assault upon their civil rights, they vigorously protested denigration, celebrated freedom, proclaimed the dignity of working people, honored the elderly and children, and collectively acted out their response to the so-called Negro problem by forming societies, clubs, business leagues, and philanthropic institutions. Galveston blacks worshipped independently, took charge of their children's education, formed labor unions, and supported their own cultural events. The great irony of this period of race relations resides in the fact that the African American community experienced a flowering in Galveston just as the Texas assembly and city government moved to restrict voting rights, to segregate public facilities, and grudgingly to provide a few social services.

Black middle-class women—teachers, doctors, and the wives of ministers, businessmen, longshoremen, and other well-paid laborers—formed a separate circle of acquaintances that actively supported community solidarity with a style that suggested cultural as well as race solidarity.[18] Having formed church societies and schools in the years between 1870 and 1900, women after the turn of the century were just beginning to find organizational strength, which they applied to Juneteenth celebrations, schools, philanthropy, and social issues via women's clubs at the local and national level. Their ability to combat increasing racism, violence, disfranchisement, and segregation needs to be told within the context of the black community, which in the first two decades of the twentieth century had grown to approximately 10,000, or one-quarter of the total population. Black women tackled issues of discrimination in a fashion that supported and complemented male endeavors toward the same end. Their campaign against the indignities of segregation led them to employ symbols of liberty and freedom in public demonstrations, while at the same time they continued to shore up their churches with fundraisers and to nurture the sick, the elderly, and children. The movement to secure independence and equality for women, a feminist response to male authority, began quietly with the establishment of their own church societies, relief associations, and civic clubs, reaching fruition with entitlement to the vote (such as it was, with a poll tax and white primaries). Much of the success of Galveston's black women, their work, their church life, and their community projects depended on the continuing prosperity of the black community.[19]

African Americans were exuberant over the economic gains made during the first years of the twentieth century and congratulated themselves in print. "Over a Quarter of a Million Dollars Paid to Colored Laborers of Galveston During This Year . . ." the *City Times* announced in December 1903. "Many a colored man is being given a chance to work and live, and not less than one thousand colored laboring men have been regularly employed on the Galveston wharf front." An estimated $332,514.30 in salaries, noted editor William H. Noble, "gives assurance that our people are enjoying their share of prosperity as well as others." In 1909, another, much longer announcement appeared in the *Times* detailing the prosperity of the African American community. An estimated $250,000 "business value to the race" was represented in three thriving groceries, sixteen hotels and restaurants (often combined), five wood dealerships, six tailor shops, two furniture dealerships, at least ten barber shops, three blacksmith shops, five ice cream parlors, two newspapers, a drugstore, a vegetable stand, a laundry, a shoemaker shop, a house-raising business, and a millinery shop. The community boasted four doctors and the Hubbard Clinic owned by Dr. Mary Moore, four lawyers, twenty-three teachers and administrators, sixteen ministers of the gospel, seven hauling contractors, thirteen policemen and street department workers, sixty federal employees, an automobile representative, nurses, midwives, and scores of longshoremen and screwmen. The article should have included servants, seamstresses, and washerwomen, who composed a significant portion of the female workforce. Also not listed were funeral homes, such as that owned by W. K. Hebert. Saloons also provided a living for quite a few residents. The Reverend Ralph Scull remembered that in the 1870s saloons and gambling were lucrative businesses, and he counted at least eight saloons and "dozens of small places in all parts of the town." The *Times* in 1909 counted some seventy-five black-owned businesses (thirty-seven different kinds) and professions, which advertised that they took pride in serving Galveston's black community. The idea that African Americans were falling behind economically or were unable to compete in the world, a view often voiced by whites, simply was not true.[20]

Churches

Churches constituted the mainstay of the African American community and the focal point for racial awareness and self-help. Activists and scholars alike have long understood that the black church pursued multifaceted objectives—as a "house of worship, . . . an agency of social control, forum of discussion and debate, promoter of education and economic cooperation, and arena for the development and assertion of leadership." Avenue L Baptist Church, founded in 1846 by slaves as an offshoot of the biracial First Baptist Church, maintained a position of strength within the black community. In the aftermath of the Civil War, the Reverend Israel S. Campbell, formerly general missionary to Baptists in Louisiana, came to Galveston and reorganized the church as the First Regular Missionary Baptist Church (on Avenue L) in 1867. Reverend Campbell had a moralizing effect on the region; he organized the Lincoln Baptist District Association, built a brick church to seat 800, baptized over 1,000 people, and saw the congregation grow from 47 to 500. Methodists in 1848 founded a church for slave members. According to the 137th anniversary program, slave owners and trustees of the Methodist Episcopal Church, South, gave property to black Methodists to form a separate place of worship. In 1866, Reedy Chapel African Methodist Episcopal Church formally organized, naming the congregation after its second pastor, Houston Reedy. Both Avenue L Baptist Church and Reedy Chapel became independent of their parent congregations and entered the New South era as rapidly growing congregations. Four other African American churches quickly sprang up and flourished out of freedom's soil: Wesley Tabernacle Methodist Church, St. Paul's Methodist Church, Shiloh A.M.E. Church, and Mt. Olive Baptist Church. Black Episcopalians from the British West Indies, members of the Church of England, formed St. Augustine Episcopal Church in 1885. Finally, the Dominican Sisters opened a school for black children, which in 1888 expanded to Holy Rosary Catholic Church and parish. Black churches ministered to the spiritual needs of a community whose faith was constantly being tested. But churches offered more than a sanctuary from the evils of the world.[21]

By 1900, fourteen black churches were listed in the city directory, with Sunday schools, youth leagues, and women's and men's church societies. The storm of September 1900, however, destroyed every black church, leaving few records, few artifacts, and no structures. Still, in time and with rebuilding campaigns, African American churches reemerged. In the immediate aftermath, more women showed up in the position of Sunday school superintendent than did men, and more women were listed in that position after 1900 than prior to it. A count in the 1890 Galveston city directory, for example, shows ten superintendents' names, nine male and one female. In 1901, out of seven superintendents listed, four were women. Probably the storm had created an immediate need for female superintendents, however, because by 1905 and 1910 the ratio returned to nine to one.[22]

By 1907, the Wesley Tabernacle Methodist Sunday school superintendent was able to announce "elaborate plans for the Easter celebration," with children's Easter exercises, a sunrise resurrection service, and a communion service. In that same year, several of the churches collectively advertised the opening of their Sunday schools in September—"all parents are kindly asked to send their children." Sunday schools provided religious education within a positive social context. Educators hoped that social events sponsored by Sunday schools would create in the minds of children a sweet connection between Bible study and nurturance. The most memorable event for one adult, who recalled the scene years later, was a Sunday school picnic to Dickinson on the mainland. The whole Sunday school took the train to Dickinson to a "lovely park up there, with swings, dance floors, . . . shade trees, . . . everything a person would want for recreation." The women teachers took basket lunches full of fried chicken, whole hams, and baked chickens, which were complemented with homemade ice cream and soft drinks. Prepared games—baseball and sack racing with prizes—were followed by dancing to a live band. The event provided "lots of fun, wonderful time." Such celebrations and enjoyments offered children the freedom to be themselves and a safe outlet away from the strictures of a biracial city. For adults Sunday school also represented a "means to save the race." With the rising tide of racism, Jim Crow laws, and violence, black mothers and fathers, clergy, and educators put their hopes for a better future on their own institutions, on Sunday schools that taught moral values, racial pride, and Christian faith. Sunday schools were a key to a future that seemed all too uncertain for black children.[23]

In an era of racial self-reliance, churches with their multiple activities became common ground for community solidarity, self-identity, and even radicalization. Galveston churches hosted sessions for the Colored Masons of Texas, state denominational conferences, and Baptist Young People's Union conventions, which brought distinction to the community and kept Galveston worshippers apprised of the internal dynamics of denominational life. For self-improvement several churches advertised literary programs. The Epworth Literary League of St. Paul's Methodist Church listed its first program of the season in 1905—a recitation, musical performance, and the reading of an essay on "Colored Authors and Their Works." The following year, St. Paul's literary society invited John R. Gibson, principal of Central High School, to advise them on "How a Literary Society May Be Helpful to a Community." Discussions such as these provided important information for men and women seeking to learn more about the history and literary achievements of African Americans. Likewise, business interests were served when Reedy Chapel hosted the organizational meeting of the Afro-American Council "to promote business enterprise, to encourage industrial and higher education." Avenue L Baptist Church held the first meeting of the National Negro Business League No. 81, an organization, chartered by Booker T. Washington, which represented more than seventy-five businesses, "giving value to nearly $250,000 of the race's business and professional" life.[24]

Churches provided a safe place for the venting of anger over crimes against the race and other injustices. The Reverend W. H. Jackson of Wesley Tabernacle Methodist Church preached a pre–Labor Day sermon on "The Revolt of Labor against Unjust Employers." When news of the 1906 lynching of a Louisiana man

FIGURE 8.1. Easter services at Shiloh African Methodist Episcopal Church, 1910. Courtesy Rosenberg Library, Galveston, Texas.

reached Galveston, the Ministers' Council held forth in St. Augustine Episcopal Church condemning the act and seeking justice that "lynching might cease." Wesley Tabernacle Church in 1914 again became the site of "the first Anti-lynching Society ever to be organized in the South." The men and women organizers planned to extend the society to work with southern legislatures, Congress, and southern "peace officers," urging them to give the same protection to black prisoners as was given to white. And finally, in 1919, the Galveston branch of the National Association for the Advancement of Colored People was founded, and its organizers launched a "spring drive for members" through six churches. The NAACP membership already included the black ministerial and educational elite of the city as well as church and club women. When it met at Avenue L Baptist Church, the members openly discussed the need for more school rooms for black children. They made plans to inform the school board of the committee's report demanding more classrooms and later held a "great educational and emancipation meeting" at the church on June 19, Juneteenth Day. Churches provided a sanctuary for positive confrontation against discrimination, violence, and injustice.[25]

Women's societies flourished in the atmosphere of church and community. They were founded well before black women's clubs had made their appearance in Galveston and served as self-help groups, as charitable associations, and as enclaves for women apart from male supervision. The Tabernacle Methodist Literary Society presented educational programs of music, recitation, and readings, yet the

Tabernacle's Ladies Advance Club prepared the sanctuary for services by lining the aisles with matting and by purchasing chairs for the podium. The women of St. Augustine Episcopal Church held an annual fair to meet the parish budget, and Mt. Pilgrim Baptist Church held concerts to benefit their congregation. The Woman's Home Missionary Society of St. Paul's Methodist Church conducted Sunday afternoon programs for the benefit of missions. Church bazaars and fairs, organized by women's societies and lasting as many as ten nights, became the main mission fundraisers. The fairs featured different stands selling seafood, hot dogs, or hayrides. At one such event, the women organized a "trip around the world," where members paid twenty-five cents to start at one house "in the East," representing China and serving tea, until they ended up "in the West," where each house represented a different country. In Germany, they served sauerkraut; in Mexico, chili; and in Italy, spaghetti. Children also raised money for churches through plays and the sale of cakes and sodas. Large fundraisers brought great benefits to Galveston's churches; in 1919, Avenue L Baptist raised more than $3,000 and Mt. Olive Baptist more than $1,500. Women's church societies offered a social outlet for good works, were crucial in building the church, and, most important, gave women a voice within their own circles, a sense of strength as women and as members of the African American community. Race pride and gender consciousness grew out of both churches and the societies that flourished within them.[26]

Schools

Equally important institutions for black pride and solidarity were schools. Immediately following the Civil War, however, public school facilities for black children across the South were few and inadequate. The Freedmen's Bureau rented classroom space in Galveston and enrolled more than 300 students. Teachers were often easier to find than rooms for black students. The Reverend Ralph A. Scull recalled that in the East End and West End of Galveston "just after emancipation there were a number of private teachers trying [to] instruct children. In the East End we first had Miss Reedy[,] who was a daughter of Rev. Reedy[,] then pastor of Reedy Chapel A. M. E. Church." The connection between church leaders and educators was a natural one, but Miss Reedy moved away, leaving several male teachers, one of whom, "a northerner, . . . used a cowhide whip quite freely." He was followed by a "Mrs. Flynn, a white widow with one son. . . . She was one of the best teachers up to about 1870." Sarah Barnes, a northern teacher with the American Missionary Association, in 1871 founded the Barnes Institute for teacher training. She also taught sixty-one students six hours a day. She and other missionary teachers conducted 112 pupils through Sunday school lessons and taught ninety more in Bible class.[27]

Education for African Americans in the postwar era not only raised literacy rates (literacy among black Texans leaped from 24.6 percent in 1880 to 61.8 percent in 1900), it also provided teaching positions for trained black men and women, some of whom would be graduating from black colleges. In 1875, as Reconstruction in the state unraveled, "politics changed," many teachers went home to the North, and schools closed. The Texas constitution written in 1875 required that schools become segregated, but the state neither gave money for new separate buildings nor allowed communities to raise funds for schools through local taxes. Although unfair, the new policies may have worked to benefit black teachers in the long run, because freedmen and women continued educating the young in churches and in private schools. A kindergarten for black children, established with private donations, opened in St. Paul's Methodist Church not long after white kindergartens sprang up. In fact, white kindergarten teachers "helped in a material way to establish the school." The driving force behind the kindergarten was Norris Wright Cuney, who served as president of the advisory board. In 1881, when the Texas legislature allowed communities to collect local taxes for schools, Galveston established its public school system. The Galveston school board of trustees created two black primary schools, East District and West District, and five white primary schools. The same teachers who had held classes for children without the aid of a public system were then hired by the school board. With the establishment of public schools, Reverend Scull noted, "there has not been many changes in the teaching force . . . except by deaths and marriages." Thus, a core of educated African Americans, who could depend on a stable income from the city, would now shape the education of black youths. Seven of these fifteen teachers were women.[28]

Galvestonians, in 1884 and 1885, chartered the city's first high schools, Ball High for whites and Central Public (High) for blacks. Children of both races who wished to continue their education beyond the sixth grade, entered their respective high schools. Even as late as 1915, most Deep South cities had no high school for black students, but Texas cities of 20,000 or larger did establish secondary schools, although separate and unequal. In 1887, total black enrollment in Galveston public schools was 1,019, of which 205 were enrolled in Central High. In the words of Central High's first principal, John R. Gibson, the man who "succeeded in inducing the board of education to establish a central [high] school for colored youth. . . . and thus to fit them for something that is really useful in life" was Norris Wright Cuney. At the school's first graduation ceremony in 1890, Maud Cuney received commendation for her essay on the "Necessity of a High School Education" and for her piano solo, which showed "an ability to interpret and execute classical music with accuracy and expression." But the most interesting part of the program, said the *Galveston News*, was the debate over woman suffrage. This first graduation ceremony represented one of the greatest singular achievements of the Galveston black community. That it was inspired by Cuney and advanced through the efforts of John Gibson, a graduate of Wilberforce University in Ohio, should surprise no one. Although dependent on whites for funding appropriation and for the hiring of teachers, African Americans, nonetheless, insisted upon designing their own education and saw black teachers and principals as role models for their children. By 1893, the school board had erected a two-story stone structure, designed by architect Nicholas Clayton, at Twenty-sixth Street and Avenue M for about $13,000. One of the finest black high schools in the South, it boasted steam heat, oak woodwork, indoor lavatories, and floors of wide pine board. Lorenzo Greene remembered it as a "large white stone building [that made] an imposing appearance from the outside." By 1895, alumni reunions replete with concerts,

FIGURE 8.2. West District School faculty in 1915. The Reverend Ralph A. Scull, front row left; Viola Scull (Fedford), second row, second from left; William N. Cummings, principal, front row center; Isabella E. Mabson, third row, third from left. Courtesy Rosenberg Library, Galveston, Texas.

solos, and speeches became part of the cultural landscape of the black community and were attended by black dignitaries. Central High School became an intellectual and cultural center for the black community; mothers' clubs gave valuable aid to the school's extracurricular needs, alumni gathered for annual celebrations, and, after 1905, when the city built an annex for a "colored library," the school became a community resource center.[29]

By 1904, whites were becoming increasingly agitated over issues of black equality and achievement, and segregation policies provided a way to address that "problem." The question of whether blacks should use the library given to the city by Henry Rosenberg took center stage. Rosenberg's will established a public library for all Galveston citizens, but the trustees decided that blacks should have separate facilities. Fearing that blacks sought social equality by asking for admission to the Rosenberg Library, the state legislature passed a library bill establishing a "Colored Branch of Rosenberg Library" as an annex to Central High School. William Noble protested the decision and the exclusion of blacks from the main library, disclaiming any desire on their part for social equality with whites. "No white person . . . need have any fear of the Negro seeking social equality because of being admitted to a library built of fine stone. . . . The negro is not seeking social equality; he

FIGURE 8.3. Central High School, Galveston, built in 1893. Courtesy Rosenberg Library, Galveston, Texas.

does not care for it, but he does insist upon being treated as an American citizen in all manner due him." Editors of the *New Idea* saw it differently, stating that "any Negro who refuses to encourage the colored library given out of the Rosenberg fund is either a fool or an ignoramus. . . . they are blocking their race's progress and standing in the way of their own intellectual light. . . . it is evident [Rosenberg] intended the Library to be a separate institution. Besides it costs the race nothing." The new library received 1,100 volumes and twenty-one periodicals the first year; about 1,500 borrowers registered and took out more than 41,500 books in 1917. By 1918, the collection had grown to 3,000 volumes. Leon Morgan, principal of Central High after 1941, remembered the branch library as a momentary victory for black students in an era of rising racism; it "meant that Central had a better library than Ball High." In 1930, when Lorenzo Greene visited Central High School, he thought that blacks had won a pyrrhic victory. "They were successful enough to secure a school library, which is also open to the public. . . . [but] naturally, it is small and inadequate for the demands made upon it."[30]

After the establishment of separate libraries, the city commissioners seemed intent on threatening black community strength. Consultants to the commissioners in 1905 recommended closing Central High School and shipping high school students to Prairie View Institute for their education. Only a handful of students

FIGURE 8.4. Central High School students, teacher, and principal, John R. Gibson in 1917. Courtesy Rosenberg Library, Galveston, Texas.

had graduated in the past several years, the consultants reported, and they implied that it was a waste of taxpayers money to keep a black high school in Galveston. Actually, seven had graduated in 1904 alone, four girls and three boys. The idea to close Central High School was an attack on one of the most important institutions in Galveston's black community and may suggest the true nature of white fears over educating black students. Should blacks become highly educated, they would seek opportunity in the community beyond manual and domestic labor. William Noble may have fed these fears when he shot off a stinging rebuke in the *City Times*. He stated that if the all-white school board would hire more black graduates to teach in the schools, more students would have an incentive to finish high school. Black parents struggled to keep their children in school, he intoned; they had to buy books twice a year and pay taxes too. "The High School was built when there was not a graduating course, and since its occupancy there has not been a year that some student has not been graduated, and next session there is a prospect of a class of nearly twelve or more. Then why should a High School for the benefit of our youth here be abolished?" Several years later, in 1907, women took the opportunity to reestablish the importance of the high school to the city. The Mothers' Club of Central High School, under the presidency of Sallie Scott, gave its first entertainment, "a good program . . . to a crowded house, perhaps the largest audience to attend an entertainment in Central school in a long time." A week later, the graduating class of 1904 held an alumni event, a concert given by one of their own, Viola A. Webber. Congratulating themselves, the graduates wrote: "The large attendance was not only complimentary to Miss Webber, our classmate, but was indeed encouraging to us, as that was our first public effort as an organization." Black Galvestonians won the argument to keep Central High. The result was that between 1891 and 1914, 121 students graduated, two-thirds of whom were girls. By 1919, the high school had one of the largest graduating classes in its history: six girls and nine boys. Central High remained an important symbol of black strength and an avenue of advancement for women as well as men.[31] White influence over the school continued, however.

In 1909, following the clamor among educators for industrial education for blacks, the school board, through the gift of two prominent white Galvestonians, Morris Lasker and Bertrand Adoue, added manual training and homemaking facilities to Central High and to two other city schools. The model for vocational education had been in place in Galveston as early as 1898, when Holy Rosary Catholic Church instituted the city's first industrial school for black girls. This complemented a belief that black children were better at "handwork" (fashioning useful articles) and domestic work than white children. In one moment of honesty, a reporter for the *Galveston Daily News* wrote that

> There are two ideas of education for the colored race in the United States, both perhaps extremes. One is a strictly literary education in an effort to raise the race in the scale of civilization; the other a strictly vocational training on the belief that the negro race as a race are only 'hewers of wood and drawers of water,' servants of the more intellectual races of the world. The real solution to the problem of negro education seems to be in the happy medium between these two extremes. This is the education given the negroes in the Galveston city school system.

In the same space, however, the writer opined that it seemed "the negro children . . . display more readiness to learn how to cook and use tools than they do to learn the literary subjects taught in the common school branches." Thus, it was not surprising that Central High was given the largest school kitchen so that the young women would become "efficient cooks or housekeepers in the best families of the country." The "cooking department" supplied a steady stream of trained servants for Galveston families. This concept of manual training was supported by black educators in the South, particularly followers of Booker T. Washington, but the black elite of Galveston seldom mentioned the merits of manual training and instead promoted the intellectual and cultural achievements of its children. As early as 1898, African Americans expressed opposition to Washington and his emphasis on "industrial training for the negro," concluding with the thought that "diversification of the mind and a varied ambition is as much a part of the negro as it is of the white race." Where white Galvestonians adhered to one standard of education for blacks, African Americans steadfastly adhered to another.[32]

Inequality of salaries was another problem for black educators. Although administrators and teachers became leaders, respected and honored in their own communities, salaries for school administrators were not equal. In 1896, the principal of Ball High earned $2,300 a year, while the principal of Central High earned $1,800. Elementary principals for three of the four white schools earned $2,200 a year—more than Central High's principal. Black elementary principals earned $1,500 a year. Salary equalization did not come to Texas teachers and principals until 1945, and then only through the courts.[33]

Despite the introduction of manual instruction and unequal wages for educators, students and parents rallied around Central High, adding a night school in 1912 and turning it into a community recreational center in 1919. The school board adopted the idea of beginning a night school by allowing use of the building, but it witheld funding from public sources. Private donations, however, sponsored the project so that sixty-five students ranging in age from fourteen to fifty-four could attend. In 1919, "the playground association of Galveston for the colored children" raised over $400 to establish a neighborhood playground on school grounds. Finally, in 1924 the school trustees expended $164,000 on Central High, adding two science laboratories, a home economics classroom, a gymnasium and auditorium, a school library, four new classrooms, and offices, teachers lounges, and new restrooms. Two years later, the school was accredited by the state, allowing graduates to enter colleges without taking entrance exams to prove eligibility.[34]

Public Celebrations

Community solidarity did not depend on churches and schools alone. Galveston's black citizens sought to encourage self-awareness and race pride by observing holidays, holding festivals and parades in a style that reflected their African American heritage. The Fourth of July, for example, was celebrated publicly for a time solely by African Americans in Galveston. The only parades held on Independence Day in 1905 were provided by the African American Loyal Knights of Progress and the Hawley Guards. On that day, blacks eulogized the contribution of Crispus Attucks, who was slain in the Boston Massacre of 1770. One must wonder what it meant to black Galvestonians when they alone celebrated the nation's independence? On Labor Day, in a racially separate celebration, men and women honored the dignity of black labor and local unions with bands, marching militia, and a festival. In 1903, nearly 1,500 black citizens—Screwmen, Teamsters, Mallory line freight haulers, railroad men, Hawley Guards, Holloman's Juvenile Light Guards, the drum corps, the Island City Brass Band, and the Women's Nineteenth of June Committee—marched or rode in decorated carriages through the streets to the

Gulf City Park. They ended the day at the Sea Wall Pavilion, "the best pleasure resort in town for colored people." Labor Day and the Fourth of July were holidays that were sometimes shared by whites and blacks, but in separate spaces. African Americans celebrated these days in a consciously public way, filling their revelry with symbolic meaning specific to their circumstances.[35]

Historians tell us that parades provided for marginalized groups (this could include women and minorities) an opportunity to "enter public life." Parades, although peaceable and often joyous, brought with them a confrontational edge, emphatically stating a right to the streets, challenging notice by dominant groups, and reinterpreting the meaning of events differently from the dominant culture. Whereas northern blacks in antebellum times often chose to celebrate emancipation day, or an end to the slave trade, rather than Independence Day, Galveston blacks reveled in the Fourth of July. For them, Union victory inserted its meaning into the commemoration. By contrast, white southerners drew a veil over Independence Day, as it reminded them of Confederate defeat. Parades announced African American solidarity and pride in an era of increasing segregation. By appropriating national symbols and national holidays and by incorporating African American themes, black Galvestonians said to whomever would listen and observe: "We too are American workers and citizens."[36]

Another summertime event celebrated by the black community was the August Children's Day Parade and Summer Night Festival at the Sea Wall Pavilion (also known as Children's and Old Folks' Day), sponsored by the managers of the city's black newspapers. The parade and festival brought the African American community together, allowed older and younger denizens to mingle, and gave hardworking laborers a rest during the hottest month of the year. Too few working-class southerners could afford the luxury of a vacation or a trip to cooler climes; thus, the Summer Night Festival gave workers a sense of escape. Young people from the Central High School Band and Holloman's Juvenile Light Guards led the way to the pavilion and park, followed by "six decorated goat wagons, . . . a number of dressed up doggies . . . [and] hundreds of ladies and little children." The Sea Wall Pavilion became the setting for a grand picnic with soda and food vendors and entertainment for 1,700 revelers. Donations for prizes and goods came from black and white merchants and tradesmen in the city. Such festivals conducted in an orderly way were meant to be observed by white Galvestonians. The day following the 1904 event, the *New Idea* editor thanked the donors and participants and remarked that "it gives us inspiration to be better citizens, set high standards for the race, and regard the interests of our friends among the white race as well as our own."[37]

By far, the most important holiday for black Texans was Juneteenth Day. It commemorated June 19, 1865, the day Texas slaves first heard the Emancipation Proclamation delivered by Union major general Gordon Granger. Because Galveston was the site of the reading, the black community took special pride in its Juneteenth Day festivities. The parade and speechmaking, which allowed participants to symbolize and explain the meaning of emancipation and the struggle for equality, was organized entirely by women. The Women's Nineteenth of June Committee invited both women and men to join the parade and, at its end, address the audience or give papers, recitations, or songs from a public podium. The planning, however, depended on the committee. Reports from the 1904 newspapers recount that the morning parade featured five divisions of mounted police, black militia, decorated vehicles "representing the race's progress in industrial, educational, commercial and laboring pursuits," a grand marshal with his assistants, and floats depicting May Pole Girls, the Goddess of Liberty, and Maids of Honor. An official program at Sea Wall Pavilion featured the Emancipation Proclamation read by Laura Austin. Her presentation was followed by a paper presented by Everlena Anderson, who posed as the Goddess of Liberty. Numerous speeches and a paper on "Solving the Negro Problem" ended the program. Women organized the symbolic portion of the celebration, while men took charge of the barbecue and afternoon festivities at San Jacinto Bay. The men planned an old fiddlers' contest as well as fishing, crabbing, boating, and bathing excursions, while ex-slaves and Union soldiers over fifty were plied with free barbecue. Ten years later, Juneteenth celebrations spread out to surrounding communities. But the Women's Nineteenth of June Committee continued to organize the Galveston parade, floats, and speeches.[38]

By 1919, Juneteenth Day had become so important that white employers gave their workers the day off and so large that the annual parade ended with celebrations in two parks. Juneteenth represented the greatest black cultural event in the city; but what did it mean that women organized that portion of the day dealing with the theoretical and ideological aspects of freedom? What did it mean to women who dressed in the clothing of Liberty and spoke on the promises of emancipation? The statue of liberty, we are told, is emblematic of the power of hope. Liberty is America's symbol, representing freedom, opportunity, and guidance to all dispossessed. By her torch Americans find a light to the future. She does not look back to the past; rather Liberty heralds what is to come. Liberty was often used by image makers to express patriotism or to legitimate political policy, but she turned her best face toward immigrants fleeing oppression and poverty. Did daughters of slaves see Liberty as the emancipator of a bonded people? Or did she represent one of the few beacons of hope in a racist age? Did Liberty's gender resonate with special meaning for those who carried the double burden of race and sex? And what of white women and Liberty? Did she not also represent them in their quest for equality of rights, for sexual equality, for emancipation from gender restrictions? Clearly Liberty transcended race, class, and even gender, but what trenchant criticism reflected upon whites as black women mirrored for them the image of emancipatory hope in a national symbol both familiar and powerful? Black women understood the power of the symbol, manipulated it to give meaning and substance to the freedom earned by ex-slaves and to the promise of freedom for themselves and their children. Wrought with allegorical hope, Juneteenth reminded Texans that freedom in any era is worth celebrating. No other public event instilled African Americans with such awareness and historic pride, and perhaps no other event so publicly managed to voice the desire for sexual equality that black women had been quietly demonstrating in their churches, schools, and clubs.[39]

Philanthropy, Health Care, and Women's Clubs

W. E. B. Du Bois wrote in 1909 that "specialized and scientific philanthropy [were] just beginning to appear among colored people." Thus, it was in keeping with this chronology that the Galveston Relief Association, chartered in 1901, announced plans to build a Home for Aged Colored People for $15,000 near the town of La Marque, thirteen miles from the island. Although the Galveston city poor farm took in elderly and infirm African Americans, the Relief Association reported that no home solely for aged blacks had ever existed. In fact, just after the 1900 storm, Magnolia Sealy sought out Clara Barton for relief of the aged homeless who were temporarily living in the ruins of Avenue L Baptist Church. Emmaline Silas, who worked as a servant for the Sealys, cared for this group. Magnolia Sealy brought Clara Barton and Emmaline Silas together and started them off with a $25 donation, to which Barton added $300. The money had come from black sympathizers in the North to be used "entirely by colored people in Galveston." A committee comprising two men and two women, including John R. Gibson, principal of Central High School, and Emmaline Silas, formed the Colored Relief Society and purchased ten acres of land where "the soil is rich enough, by proper management, to make the Home almost self-supporting." By 1912, an executive committee comprising black principals—Gibson, H. T. Davis, and W. N. Cummings—was ready to begin construction on a cottage, once it reached its fundraising goal of $1,700. Eleemosynary institutions were expensive to start up and maintain, as white women in Galveston readily concluded. While Galveston's black community was prosperous in comparison to rural black enclaves, wealthy black entrepreneurs, who would be the logical donors for such institutions, simply did not exist in the black community. Help from white donors and benefactors was slow in coming; hence, the project languished.[40]

The need to care for orphans took on an urgency that could not wait for public support. Yeager Children's Home, founded by Albertine and Charlie Yeager in 1917, was among the only surviving refuges for African American children in the city. In the entire state of Texas, only six private orphanages for black children existed, and the state built no home for black orphans until 1929. The Yeager Home was not an orphanage in the formal sense; the Yeagers took in children to their own home for forty-two years, supporting them with their own finances. Charlie Yeager worked for forty years with Armour Packing Company, while Albertine Yeager cared for the children, many of whom had been orphaned, abandoned, or neglected. They began their service to the community during World War I, when mothers who had taken wartime jobs brought their children to the Yeagers because they could not afford day care. The couple saw the need to take in on a permanent basis children who had lost their parents or who had come to them "with a plea for help." At times there were as many as forty children in the home, although the average in later years was eighteen. It was the only home to care for needy children regardless of race or religion. After years of struggle, the Yeagers found civic support from both black and white citizens. Darlene Clark Hine noted that black benevolence "usually assumed the form of small-scale, per-

FIGURE 8.5. Albertine Hall Yeager, who, with her husband, Charlie, founded the Yeager Children's Home in 1917. Courtesy Rosenberg Library, Galveston, Texas.

sonal assistance and involvement," and volunteer service was preferred to dona-tions.[41]

Health care for blacks in the South was seldom adequate, but black medical schools and black-owned hospitals continued to supply physicians and treat pa-tients. Dr. J. H. Wilkins, the first black physician to present a certificate to the Galveston county clerk from the Examining Board of the Sixth Judicial District, began his practice in 1883. The following year, R. F. Boyd, professor of physiology at Meharry Medical College in Nashville, visited Galveston to lecture on the "Needs of the Negro Race" and the "Demand for Negro Doctors." Nearly twenty years later, Dr. Mary Susan Smith Moore, one of the first women to earn a medical degree from Meharry, came to Galveston. There she set herself up in business, first by opening a meat market on the corner of Twenty-ninth Street and Avenue M, hiring a butcher to carry on the trade, and then in 1906 grandly opening the Hubbard Sanitarium as a hospital for African Americans. The advertisement announced that Dr. M. S. Moore was the physician and surgeon in charge, and the sanitarium would "be kept for operations and all sickness except contagious diseases"; cost to patients was from $1 to $4 per day. Located at 4015 Avenue N, it was hailed as the first of its kind in Texas. Dr. G. W. Hubbard, founder of Meharry Medical College, had visited Galveston the year before the sanitarium opened in his name. Declared a "noted white educator" by the *City Times*, he had come to lend support to two of his former students, Dr. Wilkins and Dr. Moore.[42]

By then, John Sealy Hospital had provided a separate wing for African Americans staffed by black doctors and nurses. As a segregated facility, it lacked many of the amenities provided white patients. In view of this, John R. Gibson raised $450 to buy new beds for the hospital. Following his example, an organization of women volunteers emerged to meet the needs of black patients and staff. The Colored Women's Hospital Aid Society, presided over for several years by Mrs. C. G. Harris and Miss I. M. Daniels, represented the elite of Galveston's black community and embodied the middle-class values of benevolence and sacrifice. But this women's group did not mirror white charitable societies, for its purpose was to ameliorate the suffocating effects of racism and to help patients claim a sense of dignity through race pride. The society, which began with thirty members in 1909, became one of the most influential black women's organizations in the city, receiving recognition from the State and National Association of Colored Women (NACW).[43]

The Hospital Aid Society met every month at the home of its various members; the meetings began with prayer and often ended with hymn singing. The women held teas in order to raise funds to buy beds for the "colored ward"; they made hospital gowns for patients, cutting them out at the meetings and taking them home to finish. They donated infant clothing, pajamas, suits for the men's ward, bed rests, wheelchairs, screens, cribs, and modern conveniences for the obstetrical room. They purchased 500 trays for serving ice cream and oranges to the patients and staff, as "there are so many sick people out to the hospital." They ended up serving eighty-nine patients and five nurses on one occasion; the average was between sixty and seventy. Members visited the hospital wards, cheering patients, answering questions, and providing amusements for children; one merchant, an ice cream vendor, donated seventy spoons for patients. The Hospital Aid Society also sponsored cultural events. Madame Ada Bell Griffin gave a dramatic recitation in Progress Hall in 1924 to raise money for the ward. Funds for their many contributions came from the dues paid by members; from Hospital Aid Day, which solicited funds through churches; and from the Community Chest, successor organization to the United Charities. In a report compiled by W. E. B. Du Bois, members of the Women's Hospital Aid Society stated that "the interest has never lagged, and as the society grows older we hope to accomplish much more."[44]

At the local level, the Hospital Aid Society belonged to a City Federation of Women's Clubs for African Americans, which brought together the presidents of the various women's clubs for coordination and sharing of information. The women met monthly at Avenue L Baptist Church, indicating the strong link between churches and women's club life. Annually the federation held a Tag Day to collect money for the "Girls' Delinquent Home" in San Antonio. The federation raised $200 on Tag Day, and members of the Hospital Aid Society pronounced it "quite a success in every way."[45]

The Hospital Aid Society belonged also to the Texas Association of Colored Women's Clubs (TACWC), which organized in 1905 "with the aim of improving the home, moral and social lives in the various communities." It held its annual convention twice in Galveston, first in 1910 and again in 1919 at Avenue L Baptist Church. Work for the state association began with just a few women representing their clubs throughout the state, but, by 1924, 100 clubs and 18,000 members had joined. Believing that "the highest ambition of the young woman should be to possess the best character of womanhood," the major project of the TACWC was a Training School for Delinquent Negro Girls begun before 1920. The 1922 fundraising drive netted $2,000, enough to put a down payment on a "ten acre plot of land with a five room house, barn and city water" in San Antonio. In 1923, the Texas Federaton of Women's Clubs and the Joint Legislative Council (or Petticoat Lobby, a coalition of white women's clubs that lobbied the state for women's issues after enfranchisement) endorsed the project, momentarily showing biracial support. By 1926, annual Tag Day drives, such as those sponsored by the Galveston Federation, raised funds to cover the total price of the school, $5,500. The state finally funded and expanded the Brady State Training School for Negro Girls in 1947, moving it to Crockett, Texas.[46] The Hospital Aid Society sent delegates, expenses partly covered, to the state and national conventions; delegate Viola Scull Fedford was on the state program and returned with "fine reports." As a member organization of the NACW, the Hospital Aid Society received information about other clubs and their activities and was exposed to the literature, the ideas, and the philosophy of uplift and service that marked the pages of the national organization. The NACW based its concerns on issues of race, gender, and poverty; hence their motto, "Lifting as We Climb," spoke of their duty to the race as well as to their sex. By 1914, the NACW was 50,000 strong, with twenty-eight federations and more than one thousand clubs. Middle-class Galveston women had tapped into a national movement, but the most vitalizing aspect of their work was their ability to actively counter the damage of segregation.[47]

Other women's clubs, following a regional example, served either as charitable, as self-help, or as civic improvement organizations. The Willing Workers Charity Club, founded in 1923 and made up mostly of churchwomen, visited the sick and elderly. Originally opposed by the founders' pastor, the women chose to disassociate from the church rather than give up the idea of a charitable society. Thus did African American women firmly assert their freedom to organize in the face of gender opposition. The members raised funds to buy fruit and cards for shut-ins by holding teas. One member had a "missionary car," which took them on their various rounds to visit and pray with the sick each Sunday afternoon. Just before Thanksgiving each year, the "Workers" presented their shut-ins with a bag of fruit; as many as 250 bags at a time passed through their hands. The Paragon

Social Club sponsored a tea and a lecture on "Women's Clubs, For What Do
They Stand?" The Women's Progressive Club, under the leadership of Laura A.
Pinkney, was organized in 1913 to "disburse charity and to improve social conditions, to bring together women interested in promoting the welfare of the city, to
care for the sick and poor, to look after juvenile offenders, and to work in the cooperation of all social forces and agencies in Galveston." The club invited Ida B.
Talbert of New York City to lecture on "the race's uplift." Pinkney, one of the
most outspoken women in the city, introduced to integrated audiences the efforts
of the Galveston Relief Association in providing a home for elderly blacks. Black
women's clubs and societies tailored their tasks toward self-improvement and service, but they also followed a Progressive Era agenda for civic activism for their
own people. They continued to be a voice for their community, which sought
moral legitimacy, better city services, and fairer treatment at a time when their
race was under attack by conservative forces.[48]

    With a stable economic base; two elementary schools; Central High School;
a myriad of churches; labor unions, and secular organizations, such as Masons
and Eastern Star, International Order of Odd Fellows and Household of Ruth,
Knights of Pythias and Order of Calanth, Knights and Daughters of Tabor, Daughters of Zion, Mosaic Templars, Pilgrim Lodges, and Sanctuaries; and mutual aid
societies, African Americans created a complex network of interlacing and connecting institutions that acted to empower black citizens as well as protect them
from the indignities of life in the segregated South. Women were more involved
than would first meet the eye when reading historial accounts. But women's in-
visibility, according to historian Glenda Gilmore, was the product of their im-
mersion in churches and in social, charitable, and civic clubs that most whites
did not see or understand. "Southern black women initiated every progressive
reform that southern white women initiated, a feat that they accomplished without
financial resources, without the civic protection of their husbands, and without
publicity." The tensions caused by disfranchisement and segregation, nonetheless,
were addressed by black women in symbolic form, in tangible aid to dependents,
and in organizations designed to alleviate the worst effects of a racist age.[49]

Black Aspirations and White Supremacy

Middle-class blacks believed in racial uplift. They wrote about the disadvantages
of slavery but spoke in hopeful tones about the "advancement of the race" and
the progress of their people. In every way they strove to provide evidence of their
education, entrepreneurship, morality, piety, and industry. They followed a genteel
code and expected to be seen as prosperous and energetic, worthy of respect by
their peers and by whites. Despite the advances made by African Americans in
education, the professions, business, church organizing, and club, band, and benevolence associations, white leaders continued to advise them to remain servile
and not to strive too hard to reach beyond their allotted place in life. They learned
that few whites had actually wanted black advancement; it represented a denial of
their notions of white supremacy.

    A good example of this came in 1905, when the Baptist Educational and

Missionary Convention meeting in Galveston chose Judge Lewis Fisher to give the welcoming address. Fisher advised this group of black educators about their morals, their homes, and their duty as citizens, but, according to observers, said nothing "of the white man's duty to the Negro." He discouraged higher learning for blacks, contending that "he saw no use for Greek and Latin." Fisher added more insult to this group of ministers and educators when he prattled that "Rastus," unlike "old slavery time darkies," was not faring well in freedom. Oblivious to the progress African Americans had made since emancipation, Fisher announced that freedom had done nothing for Rastus, had given him no school and no home and had subjected him to temptations, the result of the evils of freedom. "He was greedy as a prairie colt turned into a feed house and he ate ignorantly of every-thing. As a result the race of today has become foundered as a horse, all the doctors of the race question are advising him and he has become a very sick . . . man." W. H. Bearden, editor of the *New Idea*, incensed by the tone and language of the judge, noted that "Rastus is coming on all right, he is practicing medicine, preach-ing, lawing, teaching with his Greek and Latin; buying homes, doing business and in many instances is the leading citizen in his community. . . . What Rastus clam-ors for is life, liberty and pursuit of happiness equal under the law with other races." Protests of this sort were of no avail to a white citizenry that continued to believe in white supremacy and found little to praise in black efforts toward ad-vancement.[50]

One area of black life that whites felt worthy of praise, however, now seems ridiculously out of touch with the reality of race relations. Galveston men wanted to raise a statue to the "Old Negro Mammy" and eulogized this lost mythic char-acter with all the nostalgia of a Joel Chandler Harris writing about Uncle Remus. In the words of the proponents, it was "the beginning of a great movement throughout the South for the building of a monument to the memory of the " 'old black negro mammy.' " The first meeting in 1910, involving forty "southern men," came just in time to seek the endorsement of the United Confederate Veterans, who were convening in Mobile for Confederate Memorial Day. They remembered Mammy as "one of the grandest characters which the history of the world records"; she was "above all chronicles of pure unselfish and unfaltering devotion. . . . It was she who took up the burdens and responsibilities of the home life when the tenderly reared mistress was crushed beneath the weight of woe and uncertainty caused by the absence at the 'front' of the husband and brother fighting the battles of their country." In this instance of Old South nostalgia, not only did Mammy gain extraordinary strength of endurance but also her white mistress dis-solved into puddles of weakness. In 1910, black women were being forced to the back of the streetcar, while white southern women were beginning to fight for the right to vote. Could white men have been wishing for a different order, one that put them more firmly in control?[51]

Believing themselves to be the first in the country, elite Galveston men ini-tiated a "Mammy movement." They thought they paid black women the highest compliment when they proclaimed that "though her skin was black, her soul was white." Cheryl Thurber argues that Mammy was a character created to mollify feelings of guilt on the part of whites for their shabby treatment of African Americans at the height of the Progressive Era. She also notes that the Mammy image may have resolved sexual tensions existing between white males and young black women. Mammy was an asexual character who replaced carnality with nurture, thus making her "safe" for intimacy within the white family. Ashamed and delusional though they may have been about the true nature of the black slave nursemaid, these men, nonetheless, put forward an instructive message to the black community. It went something like this: This "good old soul" was completely loyal to her "white folks," just as her former slave owners were now being loyal to her memory. Should a black woman want the endorsement of the white community, she should become more like that "most faithful, most trustful, most devoted creature that ever served with simple faith and love sincere in the sphere in which had pleased God to place her." In her servility, they mused, Mammy was "the aristocrat of aristocrats, the patrician of patricians." Perhaps the most revealing statement of all showed that the black mammy supported no wishes for herself, sacrificed out of love her sleep for sick members of the family, denied her own children her attention, and prayed for the success of the Confederacy. In the final tribute to white male delusion, they claimed that she "did not leave her owners for freedom, because her love for her mistress was stronger than the love for freedom. . . . Was the black mammy a slave? She seemed to own her mistress as much as her mistress owned her." The meaning behind this scene of martyrdom was to suggest that if all blacks would be loyal to whites, race relations would be forever harmonious.[52]

Here one must wonder, had white Galvestonians completely missed the point of Juneteenth celebrations? Had they turned a deaf ear to the orations of young black women dressed as the goddess Liberty, upon whom hope for a future free from the fetters of oppression devolved? Or had whites been all too aware of Liberty's implications; were they frightened by the aspirations of black young people for equality? Had they calculated the pressure of black labor strikes, black Republican power, and black resistance to Jim Crow? Did they find it necessary to reply with iconographic images of beloved slave women bound, not to homes of their own, but to those of whites? Was the message still one of subordination? If the black mammy elegies were proffered as something positive toward African Americans, they entirely missed the mark. And so too, it seems, did African American celebrations of freedom seem to miscarry, bringing threatening messages to whites about freedom. Mythic imagery abounded in these years; the image of a superannuated slave unable to run away with the other slaves because of age was now heralded as a heroine at the same time that Liberty, symbol of freedom, was given new life by descendants of enslaved Americans.

It would seem as though white and black Galvestonians were talking past each other, missing an important opportunity for true communication, understanding, and eventually, cooperation. Consequently, the heart of Galveston's black community remained insular in many ways, a community within a community, little understood or appreciated by its white neighbors. Yet whites and blacks mingled on a daily basis, worked with each other in close if unequal relationship. Homer Hollier, steward of the prestigious Harmony Club and owner of a catering business, won contracts for the social events of the age, the Artillery Ball and the 1903

Kempner wedding. Reverend Scull recalled that "from the [eighteen] sixties Galveston had its brass and string bands. The Colored Cadet band served the pride of Galveston for many years and were often employed at big white funerals and in street parades." Men found themselves working in close proximity to whites in nearly every part of town, but black women more often crossed over into the private and semiprivate world of white homes and churches to work as midwives, domestics, or as maids and janitors in white churches. These women became intimately knowledgeable of the ways of whites, while whites knew little about the African American community. Margaret Sealy Burton, one of the few elite white women who left any record of her thoughts on the subject, spoke affectionately of her mother's midwife Aunt Maria. "My mother had Aunt Maria for all her babies, and many a time the old mammy was seen with a basket on her arm, covered with snow white linen, in which she insisted that she was carrying new babies to the young mothers." But Margaret became frightened when taken to Aunt Maria's funeral and remembered it as a "horrible experience." The exposure to Aunt Maria's world, her friends, and her source of support was for Margaret Burton as foreign as if she had sailed to Africa.[53]

There is evidence that whites in Galveston supported blacks through occasional donations and through the United Charities (later the Community Chest). Donating money was one thing; working together on community projects was quite another. The inability of white women in the early twentieth century to reach across the color line in sustained endeavors left black women on their own to form church societies, self-help groups, orphanages, old folks' homes, black hospitals, hospital aid societies, a Juneteenth Committee, literary and civic clubs, and a school for delinquent girls. Galveston black women, interested in securing the vote, formed the Negro Women Voters' League of Galveston. A black branch of the YWCA was finally built in the 1950s, and St. Vincent's House, a settlement house for families, emerged in 1955 under the auspices of the rector and the women of St. Augustine Episcopal Church. Finally, in the 1960s, with the passage of a civil rights act, white churchwomen joined black churchwomen in support of St. Vincent's House. Prior to that time, however, African American women managed well; forced to become responsible for their own edification and to carry on their "duty to the race," they acted in a socially and racially conscious manner.[54]

Although historians have portrayed the Progressive Era as progressive for whites only, in fact, black women created a progressive movement of their own that is only now being discovered with the mining of African American sources and careful attention to the activities and organizations of women, black and white. African American women differed from black men in their approach to reform. Sometimes they joined men in protest action, but more often they worked in gender-specific groups. Whereas prominent men, such as William Noble, Joseph Cuney, and members of the Ministers' Council, publicly and vocally challenged segregation policies, middle-class African American women formed associations to ameliorate its painful consequences. Less confrontational in their methods, they nonetheless addressed the question of the "Negro problem" with their own solutions—they commandeered help for black neighbors, children, the elderly, and victims of segregation. They sustained "an institutional infrastructure that made Black survival possible in the age of Jim Crow."[55] That this could happen within a city that at the same time saw the advancement of white women seeking cleaner alleys, vegetation for parks and esplanades, antiexpectoration laws for streetcars, paved sidewalks, trash removal, and clean markets and dairies — but without seeming to cross paths — is remarkable and sad. Yet neither racial group left much evidence of recognizing the other. Interracial cooperation among women in Galveston would have to wait a bit longer. Why this should be the case in a city as small as Galveston is part of the troubling aspect of race relations in the New South.

9

WOMEN ORGANIZING FOR THE VOTE

*This talk about women having enough moral suasion to get what political
changes they want reminds me of the dog barking at the moon.*

—C. A. T., *Galveston Tribune*

In March 1913, many of Galveston's "leading ladies" found themselves engaged in entertaining an audience at the Grand Opera House, which was filled "almost to the last seat from gallery to pit." The dramatization "of good-humored raillery and entertaining comedy," for which these women willingly shed their earnest upper-crust demeanor, was actually an appeal for the cause of woman suffrage. The three-part program featured an "Anti-Suffrage Monologue" that poked fun at the "antis"; "Lady Geraldine's Speech," a suffrage comedy that enlisted the acting talents of at least seven local suffragists; and "A Dream of Brave Women," a tableau in which the women dressed in elaborate period costumes defined by "electrical effects." This last segment, most interesting for what it reveals about local suffragists, presented female characters from the past, whom they felt most symbolized "the part . . . women have played in the world's history and progress."[1]

The women chosen to signify progress, both as historical characters and as their Galveston models, represented a curious mixture of national pride and local status. Loula Lasker, daughter of Galveston's great Jewish philanthropist, Morris Lasker, played Pocahontas; Jane Alvey, granddaughter of John and Margaret McCullough, who were among the first Presbyterian missionaries to Texas, played the role of Molly Pitcher; Elizabeth Cady Stanton was represented by Waldine Z. Kopperl, daughter-in-law of another prominent Jewish philanthropist couple, Isabella and Moritz Kopperl; Minnie Fisher Cunningham, who would become president of the local and state suffrage leagues, played Clara Barton; and, lest the audience forget that these ladies were southerners, a Daughter of the Confederacy was represented by one of the UDC's own. Then, to emphasize to Texans the urgency in joining the "suffrage states," tableaux depicting the states of Wyoming, Colorado, Utah, Idaho, Washington, California, Kansas and Arizona, which had already passed suffrage amendments, were filled by young women, many of whom were just finishing their debutant season.[2]

The affair had taken weeks of elaborate preparation by some of Galveston's wealthiest and most civically active women. It was presented in the city's cultural palace to a paying audience that, for the most part, supported the aspirations of the women on stage. The plays were humorous and light, pointed yet inoffensive. Since clubwomen had often used the technique of raising money for their causes through "entertainments" of this type, supporters and promoters were comfortable with the medium. Most important to the cause of suffrage was the fact that the tableaux and plays gave opportunity to prominent Galveston women *and their daughters* to show themselves in favor of the vote in a manner that did not make them look or seem strident.[3] The campaign for women's rights was just getting started in Galveston, but the entertainment had the air of familiarity. Suffragists, who also were much involved in other women's club activities, understood this and used the oft-familiar clubwomen's fundraising techniques subtly but persistently to purvey to male citizens the radical notion that women, too, should have the vote.

As we have already seen through the actions of members of the WHPA in the years after 1914, Galveston women were capable of confrontation and assertiveness in the cause of public health or community betterment, but they began their campaign for their own rights in a much softer tone, packaging a radical idea in comfortable wrappings. Eventually, career suffragists, women who had staked their lives on suffrage, would grow weary of these innocuous methods and would stride off to wage fiercer battles in the statehouse. But in 1913, the drive for equality in Galveston very much resembled the ways and means southern women had always used to drum up support for their goals. The presence of clubwomen in the mobilization for suffrage, the persistence of clubwomen's techniques, and the growing tension that this created is indicative of one of the enduring contradictions of southern suffragism. Without clubwomen there would have been no southern suffrage movement; with them, the movement at the local level remained torn between the conservatism of the region and the need for militant mobilization in behalf of their own rights.

Galveston suffragists came from the same ranks of women who had created a new Galveston after the 1900 storm. They formed a viable suffrage society just at the point when the WHPA was concluding its first conciliatory phase with city government and was about to launch into its second, more confrontational, phase. As the WHPA began to challenge government officials in their duties as guardians of the public welfare, members of the Equal Suffrage Association began to change their tactics as well. Suffragists would become less tolerant of political obstructions at the same time that WHPA members became more aggressive in their pursuit of pure food and milk. As the women's community grew stronger in the Progressive Era, especially with the founding of the city's first Young Women's Christian Association (YWCA) in late 1914, a newfound vitality emerged among women progressives that accelerated their energies and drive toward their own goals — whether it be safeguarding the public health, protecting working women, or expecting the right to vote. Of course, better educational and professional opportunities for women, the national and state campaign for suffrage, the continued incorporation of women into nationally affiliated women's organizations, the increased agitation among progressives for reform legislation, and then the massive

drive for women to help in the war effort also spurred women on to greater public
service, both for the city and for the women's community.

Understanding the woman suffrage movement in the South from a local perspective has not been easy. The existing articles and books on suffrage are primarily
studies of state organizations or of individuals who gave their wholehearted energies to the cause.[4] Although the subject is far from exhausted, we now have a
better picture of the politics involved at the state, regional, and national levels. In
studying the rise as well as the role and function of *local* suffrage societies in the
South, different sets of questions emerge: did the grass have any roots, for example,
and, if so, how healthy were they, and did these local roots advance or hold back
the greening of the general suffrage movement? Remembering that there were
many more foot soldiers than commanders mobilizing for suffrage, we need to ask
what kind of southern woman was willing to organize, campaign, march, and hold
meetings in her own community for the ideal of equal voting rights? How were
clubwomen, the so-called white-gloved ladies of the South, able to transcend their
domestic culture in order to emerge as "New Women" campaigners for suffrage?
What forces brought them publicly to espouse such goals? Was it religion, professional training, club work, youthful idealism, or some combination of several
influences? And, finally, how did local societies sustain suffrage in their immediate
communities while fostering state-level associations and leaders?

The answers are beginning to emerge as we explore the issue in Texas, the
first state of the former Confederacy and the ninth state in the nation to ratify the
Nineteenth Amendment. It is no doubt axiomatic to point out that strong popular
suffrage sentiment in the South was most likely to be found in cities. In Galveston,
the roots for a suffrage movement had been developing since at least the 1880s
with the growth and spectacular rise of the city as the state's leading cotton export
center. Prosperity promoted an ever more sophisticated citizenry, and as the community of 22,000 in 1880 almost doubled to 40,000 by 1900, so too did the diversity
of economic prospects.[5] Accompanying the impressive aggregation of wealth was
an equally imposing growth of clubs, societies, and private associations. By 1910,
the city directory listed no fewer than sixty-eight church and synagogue societies
(of which forty-four were women's), eight benevolent institutions (six managed by
women), thirty clubs (eight for women), forty-six fraternal associations (six for
women), and fourteen immigrant relief societies (three managed by women). All
this points to the fact that membership in societies, clubs, leagues, unions, and
associations was an important element of town life in the first decade of the twentieth century for both men and women and added a sense of integration for
individuals into community life. Discrete groups provided the necessary precon-
ditioned environment for the formation of women's *reform* associations. But the
fact that Galveston in 1910 was swimming with little clusters of self-defined groups
did not alone set the stage for the formation of a suffrage society.[6]

More essential to the process was the *type* and success of groups that women
created both before and after the turn of the century. As has already been shown,
between 1880 and 1895 four permanent benevolent institutions — two orphanages,

a home for elderly women, and a free kindergarten — were conceived and managed by white women to provide leadership and training for elite, civic-minded women. In 1891, women interested in furthering their education and broadening their intellectual horizons founded the city's first literary club, the Wednesday Club. It was followed by several more women's musical and patriotic clubs. Then, six months after the disastrous hurricane of 1900, women survivors united to form the Women's Health Protective Association (WHPA), the first citywide progressive reform association open to white women.

At the same time, male civic commercial elites were planning the nation's first commission form of government. This held great portent for white women activists who believed that the city's needs would best be met with a "progressive" form of government. The city commission system, however, eliminated city ward representation, thereby breaking up bloc voting patterns among African Americans and members of the working class. As it turned out, city government was becoming more exclusive just as female civic associations were becoming more inclusive. An opening for women of the same class with city male leaders, however, appeared at a moment when middle-class and elite women sought to influence governmental policies.

Of course, the Galveston suffrage league did not develop in a vacuum independent of the rest of the state. There had been suffrage associations earlier, and they involved Galveston women nearly from the beginning. Although petitions for woman suffrage had been sent to the Reconstruction and Redeemer constitution framers in 1868 and 1875 without success, no suffrage society came into existence in Texas until after the establishment of the National American Woman Suffrage Association (NAWSA) in 1890. In 1893, however, Galveston resident Rebecca Henry Hayes, whose background in journalism and vice presidency of the National American Suffrage Association no doubt fueled her mobilization, organized the Texas Equal Rights Association (TERA). After her election to the presidency of the TERA, Hayes articulated her thoughts on suffrage in the South: "I have met with the warmest sympathy for my views and was myself surprised at the rapid growth of equal suffrage sentiment among conservative people." Her leadership of the movement lasted for two years, from 1893 until 1895, and in that time she traveled 9,000 miles for the sake of enfranchisement. Unfortunately, the association developed ideological differences, and Hayes lost her bid for reelection. This first state suffrage association did not last beyond 1896.[7]

In the meantime, southern states began their systematic campaign to disenfranchise black voters, ending with the poll tax in Texas in 1902. Texas women supported the poll tax through the Texas Federation of Women's Clubs, which endorsed it and educated women to its advantages. The tax, they argued, would improve the electorate and purify the ballot by removing poor blacks, poor whites, and Mexicans from voting. The electorate then would be left to white middle-class men, who, presumably, were educated enough to vote. The argument that held more currency with women, however, dealt with public schools; $1 of the poll tax ($1.50 per voter) went toward education. Given the disproportionate spending on white schools — in 1910, Texas spent an average of $10 per year on white students and $5.74 on black students—the tax benefited most those who could afford to pay it. Galveston's Cornelia Branch Stone, as vice president of the TFWC in 1902, guided the Committee on Constitutional Amendments to the conclusion that voters must support the tax in order to increase funding for schools. In 1902, the poll tax amendment was ratified by voters, and state legislator Alexander W. Terrell added two additional amendments in 1903 and 1905 intended to solidify white Democratic party gains.[8] Thus, the question of black male voting was effectively eliminated, raising hopes for a woman suffrage movement that would be "for whites only."

"Electoral reform" of this nature had several results for potential women voters. Precisely because blacks held limited political power in Texas politics, being virtually eliminated from voting with legislative and municipal "reforms," there was never any real general threat to the white electorate if women were granted the vote.[9] Hence, Aileen Kraditor's notion that "Southern white women *began building* a suffrage movement [mainly to] insure the permanency of white supremacy in the South" was not true for Texas at least.[10]

Conceivably, the reality of black disfranchisement led to the next attempt to form a statewide suffrage society. In 1903, women organized another suffrage league, this time in Houston under the leadership of Annette Finnigan. The Houston society invited Carrie Chapman Catt, president of NAWSA, to come and speak, and the result was the formation of several local societies, including one in Galveston with twenty-five members. Following this success, suffragists formed a state suffrage league in Houston, and several Galveston women joined the executive board. The next year, Galveston sent delegates (among them Julia Runge, daughter of Johanna Runge, founder of Galveston's free kindergarten) to a statewide suffrage convention in Houston. All was well until Annette Finnigan left Texas for several years and the movement once again died. As long as there were individual leaders willing to stimulate interest in suffrage, the societies stayed viable. But when leadership failed, there was little on which to fall back. The reason this was so rested on the fact that few urban women's civic groups had as yet experienced politicization of their goals. Until women's civic clubs, such as the WHPA in Galveston, confronted intransigent government officials or apathetic citizens, mobilizing for the vote seemed an abstraction at best. Needing the vote to gain their civic improvement agendas and realizing the impotence of their political positions necessarily preceded the upsurge of viable local suffrage societies. And in Texas, no state association flourished until local societies had already been well established.[11]

The demise of the second state suffrage society coincided with the rise and promise of the Women's Health Protective Association in Galveston. As we know, between 1901 and 1912, WHPA members replanted the island with trees and shrubs killed by the grade raising while at the same time forming committees to inspect and report on the condition of streets, alleys, markets, bakeries, restaurants, dairies, and housing. This early period of civic activism was marked by cooperation with city officials, and the women showed more annoyance than resolve at the lack of support for clean alleys, efficient trash removal, and sidewalk construction. But after 1913, with the publication of the sanitation survey, members began to agitate for the enforcement of the pure milk and pure food and drug ordinances of 1907. Just at the point that the WHPA members were heating up in anger over governmental foot dragging, enthusiastic women formed a local suffrage society. At first, suffragists had not yet witnessed the full wrath of the WHPA and were therefore acting more like polite clubwomen than determined feminists. But as the battle for safer milk and food ensued, becoming louder and more virulent, suffragists began to feel themselves pulled into a political vortex. Consequently, suffrage strategies changed from holding "entertainments," such as that shown earlier in 1913, to lobbying directly before the public and parading in the streets. Thus, in politicizing women's domestic goals, the WHPA brought activist women directly into the political process as public policy makers and as seekers of political privileges.[12]

Another lesson learned by would-be suffragists through the WHPA concerned voting: constituent members *elected* WHPA officers. Casting votes for association officers represented the first opportunity for Galveston white women of all classes and religious backgrounds to learn about open balloting. Previously, elite groups of women confined their voting to officer elections in clubs or in church societies, neither of which had the advantage of size or openness. The democratization of the white women's progressive reform movement served to awaken women to their potential voting strength and instituted among them the habit of voting. Elected officers handled the business of domestic politics, that is, the goals of the WHPA, while city commissioners handled the business of city politics. At some point in the minds of women across the South, these two concepts merged, and city politics became women's politics. When women began to see themselves as potential city officeholders, as citizens, and certainly as voters for city office, the suffrage movement moved into high gear.

Once women experienced voting within a civic association and began to work with, then struggle against, city hall over issues of interest to women, the stage was set for the advent of a successful suffrage society. It was a great leap, and not every woman was willing to travel the distance from civic-mindedness and arguing a woman's agenda before the city commission to joining a suffrage society. Nevertheless, in February 1912, seventy-four women and seven men became charter members of the Galveston Equal Suffrage Association (GESA). The *Galveston Daily News* reported sardonically, "If the men of Galveston doubt that the cause of woman's suffrage is knocking loudly at their doors clamoring for admission they need but have peeped into the ballroom of the Hotel Galvez Thursday . . . where . . . [150] Galveston women . . . were in session to discuss the question."[13]

Just as the WHPA in 1901 had received its impetus from an "outside agitator," Anna Maxwell Jones, so the local suffrage society depended on her again for the push it needed in joining the nationwide suffrage movement. Anna M. Jones, by then described as "a leading suffragette," and her sister Etta came from New York in 1912 for the express purpose of mobilizing suffrage societies in their native state. The *Galveston Daily News* reported that the women of the city "have been informing themselves for a long time on this subject, and have been waiting for some leading spirit to call them together." Once Jones was able to bring the women out to their first organizational meeting, she addressed them about the need to begin a suffrage league. First, she enumerated the nations in the world — twenty-two — that granted the franchise to women, then she recounted the triumph of six American states, all in the West, that had provided women the vote. As Texas considered itself both a western and a southern state, she pointed proudly to the women of California as the western model to follow; 80 percent of the women of Los Angeles went to the polls at their first election. Then she described the women of the Southeast who were mobilizing their states for suffrage: Mary Johnston of Virginia, "Miss Breckenridge" of Kentucky, Mrs. Hoke Smith of Georgia. But she finally eluded to the reasons why women in general should have the vote: "As guardians of the home, protectors of the health of the family, intrusted [sic] with rearing and training of the children, we women are interested in the public welfare." Pointing to the pure milk issue, she preached that "much is being done by women's clubs and other organizations toward arousing the public conscience to the necessity for pure food laws, wholesome surroundings and sanitary uprightness." She intoned that the "physical welfare and the moral uplift of the community [would] be more quickly brought about through the direct influence of the ballot in the hands of women."[14]

Jones was not alone in speaking out at the organizing rally; several local women gave their reasons for wanting the vote. Sally Trueheart Williams, daughter of a prominent realtor and a staunch Presbyterian, went right to the heart of the conflict with city government. "Housekeeping," she reasoned,

> used to begin at home and end there. But time has changed all this. It begins now . . . in the public laundry, the grocery, the dairy, the meat market, or the candy store; it only ends in the home. . . . The woman who keeps house must in a measure also keep the laundry, the grocery, the market, the dairy, . . . and in asking for the right to vote they are following their housekeeping in the place where it is now being done, the polls.

Rebecca Brown (Miss Betty of Ashton Villa), one of the wealthiest unmarried women in the city, argued that "every property holder should have the vote." Moreover, she resented the fact that education did not lead to equality. Remembering the days when schoolchildren and Sunday school students of Trinity Episcopal Church competed for scholastic honors, she complained "that girls often carried off the highest honors, but that when each reached the age of 21 the boy had a vote in the government but the girl was not permitted to be progressive." Julia Runge, a kindergarten teacher, wanted "equal salary for men and women who do equal work." Since Galveston was a southern town, no one brought up the issue of votes for black women, nor did any woman address the more radical view that as women they were all — black and white — entitled to equal citizenship based on natural rights. Privately, Galveston suffragists wrote what they could not express in public. "I feel humiliated over the position of women," wrote Cordia Sweeny, "and the way she has been looked on in the past, as a slave or a plaything. I want to be neither, and want woman equal with man before my daughter grows up."[15]

Although Galvestonians were relatively late in organizing for suffrage compared with more western states, in Texas in 1912 they were actually riding a wave of organizational fervor as women formed local societies in San Antonio, Dallas, Waco, Tyler, San Marcos, and Houston with the return of Annette Finnigan. (Austin had already organized in 1908.) Suffragists from New York and Dr. Anna Howard Shaw, president of the National American Woman Suffrage Association, stumped the state in 1912, thus aiding Texans in their struggle to organize for suffrage. By 1913, seven local societies carried the banner; by 1915, twenty-one; by 1916, eighty; and in June 1918, one year before ratification, ninety-eight societies and leagues across Texas supported votes for women.[16] The founding of local suffrage societies was critically important to the movement as a whole. No viable, permanent state-level association in Texas existed *before* the forming of strong local societies. Sentiment for suffrage in the cities, supported by women active in local affairs, ensured the establishment and maintenance of a state organization. And support for the franchise, as demonstrated in the case of Galveston, depended upon a sufficient level of women's club activity that addressed community problems.

In 1913, Texas suffragists founded a state association. Eleanor Brackenridge of San Antonio agreed to serve as its president and to lend her own superior reputation, her family's good name, and her business acumen to the movement. But while Brackenridge gave important symbolic prestige to suffrage, the organization did not take on the efficiency of a well-oiled engine until the election of Annette Finnigan the following year. She turned it into a businesslike political organization by creating a headquarters for state work at the Brazos Hotel in Houston, by hiring a headquarters secretary who engaged in field work during the summer months, and by recruiting three nationally known lecturers to tour the state. Her first presidential report noted:

> A year ago we started without any office equipment or records. Today we have records of all correspondence, all Press, and all legislative work. We have a card catalogue system established containing the names of all organizations and their Presidents, all county committees and their chairmen; the names of suffragists in un-organized counties, and of all Representatives in the Legislature, with their ... attitude toward suffrage.... Our object ... has been to make the Texas Woman Suffrage Association a political organization, working along political lines, and conducted in a businesslike manner.[17]

Her major goal for the year was to question legislators on their position regarding the submission of a woman suffrage amendment to the people. This was followed by a petition to the legislature sent round the state for signatures asking "that a woman suffrage amendment be submitted to the voters." Then Helen Todd, a national lecturer for suffrage, made her tour of Texas cities "while the legislative campaign was attracting the attention of the state." It was a brilliant tactic, for it required the work of hundreds of local suffragists who visibly advertised their own support for woman suffrage while gathering signatures. It forced legislators, who may have hoped the issue would disappear, to declare their opposition or support. It identified the opponents of suffrage, who were then harassed by their constituents. And Helen Todd's campaign kept the issue before the public.[18]

By making woman suffrage a press item, by bringing it before the state assembly, and by encouraging the active work of local suffragists, the state organization took on its true political mission. Finnigan realized all of this and concluded: "In looking back over the work of the year, of course the legislative campaign stands out as our biggest piece of work,—it was really a brilliant success. By means of this campaign, we advanced the cause of 'Votes for Women' in a few months more than we could have done in ten years by the ordinary propaganda methods." This exciting leap into the political forum drew interest from those towns and villages where none had existed before and challenged well-established leagues to move from the parlor to the city parks for demonstrations. With a legislative proposal in place, recruiting new leaders and founding new suffrage leagues became a more realizable goal as women saw that they were no longer just talking about votes for women.[19]

The Texas Equal Rights Association (renamed the Texas Equal Suffrage Association in 1916) positioned itself to work in three major directions: first, at the national level, to support and remain under the guidance of the NAWSA; second, at the state level, to lobby the Texas legislature for passage of a state suffrage amendment; and third, at the local level, to aid and guide the activities of the local suffrage societies, particularly in organizing new suffrage leagues within their same counties. This put tremendous pressure on the state officers, especially the president and the state field workers, to give their time exclusively to suffrage work. The state association needed dedicated, energetic women who were willing to make enormous personal sacrifices for the sake of the cause and who would be able to reside in Austin when the legislature met. Texas women, such as Annette Finnigan, who were "called up" to lead the state suffrage association more closely resembled "career" suffragists, whether salaried or not. Their past lives as southern ladies quickly blurred under the demands for suffragist leadership.

Local suffrage societies differed from the state organization in their responsibilities to the movement. Their duties fell into five basic categories: to educate and agitate, not only their own members but also nonmembers and male voters; to increase membership in their own city and aid the field workers in establishing new associations within their county; to petition the legislature with as many local signatures as possible; to help raise money for their own work and for the campaign at the state level; and occasionally to send delegates to state and national meetings and to lobby the state legislature.

Local suffragists differed from state suffrage workers also in style and level of commitment. It is here that we find some white-gloved ladies and New Women acting together, although not always in concert, for the goal of enfranchisement. White-gloved ladies should be understood as a synonym for clubwomen, who respresented respectability without controversy, who took part in the round of women's teas and fundraisers for worthy causes, or who studied Shakespeare and Milton in literary clubs. Many clubwomen were content with the status quo and were unwilling to campaign for suffrage or risk their positions as community leaders even after 1912, a period when suffrage was considered safe. A few white-gloved ladies made the important decision to campaign for women's votes openly and joined the Galveston Equal Suffrage Association. But they quickly learned that the commitment to suffrage needed not only a decision to struggle for rights for women, which they made, but also a change in the way they approached the struggle. No mere conventional club tactics of endorsing national issues at the local level and then adjourning for refreshments would suffice in the campaign for political equality. Nothing less than aggressive, determined action, much like the efforts of the civic-reforming WHPA, would win the fight.

In short, suffrage demanded that New Women in both mind and deed stir the southern conscience. Anne Firor Scott offers a succinct description of the meaning of the term "New Woman" for southerners. "Like the lady, the new woman represented only a small minority of all women in the South. Unlike the lady she did not become the universal ideal. At her best, she maintained the graciousness and charm which had been the sound part of the chivalric ideal and, without losing her femininity or abandoning her responsibility for the propagation of the species, became an important force in public as well as in private life." New Women saw themselves as movers and motivators of others, not just protectors of status, convention, and the social order. All suffragists were ideologically New Women in endorsing voting rights, but those with conservative tendencies fostered by years of club work remained motivated by old patterns wherein they made few challenges to the existing order. They offered the movement respectability without innovation. State-level officers observed this when they evaluated the fire and determination of individual local suffrage societies. They clearly saw the difference between aggressive New Women and those with the habits of white-gloved ladies.[20]

Many favored the traditional white-gloved ways, while others sought more aggressive approaches to gaining the franchise — marches, outdoor rallies, and lobbying efforts at the statehouse. Yet, for the sake of the movement in the South, southern women needed to tread cautiously; too much militancy could turn voting and supporting men against the cause. Judge Robert G. Street, a suffrage supporter, cautioned the women "to be conservative, yet persistent in their methods to obtain the franchise." A *Galveston News* headline captured the dichotomy: "Galveston Ladies in Favor of Woman Suffrage Are Not Militant, but Are Deadly in Earnest." A fine tension presented itself between the usefulness of aggressive tactics and genteel confrontations of the sort southern women dispatched with grace.[21]

Local sufffragists faced another problem in their quest for political equality. Suffragists in Galveston had no "city hall" against which to struggle. Unlike the members of the WHPA, who targeted city commissioners or the city health department for reform, suffragists labored to change the attitudes of the entire male electorate. WHPA members could see immediate results, or lack of them, when confronting elected officials over issues of sanitation. But the campaign for political equality seemed diffuse and abstract compared to the fight for public health. WHPA reformers could rail against city hall without appearing altogether unladylike. After all, they were fighting for the public good. Suffragists were in the business of persuading male voters to change the law for the sake of women, which, however much they couched it in terms of the public good, still appeared self-serving. Local suffragists tried through plays, lectures, booths, and parades to convince voters of the need for equal enfranchisement. But tangible results, or lack of them, were seen most visibly at the state level, where true confrontation was waged. The consequence in Galveston was that WHPA members seemed more strident than suffragists, who hesitated to appear too forward in asking men to vote for their cause.

In cities like Galveston, women supporters contended with these conflicting ideals and processes. Many, though committed in principle to votes for women, were unable or unwilling to rearrange their lives to make the movement their sole activity or to adopt measures that would brand them as controversial. This did not mean that their efforts were nonessential or immaterial. A. Elizabeth Taylor was correct when she stated that "local societies played an important part in the votes-for-women movement, for on them rested the chief responsibility for promoting favorable sentiment in their communities."[22]

In order to gain "favorable sentiment," an image of white-gloved respectability with involvement in many other community and club activities needed to accompany their commitment to equal suffrage (white gloves symbolized both purity and activism; gloves were worn for public occasions). Local suffragists were not entirely free to abandon their club and church work, for these interests proved to male opponents that Texas suffragists were not wild-eyed harpies but civic leaders whose dedication to home, family, and community entitled them to a deferential hearing. Local suffragists also differed from their state-level sisters in their inability to remove themselves for long periods from the community or from civic work. By honoring their pledge to the city as well as to suffrage, local suffragists protected the movement from the taint of radicalism.

Most Galveston suffragists continued their involvement in the circle of women's associations. During the Progressive Era there were multiple distractions—the WHPA sanitation fight with city hall waged for five years until 1917; then the war effort commenced with Liberty Loan drives, anti-vice committees, and soldier comfort stations. During this same period women formed branches of the YWCA, the Red Cross, and the Anti-Tuberculosis Association, which required teams of women to canvass for both members and money. In a general sense, the suffragists' involvement in these varied activities supported the argument that equal dedication to community and nation earned equal voting rights. But involvement meant time away from suffrage campaigns, limiting the wholehearted advancement of the movement. This proved extremely frustrating to the women at state suffrage headquarters who wanted maximum commitment to the cause. They understood the need for credibility and respectability but also saw opportunities for suffrage slipping away.

This was understandably discouraging for some local suffragists as well. As white-gloved ladies, they wanted to maintain their involvement in the community because their work directly and tangibly affected themselves and their families. But as New Women, they often felt shackled by the very commitments that gave them access to public life. In order better to understand the problem these women faced, we need to discover who Galveston suffragists were.

The suffrage association rolls make it very clear that in an association open to white membership there were two types of members—those who supported the association nominally and those who committed themselves to work as officers. Nominal members, who composed by far the largest percentage, were willing to be listed as suffrage supporters in print and were often tapped more heavily for financial support. By 1913, the GESA had grown to 175 members and by 1915 to 300. This compares favorably with other Progressive Era women's associations in Galveston. The Woman's Christian Temperance Union (WCTU) climbed to 100 members, and the WHPA reached a maximum of 500 members in 1915; the YWCA opened with 2,000 members in 1914, a level it maintained until 1920. Of the 300 members of the GESA, 36 were men; about two-thirds of the women were active in at least one other women's group (many of the members were from other towns), and 29 were active as officers in the years 1912 to 1917.[23]

It is the officers' biographical and organizational profiles that provide the clearest picture of who southern grass-roots suffragists were (information is available for twenty-four of the twenty-nine). (See table 9.1.) At least twelve of the Galveston suffragists were native Texans; nine were born in Galveston, seven were from other states, and five were of unknown origin. With respect to age, eight (33 percent) were in their thirties in 1915, six (25 percent) were between forty and fifty, and three (13 percent) were in their fifties; only two were older, but five were in their twenties. Three-quarters of the Galveston suffragists were older than thirty (see table 9.2). The southern women who marched for votes were not necessarily young and idealistic; most were mature women in the prime of life.[24]

With respect to religious ties one might expect to see a high percentage of Methodist women, as Methodism in the South has often been linked with a lively reform tradition, including the establishment of settlement (Wesley) houses and, of course, the endorsement of prohibition. But a search through the suffrage officer rolls turned up only two Methodists and one Baptist. The majority of suffrage officers were Episcopalian (nine) and Presbyterian (four) (See table 9.3). A significant number of suffrage officers came from Episcopal and Presbyterian backgrounds because in these churches status and wealth interfaced with a strong tradition of community service. Historically, these two churches provided greater numbers of women civic leaders than any of the other congregations on the island. But it is unclear to what degree religiosity, piety, or faith motivated Episcopal or Presbyterian women to campaign for the vote. The active participation of women from these congregations in secular organizations beyond the church and their relative inactivity in church prayer groups and women's societies suggests that civic-mindedness, a sense of status, and notions of the unfairness of woman's political inequality were at heart more important motivators than faith. And perhaps the reverse was also true. Those women who maintained strong ties to the women's societies within their churches were less likely to become suffragists. Jean Morgan and Ida Austin, two extremely strong community activists, for example, who were also closely tied to their church associations and Sunday schools, did not become suffragists. Short of having a statement from each of these women regarding their faith and their acceptance or rejection of suffrage as a cause, we can only speculate as to why they made the choices they did.

Particularly striking was the fact that sixteen of the twenty-four officers (66 percent) were married. Dr. Ethel Lyon Heard combined marriage with a career as a physician and city pathologist, as well as serving a term as president of the WHPA. The fact that Dr. Heard was childless may, in part, explain her ability to

TABLE 9.1. Galveston Equal Suffrage Association Officers, 1912–1917

Name	Marital Status	Date of Birth	Religion	Profession	Age in 1915
Bettie Ballinger	S	1854	Baptist		61
Lucy K. Bornefeld	M	1886	Episcopal		29
Mary F. Bornefeld	W	1860	Swedenborgian	Piano Teacher	55
Minnie F. Cunningham	M	1882	Methodist	Pharmacist	33
Edith Fordtran	M	1887	Episcopal		29
Mary Gardner	S	1876	Episcopal	Librarian	39
Caroline Waters Garrett	M	1878	Episcopal		37
Emma Gonzales	M	1872	Episcopal		43
Bessie Grundy	M	1872	Presbyterian		43
Emma Harris	M	1868	Episcopal		47
Ethel Lyon Heard	M	1876	Episcopal	Physician	39
Ellen Hildenbrand	M	1877	Lutheran		38
Annie Hill	S	1863	Episcopal	Teacher	52
Etta Lasker	S	1886	Jewish		29
Helen McMaster	M	1863	Methodist		52
Maud Moller	M	1870	Presbyterian	Real Estate Agent	45
Pearl Penfield	S	1885		Medical Student	25
Marie Ralston	M	1879			36
Kate Rembert	W	1855	Episcopal	Teacher	60
Mrs. G. Scott Shannon	M	1882			28
Mary Steele	M	1866			49
Sadie Stubbs	M	1884	Catholic		31
Rebecca Trueheart	S	1884	Presbyterian		31
Sally T. Williams	M	1871	Presbyterian		44

Source: Galveston Women Database.

spend time with the movement outside of her professional life. But the majority of the other Galveston suffrage officers, including Minnie Fisher Cunningham, were also childless; of those who could be identified as mothers in 1915, only four had children under the age of ten at home. If anyone should wonder about birth control among southern women, one need only look at the drop in the number

TABLE 9.2. Galveston Equal Suffrage Association Officers by Age in 1915

20s = 5	21%
30s = 8	33%
40s = 6	25%
50s = 3	13%
60s = 2	8%
24	100%

N = 24

Source: Galveston Women Database.

TABLE 9.3. Galveston Equal
Suffrage Association Officers
by Religious Affiliation

Episcopal	10
Presbyterian	4
Methodist	2
Baptist	1
Lutheran	1
Jewish	1
Catholic	1
Swedenborgian	1
Unknown	3
	24

N = 24

Source: Galveston Women Database.

of children per childbearing suffragist between 1890 and 1915. Mary Fowler Borne-feld, first president of the GESA, born in 1860 and married in 1882, bore her first child in 1883 and continued to have a baby every two years thereafter until 1893, when her sixth and last child was born. By contrast, younger suffragists who married after 1900 limited their families to a maximum of three. Although the sample is too small to make generalizations about the efficacy of contraception in the South, the fact that so few suffragists had children at all is a significant factor in considering who joined the movement at the local level.[25]

Perhaps the most unifying characteristic of the married suffragists was the fact that their husbands belonged to the white-collar and professional classes: three lawyers, two physicians, two shipping agency owners, two prosperous merchants, one newspaper publisher, four transportation agents, one clerk of court, and one bookkeeper. It is safe to conclude that a comfortable middle- to upper-class lifestyle and the relative absence of maternal responsibilities provided the leisure time necessary to organize for club and suffrage work.[26]

Eight of the active suffragists in 1915 were single (two widows); here wealth clearly marked the difference in their status. Three were independently wealthy with sizable inheritances; three were teachers, one was a librarian, and one a medical student. Discrepancies in wealth did not appear to prejudice one worker against another, but every active suffragist was considered "socially acceptable." No Galveston suffrage officer came from the working class, where, for working women, finding leisure for union activities was a problem. Suffragists and labor spokeswomen lamented the absence of working women in the suffrage ranks but found few solutions to the problem.

Recruiting working women to the movement proved difficult. State suffrage president Annette Finnigan wrote to Eva Goldsmith, a member of the Legislative Committee of the State Federation of Labor, about the situation. "Galveston women of their own accord brought up the subject of reaching the working woman and said that they felt that they were not reaching the people." Finnigan asked Goldsmith if she would travel to Galveston and help the suffragists "in reaching the working women and the labor element." Goldsmith complied but recommended that the young state suffrage field-worker, Pearl Penfield, "go down and speak for them. . . . I think Miss Penfield can do some good work at this time by visiting the different shops and making the girls talks, for suffrage is being talked of more and more all the time and some outsider could do more good than my continued talk every day." But Goldsmith cautioned that not every suffragist could do the job: "Now I am going to be frank with you, do not send Mrs. [Emma] Harris to Mr. Young [president of the Galveston Labor Council], because it will do no good and may do harm. It seems that Mrs. Harris is stiff and can not reach the laboring people there."[27]

Appeals were also made to working-class mothers and homemakers, but they, too, did not join in great numbers or become part of the association's leadership. Perhaps they felt alienated from the ranks of suffrage officers, most of whom were members of the most prestigious Protestant churches. Or perhaps working-class women continued to see the vote as an abstraction divorced from the realities of their lives. Gaining the vote represented an ideal that could bring few tangible and immediate rewards to alleviate either low wages or inadequate housing. State and Galveston suffrage leaders gave the matter of organizing working-class women their attention, corresponded with labor spokeswomen, and sought solutions on how to penetrate the labor pool, but Galveston suffragists, many of whom were traditional clubwomen, had great difficulty presenting their message to working-class women. Clearly, active suffragists in Galveston were middle to upper class, and many of the leaders came with persuasive powers attached to class status and prominence. Status and elitism cut two ways, however. Apparently Texas suffragists carried their strength borne of their respectability to the statehouse, where they were well received by progressive assemblymen. But their middle- to upper-class respectability repelled working-class women whose voting menfolk were most in need of education on the issue of woman suffrage. Suffragists tended to equate working-class men with immigrants, whose votes they saw as a "counterbalance [to] the intelligent vote of Galveston."[28]

White suffragists also discussed the suffrage rights of black women only as problems that would have to be eliminated with disfranchisement measures. Indeed, Cordia Sweeny, a member of both the GESA and the WCTU, wrote Annette Finnigan that women who are "sleeping on equal rights for women . . . have one fear, of the negro woman getting the vote. I see no reason why the negro woman could not be eliminated, just the same as the negro man." Minnie Fisher Cunningham, Texas Equal Suffrage Association president, stated in 1917: "The same moral influence that prevents the negro man from gaining control of political matters can, and will, serve a similar purpose with respect to the negro woman." When an African American woman requested admission to the Texas Equal Suffrage Association, Cunningham wrote in 1918 that the idea of affiliating with African American women had never before been considered. Carrie Chapman Catt, NAWSA president, when asked about the matter, retreated to a states' rights position. The petitioning black suffragist was hence denied admission to the Texas association. Belle Critchett of El Paso shed the best light on this sordid picture when she explained: "We want to help the colored people but just now it is a rather hard question." The hard question was, of course, whether southern men would ratify votes for women if suffragists aligned themselves with black women. Pervading racism kept the question of African American women's voting rights out of the suffrage campaign.[29] The fact is that prominently placed or highly educated urban white women waged the suffrage campaign in Texas by appealing mainly to progressive white men for financial support and to progressive legislators for political support.

In Galveston, the respectability of suffrage officers did not rest exclusively on age, occupation, and their husbands' economic and social status (hence their own status). Equally important were their impressive organizational histories. Twenty-one of the twenty-four officers for whom data are available were involved in other women's clubs and church societies. The three that had no activity besides suffrage were the youngest women, all in their twenties, who had not yet had time to amass a civic leadership portfolio. It is a credit to the GESA that its members elected three eager but unproven workers. The remaining twenty-one give an impressive record of volunteer activism.

Logically, the older the woman the more associations and activities were to her credit. Among the twenty-one women with multiple associations, at least nineteen other clubs and societies were represented. Nine of the women were officers in four or more other associations. Betty Ballinger, age sixty-one, and the only Baptist, was an officer in six other clubs and associations. Eleven of the leaders held offices in from one to three other clubs. Dividing the clubs and associations into such categories as church societies, boards of lady managers for benevolent institutions, literary and performing arts clubs, patriotic-hereditary associations, and civic associations, including the WHPA, YWCA, Red Cross, and Mothers' Clubs, one finds, not suprisingly, that suffragists preferred active leadership in civic associations, followed by literary clubs, patriotic-hereditary associations, women's church societies, and benevolent institutions.

Clearly, this was an overwhelmingly active group of women. Mostly Texas born, middle-aged, patriotic, educated, well informed, industrious, and convincingly civic-minded, Galveston suffragists projected an image of unblemished respectability—an image that at times masked their political goals. The *Galveston Tribune* gave them what it considered high praise in 1915 when it wrote: "Galveston women are not the kind that go in for every fad that comes along. They are in some respects old-fashioned, meaning they are not feverishly new fashioned. They are inclined to proceed wisely, conservatively; and that is why they haven't been shouting their heads off these past 20 or 30 years about the ballot."[30]

The local women leaders may have appeared conservative to the *Tribune* editors, but the GESA differed from popular women's clubs in one respect: eight of the twenty-four officers were professional women who, undoubtedly, had seen the inequality in their paychecks and were willing to campaign for the vote in order to gain equal earning opportunities. Minnie Fisher Cunningham said that in 1901 in her first position as a prescription clerk at a Huntsville drugstore, she earned "$75 a month and everybody else $150. And now you could see what made a suffragette out of me—Equal Pay for Equal Work, only it wasn't equal work, I was the professional!" The fusion of women professionals with women volunteers who had long been prominent in civic improvement gave the GESA both a more worldly composition and certainly a more strident feminist spirit.[31]

Although we have accounted for suffragists in other types of organizations, there is one group conspicuously absent from the list of civic organizations to which suffragists were linked — the Woman's Christian Temperance Union. The WCTU flourished in other parts of Texas, but it never became a strong women's organization in Galveston. Frances Willard founded the first union in Galveston in the early 1880s; this group was reorganized in 1888. By 1906, women formed a third union with twenty members; it failed and was finally replaced by a successful union in 1914, organized not by a southerner but by Margaret Bilz, a national WCTU organizer from Michigan. In its first years, the local union focused on "working toward the suppression of the liquor traffic" and the "best interests of the community." This meant opening a chapter to the soldiers at Fort Crockett, convincing the school board to allow temperance education for children, holding a bazaar fundraiser, organizing a union among the city's African American citizens, persuading ministers to set aside special Sundays for temperance, and holding educational lectures with Minnie Fisher Cunningham as speaker on votes for women. But prohibition was not a popular topic in a city that boasted a brewery owned by local citizens and a sizable population of first- and second-generation German-speaking peoples, as well as Irish, English, Italian, and French.[32]

Suffrage was among the WCTU's several points of interest, but it was not the main item; consequently, suffragists and members of the WCTU were not close. Only one suffrage officer maintained membership in the WCTU, and the tension between the two groups was so intense that in 1915 she resigned from the GESA in a huff over perceived slights on the part of suffragists toward WCTU leaders.[33] The truth is that in Galveston suffragists and WCTU members moved in different circles bound by religion and economic status. The issues of class and religious preference in southern women's reform have often been overlooked, but in Galveston and perhaps in other urban areas, members of the WCTU belonged almost exclusively to evangelical (Baptist and Methodist) churches and were mostly middle to lower-middle class in economic status. As a rule, WCTU members joined only Protestant associations such as church missionary societies and the YWCA. The WCTU and the YWCA were the only two women's civic organizations in which at least 50 percent of the officers came from evangelical churches. In other words, when entering the public sphere, WCTU members, along with evangelical women in general, tended to confine their activism to those organizations where Christianity provided the organizing principle.

The GESA, by contrast, was more heterogeneous in membership. The officers belonged to eight different denominations, and their record of service to the community, contributed mostly through secular organizations, was far broader. Economic status varied among the suffrage officers: Miss Etta Lasker, for example, came from a family that could afford to donate a park and $35,000 to the city school system; Miss Mary Gardner, who moved to Galveston in 1903 from Montana (a suffrage state), worked all of her life as a librarian. If any link can be established between religion and suffrage in the island city, it was to those churches that had long promoted women's societies concerned with clothing and feeding the poor and that continued to emphasize community service. As discussed earlier, the women of Trinity Episcopal and First Presbyterian churches as early as the 1880s had taken charge of relief for those citizens (mainly women and children) who were in no way served by any other rescue or relief agency. Finally, suffrage officers did not confine themselves to Protestant groups; rather, they expanded upon their religious bases to embrace secular and political associations.

The evidence gathered from Galveston challenges the prevailing notions that the southern suffrage movement sprang from evangelical Protestant roots and that WCTU members who fell in line after Frances Willard's organizing tour of the South in the 1880s became suffragists when assemblymen "listened politely but refused to act" upon temperance legislation. The view advocated by some scholars of an orderly progression from Methodist missionary society to WCTU to suffrage may well be true for suffrage leaders at the state level or in other southern cities, but this view does not account for the origins of suffrage support among Galvestonians. The great storm of 1900 was a major catalyst for women's involvement in city reconstruction and political reform, but organizational experience among women had preceded the storm by twenty years. The origins of a suffrage movement in Galveston began not with Frances Willard's tour of the South but with the advent of urban problems brought on by the rapid rise of the city's population, the discrepancy in wealth among citizens, and the attendant dislocations caused by a more mobile and industrialized society. Some members of the Galveston Women's Health Protective Association and other groups that had fought city hall in order to ensure pure milk for children or parks and playgrounds for their families were the most anxious to preserve their gains by winning the vote and by entering into public office. Women in southern cities with strong progressive agendas for reform had the most to gain from access to the voting booth.[34]

Other cities need to be tested, of course. In a cursory review of the founding of suffrage societies in other southern states, a similar pattern of dependence on urban centers prevailed. In most cases, urban suffrage societies preceded permanent and viable state equal suffrage associations. A majority of the states experienced the beginning of fledgling state suffrage leagues in the 1890s, but they sputtered and died only to be resurrected after permanent local societies formed, usually after 1910. (See table 9.4.)[35]

Although urbanization acted as a catalyst in advancing suffrage, it was not the only causative agent. If that had been so, then suffrage societies would have formed in the cities of the South a decade or two earlier, especially in some cities—St. Louis, Baltimore, New Orleans, Richmond—where the population was sufficient to bring women together in cohesive groups. Margaret Nell Price observed that "suffrage agitation in the South falls roughly into three periods of time: 1) Before 1885 with individual interest, and isolated societies. 2) 1885 to 1912, when some state-level associations formed. 3) 1912 to 1920 when organizations that had disappeared revived and permanent local suffrage societies spread." The period between 1912 and 1920 coincided with the culmination in major southern cities of women's progressive civic reform activities. Prior to 1912, women worked for the betterment

TABLE 9.4. Suffrage Associations by State. (The following table shows the state, the year a permanent suffrage organization formed, whether the first association was local or state level, the cities of the first societies, and the city population at the time or at the decade closest to the time of incorporation.)

State	Year Formed	Local	First Cities	Population	
Alabama	1910	yes	Selma	13,600	(1910)
	1911		Birmingham	132,600	"
Arkansas	1911	yes	Little Rock	46,000	(1910)
Florida	1912	yes	Jacksonville	57,699	(1910)
Georgia	1890	yes	Columbus	17,300	(1890)
	1894		Atlanta	65,500	"
Kentucky	1888	no	Lexington	21,500	(1890)
Louisiana	1900	yes	New Orleans	287,000	(1900)
Maryland	1894	yes	Baltimore	434,000	(1890)
Mississippi	1906	no	Jackson	21,000	(1910)
Missouri	1910	yes	St. Louis	687,000	(1910)
North Carolina	1913	yes	Morganton	2,712	(1910)
	1913		Charlotte	34,000	"
South Carolina	1914	no	Spartanburg	17,500	(1910)
	1914		Columbia	26,300	(1910)
	1914		Charleston	58,800	(1910)
Tennessee	1910	yes	Knoxville	36,300	(1910)
	1911		Nashville	110,000	(1910)
Texas	1908	yes	Austin	29,000	(1910)
	1912		San Antonio	96,600	(1910)
Virginia	1909	no	Richmond	127,000	(1910)

Sources: Elizabeth Cady Stanton, Susan B. Anthony, Matilda Joslyn Gage, and Ida Husted Harper, eds., *History of Woman Suffrage* (6 vols., New York: J. J. Little and Ives, Co., 1881–1922; reprint edition, New York: Arno & The New York Times, 1969), Vol. 6: 1–3, 16–19, 113–116, 121–122, 207–209, 216–219, 248–250, 326–329, 342–344, 490–493, 579–580, 596–599, 630–633, 665–666. U.S. Bureau of the Census, *Thirteenth Census of the United States Taken in the Year 1910.* Vol. 1: Population (Washington, D.C.: Government Printing Office, 1913), 80–97.

of their communities and at the state-level fought for "progressive" goals to improve health, child labor, prison reform, and education. The rise of women's civic and state reforming activities actually precedes the formation of permanent local societies, which suggests a logical progression. Women had to experience some form of politicization of their goals and values before they were ready to take on the struggle for their own rights. This study argues that the WCTU was only one organization (and a weak one at that) among many by 1910 that helped Galveston women gain the political savvy necessary to mobilize. Because cities provided the most common arena for politicizing women's goals, they were essential to the suffrage movement, more essential than the ideals of the WCTU. Southern suffrage at the grass roots should perhaps be viewed first as an urban-based phenomenon supported and maintained by women with an investment in community building and only secondarily as a movement fueled by evangelical reforming sentiment.[36]

How women used their political know-how, their traditional club training, and the opportunities provided by an urban environment can be illustrated through the activities of the Galveston Equal Suffrage Association members after 1912. In the first year, suffragists made arrangements for no fewer than six speakers—from a local judge to NAWSA President Anna Howard Shaw and Mrs. Philip Snowden of Great Britain. Among the speakers was Perle Penfield, state suffrage field-worker and Galveston medical student. In her address to the women she alluded to the WHPA campaigns in Galveston for pure food and milk and the need for women to struggle for the vote in order to see that health regulations were enforced. "The present campaign being waged . . . here for pure milk has brought home to this woman the relation between disease and bad milk, and the necessity of control by enforced regulations. . . . Not only pure milk, but pure water, clean meats, pure drugs, . . . unadulterated foodstuffs . . . The housewife . . . should have the responsibility and power of requiring enforcement of the laws. . . . she must become a voter."[37]

At first GESA members held teas, but later they set up a booth at the annual Cotton Carnival and established headquarters inside a downtown store, all in order to distribute literature and gain new members. They performed in the 1913 suffrage play that entertained, educated, and brought in revenue. They raised money for the state suffrage association by soliciting pledges from wealthy men and women supporters within the city. They endorsed a married women's property rights bill in the Texas legislature. They canvassed door to door for signatures on petitions to the Texas legislature for a constitutional amendment that would enfranchise women. They placed a subscription to the *Woman's Journal* in the public library, persuaded the local press to feature weekly articles on suffrage, and edited a "Suffrage Edition" in the *Galveston Tribune*.[38]

By May 2, 1914, Galveston suffragists proved their allegiance to a national movement. They flew a new banner of white and gold representing "the flag of political freedom for women," while suffragists held demonstrations "simultaneously in all parts of the United States." This day of celebration followed a week of organized activity among the city's suffrage members and concluded with the adoption of a resolution asking Congress to grant women the franchise. *News* reporters noted "that the week has been a successful one[,] evidenced by the numbers of new converts to the cause that have been enrolled on the membership books." One of the unique features of the week's events included a voiceless speech displayed in shop windows along the Strand. "Large placards, in black and white, were turned slowly on easels . . . by members of the local suffragette organization."[39]

Later that year, Minnie Fisher Cunningham "spoke for the right of women to vote from the back seat of a touring car" in her first speech to the public. On July 4, 1914, Annette Finnigan caught the interurban from Houston at 4 P.M. and arrived about an hour later in Galveston, where she spoke to an audience at the corner of Broadway and Twenty-fifth Street. Employing Independence Day rhetoric, she addressed the crowd with the same speech she had given an hour before in Houston: "I come before you here this afternoon representing a great body of American women who are asking of the American government that the principles of the declaration of independence [sic] be applied to them. We are the mothers, wives and daughters of American men. We have been educated side by side with them. We are in sympathy with American institutions and we love our country. . . . We call this a democratic government, but we shall never have a true democracy in America until women are represented in the government." After an exhausting day of speechmaking, Finnigan and leaders of the Galveston Equal Suffrage Association dined at the Galvez Hotel.[40]

The GESA persisted in open-air activities, which had a radicalizing effect on residents. The results began to show when the Wednesday Club opted to study the suffrage movement and the rights of women at several of its meetings; the public schools used "this live topic as subject for debate," and "even at social gatherings hostesses have given their friends the opportunity of hearing experienced speakers on woman suffrage." In February 1915, Helen Todd, mentioned earlier in connection with the statewide campaign, spoke at the Grand Opera House in Galveston and frankly scolded Galveston state senator W. H. Hall for opposing the submission of a suffrage proposition to the people of Texas. Calling the attitude of the Texas senate "shameful," she passed out a resolution to be signed while the band played "Dixie." Suffrage was not the only item on her agenda; Todd spoke about "child labor, pure food and many other red hot issues . . . described as Galveston never before heard them described." Following the momentum of women's activism, in March the *Galveston Tribune* gave special coverage to the city's women's organizations, counting among the top three the WHPA, the YWCA, and the Galveston Equal Suffrage Association. In July 1916, suffragists placed a special entry in the "floral parade which was given by the women's organizations of the city."[41]

Galveston suffragists also looked beyond their community for state and national opportunities. Emma Harris represented them at the NAWSA convention in 1913; other delegates attended the state suffrage conventions through the years. The Galveston association hosted the Texas Equal Suffrage Association convention in 1915 and sent several of its own members, including its chapter president, to proselytize those parts of Texas where no suffrage leagues existed. In 1916, two suffragists from Texas City and Galveston attended their first Republican National Convention in Chicago, where they marched with the Texas suffrage delegation in a "rainy cold parade," and at the Democratic National Convention in St. Louis, where they hoped to see the endorsement of woman suffrage.[42]

All of these activities—fundraisers, lectures, booths, canvassing, open-air speaking, convention attending—were important to the development of the movement at the local level. They necessarily strengthened the resolve of suffrage supporters, helping them to focus on politicizing their goals for equality in the voting place. The power of the movement depended on just this sort of grass-roots mobilization. But local work alone could not bring voting rights to the women of Texas. It also took an intensive lobbying approach to push the Texas legislature in the direction of suffrage. This meant that a few women leaders within the state would need to give up their local agendas and assume state-level priorities. Here, local suffrage societies performed one of their most important yet unassigned tasks — the fostering and training of women who would make suffrage and politics their careers. The Galveston Equal Suffrage Association "promoted" several such women to the state level, but none was more important or influential to the movement than Minnie Fisher Cunningham.

Minnie Fisher came to Galveston from New Waverly, Texas, in 1898 as a student; she weathered the storm of 1900 and graduated with a degree in pharmacy from the University of Texas Medical Department in 1901 — the first woman in Texas to accomplish such a feat. She then left the city to work and to marry Beverly J. Cunningham, a promising young lawyer and insurance businessman. In 1907, they returned to Galveston, where Cunningham became involved in women's associational work. Just how the Galveston suffrage society and other women's clubs influenced Cunningham's decision to advance from local work to state work can be seen in a series of letters she wrote to the second state suffrage president, Annette Finnigan.[43]

Cunningham joined the GESA at its inception in 1912 but at the same time was invited to become a member of the exclusive Wednesday Club, which as we have seen was founded in 1891 and held its active roll to twenty-five members. Although Cunningham served as secretary, remained a member until 1916, and addressed the club on woman suffrage, she suspected that clubwomen in general were holding back the suffrage movement. This was confirmed for her in 1914 when the Texas Federation of Women's Clubs (TFWC) met in Galveston. First, the Wednesday Club "declined to give the Suffragists any part whatever in the entertainment of the Federation."[44] Then, the federation refused to endorse suffrage and would not allow Cunningham and other suffragists to speak openly about it. "I feel black and blue all over about that business," Cunningham wrote Finnigan. I feel so culpable in allowing myself to be bound to silence on such an important subject. . . . I can't help regretting that I didn't make a 'scene'!"[45] Later, she cast aspersions on Fort Worth's "miserable antediluvian clubwomen" but saved her most critical asides for Anna Pennybacker, a Texan and president of the General Federation of Women's Clubs, whom Cunningham regarded as a latecomer to the movement. Clearly, Cunningham was not cut out to be a literary clubwoman. Her association with the Women's Health Protective Association, it should be noted, was a happier one. In 1913, she assumed the chair of the School Hygiene Committee, which made an inspection of all the public schools. As a consequence, she reported, "conditions have been remedied, and relief has been afforded the school room." The following year, she took on a job closer to her goals; under the auspices of the WHPA, she worked toward the establishment of restrooms for women on the beaches and in the downtown area. She belonged to an age when no other avenue for women's civic activism was available. So she joined women's clubs, used them where she could to promote equal suffrage or improvements for women, and moved on.[46]

In 1914, the GESA elected Cunningham its president. She brought efficiency and zest to the organization but was compelled to leave it, too, not for its members'

FIGURE 9.1. Minnie Fisher Cunningham, president of the Galveston Equal Suffrage Association from 1914 to 1915 and the Texas Equal Suffrage Association from 1915 to 1920. Courtesy of the Austin History Center, Austin Public Library.

lack of commitment, for as already evidenced they proved their dedication to the cause, but for what seemed to her their old-fashioned methods influenced by years of traditional club work. At one time she was optimistic and wrote Finnigan that the state could "count on Galveston for teamwork."[47] Cunningham simply brimmed over with energy and ideas for how to promote the cause in Galveston. Her enthusiasm for suffrage outdistanced even her most ardent sisters in the GESA. But one frustration after another caused her to reconsider her position in local work.

The beach headquarters incident illustrates her frustrations with the GESA's foot dragging. She wrote Finnigan in May 1914,

The darling hope of my heart for three years has been a beach headquarters in the summer, and open air speaking on excursion days. It seems to me we are letting a glorious opportunity to reach all Texas slip right through our fingers. . . . Last year we had money in the bank which we had made for the express purpose of establishing a headquarters, and because the price was high we kept our money in the bank. . . . I wish you could come down . . . and see the potential readers of Suffrage literature and listeners to Suffrage speeches wandering up and down the Boulevard with nothing to do.[48]

A little later in the summer, she pleaded, "But O! *Please* worry about Galveston! We should be doing so much more than we are." The state president approved her plan for a beach headquarters but could not afford to help with even one-half the cost. The Galveston women turned down the idea again and opted instead for a less expensive booth at the Cotton Carnival for one week in August. Even then, organizers were unable to make suffrage speeches on Sunday "on account of a few *very* strict Sabbath keepers" in the association.[49] Minnie Fisher Cunningham made the most of it, but she was clearly disappointed with the GESA's fiscal and religious conservatism.

Cunningham's belief that Galveston suffragists did not do enough or spend enough on the movement was typical of the conflicts that arose between state-level and local officers, or, to put it in historical context, between women whose volunteer careers had been shaped by a "popular women's culture" found in club work and women whose lives were fully engaged in feminist politics. Actually, the GESA offered no less support than did other local groups, and its conservatism and respectability aided the cause in other ways. Cunningham, however, was unusually impatient, the mark of a leader ready to move on to larger projects. Her attitudes were bound to create tension among the more traditional suffragists, and yet, recognizing her talents, they reelected her president. She confided to Finnigan, "The Galveston organization at its annual meeting Saturday did me the honor of returning me to office for another year. In spite of my stern determination not to be returned. It makes me feel like a 'spell' of sickness to think of another year, but please don't tell on me."[50] Cunningham may have alienated some of the more traditional members, according to Cordia Sweeny, who in a letter to Annette Finnigan complained, "I can't imagine why you have not answered my letter unless I have been knifed by a party who is perfectly capable of doing such things." Referring to Cunningham, she continued, "I am not the only victim. The old executive committee was thoroughly knifed by her, especially Miss Ballinger and Mrs. Ed Harris. . . . She bites when the face is turned from her." Finnigan, disbelieving the stories, wrote back that no one had "knifed" her. Cunningham, who may have displayed her frustration with older methods, was rescued from local work by her election to the state presidency in May 1915, a position she held until the passage of the amendment. Finnigan wrote Sweeny with nothing but praise for her successor: "The women prominent in suffrage work in Galveston all backed Mrs. Cunningham, and my personal experience with her as a worker this past year, made me feel that she was the best one for the Presidency. She has the time to give to the work, the ability, and I believe, the deepest interest in the cause."[51]

By then, Cunningham's personal life was such that she was able to become a full-time servant for suffrage. She virtually took a sabbatical from her thirteen-year marriage. Putting the best face on the situation, she explained, "Mr. Cunningham and I have agreed that the fight is well worth giving up a lot for, and we will simply close the house and he will board, for as long as the State organization needs my services."[52] Thus freed from domestic responsibilities and from what was for her the cloying conservatism of the Galveston association, she became one of the South's most effective state presidents. Both she and NAWSA president Carrie Chapman Catt came into office the same year; together they provided new energy and winning leadership for the suffrage movement.[53]

The Galveston Equal Suffrage Association continued to do what it did best—educate, organize, and raise money. Although successive presidents were competent, none had Cunningham's unique leadership ability. This is not to say that the more traditional civic leaders were unnecessary to the suffrage movement; on the contrary, to mobilize for suffrage both types were critically necessary. White-gloved New Women, rooted in the soil of their native city, held the community respect that was essential to dispel the taint of radicalism. They also remained in the city to encourage and lead other women and men in the cause of suffrage, while their more peripatetic sisters canvassed the state. Local suffragists provided the home support essential to the firm planting of the movement. Women such as Minnie Fisher Cunningham, who made gaining passage of women's right to vote a career, moved on to the state level, constantly traveling, organizing, stumping, lobbying. Her leadership, drive, sacrifices, and organizational skills not only sustained her life in politics (she later ran for U.S. senator and governor) but also pushed the movement to its successful conclusion in the state of Texas.

Perhaps we should look beyond filiopietistic notions of solidarity among white women and see the campaign for the vote as it was—a complex political movement destined to bulldoze aside forever the staid traditionalism of the nineteenth century. Clearly Cunningham thought that there were major differences between individual suffragists; she felt some, after years of conventional club work, were too conservative for the good of the movement. In any such mobilization there are tensions, rifts, slights, and worse. The results of these differences were beneficial to the movement, however; eager and aggressive leaders rose to the state level, while more traditional community activists supported suffrage from their home bases. There was, it seems, room for both types in the Texas woman suffrage movement.

Historians of woman suffrage in the South have long tended to view the movement from the lofty altitudes of state and regional politics and have assumed that suffrage support stemmed from frustrated evangelical church and WCTU members determined to impose temperance reform and a women's agenda upon an unredeemed South. The Galveston case suggests that the movement for the vote among women in the South at the local level was an urban-based phenomenon and that southern or Texas women, who may have been slow to respond to the national suffrage campaign, were nonetheless stirred to action on behalf of their own communities and their equal political economic involvement in them. Galveston was a city that inspired great devotion from its women activists; some of them in return asked for the right to full electoral equality.

The Galveston Equal Suffrage Association should be credited with steering the momentum of women's public activism in two corresponding directions. First, suffragists sought to make permanent the gains made by women civic activists. After the hard won fight for government-imposed milk standards, cleaner meat markets, dairies, groceries, and restaurants, they did not want to see these gains reversed. They argued that women needed the vote in order to continue to improve the community; they saw themselves as protectors of children and the public's health, and that included guarding home, schools, streets, alleys, markets, dairies, and restaurants. In order to fulfill their responsibilities as municipal housekeepers they had to become public citizens, and by striving to implement a women's agenda they necessarily politicized their goals. Voting rights would allow them to directly elect public officials whom they would hold accountable for sanitation and civic improvement. Galveston suffragists never hesitated to remind male voters of their public service ideals.

Suffragists comprised the first Progressive Era group to promote the rights of women for the sake of their own equality. Moving away from community-oriented projects to a woman-centered agenda, the Galveston Equal Suffrage Association sharpened the focus of the progressive women's community, encouraging it to look inward toward the needs of women. Never abandoning civic outreach entirely, suffragists, nonetheless, permitted women to think in terms of their own rights, their own citizenship, their own desires, and their own limitations. They sought gains for women, in equal pay for equal work, in property rights for married women, in equal opportunity in the workplace, and in their own sense of well-being—not to be treated "as a slave or a play thing." For many, these ideas were too abstract, too unconnected to the reality of working lives to make much difference, and, consequently, the GESA constituted only one part of the women's community. But suffragists, in permitting women to see their own needs first, provided a radicalizing influence for the women of Galveston.

10

$\bullet \quad \bullet \quad \bullet \quad \bullet \quad \bullet \quad \bullet \quad \bullet \quad \bullet \quad \bullet \quad \bullet \quad \bullet \quad \bullet \quad \bullet \quad \bullet \quad \bullet \quad \bullet \quad \bullet \quad \bullet \quad \bullet$

THE YWCA AND WAGE-EARNING WOMEN

Industrial changes half a century ago altered woman's status entirely. Instead of spinning, weaving and knitting at home, girls started working away from home. Thousands are away from home today — pounding type-writers, pasting labels on bottles, cooking and earning their living. Our aim in YWCA work is to make life more complete for girls who work, to help them develop, and round out their lives.

—*Galveston Daily News*, March 4, 1916

The Young Women's Christian Association was the last major white women's organization to emerge in the Progressive Era, and it completed Galveston's white women's community. Only one other organization remained to bind the community together; by 1916, Galveston clubwomen had formed a City Federation of Women's Clubs, which brought together over 100 white women's associations representing possibly 5,000 members. Unto itself the federation offered little more than a supervisory and coordinating role over all of the many women's associations and clubs.[1] But the YWCA carried women activists in a new direction — toward acknowledging the need for an institution for young working women.

Although white women leaders ignored the problems that came with segregation as well as the existence of a black middle-class community of women activists willing to combat it, they were very much aware of the growing number of working-class white girls and women entering the city after the storm. Concerned about the safety, propriety, and piety of these newcomers, middle-class reformers turned to the Young Women's Christian Association, an organization that had penetrated the South, devoting itself to the needs of working women.

In Galveston, as in other southern cities, the YWCA served as an advocacy agency for university students and young working women. It was a much more conservative version of the New York Women's Trade Union League or Chicago's Consumers' League, associations founded by women of means to advance the economic status of working women through legislation and consumer education. The YWCA was among the first organizations to seek improvements for self-supporting women whose wages were invariably lower than men's and whose opportunities were limited by sex discrimination. When the first YWCA opened its doors in 1866 in Boston, thirty women met to consider the needs of young women who came to that city to seek jobs. By 1912, northern YWCA officers proclaimed their organization "the greatest and strongest group of women ever found . . . of

women, by women, for women." Southern cities, slower to experience industrialization, lagged behind their northern counterparts in establishing associations
that aided factory workers, clerks, telegraph and telephone operators, and shop
girls. In fact, one of the first Texas YWCAs came as a student association in 1890
to what was then called Fort Worth University. By 1914, the YWCA had already
been established in all the nation's port cities and in most of the larger southern
cities.[2]

Galveston was the last Texas city of its size to initiate a YWCA. With no
undergraduate university and few factories, city activists dallied longer than most
in establishing a branch. Once again, it took the combination of an outside agent
and about thirty interested women to launch the local chapter. Mabel K. Stafford,
executive director of the YWCA's Southwest region, came from Dallas to help
start the Galveston chapter. Once the membership drive began, it proved to be
the most successful campaign in Galveston's history. On November 30, 1914, 170
women divided the city into districts (a technique that reached back to 1875, when
Trinity Guild sought to distribute aid to storm victims) and canvassed door to door
for members. On the first day of the drive, seventeen teams of women brought in
some 440 members. The newspapers kept up the momentum as each daily issue
detailed the planning, the enthusiasm, and the gains made. By the third day the
women had secured 675 members; and by the end of the week 1,908 women had
paid at least $1 to belong to the city's most promising women's organization with
a national membership of 324,000 and with branches in fourteen countries. In the
words of the organizers, "the YWCA is striving to make actual reality 'universal
sisterhood from sea to shining sea.' " The YWCA continued to maintain its popularity; in 1920 the association remained stable at 2,000 members.[3]

A democratization process among white women's organizations that had begun with the WHPA reached new proportions with the YWCA, enlarging and
expanding the boundaries of the progressive women's community. In terms of
membership, the YWCA was the largest of the city's Progressive-Era associations.
As already noted, the WHPA never exceeded 600 members, the Galveston Equal
Suffrage Association attracted 300, and the WCTU in 1915 reached 100 members.
More important was the fact that the YWCA's first twenty-two-member board of
directors comprised an equal number of women from evangelical Protestant (four
Baptist, five Methodist, and two Disciples of Christ) and liturgical Protestant
churches (six Presbyterian and five Episcopalian). In subsequent years, Episcopal
women still predominated among the elected executive officers, but Baptist and
Methodist women, whose names had not appeared as leaders in either the WHPA
or the GESA, were found on the YWCA's elected board of directors. This may
be explained both by the broader constituency that elected them and by the fact
that the YWCA was a Christian association whose purpose was "to extend the
kingdom of God." Methodist and Baptist women, whose main outlet had been
church women's societies, no doubt felt a natural affinity toward the YWCA with
its religious committee, prayer meetings, Sunday vespers, and women missionaries
in foreign lands. Episcopal and Presbyterian women, no less ardent in their desire
for a structured program of Christian emphasis and protection for young women,
backed the organization with funds, volunteer labor, and officers. In fact, a wealthy

Episcopalian, Cornelia B. (Mrs. J. C.) League, donated $200,000 for the completion of the YWCA building in 1924. Finally, of the fifty-four YWCA board members found between 1914 and 1920, at least twenty-one (38 percent) had been actively engaged in women's church societies.[4] The opportunity for middle-class evangelical and traditional elite leaders to work together in a single organization was filled in part by the appearance of the YWCA.

Religious affiliation was not the only link to the broader community of women. Among the fifty-four YWCA board members, twenty (37 percent) were members of the WHPA, sixteen (30 percent) were suffragists, and fifteen (28 percent) had served on a board of lady managers for a benevolent institution, but only three (5 percent) were members of the WCTU. Five WHPA officers were also executive officers of the YWCA, indicating that civic reform women were elected for their experience with the hope that they might be able to institute practical advancements for women.[5]

What did the YWCA offer working women in 1915? It brought protection, especially to single working women. Mabel Stafford put it in the context of the times: the YWCA is like the Monroe Doctrine that defends America from the war in Europe; it is "a stone wall protecting unattached girls from the perils of industrial life in which so many are now engaged." The founders of the YWCA, imbued as they were with the combined ideals of motherhood and community servanthood, sought to guard unattached working girls not only from the dangers of the workplace but also from Galveston's red-light district and other evils. "The YWCA . . . may play an honorable part in properly caring for and protecting those who have been attracted to us by opportunities held out, perhaps leaving the protecting atmosphere of a pleasant home to come in contact with those influences which make the cities of the land their lurking places." Galveston was never what one would call an industrial city. It sported a few factories but was primarily a city whose economy was based on servicing the flow of goods in and out of the port. Its principal economic base was commerce, not industry. Still, the YWCA officers estimated in 1914 that the city had 1,500 self-supporting white women working in clerical positions, in shops as clerks, in professional occupations such as teaching and nursing, and in factories. In 1916, another study raised the figure to 1,700.[6]

With the establishment of the YWCA, middle-class women civic leaders believed that they had founded an institution to shield working girls from the dangers of city life. Their program aimed at encouraging newcomers to stay within the safe enclosures of a suitable home. Protection also meant the imposition of middle-class values on working-class young women whose descent into poverty or immorality was, in the minds of these women, entirely preventable. If working-class girls were able to live in decent homes or lodgings, go to church, marry and have children, they would become respectable. So thought the founders of the YWCA.[7]

Galveston women of means had long been concerned about the problem of fallen women, prostitutes, and unwed mothers but had done little to shelter these women. Galveston's problems with prostitution were notorious. Before the turn of the century, estimates for the number of bordellos reached fifty-five, and there were nearly nine times that many saloons. Although red-light districts in many cities were closed down by 1916, Galveston's "segregated district" continued through the next several decades, although it was severely limited by the antivice regulations accompanying the U.S. entry into World War I. Coupled with organized gambling, a thriving brewery, and a police force that tolerated vice, Galveston pleasure dens offered lucrative profits to owners and employment to about 1,000 prostitutes.[8]

While Galvestonians had done little to discourage women from entering the business, other Texas citizens did not shy away from the issue. At least seven institutions for prostitutes, "unfortunate women, and wayward girls" were founded in Texas before 1900. Finally, after hearing about homes for fallen women in other cities of the state, a few Galveston women opened a rescue home, Bethesda Door of Hope, in 1898. It lasted two years, was swept away in the hurricane of 1900, and never reopened. Its principal organizer and president was Hattie Carter, wife of the rector of Grace Episcopal Church, who made rescue homes her life's mission; its matron, Mrs. E. W. Nichols was a member of the Presbyterian Ladies' Aid Society and sometimes took referrals for the home from that group. Surviving with a minimum of three officers and a matron, the home struggled to maintain itself, first at 1720 Avenue O and the next year at 1311 Twenty-seventh Street, a section of the city destroyed by the storm. Little is known about this home, how many women it tried to rescue, or the way Galveston elites perceived the problem of prostitution and unwed mothers. We know that women in church societies discussed the pitfalls for young girls in the city and sought to prevent their staying in Galveston. Taking precautions against temptations for women constituted their greatest effort, which finally culminated in the opening of the YWCA in 1914.[9]

Steps were immediately taken both to champion and to aid wage-earning women. YWCA officers rented headquarters at the corner of Twenty-third and Mechanic streets and offered office space for two salaried administrators (a general secretary and an assistant secretary) and a gymnasium for "physical culture classes." A canvass committee headed by Dr. Ethel Lyon Heard, who managed to combine her medical career with volunteer work for the WHPA, the GESA, the YWCA, and the Red Cross, sought out "stranger girls" to the city through merchants and manufacturers. Minnie Fisher Cunningham and several other suffragists served on the committee to attract these girls to the YWCA's "wholesome fun and recreation." To meet newcomers to the city the officers hired a traveler's aid agent and set her up in Union Station with a desk, a chair, and a badge. Her duties were to meet every incoming train (at least twelve a day) and to counsel young women who sought lodging or employment or who were lost and in distress. With the numbers of young women increasing daily (between 300 and 400 women were aided in the first six weeks), "the railroad men are glad indeed to have us inaugurate the travelers' aid work," noted Ida Austin, the YWCA's first president.[10]

At first the travel agent gave a list of decent boarding houses to the new arrivals, who sought work and a place to live, but in 1915 she was able to direct girls to the YWCA's boarding rooms (an expansion of the headquarters), where girls found temporary or permanent shelter for $3.50 a week. By 1921, the Brewer W. Key family donated an entire house to the YWCA for boarders. Ironically, the house, at the corner of Broadway and Twenty-fourth Street, had once belonged to Rosanna Dyer Osterman, whose legacy to the city had provided for city dependents. By March 1915, just four months after the association's inception, the women opened a cafeteria selling complete meals for less than $.30 (1 cent for bread, 1 cent for butter, 10 cents for meat, 5 cents for vegetables, 5 cents for milk) and serving 6,000 people a month. The directors announced that "the new cafeteria . . . is a premeditated thrust at the high cost of living for Galveston girls and women," but it served working men as well and became the association's most popular asset.[11] An employment bureau secured jobs for women; classes for immigrants in English as well as typing, stenography, salesmanship, first aid, and mathematics attracted young women determined to improve their skills in order to earn better wages.[12]

The YWCA offered a variety of social and cultural outlets for young women: classes, parties, clubs, athletic teams, picnics, entertainments, a 100-member glee club, and an orchestra. Physical exercise classes were among the most sought after in 1915. In voting for classes, the girls chose gymnastics and swimming (in the gulf) over all other offerings, which included among others dressmaking, millinery, Bible study, china painting, sketching, Spanish, French, German, stenography and typing, bookkeeping, and elocution. Members of the various clubs and classes organized their own parties or outings. The 100-member "Young Business Women's YWCA Gymnasium Class" announced an "Old Fashioned Party" for its monthly social event. In order for working girls to practice and internalize organizational techniques, only self-governing clubs were encouraged. The officers of the Girls Athletic Club, who organized teams for boating, basketball, swimming, and tennis, included two bookkeepers, one insurance clerk, a stenographer, a hat trimmer, and one co-owner of an art supply store. Training the daughters of craftsmen and small businessmen in the art of self-government was one way that civic leaders imparted middle-class values to working girls and hence potentially broadened the progressive women's community.[13]

The YWCA also encouraged and abetted friendly meetings with the boys from the YMCA, which could be a tricky thing in this new era. The age of blue books and formal etiquette rules was giving way to informal gatherings of chaperoned young people. The workers of the YWCA recognized, no doubt, that they were dealing with the possible passionate impulses and inchoate sexual desires of adolescents and young adults, and the rules for such "promiscuous" gatherings were ill defined. Protection of young women did not mean, however, isolation from the attentions of young men; focus remained on suitability. In May 1915, some 250 youths attended a YMCA party for members of both organizations; they ate lunch, played billiards, and organized an impromptu indoor baseball game between teams of young ladies and men. YWCA members returned the favor in June by inviting the boys to a "bathing party" and beach picnic; 150 came and roasted green corn, held potato races, and were regaled with vaudeville numbers sung by the YWCA Girls' Glee Club. In these encounters with the opposite sex, middle-class and middle-aged women encouraged young men and women to mingle freely, but in a safe environment. Bringing together boys and girls of these two organizations assured the sponsors of one thing: both groups were under the auspices of Christian, that is, moral, organizations, and the hoped-for result would be for young women to find young men of suitable moral character. These outings and socials for working-class youths simulated the controlled chaperoned events of the wealthy. In the sophisticated parlors and ballrooms of the elite, daughters of privilege "came out" and announced their availability to the bachelors of their class; hence, a call for suitable marriage partners went out in another kind of protected environment, this one controlled by class as much as by moral or religious sensibilities. YWCA officers hoped to bring some semblance of order, protection, and control to the sexual lives of their young charges.[14]

While social events attracted women of different ages and classes to the YWCA, the board of directors promoted progressive causes. The YWCA observed Child Labor Sunday on January 24, 1916, and labor spokeswoman Eva Goldsmith lectured on "Street Workers," "Texas Cotton Pickers," and "State and Federal Laws on Child Labor." Nannie Webb Curtis, president of the Texas WCTU, spoke to the members about temperance. Lecturers from the GESA speaking on the benefits of woman suffrage were frequently invited to the YWCA parlors. In consultation with United Charities, a committee of women, including WHPA president Jean Morgan, opened a woman's exchange within the YWCA for the "benefit of Galveston women who must add to their incomes or depend entirely for support on handiwork created at home."[15]

Recruitment of working girls took constant effort, and a variety of techniques evolved as the needs increased. Teams of officers visited the factories, laundries, shops, and markets that employed women to give entertainment at the workers' break and encourage them to join. As a follow-up enticement, YWCA members offered excursions to young working girls: "About fifteen girls of the Model Laundry enjoyed an auto ride last evening down the west beach," read one YWCA report. "In the automobiles of Mrs. Waters S. Davis, J. E. Thompson, and Tudor Nichols, a party of YWCA girls . . . went down the island on a crabbing expedition this evening." Eventually these impromptu excursions were replaced by the YWCA's organized summer camp sessions about thirteen miles west of Galveston city. Ethel Lyon Heard taught a Red Cross class in first aid every time new classes were organized, and under the auspices of the Child Conservation League she conducted a Better Baby Conference in the YWCA parlors. The Y's finest hour came through its association with the National Red Cross during World War I. Several hundred women made hospital supplies, served in canteens, and worked in the United War Work Fund Drive. The fundraiser's projected goal was $10,000, but the women raised $12,585 in 1918. For the young women who were left behind during the war, the YWCA offered classes "to improve the earning ability of the girls and fit them to fill the places of the men who have gone to war." Although these classes were offered too late to do much good, the fact is that the YWCA stood ready to help women move into better paid male jobs. In more ways than one, the YWCA countered the limitations that surrounded women.[16]

There are, of course, limits to the claims that we may make for the Galveston YWCA. It did not include blacks, nor, unlike Ys in other parts of the South, did it make any overtures toward cooperation with black clubwomen before 1920. Construction on the Mary Patrick Branch of the YWCA for African American girls did not begin until the 1950s. Then, Jewish and Catholic girls thought that they were not welcome. Elizabeth Hyatt, general secretary of the YWCA, tried to correct this impression with a letter to the *Galveston Tribune*: "I am surprised and grieved to learn that many of the Roman Catholics and Jewish young women of the city feel that our Young Women's Christian Association is not for them — that in some way or other we discriminate against them and they can not have the same privileges here that others do. . . . I deeply regret the uncalled for and unfortunate circumstance which led to this feeling and to say that a Jewish or Roman Catholic young woman will never be known from any other religious denomination in our work together."[17]

Jews and Catholics, although eligible for membership, were not eligible for election to the board of directors, to which the Catholic clergy objected in print. Father John S. Murphy, speaking for his female parishoners wrote: "The discriminating feature of the YWCA is . . . that it is a Protestant organization and controlled as such." Office holding and voting power were "vested in those members only who [were] members of Protestant Evangelical churches." This he cited as "sufficient cause for the refusal of Catholic women to become members, for Catholics have the same sensibilities as others about what they deem their rights, and hence it is only natural that they would repudiate the offer of membership in any social organization in which they will have absolutely no voice."[18] Catholic women may well have felt as Father Murphy described, but one wonders what sort of threat an ecumenical organization such as the YWCA may have presented to the Catholic church. The absence of Catholic board members may help to explain the larger presence of evangelical women in executive positions, but Lutheran women also were not adequately represented among its officers. The YWCA did not represent trade unions, did not espouse radical designs for intensifying the class conflict to obtain social justice, did not argue for redistributing the wealth, did not challenge the business community often enough or loudly enough to give equal pay for equal work, and did not advocate racial equality.[19]

On the other hand, no other organization offered comparable opportunities for white women's independence in education, housing, social, and civic concerns. And in some cities across the South by the mid-1920s, the YWCA provided a channel for interracial activities and a forum for the exchange of ideas between black and white women. The YWCA stood at the heart of Galveston's progressive women's community by challenging women to reach beyond the strictures of their class and, in time, of their race. Ida Austin announced in 1916: "This is not an organization of one class working for the same class, but of all classes working for all classes." Working women of marginal means were subsidized through affordable room and board and were invited to improve themselves physically, intellectually, and spiritually. Women civic leaders were called upon to socialize, teach, and volunteer their administrative skills to an organization devoted to the material betterment of women. And professional women — administrators and executive secretaries — found advancement through the YWCA in ways that resembled the reformers of Hull House in Chicago, who moved into professional positions in governmental work.[20]

How much mixing occurred between the classes is difficult to reconstruct, but the opportunity for social interaction between the daughters of shopkeepers and department store owners was there. A great breakthrough was made by women of evangelical denominations into the leadership ranks of the women's community through YWCA officeholding. And, finally, it is important to remember that the opening of the YWCA doors was accomplished by the concerted efforts of the women's progressive community it offered the YWCA's services to all white women, focusing on them and their needs in a practical, tangible way as no other association had done.

CONCLUSION

Toward Progressive Women's Communities

Experience here and there indicates that women will do better than men with politics. Perhaps this is because being new to politics, they are willing to do drudgery. Perhaps it is because a great many more intelligent women than men have time for politics, or will make time. Perhaps it is because they are more sympathetic. We should like to turn more of our local politics over to women.

— *Galveston Daily News*, August 29, 1916

The summer breezes wafting off the Gulf of Mexico gently blessed the island on July 11, 1916, as white women in the city paraded their floats down Market Street. The great civic pageant associated with the Eighth Cotton Carnival featured a parade of twenty-one floats and other entries "portraying in concrete form the lines of work to which nineteen organizations of women in the city are devoting their efforts." Two squads of mounted police led the parade, but they were immediately followed by "Joan of Arc" wearing a white tunic trimmed in fleurs-de-lis and riding a stunning white horse. In historic as well as contemporary terms (France was at that time fighting for its existence), she symbolized the value of woman's patriotism and devotion to her country. As if the message would somehow be lost on male voters, the Galveston Equal Suffrage Association announced through this startling appearance that their theme, "Purity and Patriotism," represented not only heroines of the past but also the noble intentions of women who would vote and provide leadership for the city. That the GESA provided the first "special feature" of the parade speaks volumes about the importance women placed on the right to vote and govern. Other organizations exhibited their contributions to city life: the Johanna Runge Free Kindergarten and the Council of Jewish Women presented floats that showed "the kindergarten school in session, with the children playing with their lesson blocks in the class room." Representing women and culture were floats from the Girls' Musical Club, the Galveston Art League, and the Wednesday Club. The Veuve Jefferson Davis chapter of the UDC portrayed "Memories of '61," no doubt a happier year for the Confederate cause. Members of the WCTU featured the theme of "Purity" for their float, while the WHPA entered two floats symbolizing the two phases of work performed over fifteen years. One advertised the slogan, "Civic Beautification"; the other announced that "Health Is Wealth." The YWCA entry featured a white angel; "the outstretched wings symbolized the protecting spirit" of the city's newest women's organization. The *Galveston News* pronounced it "the most successful parade ever staged in the city." It celebrated the accumulated energies and the visible organized presence of Galveston's white women and was symbolic in this southern town of the great strides that women had made in advancing from home to church to public arena.[1]

Fifty years earlier, there would have been no parade, no celebration of the public roles that women had assumed in concert with one another. The "coming out" of white women's organizations in 1916 was evidence of their organizational prowess developed in the intervening years and of the city's acceptance of the public and very political nature of women's activism and their agenda for reform. Women vocally and actively sought citizenship and its attendant rights and privileges; they had persevered to prove the worthiness of their demands. For many, the parade chronicled a long history of civic activism and represented a very welcome symbolic victory. Of course, this was a white women's parade; African American women had held a much longer tradition of public celebration with floats, parades, and costumes illuminating the desires and dreams of black citizens.

In the South, women's world began with home and family, and there it might have remained had it not been for churches and synagogues, where women found a semipublic outlet for the application of their talents and interests. Imbued with artistic ideals, Protestant women sought to enhance worship through music and interior decor; they taught Sunday school, organized youth groups, and maintained last resting places. In their concern for the well-being of their churches, they provided funds through women's church and mission societies. They transformed their churches into multifaceted institutions that focused on the needs of families. After working with men in churches, they discovered patterns of systematic discrimination against their ideas and their potential leadership, so they countered this by elevating and sanctifing women's roles and values.

Galveston, the principal port of Texas until 1914, supplied an environment conducive to middle and upper-class women's advancement from congregational life into community activism and, thus, helped to extend women's issues into public forums. Proximity to one another, leisure occasioned by family income derived mainly from commerce, and compassion for the poor, who grew increasingly more prevalent as industrialization commenced, motivated white Protestant and Jewish women to establish congregation-related poor relief societies. Thus charity, which began in sacred circles in the 1870s, moved to a secular forum in the 1880s through the creation of benevolent institutions managed by women.

Women's artistic aims, first nurtured in churches via choirs and the creation of memorial windows, were given further coherency through the founding of women's music and literary clubs in the 1890s. Music clubs for the first time focused on women's talents, preparing them for public service through concerts and performances. Self-improvement associations and literary clubs educated women, eventually leading them to the study of modern problems, including the inferior position of women. The desire to venerate ancestry, expressed through family and then church graveyard tending, found secular dimension through patriotic-hereditary associations for women. These associations, involved as they were in civil religion, focused on white women in the context of heroic events, thus dispensing pride to white southern ladies who, nonetheless, kept positions of white supremacy alive.

Although white women's secular organizations before 1900 carried women into more public roles, they also manifested the hierarchies and divisions of the city's social classes. The storm, however, marked the beginning in Galveston of civic work for white women of all classes and heralded the advent of a more democratic progressive women's community made up primarily of three organizations: the Women's Health Protective Association, the Galveston Equal Suffrage Association, and the Young Women's Christian Association. These associations complemented one another, each serving different and overlapping segments of a world of women that in reality was divided by class, ethnicity, and religious affiliation. Other women's organizations that emerged in the Progressive period—the WCTU, Council of Jewish Women, mothers' clubs, the Child Conservation League, and the Juvenile Protective Association, for example—also brought progressive-minded women into civic activism and their aims into public view. But these organizations were peripheral to the core of the women's community, which resided with the three largest organizations.

The WHPA represented the first of the three women's groups to receive the approval of the *Galveston Tribune* in their 1915 special edition. Noting that theirs was a progressive town, *Tribune* editors praised the women who "labored earnestly, and successfully, for the improvement of sanitary conditions and beautification of the city."[2] Tending to the proper burial of storm victims constituted a direct connection to women's roles as guardians of family traditions. A more beautiful and healthful environment for urban citizens projected onto a larger screen women's goals of protection for city dependents. But aesthetics and sanitation do not entirely explain the surge of women's political activism in the poststorm period. White elite women moved into positions of city leadership before the creation of a separate civic reform group. By meeting the immediate and pressing needs of the city, by volunteering first through the Central Relief Committee, then through the American Red Cross, they proved to themselves and to Galveston male officeholders that women were equal to the task of energy and leadership in the midst of tragedy and loss.

The Women's Health Protective Association, which initiated the progressive women's community, after 1901 became extremely influential politically; it replaced the pre-1900 coalition of working-class and African American officeholders. WHPA entrée into city politics began in 1901, when voters eliminated the aldermanic ward system and created city commission government. Backed by a series of state laws that disfranchised black and working-class voters and then further segregated African Americans, white women reformers stepped into the political vortex. There they found allies among white male commercial elites. The WHPA endorsed the creation of city commission government by sending petitions with the names of hundreds of women to Austin. Because the WHPA leaders and city commissioners were of the same class and race, the new government presented white women with better opportunities for shaping public policy—at least toward city beautification and revegetation of the island. But as the grade raising ended and issues of sanitation, particularly the city's milk and food supply, came to the fore, WHPA members confronted commissioners about setting new standards and enforcing them. Marshaling citizen support and the endorsement of the medical, laboring, and commercial interests on the island, WHPA members finally won their case. Ordinances to inspect, grade, and pasteurize milk and ensure clean markets came five years after the women began their protests. Along with the ordinances came appointments for women — as deputy state food and drug inspectors and as city pathologist. Additionally, Eleanor Thompson won election to the School Board of Trustees, thus bringing a woman to the all-white administrative authority, where black educators before 1900 used to sit. Partly because of these gains, white women raised the flag of gender inequality. Politicizing their goals had the positive effect of creating a core of determined reformers, some of whom became suffragists. Others saw the need for a cross-class institution, especially for young women within the city.

The Galveston Equal Suffrage Association and the Young Women's Christian Association concentrated solely on women's issues. In the process of spiriting passage of a progressive agenda through official channels, women found themselves seeking political rights and better economic opportunities. On the one hand, suffragists, composed of professional women as well as civically trained white-gloved ladies, favored the advancement of the ideal of equality. On the other, officers of the YWCA moved toward the practical: protecting young white women and offering opportunities for advancement. An introduction to city problems helped women leaders realize the need for a YWCA that would protect and nurture working women and give them access to better employment as well as social events. With the emergence of the more pluralistic white YWCA, a far broader coalition of women — professional women, upper- and middle-class matrons, and wage-earning young women — worked toward progressive goals.

Baptist and Methodist women and Episcopal and Presbyterian women, nonetheless, continued to divide not only on issues of class, which, however subtly, still persisted, but on type of organization. No Episcopal women, for example, entered the officer ranks of the WCTU, which was composed almost entirely of Methodist, Baptist, and a few Presbyterian women. The one women's organization where Episcopal, Presbyterian, Methodist, and Baptist women met in nearly equal numbers as members of the board of directors was within the YWCA. The findings show that of twenty-seven voluntary organizations in Galveston studied between 1880 and 1920, two had percentages of women from evangelical Protestant churches of 50 percent or higher: the Woman's Christian Temperance Union and the Young Women's Christian Association. Prohibition legislation and the protection of young women, accompanied by a Christian message, drew more followers from among Baptists, Methodists, and, by 1914, Disciples of Christ than from all other denominations combined. The obvious Christian emphasis of the YWCA attracted members of the Baptist and Methodist churches to the board, but its goal to reach young working women appealed to Episcopalians and Presbyterians whose interest in relief for the unprotected stretched back thirty years.

It is clear that the collective actions of Galveston women differ from the model formerly provided by historians to explain the advance of white southern women from church societies to reform activism. The women's foreign mission society–WCTU–suffrage formula did not fit Galveston. Mainstream Protestant women responded first to the problems encountered in a port city. Reform was engendered for the most part, not by Baptist and Methodist women, but by Episcopal, Presbyterian, and Jewish women who responded to urban problems that accompanied the city's growth in the 1880s and 1890s and in the wake of the 1900 hurricane.

Similar patterns of movement from home to church and finally to community are discernable among middle-class African American women. Churches provided a site for community nurturance, for raising children in the faith, for Sunday school, for social, educational, and cultural events, for caring for the elderly—in short for charitable and evangelical programs. Congregations often housed and affirmed women's club efforts and encouraged fundraising for benevolent causes. But churches also fostered resistance to white supremacy in a number of ways. They reaffirmed the worthiness of followers of Christ, who was *the* suffering servant, and they bolstered black pride. Churches offered meeting places to protest lynchings, labor injustices, discrimination in school funding, and, with the founding of the NAACP, segregation and disfranchisement. Sanctuaries bore witness to the trials of women and men seeking social justice in the era of the Jim Crow South.

Galveston African Americans sought to care for the elderly through the Galveston Relief Association; they established orphanages and daycare facilities for working parents. Women, calling themselves simply "willing workers," formed charitable clubs that traveled throughout the city visiting the sick and elderly. Through the Texas Association of Colored Women's Clubs, Galveston women raised funds for the state Training School for Delinquent Negro Girls. The Hospital Aid Society met the needs of black patients at the John Sealy Hospital, while Dr. Mary Moore's Hubbard Sanitarium offered surgery and hospital care for black citizens.

The African American community rallied behind its schools and rejoiced in its celebrations. Staffed by both men and women teachers and administrators, public schools became institutions of hope for the future. Women and men defended the right to maintain Central High School—its integrity and its curriculum—in the face of white attack. Mothers' clubs and alumni associations established their presence in the schools, giving testimony to their investment in the education of children. Community celebrations—Labor Day parades, Fourth of July celebrations, Children's and Old Folks' Day—shared by women and men, projected a visible presence and gave black citizens a sense of community pride and solidarity. Juneteenth Day jubilees allowed women to reflect publicly on the multiple meanings of freedom and liberty, while men, for a change, prepared the food.

Despite the prosperity and cultural sophistication of the black community in Galveston, whites followed the South in supporting a poll tax and in segregating public facilities. Black Galvestonians did not accept disfranchisement and segregation without protest from its articulate and vocal editors, lawyers, and pastors and from its women civic activists. But just as white middle-class women confronted a recalcitrant city commission, so African American middle-class women combatted an overwhelming system of discrimination. They did so by forming self-help groups—the Colored Women's Hospital Aid Society, the Willing Workers Charity Club, the Paragon Social Club, and the Women's Progressive Club. They allied themselves with national organizations and tended to the victims of segregation. Black clubwomen, teachers, church workers, and professionals carried out a Progressive-Era agenda despite the challenges; and after 1920, under the aegis of the Negro Women Voters' League, they paid their poll tax, took themselves to the polls, and voted—for whom, we are not sure.

From the milieu of this New South city in the Progressive Era emerged two progressive women's communities. Both nurtured ameliorative and reforming sentiments; both became politically active. The African American Women's Hospital Aid Society, the Women's Progressive Club, and the Negro Women Voters' League were paralleled by the white Women's Health Protective Association, the Galveston Equal Suffrage Association, and the Young Women's Christian Association. These associations, separated as they were by race and by the pursuit of a variety of goals, nonetheless advanced women to positions of leadership, provided needed direction for a women's agenda, and announced with intentionality the demand for equal citizenship. These broader communities of politically and socially active women empowered their constituents to challenge gender and race denigrations.[3] In many ways, the first two decades of the twentieth century, thus, became women's decades, as they organized to protect health, to seek equal rights and opportunities for women, and, in the case of African American women, to combat discrimination. By aggregating their resources, talents, and civic ambitions separately—and at times at odds with each other—two progressive women's communities worked for a healthier, safer urban environment with a focus on greater political and economic benefits for women.

APPENDIX A

. . . .

AN ESSAY ON METHODOLOGY

Analysis of White Activist Women
for a Galveston Women Database

A portion of this study purports to identify those white Galveston women who were active in organizations that worked toward the good of the community or the enhancement of women in terms of education, protection, or legal rights.[1] The methodology for such a study required identifying those organizations (composed entirely of women or that allowed women to join) between the 1870s and 1920.

The search began with the women's immigrant aid societies founded in the 1870s and ended with a permanent chapter of the Red Cross, founded in 1916. I included all of the church and synagogue laywomen's societies, the secular and semireligious women's organizations, and several organizations to which both men and women belonged. The next step was to evaluate and categorize the secular organizations according to their stated goals and purposes found in club constitutions, charters, minutes, newspaper articles, and city directories. Those women's clubs that were purely social in nature were not considered for this study. But those societies that directed their energies toward community building, toward helping dependents regardless of religious affiliation, or toward promoting women's education or rights were seen to be advancing southern women into public life and were, therefore, considered activist organizations.

The selected organizations fell into seven classifications: church and synagogue benevolent societies; benevolent institutions; auxiliaries; ethnic and immigrant women's aid societies; patriotic-hereditary organizations; art, music, and literary clubs; and civic associations. Finally, forty-six church and synagogue societies and twenty-nine secular groups were chosen for study.

The next stage involved becoming acquainted with the women who served as officers of these organizations. City directories were the most useful in listing officers but at times were incomplete. Club records, when available, filled in, as did newspaper articles and state histories of associations. I created a card for each woman officer, and every time her name appeared on an officer roll or in an exclusive group where the entire membership constituted a board of directors, this information was added.[2] Her officership and years of service and membership were recorded so as to determine the strength of commitment to the organization.

At first I compiled close to 500 names but eliminated those women from consideration who belonged only to church societies and not to the secular associations chosen for consideration. To qualify for inclusion in the total number of activist women, a woman must have belonged to at least one secular organization selected for this study. Her religious affiliation and membership in a church or synagogue society was then determined after her inclusion on the list. In other words, I worked from the secular to the religious, because the purpose was to establish the religious identity of women active in secular organizations. Eventually, I was able to extract from the general population for the years 1870 to 1920 a discrete group of 370 women activists.

In order to establish their identities and possibly class and status position within the community, I added their husbands' names when appropriate and searched for biographical information such as birth and death dates, place of birth, arrival in and departure from Galveston, wedding date, number of children, number of servants, military service, and education for the women, and community and political affiliations for the men. I collected this information from community books, blue books, obituaries, and manuscript census records for 1880, 1900, and 1910. Church affiliation was gleaned from church directories, vestry and deacon minutes, and church histories. City directories provided the addresses and occupations for the years 1880, 1890, 1900, 1910, and 1921. Including the men, the number of Galvestonians under consideration totals close to 700. I then codified and entered this data into a computer, creating a database from which numerical calculations could be extracted and analyzed by SAS, a database analysis system. Most of the tables pertaining to women in organizations were assembled from this Galveston Women Database.

For a study of the social standing of the activist women and their families in Glaveston I have relied on Max Weber's tripartite definition of social power — economic status, political power, and prestige — and have concluded that the most salient dimension of his definition for women is social status or prestige.[3] By combining variables that indicate economic position and status, I have created a status index that roughly indicates social standing. When matched with religious preferences, most Episcopalians and Presbyterians are listed in the top one-third of the status index.

NOTES

A Note About Galveston City Directories.

City directories from 1870 to 1921 were used for this project. Over the years, several different printers published the directories; title changes occurred as well. The following is an attempt to represent the directories by year and by publisher without actually listing each one.

John H. Heller, *Heller's Galveston Business Directory, 1875, 1881* (Galveston, 1875, 1881).

John H. Heller, *Galveston City Directory for 1870.* (Galveston: Galveston News Steam Printing Office, 1870).

John H. Heller, *Heller's Galveston City Directory, 1874, 1875–76, 1876–77, 1879* (Galveston: Strickland and Clarke, 1874, 1875, 1877, 1879).

Morrison and Fourmy, *General Directory of the City of Galveston for 1881–1882* (Galveston: M. Strickland, 1882).

Morrison and Fourmy, *General Directory of the City of Galveston, 1884–1885* (Galveston: M. Strickland, 1885).

Morrison and Fourmy, *General Directory of the City of Galveston, 1882–1883, 1886–87, 1888–89, 1890–91, 1891–92, 1893–94, 1895–96, 1898, 1899–1900* (Galveston: Clarke and Courts, 1883, 1887, 1889, 1891, 1892, 1894, 1896, 1898, 1900).

Morrison and Fourmy, *General Directory of the City of Galveston, 1901–1902, 1903–1904* (Galveston: M & F, Publishers, 1901, 1903).

Morrison and Fourmy, *Directory of the City of Galveston, 1905, 1908–09, 1909–1910, 1911–12* (Galveston: Morrison & Fourmy Directory Co., 1905, 1908, 1909, 1911).

Morrison and Fourmy, *Directory of the City of Galveston, 1913.* (Houston: Morrison & Fourmy Directory Co., 1913.)

Morrison and Fourmy, *Directory of the City of Galveston, 1914, 1916, 1919.* (Houston: R. L. Polk & Co., 1914, 1916, 1919).

Morrison and Fourmy. *Galveston City Directory, 1921* (Houston: Morrison & Fourmy Directory Co., 1921).

Introduction   The Multiple Meanings of Culture, Community, Religion, and Reform

1. For Texas reform movements, see Alwyn Barr, *Reconstruction to Reform: Texas Politics, 1876–1906* (Austin: University of Texas Press, 1971), 86–87, 91–92; Lewis L. Gould, *Progressives and Prohibitionists: Texas Democrats in the Wilson Era* (Austin: University of Texas Press, 1973), 51; A. Elizabeth Taylor, "The Woman Suffrage Movement in Texas," *Journal of Southern History*, 17 (May 1951), 194–215; and Bradley Robert Rice, *Progressive Cities: The Commission Government Movement in America, 1901–1920* (Austin: University of Texas Press, 1977), 6–7.

2. City Population: 1860 = 7,307; 1870 = 13,818; 1880 = 22,248; 1890 = 29,084; 1900 = 37,789; 1910 = 36,981. U. S. Census Office, *Report on the Social Statistics of Cities*. Pt. 2: *The Southern and Western States* (Washington, 1887), 315; U.S. Bureau of the Census, *Thirteenth Census of the U.S. . . . 1910*. Vol. 1: *Population* (Washington, 1913), 96.

3. David G. McComb, *Galveston: A History* (Austin, 1986), 5, 33–41.

4. Ibid., 33–41, 45–49, 47 (quotation), 83. Earl Wesley Fornell, *The Galveston Era: The Texas Crescent on the Eve of Secession* (Austin: University of Texas Press, 1961), 115.

5. Don H. Doyle, *New Men, New Cities, New South: Atlanta, Nashville, Charleston, Mobile, 1860–1910* (Chapel Hill: University of North Carolina Press, 1990); Doyle, "Urbanization and Southern Culture: Economic Elites in Four New South Cities (Atlanta, Nashville, Charleston, Mobile) c. 1865–1910," in Orville Vernon Burton and Robert C. McMath, Jr., eds., *Toward a New South? Studies in Post–Civil War Southern Communities* (Westport, Conn.: Greenwood Press, 1982), 11–36. For a comparative view of southern and western cities, see Lawrence H. Larsen, *The Rise of the Urban South* (Lexington: University Press of Kentucky, 1985), 140; Larsen, *The Urban West at the End of the Frontier* (Lawrence: The Regents Press of Kansas, 1978); David R. Goldfield, *Cotton Fields and Skyscrapers: Southern City and Region, 1607–1980* (Baton Rouge: Louisiana State University Press, 1982); Blaine A. Brownell and David R. Goldfield, eds., *The City in Southern History: The Growth of Urban Civilization in the South* (Port Washington: Kennikat Press, 1977); and Blaine A. Brownell, "Urbanization in the South: A Unique Experience?" *Mississippi Quarterly*, 26 (Spring 1973), 105–120; Brownell, *The Urban Ethos in the South, 1920–1930* (Baton Rouge: Louisiana State University Press, 1975); Howard N. Rabinowitz, *The First New South: 1865–1920* (Arlington Heights, Ill.: Harlan Davidson, 1992).

6. Christian-Disciples of Christ. Doyle, *New Men, New Cities*, 96–99, 120–122.

7. Doyle, "Urbanization and Southern Culture," 25; Doyle, *New Men, New Cities*, 96–110; Larsen, *Urban South*, 51, 54. See also William G. McLoughlin, *Revivals, Awakenings, and Reform: An Essay on Religion and Social Change in America, 1607–1977* (Chicago: University of Chicago Press, 1978), 132; David Edwin Harrell, Jr., "Religious Pluralism: Catholics, Jews, and Sectarians," in Charles Reagan Wilson, ed., *Religion in the South* (Jackson: University Press of Mississippi, 1985), 70. C. Vann Woodward in *Origins of the New South, 1877–1913* (Baton Rouge: Louisiana State University, 1951), 449–451 puts the percentage of Baptists and Methodists in the rural South in 1915 at 82 percent.

8. Ira Berlin and Herbert G. Gutman, "Natives and Immigrants, Free Men and Slaves: Urban Workingmen in the Antebellum American South," *American Historical Review*, 88 (December 1983), 1175–1200; Howard Miller, "Texas," in Samuel S. Hill, ed., *Religion in the Southern States: A Historical Study* (Macon, Ga.: Mercer University Press, 1983), 321.

9. For a definition of elite status, see Appendix A. Some elite status indicators are inclusion in city "blue books," representation on corporation boards of directors, location of residence, and inclusion in city biographies or "mug books." Using church directories, comparisons were made between members of the various churches and those persons

listed in *The Galveston Blue Book: A Society Directory, 1896* (Houston: J. R. Wheat, 1896); *The International Blue Book Publications, 1912–1914: Southeast Texas* (Houston: M. J. Sullivan and Co., 1912); Samuel Chester Griffin, *History of Galveston, Texas* (Galveston: A. H. Cawston, 1931); and Sam B. Graham, ed., *Galveston Community Book: A Historical and Biographical Record of Galveston and Galveston County* (Galveston: A. H. Cawston, 1945). See James M. Russel, "Elites and Municipal Politics and Government in Atlanta, 1847–1890," in Burton and McMath, eds., *Toward A New South?*, 37–70. Also helpful was John N. Ingram, *The Iron Barons: A Social Analysis of an American Urban Elite, 1874–1965* (Westport, Conn.: Greenwood Press, 1978); and Jaher Cople, *The Urban Establishment: Upper Strata in Boston, New York, Charleston, Chicago, and Los Angeles* (Urbana: University of Illinois Press, 1982).

10. Among elite Episcopalians were the Sealy, Hutchings, League, Adoue, and Rosenberg families; elite Presbyterians included the Trueheart and Austin families; elite Jewish families included the Kempners, Laskers, Ostermans, Dyers, Lovenbergs, and Kopperls. The Moodys (Methodist) and the Ballingers (Baptist) were elite families also. U.S. Census Office, *Report on the Social Statistics of Cities*. Pt 2, 321; U.S. Bureau of the Census, *Thirteenth Census of the United States . . . 1910*. Vol. 9: *Manufactures, 1909* (Washington, 1912), 1203. Galveston in 1906 held thirty-one Protestant churches with a total reported adult membership of 5,504. White Southern Baptists = 534 (9.7 percent); African American (National Convention) Baptists = 662 (12 percent); Lutherans = 758 (13.7 percent); members of the Methodist Episcopal Church = 681 (12.3 percent); members of the Methodist Episcopal Church, South = 627 (11.3 percent); members of the African Methodist Episcopal Church = 240 (4 percent); members of the Presbyterian Church in the U.S.A. = 75 (1.3 percent); members of the Presbyterian Church in the U.S. = 400 (7.2 percent); Episcopalians = 1,278 (23.1 percent); and members of miscellaneous Protestant churches = 249 (5 percent). Membership in the Roman Catholic Church, which totaled 14,872, includes children above the age of nine. Galveston's synagogue membership included 220 heads of families. U.S. Bureau of the Census, *Religious Bodies: 1906*. Pt. 1: *Summary and General Tables* (Washington, 1910), 24.

11. Samuel S. Hill, "Religion," in Charles Reagan Wilson and William Ferris, eds. *Encyclopedia of Southern Culture* (4 vols., New York: Anchor Books, 1989), Vol. 4, 3 (quotation); James H. Smylie, "Presbyterian Church in the United States (PCUS)," ibid., 105–107. Joel A. Carpenter, "Evangelical Protestantism," in Samuel S. Hill, ed., *Encyclopedia of Religion in the South* (Macon, Ga.: Mercer University Press, 1984), 239–244. Randy J. Sparks, *On Jordan's Stormy Banks: Evangelicalism in Mississippi, 1773–1876* (Athens: University of Georgia Press, 1994). See also Samuel S. Hill, "Northern and Southern Varieties of American Evangelicalism in the Nineteenth Century," in Mark A. Noll, David W. Bebbington, and George A. Rawlyk, eds. *Evangelicalism: Comparative Studies of Popular Protestantism in North America, the British Isles, and Beyond, 1700–1990* (New York: Oxford University Press, 1994), 275–289; and Wayne Flynt, "One in the Spirit, Many in the Flesh: Southern Evangelicals," in David Edwin Harrell, Jr., and Martin E. Marty, eds., *Varieties of Southern Evangelicalism* (Macon, Ga.: Mercer University Press, 1981), 23–44.

12. Anne Firor Scott, "Women, Religion, and Social Change in the South, 1830–1930," in Samuel S. Hill, Jr., ed., *Religion and the Solid South* (Nashville: Abingdon Press, 1972), 108, 110 (first quotation), 115–117; Scott, "Historians Construct the Southern Woman," in Joanne V. Hawks and Sheila Skemp, eds., *Sex, Race, and the Role of Women in the South* (Jackson: University Press of Mississippi, 1983), 107 (second quotation); Scott, *The Southern Lady: From Pedestal to Politics, 1830–1930* (Chicago: University of Chicago Press, 1970), 144–148; Jean E. Friedman, *The Enclosed Garden: Women and Community in the Evangelical South, 1830–1900* (Chapel Hill: University of North Carolina Press, 1985), 111–118.

13. Ruth Bordin, *Frances Willard: A Biography* (Chapel Hill: University of North Carolina Press, 1986), 113–115; Barbara Leslie Epstein, *The Politics of Domesticity: Women, Evangelism, and Temperance in Nineteenth-Century America* (Middletown, Conn.: Wesleyan University Press, 1981), 118–121; Joseph R. Gusfield, *Symbolic Crusade: Status Politics and the American Temperance Movement* (Urbana: University of Illinois Press, 1970), 89; Paula Baker, "The Domestication of Politics: Women and American Political Society, 1780–1920," *American Historical Review*, 89 (June 1984), 638. See Jacquelyn Dowd Hall, *Revolt against Chivalry: Jessie Daniel Ames and the Women's Campaign Against Lynching* (New York: Columbia University Press, 1979), 22, 25, 36, 66, for a discussion of the significance of the WCTU to the Texas woman suffrage movement and of Methodist mission societies to interracial cooperation.

14. Friedman, *Enclosed Garden*, 112–118; Mrs. W. M. Baines, *A Story of Texas White Ribboners (WCTU)* (n.p., [1936]), 60–61; Epstein, *The Politics of Domesticity*, 3. Jack S. Blocker, Jr., "Separate Paths: Suffragists and the Women's Temperance Crusade," *Signs*, 10 (Spring 1985), 460–476.

15. The concept of women's culture has been a much debated topic among women's historians. As a historians' construct, it stems from the observation that industrialization separated men's work from women's household work, which led to an identification of middle-class women with domesticity. The canon of domesticity, discussed by Nancy Cott in *The Bonds of Womanhood: "Woman's Sphere" in New England, 1780–1835* (New Haven: Yale University Press, 1977), centered around work-related sex roles. Barbara Welter's notion of a cult of domesticity, based on her reading of the popular *Godey's Lady's Book*, contributed ideological concepts to women's domestic roles. See Welter, "The Cult of True Womanhood, 1820–1860," *American Quarterly*, 18 (Summer 1966), 151–174. The rise of a women's culture, historians argue, depended upon forces of modernization that first assigned women to a separate sphere, which, in turn, led to the discovery among women of common gender-related interests and sisterhood. Because of these interests, shared female experiences, and the desire to act upon their newly found resources, women created their own associations, hence their own culture. Such associations, historians have explained, compose the whole of a separate women's culture. See, for example, Friedman, *Enclosed Garden*; and Friedman, "Women's History and Revision of Southern History," in Hawks and Skemp, eds., *Sex, Race, and the Role of Women in the South*, 6; Gerda Lerner, *The Creation of Patriarchy* (New York: Oxford University Press, 1986), 242. See Ellen DuBois, Mari Jo Buhle, Temma Kaplan, Gerda Lerner, and Carroll Smith-Rosenberg, "Politics and Culture in Women's History: A Symposium," *Feminist Studies*, 6 (Spring 1980), 26–64. As the discipline of women's history moved increasingly toward the study of women of different cultures and economic stations, the notion of women's culture as a paradigm came into question. See Nancy Hewitt, "Beyond the Search for Sisterhood: American Women's History in the 1980s," *Social History*, 10 (October 1985), 299–321; Joan W. Scott, "Gender: A Useful Category of Historical Analysis," *American Historical Review*, 91 (December 1986), 1053–1075; and Joanne Meyerowitz, "American Women's History: The Fall of Women's Culture," *Canadian Review of American Studies*, Pt. 1 (1992), 27–52. A rebuttal in this debate was launched by Suzanne Lebsock at a roundtable entitled, "What Difference Does Region Make?" at the Southern Historical Association meeting in Louisville, Kentucky, November 1994. Lebsock's *The Free Women of Petersburg: Status and Culture in a Southern Town, 1784–1860* (New York: W. W. Norton, 1984) relied on the notion of women's culture to explain values and behavior of women in antebellum Petersburg. An important evolution of the concept of women's culture is the notion of a women's political culture. For an insightful history of this concept, see Kathryn Kish Sklar, "The Historical Foundations of Women's Power in the Creation of the American Welfare State, 1830–1930," in Seth Koven

and Sonya Michel, eds., *Mothers of a New World: Maternalist Politics and the Origins of Welfare States* (New York: Routledge, 1993), 43–93, 79 n.4.

16. Lawrence W. Levine, *Highbrow/Lowbrow: The Emergence of Cultural Hierarchy in America* (Cambridge: Harvard University Press, 1988); and Pierre Bourdieu, *Distinction: A Social Critique of the Judgement of Taste* (Cambridge: Harvard University Press, 1984). Richard Munch and Neil J. Smelser, eds., *Theory of Culture* (Berkeley: University of California Press, 1992). See also Victor Turner, *Blazing the Trail: Way Marks in the Exploration of Symbols* (Tucson: University of Arizona Press, 1992); Turner, *On the Edge of the Bush: Anthropology as Experience* (Tucson: University of Arizona Press, 1985); and Victor Turner and Edith Turner, *Image and Pilgrimage in Christian Culture: Anthropological Perspectives* (New York: Columbia University Press, 1978).

Chapter 1   Disaster Strikes the Island City

1. W. J. McGee, "The Lessons of Galveston," *National Geographic Magazine*, 11 (October 1900), 377.

2. Julian Ralph, "A Recent Journey through the West." Pt. 8: "Joyous Galveston," *Harper's Weekly*, November 9, 1895, 1064.

3. Edward King, *The Great South*, edited by W. Magruder Drake and Robert R. Jones (Baton Rouge: Louisiana State University Press, [1874] 1972), 101.

4. Leslie C. Brand to Mother, May 11, 1899, Galveston Vertical File (Rosenberg Library, Galveston; hereinafter cited as Rosenberg Library) (first quotation). Clarence Ousley, *Galveston in Nineteen Hundred* (Atlanta: William C. Chase, 1900), 67. Descriptions of the 1867 yellow fever epidemic may be found in the Amelia Barr Letters (Center for American History, University of Texas at Austin; hereinafter cited as Center for American History); in Amelia Edith Barr, *All the Days of My Life* (New York: Appleton, 1913), 262–284, 268 (third and fourth quotations); and in Thomas Seargent to Annie M. Seargent, August 13, 1867, Thomas Seargent Letter (Rosenberg Library) (second quotation). David G. McComb, *Galveston: A History*, (Austin: University of Texas Press, 1986), 93–96. Kathleen Davis, "Year of Crucifixion: Galveston, Texas," *Texana*, 8 No. 2, (1970), 140–153; Peggy Hildreth, "The Howard Association of Galveston: The 1850s, Their Peak Years," *East Texas Historical Journal*, 17, No. 2 (1979), 33–44. Mildred Cram, *Old Seaport Towns of the South* (New York: Dodd, Mead & Co., 1917), 325 (fifth quotation). Yellow fever, always imported by migrants to the city from other infected areas, was eventually halted altogether by the effective use of quarantines after 1870.

5. King, *Great South*, 102.

6. U.S. Census Office, *Report on the Social Statistics of Cities*. Pt. 2, 1887, 318. Barr, *All the Days of My Life*, 268. McComb, *Galveston*, 23. Margaret Sealy Burton, "I'm Telling You," typescript, Margaret Sealy Burton Letters (Center for American History).

7. King, *Great South*, 102.

8. Leslie C. Brand to Mother, May 11, 1899 (first quotation). Katherine Sherwood MacDowell to Mr. Milliken, May 7, 1877, Katherine Sherwood (Bonner) MacDowell Papers (William R. Perkins Library, Duke University; hereinafter cited as Duke University Library) (second quotation). King, *Great South*, 108; McComb, *Galveston*, 23.

9. Leslie C. Brand to Mother, May 11, 1899 (first quotation); McComb, *Galveston*, 69. Walter B. Stevens, *The Story of the Galveston Disaster* (Galveston: San Luis Press, 1975, rpt. of an article from *Munsey's Magazine*, December 1900), 5. Ralph, "A Recent Journey through the West," 1064 (quotations). Burton, "I'm Telling You" (Wollom's Lake quotations).

10. *Galveston Daily News*, June 11, 1906 (first quotation), July 4, 1926; Earl Wesley

Fornell, *The Galveston Era: The Texas Crescent on the Eve of Secession* (Austin: University of Texas Press, 1961), 16–20; McComb, *Galveston*, 61 (second quotation). *Galveston and Deep Water*, pamphlet, in Subject Files (Rosenberg Library); D. W. Meinig, *Imperial Texas: An Interpretive Essay in Cultural Geography* (Austin: University of Texas Press, 1969), 57, 61, 63; C. Vann Woodward, *Origins of the New South 1877–1913* (Baton Rouge: Louisiana State University Press, 1951), 125; Gary Cartwright, *Galveston: A History of the Island* (New York: Atheneum, 1991), 138–140. Robert H. Peebles, "The Galveston Harbor Controversy of the Gilded Age, *Texana*, 12, No. 1 (1974), 74–83; W. Maury Darst, "Galveston's Harbor Defenses," *Texana*, 10 No. l (1972), 51–54.

11. *Galveston Daily News*, April 11, 1917, June 16, 1926, December 16, 1928, December 31, 1933. Sam B. Graham, ed., *Galveston Community Book: A Historical and Biographical Record of Galveston and Galveston County* (Galveston, A. H. Cawston, 1945), 72–74, 78–80; Charles W. Hayes, *Galveston: History of the Island and the City* (2 vols, Austin: Jenkins Garrett Press, [1879], 1974), Vol. 2, 673–678, 685–688. Isaac H. Kempner, *Recalled Recollections* (Dallas: Egan Co., 1961), 15. McComb, *Galveston*, 49–53; John S. Spratt, *The Road to Spindletop: Economic Change in Texas, 1875– 1901* (Austin: University of Texas Press, 1970), Chap. 2.

12. *Galveston Daily News*, October 30, 1921, July 4, 1926, January 18, 1932; *Galveston Tribune*, March 9, 1926, July 5, 1926; John A. Downey to Ann Downey Davis, February 9, 1885, Samuel Smith Downey Papers (Duke University Library), thanks to Jane Turner Censer for this citation; McComb, *Galveston*, 70, 83, 104 (third quotation). Kenneth Lipartito, *The Bell System and Regional Business: The Telephone in the South, 1877–1920* (Baltimore, 1989); and Lipartito,"When Women Were Switches: Technology, Work, and Gender in the Telephone Industry, 1890–1920," *American Historical Review*, 99 (October 1994), 1075–1111.

13. The best account of Galveston's antebellum commercial history is found in Fornell, *The Galveston Era*, Chap. 2. John H. Heller, *Heller's Galveston Business Directory, 1880–81* (Galveston: 1881), 149–161; Walter E. Grover, "Recollections of Life in Galveston during the 1880s and 1890s," typescript, Kincy Rygaard File (Rosenberg Library). Success stories abound for Galveston entrepreneurs in the late nineteenth century. See Harold M. Hyman, *Oleander Odyssey: The Kempners of Galveston, Texas, 1854–1980s* (College Station: Texas A&M University Press, 1990), 25–37, 87; *Galveston Daily News*, November 7, 1915, July 22, 1922, July 22, 1923, June 16, July 4, 1926, April 26, 1932, September 9, 1958, February 21, 1971; *Houston Chronicle*, July 22, 1936; *Galveston Tribune*, October 25, 1922, September 14, 1932.

14. *Galveston Daily News*, November 5, 1915, September 5, 1920, January 18, 1925, March 21, 1930; April 11, 1942. The first meeting of the Galveston Cotton Exchange was held on June 18, 1873.

15. *Houston Post*, March 3, 1968 (first quotation); William T. Purviance to Belle Alderman, January 11, 1874, Alderman Family Papers (Southern Historical Collection, Chapel Hill, N.C.; hereinafter cited as Southern Historical Collection) (second quotation); *Frank Leslie's Illustrated*, March 22, 1879, *Galveston Daily News*, September 5, 1920, March 21, 1930, April 11, 1942. Samuel Chester Griffin, *History of Galveston, Texas*, (Galveston: A. H. Cawston, 1931), 159, 319–323; Graham, ed., *Galveston Community Book*, 75–77.

16. *Galveston Daily News*, November 7, 1915, October 1, 1927, April 11, 1942. Col. W. L. Moody founded the Galveston Cotton Compress and Warehouse Company in 1894; it quickly became the largest handler of cotton in the city.

17. Hayes, *Galveston*, Vol. 2, 705 (first quotation); *Galveston Daily News*, June 16, 1926 (second quotation taken from Ed Morrison's *Industries of Galveston*, published 1885), February 24, 1935, September 9, 1958. *Galveston Tribune*, November 26, 1929.

18. Gross value of industrial products climbed from $2.5 to 5 million between 1880 and 1900. Directors of the Galveston Cotton and Woolen Mills were Albert Weis, J. Reymershoffer, W. F. Ladd, H. A. Landes, D. Herlich, Bertrand Adoue, George Sealy, Morris Lasker, and Julius Runge. *Galveston Daily News*, June 16, 1926, July 7, 1929, February 28, 1932, March 8, 1932, April 11, 1942, October 26, 1958; C. W. Hayes, "Galveston's Progress," in Morrison and Fourmy's *General Directory of the City of Galveston, 1882–1883* (Galveston, 1883), 9–34; hereinafter all city directories cited as *City Directory*, with appropriate date. U.S. Census Office, *Report on the Manufactures of the U.S. . . . 1880* (Washington, 1883), 379; U.S. Census Office, *Report on Manufacturing Industries in the U.S. . . . 1890*. Pt. 2. *Statistics of Cities* (Washington, 1895), 226; U.S. Census Office. *Twelfth Census of the U.S. . . . 1900. Manufactures*, Pt. 2: *States and Territories* (Washington, 1902), 866. McComb, *Galveston*, 112–113; Hyman, *Oleander Odyssey*, 30.

19. *City Directory, 1895–96*, 66–67. U.S. Census Office, *Twelfth Census . . . 1900. Manufactures*, Pt. 2, 866, 878–879. The average female office worker earned $6 a week or $312 a year in the 1890s. McComb, *Galveston*, 112–113, 155–156. Ruth Rosen in *The Lost Sisterhood: Prostitution in America, 1900–1918* (Baltimore: Johns Hopkins University Press, 1982), 145–155, explains that the most frequently cited reasons women entered prostitution were bad home conditions, low wages, and seasonal layoffs in such industries as textiles, dressmaking, millinery, and food processing. See also Alice Kessler-Harris, *Out to Work: A History of Wage-Earning Women in the United States* (New York: Oxford University Press, 1982), 103–105, 148.

20. John H. Heller, *Heller's Galveston Business Directory, 1875* (Galveston, 1875); *Heller's Galveston Business Directory, 1880–81* (Galveston, 1881); *City Directory, 1882–1883*, 75–76. *City Directory, 1886–87*, 46–49. Unless otherwise indicated, these city directories list white businesses only.

21. Ralph Albert Scull, "Black Galveston: A Personal View of Community History in Many Categories of Life," manuscript (Rosenberg Library) (first two quotations). *Galveston Daily News*, January 8, 1889 (third quotation); *Galveston and Deep Water*, 11 (fourth quotation). McComb, *Galveston*, 99, 108–109, 112. Lawrence H. Larsen, *The Rise of the Urban South* (Lexington: University Press of Kentucky, 1985), 140; and Larsen, *The Urban West at the End of the Frontier* (Lawrence: The Regents Press of Kansas, 1978), 86–87. Larsen writes that the city with the greatest number of liquor saloons in the West was San Francisco with 8,694, but among southern cities Baltimore topped the list with 2,100; New Orleans sported 429. Whereas statistics are incomplete for the number of bordellos (they were illegal and therefore unlisted), New Orleans led among southern cities with 365; Baltimore listed 300.

22. *City Directory, 1899–1900*; U.S. Census Office, *Report on Statistics of Churches in the United States at the Eleventh Census: 1890* (Washington, 1894), 100–101.

23. In 1900, 53 percent of Galvestonians were of native parentage; 47 percent were of foreign parentage; 17 percent were foreign born, and 22 percent were black. U.S. Census Office, *Twelfth Census of the U. S. . . . 1900. Population*, Pt. 1 (Washington, 1901), 643, 681, 796–799. U.S. Census Office, *Thirteenth Census of the U.S. . . . 1910. Population*, Pt. 3 (Washington, 1913), 852–853. Fornell notes in *Galveston Era*, 115, 125, that there were 1,500 slaves in Galveston in the 1850s. Willard B. Gatewood, *Aristocrats of Color: The Black Elite, 1880–1920* (Bloomington: Indiana University Press, 1990), 19; Maud Cuney Hare, *N. W. Cuney: A Tribune of the Black People* (New York: Crisis Publishing Co., 1913); Lorenzo J. Greene, "Sidelights on Houston Negroes as Seen by an Associate of Dr. Carter G. Woodson in 1930," in Howard Beeth and Cary D. Wintz, eds., *Black Dixie: Afro-Texas History and Culture in Houston* (College Station: Texas A&M University Press, 1992), 151–153; Barr, *Black Texans: A History of Negroes in Texas, 1528–1971* (Austin: Jenkins Publishing Co., 1973), 71–73; and

Lawrence D. Rice, *The Negro in Texas, 1874–1900* (Baton Rouge: Louisiana State University Press, 1971), 35. Richard Payne and Geoffrey Leavenworth, *Historic Galveston* (Houston: Herring Press, 1985), 33–35; Hyman, *Oleander Odyssey*, 3; Don H. Doyle, *New Men, New Cities, New South: Atlanta, Nashville, Charleston, Mobile, 1860–1910* (Chapel Hill: University of North Carolina Press, 1990), 12; Howard N. Rabinowitz, *The First New South: 1865–1920* (Arlington Heights, Ill.: Harlan Davidson, 1992), 158. Howard Rabinowitz and Don Doyle mistakenly assume that Galveston's population included a great many Mexicans and Latin Americans in the early twentieth century. The 1900 census shows that this is not the case.

24. Payne and Leavenworth, *Historic Galveston*, 33–35; Burton, "I'm Telling You."

25. Ralph, "A Recent Journey through the West," 1064 (first quotation); Leslie C. Brand to Mother, May 11, 1899, Galveston Vertical File (second quotation). For a discussion of men, their work habits, and self-identity, see E. Anthony Rotundo, *American Manhood: Transformations in Masculinity from the Revolution to the Modern Era* (New York: Basic Books, 1990), Chap. 8; Ted Ownby, *Subduing Satan: Religion, Recreation, and Manhood in the Rural South, 1865–1920* (Chapel Hill: University of North Carolina Press, 1990); and Doyle, *New Men, New Cities.*

26. Payne and Leavenworth, *Historic Galveston*, 20 (first quotation); Burton, "I'm Telling You" (subsequent quotations); Doyle, *New Men, New Cities*, 240–244. For Mardi Gras in Galveston, see *Galveston Daily News*, February 21–29, March 1, 1924, March 2, 1930; *Galveston Tribune*, Magazine Section, January 30, 1932, February 14–18, 20–22, 1933, March 2, 1935.

27. John A. Downey to Ann Downey Davis, February 9, 1885, Downey Papers; McComb, *Galveston*, 106–107; Lawrence W. Levine, *Highbrow/Lowbrow: The Emergence of Cultural Hierarchy in America* (Cambridge: Harvard University Press, 1988), 18 (quotation), 88–89 for touring opera companies.

28. Kenneth Hafertepe, *A History of Ashton Villa: A Family and Its House in Victorian Galveston, Texas* (Austin: Texas State Historical Association, 1991), 6–19. Ralph A. Wooster, "Wealthy Texans, 1870," *Southwestern Historical Quarterly*, 74 (July 1970), 33–35. Howard Barnstone, *The Galveston That Was* (New York: Macmillan Co., 1966), 89; Howard Barnstone grouped Galveston's architecture into three distinct periods: classical antebellum, romantic, and Victorian Gothic, specifically under the imprint of architect Nicholas J. Clayton. Payne and Leavenworth, *Historic Galveston*, 43–45. John A. Downey to Ann Downey Davis, February 9, 1885, Downey Papers.

29. *Galveston Daily News*, September 2–8, 1900. The *News* printed on Friday, September 7, a brief story about the storm raging in the Gulf near Key West, Florida, but by then the storm was off the coast of Louisiana. Herbert Molloy Mason, Jr., *Death from the Sea: Our Greatest Natural Disaster, the Galveston Hurricane of 1900* (New York: Dial Press, 1972), 60–61.

30. John Edward Weems, *A Weekend in September* (College Station: Texas A&M University Press, 1957), 8–13. Mason, *Death from the Sea*, 71; McComb, *Galveston*, 123–124. *Houston Chronicle*, September 15, 1988.

31. Weems, *Weekend in September*, 35, 46, 53; Mason, *Death from the Sea*, 79–80; McComb, *Galveston*, 124; Ousley, *Galveston in Nineteen Hundred*, 28–29.

32. John Newman to the Editor, August 31, 1934, John Newman Letter (Center for American History); Louisa Christine Rollfing autobiography, typescript (Rosenberg Library); Ida Smith Austin, "Letter Describing the 1900 Storm," November 6, 1900 (Rosenberg Library).

33. *Galveston Daily News*, September 12, 1900. E. B. Garriott, "The West Indian Hurricane of September 1–12, 1900," *National Geographic Magazine*, 11 (October 1900), 391.

Louisa C. Rollfing autobiography; Henry W. Wolfram to Dear George, September 21, 1900, Henry M. Wolfram Letter (Center for American History).

34. Ousley, *Galveston in Nineteen Hundred*, 28, 43–44 (quotation); McComb, *Galveston*, 125; *Houston Chronicle*, September 8, 1934; Weems, *Weekend in September*, 104, 115. Cartwright, *Galveston*, 168.

35. Hafertepe, *Ashton Villa*, 39; Weems, *Weekend in September*, 80–81, 90, 122; Cartwright, *Galveston*, 168. George P. Rawick, ed., *The American Slave: A Composite Autobiography*, Supp., Ser. 2, Vol. 8, Pt. 7 (Westport, Conn.: Greenwood Press, 1979), 3244 (third quotation); ibid. Ser. 2, Vol. 6, Pt. 5, 2010–2011 (first two quotations); John Newman to the Editor, August 31, 1934 (last two quotations).

36. Ousley, *Galveston in Nineteen Hundred*, 110–113.

37. Sarah Helen Littlejohn, "My Experiences in the Galveston Storm, September 8, 1900" (Rosenberg Library); Ousley, *Galveston in Nineteen Hundred*, 35; *Galveston Daily News*, August 9, 1978; Louisa Rollfing autobiography; Gid Scherer to Mary Hutson, September 28, 1900, Charles Woodward Hutson Papers (Southern Historical Collection); Henry W. Wolfram to Dear George, September 21, 1900, Henry M. Wolfram Letter.

38. John Newman to the Editor, August 31, 1934.

39. Mason, *Death from the Sea*, 90, 107, 110, 116; McComb, *Galveston*, 124–128; Ousley, *Galveston in Nineteen Hundred*, 30–32; *Galveston Daily News*, September 12, 1900.

40. Ousley, *Galveston in Nineteen Hundred*, 47–50; Stevens, *Galveston Disaster*, 12–15. McComb, *Galveston*, 127. Scull, "Black Galveston." [Galveston] *City Times*, August 17, 1901.

41. "Reminiscences of Mrs. Martha H. Poole," typescript, 7 (Rosenberg Library); William Manning Morgan, *Trinity Protestant Episcopal Church, Galveston, Texas, 1841–1953* (Houston: Anson Jones Press, 1954), 102. Ousley, *Galveston in Nineteen Hundred*, 95–97, 100, 119 (second quotation); Weems, *Weekend in September*, 158.

42. Mason, *Death from the Sea*, 90, 107, 110, 116; McComb, *Galveston*, 124–128; Ousley, *Galveston in Nineteen Hundred*, 30–32; *Galveston Daily News*, September 12, 1900.

43. Rawick, ed., *American Slave*, Supp. Ser. 2, Vol. 8, Pt. 7, 3235 (first quotation); Ousley, *Galveston in Nineteen Hundred*, 31, 110–120 (last quotations); Weems, *Weekend in September*, 135–145.

44. *Galveston Daily News*, September 12, 1900. Austin, "Letter Describing the 1900 Storm." Mason, *Death from the Sea*, 194, 198, 200, 209–210, 217–218; McComb, *Galveston*, 126–127; Ousley, *Galveston in Nineteen Hundred*, 31, 36–37, 120; Weems, *Weekend in September* 145; *Galveston Tribune*, September 12, 1900.

45. Rawick, ed., *American Slave*, Supp. Ser. 2, Vol. 8, Pt. 7, 3245 (first quotation). Red Cross, "Report of Fannie B. Ward," in *Report of Red Cross Relief, Galveston, Texas* (Washington, D.C., 1900–1901), 48 (second quotation). Mason, *Death from the Sea*, 209–210, 217–218; McComb, *Galveston*, 126–127; Ousley, *Galveston in Nineteen Hundred*, 37–38; *Galveston Daily News*, September 16, 1900 (third quotation).

46. *Galveston Daily News*, September 14, 1900.

47. Austin, "Letter Describing the 1900 Storm."

Chapter 2   Women, Culture, and the Church: Memorials, Cemeteries, and Music

1. *Galveston Daily News*, September 2, 1895, May 30, 1917; *Henry Rosenberg: 1824–1893* (Galveston: Board of Directors of the Rosenberg Library, 1918); *Galveston City Directories*, 1898, 1908–09, 1921. "Mrs. Mollie R. Rosenberg, 'Patron Saint' of Texas Division U.D.C," photograph with play description, Grace Episcopal Church Records (Rosenberg

Library). Margaret Sealy Burton, "I'm Telling You," typescript, Margaret Sealy Burton Letters (Center for American History).

2. The literature on the change in family life and the role of women as a result of commercial and industrial revolutions is now voluminous. For a sampling, see Steven Mintz and Susan Kellogg, *Domestic Revolutions: A Social History of American Family Life* (New York: The Free Press, 1988), 55 (quotation); Carl Degler, *At Odds: Women and the Family in America from the Revolution to the Present* (New York: Oxford University Press, 1980); Barbara Welter, "The Cult of True Womanhood, 1820–1869," *American Quarterly,* 18 (Summer 1966), 151–174. Kathleen D. McCarthy, *Women's Culture: American Philanthropy and Art, 1830–1930* (Chicago: University of Chicago Press, 1991), 5–8. For a description of the change in household production and consumption, see Ruth Schwartz Cowan, *More Work for Mother: The Ironies of Household Technology from the Open Hearth to the Microwave* (London: Basic Books, 1983); and Harvey Green, *The Light of the Home: An Intimate View of the Lives of Women in Victorian America* (New York: Pantheon Books, 1983). See also Robert N. Bellah, Richard Madsen, William M. Sullivan, Ann Swidler, and Steven M. Tipton, *Habits of the Heart: Individualism and Commitment in American Life* (New York: Harper and Row, 1985), 85–90.

3. Colleen McDannell, *The Christian Home in Victorian America, 1840–1900* (Bloomington: Indiana University Press, 1986), 9, 21, 42–45. McDannnell writes that Catherine Beecher went so far as to design a home "that doubled as a church and a school" (37); Green, *Light of the Home,* 174.

4. Rima Lunin Schultz, "Woman's Work and Woman's Calling in the Episcopal Church: Chicago, 1880–1989," in Catherine Prelinger, ed., *Episcopal Women: Gender, Spirituality, and Commitment in a Mainline Denomination* (New York: Oxford University Press, 1992), 19–71, 20 (quotation). Much of this discussion of the value of women's roles in church life differs from Ann Douglas's interpretation of the feminization of religion as found in Chap. 4, "The Loss of Theology," in *The Feminization of American Culture* (New York: Avon Books, 1977). For an interpretation that complements the one presented here, see McDannell, *Christian Home,* 18.

5. Anne Firor Scott, *The Southern Lady: From Pedestal to Politics, 1830–1930* (Chicago: University of Chicago Press, 1970), 141. Evelyn Brooks Higginbotham, *Righteous Discontent: The Women's Movement in the Black Baptist Church, 1880–1920* (Cambridge: Harvard University Press, 1993), 229. Du Bois et al., "Politics and Culture in Women's History: A Symposium," *Feminist Studies,* 6 (Spring 1980), 41.

6. John B. Boles, *The Great Revival: The Origins of the Southern Evangelical Mind* (Lexington: University Press of Kentucky, 1972); and Donald G. Mathews, *Religion in the Old South* (Chicago: University of Chicago Press, 1977), 47–49. Mathews estimates that 27 percent of the white adult population were church members, and "southern women outnumbered men in the churches (65:35), though men outnumbered women in the general population (51.5:48.5), 47, 102–105.

7. Between 1865 and World War I, church membership increased to 43 percent of the total population; 150,000 new churches were constructed nationwide. Robert Wuthnow and William Lehrman, "Religion: Inhibitor or Facilitator of Political Involvement among Women?" in Louise Tilly and Patricia Gurin, eds., *Women Politics, and Change* (New York: The Russell Sage Foundation, 1990), 301. U.S. Census Office, *Report on Statistics of Churches . . . 1890,* 112–113; U.S. Bureau of the Census, *Religious Bodies,* 1906. Pt. 1: *Summary and General Tables* (Washington, 1910), 442; U.S. Bureau of the Census, *Religious Bodies: 1916.* Pt. 1. *Summary and General Tables* (Washington, 1919), 404–406.

8. Rosemary Skinner Keller, "Creating a Sphere for Women," in Hilah F. Thomas

and Rosemary Skinner Keller, eds., *Women in New Worlds: Historical Perspectives on the Wesleyan Tradition* (2 vols., Nashville: Abingdon Press, 1982), Vol. 1, 246–260.

9. The exceptions were memorials to fallen war heroes and storm victims raised by women's groups such as the Daughters of the Republic of Texas or the Women's Health Protective Association.

10. Beside the contributions of Henry Rosenberg to Galveston, George Ball donated money for a high school; John Sealy bequeathed $50,000 for a hospital; Bertrand Adoue left part of his fortune to build the Adoue Seamen's Bethel; Morris Lasker funded the Lasker Home for Homeless Children and a Manual Training School. *Monuments of Galveston: A Guide*, pamphlet, n.d. (Rosenberg Library).

11. T. J. Jackson Lears, *No Place of Grace: Antimodernism and the Transformation of American Culture, 1880–1920* (New York: Pantheon Books, 1981), 193. McDannell, *Christian Home*, 28–31.

12. McCarthy, *Women's Culture*, 44, 46 (quotation), 53–55, 60. Green, *Light of the Home*, 90–115; McDannell, *Christian Home*, 29, 50. Eileen Boris, *Art and Labor: Ruskin, Morris, and the Craftsman Ideal in America* (Philadelphia: Temple University Press, 1986), xiii.

13. Boris, *Art and Labor*, Chap. 4. Lears, *No Place of Grace*, 66–69. McDannell, *Christian Home*, 49–50. Much of what is discussed here is tangentially related to the American Arts and Crafts movement, which had its formal beginnings in this country in 1897. This movement placed emphasis not only on simplicity of design and authenticity of material but on the "craftsman ideal." See also Lawrence W. Levine, *Highbrow/Lowbrow: The Emergence of Cultural Hierarchy in America* (Cambridge: Harvard University Press, 1988), esp. Chap. 2.

14. James L. Sturm, *Stained Glass from Medieval Times to the Present: Treasures to Be Seen in New York* (New York: E. P. Dutton, 1982), 34–55. Weber Wilson, *Great Glass in American Architecture: Decorative Windows and Doors before 1920* (New York: E. P. Dutton, 1986), 100–103. L. A. Richards, "An Unworthy Obscurity," *Stained Glass Quarterly*, 89 (Spring 1994), 35–52. Russell Lynes, *The Tastemakers* (New York: Harper and Brothers, 1949), 172–175.

15. Suzanne Lebsock, *The Free Women of Petersburg: Status and Culture in a Southern Town, 1784–1860* (New York: W. W. Norton, 1984), 198. Bequests and gifts by women changed after 1900 to include structures specifically for women's organizations and the poor.

16. "Reminiscences of Mrs. Martha H. Poole," typescript, 7 (Rosenberg Library). Clarence Ousley, *Galveston in Nineteen Hundred* (Atlanta: William C. Chase, 1900), 84. Mrs. J. E. Murphy, "The History of Methodism in Galveston, 1839–1942," 31–39, typescript (Moody Memorial Methodist Church, Galveston). *A Brief Historical Introduction to the First Presbyterian Church, Galveston, Texas*, brochure, First Presbyterian Church Records (Rosenberg Library); hereinafter cited as FPC Records.

17. E. Anthony Rotundo, *American Manhood: Transformations in Masculinity from the Revolution to the Modern Era* (New York: Basic Books, 1990), 104. William Manning Morgan, *Trinity Protestant Episcopal Church, Galveston, Texas, 1841–1953* (Houston: Anson Jones Press, 1954), 594–617. For an especially thought provoking explication of the Victorian use of angel imagery for women, see Nina Auerbach, *Woman and the Demon: The Life of a Victorian Myth* (Cambridge: Harvard University Press, 1982), 63–88.

18. Morgan, *Trinity*, 594–617. Pauline Spurway, "Trinity Protestant Episcopal Church of Galveston, Texas" (M.A. thesis, Sam Houston State Teachers College, 1940), 39–46.

19. Voting rights for women in churches varied by denomination, but in no case did women hold church office beyond appointment to church committees.

20. See Auerbach, *Woman and Demon*, esp. Chap. 5; Norma Broude and Mary D. Garrard, eds., *Feminism and Art History: Questioning the Litany* (New York: Harper and Row, 1982); Helena Waddy Lepovitz, *Images of Faith: Expressionism, Catholic Folk Art, and the Industrial Revolution* (Athens: University of Georgia Press, 1991), 125–130; Linda Nochlin, *Women, Art, and Power and Other Essays* (New York: Harper and Row, 1988); and most especially, Joy S. Kasson, *Marble Queens and Captives: Women in Nineteenth-Century American Sculpture* (New Haven: Yale University Press, 1990), 1–4, 18–19, 68–69, 72–73, 87, 158, 166.

21. *Henry Rosenberg*, 3–13; *Henry Rosenberg: Benefactor*, brochure, June 1943, Rosenberg Family Papers (Rosenberg Library).

22. *Henry Rosenberg*, 17–21.

23. *Henry Rosenberg*, 91–96. To Mollie he left the family home and $150,000 in bonds. Will of Henry R. Rosenberg, May 31, 1892, Rosenberg Family Papers; *Henry Rosenberg: Benefactor*.

24. Silas McBee to William V. R. Watson, fifteen letters dated June 16, 1893, to January 25, 1894, Silas McBee Papers (Southern Historical Collection).

25. *Galveston Daily News*, September 2, 1895; *Galveston Daily News*, November 1895, clipping, Grace Episcopal Church Records (quotation); *Henry Rosenberg*, 109–111. *Grace Episcopal Church: A Hundred Years of Grace* (Galveston: Limited Edition Printed for Grace Church, 1974), 6–10. The reredos and altar cost $4,000. Silas McBee to Mrs. Henry Rosenberg, December 23, 1895, Rosenberg Family Papers. Mollie Rosenberg spent approximately $20,000 on the interior furnishings, *Galveston Tribune*, November 17, 1926.

26. The center window above the altar was destroyed in a 1943 storm and was replaced with a new window depicting an ascending Christ.

27. Mary Magdalene, Mary the mother of James, and Salome were among those mentioned in Mark 16:1–7, while Luke 24:1–12 mentions the two Marys but adds Johanna. Matthew 28:1–10 speaks of the two Marys alone. Luke (24:10–11) writes that the women "told this to the disciples; but these words seemed to them an idle tale, and they did not believe them." Elisabeth Schüssler Fiorenza, *In Memory of Her: A Feminist Theological Reconstruction of Christian Origins* (New York: Crossroad Publishing, 1989), 139–140 (first quotation), 321(second quotation). See also Fiorenza, *But She Said: Feminist Practices of Biblical Interpretation* (Boston: Beacon Press, 1992), esp. Chap. 3; and Karen Jo Torjesen, *When Women Were Priests: Women's Leadership in the Early Church and the Scandal of Their Subordination in the Rise of Christianity* (San Francisco: Harper Collins, 1993), 33–37.

28. On the meaning of symbols in historic interpretation, see Joan W. Scott, "Gender: A Useful Category of Historical Analysis," *American Historical Review*, 91 (December 1986), 1053–1075, 1067.

29. Book of Remembrance for Grace Episcopal Church (Grace Episcopal Church, Galveston). In Deuteronomy 10:18, God promises to "execute justice for the fatherless and the widow." The phrase is repeated in Psalms 68:5 and 146:9. But the exact passage of scripture cited here is from James 1:27. "Religion that is pure and undefiled before God and the Father is this: to visit orphans and widows in their affliction, and to keep oneself unstained from the world." For the description of Tabitha, see Acts 9:36–43. The apostle Peter found Tabitha of Joppa dead, but with the power of the Holy Spirit raised her to life. "Now there was at Joppa a *disciple* named Tabitha, which means Dorcas or gazelle. She was full of good works and acts of charity." (emphasis mine).

30. Luke 10:40. Helene Weis, "Those Old, Familiar Faces," *Stained Glass Quarterly*, 86 (Fall 1991), 204–217. Although Mollie Rosenberg was the principal donor of the windows, carpeting, altar, and most of the church furnishings at the time of its dedication in 1895; other donors provided windows to memorialize loved ones—the wise virgins donated by

Julia B. Southwick and the adolescent Jesus and his mother donated by the League family are two examples. The rose window on the east side, depicting Christ surrounded by serenading angels, was given in memory of Sarah Pearson by her friends, and the pipe organ was donated by the congregation in memory of its benefactor Henry Rosenberg.

31. *Galveston Daily News*, September 2, 1895.

32. Quotation from Carroll Smith-Rosenberg, *Disorderly Conduct: Visions of Gender in Victorian America* (New York: Oxford University Press, 1985), 45.

33. Mary S. Donovan, *A Different Call: Women's Ministries in the Episcopal Church, 1850–1920* (Wilton, Conn.: Morehouse-Barlow, 1986), 20.

34. Galveston Screwmen's Benevolent Association Records, Vol. 1, 1866–1889, June 7, 1867, October 21, 1879, February 2, 21, 1881, June 8, 1888 (Center for American History); Lynn Dumenil, *Freemasonry and American Culture, 1880–1930* (Princeton: Princeton University Press, 1984), 40–41. For private mourning rituals practiced by women, see Douglas, *Feminization of American Culture*, 240–272.

35. Green, *Light of the Home*, 170–175. Shirley Abbot, *Womenfolks: Growing Up Down South* (New York: Ticknor and Fields, 1983), 1–3; Terry G. Jordan, *Texas Graveyards: A Cultural Legacy* (Austin: University of Texas Press, 1982), 13–40.

36. Rosanna Dyer Osterman died in the explosion of the steamship *W. R. Carter* on the Mississippi River near Vicksburg. Her estate, valued at $204,000, was divided among charities in Galveston, Houston, New Orleans, Cincinnati, and New York. Charles W. Hayes, *Galveston: History of the Island and the City*, Vol. 2, 892; Henry Cohen, David Lefkowitz, and Ephraim Frisch, *One Hundred Years of Jewry in Texas* (Dallas: Jewish Advisory Committee, 1936), 9–10; Record Ledger of Association Secretary, 1854–1882, May 6, 1867, Howard Association of Galveston Records (Rosenberg Library); Rosanna Dyer Osterman's will, filed March 26, 1866, Will Book 2, 229–244; Rosanna Dyer Osterman's inventory, Inventories Book 1, 405–411, Galveston County Courthouse; *Galveston Tri-Weekly News*, February 14, 1866; A. Stanley Dreyfus, "Hebrew Cemetery No.1 of Galveston," and "The Hebrew Benevolent Society: A Saga of Service," typescripts, A. Stanley Dreyfus Papers (Rosenberg Library).

37. Dreyfus, "Hebrew Benevolent Society." Beth Ann Bassein, *Women and Death: Linkages in Western Thought and Literature* (Westport, Conn.: Greenwood Press, 1984), 205.

38. Morgan, *Trinity*, 709; Willis W. Pratt, ed., *Galveston Island; or, A few Months off the Coast of Texas: The Journal of Francis C. Sheridan, 1839–1840* (Austin: University of Texas Press, 1954), 49.

39. Vestry Minutes, January 16, 1878, Trinity Episcopal Church Records (Rosenberg Library); hereinafter cited as Vestry Minutes, TEC; Morgan, *Trinity*, 711.

40. Morgan, *Trinity*, 713.

41. Vestry Minutes, TEC, June 6, 1881, July 8, 1884 (first quotation), April 5, 1885, April 6, 1886 (second quotation).

42. Vestry Minutes, TEC, April 6, 1904; Morgan, *Trinity*, 714–715 (quotations).

43. Vestry Minutes, TEC, August 1901, November 1902, December 4, 1907, April 12, 1910; Morgan, *Trinity*, 714–715, 716 (quotation), 627–628.

44. "Reminiscences of Mrs. Martha H. Poole." Randy J. Sparks in *On Jordan's Stormy Banks: Evangelicalism in Mississippi, 1773–1876* (Athens: University of Georgia Press, 1994) notes that by singing, women "acquired their first major liturgical role in worship services" (45).

45. Karen J. Blair, *The Torchbearers: Women and Their Amateur Arts Associations in America, 1890–1930* (Bloomington: Indiana University Press, 1994), 3, 12–16. Green, *Light of the Home*, 13, 93.

46. *Galveston Daily News,* December 26, 1884, quoted in Morgan, *Trinity,* 482–483.

47. "Etheldreda Aves," Subject Files (Rosenberg Library); *Galveston Daily News,* April 18, 1942.

48. Morgan, *Trinity,* 478; The Methodists, on the other hand, retained the same woman organist for thirty-two years. Murphy, "The History of Methodism in Galveston," 28.

49. Morgan, *Trinity,* 478; *Galveston Daily News,* March 1, 1914, November 14, 1925; "Mrs. William Francis Beers," typescript, Beers Family Papers (Rosenberg Library).

50. Louise F. Parker was hired as choir director of Trinity Church probably before January 1904. Morgan, *Trinity,* 111, 235 (quotation), 443; Programs, Ladies' Musical Club of Galveston, 1899–1905, Subject Files (Rosenberg Library).

51. *Galveston Daily News,* March 1, 1914. All the Fowlers were supporters of woman suffrage, but Louise Parker died in 1910 before a permanent suffrage society was formed in Galveston. By choosing paid work in a field where talent and training mattered, she may have been pioneering the path she felt women should take.

52. Vestry Minutes, TEC, April 22, 1901 (quotation), April 12, 1910. Clifford Groce is Mrs. Thomas Groce's given name. The other vestry committees included finance, pew, envelope (stewardship), and church property.

Chapter 3   Church Programs: Sunday School, Bible Classes, and Women's Societies

1. William McCullough to Mrs. Margaret Jane McCullough, August 3, 1870, in William Wallace McCullough, Jr., "John McCullough 'Grandfather,' 1805–1870: Pioneer Presbyterian Missionary and Teacher in the Republic of Texas," typescript, Subject Files (Rosenberg Library); hereinafter cited as McCullough Biography.

2. Ibid.

3. Mary Beth Norton, "The Evolution of White Women's Experience in Early America," *American Historical Review,* 89 (June 1984), 606. For a description of the importance of the mother in Methodist Sunday school literature see Joanna Bowen Gillespie, " 'The Sun in Their Domestic System,' " in Rosemary Skinner Keller, Louise L. Queen, and Hilah F. Thomas, eds., *Women in New Worlds: Historical Perspectives on the Wesleyan Tradition* (2 vols., Nashville: Abingdon Press, 1982), Vol. 2, 45–59. For a more secular version of the "democratic family" and the role of mothers in raising children to become independent adults, see Steven Mintz and Susan Kellogg, *Domestic Revolutions: A Social History of American Family Life* (New York: The Free Press, 1988), 45–48, 58–60.

4. Lucy P. Shaw to Mrs. Jane N. Weston, March 1, 1840, Lucy P. Shaw Papers (Rosenberg Library) (quotation); *Texas Presbyterian,* June 9, 1876; *Galveston Daily News,* January 1, 1939; *Galveston Tribune,* April 14, 1936; *Echoes from the Past: A Brochure of Brief Historical Sketches Connected with Presbyterianism in the South and Its God-given Work in the World* (Galveston: Presbytery of Brazos, 1936), 11–13.

5. William McCullough to John W. Riddell, June 8, 1878, McCullough Biography (quotation). Manuscript Census Returns, Galveston County, 1880.

6. William McCullough to John W. Riddell, June 8, 1878, McCullough Biography.

7. Sunday School Records, 1877–1879, 1895–1899, FPC Records; *Echoes from the Past,* 15.

8. By 1900, Margaret no longer took in boarders; she lived in the same home with her youngest daughter and a woman friend. Manuscript Census Returns, Galveston County, 1900.

9. Sydney E. Ahlstrom, *A Religious History of the American People* (New Haven: Yale University Press, 1972), 741–742.

10. Walter N. Vernon, Robert W. Sledge, Robert C. Monk, Norman W. Spellmann, *The Methodist Excitement in Texas: A History* (Dallas: Texas United Methodist Historical Society, 1984), 177. See also Anne M. Boylan, *Sunday School: The Formation of an American Institution, 1790–1880* (New Haven: Yale University Press, 1988), 138; Ahlstrom, *Religious History*, 741.

11. John B. Boles, *The Great Revival: The Origins of the Southern Evangelical Mind* (Lexington: University Press of Kentucky, 1972), 91 (quotation); and Donald G. Mathews, *Religion in the Old South* (Chicago: University of Chicago Press, 1977), 49–50, 243–245. Randy J. Sparks, *On Jordan's Stormy Banks: Evangelicalism in Mississippi, 1773–1876* (Athens: University of Georgia Press, 1994), 18–19, 24–25, 79. For Civil War revivals, see Drew Gilpin Faust, "Christian Soldiers: The Meaning of Revivalism in the Confederate Army," *Journal of Southern History*, 53 (February 1987), 63–90. Kenneth K. Bailey, *Southern White Protestantism in the Twentieth Century* (New York: Harper and Row, 1964), 20–28. Rufus B. Spain, *At Ease in Zion: Social History of Southern Baptists, 1865–1900* (Nashville: Vanderbilt University Press, 1961), vii–x.

12. Kenneth K. Bailey, Rufus B. Spain, and John Eighmy, author of *Churches in Cultural Captivity: A History of the Social Attitudes of Southern Baptists*, (Knoxville: University of Tennessee Press, 1972), are all silent on the subject of Sunday schools. See Vernon et al., *Methodist Excitement in Texas*, 176–180; Edward L. Ayers, *The Promise of the New South: Life After Reconstruction* (New York: Oxford University Press, 1992), esp. Chap. 7; William A. Link, *The Paradox of Southern Progressivism, 1880–1930* (Chapel Hill: University of North Carolina Press, 1992), 79–83; Anne M. Boylan, "Evangelical Womanhood in the Nineteenth Century: The Role of Women in Sunday Schools," *Feminist Studies*, 4 (October 1978), 62–80; Boylan, *Sunday School: The Formation of an American Institution 1790–1880* (New Haven: Yale University Press, 1988), 114–124; and Thomas Walter Laqueur, *Religion and Respectability: Sunday Schools and Working Class Culture, 1780–1850* (New Haven: Yale University Press, 1976). For one of the best discussions of Christian youth organizations, see Joseph F. Kett, *Rites of Passage: Adolescence in America, 1790 to the Present* (New York: Basic Books, 1977), 189–198.

13. Sally G. McMillen, "To Train Up a Child: Southern Baptist Sunday Schools and the Socialization of Children, 1870–1900," paper presented to the annual meeting of the Southern Historical Association, November 1986; Sally McMillen's work-in-progress, " 'An Answer for Our Future': Black and White Sunday Schools in the South, 1865–1915," promises to fill this gap in the literature.

14. Ayers, *Promise of the New South*, 182; Link, *Paradox of Southern Progressivism*, 51–54. *City Directory, 1899–1900*, 282–285. See also Ted Ownby, *Subduing Satan: Religion, Recreation, and Manhood in the Rural South, 1865–1920* (Chapel Hill: University of North Carolina Press, 1990), Chap. 7; and Kett, *Rites of Passage*, 131.

15. Vernon et al., *Methodist Excitement*, 178. *City Directory, 1899–1900* , 282–285. Kett, *Rites of Passage*, 190.

16. It is quite likely that fewer teachers in Catholic Sunday schools was the consequence of the lower numbers of laywomen active in parishes generally; 3,254 Protestant, 1,398 Catholic, 150 Jewish (10 teachers), and 25 Spiritualist (1 teacher) Sunday school students were enumerated in the 1906 census. U.S. Census, *Religious Bodies*, 1906, 442–443; and U.S. Bureau of the Census, *Religious Bodies: 1916*, 405–407.

17. *Echoes from the Past*, 16; "Lessons of the First Presbyterian Church Sabbath School of Galveston, April 4 to June 27, 1869"; Sunday School Reports, July 8, 1875, April 28, 1877, all in FPC Records.

18. Church Minutes, First Baptist Church, Galveston, July 10, 1842, April 10, 1846, August 3, 1860, March 6, 1866, January 29, April 30, December 3, 1874, January 3, 1878,

March 3, 1881, First Baptist Church Records; hereinafter cited as Minutes, FBC and FBC Records; James P. Cole to Gail Borden, March 11, 1855, Gail Borden Papers, (both in Rosenberg Library). *Historical Sketch of the First Baptist Church of Galveston, Texas, Organized January 30, 1840* (Galveston: New Steam Press, 1871).

19. A. Branch Norman, *History of Central Methodist Episcopal, South of Galveston, Texas*, pamphlet, Subject Files (Rosenberg Library). The church's name began as West End Methodist Church, South, until 1914, then became Thirty-Third Street Methodist Episcopal Church, South, until 1927, when the name was finalized with Central Methodist Church, South. *Galveston Daily News*, September 2, 1929, April 13, 1941. Mrs. J. E. Murphy, "The History of Methodism in Galveston, 1839–1942," 12–13 typescript (Moody Memorial Methodist Church, Galveston); Vernon et al., *Methodist Excitement*, 104–106. Link, *Paradox of Southern Progressivism*, 79–85.

20. *Grace Episcopal Church: A Hundred Years of Grace* (Galveston: Limited Edition Printed for Grace Church, 1974), 5–15. William Manning Morgan, *Trinity Protestant Episcopal Church, Galveston, Texas, 1841–1953* (Houston: Anson Jones Press, 1954), 654–677. For a history of Texas's African American Episcopal churches, see Lawrence L. Brown, *The Episcopal Church in Texas: The Diocese of Texas, 1875–1965* (Austin: Eakin Press, 1985), 9–11.

21. Boylan, *Sunday School*, 147–150, Ann Douglas, *The Feminization of American Culture* (New York: Avon Books, 1977), 59–62. Susan Dye Lee, "Evangelical Domesticity," in Keller, Queen, and Thomas, eds., *Women in New Worlds*, Vol. 2, 293–309. Colleen McDannell, *The Christian Home in Victorian America, 1840–1900* (Bloomington: Indiana University Press, 1986), 18–19; Kett, *Rites of Passage*, 119–121.

22. "Reminiscences of Mrs. Martha H. Poole," typescript (Rosenberg Library) (quotation). Sunday Bulletin, First Baptist Church, Galveston, February 13, 1927, FBC Records.

23. Morgan, *Trinity*, 451 (quotation), 465. Equally uninvolved was the vestry, which in the years before 1920 allocated no money to the maintenance of Trinity's Sunday school. The school ran on its own resources, which meant that the tithes of children and fundraisers promoted by the women were the only income granted to this important church institution.

24. Lawrence L. Brown, *The Episcopal Church in Texas, 1838–1874: From Its Foundation to the Division of the Diocese* (Austin: The Church Historical Society, 1963), 143 (first quotation). Second and third quotations are from Alexander Gregg, bishop of the Diocese of Texas, writing in the *Texas Journal*, 1869, 33; and from Ephesians 4:15–16. Mary S. Donovan, in *A Different Call: Women's Ministries in the Episcopal Church, 1850–1920* (Wilton, Conn.: Morehouse-Barlow, 1986), 20, makes the case that an unusually high number of prominent American women writers and educators in the mid-nineteenth century converted to the Episcopal Church because "they preferred the way Episcopalians treated children," offering education and training. Among those who converted were Catherine Beecher, Harriet Beecher Stowe, Emma Willard, and Sarah Josepha Hale, editor of *Godey's Lady's Book*. See also Kathryn Kish Sklar, *Catherine Beecher: A Study in American Domesticity* (New York: W. W. Norton, 1973), 79.

25. Donovan, *A Different Call*, 20.

26. Morgan, *Trinity*, 450–452; Vestry Minutes, TEC, 1852–1893.

27. Morgan, *Trinity*, 458–459. Ownby, *Subduing Satan*, 141. First Presbyterian Sunday school also held an annual summer picnic, as did most Protestant churches in the South.

28. Morgan, *Trinity*, 452–465. Minutes, TEC, October 6, 1885. Trinity and its two city missions reached their peak Sunday school enrollment in 1894 with 667 students and forty-one teachers (thirty-six were women, twenty-two were single women). By 1911, in keeping with the increasing feminization of the teaching staff, all twenty-two teachers were women, eighteen of them single.

29. Morgan, *Trinity*, 461.

30. For further discussion of Muscular Christianity, see E. Anthony Rotundo, *American Manhood: Transformations in Masculinity from the Revolution to the Modern Era* (New York: Basic Books, 1990), 224–226; and Evelyn Brooks Higginbotham, *Righteous Discontent: The Women's Movement in the Black Baptist Church, 1880–1920* (Cambridge: Harvard University Press, 1993), 140–142. For evangelicalism and the working classes, see E. P. Thompson, *The Making of the English Working Class* (New York: Random House, 1966); Thomas W. Laqeuer, *Religion and Respectability*; and Paul E. Johnson, *A Shopkeeper's Millennium: Society and Revivals in Rochester, New York, 1815–1837* (New York: Hill and Wang, 1978).

31. Peter G. Filene states that between 1890 and 1910 female enrollment in colleges increased threefold and by 1900, 40 percent of all undergraduates were women. *Him/Her/Self: Sex Roles in Modern America* (Baltimore: Johns Hopkins University Press, 1986), 26. See also Rosalind Rosenberg, *Beyond Separate Spheres: Intellectual Roots of Modern Feminism* (New Haven: Yale University Press, 1982), 4, 18; and Barbara Miller Solomon, *In the Company of Educated Women: A History of Women and Higher Education in America* (New Haven: Yale University Press, 1985), esp. Chap. 4.

32. Morgan, *Trinity*, 457. Kett, *Rites of Passage*, 138.

33. Out of twenty-one Sunday school superintendents listed in the 1900 Galveston City Directory, two were women, one from the Swedenborgian New Church and the other from the Christian Scientists.

34. Minutes, FBC, 1850–1861, February 1, 1861; "Reminiscences of Mrs. Martha H. Poole" (quotation).

35. Minutes, FBC, February 1, 1861; "Reminiscences of Mrs. Martha H. Poole."

36. Mathews, *Religion in the Old South*, 109 (quotation). When Martha Poole joined the church, membership had fallen to thirty and white women outnumbered white men by two to one. The Ladies' Sewing Society raised money for the church and continued to teach and attract students to Sunday school classes—the church's most valuable hope for the future. No church meeting was held without women in attendance, often in greater numbers than the men. On the eve of the Civil War, Baptist women literally rescued the church from demise. Minutes, FBC, 1850–1861; "Reminiscences of Mrs. Martha H. Poole."

37. Minutes, FBC, March 6, 11, 1866; Vernon E. Bennett, *An Informal History of the First Baptist Church, Galveston, Texas* (Galveston: Privately Printed, n.d.), 36; "Reminiscences of Mrs. Martha H. Poole." The first Freedmen's Bureau school in Texas was established in Galveston in 1865. Barr, *Black Texans: A History of Negroes in Texas, 1528–1971* (Austin: Jenkins Publishing Co., 1973), 60.

38. "Reminiscences of Mrs. Martha H. Poole." She added importance to the class not only by her presence but also by choosing the class song, "Am I a Soldier of the Cross?"; the flower, white carnation; the colors, white and green; and the motto, "Always Abounding" from I Corinthians 15:58. Church bulletin, FBC, February 13, 1927, FBC Records. *Galveston Tribune*, May 12, 1926, January 19, 1927; *Galveston Daily News*, January 19, 1927.

39. Sparks, *On Jordan's Stormy Banks*, 41. I am grateful to Margaret R. Miles of Harvard Divinity School for her insights regarding power and privilege. See Margaret R. Miles, "Theory, Theology, and Episcopal Churchwomen," in Catherine M. Prelinger ed., *Episcopal Women: Gender, Spirituality, and Commitment in an American Mainline Denomination* (New York: Oxford University Press, 1992), 330–344, 330–31 (quotations). Matthew 6:19–21.

40. Boles, *Great Revival*, 113–115. See also Anne Loveland, *Southern Evangelicals and the Social Order, 1800–1860* (Baton Rouge: Louisiana State University Press, 1980). I Corinthians 14:1, 13:4.

41. Miles, "Theory, Theology, and Episcopal Churchwomen," 331.

42. Ida Smith Austin, "Story of the Ida Austin Bible Class," Ida Austin Bible Class Scrapbook, FPC Records.

43. *Echoes from the Past*, 16–17; *Galveston Daily News*, December 28, 1912. "Fiftieth Anniversary, Ida Austin Bible Class of the Sunday School of the First Presbyterian Church, Galveston, Texas, March 2, 1934," bulletin, FPC Records; Austin, "Story of the Ida Austin Bible Class."

44. "Fiftieth Anniversary, Ida Austin Bible Class."

45. Austin, "Story of the Ida Austin Bible Class" (quotation). Frank H. Austin to John W. McCullough, August 5, 1975, Box 7, File 5, FPC Records. *Galveston Daily News*, August 7, 1938; Will of Ida Austin, FPC Records; "Fiftieth Anniversary." Ida Austin joined the Wednesday Club, the United Daughters of the Confederacy, the Daughters of the American Revolution, the Daughters of the War of 1812, and the Women's Health Protective Association; she served as president of the YMCA auxiliary for twenty years and president of the YWCA for two. She left $5,000 to the Ida Austin Bible Class in her will.

46. *Galveston News*, February 8, 1927; *Galveston Tribune*, February 14, 1927. Martha Poole taught in the public schools and raised one son, the only survivor of five children. She served on the board of lady managers for the Galveston Orphans' Home for a short time and held membership in Colonial Dames and the Daughters of the American Revolution.

47. Rosemary Skinner Keller, "Lay Women in the Protestant Tradition," in Rosemary Radford Ruether and Rosemary Skinner Keller, eds., *Women and Religion in America.* Vol. 1: *The Nineteenth Century* (San Francisco: Harper and Row, 1981), 242–253, 242 (quotation).

48. The women of Temple B'nai Israel by 1870 had formed the Ladies' Hebrew Benevolent Society, which will be discussed in Chapter 4.

49. Thirty-four church-related women's societies were listed in the 1913 Galveston city directory. At least fourteen national women's missionary societies formed between 1861 and 1884. Added to these were three southern societies: Woman's Board of Foreign Mission, MEC, South (1878); Woman's Missionary Union, Auxiliary to the SBC (1888); and Woman's Auxiliary, Presbyterian Church in the U.S. (1912). Virginia Lieson Brereton and Christa Ressmeyer Klein, "American Women in Ministry: A History of Protestant Beginning Points," in Janet Wilson James, ed., *Women in American Religion* (Philadelphia: University of Pennsylvania Press, 1980), 171–190, 174.

50. *City Directories 1880–1910*; Morgan, *Trinity*, 540. "In 1910 the [Baptist Young Ladies] Guild purchased an Individual Lord's Supper Service. . . . Mrs. Chas. Scrimgeour had been appointed to the Lord's Supper Committee." "Women's Work in the First Baptist Church, Galveston, Texas," typescript, 8 (First Baptist Church, Galveston).

51. *Galveston Daily News*, February 26, April 2, 1922. *History of the Diocese of Galveston and St. Mary's Cathedral*, Compiled by the Priests of the Seminary (Galveston [1922]), 102, 110; Carlos E. Castaneda, *Our Catholic Heritage in Texas, l519–1936* (7 vols.; Austin: Von Boeckmann-Jones Co., 1958), Vol. 7, 285, 361–365; Catholic Youth Organization, *Centennial: The Story of the Development of the . . . Diocese of Galveston* (Houston: Catholic Youth Organization, 1947), 159, 163.

52. Sheila Hackett, *Dominican Women in Texas: From Ohio to Galveston and Beyond* (Houston: Sacred Heart Convent of Houston, Texas, 1986), 65. McDannell, *Christian Home*, 14–15.

53. James J. Kenneally, "Eve, Mary, and the Historians: American Catholicism and Women," in James, ed., *Women in American Religion*, 191–206. Antagonism to Roman Catholicism had its roots among Protestants in the antebellum era, when great numbers of Irish Catholics immigrated to this country. The Know Nothing Party of the 1840s presented

the most virulent anti-Catholic rhetoric, claiming that Catholics hoped to take over control of the nation with the Pope at its head. The American Protective Association organized in the postbellum era primarily to persuade Congress to limit immigration of Catholics and other foreigners. Southerners, especially Tom Watson of Georgia, from the "Bible Belt" provided some of the most vicious anti-Catholic pronouncements, which led to the formation of the second Ku Klux Klan in 1915. Protestant Galvestonians showed a milder form of discrimination—not brutality, but rather a hurtful type of snobbery that excluded as much for reasons of class as for religion. See Leonard Dinnerstein, Roger L. Nichols, and David M. Reimers, *Natives and Strangers: Ethnic Groups and the Building of America* (New York: Oxford University Press, 1979), 114–18, 238; and Milton M. Gordon, *Assimilation in American Life: The Role of Race, Religion, and National Origins* (New York: Oxford University Press, 1964), 208.

54. John O'Grady, *Catholic Charities in the United States: History and Problems* (Washington, D.C.: National Conference of Catholic Charities, 1930), 405–406; and Jay P. Dolan, *The American Catholic Experience: A History from Colonial Times to the Present* (Garden City, N.Y.: Image Books, 1985), 324, 328. McDannell, *Christian Home*, 14.

55. The body of literature for women in home and foreign mission societies nationwide is large but should certainly include R. Pierce Beaver, *American Protestant Women in World Mission: History of the First Feminist Movement in North America* (Grand Rapids: William B. Eerdmans Publishing Co., 1968); Patricia R. Hill, *"The World Their Household": The American Woman's Foreign Mission Movement and Cultural Transformation, 1870–1920* (Ann Arbor: University of Michigan Press, 1985); Barbara Welter, "She Hath Done What She Could: Protestant Women's Missionary Careers in Nineteenth-Century America," in James, ed., *Women in American Religion*, 111–125; Lois A. Boyd and Douglas Brackenridge, *Presbyterian Women in America: Two Centuries of a Quest for Status* (Westport, Conn.: Greenwood Press, 1983), 217–224; Mary S. Donovan, "Women and Mission: Towards a More Inclusive Historiography," *Historical Magazine of the Protestant Episcopal Church*, 53 (December 1984), 297–305; Catherine M. Prelinger, "Women as Episcopalians: Some Methodological Observations," *Historical Magazine of the Protestant Episcopal Church*, 52 (June 1983), 141–152. For a view of southern home and foreign mission societies, see Noreen Dunn Tatum, *A Crown of Service: A Story of Woman's Work in the Methodist Episcopal Church, South, from 1878 to 1940* (Nashville: Parthenon Press, 1960); John Patrick McDowell, *The Social Gospel in the South: The Woman's Home Mission Movement in the Methodist Episcopal Church, South, 1886–1939* (Baton Rouge: Lousiana State University Press, 1982); Sara Estelle Haskin, *Women and Missions in the Methodist Episcopal Church, South* (Nashville: Abingdon Press, 1923); Ernest Trice Thompson, *Presbyterians in the South* (3 vols., Richmond, Va.: John Knox Press, 1973), Vol. 3, 385–391. Histories of Texas women in mission work include Inez Boyle Hunt, *Century One, A Pilgrimage of Faith: Woman's Missionary Union of Texas, 1880–1980* (n.p.: Woman's Missionary Union of Texas, 1979); Mrs. W. J. J. Smith, *A Centennial History of the Baptist Women of Texas, 1830–1930* (Dallas: Woman's Missionary Union of Texas, 1933); Katherine L. Cook, "Texas Baptist Women and Missions, 1830–1900," *Texas Baptist History*, Vol. 3 (1983), 31–43; and Patricia Summerlin Martin, "Hidden Work: Baptist Women in Texas, 1880–1920" (Ph.D. dissertation, Rice University, 1982).

56. By 1918, Baptist women reorganized into the Woman's Auxiliary "to work along the lines of the Woman's Missionary Union," a conventionwide women's organization whose main goal, support of foreign and home missions, was achieved through personal service, mission study, and literary programs. Minutes, FBC, May 3, 1886; "Women's Work in the FBC," 5–8; Minutes of the Woman's Auxiliary of the First Baptist Church, Galveston, Texas, December 2, 1918, December 9, 1918, January 6, 13, 20, February 10, March 17, 24,

30, May 5, July 21, October 27, December 15, December 29, 1919, January 7, 1924 (First Baptist Church, Galveston).

57. Edith Park's grandmother, Mrs. S. S. Park, founded Laredo Seminary. *City Directories, 1880–1900*; Mrs. J. E. Murphy, "History of the Woman's Missionary Society of First Methodist Church South," 3–5, typescript (Moody Memorial Methodist Church, Galveston). Brereton and Klein, "American Women in Ministry," 177. For a description of Laredo Seminary in Laredo, Texas, the Saltillo school for children and Normal School, Virginia Atkinson's mission work in Soochow, China, and Scarritt College, see Haskin, *Women and Missions in the Methodist Episcopal Church, South*, 53–55, 136–144, Chap. 11; and Tatum, *Crown of Service*, 84–88, Chap. 18. On home missions, see Virginia A. Shadron, "Out of Our Homes: The Woman's Rights Movement in the Methodist Episcopal Church, South, 1890–1918" (M.A. thesis, Emory University, 1976); and Elaine Magalis, *Conduct Becoming to a Woman: Bolted Doors and Burgeoning Missions* (Nashville: United Methodist Church, 1973).

58. Brereton and Klein, "American Women in Ministry," 178 (quotation); Keller, "Lay Women in the Protestant Tradition," 245.

59. Martin, "Hidden Work," 107–108. See also Beaver, *American Protestant Women*, 100–104, for a description of men's opposition to women's ministries and the church as "the bastian of male arrogance and power" (104).

60. Suzanne Lebsock, *The Free Women of Petersburg: Status and Culture in a Southern Town, 1784–1860* (New York: W. W. Norton, 1984), 223.

61. Interest by women in missionary activities followed much later when Lutheran churches had the means to invest in missions abroad. In 1921, the Ladies' Auxiliary voted to study missionary activities of the American Lutheran Church. *One Hundredth Anniversary of the First Evangelical Lutheran Church* (Galveston, 1950), 55–59 (quotation on p. 55); *A Brief Review of the Past and Survey of the Present of the First Evangelical Lutheran Church of Galveston* (Galveston, 1925), 19; H. C. Ziehe, *A Centennial Story of the Lutheran Church* (2 vols. in 1; Seguin, Tex.: 1951), Vol. 2, 325–326; Minutes [Protokoll-Buch], First Evangelical German Lutheran Church, January 1893 to 1912 (Rosenberg Library); microfilm.

62. Minutes, Ladies' Aid Society of the First Presbyterian Church, March 27, April 24, 1890, FPC Records; hereinafter cited as Minutes, LASFPC. Most of the minutes for this society are available from 1890 until 1915. The description of the annual missionary tea from Minutes, LASFPC, February 23, 1893.

63. Minutes, LASFPC, March 12, 1891 (first and second quotations). Italics in the original. Minutes, LASFPC, May 7, 1891, January 28 (third quotation), February 4, 11, March 3, 1892.

64. Vestry minutes, TEC, February 16, 1882. Italics not in the original.

65. Vestry minutes, TEC, May 5, 1885 (first quotation), April 6, 1886 (second quotation), March 4, 1890, June 6, 1891. After the hurricane of 1900, Guild members divided their time between charity and church repairs. Minutes, Trinity Church Guild, June 1, 1902, TEC Records; hereinafter cited as Minutes, TCG. Vestry minutes, TEC, June, August 1901, September 2, 1902. Between 1903 and 1915 they paid for electric wiring in the church, made the choir robes, fitted up the Guild room, built a green house in order to have flowers for the sanctuary, and repaired the Sunday school rooms; they fixed the rectory, underwrote the organ fund, again repaired the sanctuary after the 1915 storm, and during the war years provided a resting place for servicemen stationed on the Gulf Coast. They also assumed responsibility for collecting Trinity's share of the Bishop's stipend. Morgan, *Trinity*, 567. Minutes, TCG, March 2, December 7, 1903, December 5, 1904, January 10,

1905, March 19, November 12, 1906, June 3, 1907, December 20, 1915, December 3, 1917. Vestry minutes, TEC, February 3, 1916, September 1918.

66. Vestry minutes, TEC, February 17, 1915. Joan R. Gundersen, "Women and the Parallel Church: A View from the Congregations," in Catherine M. Prelinger, ed., *Episcopal Women: Gender, Spirituality, and Committment in a Mainline Domination* (New York: Oxford University Press, 1992), 111–132.

67. Minutes, Ladies' Aid Society, Grace Episcopal Church, June 1, November 9, December 7, 1915, January 11, October 10, December 3, 1916, January 15, 22, April 17, 23, September 24, 1917, Grace Episcopal Church Records (Rosenberg Library); hereinafter cited as Minutes, LASGEC. *One Hundred Years of Grace,* 9. Invoices for the Ladies' Aid Society, Grace Episcopal Church, undated and 1896, File 10, Box 3, Rosenberg Family Papers.

68. Minutes, LASGEC, September 24, 1917 (quotation), April 17, 1917. To add injury to insult, in the 1920s a rector sold the rental house owned by the Ladies' Aid and used the money to pay for a family trip to Europe. Aunt Ida to Mrs. L. Fox, February 11, 1949, Grace Episcopal Church Records; *One Hundred Years of Grace,* 12–13.

69. Women's laity rights were more difficult to achieve within the church, however. Male delegates to the Diocesan Council in 1919, sensing the need to affirm women's rights, moved to endorse woman suffrage. The motion failed, but three years later delegates felt they owed women representation and voted "for changing the constitution to permit women to be delegates to the [Diocesan] Council. . . ." It must have seemed an unusually unfair blow when this was vetoed by Bishop George H. Kinsolving, ending for the time being hope of women's representation to decision making at the diocesan level. Despite the setback, the time would come in 1971 when churchwomen would vote in parish meetings and serve as vestry members. Vestry minutes, TEC, February 13, 1919, February 3, 1921.

70. Anne Firor Scott, *The Southern Lady: From Pedestal to Politics, 1830–1930* (Chicago: University of Chicago Press, 1970), 141. The figure includes Jewish women who comprised 25, or 13 percent, of women in congregational societies.

Chapter 4   "A Blessing upon Our Labors": Women's Benevolent Societies and Poor Relief

1. Minutes LASFPC, July 6, 1893.

2. Ibid., August 3, 1893.

3. Ibid., November 2, (first quotation), 23 (second quotation), 1893, January 25, 1894 (third quotation).

4. The Howard Association was a notable exception. In existence since 1845 and incorporated in 1854, it gave aid to all victims of yellow fever, nursing them and burying the indigent dead. Record Ledger of Association Secretary, 1854–1882, Howard Association of Galveston Records (Rosenberg Library). Peggy Hildreth, "The Howard Association of Galveston: The 1850s, Their Peak Years," *East Texas Historical Journal,* 17, no. 2 (1979), 33–44; Kathleen Davis, "Year of Crucifixion: Galveston, Texas," *Texana,* 8, no. 2 (1970), 140–153; and Charles W. Hayes, *Galveston: History of the Island and the City* (2 Vols., Austin: Jenkins Garrett Press [1879] 1974), Vol. 2, 705, writes, "All nationalities in Galveston have their benevolent associations, which are organized and maintained for the purpose of extending aid and relief to their fellow countrymen when sick or destitute. Prominent among these are the French, German, Spanish, Italian, Caledonian, Hibernian and B'nai Brith, besides the colored people, who have well organized benevolent associations."

5. Samuel Chester Griffin, *History of Galveston, Texas* (Galveston: A. H. Cawston, 1931), 38–39; *City Directory, 1891–92,* 56–60. *Galveston Daily News,* June 21, 1959; *Galveston Tribune,* April 27, 1915. For a discussion of the function of fraternal orders in community

life, see Don Harrison Doyle, *The Social Order of a Frontier Community: Jacksonville, Illinois, 1825–70* (Urbana: University of Illinois Press, 1978), 188.

6. *By-Laws and Rules of Order of Tucker Lodge of Free and Accepted Masons* (Galveston, 1882), 13, chartered in 1867 (Rosenberg Library). See also Joseph W. Hale, "Masonry in the Early Days of Texas," *Southwestern Historical Quarterly*, 49 (1945–1946), 374–383; and Lynn Dumenil, *Freemasonry and American Culture: 1880–1930* (Princeton: Princeton University Press, 1984), 19–20, 62–63, 70–71, 73–75, 103–107. Doyle, *Social Order of a Frontier Community*, 188 (life insurance quotation).

7. Doyle, *Social Order of a Frontier Community*, 131. Leonard Dinnerstein, Roger L. Nichols, and David M. Reimers, *Natives and Strangers: Ethnic Groups and the Building of America* (New York: Oxford University Press, 1979), 106–108, 159–162 (quotation on p. 160). The French Benevolent Society's charter, for example, intended "to aid and assist its members in case of need or sickness and to perform the funeral duties in case of their death." Every year since its founding in 1860, the society elected one of its own to serve as physician "to attend to the members in case of sickness" and a pharmicist to fill drug orders. Charter of the French Benevolent Society of Galveston, May 2, 1871, French Benevolent Society of Galveston Records (Rosenberg Library).

8. The early ethnic benevolent societies of Galveston included: *Freundschaftsbund* (1842), French Benevolent Society (1860), Spanish Benevolent Society (1873), Irish Benevolent Society (1875), Italian Benevolent Society (1876). *City Directories, 1870–1878*.

9. *City Directories, 1881–82, 1882–83. Galveston Daily News*, July 2, 1880. The 1880–1881 city directory was for whites only, and as if to emphasize segregation, after 1884 city directories listed black churches but no black organizations. Barr, *Black Texans* (Austin: Jenkins Publishing Co., 1973), 106. For a discussion of postbellum black organizations southwide see Howard N. Rabinowitz, *Race Relations in the Urban South, 1865–1890* (New York: Oxford University Press, 1978).

10. *City Directories, 1871–1895*. This does not include the forty-seven chapters of labor organizations and unions that also may have used dues for workers' relief. Screwmen were skilled laborers who through teamwork loaded the ships with cotton, adroitly packing the bales into the holds and then using a jackscrew to squeeze the bales tight. Shippers employed screwmen in order to increase the shipload by as much as 15 percent. After 1910 and the invention of cotton compresses, which through high density pressure reduced a 500 pound bale from 22 to 15 cubic feet, the need for screwmen declined and the labor organization died. See Allen Clayton Taylor, "A History of the Screwmen's Benevolent Association from 1866 to 1924" (M.A. thesis, University of Texas, Austin, 1968), 109.

11. Galveston Screwmen's Benevolent Association Records, Vol. 1, 1866–1889; Vol. 2, 1890–1900; Vol. 3, 1900. Vol. 1: September 11, 26, October 5, December 1866, June 7, 1867, February 28, 1868, July 9, 1875, July 25, 1879 (quotation), April 9, 1979, January 14, 1880; Vol. 2: January 9, 1891, February 24, 1899; Vol. 3: September 11, 1900 (Center for American History); Taylor, "A History of the Screwmen's Benevolent Association," 30, 49. David G. McComb, *Galveston: A History* (Austin: University of Texas Press, 1986), 113–114.

12. By 1885, some of these dock workers earned $500 a year and apparently could afford union dues. Lorenzo J. Greene, "Sidelights on Houston Negroes as Seen by an Associate of Dr. Carter G. Woodson in 1930," in Howard Beeth and Cary D. Wintz, eds. *Black Dixie: Afro-Texas History and Culture in Houston* (College Station: Texas A&M University Press, 1992), 152; Barr, *Black Texans*, 59–60, 93; Lawrence D. Rice, *The Negro in Texas, 1874–1900* (Baton Rouge: Louisiana State University Press, 1971), 189–190.

13. For example, Episcopal Rector Benjamin Eaton reserved a portion of the offering for individual relief. "Records of Trinity Episcopal Church, Galveston, Texas, December 4, 1865–April 9, 1871," typescript, TEC Records. One of the most generous religious leaders

on the island was Temple B'nai Israel's Rabbi Henry Cohen, who remained at his post for fifty years before retirement.

14. Rosanna Dyer Osterman died in 1866 leaving in her will $5,000 for a synagogue, $1,000 for a Jewish school, and $1,000 for a cemetery, as already noted, in addition to the benevolent society. A. Stanley Dreyfus, "The Hebrew Benevolent Society: A Saga of Service," typescripts, A. Stanley Dreyfus Papers (Rosenberg Library) (quotation p. 9); Rosanna Dyer Osterman's will, filed March 26, 1866, Will Book 2, 229–244, Galveston County Courthouse.

15. The Hebrew Benevolent Society did not meet but once a quarter, its business presumably handled by subcommittees on a more frequent basis. By 1900, the society numbered 153 members and comprised nearly all the men in the congregation. *City Directories, 1875–76, 1881–82, 1898, 1899–1900.* Dreyfus, "The Hebrew Benevolent Society." The Hebrew Orthodox Benevolent Society formed in 1897 and was associated with Congregation Ahavas Israel first listed in the *City Directory, 1898.*

16. *City Directory, 1870, 1879, 1895–96.* Dreyfus, "The Hebrew Benevolent Society"; William Manning Morgan, *Trinity Protestant Episcopal Church, Galveston, Texas, 1841–1951* (Houston: Anson Jones Press, 1954), 563 (quotation).

17. Minutes, FBC, December 2, 1869 (quotation), February 3, 1870, May 8 1873, April 15, 1880, February 5, 1888. Anne Loveland, *Southern Evangelicals and the Social Order 1800–1860* (Baton Rouge: Lousiana State University Press, 1980), 162, 167–171. Inspiration for benevolence from Texas Baptists was also minimal; the first program for relief within the Baptist General Convention of Texas was the creation of a Committee on Christian Beneficence in 1883, which took no action other than to direct pastors and laity "to practice the benevolent spirit in dealing with those in need of Christian sympathy and helpfulness." Baptist Texas General Convention, *Centennial Story of Texas Baptists* (Dallas, 1936), 173. See also Samuel S. Hill, "Northern and Southern Varieties of American Evangelicalism in the Nineteenth Century," in Mark A. Noll, David Bebbington, and George A. Rawlyk, eds., *Evangelicalism: Comparative Studies of Popular Protestantism in North America, the British Isles, and Beyond, 1700–1990* (New York: Oxford University Press, 1994), 275–289.

18. *Charter of the City of Galveston with the Amendments thereto and the Revised Ordinances,* Art. 386 (Galveston: Clarke and Courts, 1888) (first quotation); ibid, 1893, Art. 67 (second quotation). *Lee County v. Lackie,* 30 Arkansas, 764 (1875), (third quotation); Elizabeth Wisner, *Social Welfare in the South: From Colonial Times to World War I* (Baton Rouge: Louisiana State University Press, 1970), 30.

19. Raymond A. Mohl, *The New City: Urban America in the Industrial Age, 1860–1920* (Arlington Heights, Ill.: Harland Davidson, 1985), 156. Michael B. Katz, *In the Shadow of the Poor House: A Social History of Welfare in America* (New York: Basic Books, 1986), 66–84. Walter I. Trattner explains that a combination of beliefs in Social Darwinism and the notion that the poor were being punished for their lack of ambition and morality contributed to the decline in public assistance. *From Poor Law to Welfare State: A History of Social Welfare in America* (New York: The Free Press [1974], 1989) 83.

20. Minutes, County Commissioners Court, Galveston, Texas, Galveston County Courthouse, December 13, 1886, June 28, 1887, December 14, 1916; hereinafter cited as Commissioners' Minutes. State statutes concerning relief for the poor did not stipulate if the county should give outdoor (money given directly to the supplicant) or indoor (institutional) relief; in the case of Galveston County both were tried. Helen Evans, "Provisions for Public Relief in Texas, 1846–1937" (M.S. thesis, Tulane University School of Social Work, 1941), 23. Philip Klein, *From Philanthropy to Social Welfare: An American Cultural Perspective* (San Francisco: Jossey-Bass Publishers, 1968), 15–18.

21. David J. Rothman, *The Discovery of the Asylum: Social Order and Disorder in the New Republic* (Boston: Little, Brown and Co., 1971), 42–44, 293–294. Katz, *In the Shadow of the Poorhouse*, 10–33; *Texas Constitution*, 1876, General Provisions, Sec. 9 (quotation).

22. Commissioners hired a superintendent and manager at a salary of $75 per month, and they called for bids from contractors to build a dormitory for white paupers, "colored" paupers, the insane, and convicts. Commissioners' Minutes, June 28, July 14, 19, 20, 27, August 9, September 14, 1887 (quotations).

23. Commissioners' Minutes, December 14, 1886, July 9, January 15, March 26, June 22, 28, July 14, 16, 19, 20, 21, 27, 28, August 9, 1887, August 15, 1888. Report and Account of County Patients at St. Mary's Infirmary, December, 1887; Report of Sheriff of Galveston County for the Feeding and Keeping of County Prisoners, June 1875, both in Uncatalogued County Records (Houston Metropolitan Research Center, Houston Public Library).

24. Minutes, LASFPC, April 3, 1890.

25. Joe Meyers, Superintendent County Farm, to the Honorable Judge and Board of Commissioners, January 6, 1888, Uncatalogued County Records (Houston Metropolitan Archives). Commissioners' Minutes, December 13, 1887, January 9, February 13, 14 (quotations), March 12, May 14, June 11, 1888, March 11, 1889.

26. LeeAnn Whites, "The Charitable and the Poor: The Emergence of Domestic Politics in Augusta, Georgia, 1860–1880," *Journal of Social History*, 17 (Summer 1984), 601–616. See also Anne Firor Scott, *The Southern Lady: From Pedestal to Politics, 1830–1930* (Chicago: University of Chicago Press, 1970), 81–84; and Mary Elizabeth Massey, *Bonnet Brigades* (New York: Knopf, 1966); George C. Rable, *Civil Wars: Women and the Crisis of Southern Nationalism* (Urbana: University of Illinois Press, 1989), 120–125, 144, 236.

27. Hayes, *Galveston*, Vol. 2, 892–893; Henry Cohen, David Lefkowitz, and Ephraim Frisch, *One Hundred Years of Jewry in Texas* (Dallas: Jewish Advisory Committee, 1936), 9–10; Howard Association of Galveston Ledger, May 6, 1867; *Galveston Tri-Weekly News*, February 14, 1866. Carlos E. Castaneda, *Our Catholic Heritage in Texas, 1519–1936* (7 vols., Austin: Von Boeckmann-Jones Co., 1958), Vol. 7, 288–289; *Diamond Jubilee, 1847–1922, of the Diocese of Galveston and St. Mary's Cathedral* Compiled by the Priests of the Seminary (Galveston, [1922]), 110; Sister Francis Johnston, *Builders by the Sea: A History of the Ursuline Community of Galveston, Texas* (New York: Exposition Press, 1970); Robert M. Franklin, *Battle of Galveston, January 1, 1863* (Houston: Privately Printed, 1940); and Sam B. Graham, ed., *Galveston Community Book: A Historical and Biographical Record of Galveston and Galveston County* (Galveston: A. H. Cawston, 1945), 42.

28. The islanders also suffered a yellow fever epidemic in 1864. Ruby Garner, "Galveston during the Civil War" (M.A. thesis, University of Texas, 1927), 99–103, 131–134; Hayes, *Galveston*, Vol. 2, 621, 623–628. *Galveston Daily News*, March 1, 10, 1865; April 30, May 5, 1865. See also John Edwards, "Social and Cultural Activities of Texans during Civil War and Reconstruction, 1861–73" (M.A. thesis, Texas Tech University, 1985), 241–242. McComb, *Galveston*, 72–83.

29. *City Directories, 1878–1921; Galveston Daily News*, September 22, 1875, Morgan, *Trinity*, 737. U.S. Census Office, *A Compendium of the Ninth Census* (Washington, 1872), 343. U.S. Census Office, *Report on the Social Statistics of Cities*. Pt. 2, 1887, 315.

30. *Constitution and By-Laws of the Ladies Hebrew Benevolent Society of Galveston, Texas* (Galveston, 1903), 7 (quotation), 9.

31. The dues were somewhat steep at $.50 a month and no doubt helped to defray the expenses of their charity. Minutes, Ladies' Hebrew Benevolent Society, May 5, 1881, May 5, 1883, March 10, April 30, 1885, February 11, 1886, November 15, 1888 to November 8, 1893, February 7, June 7, 1894, February 18, 1897, December 21, 1898 (Congregation B'nai Israel, Galveston); hereinafter cited as Minutes, LHBS.

32. Ibid., first entry in 1903. Galveston Women Database.

33. Morgan, *Trinity*, 558, 563–565.

34. *Galveston Daily News*, September 22, 1875 (first quotation). Hayes, *Galveston*, Vol. 2, 731 (second quotation); *Galveston Daily News*, March 4, 1979 (third quotation). Isaac H. Kempner, *Recalled Recollections* (Dallas: Egan Co., 1961), 1.

35. Although the death toll was low, Dr. George W. Peete, the city's health and quarantine officer, and his grandson were drowned while at the quarantine station on Bolivar Point across the entrance to the bay. *Galveston Daily News*, September 19, 22, 1875, March 4, 1979. Hayes, *Galveston*, Vol. 2, 732 (quotations), 733–734.

36. *Galveston Daily News*, September 22 (first quotation), 23, 24 (second quotation), 1875.

37. Ibid., September 22, 1875.

38. Ibid., September 24, 1875 (quoted words); McComb, *Galveston*, 30, 59–61.

39. Morgan, *Trinity*, 564.

40. "Trinity Church Guild, 1873–1941," typescript, Box 8, TEC Records (first quotation); Morgan, *Trinity*, 558, 563, 565, quoting the *Galveston Daily News*, March 24, 1880.

41. Of the twenty-three women's religious societies formed in this period, only the three mentioned appear to have chosen poor relief as their principal activity.

42. *A Brief Review of the Past and Survey of the Present of the First Evangelical Lutheran Church of Galveston* (Galveston: n.p., 1925), 19.

43. Fuller accounts of the origins of northern benevolent societies may be found in Keith Melder, "Ladies Bountiful: Organized Women's Benevolence in Early Nineteenth-Century America," *New York History*, 48 (July 1967), 231–254; Lori D. Ginzberg, *Women and the Work of Benevolence: Morality, Politics, and Class in the Nineteenth-Century United States* (New Haven: Yale University Press, 1990); Rosenberg, *Religion and the Rise of the American City: The New York City Mission Movement, 1812–1870* (Ithaca: Cornell University Press, 1971); Christine Stansell, *City of Women: Sex and Class in New York, 1789–1860* (New York: Alfred Knopf, 1986), 14, 30–33; Paul Boyer, *Urban Masses and Moral Order in America, 1820–1920* (Cambridge: Harvard University Press, 1978). See also Barbara Berg, *The Remembered Gate: Origins of American Feminism* (New York: Oxford University Press, 1978); Mary P. Ryan, *Cradle of the Middle Class: The Family in Oneida County, New York, 1790–1865* (Cambridge, Eng.: Cambridge University Press, 1981); Nancy Cott, *The Bonds of Womanhood: "Woman's Sphere" in New England, 1780–1835* (New Haven: Yale University Press, 1977). An excellent study of midwestern female benevolence is Kathleen McCarthy, *Noblesse Oblige: Charity and Cultural Philanthropy in Chicago, 1849–1929* (Chicago: University of Chicago Press, 1982), 3–23.

44. U.S. Census Office, *Report on the Manufactures of the United States at the Tenth Census, 1880* (Washington, 1883), 379, 403; and *Compendium of the Eleventh Census: 1890. Part II: Vital and Social Statistics* (Washington, 1894), 820–821. In 1880, there were 170 manufacturing establishments with 684 employees, earning an average of $730 a year. In 1890, there were 190 manufacturing establishments with 1,932 employees earning $642.50 average a year. Although this is a brief sketch of a complex phenomenon, it indicates that factories, especially garment industries that increased by twenty-four in the decade, were hiring more people at lower wages, thus creating a larger population of working poor. Pauperism, as indicated by the Census Bureau, more than doubled in Texas between 1880 and 1890. Figures for Galveston County show that of the 75 white inmates in St. Mary's Infirmary, 54 were children of immigrants. U.S. Census Office, *Report on Crime, Pauperism, and Benevolence in the United States: 1890* (Washington, 1895), 658, 933.

45. McCarthy, *Noblesse Oblige*, 3. U.S. Census Office, *Compendium of the Eleventh Census, 1890. Pt. 1: Population* (Washington, 1892), 556. A compilation of Galveston by its

twelve wards in 1890 indicates that there were no overwhelmingly African American or ethnic neighborhoods.

46. Matthew 25:40. Minutes, LASFPC, October 1, 1891. Mary Donovan, in *A Different Call: Women's Ministries in the Episcopal Church, 1850–1920* (Wilton, Conn.: Morehouse-Barlow, 1986), argues that Episcopal women were far more likely to be "social servants" out of a sense of noblesse oblige. They had the means to hire domestic servants and the education to teach those with fewer advantages. But, because of the church's episcopal governmental and theological structure, Episcopal women did not feel that they were given priestly authority or were qualified to effect conversions among the poor. "Education rather than evangelism was the primary focus" (16).

47. Reverend S. M. Bird, *Twenty Years in Trinity Parish* (Galveston: Press of J. W. Burson Co., 1891), 25, 27 (quotation). After the Reverend Bird's death, members of St. Augustine's Episcopal Church remembered him as "the friend of the poor and oppressed and unfortunate." Reverend Benjamin A. Rogers, *Memorial Serman on the Rev. Stephen Moylan Bird, D. D.* (Galveston: Printed by Order of the Vestry, 1894), 13–14.

48. Ralph Luker, *A Southern Tradition in Theology and Social Criticism, 1830–1930: The Religious Liberalism and Social Conservatism of James Warley Miles, William Porcher Dubose and Edgar Gardner Murphy* (New York: Edwin Mellon Press , 1984), 303 (first two quotations), 308 (last quotation). See Grantham, *Southern Progressivism: The Reconciliation of Progress and Tradition* (Knoxville: The University of Tennessee Press, 1983), 181–187; and Hugh C. Bailey, *Edgar Gardner Murphy: Gentle Progressive* (Coral Gables, Fla., 1968).

49. Donovan, *A Different Call*, 5 (first quotation), 9, 16 (second quotation), 66, 93–95. Episcopal women founded hospitals, children's homes, and schools; the creation of a Woman's Auxiliary to Foreign Missions in 1872 permitted every laywoman to invest in the church's missionary efforts; and with the office of deaconess devised in the 1870s, women were finally given official wage-earning status within parishes to serve as caretakers to widows, orphans, the sick, and the destitute.

50. Minutes, LASFPC, October 7, 1897. Minutes, LHBS, June 11, 1908.

51. For a discussion of the establishment of the virtues of womanhood in the construct of charity at the beginning of the nineteenth century, see Stansell, *City of Women*, 35–36.

52. J. Frederick Roeck to Rosanna Summers Hair, May 31, 1891, Waters-Roeck-Thompson Papers, in the possession of Mrs. Henry W. Cave, New York, New York.

53. Nellie Roeck, "Nino," manuscript, Waters-Roeck-Thompson Papers; Editors, *The Youth's Companion*, to Nellie W. Roeck, December 1, 1892, ibid.

54. Morgan, *Trinity*, 570; Minutes, TCG, 1902–1920.

55. Kempner, *Recalled Recollections*, 7; Harold M. Hyman, *Oleander Odyssey: The Kempners of Galveston, Texas, 1854–1980s* (College Station: Texas A&M University Press, 1990), 34; McComb, *Galveston*, 101–102.

56. Minutes, LASFPC, 1890–1897, 1900.

57. Ibid., March 27, 1890, May 29, 1890, February 5, (second quotation), 19, 26, March 5, 19, May 14, 1891 (first quotation), December 22, January 5, 1893, October 26, 1893.

58. Ibid., January 22, February 5, 12, 19, 1891. See Stansell, *City of Women*, 70.

59. Minutes, LASFPC, May 28, 1891 (first quotation), March 24, 1892 (second quotation), April 23, 1896. *City Directories, 1898–1900*.

60. Minutes, LASFPC, March 23, 1893 (first quotation), October 4, 1894 (second quotation), April 23, 1896 (third quotation), November 10 (fourth quotation), December 1, December 8, December 29, 1892, January 5, February 9, 1893 (fifth quotation), March 16, March 23, 1893 (last quotation).

61. Morgan, *Trinity*, 563–565; Minutes, LASFPC, April 3, April 10, May 1, 1890, July

6, August 3, November 2, 1893. The Ladies' Hebrew Benevolent Society also tried to find employment for workers.

62. Minutes, LASFPC, October 6, 1892.

63. Minutes, TCG, February 3, 1902 (first quotation); LASFPC, December 20, 1906 (second quotation). Minutes, LHBS, November 1911 to February 16, 1916; members of the Ladies' Hebrew Benevolent Society increased their endowment from $1,500 to $2,272 between 1911 and 1916, all the while contributing funds to the needy.

64. Roy Lubove, *The Professional Altruist: The Emergence of Social Work as a Career, 1880–1930* (Cambridge: Harvard University Press, 1965). Nathan Irvin Huggins, *Protestants Against Poverty: Boston's Charities, 1870–1900* (Westport, Conn.: Greenwood Press, 1971), 17, 71; Trattner, *From Poor Law to Welfare State*, 71; Rothman, *The Discovery of the Asylum*, 177–179; Frank Dekker Watson, *The Charity Organization Movement in the United States: A Study in American Philanthropy* (New York: Macmillan Co., 1922), 70–76.

65. Minutes, LASFPC, "List of Members in 1883 and Charity Committees." "Constitution and By-Laws of the Ladies' Aid Society of the First Presbyterian Church of Galveston," FPC Records. Alcoholics, derelicts, and prostitutes found help in Galveston from a branch of the Salvation Army organized in 1896. For a discussion of systematic visiting in the antebellum North see Ginzberg, *Women and the Work of Benevolence*, 41.

66. Treasurer's Report for the Ladies' Aid Society, 1893–1896, FPC Records. The Presbyterians had two funds from which to give aid: the Charity Fund, which came from the sale of items sewn by the members, and the [George] Ball Charity Fund (Sarah Ball was a member), which was a charitable trust set up to aid the poor through various relief agencies including Trinity Church Guild. The Ball Fund distributed $500 each year to the benevolent societies that helped the deserving poor.

67. Minutes, LASFPC, 1890–1896, August 3, 1893 (quotation).

68. Ibid., November 5, 1891 (quotation). Perhaps that explains why so many widows carried on their work for decades as presidents of benevolent societies. In the German Ladies' Benevolent Society, the Ladies' Hebrew Benevolent Society, and the Presbyterian Ladies' Aid Society, Presidents Agnes Erhard, 1901–1921(?), Caroline Block, 1870–1902, and Margaret McCullough, 1890–1911, were widows who occupied their posts for over twenty years. Widows knew firsthand the unfortunate side of "independence," the insecurity, the hopelessness. Charitable "tenure" gave widows a position of power and authority in the community after their roles as wives and mothers ended. See Suzanne Lebsock, *Free Women of Petersburg: Status and Culture in a Southern Town, 1784–1860* (New York: W. W. Norton, 1984), 142–143. Anne Firor Scott, "Women's Voluntary Associations: From Charity to Reform," 36–37; and Kathleen D. McCarthy, "Parallel Power Structures," both in Kathleen D. McCarthy, ed., *Lady Bountiful Revisited: Women, Philanthropy, and Power* (New Brunswick: Rutgers University Press, 1990), 2–5; Anne Firor Scott, *Natural Allies: Women's Associations in American History* (Urbana: University of Illinois Press, 1991), 15.

69. The debate over social control and moral stewardship is summarized in Lois W. Banner, "Religious Benevolence as Social Control: A Critique of an Interpretation," *Journal of American History*, 60 (June 1973), 23–41; and Trattner, *From Poor Law to Welfare State*, Preface to the Third Edition, vii–ix. For a discussion of the imposition of "moral order" on the urban poor through organizations such as the Charity Organization Movement see Boyer, *Urban Masses and Moral Order*, 148–155; and Katz, *Shadow of the Poorhouse*, 68–84.

70. Minutes, LASFPC, November 5, 1891 (first quotation). Ginzberg, *Women and the Work of Benevolence*, 7 (second quotation). On class differences, see McCarthy, "Parallel Power Structures," 10–11; Peggy Pascoe, *Relations of Rescue: The Search for Female Moral Authority in the American West, 1874–1939* (New York: Oxford University Press, 1990), 6–

7; Nancy A. Hewitt, *Women's Activism and Social Change: Rochester, New York, 1822–1872* (Ithaca: Cornell University Press, 1984).

71. Minutes, LASFPC, November 12, 1891, October 6, 1892, February 2, 1893.

72. Ibid., January 4, 1894, December 27, 1894, February 28, March 7, 1895, March 19, (second quotation), April 29, 1897, July 1, 1897. McComb, *Galveston*, 112 (first quotation).

73. Minutes, LASFPC, October 25, 1900; Morgan, *Trinity*, 565–567; *One Hundredth Anniversary of the First Evangelical Lutheran Church* (Galveston, 1950), 56–57.

74. *Anniversary of the First Evangelical Lutheran Church*, 56.

75. Minutes, LHBS, May 2, November 19, 1913, February 20, 1914, April 16, 1915, February 16, November 11, 1916, December 1917, March 1, June 18, November 29, 1918. The society continued to maintain a membership of between sixty and seventy members. When asked to "amalgamate" with the Council of Jewish Women, despite the strong endorsements of their president, Henrietta Kempner, and of Rabbi Cohen, who thought the ladies "would be brought in closer touch with things in general," the members voted to remain independent. Minutes, LHBS, November 29 (quotation), December, 1918.

76. Minutes, TCG, February 1, 1904, May 1909, February 5, 1912, January, February 26, March, December 1913, May 3, November 1, 1915, January 3, April 1916. The treasurer's report for 1916 showed the amount spent on charity equaled $51, while the total expenses were $1,421. The only item larger than charity was $1,150 for church repairs, but it was twenty-two times larger.

77. Minutes, TCG, January 3, 1918, December 1918 (quotation), January 6, 13, 1919.

78. Minutes, LASFPC, October–December 1900, and between 1900 and 1923. Annual Report of the Secretary, LASFPC, 1908–1909, 1909–1910, 1911, 1912–1913. Minutes, Ladies' Aid Circle, April 17, 1923, FPC Records.

79. Mrs. J. E. Murphy, "The History of Methodism in Galveston 1839–1942," typescript (Moody Memorial Methodist Church, Galveston), 24; *Galveston Tribune*, November 29, 1916; Olin W. Nail, *History of Texas Methodism, 1900–1960* (Austin: Capital Printing Co., 1961), 275.

80. McCarthy, *Noblesse Oblige*, 28–29.

81. Ibid., 30–31.

82. *Galveston Daily News*, May 7, 22, 23, August 15, September 17, 1914, November 3, 1916.

83. Constitution, United Charities of Galveston; Mary E. Wood to Jean S. Morgan, November 4, 1916; Circular sent to all clergymen in the city, United Charities (quotation), all in Morgan Family Papers. *Galveston Daily News*, July 10, 1914.

84. For an overview and bibliography of the extensive writings of the social gospel, see Ronald C. White, Jr., and C. Howard Hopkins, *The Social Gospel: Religion and Reform in Changing America* (Philadelphia: Temple University Press, 1976), xi–xix. Three historians of religion in the South have assumed different positions on southern churches' involvement in the social gospel movement. Samuel S. Hill in *The South and North in American Religion* (Athens: University of Georgia Press, 1980), 130–131, states that while southern churches were aware of social problems and the need to take action, "yet by no stretch of the imagination can it be said that a strong Social Gospel tradition lived as an element in regional religious life." (130). Kenneth Bailey, in *Southern White Protestantism in the Twentieth Century* (New York: Harper and Row, 1964), notes that, "although the social gospel movement was much weaker in the South than in the North, yet social concern was more manifest among southern religious leaders than has been generally recognized" (43n). By contrast, John Patrick McDowell in *The Social Gospel in the South* (Baton Rouge: Louisiana State University Press, 1982), challenges these positions by arguing vehemently for the existence of a social gospel movement within the Methodist

church. This is a question of supreme importance to the study of women and the churches as their influence and role in mission outreach is surprising even to religious historians. To tag this activity as social gospel, however, may confuse and distort what seems to have been a female or gender-related manifestation of the churches' long-held tradition of charitable works.

85. Scott, "Historians Construct the Southern Woman," in Joanne V. Hawks and Sheila Skemp, eds., *Sex, Race, and The Role of Women in the South* (Jackson: University Press of Mississippi, 1983), 107.

Chapter 5   Benevolent Institutions and Their Lady Managers

1. This is not uncommon, as churches in the South, the Catholic church excepted, were reluctant to build and sponsor benevolent institutions. Southern states, with the exception of Louisiana with its large Catholic population, had the lowest number of such institutions under church management of any part of the nation. U.S. Bureau of the Census, *Benevolent Institutions, 1904* (Washington, 1905), 14.

2. The four institutions featured here were both permanent and nonsectarian. One other institution founded by women will be mentioned in this chapter: the Jewish Free Kindergarten (1913), which was a sectarian enterprise.

3. Although Catholics formed an important segment of the community, there are two reasons why a more detailed study of their activities has not been presented here. First, charitable work in the fields of education, hospitals, and asylums were almost entirely in the hands of the female religious orders. Therefore, opportunities for Catholic laywomen to become involved in benevolent institution building (an important first step to civic involvement) was almost nonexistent. Until 1914 Catholic laywomen performed only primary parochial duties for their parish churches. Second, it is clear that Protestant and Jewish women did not encourage Catholic laywomen to join them in managing their orphanages, kindergarten, and old-age home; only a handful ended up on the board of lady managers of the non-Catholic institutions. Consequently, very few Catholic women were found in the post-1900 secular civic leadership. It is difficult to conclude, therefore, that Catholic laywomen advanced from their church societies to the secular world as Protestant and Jewish women did. *History of the Diocese of Galveston*, Compiled by the Priests of the Seminary (Galveston, [1922]), 102, 110; Carlos E. Castaneda, *Our Catholic Heritage in Texas, 1519–1936* (7 vols., Austin: Von Boeckmann-Jones Co., 1958), Vol. 7, 285, 361–365; Catholic Youth Organization, *Centennial* (Houston: Catholic Youth Organization, 1947), 159, 163; Sam B. Graham, ed., *Galveston Community Book* (Galveston: A. H. Cawston, 1945), 20–21; *Galveston Daily News*, February 26, April 2, 1922; John O'Grady, *Catholic Charities in the United States: History and Problems* (Washington, D.C.: National Conference of Catholic Charities, 1930), 405–406; and Jay P. Dolan, *The American Catholic Experience: A History from Colonial Times to the Present* (Garden City, N.Y.: Image Books, 1985), 324, 328.

4. Lawrence H. Larsen, *The Urban West at the End of the Frontier* (Lawrence: The Regents Press of Kansas, 1978), 15; U.S. Bureau of the Census, *Abstract of the Twelfth Census of the United States, 1900* (Washington, 1901), 100.

5. Samuel Chester Griffin, *History of Galveston, Texas* (Galveston: A. H. Cawston, 1931), 112–115.

6. Ibid., 115, 122; Graham, ed., *Galveston Community Book*, 144. *Henry Rosenberg: Benefactor*, brochure, June 1943, Rosenberg Family Papers, (Rosenberg Library). The Adoue Seamen's Bethel organized in 1899 and gained a structure in 1913; the YWCA organized in 1914 and obtained its own structure (rented at first) in 1924. *Galveston Tribune*, September

10, 1927, October 25, 1930; *Galveston Daily News*, March 12, 1918, March 17, 1924. Griffin, *History of Galveston*, 118–119, 122–123.

7. David J. Rothman, *The Discovery of the Asylum: Social Order and Disorder in the New Republic* (Boston: Little, Brown and Co., 1971), 206; Carole Haber, *Beyond Sixty-Five: The Dilemma of Old Age in America's Past* (Cambridge, Eng.: Cambridge University Press, 1983), 28, 36, 82–83; Kathleen McCarthy, *Noblesse Oblige: Charity and Cultural Philanthropy in Chicago, 1849–1929* (Chicago: University of Chicago Press, 1982), 5–7; Trattner, *From Poor Law to Welfare State* (New York: The Free Press, [1974], 1989), Chap. 6; Lewis L. Gould, *Progressives and Prohibitionists: Texas Democrats in the Wilson Era* (Austin: University of Texas Press, 1973), 42.

8. By 1904, Galveston, Houston, San Antonio, and Dallas each had three orphanages. U.S. Bureau of the Census, *Benevolent Institutions, 1904*, 14, 15, 122.

9. Lawrence D. Rice, *The Negro in Texas, 1874–1900* (Baton Rouge: Louisiana State University Press, 1971), 237; Barr, *Black Texans* (Austin: Jenkins Publishing Co., 1973), 141. Howard N. Rabinowitz, *The First New South; 1865–1920* (Arlington Heights, Ill.: Harlan Davidson, 1992), 133–140. *Galveston Daily News*, July 23, 1881 (quotation); September 27, 1881.

10. Minutes, FBC, April 15, 1880, July 6, 1882, February 7, 1884. *Galveston Daily News*, September 23, 1894, November 22, 1925; *Galveston Tribune*, September 28, 1925, November 5, 1926, November 14, 1928.

11. *Galveston Daily News*, September 23, 1894 (quotation), April 21, 1897. At this point, another version of the founding enters the story. According to a different source, the orphanage originated with Mrs. Clara Ritter, who began taking care of orphan children in her own home at Seventeeth Street and Avenue F. Her work drew the interest of the same group of men who supported George Dealey's home. Possibly the two were combined and a new organization adopted. Ibid., November 13, 1921.

12. Ibid., April 21, 1897, *Galveston Tribune*, October 30, 1926. *City Directory, 1884–1885*. The board of trustees elected in 1880 included Moritz Kopperl, president; Judge Charles Cleveland, vice president; George Sealy, treasurer; J. S. Montgomery, secretary; members, Leander Cannon, Henry M. Trueheart, George W. Briggs, John Hendrick, William H. Stewart, F. W. Brittingham, A. W. Fly, S. T. Blessing, and Abraham Fly. This was an ecumenical body representing the various denominations, excepting Lutheran and Catholic.

13. *Galveston Daily News*, April 21, 1897. The executive officers included Hallie Ballinger, Ella Goldthwaite, Sarah Ball, Martha (Mrs. S. S.) Park, Martha Poole, and Magnolia Sealy. "Officers and Standing Committees," Island City Protestant and Israelitish Orphans' Home, no date, Galveston Orphans' Home Records (Rosenberg Library); hereinafter cited as GOH Records.

14. For a listing of donors before 1931, see Annual Report of Galveston Orphans' Home, January 1931, GOH Records.

15. *Galveston Daily News*, April 21, 1897, November 13, 1921.

16. Isabella Dyer Kopperl lived with her aunt before Rosanna's untimely death in 1866. Rosanna Osterman left a legacy not only for the Jewish communities of Galveston and Houston but also for the widows and orphans of her adopted city. Accounts, Osterman Widows and Orphans Home Fund of Galveston Records (Rosenberg Library).

17. The Galveston Orphans' Home was incorporated as a "permanent, benevolent, non-sectarian institution" by the state of Texas and by lawmakers and trustees whose vision of the duties of men and women was limited by the conventional notions of separate spheres. Charter and By-laws of the Galveston Orphans' Home, 1913, Morgan Family Pa-

pers. Charter and By-laws of the Galveston Orphans' Home, 1930, GOH Records (both in Rosenberg Library).

18. Minutes, Board of Managers Galveston Orphans' Home, January 14, 28 (first and second quotations), February 11, April 22, July 29, December 30, 1885, March 10, 1886, April 21, 1891, GOH Records; hereinafter cited as Minutes, GOH.

19. Minutes, GOH, January 14, 1885; Women teachers earned about $30 a month. Report of the Board of Trustees, Galveston Public Schools, 1897, Uncatalogued County Records (Houston Metropolitan Research Center).

20. Annual Reports, January 14, 1885, January 13, 1886, January 8, 1890, in Minutes, GOH.

21. Minutes, GOH, June 3 (first quotation), March 25 (second quotation), April 8 (third quotation), July 15, (fifth quotation), August 12 (fourth quotation), October 7, 1885.

22. Rothman, Discovery of the Asylum, 223; Barbara L. Bellows, " 'My Children, Gentlemen, Are My Own' ": Poor Women, the Urban Elite, and the Bonds of Obligation in Antebellum Charleston," in Walter J. Fraser, Jr., R. Frank Saunders, Jr., Jon L. Wakelyn, eds., The Web of Southern Social Relations: Women, Family, and Education (Athens: University of Georgia Press, 1985), 52–71, 57–58.

23. Adolescent girls who were old enough to help with the younger children and who prepared themselves for independence after release from the orphanage were the best at living up to the ladies' expectations. Minutes, GOH, May 6, June 17, July 29, September 23, 1885, July 27, October 5, 19, 1887, June 12, 1889, November 13, 1890, September 28, 1892.

24. Minutes, GOH, January 28, February 11, July 1, November 4, December 2, 1885, August 26 (quotation), September 1886, October 5, 1887.

25. Apprenticeships were difficult to obtain in Texas in the 1880s and undoubtedly no little anxiety was felt by the youths about their future as they waited for an assignment. Joseph F. Kett, Rites of Passage: Adolescence in America, 1790 to the Present (New York: Basic Books, 1977), 147–149.

26. Minutes, GOH, February 25, April 22, May 6 (quotation), 1885. Priscella Ferguson Clement in "Children and Charity: Orphanages in New Orleans, 1817–1914," Louisiana History, 27 (Fall 1986), 337–353, explains that managers often refused to admit older children because they were more frequent runaways. She also found that children ran away "only after they had been punished for other offenses" (343).

27. Minutes, GOH, June 17 (quotation), 1885, March 15, 1893. E. Anthony Rotundo, American Manhood: Transformations in Masculinity from the Revolution to the Modern Era (New York: Basic Books, 1990), 48–50. Minor infractions brought banishment to the closet where air holes had been drilled. Girls could behave badly, too. When the matron complained that several large girls had tried to set the house afire, the managers separated the girls, gave them different tasks, and informed the parents. They did not remove them, perhaps because girls were seen as less overtly rebellious and were, therefore, treated more leniently than boys.

28. Minutes, GOH, July 29, 1885, August 26, September 1886, November 26, 1890, March 20, 1893. In September 1886, when Pat Newport came back to the home after being rejected by the woman who had given him sanctuary for over a year, he, along with four other boys, ran away again, and this time the managers lost patience. Three boys were sent to their relatives, Pat Newport was kicked out, and John Whittaker was apprenticed to a baker. But John was one of their successes, for within five years he was able to support his orphan sister, who also had been in the home.

29. Kathleen McCarthy notes that in the Chicago Orphan Asylum before 1860 punishments were mild, no whippings or solitary confinement, Noblesse Oblige, 9; Steven

Mintz and Susan Kellogg, *Domestic Revolutions: A Social History of American Family Life* (New York: The Free Press, 1988), 58–59. For a discussion of southern self-control see Ted Ownby, *Subduing Satan: Religion, Recreation, and Manhood in the Rural South, 1865–1920* (Chapel Hill: University of North Carolina Press, 1990), Chap. 6. For southern violence, see Carl N. Degler, *Place Over Time: The Continuity of Southern Distinctiveness* (Baton Rouge: Louisiana State University Press, 1977), 24–25; Bertram Wyatt-Brown, *Honor and Violence in the Old South* (New York: Oxford University Press, 1986); and Dickson D. Bruce, in *Violence and Culture in the Antebellum South* (Austin: University of Texas Press, 1979).

30. Linda Gordon, *Heroes of Their Own Lives: The Politics and History of Family Violence, Boston, 1880–1960* (New York: Viking, 1988), 177–180. James E. Thompson to Eleanor Waters Roeck, July 13, 1895, Waters-Roeck-Thompson Papers. Bruce, *Violence and Culture in the Antebellum South*, 78–79.

31. Minutes, GOH, 1887–1893. Calculating the costs of admitting charity cases, most of whom belonged to women, went beyond simple acceptance. Charity cases required more work, mainly in fundraising by the women managers. Thus, their decision to admit in overwhelming numbers children of poor women was a conscious effort on their part to right society's wrongs of economic discrimination toward women.

32. Not until a constitutional amendment was passed in 1937 that allowed Texas to claim aid to dependent children through the Federal Security Act did the state authorize aid directly to indigent children. Before that, the only aid allowed was in the form of institutional care at the state's three institutions: the State Orphan's Home in Corsicana, the State Colored Orphan's Home at Gilmer, and the Home for Dependent and Neglected Children at Waco. No state institution for orphans existed before 1887, however, making the Galveston Orphans' Home one of the early few in the state. Mothers' Pension laws, passed by the legislature in 1917 relieved poor mothers of institutionalizing their children. Helen Evans, "Provisions for Public Relief in Texas, 1846–1937" (M.S. thesis, Tulane Univ. School of Social Work, 1941), 52–61. See also Theda Skocpol, *Protecting Soldiers and Mothers: The Political Origins of Social Policy in the United States* (Cambridge: Harvard University Press, 1992), 554.

33. *City Directory*, 1895–96, 66–67. U.S. Census Office, *Twelfth Census . . . 1900. Manufactures*, Pt. 2, 866, 878–879. In 1895, cotton mill factory owners lengthened the work day from eleven hours to thirteen. David G. McComb, *Galveston: A History* (Austin: University of Texas Press, 1986), 112–113, 155–156. Bellows, "My Children, Gentlemen, Are My Own," 55. For a critical view of women reformers of schools in a later period see James L. Leloudis II, "School Reform in the New South: The Woman's Association for the Betterment of Public School Houses in North Carolina, 1902–1919," *Journal of American History*, 69 (March 1983), 886–909.

34. Griffin, *History of Galveston*, 313; McComb, *Galveston*, 92; "George Ball," typescript, Ball Family Papers (Rosenberg Library); "Complete Roster of Alumnae and Alumni of Ball High School," Historical Mounts (Rosenberg Library); Charter and By-laws of the Galveston Orphans' Home, 1930.

35. Galveston Women Database. Among the executive officers, Episcopal women — Magnolia Sealy, Lucy Mills, Sarah Davis, and Clifford Groce — served more than four times. Isabella Kopperl, from Temple B'nai Israel, served as president twice and five times on the executive board. Mary Landes, of the Presbyterian Ladies' Aid Society, served four times on the board, each time as president.

36. The Ladies' Aid Society of the First Presbyterian Church was instrumental in admitting at least four children between 1891 and 1896. The Ladies' Hebrew Benevolent Society, the Lutheran Ladies' Aid Society, the Baptist Ladies' Aid Society, and the Meth-

odist Home Mission Society also contributed to the Home. Minutes, LASFPC, April 9, 1891, January 18, 1894, February 6, 1896. Minutes, GOH, 1891. Galveston Women Database.

37. McCarthy, *Noblesse Oblige*, 27–30; Minutes, GOH, April 9, 21, 1891, February 10, April 18, 1912. *Galveston Tribune*, April 18, 1906.

38. *New York Times*, October 16, 18, 1900. *Galveston Daily News*, March 27, 31, 1902.

39. *City Directory, 1899–1900*, 285. Kathleen D. McCarthy, "Parallel Power Structures: Women and the Voluntary Sphere," in Kathleen D. McCarthy, ed., *Lady Bountiful Revisited: Women, Philanthropy, and Power* (New Brunswick: Rutgers University Press, 1990), 1–31.

40. Unidentified clipping, 1896, Minutes, Board of Lady Managers, 1894–1896, Letitia Rosenberg Women's Home Records (Rosenberg Library); hereinafter Minutes, Women's Home.

41. Haber, *Beyond Sixty-Five*, 90–93.

42. *Galveston Daily News*, December 5, 1926. A Woman's Home in Dallas and similar institutions in Fort Worth, Palestine, and Waco, Texas, all appeared in the years between 1886 and 1902. U.S. Bureau of the Census, *Benevolent Institutions*, 1904 122, 210, 292. Galveston Women Database.

43. Henry Rosenberg's will, 1893. *Galveston Daily News*, July 18, 1965. Isabella Kopperl, Emma Fellman, and Lucy Gregory served on the board of lady managers for both the Orphans' Home and the Women's Home in 1889.

44. Finally, the home became a beneficiary of the Community Chest, successor organization to the United Charities. Minutes, Women's Home, March 9, 19, 29, 1894; Charles Fowler to the Executrix of the Estate of Julia B. Southwick, July 23, 1896, Rosenberg Family Papers; *Galveston Tribune*, March, April 1895 (clippings in Minutes, Women's Home), May 8, 1896; *Galveston Daily News*, August 2, 1925, December 5, 1926.

45. *Galveston Daily News*, August 2, 1925 (quotation); *City Directories, 1889–1921*.

46. Unidentified clipping, 1896, Minutes, Women's Home.

47. Frank Dekker Watson, *The Charity Organization Movement in the United States: A Study in American Philanthropy* (New York: Macmillan Co., 1922), 527–529.

48. Almira Nichols, Agnes Griffin, Mrs. George Wilson, Hannah Pollard, Annie Rowena Kauffman, Rebecca Henry Hayes, Mary A. Nichols, Mary Burns. Charter Constitution and By-Laws of the Society for the Help of Homeless Children of Galveston, Texas, February 2, 1894, Morgan Family Papers.

49. Annual Reports, January 13, 1886, Minutes, GOH.

50. Constitution of the Society for . . . Homeless Children. The standing committees were: Investigating (each case before admission), Employment (of staff), Finance, Collecting (money owed), Nursery, House, Clothing, and School. Eleven women also served on the Galveston Orphans' Home Board and the Rosenberg Women's Home Board, with two, Jean Morgan and Lucy Gregory, serving on all three boards. Galveston Women Database.

51. Taylor, "The Woman Suffrage Movement in Texas," in Winegarten and McArthur, eds., *Citizens at Last: The Woman Suffrage Movement in Texas* (Austin: Ellen C. Temple, 1987), 16–23. *City Directory, 1898*.

52. *Galveston Daily News*, October 8, 1904.

53. Manuscript Census Returns, Galveston County, 1900, Population. Minutes, Lasker Home for Homeless Children, February 2, 1904, Lasker Home for Children Records (Rosenberg Library); Clarence Ousley, *Galveston in Nineteen Hundred* (Atlanta: William C. Chase, 1900), 293–297.

54. *Galveston Daily News*, April 15, 1908 (quotations), April 10, 1910. The efficacy of this means of fundraising lost its novelty, and subsequent years saw declining receipts of $1,700 and $1,400.

55. John Gunther, *Taken at the Flood: The Story of Albert D. Lasker* (New York: Harper and Row, 1960), 19–22, 25–26; *Galveston Daily News*, February 28, 29, March 4, 1916.

56. Inventory, Lasker Home for Children Records. Griffin, *History of Galveston*, 121. Lasker's charitable donations list all of the major city institutions; he served on the board of trustees for the Women's Home and gave funds for teacher training for the Free Kindergarten. Nettie, his wife, served on the board of directors for the Galveston Orphans' Home. Of his six children, the three sons became ardent entrepreneurs and the three daughters became active social reformers. Morris Lasker, along with his children, joined the Galveston Equal Suffrage Association, and after his death in 1916 his family (the daughters all received training in social welfare work from the New York School of Philanthropy) continued to remember Galveston with gifts to the Morris Lasker Playground and to the Home for Homeless Children. *Galveston Tribune*, February 20, 1915; *Galveston Daily News*, January 23, 1909, March 15, 1912, October 1, 1921, August 9, 1936, March 25, 1961. Nettie Davis Lasker bequeathed $5,000 to the Lasker Home for Homeless Children and $2,500 to the Lasker Playground in 1930. Their son Edward equipped and improved Lasker Playground as a tribute to his father. *Galveston Tribune*, June 19, 1930.

57. *Galveston Daily News*, May 29, 1899.

58. Probably Johanna Runge entered Factory Row, a housing project for the workers near Fortieth Street and Avenue G. The Galveston Cotton and Woolen Mills was established in 1889 and employed about 650 men and women workers. *Galveston Daily News*, April 11, 1942. Settlement house literature abounds, but Allen F. Davis, *Spearheads for Reform: The Social Settlements and the Progressive Movement, 1890–1914* (New York: Basic Books, 1967), should head the list. McComb, *Galveston*, 112.

59. Galveston Women Database. Twelve, or 50 percent, belonged to congregational societies.

60. *Galveston Daily News*, May 29, 1899. Runge does not name the eight influential ladies, but the 1898 board of managers lists Minna W. Fowler, Rebecca H. Harris, Betty Ballinger, Anna Wilkens, Isabella Kopperl, Pearl Burck Selby, Cecile J. Blum, Margaret Focke, Bettie C. Austin, Reba B. McClanahan, Nellie Ball League, and Mary Davis. *Galveston Daily News*, June 16, 1921.

61. *Galveston Daily News*, May 29, 1899.

62. Ibid.

63. Ibid. October 4, 1904.

64. Ibid., February 7, 1895, November 12, 1916, September 5, 1952.

65. Ibid., June 16, 1921. *Galveston Daily News*, October 8, 1904. See Trattner, *From Poor Law to Welfare State*, 105–106.

66. Katz, *Shadow of the Poorhouse* (New York: Basic Books, 1986), 69. For an excellent discussion of the attempts by middle-class reformers and factory owners to ameliorate the conditions surrounding the mills without changing the wage scale in the Southeast, see Jacquelyn Dowd Hall, James Leloudis, Robert Korstad, Mary Murphy, LuAnn Jones, and Christopher B. Daly, *Like a Family: The Making of a Southern Cotton Mill World* (New York: W. W. Norton, 1987), 131–139.

67. Minutes, LHBS, May 2, 1913. On June 15, 1917, the ladies gave an additional $150 to the Jewish Free Kindergarten. Marilyn Gittell and Teresa Shtob, "Changing Women's Roles in Political Volunteerism and Reform of the City," in Catharine R. Stimpson, Elsa Dixler, Martha J. Nelson, and Kathryn B. Yatrakis, eds., *Women and the American City* (Chicago: University of Chicago Press, 1980), 66–67. See also Bernard Marinbach, *Galveston: Ellis Island of the West* (Albany: State University of New York Press, 1983).

68. *Galveston Daily News*, October 18, 1914.

69. Ibid., October 18, 1914, November 12, 1916 (quotation).

70. Minutes, LHBS, November 11, 1916, December 1917, March 1, June, November 1918; Minutes, FBC Woman's Auxiliary, April 21, May 5, November 24, December 29, 1919; Mrs. J. E. Murphy, "The History of Methodism in Galveston, 1839–1942," typescript (Moody Memorial Methodist Church, Galveston), 24; Minutes, TCG, January 6, 1908, December 1913, April 1916, May 3, November 1, 1915; Minutes, LASFPC, November 1, December 6, 1894.

71. Among the Galveston Orphans' Home Board of Managers, 46 percent belonged collectively to women's congregational societies: Trinity Guild (24 percent), Presbyterian Ladies Aid (14 percent), and the Ladies' Hebrew Benevolent societies(8 percent); 37 percent belonged to women's congregational societies from the Rosenberg Women's Home board (26 percent, 7 percent, 4 percent); 34 percent belonged to women's congregational societies from the Lasker Home for Homeless Children board (13 percent, 19 percent, 2 percent); and 40 percent belonged to women's congregational societies from the Johanna Runge Kindergarten board (2 percent, 1 percent, 0 percent). Galveston Women Database.

Chapter 6 Women's Clubs

1. According to Barbara Miller Solomon, *In the Company of Educated Women: A History of Women and Higher Education in America* (New Haven: Yale University Press, 1985), 52–54, 56, 62–63, the eight state universities to admit women by 1870 were Iowa, Wisconsin, Kansas, Indiana, Minnesota, Missouri, Michigan, and California. Some Virginia state-supported universities did not accept women until 1970.

2. Amy Thompson McCandless, "Progressivism and the Higher Education of Southern Women," *North Carolina Historical Review*, 70 (July 1993), 302–325.

3. *Galveston Tribune*, October 22, 1898 (quotation).

4. *Dallas Morning News*, October 18, 1897 (quotation). Anne Firor Scott, *The Southern Lady: From Pedestal to Politics, 1830–1930* (Chicago: University of Chicago Press, 1970), 152–162. For a description of the earliest women's clubs, black and white, see Scott, *Natural Allies* (Urbana: University of Illinois Press, 1991), Chap. 5, 112–113.

5. Karen J. Blair, *The Clubwoman as Feminist: True Womanhood Redefined, 1868–1914* (New York: Holmes and Meier Publishers, 1980), 12, 20, 25. With the founding of Sorosis and the New England Woman's Club in the same year and with the establishment of the Association for the Advancement of Women, which met annually after 1873 to proselitize "organized womanhood," a movement was launched that within two decades reached even remote towns in Texas. Jennie June (Mrs. J[ane]. C[unningham].) Croly, *The History of the Woman's Club Movement in America* (New York: Henry G. Allen and Co., 1898), 15–16. Scott, *Natural Allies*, 114–118. Kathleen D. McCarthy in *Women's Culture: American Philanthropy and Art, 1830–1930* (Chicago: University of Chicago Press, 1991), 44–45, points to Sorosis as the forerunner of women's art clubs and the decorative arts movement.

6. *Galveston Daily News*, April 26, 1899. Megan Seaholm, "Earnest Women: The White Woman's Club Movement in Progressive Era Texas, 1880–1920" (Ph.D. dissertation, Rice University, 1988), 190. The largest cities of the former Confederate South in 1900 were New Orleans (287,000), Memphis (102,000), Atlanta (89,000), Richmond (85,000), Charleston (55,000), San Antonio (53,000), Houston (44,000), and Dallas (42,000). Galveston's population in 1900 stood at 38,000.

7. Sheila M. Rothman, *Woman's Proper Place: A History of Changing Ideals and Practices, 1870 to the Present* (New York: Basic Books, 1978), 64. Cynthia Neverdon-Morton, *Afro-American Women of the South and the Advancement of the Race, 1895–1925* (Knoxville: University of Tennessee Press, 1989), 192–193, Chap. 10; Scott, *Natural Allies*,

127. Suzanne Lebsock, "Women and American Politics, 1880–1920," in Louise Tilly and Patricia Gurin, eds., *Women, Politics, and Change* (New York: The Russell Sage Foundation, 1991), 42; Ruthe Winegarten, *Texas Women: A Pictorial History* (Austin: Eakin Press, 1986), 101; Winegarten, *Black Texas Women: 150 Years of Trial and Triumph* (Austin: University of Texas Press, 1995), 187–190. For Galveston's club movement among black women, see chapter 8.

8. Seaholm, "Earnest Women," 85 (quotation); Blair, *Clubwoman as Feminist*, 15, 118.

9. Blair, *Clubwoman as Feminist*, 25 (quotation). The term "woman's domain" is taken from Blair, *The Torchbearers: Women and Their Amateur Arts Associations in America, 1890–1930* (Bloomington: Indiana University Press, 1994), 2.

10. Blair, *Clubwoman as Feminist*, 27. Lawrence W. Levine, *Highbrow/Lowbrow* (Cambridge: Harvard University Press, 1988), 173–177, 200.

11. Grantham, *Southern Progressivism*, (Knoxville: The University of Tennessee Press, 1983), 269; Rosalind Rosenberg, *Beyond Separate Spheres: Intellectual Roots of Modern Feminism* (New Haven: Yale University Press, 1982), 4; Lois W. Banner, *Women in Modern America: A Brief History* (New York: Harcourt Brace Jovanovich, 1974), 4; Solomon, *In the Company of Educated Women*, 54–55; Winegarten, *Texas Women*, 65–68.

12. *Galveston Tribune*, December 13, 1930 (quotation). Blair, *Torchbearers*, 23–27; Janet Wolff, "The Culture of Separate Spheres: The Role of Culture in Nineteenth-Century Public Life," in Janet Wolff and John Seed, eds., *The Culture of Capital: Art, Power, and the Nineteenth-Century Middle Class* (New York: St. Martin's Press, 1988), 117–134.

13. *Galveston Daily News*, March 1, 1914. For some their early training had little to do with their adult "careers." Jean Scrimgeour Morgan, who spent her life in civic activism, trained as a young woman under New York artists at the Art Student's League. While she continued her artwork as an avocation, the importance of her involvement in women's civic reform groups—the Red Cross, the Women's Health Protective Association, and the Public Health Nursing Service—far outweighed her artistry. Margaret Sealy Burton received training in music from Hernoni Bjorksten and Francis Fisher Powers of New York, yet she presided over the Women's Civic League, making city beautification her principal life's work. Rebecca Brown of Ashton Villa, daughter of railroad magnate James Moreau Brown, studied music in the major European capitals yet spent her most useful days presiding over the Letitia Rosenberg Women's Home.

14. As mentioned in chapter 2, New York Metropolitan Opera soloist Etheldreda Aves began her musical career in Trinity Episcopal Church choir.

15. Frederick Roeck to Kate Waters Roeck, July 23, 1881, Waters-Roeck-Thompson Papers.

16. Eleanor Roeck to Kate Waters Roeck, September 8, 1889, ibid.

17. For a discussion of the democratization of the goal of women's music clubs to bring fine music to the many, see Blair, *Torchbearers*, Chap. 3, 45–48. Levine, *Highbrow/Lowbrow*, 122–125.

18. *City Directories*, 1886–1910; By-Laws of the Ladies' Musical Club; Programs, Ladies' Musical Club, 1899–1905, Subject Files (Rosenberg Library). See Blair, *Torchbearers*, esp. Chap. 3 on women's amateur musical societies.

19. *Galveston Tribune*, November 14, 1925, December 13, 1930; *Galveston Daily News*, March 1, 1914 (quotation), December 3, 1916, May 11, 1930, October 7, 1956.

20. Blair, *Clubwoman as Feminist*, 27 (quotation).

21. W. P. Ballinger received the first license to practice law issued by the state of Texas in 1846. He was appointed U.S. district attorney for the Texas District in 1850. He and his partners set up a successful law practice in Galveston, where he settled into a comfortable

life until his death in 1888. His wife, Hallie Jack Ballinger, served as president of the Galveston Orphans' Home at its incorporation in 1880. Emma Barrett Reeves, comp., *Three Centuries of Ballingers in America* (n.p: Texian Press, 1977), 91–98a; "William Pitt Ballinger," *Handbook of Texas* (3 vols., Austin: Texas State Historical Association, 1952), Vol. 1, 104; John A. Moretta, "Biographical Study of a Texan: William Pitt Ballinger" (Ph.D. dissertation, Rice University, 1985); Maxwell Bloomfield, *American Lawyers in a Changing Society, 1776–1876* (Cambridge: Harvard University Press, 1976).

22. *Fifty Years of Achievement: History of the Daughters of the Republic of Texas* (Dallas: Banks Upshaw and Co., [1942]), 15–17. "The Wednesday Club of Galveston, Texas," compiled in 1948 by Corinne Smith and revised in 1978 by Mrs. Elizabeth Head, Mrs. James E. Johnson, and Mary Tramonte, typescript history, in the possession of Elizabeth Head, Galveston.

23. *Galveston Daily News*, April 26, 1899 (quotations), May 30, 1941. See also Stella L. Christian ed., *The History of the Texas Federation of Women's Clubs* (Houston: Texas Federation of Women's Clubs, 1919), 36; and Croly, *History of the Woman's Club Movement*, 1094–1098.

24. *Galveston Daily News*, May 30, 1941 (first quotations). Blair, *Torchbearers*, 39 (last quotations). For a description of women's interest in art in schools in Dallas see Elizabeth York Enstam, "They Called It 'Motherhood': Dallas Women and Public Life, 1895–1918," in Virginia Bernhard, Betty Brandon, Elizabeth Fox-Genovese,Theda Perdue, and Elizabeth H. Turner, eds., *Hidden Histories of Women in the New South* (Columbia: University of Missouri Press, 1994), 71–95.

25. Limerick Book, 1904, Wednesday Club Records (Rosenberg Library).

26. Wednesday Club Constitution, Wednesday Club Program, 1904–1905, Morgan Family Papers (Rosenberg Library).

27. The members met twice monthly; at each meeting they reserved one-half hour for business and the rest for paper readings and discussion.

28. Seaholm, "Earnest Women," 130–138, 144–148, 291–311, 360–382, 387–405. Winegarten, *Texas Women*, 66.

29. Minutes, Wednesday Club, March 16, 1904, to May 19, 1909, Wednesday Club Records. Quotations from April 7, 1909.

30. "The Wednesday Club of Galveston"; Wednesday Club Program, 1904–1905, Morgan Family Papers; Wednesday Club Programs, 1905–1906, 1909–1910, 1912–1913, 1913–1914, 1916–1917, 1918–1919, 1919–1920, Wednesday Club Records.

31. Christian, *History*, 42. Jacquelyn McElhaney, "Pauline Periwinkle: Prodding Dallas into the Progressive Era," in Fane Downs and Nancy Baker Jones, eds., *Women and Texas History: Selected Essays* (Austin: Texas State Historical Association, 1993), 42–56.

32. Wednesday Club Minutes, December 4, 1907.

33. Wednesday Club Program, 1905–1906.

34. Wednesday Club Programs, 1914–1915, 1916–1917.

35. Wednesday Club Program, 1912–1913.

36. Ibid.

37. Wednesday Club Programs, 1912–1913, 1913–1914.

38. *The Galveston Blue Book, a Society Directory* (Houston, 1896), 4, 6. See also John F. Kasson, *Rudeness and Civility: Manners in Nineteenth-Century Urban America* (New York: Hill and Wang, 1990), 129.

39. *Galveston Blue Book*, 137.

40. Ibid., 142 (subsequent quotations). E. Anthony Rotundo, *American Manhood: Transformations in Masculinity from the Revolution to the Modern Era* (New York: Basic Books, 1990), 101 (first quotation).

41. Don H. Doyle, "Urbanization and Southern Culture: Economic Elites in Four New South Cities (Atlanta, Nashville, Charleston, Mobile), c. 1865–1910," in Orville Vernon Burton and Robert C. McMath, Jr., eds., *Toward a New South? Studies in Post–Civil War Southern Communities* (Westport, Conn.: Greenwood Press, 1982), 11–36.

42. David G. McComb, *Galveston: A History* (Austin: University of Texas Press, 1986), 138. Ironically, Henry M. Robert, a civil engineer, had worked in Galveston on various projects from the harbor to the seawall between 1899 and 1901.

43. *The International Blue Book Publications: 1912–1914*; Samuel Chester Griffin, *History of Galveston, Texas* (Galveston, A. H. Cawston, 1931); Sam B. Graham, ed., *Galveston Community Book: A Historical and Biographical Record of Galveston and Galveston County* (Galveston: A. H. Cawston, 1945).

44. For the best study on the socialization of young southern women, see Florence Elliott Cook, "Growing Up White, Genteel, and Female in a Changing South, 1865–1915" (Ph.D. dissertation, University of California at Berkeley, 1992). For a discussion of the fears most Anglo-Americans felt over "aliens" at the end of the nineteenth century, see Levine, *Highbrow/Lowbrow*, 173–177.

45. For hard-working plantation mistresses, see Catherine Clinton, *The Plantation Mistress: Woman's World in the Old South* (New York: Pantheon, 1982); and Scott, *Southern Lady*, 22–44. For the sacrifices made by Confederate women, see Drew Gilpin Faust, "Altars of Sacrifice: Confederate Women and the Narratives of War," *Journal of American History*, 76 (March 1990), 1200–1228; and George C. Rable, *Civil Wars: Women and the Crisis of Southern Nationalism* (Urbana: University of Illinois Press, 1989).

46. Charles Wilson Reagan, *Baptized in Blood: The Religion of the Lost Cause, 1865–1920* (Athens: University of Georgia Press, 1980), 25.

47. Helen Dow Baker, comp. and ed., *Texas State History of the Daughters of the American Revolution* (n.p., 1929), 27, 42–42, 161–162; *Galveston Tribune*, June 17, 1927, November 3, 1928; *Galveston Daily News*, February 22, 1970. Maria Meade Davenport married George Seeligson, son of Michael Seeligson, one of the founding fathers of the city and mayor in 1853.

48. Baker, ed., *Texas DAR*, 26 (quotations), 60. Laura Ballinger Randall, Betty Ballinger's sister, served as regent of the local chapter and as national vice president general of the DAR from 1910 to 1912. During that time she made a gift of a large U.S. flag to each of the public schools of Galveston.

49. Elliott J. Gorn writes of the cultural adaptations of southern backcountrymen to the hardships of the frontier and to their exclusion from gentry dueling culture. Although there is little resemblance between postbellum urban ladies and his antebellum backcountrymen, their mutual needs to participate in the national culture led them to invent patterns of behavior that enhanced their egos. " 'Gouge and Bite, Pull Hair and Scratch': The Social Significance of Fighting in the Southern Backcountry," *American Historical Review* 90 (February 1985), 18–43, quotation on p. 30.

50. *Fifty Years of Achievement*, 50–51, 105–106.

51. Ibid., 50–51. Henderson King Yoakum, *History of Texas from Its First Settlement in 1685 to Its Annexation to the United States in 1846* (2 vols., 1855). William Pitt Ballinger's home was called simply "The Oaks."

52. *Fifty Years of Achievement*, 51–52; *Galveston Tribune*, August 29, 1924; *Galveston Daily News*, December 18, 1921. *Constitution and By-laws of the Daughters of the Republic of Texas* (Houston: Gray's Printing Press, 1892) (quotation).

53. Ibid., *Proceedings of the Daughters of the Republic of Texas Held at Houston, Harris County, Texas, April 20th and 21st, 1893* (Houston, 1893).

54. *Proceedings, DRT*, 1893, 2.

55. Ibid.

56. Ibid., 2–3 (first quotations). Rotundo, *American Manhood*, 3, 4 (subsequent quotations).

57. General Sherman fought at the Battle of San Jacinto, made his home in Galveston, and sacrificed a son in the Battle of Galveston in 1863. The chapter began November 1891 with eight women. By the following year, the chapter claimed forty-two members, by 1894, forty-seven. *Constitution and By-Laws, DRT, 1892. Proceedings, DRT,* 1893, 4.

58. Sidney Sherman chapter, DRT, *Memorial of the Unveiling Ceremonies of the Monument to David G. Burnet and Sidney Sherman* (Galveston: Clarke and Courts, 1894), 3, 8–9 (quotation).

59. *Proceedings, DRT,* 1898; 1899, 1900, 1901, 1902, 1903; *Fifty Years of Achievement,* 107–110; *Galveston Daily News,* December 18, 1921. According to the *Galveston Tribune,* February 2, 1923.

60. "Brief History of the Work of Placing in the Hall at Washington D.C., the Statues of General Houston and Stephen F. Austin," typescript, Cornelia Branch Stone Scrapbook (Rosenberg Library).

61. *Proceedings of the Tenth Annual Convention of the Texas Division of the United Daughters of the Confederacy . . . 1905* (Weatherford, Tex.: Herald Publishing Co., 1906), 50 (quotation). See Fred Arthur Bailey, "Free Speech and the 'Lost Cause' in Texas: A Study of Social Control in the New South," *Southwestern Historical Quarterly,* 97 (January 1994), 543–577.

62. *Proceedings of the Texas UDC,* 1905, 52 (first quotation), 50 (second quotation). Gaines M. Foster, *Ghosts of the Confederacy: Defeat, the Lost Cause, and the Emergence of the New South* (New York: Oxford University Press, 1987), 186–188. In minutes to the Galveston UDC chapter, a letter to the local president from J. William Jones, secretary and superintendent of the Confederate Memorial Association in Richmond, listed "suitable Confederate books to be used in the libraries." Minutes, Veuve Jefferson Davis chapter, March 3, 1905, United Daughters of the Confederacy Veuve Jefferson Davis chapter #17 Records (Rosenberg Library); hereinafter cited as Galveston UDC Records. See also Fred Arthur Bailey, "Textbooks of the 'Lost Cause': Censorship and the Creation of Southern State Histories," *Georgia Historical Quarterly,* 75 (Fall 1991), 507–533; and Angie Parrott, " 'Love Makes Memory Eternal': The United Daughters of the Confederacy in Richmond, Virginia, 1897–1920," in Edward L. Ayers and John C. Willis, eds., *The Edge of the South: Life in Nineteenth-Century Virginia* (Charlottesville: University Press of Virginia, 1991), 219–238.

63. *Proceedings of the Texas UDC,* 1905, 52.

64. Ibid., 51.

65. Cornelia Branch Stone, "U. D. C. Catechism for Children," Galveston UDC Records.

66. Bertram Wyatt-Brown, *Southern Honor: Ethics and Behavior in the Old South* (New York: Oxford University Press, 1982). LeeAnn Whites, *The Civil War as a Crisis in Gender: Augusta, Georgia, 1860–1890* (Athens: University of Georgia Press, 1995), 163.

67. Mildred Lewis Rutherford, "The Civilization of the Old South: What Made It: What Destroyed It: What Has Replaced It," printed address, November 9, 1916, Dallas, Texas, 26, 30, Galveston UDC Records. Rutherford was historian general from 1911 to 1916. See also Fred Arthur Bailey, "Mildred Lewis Rutherford and the Patrician Cult of the Old South," *Georgia Historical Quarterly,* 77 (Fall 1994), 509–535.

68. James S. Hanna, *What Life Was Like When I Was a Kid* (San Antonio: Naylor Co., 1978), 74.

69. *Proceedings of the Texas UDC,* 1905, 51.

70. *City Directories, 1898, 1908–09, 1921.* By 1921 the Galveston UDC had 100 members.

71. "Mrs. Mollie R. Rosenberg, 'Patron Saint' of Texas Division U.D.C." photograph, Grace Episcopal Church Records (Rosenberg Library).

72. Minutes, Veuve Jefferson Davis chapter, August 24, 1901, Galveston UDC Records.

73. Cornelia Branch Stone, "Mrs. Rosenberg's Gift: A Hall for the Daughters of the Confederacy," unidentified clipping in Cornelia Branch Stone Scrapbook.

74. Blair, *Torchbearers,* 178, Chap. 7.

75. *City Directories, 1898–1921;* Mary B. Poppenheim, *The History of the United Daughters of the Confederacy* (2 vols., Richmond: Garret and Massey, 1938), Vol. 1, 3.

76. For a full explanation of the connection between religion and the Lost Cause, see Wilson, *Baptized in Blood,* 32–33; and Faust, "Altars of Sacrifice," 1200–1228.

77. *Proceedings of the Texas UDC,* 1905, 86. "Confederate Women's Home," unidentified news clipping in Cornelia Branch Stone Scrapbook.

78. *Proceedings of the Texas UDC,* 1905, 46–47 (quotations). *Proceedings of the Eleventh Annual Convention of the Texas Division, United Daughters of the Confederacy...* 1906 (Weatherford, Texas: Herald Publishing Co., 1907), 58; *Proceedings of the Fourteenth Annual Convention of the Texas Division of the United Daughters of the Confederacy...* 1909 (Austin: Von Boeckmann Jones Co., 1910), 40–47. Eventually maintenance of the home was assumed by the state.

79. Mrs. James Britton Gantt, "Mrs. Cornelia Branch Stone," clipping from *The Confederate Veteran* in Cornelia Branch Stone Scrapbook.

80. Mollie M. Rosenberg to Ida Austin, August 24, 1901, Galveston UDC Records (quotations). Grantham, *Southern Progressivism,* 203. Scott, *Southern Lady,* 221. Foster, *Ghosts of the Confederacy,* 173; Cameron Freeman Napier, "United Daughters of the Confederacy," in Charles Reagan Wilson and William Ferris, eds., *Encyclopedia of Southern Culture* (4 vols., New York: Anchor Books, 1989), 706.

81. Minutes, Veuve Jefferson Davis chapter, January 5, 1906, February 2, 1906. Scott, *Southern Lady,* 162.

82. A few women from Galveston campaigned and won election to associational offices at the state and national levels. Cornelia Branch Stone, Ida Smith Austin, Betty Ballinger, and Julia Washington sucessfully advanced beyond their local clubs to associate, plan, and coordinate on a greater scale. Indicative of the conservative nature of these women, however, was the fact that only Betty Ballinger joined in the struggle for women's right to vote.

Chapter 7   After the Storm: Women, Public Policy, and Power

1. Jimmy Webb, "Galveston," (New York: Ja-Ma Music, 1968) sung by Glenn Campbell. Bradley Robert Rice, *Progressive Cities: The Commission Government Movement in America, 1901–1920* (Austin: Unveristy of Texas Press, 1977), xiv. Richard G. Miller, "Fort Worth and the Progressive Era: The Movement for Charter Revision, 1899–1907," in Margaret Francine Morris and Elliott West, eds., *Essays on Urban America: The Walter Prescott Webb Memorial Lectures* (Austin: University of Texas Press, 1975), 89–121; James Weinstein, "Organized Business and the City Commission and Manager Movements," *Journal of Southern History,* 27 (May 1962), 166–182.

2. Hewitt and Lebsock, eds., *Visible Women: New Essays in American Activism* (Urbana: University of Illinois Press, 1984), 3.

3. David C. Hammack, "Problems in the Historical Study of Power in the Cities and Towns of the United States, 1800–1960," *American Historical Review,* 83 (April 1978), 325, quoting Max Weber.

4. Exceptions in southern history include William A. Link, *The Paradox of Southern Progressivism, 1880–1930* (Chapel Hill, University of North Carolina Press, 1992), esp. Chap. 6; and Grantham, *Southern Progressivism* (Knoxville: The University of Tennessee Press, 1983). For studies of women and politics, see Marlene Stein Wortman, "Domesticating the Nineteenth-Century American City," *Prospects: An Annual of American Cultural Studies*, 3 (1977), 531–572; Paula Baker, "The Domestication of Politics: Women and American Political Society, 1780–1920," *American Historical Review*, 89 (June 1984), 620–647; and Suellen M. Hoy, " 'Municipal Housekeeping': The Role of Women in Improving Urban Sanitation Practices, 1880–1917," in Martin V. Melosi, ed., *Pollution and Reform in American Cities, 1870–1930* (Austin: University of Texas Press,1980). Kathryn Kish Sklar, "Organized Womanhood: Archival Sources on Women and Progressive Reform," *Journal of American History*, 75 (June 1988), 176–183, states that "power . . . was more evident in women's activities in the Progressive Era than at any time previous or, some would say, since" (176).

5. Hewitt and Lebsock, eds., *Visible Women*, 3. See also Lebsock, "Women and American Politics, 1880–1920," in Louise Tilly and Patricia Gurin, eds., *Women, Politics, and Change* (New York: The Russell Sage Foundation, 1990), 35–62, 37.

6. For a fuller discussion of the debate see Hammack, "Problems in the Historical Study of Power"; and Hammack, *Power and Society: Greater New York at the Turn of the Century* (New York: Russell Sage Foundation, 1982), 3–21. Samuel P. Hays, "The Politics of Reform in Municipal Government in the Progressive Era," *Pacific Northwest Quarterly*, 55 (1965), 157–169; Hays, "The Changing Political Structure of the City in Industrial America," *Journal of Urban History*, 1 (1974), 6–38; and Robert R. Dykstra, *The Cattle Towns* (New York: Alfred A. Knopf, 1968).

7. Howard N. Rabinowitz, "Continuity and Change: Southern Urban Development, 1860–1900," in Brownell and Goldfield, eds., *The City in Southern History: The Growth of Urban Civilization in the South* (Port Washington: Kennikat Press, 1977), 109–110; Brownell, "The Urban South Comes of Age, 1900–1940," ibid., 141–142.

8. Weems, *A Weekend in September* (College Station: Texas A&M University Press, 1957), 139–140; *Galveston Daily News*, September 10, 1900.

9. *Galveston Daily News*, September 10, 1900 (quotation). "1900 Storm Meetings, September 9, 1900–September 14, 1900," City Council Minutes (Galveston City Hall, Galveston). Clarence Ousley, *Galveston in Nineteen Hundred* (Atlanta: William C. Chase, 1900), 255–264. Bradley R. Rice, "The Galveston Plan of City Government by Commission: The Birth of a Progressive Idea," *Southwestern Historical Quarterly*, 78 (April 1975), 365–408. The committee members listed in the *News* September 10 were: Mayor Jones (chair), Bertrand Adoue (finance member), John Sealy (finance chair), I. H. Kempner (finance member), Jens Moller (finance member), W. A. McVitie (relief chair), Ben Levy (burial chair), Morris Lasker (correspondence chair), Daniel Ripley (hospital chair), and J. H. Hawley (property protection).

10. *Galveston Daily News*, September 25, 1900. Red Cross, "Report of Clara Barton, President of the American National Red Cross," in *Report of Red Cross Relief*, 6 (quotation), 31, 51.

11. *Galveston Daily News*, September 28 (quotations), 29, 1900. Ousley, *Galveston in 1900*, 255–264.

12. *Galveston Daily News*, September 30, 1900 (quotation). Red Cross, *Report of Red Cross Relief*, 51.

13. The ward leaders were: Annie B. Hill, Mollie Settle, Margaret Griffin, Ella Goldthwaite, Lucy Quarles, Mrs. J. W. Keenan, Mrs. Forster Rose, Lucy Ballinger Mills, Mary E. Reading, Iola Barns Beers, and Lucy Gregory. Later, Ellen Kenison, Mary J. Scrimgeour,

and Mrs. J. H. Miller replaced some of the women who fell ill. *Galveston Daily News,* September 28, 30, 1900.

14. Ibid., October 1, 2 (quotations), 1900. Ousley, *Galveston in Nineteen Hundred,* 259; David G. McComb, *Galveston: A History* (Austin: University of Texas Press, 1986), 134; Mason, *Death from the Sea,* 222–226.

15. *Galveston Daily News,* September 12, 14, 1900; McComb, *Galveston,* 132; Herbert Molloy Mason, Jr., *Death from the Sea: Our Greatest Natural Disaster, the Galveston Hurricane of 1900* (New York: Dial Press, 1972), 230.

16. *Galveston Daily News,* September 12, (first two quotations), 14, 16, (subsequent quotations) 1900; Ousley, *Galveston in 1900,* 90–91, 110; Galveston *City Times,* September 29, 1900 (last quotation), November 21, 1908.

17. *Galveston Daily News,* September 14 (first quotation), 17, 18 (subsequent quotations), 1900. It is unlikely that any women were detained or impressed. The papers do not mention it again, and martial law was lifted on September 21.

18. *Galveston Daily News,* September 30, 1900. For an explanation of disorderly conduct among women during the Civil War, see Victoria E. Bynum, *Unruly Women: The Politics of Social and Sexual Control in the Old South* (Chapel Hill: University of North Carolina Press, 1992), esp. Chap. 6.

19. Rice, *Progressive Cities,* 4–15; McComb, *Galveston,* 134–137; Mason, *Death from the Sea,* 234–236; Grantham, *Southern Progressivism,* 115, 283–286; Joe B. Frantz, *Texas: A History* (New York: W. W. Norton, 1984), 160; J. Morgan Kousser, *The Shaping of Southern Politics: Suffrage Restriction and Establishment of the One-Party South, 1880–1910* (New Haven: Yale University Press, 1974), 208. See also Weinstein, "Organized Business and the City Commission and Manager Movements," 166–182; and Clinton Rogers Woodruff, ed., *City Government by Commission* (New York: D. Appleton and Co., 1914). The constitutionality of the reform was challenged in court, and in March 1903 a new charter was adopted that removed the governor's appointive power. The five commissioners were then elected at large by voters. Isaac H. Kempner, age twenty-seven, became a sustaining link between all of the groups interested in municipal government. He served first as city treasurer, was a member of the Central Relief Committee, and the Deep Water Committee, and was appointed to the City Commission by Governor Sayers in 1901.

20. Rice, *Progressive Cities,* 4 (quotation), 5–13. The five city commissioners represented varying occupational, religious, and ethnic groups — an Episcopalian judge (William T. Austin, mayor, elected), a Presbyterian realtor (Valery Austin, appointed), a Methodist livestock dealer (A. P. Norman, elected), a Jewish financier (Isaac H. Kempner, appointed), and a German Lutheran wholesale grocer (Herman C. Lange, appointed). Among those not represented directly were blacks, Catholics, Baptists, laborers, and, of course, women. Barr in *Black Texans* (Austin: Jenkins Publishing Co., 1973), 80.

21. Although the advent of city commission government, also known as the Galveston Plan, brought with it a reduction in representation by working-class voters through the elimination of the ward system, it was considered a reform over the (possibly corrupt) ward-based boss and his machine in some cities and over the mayor-alderman system in Galveston. Rice, *Progressive Cities,* xii, 98. Samuel P. Hays, "The Politics of Reform in Municipal Government," 228, notes the paradox in the use of the term "reform."

22. E. Anthony Rotundo, *American Manhood: Transformations in Masculinity from the Revolustion to the Modern Era* (New York: Basic Books, 1990), 3, 4, 24, 30. See Theda Skocpol, *Protecting Soldiers and Mothers: The Political Origins of Social Policy in the United States* (Cambridge: Harvard University Press, 1992), 20; Seth Koven and Sonya Michel, eds., *Mothers of a New World: Maternalistic Politics and the Origins of the Welfare State* (New York: Routledge, 1993); and Eileen Boris, *Home to Work: Motherhood and the Politics*

of Industrial Homework in the United States (Cambridge, Eng: Cambridge University Press, 1994).

23. The four women officers were Mary Scrimgeour, Iola Barns Beers, Lucy Ballinger Mills, and Mary E. Reading.

24. *Galveston Daily News*, October 2 (first quotation), 3 (second, third, and fourth quotations), 9 (last quotation), 1900.

25. Ibid., March 3, 1901, December 3, 1902, May 20, 1904, May 12, 1906, December 11, 1921. The WHPA joined the Texas Federation of Women's Clubs for a few years in 1902. Suellen M. Hoy, "'Municipal Housekeeping'," 175. Mary Ritter Beard, *Woman's Work in Municipalities* (New York: Arno Press, [1915], 1972), 76; Scott, *Natural Allies* (Urbana: University of Illinois Press, 1991), 143–144. See also Hammack, *Power and Society*, 143, for a discussion of the Ladies' Sanitary Reform Association of New York.

26. Margaret Sealy Burton, "I'm Telling You," typescript, Margaret Sealy Burton Letters (Center for American History) (quotation). *Galveston Daily News*, February 8, 1932.

27. *Galveston Daily News*, March 3, 1901.

28. Ibid., May 22, 1904 (first three quotations); September 9, 1901 (fourth quotation). *Constitution and By-laws of the Women's Health Protective Association of Galveston* (Galveston: Clarke and Courts, 1901), 1 (last quotation).

29. Galveston Women Database. The other WHPA presidents include: Dr. Ethel Lyon Heard (1916–1918), city pathologist and vice president of the Galveston Equal Suffrage Association, who joined Trinity Episcopal in 1908 but was far more active in YWCA first aid training, the Better Baby campaign, and teaching medicine at the University of Texas Medical Branch (UTMB); Clara J. Ujffy (1913–1914), a director of the Galveston Playground Association, who was active in the Galveston Equal Suffrage Association; and Maud Wilson Moller (1915–1916, 1919–1920), member of a number of women's organizations, served also as president of the Galveston Equal Suffrage Association in 1917 and, while identified as a Presbyterian, converted to the Episcopal faith shortly before her death in 1925.

30. Studies of northern women's antebellum societies have found little indication that individual women progressed from church to benevolent to reform societies, yet in postbellum Galveston there is sufficient evidence to suggest that this was the case. See Anne M. Boylan, "Women in Groups: An Analysis of Women's Benevolent Organizations in New York and Boston, 1797–1840," *Journal of American History*, 71 (December 1984), 502, 514; and Nancy A. Hewitt, *Women's Activism and Social Change: Rochester, New York, 1822–1872* (Ithaca: Cornell University Press, 1984), 22.

31. William Manning Morgan, *Trinity Protestant Episcopal Church, Galveston, Texas, 1841–1953* (Houston: Anson Jones Press, 1954), 428–431. Jean Morgan did not support votes for women, even though many suffrage officers were Episcopalian.

32. Report of the Social Service Department to the Church Service League, December 21, 1922, TEC Records (first quotation). Jean S. Morgan, "Social Service in the Parish," manuscript speech presented to the Woman's Auxiliary of Trinity Episcopal Church, October 21, 1932, Morgan Family Papers (second quotation).

33. Report of the Social Service Department to the Church Service League, [1921].

34. *Galveston Daily News*, July, 1901, clipping, WHPA File, Morgan Family Papers; *Constitution and By-laws of the Women's Health Protective Association of Galveston*, 10–16. The periodicals mentioned were found in the Anna Pennybacker Papers and the Mrs. Walter B. Sharp Collection (Barker Texas History Center). Additional papers from the Texas Federation of Women's Clubs are archived at Texas Woman's University in Denton, Texas.

35. *Galveston Daily News*, September 9, 1901.

36. Ibid., July 1901, clipping (second quotation); December 3, 1902 (first quotation);

unidentified news clipping, 1908; W. L. Ratisseau to Jean S. Morgan, June 6, 1902, all in WHPA File, Morgan Family Papers.

37. *Galveston Daily News*, July, 1901, clipping; *Galveston Tribune*, May 12, 1906.

38. McComb, *Galveston*, 138–143, Mason, *Death from the Sea*, 238–241 (quotation on 241).

39. David R. Goldfield and Blaine A. Brownell, *Urban America: A History* (Boston: Houghton Mifflin, 1990), 274–277; Jon A. Peterson, "The City Beautiful Movement: Forgotten Origins and Lost Meaning," *Journal of Urban History*, 2 (August 1976), 425.

40. *Galveston Tribune*, February 6, 13, 1906; *Galveston Daily News*, May 22, 1904 (subsequent quotations), May 2, 8, November 17, 1906 (first quotation).

41. *Galveston Daily News*, July 1901, clipping, WHPA File. *Galveston Tribune*, February 6, 13, May 2, 11, 12, 17, 1906, April 25, November 12, 13, 1907, March 3, October 10, 1908; *Galveston Daily News*, May 2, 8, November 6, 10, 17 (quotation) 1906, March 10, November 3, 14, 1907, March 15, October 7, 17, 1908, April 8, 1908. October 4, 8, 15, October 25, 27, 31, November 2, 5, 13, December 11, 12, 16, 1911; December 11, 1921. Galveston *City Times*, May 12, 1906.

42. *Galveston Daily News*, December 11, 1921.

43. *Galveston Daily News*, November 10, 1906 (quotations), November 16, 1906, December 11, 1921 (last quotation); *Galveston Daily News*, October 1909 clipping, WHPA File; *Galveston Tribune*, October 9, 10, 1908.

44. *Galveston Daily News*, November 17, 1906, October 17, 1908, October 21, November 11, 1911. News clippings, 1911, WHPA File (quotation about lights).

45. WHPA Report to the TFWC Fourth District Meeting, 1905–1906, WHPA File.

46. *Galveston Daily News*, June 3, 1903, May 2, 1906, October 7, 1911, December 3, 1912. Clippings, 1908, 1912; I. H. Kempner to Mrs. M. S. Ujffy, March 27, 1913; Jean S. Morgan to Honorable Board of City Commissioners, April 18, 1913, all in WHPA File.

47. *Christian Science Monitor*, November 14, 1911.

48. *Galveston Daily News*, September 22, October 4 (first two quotations), October 6 (third and fourth quotations), October 7, 1911 (last quotation).

49. *Galveston Daily News*, October 9, (first two quotations), October 15, (third and fourth quotations) 27, November 5, 1911. Draft Letter [1911], WHPA Files.

50. *Galveston Daily News*, November 5 (first three quotations), December 12, 16 (fourth quotation), 1911, January 7, 10 (second quotation), 1912.

51. *Galveston Daily News*, October 9, November 5, 1911 (quotation). See also Ibid., October 15, 19, 21, 22, 25, 26, 27, 31, November 2, 12, 13, 16, 23, December 11, 1911. "How They Are Doing It in Galveston," *Tradesman*, November 16, 1911, in WHPA File.

52. *Galveston Daily News*, November 15 (first and last quotations), November 24, 1911 (second quotation), January 10, 1912, January 10, 1913.

53. *Galveston Daily News*, January 1, March 5, 6, 7, May 7, 8, 1912, November 3, December 3, 1912, January 10, February 5, 1913, February 4, June 30, 1914, December 11, 1921. *Galveston Tribune*, May 7, December 3, 1912, December 4, 1913, May 4, 1915. Jean S. Morgan to Mr. Sewell, Sept. 10, 1913; Jean S. Morgan to H. S. Cooper [1913]; Jean S. Morgan to A. P. Norman [1913] (quotation); R. J. Newton to Mrs. G. D. Morgan, March 24, 1914; unidentified clippings, 1906, 1912, all in WHPA File. The WHPA did not go as far in its demands or expectations for child welfare as some northern women's clubs did, or as some communities such as New York and Cincinnati did. For more information about "progressive" programs for combined milk stations and well-baby clinics, see Patricia Melvin Mooney, *The Organic City: Urban Definition and Neighborhood Organization, 1880–1920* (Lexington: University Press of Kentucky, 1987); and Beard, *Woman's Work in Municipalities*, 59–61.

54. *Galveston Daily News*, January 12, March 5 (quotation), 6, 7, May 7, 8, 1912, January 10, February 5, February 22, 23, 1913, January 6, 7, 9, 10, 17, February 4, 7, 10, 12, 15, March 15, 21, April 11, May 6, 31, June 4, July 3, November 4, 1914, January 6, February 2, 3, April 7, May 5, July 6 1915, October 5, November 3, December 1, 7, 1916 ; *Galveston Tribune*, December 3, 1912, February 2, 4, 12, 20, 21, December 1, 1914, January 5, March 2, April 11, May 4, 1915, October 4, 21, 1916, July 11, 1917. Mazyck Porcher Ravenel, ed., *A Half Century of Public Health* (New York: American Public Health Association, 1921), 241.

55. Ravenel, ed., *Half Century of Public Health*, 238, 239, 266, 283.

56. Ibid., 240–242, 250.

57. Megan Seaholm, "Earnest Women: The White Woman's Club Movement in Progressive Era Texas, 1880–1920" (Ph.D. dissertation, Rice University, 1988), 144–147; see also Mitchell Okun, *Fair Play in the Marketplace: The First Battle for Pure Food and Drugs* (Dekalb, Ill.: Northern Illinois University Press, 1986), for a description of New York's fight in the 1880s for pure food and drug laws.

58. Hoy, "Municipal Housekeeping," 178–188. *Galveston Daily News*, February 22 (quotation), 23, 1913. Later, city health officials endorsed the survey.

59. *Report of a Sanitary Survey of the City of Galveston, Texas* (Galveston, 1913) copy in WHPA File, 20 (first quotation), 14 (second two quotations), 16 (third quoted word), 19 (fourth quotation), 25 (fifth quotation).

60. Ibid., 6 (first quotation), 9 (second quotation), 4–13. Deaths from tuberculosis ranged from 64 in 1910 to 78 in 1912; deaths form diarrheal diseases reached a high of 99 in 1907 to a low of 23 in 1910; cases of typhoid fever ranged from a low of 42 in 1906 to a high of 132 in 1909. Galveston's population was 37,789 in 1900. U.S. Census Office, *Twelfth Census of the United States . . . 1900* (Washington, 1902), 8, 22. For a discussion of changing maternal attitudes toward prevention of infant mortality through guardianship of pure food and milk, see Nancy Shrom Dye and Daniel Blake Smith, "Mother Love and Infant Death, 1750–1920," *Journal of American History*, 73 (September 1986), 347–349.

61. *Galveston Daily Herald*, March 5, 1913; *Galveston Daily News*, January 7, 9, 1914.

62. *Galveston Daily News*, August 3, 1913.

63. Ibid., August 7 (first quotation), October 4, 1913 (subsequent quotations).

64. *Galveston Daily News*, August 7, 26, October 4 (first quotation), 19, 1913, January 9, 10, 1914; *Galveston Tribune*, January 6, 1914 (second quotation).

65. *Galveston Tribune*, February 17, 1914 (quotation); *Galveston Daily News*, January 9, February 10, March 15, 21, June 30, July 3, November 4, 1914.

66. "Milk Situation Subject of Talk," unidentified news clipping [1914], WHPA File (quotations); *Galveston Daily News*, December 2, 1914.

67. *Galveston Daily News*, January 9, November 4, 1914 (second quotation), December 1, 2 (first quotation), 1914; *Galveston Tribune*, March 2, 1915.

68. *Galveston Daily News*, December 4, 1914, January 21, 1915 (first quotation), "WHPA Outlines Market Standards," clipping [January 1915]; "WHPA Committee Sets Food Standard," clipping [January 1915], both in WHPA File. *Galveston Tribune*, March 18, 1915 (subsequent quotations).

69. *Galveston Daily News*, April 11, 1915; January 1915, clipping, WHPA File; *Galveston Tribune*, December 1, 1914, January 5, 1915 (first quotation), March 18, May 4, 1915 (court quotations).

70. *Galveston Tribune*, December 1, 1914, May 4, 1915; February 3, 1915, clipping, WHPA File; *Galveston Daily News*, May 5, 1915 (quotation).

71. *Galveston Daily News*, February 3, April 7, 11, November 3 (subsequent quotations), December 1, 7, 1916. *Galveston Tribune*, July 6, 1915 (first quotation), October 21, 1916. City Commission Minutes, December 1, 21, 1916.

72. *Galveston Daily News*, November 3 (quotations), December 1, 7, 1916. *Galveston Tribune*, October 21, 1916. City Commission Minutes, December 1, 21, 1916.

73. *Galveston Tribune*, March 18, 1915.

74 *Galveston Daily News*, April 11, 1915.

75. Ibid., January 7, 1914.

76. Ibid., January 21, 1914 (quotations); *Galveston Tribune*, January 20, 1914.

77. *Galveston Daily News*, February 4, 1914.

78. The black population in Galveston in 1900 was 22 percent; the foreign-born population was 17 percent. U. S. Census Office, *Twelfth Census of the United States . . . 1900: Population*, 643. Galveston *Daily News*, June 3, 1903. Mrs. Frederick M. Burton to Mrs. George D. Morgan, February 10, 1914; unidentified news clipping, "Type of Ornamental Concrete Bench Proposed for Seawall Boulevard Facing Gulf and Drive," both in WHPA File. See Bernard Marinbach, *Galveston: Ellis Island of the West* (Albany: State University of New York Press, 1983).

79. *Galveston Tribune*, July 11, 1917.

80. *Galveston Daily News*, December 11, 1921, February 13, May 22, 1949; *Galveston Tribune*, September 30, 1925. Mrs. John Archer Davis to WHPA Member, February 28, 1920, WHPA File.

81. *Galveston Daily News*, January 21, 1914.

Chapter 8   "The Interest Never Lagged": African American Women and the Black Community

1. Maud Cuney Hare, *N. W. Cuney: A Tribune of the Black People* (New York: Crisis Publishing Co., 1913), 12–13. Maud Cuney Hare (1874–1936). Another black politician, George T. Ruby, who came to Galveston during Reconstruction, secured Cuney's appointment and helped him in his subsequent rise in Republican party politics. Lawrence D. Rice, *The Negro in Texas, 1874–1900* (Baton Rouge: Lousiana State University Press, 1971), 36–37.

2. Hare, *Cuney*, 10, 14, 79–83. *Galveston Daily News*, October 2, 1896.

3. Hare, *Cuney*, 16, 22, 28–29, 33–34, 42, 44–45, 48–49, 56, 60, 64, 72, 74; Rice, *Negro in Texas*, 95–96. *Galveston Daily News*, March 21, 1883, April 3, 1883, April 8, 10, 11, 23–30, 1885. Cuney ran against R. L. Fulton in the mayoral race of 1875. The Twelfth Ward in 1890 had a slight white majority—1,445 white to 1,089 black. U.S. Census Office, *Compendium of the Eleventh Census: 1890. Pt. 1. Population* (Washington, 1892), 576.

4. Hare, *Cuney*, 107–108, 118–128, 144, 150, 156, 164, 169–203; Rice, *Negro in Texas*, 43–50. *Galveston Daily News*, July 21, 25, 1889; August 24, 1889; March 9, 1892; May 17, 19, 1893; July 6, 1893; September 24, 1893; February 21, 27, 28, 1894; May 13, 1894; September 10, 1896; March 4, 1898. N. W. Cuney sued the Pullman Company for $5,000 damages. Ibid., February 21, 1894.

5. Hare, *Cuney*, 45–46, 67–68, 131–133 (first two quotations). *Galveston Daily News*, October 2, 1896, March 4, 1989. Adelina died of tuberculosis in 1896; Wright died of the same disease in 1898 at age fifty-two. See also Maud Cuney Hare, *Negro Musicians and Their Music* (Washington, D.C.: Associated Publishers, 1936). Galveston *City Times*, March 14, 28, 1914 (last quotation).

6. Bradley Robert Rice, *Progressive Cities: The Commission Government Movement in America, 1901–1920* (Austin: University of Texas Press, 1977), 5–13. *Galveston Daily News*, August 25, 1891.

7. U.S. Census Office, *Report on the Social Statistics of the Cities. Pt. 2*, 1887, 315–318, 321. Rice, *Negro in Texas*, 189–190; Barr, *Black Texans* (Austin: Jenkins Publishing Co.,

1973), 93; *Galveston Daily News*, March 16, 1883 (quotations), April 3, 1883. Lawrence Rice calculates a $500 yearly income for a black longshoreman.

8. In the meantime, forty black pressmen and heatermen at the Galveston Oil mills walked out and struck at the plant, not for higher wages but for a half-hour for dinner and a half night's work on Saturday night. The mill superintendent simply hired white men, and the strikers were arrested. *Galveston Daily News*, September 14, 15, 1887, August 31, 1898 (quotation), September 1, 2, 3, 4, 11, 13, 17, 18, 19, 23, 24, 25, 27, 1898. Galveston white longshoremen made 40 cents a day for day work and 50 cents a day for night work; black longshoremen at the Mallory wharves made 30 cents and 40 cents, respectively. Black screwmen working for William Parr and Company earned the 10-cent-higher wage per day demanded by the strikers. Rice, *Negro in Texas*, 190–191.

9. Rice, *Negro in Texas*, 250–254, Barr, *Black Texans*, 84–85, 136; *Galveston Daily News*, August 25, December 7, 12, 1881; November 19, December 24, 1895. Despite prejudice, African Americans signed up in record numbers to enlist in the army after a call to serve in a war against Spain, filling the recruitment hall with "enthusiatic and patriotic speeches." Ibid., April 27, 1898; June 10, 1898.

10. *Galveston Daily News*, August 8, 1884 , August 23, 1889 (first quotation); June 21, 1891 (second quotation); September 3, 1891 (third quotation).

11. Rice, *Negro in Texas*, 145. *Galveston Daily News*, November 3, 1891 (first quotation). The plaintiffs listed in the *News* were Charlotte Mestre and Felicia Walton. Ibid., November 19, 1898 (second quotation). *City Directory*, 1903–1904, 40.

12. *Galveston City Times*, January 9 (first quotation), February 6, 1904, December 26, 1908 (second quotation). Creation of a poll tax did not stop vote buying since employers bought poll taxes for employees. Texas did not adopt literacy tests and grandfather clauses mainly because of its smaller black population. Barr, *Black Texans*, 79–80.

13. Grantham, *Southern Progressivism* (Knoxville: The University of Tennessee Press, 1983), 123–127. Barr, *Black Texans*, 76, 79, 82, 88.

14. Galveston *New Idea*, July 15, 1905 (first quotation). Galveston *City Times*, April 28, 1906 (second and third quotations). Although Noble thought there was more power among blacks outside the South, that may have been idealistic. In August 1906, after an alledged raid on the town of Brownsville by black troops stationed at Fort Brown, President Theodore Roosevelt dismissed the three companies in the face of demands for removal of all black enlistments from the U.S. Army. Garna L. Christian, *Black Soldiers in Jim Crow Texas, 1899–1917* (College Station: Texas A&M University Press, 1995), Chap. 4. Barr, *Black Texans*, 86–88.

15. Galveston *City Times*, December 19, 1903. *Galveston Daily News*, June 29, 1906.

16. Galveston *City Times*, May 15, 1906. Galveston *New Idea*, July 15, December 23, 1905, March 31, 1906. *Galveston Daily News*, June 29, 1906 (Noble commissioners' quotations). Harold M. Hyman, *Oleander Odyssey: The Kempners of Galveston, Texas, 1854–1980s* (College Station: Texas A&M University Press, 1990), 156.

17. "Mrs. H. Smith and Mrs. L. Harrison," Oral History (Rosenberg Library). *Galveston Daily News*, June 29, 1906, October 5, 11 (bathhouse quotations), 27, 1907.

18. Deborah Gray White, "The Cost of Club Work, the Price of Black Feminism," in Hewitt and Lebsock, eds., *Visible Women*, 259, 249–269. Willard B. Gatewood, *Aristocrats of Color: The Black Elite, 1880–1920* (Bloomington: Indiana University Press, 1990), 21–29. For studies of black women activists in Atlanta, see Jacqueline A. Rouse, "Atlanta's African-American Women's Attack on Segregation, 1900–1920," in Noralee Frankel and Nancy S. Dye, eds., *Gender, Class, Race, and Reform in the Progressive Era* (Lexington: University Press of Kentucky, 1991), 10–23; and Rouse, *Lugenia Burns Hope: Black Southern Reformer* (Athens: University of Georgia Press, 1989).

19. Elsa Barkley Brown, "Womanist Consciousness: Maggie Lena Walker and the Independent Order of Saint Luke," *Signs*, 14, No. 3 (1989), argues for understanding the black woman's struggle for equal rights in the context of the struggle for racial equality.

20. Galveston *City Times*, December 26, 1903, May 1, 1909. Ralph Albert Scull, "Black Galveston: A Personal View of Community History in Many Categories of Life," manuscript (Rosenberg Library).

21. W. E. B. Du Bois, ed., *Efforts for Social Betterment among Negro Americans* (Atlanta: Atlanta University Press, 1909), 16–28. Evelyn Brooks Higginbotham, *Righteous Discontent: The Women's Movement in the Black Baptist Church, 1880–1920* (Cambridge: Harvard University Press, 1993), 5 (quotation). First Baptist Church, Galveston, was chartered in 1840 as a biracial church; in 1846, slave members began to worship separately from whites, but they maintained the same church name until after the Civil War. "Reminiscence of a Church in Galveston: The Avenue L Baptist Church," typescript; "Avenue L Missionary Baptist Church," typescript, both in Bert Armstead Papers (Rosenberg Library); Minutes of the First Baptist Church of Galveston, February 1, 1846, FBC Records; Scull, "Black Galveston." William Manning Morgan, *Trinity Protestant Episcopal Church, Galveston, Texas, 1841–1953* (Houston: Anson Jones Press, 1954), 673–677; Brown, *The Episcopal Church in Texas, 1875-1965*, 9–10, 233–334. Sheila Hackett, *Dominican Women in Texas: From Ohio to Galveston and Beyond* (Houston: Sacred Heart Convent of Houston, Texas, 1986), 64. Wesley Tabernacle Methodist Church is also listed in city directories as Tabernacle Methodist and West Tabernacle M. E. Church; I have consistantly used the first name.

22. *City Directory, 1896* lists eleven superintendents, ten male and two female. One position was shared by both a man and a woman. *City Directories, 1890, 1900–1901, 1905, 1910.*

23. *City Directory, 1899–1900*, 282. Galveston *New Idea*, March 30, 1907 (Wesley Tabernacle M.E.).[Galveston] *City Times*, September 15, 1907 (Sunday school quotation). "Mrs. H. Smith and Mrs. L. Harrison," Oral History (picnic quotations). Sally G. McMillen, " 'An Answer for Our Future': Goals and Concerns of the Black Sunday School Movement, 1865–1915," paper presented to the Southern Historical Association meeting, 1993.

24. *Galveston Daily News*, "A.M.E. Conference," December 18, 1881, August 19, 1896, December 10, 1898 (conventions), April 15, 1900 (Afro-American Council), August 15, 1900. Galveston *City Times*, May 1, 1909 (Business League).

25. Galveston *City Times*, March 3, April 28, 1906, August 22, 1914 (lynching), April 12, June 7, 1919 (NAACP). *Galveston Daily News*, August 2, 1914. At the NAACP meeting were E. M. Henderson, P. B. Phelps, Thomas H. Love, Rev. H. M. Williams, Professors H. T. Davis, J. R. Gibson (principal of Central High School), W. N. Cummings (principal of West District School and superintendent of Sunday school, Reedy Chapel), H. M. Earles, Dr. R. H. Stanton, Mrs. W. N. Cummings, L. Justice, Shelton Banks, A. J. Johnson, and Mrs. Laura A. Pinckney (president of Women's Progressive Club). For a discussion of women and the NAACP, see Dorothy Salem, *To Better Our World: Black Women in Organized Reform, 1890–1920* (Brooklyn: Carlson Publishing, 1990), Chap. 5.

26. An advertisement for a supper to benefit Avenue L Sunday School at Mrs. Hallies Whistnant's home on twenty-fifth Street between Avenues I and H was given extra large type in the *New Idea*. August 20, 1904. [Galveston] *New Idea*, February 27, 1909. [Galveston] *City Times*, December 19, 1903, July 29, 1905, May 12, 1906, July 4, 1908, November 29, 1919. "Mrs. H. Smith and Mrs. L. Harrison," Oral History. Higginbotham, *Righteous Discontent*, 67–75.

27. Barr, *Black Texans*, 98–101; Winegarten, *Black Texas Women: 150 Years of Trial and Triumph* (Austin: University of Texas Press, 1995), 86–87, 93, 106. Rice, *Negro in Texas*, 211–213. Scull, "Black Galveston"; Typescript of Barnes's Diary, March 14, 1868, American

Missionary Association Register and Daily Record Book (1868–1869), Sarah M. Barnes Papers (Rosenberg Library).

28. Barr, *Black Texans*, 101; Rice, *Negro in Texas*, 216; Howard N. Rabinowitz, *The First New South: 1865–1920* (Arlington Heights, Ill.: Harlan Davidson, 1992), 136. *Galveston Daily News*, February 7, 1895 (first quotation). Scull, "Black Galveston" (second quotation). Izola Fedford Collins, granddaughter of Ralph Albert Scull (1860–1949), indicated the importance of education and religion in her family's history: Clara Scull, Ralph's sister, was among the first female teachers hired by the city. Ralph Scull was educated in Indiana, taught fifty-two years at East District and West District schools, was superintendent, teacher, trustee, and class leader at Reedy Chapel AME Church, joined the ministry in 1919, and pastored St. Andrews Missionary Church in Galveston, later named Scull Chapel. His children graduated from Central High School; his daughter Viola Cornelia Scull Fedford (1888–1974) attended Prairie View A&M University and taught at West District and East District schools, Booker T. Washington Elementary, and Central High, retiring in 1959. Ralph Scull's granddaughters, Izola Collins and Florence Carlotta Fedford Henderson both graduated from Central High School and taught in public schools in Galveston. Izola Collins was elected president of the Galveston Independent School District Board of Trustees from 1994–1995. The Scull family has given a total of 215 years to teaching. Izola Fedford Collins to Elizabeth Turner, March 29, 1995, in author's possession.

29. By 1900, Texas had nineteen black high schools; Barr, *Black Texans*, 100. *City Directory, 1886–1887*, 46–47. Total white enrollment for 1886–1887 was 2,676, of which 585 were high school students. *Galveston Daily News*, June 2, 1890 (first and second quotations), March 8, 1895. Hare, *Cuney*, 14; Leon A. Morgan, *Public Education for Blacks in Galveston, 1838–1968* (Galveston: Old Central Cultural Center, 1978), 4–19, 20 (third quotation). Lorenzo J. Greene, "Sidelights on Houston Negroes as Seen by an Associate of Dr. Carter G. Woodson in 1930," in Howard Beeth and Cary D. Wintz, eds., *Black Dixie: Afro-Texas History and Culture in Houston* (College Station: Texas A&M University Press, 1992), 153. James D. Anderson, *The Education of Blacks in the South, 1860–1935* (Chapel Hill: University of North Carolina Press, 1988), 193–199. In 1916, Central High School was one of fifty-eight high schools in the former slave states (197).

30. [Galveston] *City Times*, January 2, 9, 1904 , February 6, 1904, January 28, 1905 (Noble quotations), [Galveston] *New Idea*, February 18, 1905 (quotation). *Houston Post*, February 22, 1987 (Morgan quotation). Rosenberg Library, "Handbook, Colored Branch," 1918; Minutes, Rosenberg Library Association, March 30, 1904, both in Rosenberg Library Papers (Rosenberg Library). Greene, "Sidelights on Houston Negroes," 134–154, 154 (quotation).

31. [Galveston] *City Times*, June 11, 1904, July 22, 1905 (first quotation), June 7, 21, 1919. Galveston *New Idea*, March 30, 1907 (subsequent quotations).

32. *Galveston Daily News*, October 2, 3, December 10, 1898 (subsequent quotations), February 11, 1901, February 18, 1912 (first and second quotations).

33. *City Directory, 1895–96*, 53. *City Directory, 1897–98*, 275. Winegarten, *Black Texas Women*, 255. Thelma Paige of Dallas and Jessie Dent of Galveston filed suit in separate cases and won salary adjustments.

34. [Galveston] *City Times*, May 31, 1919. *Galveston Daily News*, October 15, 22, 1912, May 21, 1933. Morgan, *Public Education for Blacks in Galveston*, 20.

35. [Galveston] *City Times*, September 3, 1903 (quotation), September 10, 1904.

36. Shane White, " 'It Was a Proud Day': African Americans, Festivals, and Parades in the North, 1741–1834," *Journal of American History* 81 (June 1994), 13–50 (quotation p. 49).

37. [Galveston] *New Idea*, August 27, 1904 (quotations), July 29, 1905. *Galveston Daily News*, August 19, 1910.

38. [Galveston] *City Times*, May 28, 1904, June 11, 1904 (quotation), June 10, 17, July 8, 1905, June 20, 1914 , June 21, 1919. [Galveston] *New Idea*, March 4, 1905. For a description of Juneteenth as celebrated in Rockdale, Texas, in 1972, see William H. Wiggins, O *Freedom! Afro-American Emancipation Celebrations* (Knoxville: University of Tennessee Press, 1987), 1–7.

39. [Galveston] *City Times*, June 21, 1919. [Galveston] *New Idea*, March 4, 1905. Shane White notes that antebellum northern parades were "typically all-male affairs," suggesting the narrowed role of black women in public celebrations. White, " ' It Was a Proud Day,' " 47–48. For variations on the meaning of Liberty, see Marina Warner, *Monuments and Maidens: The Allegory of the Female Form* (New York: Atheneum, 1985), 14–15. For a discussion of symbolic protest as a vital part of African American identity, see James Oliver Horton, *Free People of Color: Inside the African American Community* (Washington: Smithsonian Institution Press, 1993), 164.

40. *Galveston Daily News*, July 21, 1912, October 9, 1927 (second quotation); Du Bois, *Efforts for Social Betterment*, 45 (first quotation).

41. Barr, *Black Texans*, 141; Rice, *Negro in Texas*, 237–239. *Galveston Daily News*, June 26, 1960, June 12, 1970 (quotation). Betty Massey, ed., *Black Galvestonians: A Glimpse of the Past, a Challenge for the Future* (Galveston: Galveston Historical Foundaiton, n.d.), 10. For books and articles on African American benevolence, see Hine, " 'We Specialize in the Wholly Impossible': The Philanthropic Work of Black Women," in Kathleen D. McCarthy, ed., *Lady Bountiful Revisited: Women, Philanthropy, and Power* (New Brunswick: Rutgers University Press, 1990), 70–93 (quotation p. 71); Neverdon-Morton, *Afro-American Women of the South and the Advancement of the Race, 1895–1925* (Knoxville: University of Tennessee Press, 1989), 105–201; Kathleen C. Berkeley, "Colored Ladies Also Contributed: Black Women's Activities from Benevolence to Social Welfare, 1866–1896," in Walter J. Fraser, Jr., R. Frank Saunders, Jr., and Jon L. Wakelyn, eds., *The Web of Southern Social Relations: Women, Family and Education* (Athens: University of Georgia Press, 1985), 181–203.

42. *Galveston Daily News*, November 25, 1883, November 10, 1884. [Galveston] *City Times*, December 26, 1903, May 6, 1905 (second quotation), May 19, 1906 (first quotation). Winegarten, *Black Texas Women*, 158–159.

43. *Galveston Tribune*, September 9, 1963, "Women's Hospital Aid Unit in Action Here 66 Years." Although this article places the founding date at about 1897, I was unable to confirm its existence earlier than 1909. A report submitted by the Colored Women's Hospital Aid Society to W. E. B. Du Bois's edited social survey indicated that the society organized in January 1909. Du Bois, *Efforts for Social Betterment*, 87. [Galveston] *City Times*, March 1, 1902 (for John Gibson); [Galveston] *New Idea*, February 27, 1909. The Society is mentioned in the Eighth Bienniel Report to the NACW in 1914. Elizabeth Lindsay Davis, *Lifting as They Climb: The National Association of Colored Women* (Washington, D.C.: National Assocation of Colored Women, 1933), 55. *Galveston Daily News*, June 22, 1913, May 3, 1914, October 18, 1965. The National Association of Colored Women was founded in 1896.

44. Minutes, Hospital Aid Society, 1924 to 1954 (in the possession of Izola Collins, Galveston); June 2, 1923, November 15, 1923 (quotation), April 12, 1924, October 4, November 1, 1924, February 26, March 7, May 2, 1925. [Galveston] *New Idea*, February 27, 1909 ("colored ward" quotation); *Galveston Daily News*, June 22, 1913, May 3, 1914, Oct. 18, 1965; *Galveston Tribune*, September 9, 1963. Du Bois, *Efforts for Social Betterment*, 87. I wish to

acknowledge Mrs. Izola Collins's generosity in allowing me to read her family's private records.

45. Minutes, Hospital Aid Society, June 2, 1923 (quotation), May 2, 1925 . For the core position that black churches held in connection with women's club work, see Higginbotham, *Righteous Discontent*, 14.

46. "The Texas Federation of Colored Women's Clubs, Annual Review, 1923–24," (quotation) in possession of Izola Collins. Winegarten, *Black Texas Women*, 195–96. [Galveston] *City Times*, October 17, 1908 (womanhood quotation), June 7, July 5, 1919.

47. Minutes, Hospital Aid Society, June 2, 1923, June 7, 1924 (that year twenty members were counted in the society), October 4, 1924 (quotation). [Galveston] *City Times*, June 7, 1919. See Paula Giddings, *When and Where I Enter: The Impact of Black Women on Race and Sex in America* (New York: William Morrow and Co., 1984), 97–98; Scott, *Natural Allies* (Urbana: University of Illinois Press, 1991), 147–148. Deborah Gray White argues that black club women "took the helm of race leadership" in "The Cost of Club Work," 257.

48. [Galveston] *New Idea*, August 20, 1904. *Galveston Daily News*, March 4, 1913 (quotation); [Galveston] *City Times*, September 15, 1907, May 31, 1919. Winegarten, *Black Texas Women*, 195. "Mrs. H. Smith and Mrs. L. Harrison," Oral History. Other Willing Workers Clubs existed in Detroit and Stamford, Connecticut. Du Bois, *Efforts for Social Betterment*, 45. For a further discussion of black women's clubs see Davis, ed., *Lifting as We Climb*; Salem, *To Better Our World*; Stephanie J. Shaw, "Black Club Women and the Creation of the National Association of Colored Women," *Journal of Women's History*, 3 (Fall 1991), 10–25.

49. [Galveston] *City Times*, March 1, 1902; Greene, "Sidelights on Houston Negroes," 153. Scull, "Black Galveston." Ledger #2, W. K. Hebert and Company Records (Rosenberg Library, Galveston). The Hebert Company ledgers also list an Old Folks Home and an Ever Ready Charity Club in 1916; Rice, *Negro in Texas*, 37–43. Glenda Elizabeth Gilmore, "Gender and Jim Crow: Women and the Politics of White Supremacy in North Carolina, 1896–1920" (Ph.D. dissertation, University of North Carolina, 1992), 358–359 (quotation). Merline Pitre, *Through Many Dangers, Toils and Snares: The Black Leadership of Texas, 1868–1900* (Austin: Eakin Press, 1985), 188–197. Gatewood, *Aristocrats of Color*, 19. Massey, ed., *Black Galvestonians*, 6. Besides Norris Wright Cuney several other members of Galveston's black community achieved national recognition. Central High School principal John R. Gibson, who served from 1888 to 1936, was a native of Ohio and a graduate of Wilberforce University. He was appointed consul for Liberia in 1901 by President William McKinley and served for twenty years. That same year he was appointed to the local board of the biracial American Red Cross. William H. Noble, editor of the *City Times*, served with Booker T. Washington on the committee to memorialize William McKinley and was elected secretary for the southern Negro Congress in 1904.

50. [Galveston] *New Idea*, October 14, 1905. See also Janette Greenwood, *Bittersweet Legacy: The Black and White "Better Classes" in Charlotte, 1850–1910* (Chapel Hill: University of North Carolina Press, 1994), 205.

51. *Galveston Daily News*, April 24, 1910.

52. Ibid., April 28, 1910 (first quotation). Cheryl Thurber, "The Development of the Mammy Image and Mythology," in Virginia Bernhard, Betty Brandon, Elizabeth Fox-Genovese, and Theda Perdue, eds., *Southern Women: Histories and Identities* (Columbia: University of Missouri Press, 1992), 87–108. *Galveston Daily News*, April 28, 1910 (aristocrats quotation); May 14, 1910 (good old soul, faithful quotations); November 12, 1911 (last quotation). See also Kenneth W. Goings, *Mammy and Uncle Mose: Black Collectibles and American Stereotyping* (Bloomington: Indiana University Press, 1994). For a description of

the southwide movement to seek the testimonials of "faithful slaves," see Fred Arthur Bailey, "Mildred Lewis Rutherford and the Patrician Cult of the Old South," *Georgia Historical Society*, 77 (Fall 1994), 509–535.

53. [Galveston] *City Times*, December 19, 1903. Horace Hollier married Lillie Scull, the sister of Ralph Scull. Scull, "Black Galveston." Burton, "I'm Telling You."

54. *Galveston Daily News*, July 10, 1914; Galveston *City Times*, November 29, 1919. Stephanie Shaw, "Black Club Women," 14; Rosalyn Terborg-Penn, "Discontented Black Feminists: Prelude and Postscript to the Passage of the Nineteenth Amendment," in Lois Scharf and Joan M. Jensen, eds., *Decades of Discontent: The Woman's Movement, 1920–1940* (Westport, Conn., Greenwood Press, 1983). Elizabeth Hayes Turner, "Episcopal Women as Community Leaders: Galveston, 1900–1989," in Catherine Prelinger, ed., *Episcopal Women: Gender, Spirituality, and Committment in a Mainline Denomination* (New York: Oxford University Press, 1992), 72–110, 96. See also Linda Gordon, "Black and White Visions of Welfare: Women's Welfare Activism, 1890–1945," *Journal of American History*, 78 (September 1991), 559–590.

55 Darlene Clark Hine, "Black Women's History, White Women's History: The Juncture of Race and Class," *Journal of Women's History*, 4 (Fall 1992), 127 (quotation), 125–133.

Chapter 9   Women Organizing for the Vote

A version of this chapter appeared as " 'White-Gloved Ladies' and 'New Women' in the Texas Woman Suffrage Movement," in Virginia Bernhard, Betty Brandon, Elizabeth Fox-Genovese, and Theda Perdue, eds., *Southern Women: Histories and Identities* (Columbia: University of Missouri Press, 1992), 129–156

1. *Galveston Daily News*, March 29, 1913. Playbill, "The Equal Suffrage Association presents 'A Dream of Brave Women,' 'An Anti-Suffrage Monologue,' and 'Lady Geraldine's Speech.' " March 28, 1913, Galveston Equal Suffrage Association Records (Rosenberg Library); hereinafter cited as GESA Records.

2. *Galveston Daily News*, March 29, 1913.

3. I counted at least seventeen teenage girls participating in this play, indicating the desire on the part of suffrage mothers to introduce their daughters to the concept of voting equality.

4. Marjorie Spruill Wheeler, *New Women of the New South: The Leaders of the Woman Suffrage Movement in the Southern States* (New York: Oxford University Press, 1993); Winegarten and McArthur, eds., *Citizens at Last: Diaries and Writings of Jane Y. McCallum* (Austin: Ellen C. Temple, 1987); Janet G. Humphrey, ed., *A Texas Suffragist: Diaries and Writings of Jane Y. McCallum* (Austin: Ellen C. Temple, 1988). See also Judith Nichols McArthur, "Motherhood and Reform in the New South: Texas Women's Political Culture in the Progressive Era" (Ph.D. dissertation, University of Texas, 1992); Patricia B. Nieuwenhuizen, "Minnie Fisher Cunningham and Jane Y. McCallum: Leaders of Texas Women for Suffrage and Beyond" (Senior Thesis, University of Texas at Austin, 1982); and Anastatia Sims, "The Woman Suffrage Movement in Texas" (Senior Thesis, University of Texas at Austin, 1974).

5. David G. McComb, *Galveston: A History* (Austin: University of Texas Press, 1986), 112.

6. *City Directory*, 1909–1910. For a discussion of the specialization represented in clubs and societies see Robert H. Wiebe, *The Search for Order, 1877–1920* (New York: Hill and Wang, 1967), 123; and Don H. Doyle, *New Men, New Cities, New South: Atlanta, Nashville, Charleston, Mobile, 1860–1910* (Chapel Hill: University of North Carolina Press, 1990), 205–59. For a women's history perspective, see Suzanne Lebsock, "Women and

American Politics, 1880–1920," in Louise Tilly and Patricia Gurin, eds., *Women, Politics, and Change* (New York: The Russell Sage Foundation, 1990), 35–62.

7. A. Elizabeth Taylor, "The Woman Suffrage Movement in Texas," reprinted from the *Journal of Southern History*, 27 (May 1951), in Winegarten and McArthur, eds., *Citizens at Last*, 16–23 (hereinafter cited with reprinted page numbers). "Minutes of the First Session of the Texas Equal Rights Association, May 10, 1893," in ibid., 89 (quotation). Letters explaining Hayes's involvement in the split may be found in Rebecca Henry Hayes to Laura Clay, November 8, 1894; and July 1, 1895; Grace Danforth to Laura Clay, August 3, 1894, Laura Clay Papers (Special Collections, University of Kentucky Libraries, Lexington, Ky.). Thanks to Judith McArthur for copies of these letters.

8. Lewis L. Gould, *Progressives and Prohibitionists: Texas Democrats in the Wilson Era* (Austin: University of Texas Press, 1973), 6–7, 48; McArthur, "Motherhood and Reform in the New South," 315–322. Barr, *Black Texans* (Austin: Jenkins Publishing Co., 1973), 157; C. Vann Woodward, *Origins of the New South, 1877–1913* (Baton Rouge: Louisiana State University Press, 1951), Chap. 14; and J. Morgan Kousser, *The Shaping of Southern Politics: Suffrage Restriction and Establishment of the One-Party South, 1880–1910* (New Haven: Yale University Press, 1974), 260–263. Kousser states that "Southern political institutions . . . gained legitimacy not by expanding, but by contracting the electorate" (263). His research does not go beyond 1910, so he is not forced to address the question of why the legislature in Texas in 1918 extended the franchise to women and thus expanded the electorate.

9. There were, however, specific instances of black women registering to vote in Texas, which caused discriminatory backlashes. See Rosalyn Terborg-Penn, "Discontented Black Feminists: Prelude and Postscript to the Passage of the Nineteenth Amendment," in Lois Scharf and Joan. M. Jensen, eds., *Decades of Discontent: The Woman's Movement, 1920–1940* (Westport, Conn.: Greenwood Press, 1983).

10. Aileen S. Kraditor, "Tactical Problems of the Woman-Suffrage Movement in the South," *Louisiana Studies* (Winter, 1966), 289–307; and *The Ideas of the Woman Suffrage Movement, 1890–1920* (New York: Columbia University Press, 1965), 165.

11. Taylor, "Woman Suffrage Movement," in *Citizens at Last*, 23–25. See also Jane Y. McCallum, "Activities of Women in Texas Politics, I," in ibid., 203.

12. *Galveston Daily News*, December 11, 1921.

13. Ibid., February 16, 1912. For a discussion of feminism and woman suffrage see Gerda Lerner, who defines the term "feminism" as "a doctrine advocating social and political rights for women equal to those of men . . . [and] an organized movement for the attainment of these rights" (236). Lerner, *The Creation of Patriarchy* (New York: Oxford University Press, 1988). See also Ellen Carol DuBois, *Feminism and Suffrage: The Emergence of an Independent Women's Movement in America, 1848–1869* (Ithaca: Cornell University Press, 1978), 18. For the history of twentieth-century feminism, see Nancy F. Cott, *The Grounding of Modern Feminism* (New Haven: Yale University Press, 1987).

14. *Galveston Daily News*, February 16, 1912 (quotations); *Galveston Tribune*, June 14, 1913.

15. *Galveston Daily News*, February 16, 1912 (first four quotations). Cordia [Mrs. John S.] Sweeny to Annette Finnigan, February 25, 1915, Jane Y. McCallum Papers (Austin Public Library, Austin). Some Galveston men used the natural rights argument for women's right to vote. See *Galveston Daily News*, February 16, 1912; and Edmund R. Cheesborough to Minnie Fisher Cunningham, November 18, 1916, McCallum Papers.

16. Taylor, "Woman Suffrage Movement," in *Citizens at Last*, 16, 26, 30; see also "Austin Woman Suffrage Association Minutes," March 1, 1912, in ibid., 124; Jacquelyn Dowd Hall, *Revolt Against Chivalry: Jessie Daniel Ames and the Women's Campaign against Lynching* (New York: Columbia University Press, 1979), 21–26; and Elizabeth Cady Stanton

et al., eds., *History of Woman Suffrage* (6 vols., New York: Arno & *The New York Times* ob1881–1922] 1969), Vol. 6, 631–632.

17. President's Report, 1914, File 8, Box 11, Pt. 2, McCallum Papers. The three lecturers hired were: Mrs. Desha Breckinridge, Miss Helen Todd, and Dr. Anna Howard Shaw.

18. Ibid.

19. Ibid. Paula Williams Webber, "The Early Houston Woman Suffrage Movement, 1903–1917" (M.A. thesis, University of Houston–Clear Lake, 1995), 75.

20. Scott, *Making the Invisible Woman Visible* (Urbana: University of Illinois Press, 1984), 220.

21. *Galveston Tribune*, June 14, 1913 (first quotation). *Galveston Daily News*, May 6, 1914 (second quotation).

22. Taylor, "Woman Suffrage Movement," in *Citizens at Last*, For a study that discusses the consciousness of women relevant to their public activism, see Nancy F. Cott, "What's in a Name? The Limits of 'Social Feminism': or, Expanding the Vocabulary of Women's History," *Journal of American History*, 76 (December 1989): 809–829, esp. 827.

23. *Galveston Tribune*, March 11, and Special Edition between March 17 and 18, 1915.

24. Biographical entries for these twenty-four suffragists were acquired from the Galveston Women Database. A similar project using the *Woman's Who's Who of America, 1914–1915* can be found in Barbara Campbell, *The "Liberated" Woman of 1914: Prominent Women in the Progressive Era* (Ann Arbor: UMI Research Press, 1979). The roll of officers for the GESA in its first year (1912) contains the names of women who were known in the community for the prominence of their families and for their involvement in other areas of municipal housekeeping. Nine of the seventeen officers of the GESA in 1912 had held or would hold executive positions in the WHPA; seven of the seventeen belonged to commercially wealthy families that practiced civic philanthropy (five male members of these families became charter members of the GESA, as did Rabbi Henry Cohen). The nine suffragist officers who were also officers for the WHPA were: Betty Ballinger, Minnie Fisher Cunningham, Caroline Waters Garrett, Emma Davis Gonzales, Bessie Grundy, Emma Harris, Dr. Ethel Lyon Heard, Helen McMaster, and Maud Moller. Suffragists from wealthy families included: Betty Ballinger, Lucy Kenison Bornefeld, Mary Fowler Bornefeld, Emma Davis Gonzales, Etta Lasker, Rebecca Trueheart, and Sally Trueheart Williams.

25. Of the twenty-four officers for whom data are available, seven bore children. I was unable to verify if four of the twenty-four suffragists had children or not.

26. Surprisingly few suffragists hired live-in help. Only three suffragists employed live-in servants, but, of these, two also kept boarders. Manuscript Census Returns, 1910, Galveston County.

27. Annette Finnigan to Eva Goldsmith, July 7, 1914 (first two quotations); Goldsmith to Finnigan, July 20, 1914 (third quotation), February 3, 1916 (fourth quotation), all in McCallum Papers. There were virtually no farm women active in Galveston civic affairs.

28. This was borne out in 1919 when the Texas legislature introduced a woman suffrage referendum to Texas voters. Working-class immigrant, Catholic, and antiprohibition voters rejected the amendment. One month later, progressive assemblymen ratified the Nineteenth Amendment. Eva Goldsmith to Annette Finnigan, February 3, 1915, McCallum Papers. Larry J. Wygant, " 'A Municipal Broom': The Woman Suffrage Campaign in Galveston, Texas," *Houston Review*, 6, No. 3 (1984), 117–134, quoting *Galveston Tribune*, June 14, 1913.

29. Cordia Sweeny to Annette Finnigan, February 28, 1915, McCallum Papers (first quotation). Nieuwenhuizen, "Minnie Fisher Cunningham and Jane Y. McCallum," 61–62 (second quotation), 63 (third quotation). For a discussion of the strategies employed by southern suffragists with respect to race, see Kraditor, "Tactical Problems of the Woman-

Suffrage Movement in the South," 289–307; *The Ideas of the Woman Suffrage Movement*, Chap. 7; and Wheeler, *New Women of the New South*, 19–21, esp. Chap. 4.

30. *Galveston Tribune*, Special Edition, March 17 and 18, 1915.

31. Ronnie Dugger, "Spanning the Old to the New South: Minnie Fisher and Her Heroine Mother," *Texas Observer*, November 21, 1958; Patricia Ellen Cunningham, "Too Gallant a Walk: Minnie Fisher Cunningham and Her Race for Governor of Texas in 1944" (M.A. thesis, University of Texas, 1985), 24 (quotation). Thanks to Patricia Cunningham for this citation. See also John Carroll Eudy, "The Vote and Lone Star Women: Minnie Fisher Cunningham and the Texas Equal Suffrage Association," *East Texas Historical Journal*, 14 (Fall 1976), 52–59.

32. Mrs. W.M. Baines, A *Story of Texas White Ribboners* [WCTU] (n.p.[1935]), 66, 122, 125; *Galveston Daily News*, October 22, 1922 (quotations).

33. Cordia Sweeny to Annette Finnigan, March 26, 1915, McCallum Papers. Marjorie S. Wheeler makes the point that association between woman suffrage and temperance was "less automatic" in the South, as there were also many temperance followers who did not support suffrage. *New Women of the New South*, 11.

34. For a discussion of the links connecting Methodism, the WCTU, and suffrage see Anne Firor Scott, *The Southern Lady: From Pedestal to Politics, 1830–1930* (Chicago: University of Chicago Press, 1970), 144–148 (quotation on p. 148); Jean E. Friedman, *The Enclosed Garden: Women and Community in the Evangelical South, 1930–1900* (Chapel Hill: University of North Carolina Press, 1985), 111–120; and Hall, *Revolt Against Chivalry*, 22, 25, 36, 66.

35. In table 9.4, the smaller towns cited as forming first suffrage societies (Selma, Ala.; Columbus, Ga.; Morganton, N.C.; Spartanburg, S.C.; Austin, Tex.) were soon followed by the state's more populated cities. Margaret Nell Price, "The Development of Leadership by Southern Women through Clubs and Organizations" (M.A. thesis, University of North Carolina, 1945), 97.

36. Price, "The Development of Leadership by Southern Women," 96. Grantham, *Southern Progressivism* (Knoxville: University of Tennessee Press, 1983), 200–217. Jean Friedman in *The Enclosed Garden*, Chap. 6, also maintains that a strong suffrage movement in the South was not possible until modernization triumphed over ties of kinship that prevented women from forming independent women's societies.

37. *Galveston Tribune*, June 14, 1913. Perle P. Penfield, "Woman Suffrage: Do Household Duties Interfere with Politics for American Women," clipping, GESA Records (quotation).

38. *Galveston Tribune*, June 14, 1913, February 3, 1915, Special Edition, March 17,18, 1915. Playbill, "The Equal Suffrage Association presents 'A Dream of Brave Women,' 'An Anti-Suffrage Monologue,' and 'Lady Geraldine's Speech.'" March 28, 1913, GESA Records.

39. *Galveston Daily News*, May 2, 1914. A large crowd of Galveston women joined in singing a suffragist anthem to the tune of "My Country 'tis of Thee."

40. Dugger, "Minnie Fisher and Her Heroine Mother," (first quotation); *Galveston Daily News*, July 5, 1914 (second quotation). *Houston Daily Post*, July 4, 5, 1914. Annette Finnigan to Minnie Fisher Cunningham (MFC), June 22, 29, 1914; MFC to Finnigan, June 24, 1914, both in Galveston File, Pt. 2, McCallum Papers.

41. *Galveston Tribune*, June 14, 1913 (first and second quotations), February 3, 1915 (third quotation) Special Edition, March 17,18, 1915; *Galveston Daily News*, May 2, 1914, July 12, 1916 (fourth quotation), October 22, 1922. Wednesday Club Program, 1912–1913, Wednesday Club Records (Rosenberg Library).

42. *Galveston Tribune*, June 14, 1913; Wygant, "A Municipal Broom," 117–127; Taylor,

"The Woman Suffrage Movement in Texas," in *Citizens at Last*, 27–28. H. B. Moore to Hon. James B. Stubbs, June 7, 1916; H. B. Moore to Charles J. Kirk, June 9, 1916; Helen Moore to Minnie Fisher Cunningham, June 8, 1916; Helen Moore to MFC, June 19, 1916; Helen Moore to MFC, August 19, 1916, all in McCallum Papers. Eleanor Flexner, *Century of Struggle: The Woman's Rights Movement in the United States* (New York: Atheneum, 1959), 277–278.

43. Cunningham, "Too Gallant a Walk," 24. Dugger, "Minnie Fisher and Her Heroine Mother."

44. Membership roll, 1903–1919, Program 1912–1913, Wednesday Club Records. Mary Fowler Bornefeld to Annette Finnigan, n.d. [October or November 1914], McCallum Papers (quotation).

45. MFC to Annette Finnigan, n.d. [November or December 1914], McCallum Papers.

46. MFC to Annette Finnigan, n.d. [January 1915], ibid. (first quotation). *Galveston Daily News*, February 4 (second quotation), November 4, 1914. MFC to Carrie Chapman Catt, April 27, 1917, Minnie Fisher Cunningham Papers (Houston Metropolitan Research Center, Houston). Houston).

47. MFC to Finnigan, July 15, 1914, McCallum Papers.

48. MFC to Finnigan, May 8, 1914, ibid.

49. MFC to Finnigan, June 2, 1914 (first quotation); MFC to Perle Penfield, n.d. [July 16, 1914], (second quotation), ibid.

50. Jacquelyn Dowd Hall and Anne Firor Scott, "Women in the South," in John B. Boles and Evelyn Thomas Nolen, eds., *Interpreting Southern History: Historiographical Essays of Sanford W. Higginbotham* (Baton Rouge: Louisiana State University Press, 1987), 491(first quotation). MFC to Finnigan, n.d. [January 1915] (second quotation), McCallum Papers.

51. Cordia Sweeny to Finnigan, March 26, 1915 (first quotation); Finnigan to Sweeny, March 28, 1915; Finnigan to Sweeny, June 5, 1915, Box 11, McCallum Papers.

52. MFC to Finnigan, n.d. [January 1915], ibid.

53. Flexner, *Century of Struggle*, 272–273. Michael McGerr, "Political Style and Women's Power, 1830–1930," *Journal of American History*, 77 (December 1990), 876–878.

Chapter 10   The YWCA and Wage-Earning Women

1. *Galveston Daily News*, September 1, 1916.

2. Helen Bittar, "The Y.W.C.A. of the City of New York: 1870 to 1920" (Ph. D. dissertation, New York University, 1979), 34 (quotation); *Galveston Daily News*, November 23, 1914; clipping, February 1916, YWCA Scrapbook, 1916, Galveston YWCA Records (Rosenberg Library); hereinafter cited as YWCA Records. Carl Degler, *At Odds: Women and the Family in America from the Revolution to the Present* (New York: Oxford University Press, 1980), 322. For background information on the national YWCA, see Mary Sims, *The Natural History of a Social Institution: The Young Women's Christian Association* (New York: Columbia University Press, 1936); Sims, *The YWCA: An Unfolding Purpose* (New York, 1950); Grace H. Wilson, *The Religious and Educational Philosophy of the Young Women's Christian Association* (New York, 1933). A "Colored Women's Branch" of the New York YWCA was not organized until 1905, and no facility was built for them until 1911. In Galveston, a branch for black women was not established until 1954; Plans for the Mary Patrick Branch YWCA for Black Women, File 14, Box 1, YWCA Records. YWCAs for black women existed in only four Texas cities, Beaumont, Dallas, Houston, and San Antonio, by 1931. Barr, *Black Texans* (Austin: Jenkins Publishing Co., 1973), 168.

3. *Galveston Daily News*, November 23, 24, December 1, 3, 4, 7, 1914; *Galveston Tribune*, December 7, 1914, all in YWCA Scrapbook, 1914–1915. *City Directory*, 1921.

4. Percentages compiled by matching officers found in the YWCA Records with religious affiliation found in church records, Galveston Women Database. Sims, *Natural History of a Social Institution*, 28. *Galveston Tribune*, January 20, 1955.

5. Percentages were compiled from YWCA records and from WHPA and GESA lists of officers and members found in local newspapers.

6. *Galveston Daily News*, November 30, 1914 (first quotation), November 24, 1914 (second quotation), YWCA Scrapbook, 1914–1915, YWCA Records; *Galveston Journal*, January 2, 1915; U.S. Census Office, *Census Reports*. Vol. 8: *Twelfth Census of the United States . . . 1900. Manufactures* (Washington, 1902), 866. Between 1890 and 1900, Galveston "industrial establishments" increased from 190 to 295 (55.3 percent) but dropped to 64 in 1904. By 1909, manufactories had risen to 81. U.S. Bureau of the Census, *Thirteenth Census of the United States . . . 1910*. Vol. 9: *Manufactures, 1909* (Washington, 1912), 1204. *Galveston Daily News*, Decemer 1, 1914, May 8, 1915; clipping February 2, 1916, YWCA Scrapbook, 1916.

7. Susan Estabrook Kennedy, *If All We Did Was to Weep at Home: A History of White Working-Class Women in America* (Bloomington: Indiana University Press, 1979), 155–156.

8. Granville Price, "A Sociological Study of a Segregated District" (M.A. thesis, University of Texas at Austin, 1930), 61–71. Lawrence H. Larsen, *The Urban West at the End of the Frontier* (Lawrence: The Regents Press of Kansas, 1978), 86–87.

9. U.S. Bureau of the Census, *Benevolent Institutions, 1904* (Washington, 1905), 292 (quotation). Texas cities with rescue homes included Arlington, Dallas, Fort Worth, Houston, Pilot Point, and San Antonio (2); *City Directories, 1898–1900*; Minutes, LASFPC, March 24, 1892, March 23, May 4, June 1, 1893, October 4, 1894. For a discussion of rescue homes, their mission, and moral action, see Peggy Pascoe, *Relations of Rescue: The Search for Female Moral Authority in the American West, 1874–1939* (New York: Oxford University Press, 1990), 31 ff.

10. *Galveston Tribune*, December 17, 18, January 2, February 19, 1915 (third quotation); clipping, February 2, 1916, YWCA Scrapbook, 1916 (first and second quotations).

11. *Galveston Tribune*, March 10, 1915. Samuel Chester Griffin, *History of Galveston, Texas* (Galveston: A. H. Cawston, 1931), 402. Facilities in this period were for whites only.

12. Clipping, December 31, 1914, YWCA Scrapbook, 1914–1915; *Galveston Daily News*, July 9, 1915; *Galveston Tribune*, February 11, 1915, September 23, 1915, ibid.; clipping, March 1, 1916, YWCA Scrapbook, 1916.

13. Clipping, June 28, 1915, YWCA Scrapbook, 1914–1915; *Galveston Tribune*, March 3, 1915. *City Directory*, 1916.

14. *Galveston Daily News*, May 8, June 17, 1915. See E. Anthony Rotundo, *American Manhood: Transformations in Masculinity from the Revolution to the Modern Era* (New York: Basic Books, 1990), 100; Don H. Doyle, *New Men, New Cities, New South: Atlanta, Nashville, Charleston, Mobile, 1860–1910* (Chapel Hill: University of North Carolina Press, 1990), 216–220.

15. *Galveston Tribune*, March 24, 1915; clipping, February 1916 (woman's exchange quotation), YWCA Scrapbook, 1916.

16. Clippings, March 24, 1917, October 26, 1918, YWCA Scrapbook, 1917–1918; *Galveston Tribune*, June 30, 1916 (first quotation); clipping, January 2, 1918, YWCA Scrapbook, 1918; *Galveston Tribune*, November 5, 1918 (second quotation); *Galveston Daily News*, June 3, 1919. Nellie B. League to Mrs. Charles Fowler, January 27, 1918, File 3, Box 1, YWCA Records.

17. T. W. Patrick and Mary Patrick to Dear Friends, October 23, 1951, YWCA for Black Women, File 14, Box 1, YWCA Records. *Galveston Tribune*, February 26, 1915 (quotation). In a speech to the Galveston YWCA, Edith Stanton of the New York YWCA explained to this audience of white women that "three secretaries have been appointed to direct the activities in a branch of the organization for colored women. In a number of Northern cities, and in the South, these institutions have been started and are of course conducted separately from the associations for white girls and women," Clipping [November 1915], YWCA Scrapbook 1914–1915.

18. *Galveston Daily News*, February 27, 1915.

19. See Jacquelyn David Hall, *Revolt Against Chivalry: Jessie Daniel Ames and The Women's Campaign against Lynching* (New York: Columbia University Press, 1979), 82–83, 103; and Marion W. Roydhouse, "Bridging Chasms: Community and the Southern YWCA," in Hewitt and Lebsock, eds., *Visible Women* (Urbana: University of Illinois Press, 1984), 270–295.

20. *Galveston Tribune*, March 15, 1916 (quotation). For a discussion of Hull House graduates, see Robyn Muncy, *Creating a Female Dominion in American Reform, 1890–1935* (New York: Oxford University Press, 1991).

Conclusion   Toward Progressive Women's Communities

1. *Galveston Daily News*, July 12, 1916.

2. *Galveston Tribune*, March 11, and Special Edition between March 17 and 18, 1915.

3. For a discussion of a women's community as seen through Chicago's settlement house, see Kathryn Kish Sklar, "Hull House in the 1890s: A Community of Women Reformers," *Signs*, 10, No. 4 (1985), 658–677; and for the political potential of the woman's sphere, Estelle Freedman, "Separatism as Strategy: Female Institution Building and American Feminism, 1870–1930," *Feminist Studies*, 5 (Fall 1979), 512–529.

Notes on Methodology

1. Although mention will be made of religious women in Roman Catholic orders, their organizations were not included for evaluation in this study. Analysis for this study includes only laywomen and their organizations.

2. Names are a problem in women's history. A woman, if she marries once, will have three names; her name before marriage, e.g., Miss Lucy Ballinger; her given maried name, e.g., Mrs. Lucy Mills; and her husband's name, e.g., Mrs. Andrew G. Mills. If she marries more than once, the possibilities are unlimited. Wherever possible I have used a married woman's given name and her married name. In some cases, a given name has been impossible to find.

3. Max Weber, *The Theory of Social and Economic Organization* (New York: Oxford University Press, 1947), 428; Max Weber, "Class, Status, Party," from *Max Weber: Essays in Sociology*, trans. and ed. H. H. Gerth and C. Wright Mills (New York: Oxford University Press, 1946), chap. 7.

INDEX